CASES IN
COMPARATIVE
POLITICS

SIXTH EDITION

CASES IN
COMPARATIVE
POLITICS

SIXTH EDITION

PATRICK H. O'NEIL | KARL FIELDS | DON SHARE

W. W. NORTON & COMPANY
NEW YORK · LONDON

W. W. Norton & Company has been independent since its founding in 1923, when William Warder Norton and Mary D. Herter Norton first published lectures delivered at the People's Institute, the adult education division of New York City's Cooper Union. The firm soon expanded its program beyond the Institute, publishing books by celebrated academics from America and abroad. By midcentury, the two major pillars of Norton's publishing program—trade books and college texts—were firmly established. In the 1950s, the Norton family transferred control of the company to its employees, and today—with a staff of four hundred and a comparable number of trade, college, and professional titles published each year—W. W. Norton & Company stands as the largest and oldest publishing house owned wholly by its employees.

Editor: Peter Lesser
Project Editor: Linda Feldman
Associate Editor: Samantha Held
Managing Editor, College: Marian Johnson
Managing Editor, College Digital Media: Kim Yi
Production Manager: Elizabeth Marotta
Media Editor: Spencer Richardson-Jones
Media Associate Editor: Michael Jaoui
Media Editorial Assistant: Ariel Eaton
Marketing Manager, Political Science: Erin Brown
Design Director: Hope Miller Goodell
Text Design: Faceout Studio
Map Design: Mapping Specialists
Photo Editor: Catherine Abelman
Permissions Manager: Megan Schindel
Composition: Six Red Marbles
Manufacturing: TC-Transcontinental Printing

Permission to use copyrighted material is included on page A-1.

Names: O'Neil, Patrick H., 1966- author. | Fields, Karl J., author. | Share, Donald, author.
Title: Cases in comparative politics / Patrick H. O'Neil, Karl Fields, Don Share.
Description: Sixth edition. | New York : W. W. Norton & Company, [2018] |
   Includes bibliographical references and index.
Identifiers: LCCN 2017046475 | ISBN 9780393624595 (pbk.)
Subjects: LCSH: Comparative politics—Case studies.
Classification: LCC JF51 .O538 2018 | DDC 320.3—dc23 LC record available at
https://lccn.loc.gov/2017046475

W. W. Norton & Company, Inc., 500 Fifth Avenue, New York, NY 10110-0017
wwnorton.com

W. W. Norton & Company Ltd., Castle House, 15 Carlisle Street, London W1D 3BS

3 4 5 6 7 8 9 0

BRIEF CONTENTS

CONTENTS

4.   FRANCE   150

7.   RUSSIA   336

11. MEXICO 560

12. BRAZIL   620

ABOUT THE AUTHORS

PATRICK H. O'NEIL is Distinguished Professor of Politics and Government at the University of Puget Sound in Tacoma, Washington. He received his Ph.D. in political science from Indiana University. Professor O'Neil's teaching and research interests are in the areas of authoritarianism and democratization. His past research focused on Eastern Europe, and his current research deals with the Middle East, particularly Iran. His publications include the books *Revolution from Within: The Hungarian Socialist Workers' Party and the Collapse of Communism* and *Communicating Democracy: The Media and Political Transitions* (editor).

KARL FIELDS is Distinguished Professor of Politics and Government and former Director of Asian Studies at the University of Puget Sound in Tacoma, Washington. He has a Ph.D. in political science from the University of California, Berkeley. Professor Fields' teaching and research interests focus on various topics of East Asian political economy, including government-business relations, economic reform, and regional integration. His publications include *Enterprise and the State in Korea and Taiwan.*

DON SHARE is Professor Emeritus of Politics and Government at the University of Puget Sound in Tacoma, Washington. He has a Ph.D. in political science from Stanford University. He has taught comparative politics and Latin American politics, and has published widely on democratization and Spanish politics. His published books include *The Making of Spanish Democracy* and *Dilemmas of Social Democracy.*

PREFACE

Cases in Comparative Politics can be traced to an ongoing experiment undertaken by the three comparative political scientists in the Department of Politics and Government at the University of Puget Sound. Over the years the three of us spent much time discussing the challenges of teaching our introductory course in comparative politics. In those discussions we came to realize that each of us taught the course so differently that students completing our different sections of the course did not really share a common conceptual vocabulary. Over several years we fashioned a unified curriculum for Introduction to Comparative Politics, drawing on the strengths of each of our particular approaches.

All three of us now equip our students with a common conceptual vocabulary. All of our students now learn about states, nations, and different models of political economy. All students learn the basics about nondemocratic and democratic regimes, and they become familiar with characteristics of communist systems and advanced democracies. In developing our curriculum, we became frustrated trying to find cases that were concise, sophisticated, and written to address the major concepts introduced in Patrick H. O'Neil's textbook *Essentials of Comparative Politics*. Thus, we initially coauthored six cases adhering to a set of criteria:

- Each case is concise, making it possible to assign an entire case, or even two cases, for a single class session.
- All cases include discussion of major geographic and demographic features, themes in the historical development of the state, political regimes (including the constitution, branches of government, the electoral system, and local government), political conflict and competition (including the party system and civil society), society, political economy, and current issues. This uniform structure allowed us to assign specific sections from two or more cases simultaneously.
- The cases follow the general framework of *Essentials of Comparative Politics*, but can also be used in conjunction with other texts.

After the publication of the initial six cases (the United Kingdom, Japan, China, Russia, Mexico, and South Africa), we received positive feedback from teachers of comparative politics. Drawing on their comments and suggestions, we wrote new cases to accommodate individual preferences and give instructors more choice. We subsequently added cases on Brazil, France, India, Iran, the United States, and Nigeria. Based on feedback from instructors, the third edition added Germany, bringing the total number of cases to thirteen.

Selecting only thirteen cases is, of course, fraught with drawbacks. Nevertheless, we believe that this collection represents countries that are both important in their own right and representative of a broad range of political systems. Each of the thirteen cases has special importance in the context of the study of comparative politics. Five of our cases (France, Germany, Japan, the United States, and the United Kingdom) are advanced industrial democracies, but they represent a wide range of institutions, societies, political-economic models, and relationships with the world. Japan is an important instance of a non-Western industrialized democracy and an instructive case of democratization imposed by foreign occupiers. Though the United Kingdom and the United States have been known for political stability, France and Germany have fascinating histories of political turmoil and regime change.

Two of our cases, China and Russia, share a past of Marxist-Leninist totalitarianism. Communism thrived in these two large and culturally distinct nations. Both suffered from the dangerous concentration of power in the hands of communist parties and, at times, despotic leaders. The Soviet Communist regime imploded and led to a troubled transition to an authoritarian regime with a capitalist political economy. China has retained its communist authoritarian political system but has experimented with a remarkable transition to a largely capitalist political economy.

The remaining six cases illustrate the diversity of the developing world. Of the six, India has had the longest history of stable democratic rule, but like most countries in the developing world, it has nevertheless struggled with massive poverty and inequality. The remaining five have experienced various forms of authoritarianism. Brazil and Nigeria endured long periods of military rule. Mexico's history of military rule was ended by an authoritarian political party that ruled for much of the twentieth century through a variety of nonmilitary means. South Africa experienced decades of racially based authoritarianism that excluded the vast majority of its population. Iran experienced a modernizing authoritarian monarchy followed by its current authoritarian regime, a theocracy ruled by Islamic clerics.

In this sixth edition we have extensively rewritten and updated each chapter, and we are proud to feature up-to-date photographs and political cartoons, and an all-new comparative data chart at the front of the book.

In writing the cases we have incurred numerous debts. First, and foremost, we wish to thank our wonderful colleagues in the Department of Politics and Government at the University of Puget Sound. By encouraging us to develop a common curriculum for our Introduction to Comparative Politics offering, and by allowing us to team-teach the course in different combinations, they allowed us to learn from each other. These cases are much stronger as a result. The university has also been extremely supportive in recognizing that writing for the classroom is as valuable as writing scholarly publications, and in providing course releases and summer stipends toward that end. Student assistants Brett Venn, Jess Box, Liz Kaster, and Céad Nardi-Warner proved extremely helpful in conducting research for our various cases; Irene Lim has, as always, supported us with her amazing technical and organizational skills. Our colleagues Bill Haltom, Robin Jacobsen, and David Sousa provided very helpful input throughout the project.

We very much appreciate the many helpful comments we have received from fellow instructors of comparative politics and area experts, including Emily Acevedo (California State University, Los Angeles), Josephine Andrews (University of California, Davis), Jason Arnold (Virginia Commonwealth University), Alex Avila (Mesa Community College), Gregory Baldi (Western Illinois University), Caroline Beer (University of Vermont), Marni Berg (Colorado State University), Prosper Bernard Jr. (College of Staten Island), Jeremy Busacca (Whittier College), Anthony Butler (University of Cape Town), Roderic Camp (Claremont McKenna College), Robert Compton (SUNY Oneonta), Isabelle Côté (Memorial University of Newfoundland), Lukas K. Danner (Florida International University), Bruce Dickson (George Washington University), Emily Edmonds-Poli (University of San Diego), Kenly Fenio (Virginia Tech), John Gaffney (Aston Centre for Europe), Sumit Ganguly (Indiana University), Sarah Goodman (University of California at Irvine), Ivy Hamerly (Baylor University), Rongbin Han (University of Georgia), Holley Hansen (Oklahoma State University), Cole Harvey (University of North Carolina, Chapel Hill), William Heller (Binghamton University), Yoshiko Herrera (University of Wisconsin at Madison), Robert Jackson (University of Redlands), Maiah Jaskoski (Northern Arizona University), John Jaworsky (University of Waterloo), Arang Keshavarzian (New York University), Peter Kingstone (King's College), Tamara Kotar (University of Ottawa), Brian Kupfer (Tallahassee Community College), Ahmet Kuru (San Diego State University), Ricardo Larémont (Binghamton University), Jeffrey Lewis (Cleveland State University), Peter H. Loedel (West Chester University), Mary Malone (University of New Hampshire), Pamela Martin (Coastal Carolina University), Rahsaan Maxwell (University of North Carolina, Chapel Hill),

Mark Milewicz (Gordon College), Michael Mitchell (Arizona State Univerity), Christopher Muste (University of Montana), John Occhipinti (Canisius College), Omobolaji Olarinmoye (Hamilton College), Anthony O'Regan (Los Angeles Valley College), T. J. Pempel (University of California, Berkeley), Paul Rousseau (University of Windsor), Steve Sharp (Utah State University, Logan), Jennifer Smith (University of Wisconsin, Milwaukee), Aaron Stuvland (George Mason University), Emmanuel J. Teitelbaum (George Washington University), John Tirman (Massachusetts Institute of Technology), Hubert Tworzecki (Emory University), José Vadi (Cal Poly, Pomona), Sydney Van Morgan (Cornell University), Steven Vogel (University of California, Berkeley), Stacey Philbrick Yadav (Hobart & William Smith Colleges), and Lyubov Zhyznomirska (Saint Mary's University).

Many thanks to all the folks at Norton—Peter Lesser, Ann Shin, Roby Harrington, Aaron Javsicas, and Jake Schindel among others—who have contributed to the success of this project over many years. For this sixth edition we want to give our special thanks for the extraordinary hard work and attention to detail of Samantha Held. Finally, we thank our students at the University of Puget Sound who inspired us to write these cases and provided valuable feedback throughout the entire process.

Don Share
Karl Fields
Patrick H. O'Neil
Tacoma, WA 2017

A note about the data: The data that are presented throughout the text in numerous tables, charts, and other figures are drawn from the *CIA World Factbook* unless otherwise noted.

	UNITED KINGDOM	UNITED STATES	FRANCE	GERMANY	JAPAN	RUSSIA
Geographic Size Ranking	80	3	43	63	62	1
Population Size Ranking	22	3	21	18	10	9
GDP per Capita at PPP, $	$42,600	$57,500	$41,500	$48,700	$41,500	$23,200
GDP per Capita at PPP, Ranking (Estimated)	38	20	39	30	43	71
UN Human Development Index Ranking	16	10	21	4	17	49
Freedom House Rating	Free	Free	Free	Free	Free	Not free
Transparency International Corruption Score Ranking	10	18	23	10	20	131
Capital City	London	Washington, D.C.	Paris	Berlin	Tokyo	Moscow
Head of State	Queen Elizabeth II	Donald Trump	Emmanuel Macron	Joachim Gauck	Akihito	Vladimir Putin
Head of Government	Theresa May	Donald Trump	Édouard Philippe	Angela Merkel	Shinzō Abe	Dimitri Medvedev
Legislative-executive System	Parliamentary	Presidential	Semi-Presidential	Parliamentary	Parliamentary	Semi-Presidential
Unitary or Federal?	Unitary	Federal	Unitary	Federal	Unitary	Federal
Electoral System for Lower House of Legislature	Single-member districts with plurality	Single-member districts with plurality	Single-member districts with two rounds of voting	Mixed proportional representation and single-member districts with plurality	Mixed proportional representation and single-member districts with plurality	Proportional representation
Political-economic System	Liberal	Liberal	Social democratic	Social democratic	Mercantilist	Mercantilist

CHINA	INDIA	IRAN	MEXICO	BRAZIL	SOUTH AFRICA	NIGERIA
4	7	18	14	5	25	32
1	2	16	11	5	25	7
$15,500	$6,600	$17,000	$17,900	$15,100	$13,200	$5,900
111	157	91	89	110	117	162
90	131	69	77	79	119	152
Not free	Free	Not free	Partly free	Free	Free	Partly free
79	79	131	123	79	64	136
Beijing	New Delhi	Tehran	Mexico City	Brasília	Pretoria, Cape Town, Bloemfontein	Abuja
Xi Jinping	Ram Nath Kovind	Ali Khamenei	Enrique Peña Nieto	Michel Temer	Jacob Zuma	Muhammadu Buhari
Li Keqiang	Narendra Modi	Hassan Rouhani	Enrique Peña Nieto	Michel Temer	Jacob Zuma	Muhammadu Buhari
Communist Party authoritarian regime	Parliamentary	Semi-presidential theocracy	Presidential	Presidential	Parliamentary	Presidential
Unitary	Federal	Unitary	Federal	Federal	Unitary	Federal
Not applicable	Single-member districts with plurality	Single- and multimember districts	Mixed proportional representation and single-member districts with plurality	Proportional representation	Proportional representation	Single-member districts with plurality
Mercantilist	Liberal	Mercantilist	Liberal	Liberal	Liberal	Liberal

CASES IN
COMPARATIVE
POLITICS

SIXTH EDITION

1

Light emissions from North and South Korea. Whereas South Korea has experienced democratization and development over the past fifty years, North Korea remains a much poorer, communist state. What can comparative politics tell us about the different trajectories of North and South Korea?

INTRODUCTION

What Is Comparative Politics?

Comparative politics is the study and comparison of politics across countries. Studying politics in this way helps us examine major questions of political science: For example, why do some countries have democratic regimes whereas others experience authoritarianism? Why and how do regimes change? Why do some countries experience affluence and growth, but others endure poverty and decline? In this volume, we describe and analyze the political systems of 13 countries. We focus on their major geographic and demographic features; the origins and development of their state; and their political regimes, patterns of political conflict and competition, societies, political economies, and relationships with the world. This brief introduction seeks to familiarize students with the very basic vocabulary of comparative politics. The concepts and terms described here will be extremely useful in an examination of any of the country cases contained in this book. Moreover, this vocabulary is an essential tool for making comparisons *among* the cases.

Comparing States

States are organizations that maintain a monopoly of violence over a territory. The term *state* can be confusing because it sometimes refers to a subnational government (for example, any of the 50 states in the United States). Political scientists, however, use *state* to refer to a national organization. In this book, *state* is used in the latter, broader sense. Still, the concept of state is narrower than the notion of country, which encompasses the territory and people living within a state. As illustrated by our collection of cases, states can differ in many ways, including in origin, length of existence, strength, and historical development.[1] Political

MAP OF THE WORLD

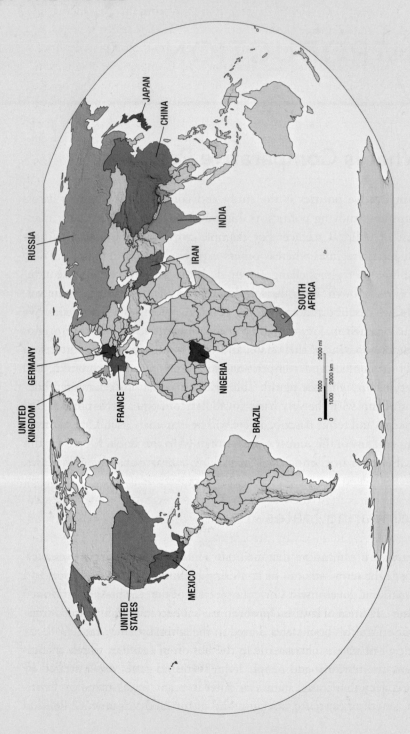

JAPAN

CHINA

INDIA

RUSSIA

IRAN

SOUTH
AFRICA

GERMANY

NIGERIA

UNITED
KINGDOM

FRANCE

BRAZIL

UNITED
STATES

MEXICO

2000 mi

1000   2000 km

0

1000

0

scientists also distinguish between the state and the **government**, considering the government to be the leadership or elite that administers the state.

Two of the most obvious differences among states are their size and population (see "In Comparison: Total Land Size" and "In Comparison: Population," pp. 6 and 7). The 13 countries included in this book vary considerably in both respects. States also vary in their natural endowments, such as arable land, mineral resources, navigable rivers, and access to the sea. Well-endowed states may have advantages over poorly endowed ones, but resource endowments do not necessarily determine a state's prosperity. Japan, for example, has become one of the world's dominant economic powers despite having relatively few natural resources. Russia and Iran, in contrast, are rich in natural resources but have struggled economically.

States also differ widely in their origins and historical development.[2] Some countries (for example, China, France, and the United Kingdom) have long histories of statehood. Other political systems, such as Germany, experienced the creation of a unified state only after long periods of division. Many countries in the developing world became states after they were decolonized. Nigeria, for example, became an independent state relatively recently, in 1960. With the end of the Cold War in 1989 and the collapse of the Soviet Union two years later, a number of states emerged or reemerged. At the same time, Germany, which had been divided into two states during the Cold War, became a single state in 1990. It is important to point out that in today's world, we continue to witness both the erosion of existing states (for example, Somalia) and the emergence of new ones, such as the Republic of South Sudan, which was established in 2011.

States differ, too, in their level of organization, effectiveness, and stability. The power of a state depends in part on its **legitimacy**, or the extent to which its authority is regarded as right and proper. Political scientists have long observed that there are different sources of a state's legitimacy. State authority may draw on **traditional legitimacy**, in which the state is obeyed because it has a long tradition of being obeyed. Alternatively, a state may be considered legitimate because of **charismatic legitimacy**—that is, its identification with the magnetic appeal of a leader or movement. Finally, states may gain legitimacy on the basis of **rational-legal legitimacy**, a system of laws and procedures that becomes highly institutionalized. Although most modern states derive their legitimacy from rational-legal sources, both traditional and charismatic legitimacy often continue to play a role. In Japan and the United Kingdom, for example, the monarchy is a source of traditional legitimacy that complements the rational-legal legitimacy of the state. Some postcolonial states in the developing world have had considerable trouble

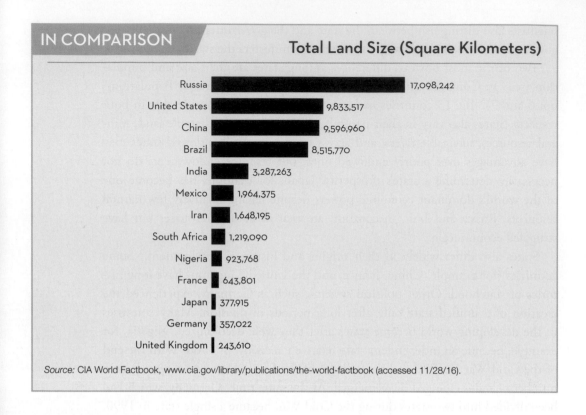

establishing legitimacy. Often colonial powers created states that cut across ethnic boundaries or contain hostile ethnic groups, as in Nigeria and Iran.

States differ in their ability to preserve their sovereignty and carry out the functions of maintaining law and order. **Strong states** can perform the tasks of defending their borders from outside attacks and defending their authority from internal nonstate rivals. **Weak states** have trouble carrying out those basic tasks and often suffer from endemic internal violence, poor infrastructure, and the inability to collect taxes and enforce the rule of law. High levels of corruption are often a symptom of state weakness. Taken to an extreme, weak states may experience a complete loss of legitimacy and power and may be overwhelmed by anarchy and violence. Political scientists refer to those relatively rare cases as **failed states**.[3]

Finally, states differ in the degree to which they centralize or disperse political power. **Unitary states** concentrate most of their political power in the national capital, allocating little decision-making power to regions or localities. **Federal states** divide power between the central state and regional or local

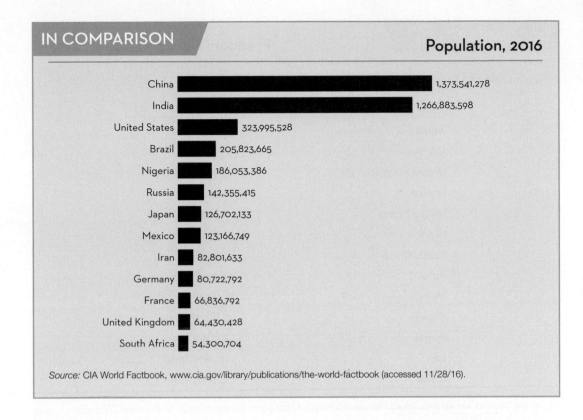

China	1,373,541,278
India	1,266,883,598
United States	323,995,528
Brazil	205,823,665
Nigeria	186,053,386
Russia	142,355,415
Japan	126,702,133
Mexico	123,166,749
Iran	82,801,633
Germany	80,722,792
France	66,836,792
United Kingdom	64,430,428
South Africa	54,300,704

Source: CIA World Factbook, www.cia.gov/library/publications/the-world-factbook (accessed 11/28/16).

authorities (such as provinces, counties, and cities). Unitary states, such as the United Kingdom and South Africa, may be stronger and more decisive than federal states, but the centralization of power may create local resentment and initiate calls for a **devolution** (handing down) of power to regions and localities. Federal states, such as India, Brazil, Germany, Mexico, Nigeria, Russia, and the United States, often find that their dispersal of power hampers national decision making and accountability, and can even increase corruption by giving local officials greater access to resources.

Comparing Regimes

Political regimes are the norms and rules regarding individual freedoms and collective equality, the locus of power, and the use of that power. It is easiest to think of political regimes as the rules of the game governing the exercise of power. In

Freedom House Rankings, 2017

On a scale of 1 to 100, with 100 representing the most free.

COUNTRY	RANKING
Japan	96 (Free)
Germany	95 (Free)
United Kingdom	95 (Free)
France	90 (Free)
United States	89 (Free)
Brazil	79 (Free)
South Africa	78 (Free)
India	77 (Free)
Mexico	65 (Partly Free)
Nigeria	50 (Partly Free)
Russia	20 (Not Free)
Iran	17 (Not Free)
China	15 (Not Free)

Source: Freedom House, https://freedomhouse.org/report/freedom-world/freedom-world-2017 (accessed 7/21/17).

modern political systems, regimes are most often described in written constitutions. In some countries, however, such as the United Kingdom, the regime consists of a combination of laws and customs that are not incorporated into any one written document. In other countries, such as China and Iran, written constitutions do not accurately describe the extra-constitutional rules that govern the exercise of power.

Democratic regimes have rules that emphasize a large role for the public in governance, protect basic rights and freedoms, and attempt to ensure basic transparency of and accountability for government actions. **Authoritarian regimes** limit the role of the public in decision making, often deny citizens' basic rights, and restrict their freedoms. In the past quarter century, the world has witnessed a dramatic rise in the number of democratic regimes.[4] Over half the world's population, however, is still governed by regimes defined as "partly free," or illiberal (meaning that some personal liberties and democratic rights are limited while others are protected), or "not free," or authoritarian (meaning that the public has very little individual freedom).[5] Freedom House, a U.S. research organization, regularly measures the amount of freedom in different political systems, and the "In Comparison: Freedom House Rankings, 2017" table on p. 8 provides those measures for the cases included in this volume.

COMPARING DEMOCRATIC POLITICAL INSTITUTIONS

Most political regimes, whether democratic or not, establish a number of political institutions. Students of comparative politics must learn to identify and distinguish these institutions precisely. The **executive** is the branch of government that carries out the laws and policies of a given state. We can think of the executive branch as performing two separate sets of duties. On the one hand, the **head of state** symbolizes and represents the people, both nationally and internationally, embodying and articulating the goals of the regime. On the other hand, the **head of government** deals with the everyday tasks of running the state, such as formulating and executing policy. The distinction between those roles is most easily seen in, for example, France, Germany, India, Japan, and the United Kingdom, which have separate heads of state and heads of government. Other regimes, such as those of Brazil, Mexico, Nigeria, South Africa, and the United States, assign the two roles of the executive branch to a single individual.

The **legislature** is the branch of government formally charged with making laws. The organization and power of legislatures differ considerably from country to country. In some political regimes, especially authoritarian ones such as China and Russia, the legislature has little power or initiative and serves mainly to rubber-stamp government legislation. In other systems, such as those of Germany and India, the legislature is relatively powerful and autonomous. **Unicameral legislatures** (often found in smaller countries) consist of a single chamber; **bicameral legislatures** consist of two legislative chambers. In the latter systems, one chamber often represents the population at large and is referred to as the **lower house**, and the other chamber (referred to as the **upper house**) reflects the geographical subunits.

The **judiciary** is the branch of a country's government that is concerned with dispensing justice. The **constitutional court** is the highest judicial body to rule on the constitutionality of laws and other government actions; in most political systems, the constitutional court also formally oversees the entire judicial structure. The power of a regime's judiciary is determined in part by the nature of its power of **judicial review**, the mechanism by which the court reviews laws and policies and overturns those seen as violations of the constitution. Some regimes give the judiciary the power of **concrete review**, allowing the high court to rule on constitutional issues only when disputes are brought before it. Other regimes give the judiciary the power of **abstract review**, allowing it to decide questions that do not arise from legal cases, sometimes even allowing it to make judgments on legislation that has not yet been enacted. In France, the Constitutional Council has the power of abstract review, whereas in the United States the Supreme Court has the power of concrete review. The highest courts in the United Kingdom, by contrast, do not have the power to overturn legislation passed by the national legislature under any circumstances.

The powers of these political institutions and the relationships among them vary considerably across regimes. The most important variation concerns the relationship between the legislature and the executive. There are three major models of **legislative–executive relations** within democratic regimes: parliamentary, presidential, and semi-presidential. The **parliamentary system** (seen among our cases in Germany, India, Japan, and the United Kingdom) features an executive head of government (often referred to as a prime minister) who is usually elected from within the legislature. The prime minister is usually the leader of the largest political party in the legislature. The prime minister and the **cabinet** (the body of chief ministers or officials in government in charge of such policy areas as defense, agriculture, and so on) are charged with formulating and executing policy. The head of state in such systems has largely ceremonial duties and is usually either an indirectly elected president or a hereditary monarch.

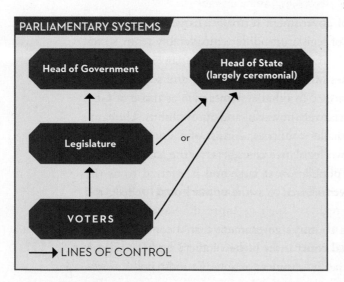

The **presidential system**, used by Brazil, Mexico, and the United States, combines the roles of head of state and head of government in the office of the president. These systems feature a directly elected president who holds most of the government's executive powers. Presidential systems have directly elected legislatures that to varying degrees serve as a check on presidential authority.

Scholars debate the advantages and disadvantages of these legislative–executive models.[6] Parliamentary systems are often praised for reducing conflict between the legislature and the executive (since the executive is approved by the legislature), thus producing more efficient government. In addition, when parliamentary legislatures lack a majority, political parties must compromise to create a government supported by a majority of the legislature. Parliamentary systems are also more flexible than presidential systems because when prime ministers lose the support of the legislature, they can be swiftly removed through a legislative **vote of no confidence**. Coalition governments are often formed as a result of negotiations and compromise between political parties. The appointment of a new prime minister, or the convocation of new elections, can often resolve political deadlocks. But critics point out that parliamentary systems with a strong majority in the legislature can produce a very dominant, virtually unchecked government. Moreover, in fractious legislatures, it can be difficult to cobble together a stable majority government, and coalitions, when they result, can be unstable.

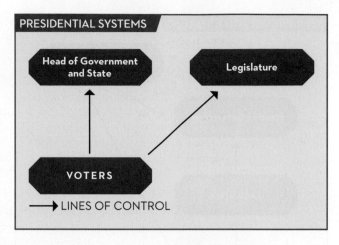

Presidential systems are often portrayed as more stable than parliamentary systems. There are fixed terms of office for the president and the legislature, which is not the case in most parliamentary systems. Moreover, presidents are directly elected by the public and can be removed only by the legislature and only in cases of criminal misconduct. Nonetheless, presidential systems have been criticized for producing divisive winner-take-all outcomes, lacking the flexibility needed to confront crises, and leading to overly powerful executives in the face of weak and divided legislatures.[7] Also, presidential systems can experience gridlock when the presidency and legislature are controlled by different parties.

In an attempt to avoid the weaknesses of parliamentary and presidential systems, some newer democratic regimes, such as those of France and Russia, have adopted a third model of legislative–executive relations, called the **semi-presidential system**. This system includes a prime minister approved by the legislature and a directly elected president, both of whom share executive power.

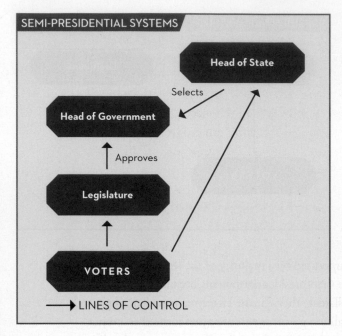

SEMI-PRESIDENTIAL SYSTEMS

Head of State

Selects

Head of Government

Approves

Legislature

VOTERS

→ LINES OF CONTROL

In practice, semi-presidential systems tend to produce strong presidents akin to those in pure presidential systems, but the exact balance between the executives varies from case to case.

Another influential political institution is the **electoral system**, which determines how votes are cast and counted. Most democratic regimes use one of two models. The most commonly employed is **proportional representation (PR)**. Among our 13 cases, Brazil and South Africa employ this system. The PR model relies upon **multi-member districts (MMDs)**, in which more than one legislative seat is contested in each electoral district. Voters cast their ballots for a list of party candidates rather than for a single representative, and the percentage of votes a party receives in a district determines how many of that district's seats the party will win. Thus, the percentage of votes each party wins in each district should closely correspond to the percentage of seats allocated to each party. PR systems produce legislatures that often closely reflect the percentage of votes won nationwide by each political party. As a result, they tend to foster multiple political parties, including small ones.

A minority of the world's democracies (mainly France, the United Kingdom, and the former British colonies such as India, Nigeria, and the United States, among the cases in this volume) rely upon **single-member districts (SMDs)**. In these systems, there is only one representative for each constituency, and in each district the candidate with the greatest number of votes (not necessarily a majority) wins the seat. Unlike PR systems, in SMD systems the votes cast for all but the sole winning candidate are, in effect, wasted because they do not count toward any representation in the legislature. SMD systems tend to discriminate against small parties, especially those with a national following rather than a geographically concentrated following.

As with the legislative–executive models, there is vigorous debate about which electoral system is most desirable.[8] PR systems are considered more democratic, since they waste fewer votes and encourage the expression of a wider range of political interests. The PR model increases the number of parties able to win seats in a legislature and allows parties concerned with narrow or minority interests to gain representation. SMD systems are often endorsed because they allow voters in each district to connect directly with their elected representatives instead of their party, making the representatives more accountable to the electorate. Supporters of SMD systems argue that they are beneficial for eliminating narrowly based or extremist parties from the legislature. They view SMD systems as more likely to produce stable, centrist legislative majorities.

Some countries, including Germany, Japan, Russia, and Mexico, have combined SMD and PR voting systems in what is known as a **mixed electoral system**. Voters are given two votes, one for a candidate and the other for a party. Candidates in the SMDs are elected on the basis of a plurality; other seats are elected from MMDs and are allocated using PR.

Much of the diversity of comparative politics is the result of different combinations of the political institutions just described (see "Combinations of Political Institutions," p. 14). Even among the 10 democratic regimes studied in this volume, different combinations of political institutions result in considerable diversity. For example, Germany and the United States are federal states, but the United States has a presidential legislative–executive system, while Germany uses a parliamentary system. Germany and the United Kingdom both use parliamentary legislative–executive systems, but their electoral systems differ.

COMPARING NONDEMOCRATIC REGIMES

Many nondemocratic regimes have institutions that on paper appear quite similar to those in democratic regimes. In most authoritarian regimes, however, a study of the legislature, the judiciary, and the electoral system may not reveal much about the exercise of political power.

Nondemocratic regimes differ from one another in a number of important ways. Common forms of nondemocratic regimes include personal dictatorships, monarchies, military regimes, one-party regimes, theocracies, and illiberal regimes. A **personal dictatorship**, such as that of Porfirio Díaz in Mexico (1876–1910), or Vladimir Putin in Russia, is based on the power of a single strong leader who usually relies on charismatic or traditional authority to maintain power. In a **military regime** (such as Brazil from 1964 to 1985 or Nigeria from 1966 to 1979), the institution of the military dominates politics. A **one-party regime** (such as that

Combinations of Political Institutions

COUNTRY	TYPE OF REGIME	TYPE OF STATE	LEGISLATIVE-EXECUTIVE SYSTEM	ELECTORAL SYSTEM
Brazil	Democratic	Federal	Presidential	PR
China	Authoritarian	Unitary	N/A	N/A
France	Democratic	Unitary	Semi-presidential	SMD
Germany	Democratic	Federal	Parliamentary	Mixed
India	Democratic	Federal	Parliamentary	SMD
Iran	Authoritarian	Unitary	N/A	Mixed
Japan	Democratic	Unitary	Parliamentary	Mixed
Mexico	Democratic	Federal	Presidential	Mixed
Nigeria	Democratic	Federal	Presidential	SMD
Russia	Authoritarian	Federal	Semi-presidential	PR
South Africa	Democratic	Unitary	Parliamentary	PR
United Kingdom	Democratic	Unitary	Parliamentary	SMD
United States	Democratic	Federal	Presidential	SMD

in Mexico from 1917 to 2000) is dominated by a strong political party that relies upon a broad membership as a source of political control. In a **theocracy**, a rare form of government (though one that best characterizes present-day Iran), a leader claims to rule on behalf of God. An **illiberal regime**, such as in Nigeria, retains the basic structures of a democracy but does not protect civil liberties. In the real world, many nondemocratic regimes combine various aspects of these forms.

Communist regimes are one-party regimes in which a Communist party controls most aspects of a country's political and economic system. Specific

Communist regimes (such as China under Mao Zedong or the Soviet Union under Joseph Stalin) have sometimes been described as **totalitarian**. Totalitarian regimes feature a strong official ideology that seeks to transform fundamental aspects of the state, society, and economy, using a wide array of organizations and the application of force. As the case of Nazi Germany illustrates, totalitarian regimes need not be communist.

Nondemocratic regimes use various tools to enforce their political domination. The most obvious mechanisms are state violence and surveillance. The enforcement ranges from systematic and widespread repression (for example, the mass purges in the Soviet Union or contemporary Iran) to sporadic and selective repression of the regime's opponents (as in Brazil during the 1960s). Another important tool of nondemocratic regimes is **co-optation**, whereby members of the public are brought into a beneficial relationship with the state and the government. Co-optation takes many forms, including **corporatism**, in which citizen participation is channeled into state-sanctioned groups; **clientelism**, in which the state provides benefits to numerous political supporters; or patrimonialism, where benefits are dispersed among a more narrow group of ruling elites. These forms of co-optation typically rely on **rent seeking**, in which the government allows its supporters to occupy positions of power in order to monopolize state benefits. The nondemocratic regime that dominated Mexico for much of the twentieth century skillfully employed all these forms of co-optation to garner public support for the governing party, minimizing its need to rely upon coercion. Finally, an additional mechanism of control that is most often employed in totalitarian regimes is the **personality cult**, or the state-sponsored exaltation of a leader. The personality cult of Stalin in the Soviet Union and that of Mao in China are prime examples, as is the cult of personality that developed around Ayatollah Ruhollah Khomeini, the leader of the 1979 Iranian Revolution. Vladimir Putin in Russia has also attempted to consolidate control with elements of a personality cult.

Comparing Political Conflict and Competition

Political scientists can compare and contrast patterns of political conflict and competition in both democratic and authoritarian regimes. In democratic regimes, for example, it is common to compare the nature of elections and other forms of competition among political parties (often referred to as the **party system**).

On the most basic level, political scientists can compare the nature of **suffrage**, or the right to vote. In democratic regimes and even in many nondemocratic ones,

IN COMPARISON

Comparative Voter Turnout for Legislative Elections

COUNTRY	PERCENTAGE
Brazil (2014)	80
South Africa (2014)	74
Germany (2013)	72
India (2014)	66
United Kingdom (2015)	66
Iran (2016)	60
France (2012)	55
Japan (2014)	53
Russia (2016)	48
Mexico (2015)	47
United States (2014)	43
Nigeria (2015)	43
China	N/A

Source: International Institute for Democracy and Electoral Assistance, www.idea.int (accessed 11/28/16).

such as China and Iran, that right is often guaranteed to most adult citizens.[9] Another important feature of elections is the degree to which citizens actually participate by voting and by engaging in campaign activities (see "In Comparison: Comparative Voter Turnout for Legislative Elections"). Party systems also can be compared on the basis of the number of parties, the size of their membership, their organizational strength, their ideological orientation, and their electoral strategies.

A comparative analysis of political conflict and competition cannot focus solely on elections, though. In most political systems, much political conflict and competition takes place in **civil society**, which comprises the organizations outside the state that help people define and advance their own interests. In addition to political parties, the organizations that make up a country's civil society often include a host of groups as diverse as gun clubs and labor unions. Many scholars believe that these autonomous societal groups are vital to the health of democratic regimes.[10]

Ethnic and Religious Diversity

COUNTRY	LARGEST ETHNIC GROUP (%)	LARGEST RELIGIOUS GROUP (%)
Brazil	48	65
China	92	18
France*	N/A	66
Germany	92	29
India	72	80
Iran	61	99
Japan	99	79
Mexico*	N/A	83
Nigeria	29	50
Russia	78	20
South Africa	80	37
United Kingdom	87	60
United States	62	47

*Mexico and France do not collect data on ethnicity.

Source: CIA World Factbook, www.cia.gov/library/publications/the-world-factbook (accessed 11/28/16); U.S. Census Bureau Quickfacts, www.census.gov/quickfacts (accessed 2/7/17).

Comparing Societies

The state and the regime exist in the context of their society, and societies differ from one another in ways that can strongly influence politics. For example, ethnic divisions exist within many states. **Ethnicity** refers to the specific attributes that make one group of people culturally different from others—customs, language, religion, geographical region, history, and so on. Some states, such as China, Germany, Japan, and Russia, are relatively homogeneous: one ethnic group makes up a large portion of the society. At the other extreme, countries such as India, Iran, Mexico, Nigeria, and South Africa have a great deal of ethnic diversity. Ethnic diversity can often be a source of political conflict, and even in relatively homogeneous societies the presence of ethnic minorities can pose political challenges.[11]

Societies also differ in terms of their political cultures. **Political culture** can be defined as the patterns of basic norms relating to politics. Political scientists have learned a great deal about how political cultures differ in a variety of areas, including citizens' trust in government, respect for political authority, knowledge about politics, and assessment of their political efficacy (the ability to influence political outcomes).[12]

Political scientists also consider **national identity**, or the extent to which citizens of a country are bound together by a common set of political aspirations (most often self-government and sovereignty). Countries with a long history as consolidated states often have higher levels of national identity than do states with a shorter history. Political scientists use the term **nationalism** to refer to pride in one's people and the belief that they share a common political identity. Individuals who believe they have a common political destiny, or **nationalists**, often seek the creation of a new state for individuals sharing that identity. Scottish nationalists, who seek an independent Scottish state, or Tibetan nationalists, who want Tibet to be independent from China, are excellent examples of nationalism in contemporary politics.

One interesting difference among societies is in the importance they place on religion. In most societies, religiosity has declined with economic prosperity and with the growth of secular (nonreligious) values. France, Japan, Russia, and the United Kingdom are relatively secular societies in which most people do not view religion as an important part of their lives beyond a cultural identity; the United States continues to be an interesting exception in this regard. In Nigeria and Iran, nearly all citizens view religion as important.

Individuals and groups within a society can also be distinguished according to their political attitudes and ideologies. **Political attitudes** describe views regarding the status quo in a society—specifically, the desired pace and methods of political change. **Radical attitudes** support rapid, extensive, and often revolutionary change. **Liberal attitudes** promote evolutionary change within the system. **Conservative attitudes** support the status quo and view change as risky. **Reactionary attitudes** promote rapid change to restore political, social, and economic institutions that once existed. Since political attitudes are views of the status quo, radicals, liberals, conservatives, and reactionaries differ according to their setting. A reactionary in Iran, for example, might support the restoration of the monarchy overthrown in 1979; a reactionary in Germany might desire a return to Nazism; and a reactionary in China might call for a return to Maoist communism.

Whereas political attitudes are particular and context-specific, **political ideologies** are universal sets of political values regarding the fundamental goals of politics.[13] A political ideology prescribes an ideal balance between freedom and equality. The ideology of **liberalism** (as opposed to a liberal political attitude)

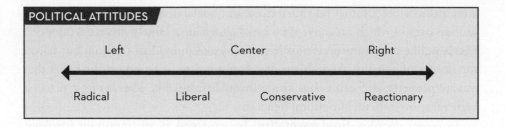

Left   Center   Right

Radical   Liberal   Conservative   Reactionary

places a high priority on individual political and economic freedoms, favoring them over any attempts to create economic equality. Private **property**, capitalism, and protections for the individual against the state are central to liberal ideology. In the United States, such views tend to be called "libertarian," though increasingly Americans are using the term in the same manner as found elsewhere around the world. **Communism**, in contrast, emphasizes economic equality rather than individual political and economic freedoms. Collective property (state ownership) and a dominant state are cornerstones of communism. **Social democracy** (often referred to as democratic socialism) is in some ways a hybrid of liberalism and communism in that it places considerable value on equality but

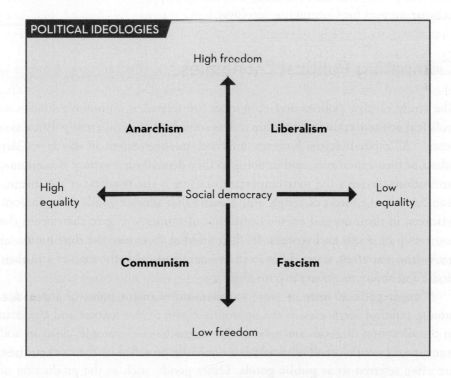

POLITICAL IDEOLOGIES

High freedom

Anarchism   Liberalism

High
equality   Social democracy   Low
equality

Communism   Fascism

Low freedom

attempts to protect some individual freedoms. Social democrats advocate a mixed welfare state in which an active state exists alongside a largely private economy.[14] **Fascism**, like communism, is hostile to the idea of individual freedom but rejects the notion of equality. **Anarchism**, like communism, is based on the belief that private property and capitalism create inequality, but like liberalism, it places a high value on individual political freedom.

In recent decades, **fundamentalism** has emerged as an important ideology. It differs from the five ideologies just mentioned in that it seeks to unite religion with the state and to make faith the sovereign authority. Fundamentalists thus view some form of theocracy (or rule by clerics) as the way to implement their ideology. Among the cases studied in this text, Iran's political regime is most inspired by fundamentalist ideology, though there are strong fundamentalist movements in India as well.

The strength of each ideology differs across political systems. For example, opinion research demonstrates that citizens in the United States and United Kingdom have a strong commitment to liberal ideology; though this has eroded somewhat of late, evidenced by declining support for democracy. French and Japanese citizens tend to be less individualistic and are more supportive of an active role for the state in the economy. In China, the rise of capitalist economics has eroded popular support for Communist ideology.

Comparing Political Economies

The study of how politics and economics are related is commonly known as **political economy**; this relationship differs considerably in different political systems.[15] All modern states, however, intervene to some extent in the day-to-day affairs of their economies, and in doing so they depend on a variety of economic institutions. Perhaps the most important of these is the **market**, or the interaction between the forces of supply and demand that allocate goods and resources. Markets, in turn, depend on the institution of property, a term that means the ownership of goods and services. In their attempt to ensure the distribution of goods and resources, states differ in their interaction with the market and their desire and ability to protect private property.

A major political issue in most societies, and a major point of contention among political ideologies, is the appropriate role of the market and the state in the allocation of goods and services. Some goods—for example, clean air and water—are essential to all of society but not easily provided by the market; these are often referred to as **public goods**. Other goods, such as the production of food and automobiles, are more feasibly provided by private producers using the market. Between those extremes is a large gray area. States differ in the degree to which they define a wide array of goods and services as public goods. As a result, government **social expenditures** (state provision of public benefits, such as education, health care, and transportation) vary widely among countries.

In the political-economic systems of countries such as the United States and the United Kingdom, where liberal ideology is dominant, the state plays a significant but smaller role. In France, Germany, and Japan, however, the state has played a much larger role in the economy through state ownership (especially in France) and state direction of the economy (especially in Japan). Authoritarian regimes have typically had a heavy hand in economic matters, as has certainly been the case in Russia, China, and Iran. Whereas China's Communist regime has gradually allowed growth in the private sector, the Iranian Revolution of 1979 led to an increase in that state's involvement in the economy.

Economies also differ markedly in their size, affluence, rates of growth, and levels of equality. The most commonly used tool for comparing the size of economies is the **gross domestic product (GDP)**, the total market value of goods and services produced in a country in one year. GDP is often measured in U.S. dollars at **purchasing power parity (PPP)**, a mechanism that attempts to estimate the real buying power of income in each country using prices in the United States as a benchmark (see "In Comparison: Total GDP at Official Exchange Rates (USD), 2016," p. 22). In overall size of the 13 economies considered in this volume, China and the United States dwarf the other cases. It is sometimes more useful, however, to look at **GDP per capita**, which divides the GDP by total population (see "In Comparison: Total per Capita GDP at Purchasing Power Parity (USD), 2016," p. 23). Because GDP is rarely distributed evenly among the population, the **Gini index** is the most commonly used measure of economic inequality. The index gives perfect equality a score of 0, and perfect inequality a score of 100. Endemic inequality has long been a characteristic of developing countries, such as Brazil, India, Mexico, and South Africa, though some developing countries (like Brazil and India) recently have made progress in reducing inequality. In wealthy countries such as the United States, the economic boom of the 1980s and 1990s led to a growing gap between the rich and the poor and among some populations a declining life expectancy more in keeping with developing countries.

It is also important to compare the GDP growth rate, often expressed as an average of GDP growth over a number of years. Nine of the 13 countries considered in this volume enjoyed economic growth between 1975 and 2005, and China and India grew fastest (see "In Comparison: GDP Growth Rate, 1990–2011," p. 24).

The size and wealth of an economy, and even the distribution of wealth, are not necessarily correlated with the affluence or poverty of its citizens. The United Nations produces a Human Development Index (HDI) that considers various indicators of affluence, including health and education (see "In Comparison: Human Development Index Scores, 2015," p. 25). When considering GDP per capita and the HDI, one sees that the United States, the United Kingdom, Japan, Germany, and France are clearly the most affluent of the countries discussed in this volume. However, since 1980 the developing nations have made the most dramatic improvements in their HDI, with China, Iran, and India leading the way. In the last decade, India and China have seen impressive growth in their HDI (see "In Comparison: Average Annual HDI Growth Rates, 1990–2015," p. 26). Developed countries may see much lower increases simply because their levels of development are already high, though the United States remains a laggard in comparison with countries like Japan and the United Kingdom.

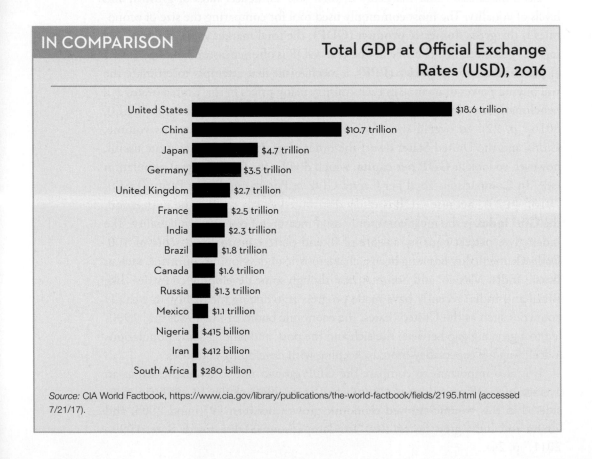

IN COMPARISON

Total GDP at Official Exchange Rates (USD), 2016

Country	GDP
United States	$18.6 trillion
China	$10.7 trillion
Japan	$4.7 trillion
Germany	$3.5 trillion
United Kingdom	$2.7 trillion
France	$2.5 trillion
India	$2.3 trillion
Brazil	$1.8 trillion
Canada	$1.6 trillion
Russia	$1.3 trillion
Mexico	$1.1 trillion
Nigeria	$415 billion
Iran	$412 billion
South Africa	$280 billion

Source: CIA World Factbook, https://www.cia.gov/library/publications/the-world-factbook/fields/2195.html (accessed 7/21/17).

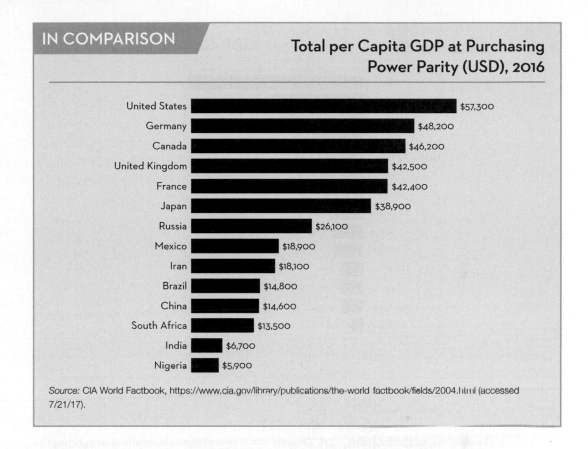

Total per Capita GDP at Purchasing Power Parity (USD), 2016

Country	GDP
United States	$57,300
Germany	$48,200
Canada	$46,200
United Kingdom	$42,500
France	$42,400
Japan	$38,900
Russia	$26,100
Mexico	$18,900
Iran	$18,100
Brazil	$14,800
China	$14,600
South Africa	$13,500
India	$6,700
Nigeria	$5,900

Source: CIA World Factbook, https://www.cia.gov/library/publications/the-world factbook/fields/2004.html (accessed 7/21/17).

Governments often struggle with myriad challenges within their economic systems. One concern is the danger of **inflation**, a situation characterized by sustained rising prices. Extremely high levels of inflation (**hyperinflation**) can endanger economic growth and impoverish citizens who live on a fixed income. Governments also fear the consequences of high levels of unemployment, which can place a large burden on public expenditures and reduce the tax base.

The Global Context

A country's politics is not determined solely by domestic factors. Increasingly, international forces shape politics in the context of a rapidly expanding and intensifying set of links among states, societies, and economies. This phenomenon,

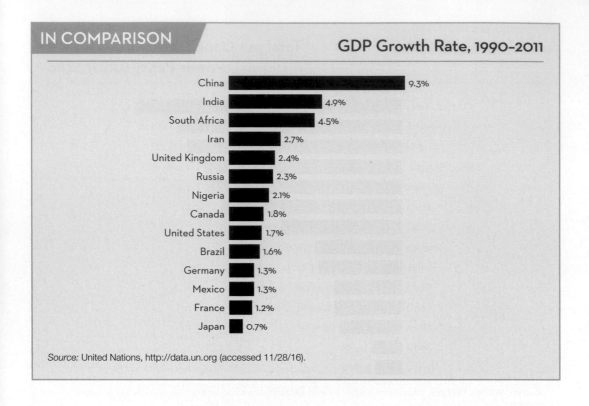

GDP Growth Rate, 1990–2011

China 9.3%
India 4.9%
South Africa 4.5%
Iran 2.7%
United Kingdom 2.4%
Russia 2.3%
Nigeria 2.1%
Canada 1.8%
United States 1.7%
Brazil 1.6%
Germany 1.3%
Mexico 1.3%
France 1.2%
Japan 0.7%

Source: United Nations, http://data.un.org (accessed 11/28/16).

known as **globalization**, has created new opportunities while posing important challenges to states. Cross-border interactions have long existed, but the trend toward globalization has created a far more extensive and intensive web of relationships among many people across vast distances. People are increasingly interacting regularly and directly through sophisticated international networks involving travel, communication, business, and education.

It is too early to predict the consequences of globalization for governments and citizens of states. Some observers have argued that globalization may eclipse the state, resulting in global political institutions, whereas others contend that states will continue to play an important, albeit changed, role.[16] Governments are increasingly restricted by the international system, both because of international trade agreements (such as those promoted by the World Trade Organization) and because of the need to remain competitive in the international marketplace.

As a result of globalization, a host of international organizations regularly affects domestic politics, economics, and society. **Multinational corporations**

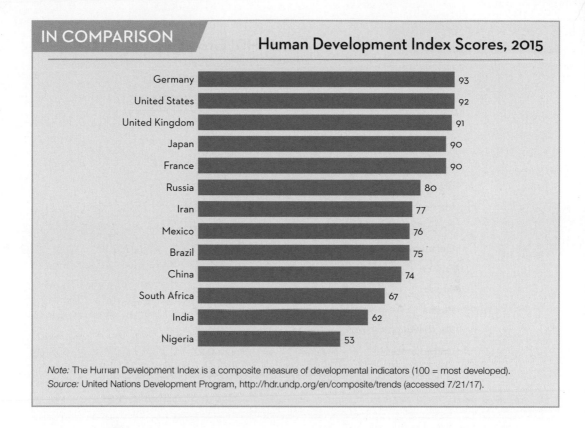

Human Development Index Scores, 2015

Country	Score
Germany	93
United States	92
United Kingdom	91
Japan	90
France	90
Russia	80
Iran	77
Mexico	76
Brazil	75
China	74
South Africa	67
India	62
Nigeria	53

Note: The Human Development Index is a composite measure of developmental indicators (100 = most developed).
Source: United Nations Development Program, http://hdr.undp.org/en/composite/trends (accessed 7/21/17).

(MNCs), firms that produce, distribute, and market goods or services in more than one country, are increasingly powerful. They are an important source of **foreign direct investment**, or the purchase of assets in one country by a foreign firm. An array of **nongovernmental organizations (NGOs)**—Amnesty International and the International Red Cross, for example—are increasingly visible. Also active are **intergovernmental organizations (IGOs)**, which are groups created by states to serve particular policy ends. Some important examples of IGOs are the United Nations, the World Trade Organization, the European Union, the Group of 8 (G8), and the Organization of American States.

A final dimension of globalization, and another example of the growing interconnectedness of states, is the increasing movement of people both within and across borders. Relatively homogeneous societies such as France and the United Kingdom have struggled in recent decades to integrate their growing immigrant populations, while Japan faces a demographic crisis because of its failure

Average Annual HDI Growth Rates, 1990–2015

COUNTRY	AVERAGE ANNUAL HDI GROWTH RATE, 1990–2015
China	1.57
India	1.52
Iran	1.22
Brazil	0.85
Mexico	0.65
United Kingdom	0.64
Germany	0.58
France	0.57
Japan	0.42
Russia	0.37
South Africa	0.28
United States	0.27
Nigeria	N/A

Source: United Nations Development Program, http://hdr.undp.org/en/composite/trends (accessed 7/21/17).

to encourage immigration (an issue explored in the Japan case in this book). The United States has become dependent on immigrant labor from Mexico and elsewhere. China's opening to the world economy has drawn millions of rural citizens to its booming coastal cities. More than ever, states find that the environment of globalization limits the policy options open to their governments.

Globalization presents numerous challenges, but the cases in this volume also suggest that globalization has delivered enormous benefits. After World War II, Germany's integration into the European Union led to peace in a region often characterized by war, and it contributed to the rapid economic growth of Germany and France. After the United Kingdom joined the European Union in 1973, its economy boomed. Japan's spectacular postwar recovery was based on global trade. In China and India, integration into the world economy has lifted millions out of poverty.

Conclusion

This introduction briefly summarized some key concepts and terms used by political scientists to compare political systems. The inquisitive student of comparative politics will find fascinating similarities in the 13 cases that follow. The commonalities across cases give credence to the utility of the comparative enterprise and justify the analytic comparisons offered. But these countries are also diverse and always changing, reminding us of the daunting challenges facing comparative political study.

NOTES

1. For an excellent collection of essays on the state, see Peter B. Evans, Dietrich Rueschemeyer, and Theda Skocpol, eds., *Bringing the State Back In* (Cambridge: Cambridge University Press, 1985).
2. On the origins of the state and forms of authority preceding the state, see Francis Fukuyama, *The Origins of Political Order* (New York: Farrar, Straus and Giroux, 2011).
3. Robert I. Rotberg, "Failed States in a World of Terror," *Foreign Affairs* 81, no. 4 (July/August 2002): 127–40; see also Charles T. Call, "Beyond the 'Failed State': Toward Conceptual Alternatives," *European Journal of International Relations* 17, no. 2 (2011): 303–26.
4. Renske Doorenspleet, "Reassessing the Three Waves of Democratization," *World Politics* 52, no. 3 (April 2000): 384–406.
5. Freedom House issues a yearly report card rating political regimes; see www.freedomhouse.org.
6. See, for example, Alfred Stepan with Cindy Skach, "Constitutional Frameworks and Democratic Consolidation: Parliamentarism versus Presidentialism," *World Politics* 46, no. 1 (January 1993): 1–22.
7. Juan J. Linz and Arturo Valenzuela, eds., *The Failures of Presidential Democracy: The Case of Latin America* (Baltimore, MD: Johns Hopkins University Press, 1994); Jose Antonio Cheibub, Zachary Elkins, and Tom Ginsburg, "Beyond Presidentialism and Parliamentarism," *British Journal of Political Science* 44, no. 3 (July 2014): 515–44.
8. Josep Colomer, ed., *The Handbook of Electoral System Choice* (New York: Palgrave Macmillan, 2004).
9. Nondemocratic regimes such as the former Soviet Union or contemporary Iran often feature elections that impose serious limits on the political opposition. In the Soviet Union, only the Communist Party could run candidates. In Iran, the government has often excluded opposition candidates.
10. See, for example, Robert D. Putnam, *Bowling Alone: The Collapse and Revival of American Community* (New York: Simon and Schuster, 2001).
11. For a good overview, see Donald Horowitz, *Ethnic Groups in Conflict* (Berkeley: University of California Press, 2000); also Rogers Brubaker, *Ethnicity without Groups* (New Haven: Harvard University Press, 2004).

12. Among the many works on public opinion and political participation, see Russell Dalton, *The Civic Culture Transformed: From Allegiant to Assertive Citizens* (Cambridge: Cambridge University Press, 2014).

13. For a good overview of political ideologies, see Leon Baradat, *Political Ideologies*, 11th ed. (Upper Saddle River, NJ: Prentice Hall, 2012).

14. Confusingly for U.S. and Canadian students, in those countries such views are usually called "liberal." Thus, the U.S. Democratic Party and the Liberal Party in Canada are best thought of as social-democratic parties. In Europe, "liberal" parties are free-market and small-government parties.

15. One notable recent work in the area of political economy is Thomas Piketty, *Capital in the Twenty-First Century* (New York: Belknap Press, 2014).

16. See, for example, Dani Rodrik, *The Globalization Paradox: Democracy and the Future of the World Economy* (New York: W. W. Norton, 2012).

KEY TERMS

abstract review The power of judicial review that allows courts to decide on questions that do not arise from actual legal cases; sometimes occurs even before legislation becomes law

anarchism An ideology based on the belief that private property and capitalism lead to inequality; however, like liberals, anarchists place high value on individual political freedom

authoritarian regimes Regimes that limit the role of the public in decision making and often deny citizens basic rights and restrict their freedoms

bicameral legislatures Legislatures with two chambers

cabinet The chief government ministers or officials in government, in charge of such policy areas as defense and agriculture

charismatic legitimacy Legitimacy based on a state's identification with an important individual

civil society The collection of organizations outside of the state that help people define and advance their own interests

clientelism The mechanism whereby the state provides benefits to groups of its political supporters

communism An ideology that emphasizes creating economic equality instead of ensuring individual political and economic freedoms

Communist regimes One-party authoritarian regimes in which a Communist party controls most aspects of a country's political and economic system

comparative politics The study and comparison of politics across countries

concrete review The power of judicial review that allows the high court to rule on constitutional issues only on the basis of disputes brought before it

conservative attitudes Attitudes that support the status quo and view change as risky

constitutional court The highest judicial body that rules on the constitutionality of laws and other government actions and, in most political systems, formally oversees the entire judicial structure

co-optation The mechanism by which members of the public are brought into a beneficial relationship with the state and government

corporatism The mechanism by which citizens are forced to participate in state-sanctioned groups

democratic regimes Regimes with rules that emphasize a large role for the public in governance and that protect basic rights and freedoms

devolution The process by which central states hand down power to lower levels of government

electoral system The system that determines how votes are cast and counted

ethnicity The specific attributes and societal institutions that make one group of people culturally different from others

executive The branch of government that carries out the laws and policies of a given state

failed states States that experience a complete loss of legitimacy and power and so are overwhelmed by anarchy and violence

fascism An ideology that is hostile to the idea of individual freedom and rejects the notion of equality

federal states States whose power is divided between the central state and regional or local authorities (such as provinces, counties, and cities)

foreign direct investment The purchase of assets in one country by a foreign firm

fundamentalism An ideology that seeks to unite religion with the state so as to make religion the sovereign authority

Gini index The most commonly used measure of economic inequality

globalization The process of expanding and intensifying linkages among states, societies, and economies

government The leadership or elite that operates the state

gross domestic product (GDP) The total market value of goods and services produced within a country over a period of one year

gross domestic product (GDP) per capita A measure of affluence that divides gross domestic product by total population

head of government The individual who deals with the everyday tasks of running the state, such as formulating and executing policy

head of state The individual who symbolizes and represents the people, both nationally and internationally, embodying and articulating the goals of the regime

hyperinflation Extremely high levels of inflation

illiberal regime An authoritarian regime that retains the basic structures of democracy but does not protect basic civil liberties

inflation A situation of sustained rising prices

intergovernmental organizations (IGOs) Groups created by states to serve particular policy ends

judicial review The mechanism by which a court can review laws and policies and overturn those that are seen as violations of the state's constitution

judiciary The branch of a country's central administration that is concerned with dispensing justice

legislative–executive relations The relationship between legislatures and the executive

legislature The branch of government that is formally charged with making laws

legitimacy State authority that is regarded as right and proper

liberal attitudes Attitudes that promote evolutionary change within a system

liberalism An ideology that places a high priority on individual political and economic freedoms, favoring them over any attempts to create economic equality

lower house The legislative chamber that usually represents the population at large

market The interaction between the forces of supply and demand that allocates goods and resources

military regime An authoritarian regime in which the institution of the military dominates politics

mixed electoral system An electoral system that combines single-member districts and proportional representation

multimember districts (MMDs) Districts in which more than one legislative seat is contested

multinational corporations (MNCs) Firms that produce, distribute, and market in more than one country

national identity The common set of political aspirations that bind citizens of a country together

nationalism Pride in one's people and the belief that they share a common political identity

nationalists Individuals who believe they have a common political destiny

nongovernmental organizations (NGOs) National or international groups, independent of any state, that pursue policy objectives and foster public participation

one-party regime An authoritarian regime that is dominated by a strong political party able to create a broad membership as a source of political control

parliamentary system A legislative–executive system that features a head of government (often referred to as a prime minister) elected from within the legislature

party system A system characterized by competition among political parties

personal dictatorship An authoritarian regime that is based on the power of a single strong leader who usually relies on charismatic or traditional authority to maintain power

personality cult State-sponsored exaltation of an authoritarian leader

political attitudes Views regarding the status quo in any society, specifically the desired pace and methods of political change

political culture Societal pattern of basic norms about politics

political economy The study of how politics and economics are related

political ideologies Sets of political values regarding the fundamental goals of politics

political regimes The norms and rules regarding individual freedom and collective equality, the locus of power, and the use of that power

presidential system A legislative–executive system that features a directly elected president with most executive powers

property Ownership of goods and services

proportional representation (PR) An electoral system where the percentage of votes a party receives in a district determines how many of that district's seats the party will gain

public goods Goods and services that benefit all society and are not easily provided by the market

purchasing power parity (PPP) A mechanism that attempts to estimate the real buying power of income in each country, using U.S. prices as a benchmark

radical attitudes Attitudes that support rapid, extensive, and often revolutionary change

rational-legal legitimacy Legitimacy based on a system of laws and procedures that become highly institutionalized

reactionary attitudes Attitudes that promote rapid change to restore political, social, and economic institutions that once existed

rent seeking A process whereby the government allows its supporters to occupy positions of power in order to monopolize state benefits

semi-presidential system A legislative–executive system that features a prime minister approved by the legislature *and* a directly elected president

single-member districts (SMDs) Districts in which only one representative for each constituency and the candidate with the largest number of votes—and not necessarily a majority—wins the seat

social democracy An ideology that places considerable value on equality, but also attempts to protect some individual freedoms

social expenditures State provision of public benefits, such as education, health care, and transportation

states Organizations that maintain a monopoly of violence over a territory

strong states States that perform the basic tasks of defending their borders from outside attacks and defending their authority from internal nonstate rivals

suffrage The right to vote

theocracy An authoritarian regime that has leaders who claim to rule on behalf of God

totalitarian Characterized by a strong, official ideology that seeks to transform fundamental aspects of the state, society, and the economy using a wide array of organizations and the application of force

traditional legitimacy Legitimacy in which the state is obeyed because it has a long tradition of being obeyed

unicameral legislatures Legislatures with a single chamber

unitary states States that concentrate most political power in the national capital, allocating very little decision-making power to regions or localities

upper house The legislative house that often represents geographic subunits

vote of no confidence Legislative check on government whereby a government deems a measure to be of high importance, and if that measure fails to pass the legislature, either the government must resign in favor of another leader or new parliamentary elections must be called

weak states States that have trouble carrying out the basic tasks of defending themselves against external and internal rivals; weak states often suffer from endemic violence, poor infrastructure, weak rule of law, and an inability to collect taxes

WEB LINKS

- CIA World Factbook (www.cia.gov/library/publications/the-world-factbook)
- Freedom House (www.freedomhouse.org)
- Inter-Parliamentary Union (www.ipu.org/english/home.htm)
- *Journal of Democracy* (www.journalofdemocracy.org)
- Political Science Resources (www.psr.keele.ac.uk/area.htm)
- World Bank (www.worldbank.org)
- WWW Virtual Library: International Affairs Resources (www2.etown.edu/vl)

2

British supporters of the United Kingdom's exit, or "Brexit," from the European Union celebrate their surprise victory in the June 2016 referendum.

UNITED KINGDOM

Why Study This Case?

For many reasons, most introductory works about comparative politics begin with a study of the United Kingdom. As the primogenitor of modern democracy, the UK political system is at once strikingly unique and a model for many other liberal democracies. The United Kingdom is the world's oldest democracy. Its transition to democracy was gradual, beginning with thirteenth-century limitations on absolute monarchs and continuing incrementally to the establishment of the rule of law in the seventeenth century and the extension of suffrage to women in the twentieth century. This democratization process persists today with reforms of the anachronistic upper house of the legislature, decentralization of power, and two recent popular referenda on Scottish independence in 2014 and British exit (**Brexit**) from the European Union (EU) in 2016. Unlike many other democracies, the United Kingdom cannot attach a specific date or event to the advent of its democracy. It is also unusual in that the main political rules of the game in that country have not been seriously interrupted or radically altered since the mid-seventeenth century.

The United Kingdom is one of only a handful of democracies without a written constitution. The longevity and stability of its democracy have thus depended largely on both traditional legitimacy and a unique political culture of accommodation and moderation. Although its constitution is unwritten, many aspects of its "Westminster system" of democracy have been adopted by a number of the world's other democracies, especially in areas of the globe that were once part of the far-flung British Empire.

Finally, the United Kingdom deserves careful study because it is the birthplace of the Industrial Revolution, which fueled British economic and political dominance during the nineteenth century. Some have attributed the United Kingdom's early industrialization to the emergence of its liberal political ideology. The United Kingdom was also the

UNITED KINGDOM

ATLANTIC
OCEAN

North
Sea

N

SCOTLAND

Glasgow Edinburgh

NORTHERN
IRELAND
Belfast

ISLE
OF
MAN

REPUBLIC
OF
IRELAND

Irish Sea

Liverpool Manchester
Sheffield

ENGLAND

Birmingham

WALES

Cardiff

LONDON
Bristol Thames

Celtic Sea

English Channel

0   50   100 mi
0   50   100 km

CHANNEL
ISLANDS

FRANCE

first major industrialized country to experience an extended economic decline after World War II, for reasons that have been much debated.

The United Kingdom remains a fascinating case. In 1979, **Margaret Thatcher** of the Conservative Party was the first leader of an industrial democracy to experiment with **neoliberal** economic policies in an attempt to stem economic decline. The policies were very controversial within the United Kingdom but widely emulated in other democracies, including the United States. Even with Thatcher's resignation in 1990, the **Conservatives (Tories)** remained in power until the 1997 election, when they were ousted by the **Labour Party**. Under the leadership of **Tony Blair** and his successor, Gordon Brown, the Labour Party sought to soften some of the harder edges of Thatcher's neoliberalism while still embracing many of the policies executed by her and her Conservative successors. These policies became known as the **Third Way**, a political compromise between the right and the left that also informed the improbable coalition that governed Britain from 2010 to 2015. **David Cameron** and the Conservatives won an outright majority in the 2015 election and pursued a more neoliberal platform, policies that Cameron's successor and current Conservative Prime Minister **Theresa May** has once again tempered. However, the capacity of May's government to carry out domestic reforms as well as its ability to negotiate Britain's departure from the European Union have been severely weakened by the Conservative Party's losses in a 2017 election that deprived the government of its majority in parliament.

Major Geographic and Demographic Features

Since 1801, the **United Kingdom of Great Britain and Northern Ireland** has been the formal name of the United Kingdom. Separated from France by the English Channel, Great Britain itself consists of three nations (England, Scotland, and Wales). These three nations plus the northeastern part of the island of Ireland constitute the United Kingdom. The remainder of Ireland is called the Republic of Ireland. Although it is confusing, citizens of the United Kingdom are often referred to as British or Britons even if they live in Northern Ireland. Most Welsh, Scots, and Northern Irish consider themselves British, but it would be unwise (and inaccurate) to call a resident of Edinburgh (in Scotland) or Cardiff (in Wales) English.

The United Kingdom is roughly the size of Oregon in the United States and about two-thirds the size of Japan. It has approximately 64 million residents, about half the population of Japan. With five of six Britons living in England, the country's population is not equally distributed among its constituent members. The United Kingdom can be considered a multiethnic state because it contains Scottish, Welsh, and English citizens, who have distinct cultures and languages. Racially, however, it is relatively homogeneous; its nonwhite population, composed mainly of immigrants from the United Kingdom's former colonies, makes up about 13 percent of the total. Roughly a third of those immigrants come from the Indian subcontinent and another fourth from the Caribbean.

The United Kingdom's physical separation from the European mainland ended in 1994 with the inauguration of the Channel Tunnel, which links Britain and France. For much of British history, the country's isolation provided some protection from the conflicts and turmoil that afflicted the rest of Europe. A diminished fear of invasion may help explain the historically small size and minimal political importance of the United Kingdom's standing army (and the relative importance and strength of its navy). In addition, it may help explain its late adherence to the European Union, its unwillingness to replace the British pound with the euro (the single European currency), and its decision in 2016 to leave the European Union.

Historical Development of the State

British citizens owe their allegiance to the Crown, the enduring symbol of the United Kingdom's state, rather than to a written constitution. The Crown symbolizes far more than just the monarchy or even Her Majesty's government. It represents the ceremonial and symbolic trappings of the British state. In addition, it represents the rules governing British political life (the regime) and the unhindered capacity (the sovereignty) to enforce and administer these rules and to secure the country's borders.

The evolutionary changes of the state over the past eight centuries have been thoroughgoing and not without violence. But in comparison with political change elsewhere in the world, the development of the modern British state has been gradual, piecemeal, and peaceful.

Early Development

Although we commonly think of the United Kingdom as a stable and unified nation-state, the country experienced repeated invasions over a period of about 1,500 years. Celts, Romans, Angles, Saxons, Danes, and finally Normans invaded

TIMELINE OF POLITICAL DEVELOPMENT

YEAR	EVENT
1215	King John I forced to sign Magna Carta, thereby agreeing to a statement of the rights of English barons.
1295	Model Parliament of Edward I is convened, the first representative parliament.
1529	Reformation Parliament is summoned by Henry VIII, beginning process of cutting ties to the Roman Catholic Church.
1628	Charles I is forced to accept Petition of Right, Parliament's statement of civil rights, in return for funds.
1642–51	English Civil War is fought between Royalists and Parliamentarians.
1649	Charles I is tried and executed.
1689	Bill of Rights is issued by Parliament, establishing a constitutional monarchy in Britain.
1707	Act of Union is put into effect, uniting kingdoms of England and Scotland.
1721	Sir Robert Walpole is effectively made Britain's first prime minister.
1832, 1867	Reform Acts are passed, extending right to vote to virtually all urban males and some in the countryside.
1916–22	Anglo-Irish War is fought, culminating in establishment of independent Republic of Ireland; Northern Ireland remains part of the United Kingdom.
1973	United Kingdom is made a member of the European Economic Community (now the European Union).
1979–90	Margaret Thatcher serves as Conservative prime minister.
1982	Falklands War is fought with Argentina.
1997–2007	Tony Blair serves as Labour prime minister.
2007–10	Gordon Brown serves as Labour prime minister.
2010–16	David Cameron serves as Conservative prime minister.
2016	Referendum calling for Britain to leave the EU passes, and Theresa May replaces Cameron as Conservative prime minister.
2017	Theresa May's Conservatives suffer losses in a "snap" election, forcing the party to form a minority government.

the British Isles, each leaving important legacies. For example, the Germanic Angles and Saxons left their language—except in Wales, Scotland, and other areas they could not conquer. Local languages remained dominant there until the eighteenth and nineteenth centuries. Today, we still refer to those areas on Britain's northern and western perimeter as the United Kingdom's **Celtic fringe**.

As part of the United Kingdom's political development, another important legacy was the emergence of **common law**, a system based on local customs and precedent rather than formal legal codes. That system forms the basis of the contemporary legal systems of the United Kingdom (with the exception of Scotland), the United States, and many former British colonies.[1]

The last wave of invasions, by the Normans, occurred in 1066. The Normans were Danish Vikings who occupied northern France. In Britain, they replaced the Germanic ruling class and imposed central rule. Politically, their most important legacy was the institution of feudalism, which they brought from the European continent. Under feudalism, lords provided vassals with military protection and economic support in exchange for labor and military service. Though hardly a democratic institution, feudalism did create a system of mutual obligation between lord and peasant on one level, and between monarch and lord on another level. Indeed, some scholars have seen in these obligations the foundation for the eventual limits on royal power. The most important initial document in this regard is the **Magna Carta**, which British nobles obliged King John to sign in 1215. The Magna Carta became a royal promise to uphold feudal customs and the rights of England's barons. It set an important precedent by limiting the power of British monarchs and subjecting them to the rule of law. As a result, the United Kingdom never experienced the type of royal absolutism that was common in other countries (for example, in Russia), and this in turn helped pave the way for public control over government and the state.

The United Kingdom was fortunate to resolve relatively early in its historical development certain conflicts that other states would experience later in the modern era. A prime example is the religious divide. During the reign of Henry VIII (1509–47), a major dispute between the British monarch and the Vatican (the center of the Roman Catholic Church) had unintended consequences. When the Catholic Church failed to grant Henry a divorce, he used **Parliament** to pass laws that effectively took England out of the Catholic Church and replaced Catholicism with a Protestant Church that could be controlled by the English state instead of by Rome.

The creation of a state-controlled Anglican Church led to a religious institution that was weaker and less autonomous than its counterparts in other European countries. Supporters of Catholicism fought unsuccessfully to regain power, and religion never plagued the United Kingdom as a polarizing force the way it did in so many other countries. Northern Ireland, where the split between Protestants and Catholics continues to create political division, is the bloody exception to the rule. A second unintended consequence of creating the Anglican Church was that Henry VIII's reliance on Parliament to sanction the changes strengthened and legitimized Parliament's power. As with the Magna Carta, piecemeal institutional changes helped pave the way for democratic control—even if that result was not foreseen at the time.

Emergence of the Modern British State

Compared with its European neighbors, the United Kingdom had a more constrained monarchy. This is not to say that British rulers were weak, but in addition to the early checks on monarchic rule, three major developments in the seventeenth and eighteenth centuries decisively undermined the power of British sovereigns and are crucial for our understanding of why the United Kingdom was one of the first nations to develop democratic control.

First, the crowning of James I (a Scot) in 1603 united Scotland and England but created a political crisis. James was an absolutist at heart and resisted limits on his power imposed by Parliament. He sought to raise taxes without first asking Parliament, and his son Charles I, whose reign began in 1625, continued this flaunting of royal power, eventually precipitating civil war. The **English Civil War** (1642–51) pitted the defenders of Charles against the supporters of Parliament, who won the bitter struggle and executed Charles I in 1649.

For eleven years (1649–60), England had no monarch. It functioned as a republic led by Oliver Cromwell, whose rule soon became a military dictatorship. Parliament restored the monarchy in 1660 with the ascension of Charles II, but its power was forever weakened.

Second, when James II, a brother of Charles II, inherited the throne in 1685, the monarchy and Parliament again faced off. James was openly Catholic, and Parliament feared a return to Catholicism and absolute rule. In 1688, it removed James II and sent him into exile. In his place, it installed James's Protestant daughter Mary and her Dutch husband, William. A year later, Parliament enacted the Bill of Rights, institutionalizing its political supremacy. Since that time, monarchs have owed their position to Parliament. This so-called Glorious Revolution was a key turning point in the creation of the constitutional monarchy.

Third, in 1714, Parliament installed the current dynastic family by crowning George I (of German royalty). The monarch, who spoke little English, was forced to rely heavily on his **cabinet** (his top advisers, or ministers) and, specifically, his **prime minister**, who coordinated the work of the other ministers. From 1721 to 1742, Sir Robert Walpole fashioned the position of prime minister into much of what the office is today. By the late eighteenth century, largely in reaction to the loss of the colonies in America, prime ministers and their cabinets were no longer selected by monarchs but were instead appointed by Parliament. Monarchs never again had the power to select members of the government.[2]

The British Empire

The United Kingdom began its overseas expansion in the sixteenth century, and by the early nineteenth century it had vanquished its main European rivals to become the world's dominant military, commercial, and cultural power. Its navy helped open new overseas markets for its burgeoning domestic industry, and by the empire's zenith in 1870 the United Kingdom controlled about a quarter of all world trade and probably had the globe's wealthiest economy. The dimensions of the British Empire were truly exceptional. In the nineteenth century, it governed one-quarter of the world's population, directly ruled almost 50 countries, and dominated many more with its commercial muscle.

Paralleling the gradual process of democratization in the United Kingdom, the erosion of the British Empire was also slow and incremental. It began with the loss of the American colonies in the late eighteenth century, though subsequently the empire continued to expand in Asia and Africa. By the early twentieth century, however, it had begun to shrink. Following World War I, the United Kingdom granted independence to a few of its former colonies, including Egypt and most of Ireland. With the conclusion of World War II, the tide turned even more strongly against the empire. Local resistance in many colonies, international sentiment favoring self-determination for subject peoples, the cumulative costs of two World Wars, and the burden of maintaining far-flung colonies helped spell the end of the British Empire. Independence was willingly granted to most of the remaining colonial possessions throughout Southeast Asia, Africa, and the Caribbean.

The United Kingdom managed to retain control of a few small colonies, and in 1982 it fought a brief war with Argentina to retain possession of the remote Falkland Islands. One of the United Kingdom's last colonial possessions, Hong Kong, was returned to China in 1997. Today, the **Commonwealth** includes the United Kingdom and 54 of its former colonies and serves to maintain at least some of the economic and cultural ties established during its long imperial rule.

The Industrial Revolution

The United Kingdom lays claim to being the first industrial nation, and industrialization helped support the expansion of its empire. The country's early industrialization, which began in the late eighteenth century and developed slowly, was based on its dominance in textiles, machinery, and iron production. By the mid-nineteenth century, most of the United Kingdom's workforce had moved away from the countryside to live in urban areas. While industrialization dramatically changed British politics and society, the process did not create the kind of political upheaval and instability that was seen in many late-developing nations, where it occurred more rapidly. Because the British were the first to industrialize, the United Kingdom faced little initial competition and therefore amassed tremendous wealth. Moreover, the rise of a prosperous and propertied middle class demanding a stronger political voice also facilitated the country's first steps toward democracy.[3]

But the benefits of early industrialization may also have been factors in its economic decline. As a world leader, the United Kingdom spent lavishly on its empire and led the Allied forces in World Wars I and II. Although the Allies won both wars, the United Kingdom was drained economically. The end of World War II also signaled the end of colonial rule, and the United Kingdom began to relinquish its empire. Finally, as the first industrialized country, it would also be one of the first nations to experience economic challenges inherent in "first-mover" industrialization. When British industries faced new competition and the obsolescence of some of their technologies after World War II, the country found it increasingly difficult to reform its economy, which began to decline.

Gradual Democratization

We have seen how Parliament weakened the power of the British monarchs, but at the same time we should note that Parliament itself originally represented the interests of the British elite: only the wealthy could vote. The United Kingdom had an "upper" **House of Lords**, which represented the aristocracy, and a "lower" **House of Commons**, which represented the interests of the lower nobility and the merchant class. In addition, by the time Parliament was established, British monarchs were no longer absolute rulers, although they continued to wield considerable political power. Two factors gradually democratized Parliament and further weakened monarchical power.

The first was the rise of political parties, which emerged in the eighteenth century as cliques of nobles but eventually reached out to broader sectors of society for support. The two largest cliques became the United Kingdom's first parties: the Conservatives (Tories) supported the monarch, and the **Liberals (Whigs)** opposed the policies of the monarch. The Whigs were the first to cultivate support among members of the United Kingdom's burgeoning commercial class, many of whom were still excluded from the political system.

The second factor was the expansion of suffrage. In 1832, the Whigs were able to push through a Reform Act that doubled the size of the British electorate, though it still excluded more than 90 percent of British adults. Over the next century, both parties gradually supported measures to expand suffrage, hoping in part to gain a political windfall. This process continued in 1928, when women over the age of 21 were granted the right to vote, and culminated in 1969 when the voting age was reduced to 18.

The gradual expansion of the vote to include all adult citizens forced the political parties to respond to demands for additional services. The new voters wanted the expansion of such public goods as improved working conditions, health care, education, and housing, and they looked to the state to provide them. The Labour Party, formed in 1900 as an outgrowth of the trade union movement, had become by the end of World War I the main representative of the working class and the primary beneficiary of expanded suffrage. By the 1920s, Labour became the United Kingdom's largest center-left party and pushed for policies that would develop basic social services for all citizens, or what we commonly call the welfare state. The British workers who defended the United Kingdom so heroically during World War II returned from that conflict with a new sense of entitlement, electing Labour to power in 1945. Armed with a parliamentary majority, the Labour government quickly moved to implement a welfare state. This was accompanied by the nationalization of a number of sectors of industry, such as coal, utilities, rail, and health care.

Postwar Politics and Debates on National Identity and State Sovereignty

The Labour Party initiated the welfare state, but British Conservatives generally supported it during much of the postwar period in what has been called the postwar **collectivist consensus**. By the 1970s, however, the British economy was in crisis, and a new breed of Tories (dubbed *neoliberals* due to their embrace of classical liberal values of limited state intervention) began to blame the United Kingdom's economic decline on the excesses of the welfare state. When Margaret

Thatcher became prime minister in 1979, she broke with traditional Tory support for what she derided as the United Kingdom's "nanny" state and pledged to diminish government's role in the economy. She lowered taxes and cut state spending on costly social services, and she replaced some state services (in areas as diverse as housing and mass transit) with private enterprise. Her government thus marked the end of the postwar collectivist consensus.

Yet in some ways, a new consensus emerged around Thatcher's reforms.[4] Although the Labour Party's landslide victory over the Tories in 1997 can be seen as a rejection of some aspects of Thatcher's rollback of the state, the Labour Party returned to office that year under the banner of "New Labour." By adopting this new name, Prime Minister Tony Blair sought to rebrand the party and distinguish his government's "Third Way" centrist program from both Thatcher's hard-edged laissez-faire policies and Labour's more traditional platform as staunch defender of an elaborate welfare state. New Labour held government for 13 years, balancing popular progressive social reforms with policies of devolution and continued limits on social expenditures. The 2010 parliamentary election resulted in a **hung parliament** in which no party obtained a majority of seats. In what can be seen as a nod to both Thatcher and Blair, Prime Minister David Cameron and the Conservatives formed a coalition government with the center-left Liberal Democrats, calling for "fairness," but also "freedom" and "responsibility."

In the 2015 election, voters rewarded the Tories with an outright majority, signaling a conservative shift in the electorate on policies from government spending to immigration. Although his party won the election handily, Cameron struggled with controversial issues involving national identity and state sovereignty both at home and abroad. In 2014, Scotland held a referendum calling for independence from Britain, with Cameron leading the successful effort to reject independence and retain Scotland as a part of Great Britain. Two years later, the entire United Kingdom held a referendum on Britain's membership in the European Union, with Cameron once again leading the campaign for Britain to remain in the Union. In this case, those favoring an exit from the EU and greater sovereignty for Britain prevailed, leading to Cameron's resignation and triggering the process of Britain's departure from the Union after more than four decades of participation in the European project. Cameron was replaced by Theresa May in 2016 as leader of

Theresa May replaced David Cameron in 2016 as leader of the Conservative Party and prime minister.

the Conservatives and as Britain's second female prime minister. In a failed effort to strengthen her government's Brexit bargaining position, May called an early "snap" election in 2017, in which her Conservatives ultimately lost seats. This returned the United Kingdom to a hung parliament and left the Conservatives with a minority government.

Political Regime

The political regime of the United Kingdom is notable among the world's democracies because of its highly **majoritarian** features. Under the rules of British politics, the majority in Parliament has virtually unchecked power. Unlike political parties in other democracies, even parliamentary democracies, the majority party in the United Kingdom can enact policies with few checks from other branches of government. Also unlike other democracies, in the United Kingdom there are no formal constitutional limits on the central government, few judicial restraints, and no constitutionally sanctioned local authorities to dilute the power of the government in London. Only the historical traditions of democratic political culture and, while retaining membership in the European Union, restrictions imposed by that body have checked the possibility of the British government abusing its power.

Political Institutions

THE CONSTITUTION

The United Kingdom has no single document that defines the rules of politics, but the constitution is generally understood to include a number of written documents and unwritten rules that most British citizens view as inviolable.[5] In 1215, the Magna Carta set a precedent for limits on monarchical power. Other documents include the 1689 Bill of Rights and the 1707 Act of Union, which united Scotland and England. What makes the United Kingdom's constitution particularly unusual is that it also consists of various acts of Parliament, judicial decisions, customs, and traditions. Since Parliament is viewed as sovereign, the democratically elected lower house of the legislature can amend any aspect of the constitution by a simple majority vote. This power extends to the very existence of the monarchy, the powers of regions or local governments, and the powers of the houses of Parliament. Therefore, unlike most other democratic regimes, the

United Kingdom has no constitutional court, because any law passed by Parliament is by definition constitutional.

The absence of written constitutional guarantees has consistently alarmed human rights advocates and has given rise to demands for a more formal constitution or, at the very least, *written* constitutional protections of basic rights. Since 1973, when the United Kingdom became a member of the European Union, British citizens have increasingly appealed to European laws to protect their rights. In response to such concerns, in 1998 the government incorporated into law the European Convention on Human Rights, a document that now serves as a basic set of constitutional liberties. In 2007, signatories to the European Union's Lisbon Treaty agreed, among other things, to make this bill of rights legally binding. As with other aspects of its EU membership, however, Britain negotiated the ability to choose which judicial matters would be ceded to the authority of the European Union's constitutional court and those over which it would retain national sovereignty. This stance has led to debate between political conservatives who have largely favored the current accumulation of conventions and statutes and liberals who have argued for the value of a written, codified constitution.[6] It is uncertain what long-run consequences the voters' decision in 2016 to end British membership in the EU will have on constitutional liberties and other judicial matters.

Although it is a source of concern to some political analysts, others have lauded the United Kingdom's unwritten constitution for its unparalleled flexibility and responsiveness to the majority. Changing the constitution in most democracies is a cumbersome and often politically charged process. In the United Kingdom, however, changes can be implemented more quickly and without lengthy political battles. Blair's Labour government (1997–2007) carried out piecemeal constitutional reforms that have proven so significant in their effects that they have been compared to the Great Reform Act of 1832.[7] Likewise, concessions offered by Parliament to persuade Scottish voters to reject independence in 2014 and the government's efforts to unwind Britain from the EU have also required significant constitutional reforms. Admirers of the British constitution argue that it has delivered both political stability and flexibility since the late seventeenth century; in their view, a formal document does not necessarily make for a more democratic government.

THE CROWN

We can think of the **Crown**, the legislature, the prime minister, the cabinet, and the judiciary as the main branches of government in the United Kingdom. In most respects, we can think of the British Crown as the head of state. The Crown, embodied by the monarch, is the symbolic representative of the continuity of the British state. The monarch (currently Queen Elizabeth II) thus acts as a purely ceremonial figure; and on matters of importance, she can act only at the behest of the cabinet even though the cabinet is referred to collectively as Her Majesty's government. The British monarchy is a continual source of popular fascination, in part because the institution and all its pomp and circumstance appear to be a relic in the twenty-first century. The reality, however, is less glamorous. The British monarch today is essentially a paid civil servant: the government allocates a budget to cover the royal family's expenses, and the queen spends much of her time signing papers, dedicating public works, and performing diplomatic functions.

The UK monarchy has survived for centuries precisely because it has agreed to act constitutionally. Since the nineteenth century, this has meant that it must always follow the orders of elected representatives. For example, although the monarch always selects the head of government, the choice must always be the leader of the majority party in the lower house of Parliament. Only in the unlikely event that the legislature found itself deadlocked and unable to form a government could a monarch have any real influence on politics, and even in that case her choice would be severely constrained. Likewise, the monarch is officially the commander of the British armed forces, but it is the prime minister who has the power to declare wars and sign treaties.

The British monarchy is a hereditary institution that until recently followed the rule of primogeniture—the oldest son (or oldest daughter if there were no sons) inherited the throne. In an effort to modernize this most traditional of institutions, however, the Cameron government secured passage of a bill in 2011 abolishing male precedence in royal succession. Approved by the 16 other countries in the British Commonwealth that recognize the British monarch as their head of state, this reform means that the eldest born of each generation, regardless of gender, is entitled to inherit the throne. However, the cardinal constitutional principle of parliamentary supremacy means that Parliament itself may actually choose the monarch. In 1701, for example, Parliament imposed a new dynastic family (the Hanovers) to replace the reigning Stuarts. Since that time, only Protestants have been allowed to succeed to the throne. For more than six decades, since 1952, Elizabeth II has been queen, succeeding her father, George VI.

Despite the series of high-profile scandals that have rocked the monarchy during her reign, polls consistently show that the institution remains highly popular, as evidenced by the public celebrations of the queen's diamond jubilee (60 years on the throne) in 2012 and the great national interest in the 2011 wedding of Prince William (the queen's eldest grandson) and Catherine Middleton and the birth of their son and daughter, George and Charlotte, respectively (third and fourth in line after their grandfather and father). There have been occasional movements in the United Kingdom to eliminate the monarchy, but these have failed to garner much support. Despite scandals and the costs of royalty, public support for the institution remains strong. A 2016 poll, for example, placed confidence in the monarchy at an all-time high: three-fourths of Britons were in favor of retaining the monarchy, and only 17 percent preferred its elimination.[8]

The Branches of Government

THE PRIME MINISTER

Parliament is supreme in the United Kingdom's political system, but real power is concentrated in the prime minister and the cabinet, which together constitute the government. The prime minister is the head of government and, as in all parliamentary systems, must be an elected member of the legislature. She or he is the head of the largest party in the lower house, the House of Commons (selection as party leader is handled in a party convention held before a general election). Once named prime minister by the monarch (a mere formality), this individual selects the cabinet.

British prime ministers are probably the most powerful heads of government of any contemporary democracy. Because they can expect their parliamentary majority to approve all legislation, because party discipline in the United Kingdom is very strong, and because there are few checks on the power of the central government, prime ministers usually get their way. They wield less power, though, when their parties hold a slim majority (as was the case with John Major from 1990 to 1997) or when they are forced to depend on a coalition of parties (as was the case with the Conservative–Liberal Democrat coalition from 2010 to 2015). As with any other **Member of Parliament (MP)**, prime ministers in the United Kingdom are elected to a maximum term of five years. Before the passage of the 2011 Fixed-term Parliaments Act, the prime minister could choose to call elections at any time before that term had expired and would commonly do so to take advantage of favorable political conditions. The 2011 act fixed the date of subsequent elections for every five years beginning in 2015. The Conservative government's decision to call an early election in 2017 required a two-thirds parliamentary "supermajority" in order to override the Fixed-term Parliaments Act.

Of course, prime ministers are still subject to a legislative **vote of no confidence**, which can occur when the chamber rejects a measure deemed of high importance to the government. In such situations, either the entire cabinet must resign (and be replaced by a new one) or new elections must be called. Although such a check on the government exists, it is rarely used; over the past century, only two governments have been toppled by a legislative vote of no confidence. In fact, the prime minister can use the threat of a no-confidence vote as a way to rally support. In 2003, Tony Blair submitted a motion to the House of Commons to support the use of force against Iraq even though a prime minister may take the country to war without parliamentary approval. Yet he chose to submit his decision to the House of Commons, threatening to resign if he failed to win support. The tactic worked: despite widespread opposition to the war among his Labour Party backbenchers (MPs holding no government office), a large majority in Parliament supported the war.

Prime ministers play a number of roles. As leaders of their party, they must maintain the support of their fellow MPs, a condition that has plagued every prime minister since Thatcher. They must appear in the legislature weekly for a televised question period, during which they must defend government policies and answer questions from MPs—and in so doing, display strong oratorical skills.[9] As head of government, the prime minister must direct the activity of the cabinet and smooth over differences among cabinet members. As a politician, she is expected to guide her party to victory in general elections and, in some cases, manage to hold together a fractious coalition. Even though the monarch is head of state and the nation, the prime minister is expected to provide national leadership. British prime ministers are also diplomats and world leaders, roles that Tony Blair, for example, especially relished—despite the objections of many of his own party members, particularly regarding the war in Iraq.

Prime ministers are always seasoned political veterans with, on average, more than two decades of experience in the House of Commons. As a result, British prime ministers are usually outstanding debaters, effective communicators, and skilled negotiators. In the British system, a political outsider has virtually no chance of becoming prime minister; those aspiring to this title must move up the ranks of the party before gaining the highest office.

Margaret Thatcher and Tony Blair are arguably the United Kingdom's most important and controversial prime ministers since the end of World War II. Although Thatcher, who served from 1979 to 1990, was a Conservative and Blair, who served from 1997 to 2007, was a Labourite, they share some remarkable similarities. Defying the Conservative Party's traditional ties to the aristocracy, Thatcher was a grocer's daughter who came to political power through sheer force of will. She steered the Tories away from the party's traditional social paternalism and toward a more free-market economy. Blair reoriented the Labour Party away from its traditional hostility toward the free market and sought to make the party less dependent on its trade union supporters. Both of these leaders are credited with reinvigorating political parties that were in crisis after having suffered from long periods of being out of government.

Once in office and armed with large majorities in the House of Commons, both leaders implemented important domestic reforms that were radical departures from the past. The Iron Lady, as Thatcher was dubbed, undertook a series of dramatic steps to reverse Britain's economic stagnation and to repeal the social-democratic policies that had been created under the collectivist consensus. Her government privatized many state-owned businesses and allowed numerous ailing firms to go bankrupt. Thatcher also confronted and eventually defeated powerful trade unions during widespread strikes by unions opposed to her policies. One particularly controversial but popular policy was her decision to sell millions of public housing units to their occupants in order to create more private homeowners in the United Kingdom. Her boldest policy was the ill-advised introduction of the so-called poll tax, designed to move local governments' tax burden from property owners to all citizens. This legislation generated widespread resentment and even rioting.

Blair's domestic reforms were no less dramatic, although they were less controversial. Although he continued most of Thatcher's economic policies, he implemented an ambitious set of constitutional reforms. He devolved power to regional and local governments (some of which had lost power under Thatcher), creating new legislatures in Scotland and Wales. He began to reform the archaic House of Lords, established a Supreme Court, and made the central bank (the Bank of Britain) independent of the government.

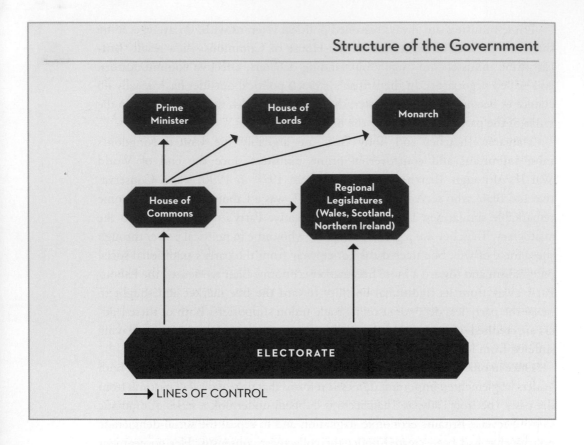

Structure of the Government

Prime Minister

House of Lords

Monarch

House of Commons

Regional Legislatures (Wales, Scotland, Northern Ireland)

ELECTORATE

→ LINES OF CONTROL

In their foreign policies, both leaders favored an extremely close relationship with the United States, often at the expense of relations with the United Kingdom's European allies. Thatcher and Blair also took the country into controversial wars. Thatcher launched a costly war against Argentina in 1982 to retake the distant Falkland Islands, and the United Kingdom's victory in that war temporarily buoyed her political success. In 2003, Blair joined the United States in the Iraq War—a move bitterly opposed by many within his own party and by a large majority of the UK public. As the war bogged down, Blair's popularity plummeted.

Thatcher and Blair were exceptional communicators whose charismatic personalities charmed the public. Thatcher was known for her tough, often blunt public statements and her fierce debating skills. Blair had wit and charm that captivated Britons for over a decade. However, both were unpopular by the end of their time in office. Many people viewed Thatcher as insensitive and out of touch, and Blair increasingly as a spinmaster who often skirted the truth. Both of them stubbornly refused to budge from policies that the British public bitterly opposed (such as Thatcher's poll tax and Blair's stance on the Iraq War).

After over a decade in power, Thatcher and Blair each resigned their positions without ever having lost an election. Thatcher quit when she faced growing opposition and a challenge to her leadership within the Conservative Party. After Labour won its third consecutive majority in the Commons, the increasingly beleaguered Blair agreed to step down and hand power to his longtime chancellor of the exchequer, Gordon Brown. One final similarity is worth noting: Thatcher and Blair both handed power to competent but less charismatic party leaders who proved less controversial and less successful.[10]

THE CABINET

Cabinets evolved out of the group of experts who originally advised Britain's monarchs. Contemporary British cabinets have about 20 members (called *ministers*), all of whom must be MPs. They are usually from the lower house but occasionally are members of the upper house, the House of Lords. The prime minister generally appoints leading party officials to the top cabinet positions. Although the prime minister and the cabinet emerge from the Parliament, they stand apart from the legislature as a separate executive branch and have few checks on their powers.

As in most democracies, cabinet ministers in the United Kingdom preside over their individual government departments and are responsible for answering to Parliament (during question time) about actions of the bureaucracies they oversee. The most important ministries are the Foreign Office (which conducts foreign policy), the Home Office (which oversees the judiciary), and the Exchequer (whose minister, called the chancellor, oversees financial policy).

One unwritten rule of cabinet behavior in the United Kingdom is **collective responsibility**—even when individual cabinet ministers oppose a given policy, the entire cabinet must appear unified and take responsibility for the policy. Cabinet ministers who cannot support a decision must resign and return to the legislature. For example, three members of Blair's cabinet resigned in 2003 over opposition to the war in Iraq, and a member of Cameron's cabinet resigned in 2016 in protest over government cuts to disability benefits.

THE LEGISLATURE

The British legislature, called Parliament, is perhaps the most powerful legislature on earth, due largely to the lack of constitutional constraints, which we have just discussed. The concentration of power is even more impressive when it is considered that of the two chambers of the legislature, the House of Commons and the House of Lords, only the former has any real power.

The House of Commons currently consists of 650 members representing individual districts in the United Kingdom of Great Britain and Northern Ireland. Members are elected for a maximum term of five years, though new elections may be called before the expiration of the term in the event of a successful vote of no confidence or vote to override the Fixed-term Parliaments Act. Government and opposition parties face each other in a tiny rectangular chamber, where members of the government and leaders of the opposition sit in the front rows. The other MPs, called backbenchers, sit behind their leaders. A politically neutral Speaker of the House presides.

Despite the enormous power of the House of Commons, individual legislators are far less powerful than their counterparts in the United States. They receive relatively paltry salaries and have very small staffs and few resources. In parliamentary systems in general, the largest party elects the prime minister as head of government; as a result, political parties, not individual members, are what matter. Thus British legislators follow the lead of their party and, for fear of weakening party cohesion, do not undertake the type of individual initiative common to representatives in the United States. Moreover, parties designate certain members to serve as whips, who are charged with enforcing the party line. Nevertheless, MPs are typically more accessible than American legislators and offer frequent "clinics," or face-to-face meetings, with individual constituents to hear their concerns.

Even with these limitations, MPs do perform important tasks. They actively debate issues, participate in legislative committees (though these are less powerful than their U.S. counterparts), vote on legislation proposed by the government, and have the power to remove the prime minister through a vote of no confidence. Finally, although the government initiates the vast majority of legislation, individual members propose measures from time to time.

Thus, despite the doctrine of parliamentary supremacy, the legislature in the United Kingdom mostly deliberates, ratifies, and scrutinizes policies that are proposed by the executive. The government is usually able to impose its will on its majority in the House of Commons. MPs have traditionally voted with their parties more than 90 percent of the time, though both the coalition government (2010–15) and the current Conservative minority government have been predictably less disciplined. Weaker governments can embolden backbenchers in their own parties to defy party whips and vote against their own governments. Nevertheless, even governments with large majorities occasionally lose the vote in the lower house, which suggests that MPs sometimes act independently.

The House of Lords is another uniquely British institution. It was considered the *upper* house not only because it represented the top aristocracy but also because it was at the time considered the more powerful of the two chambers. As the United Kingdom underwent democratization, however, it made sense for a chamber of appointed members of the aristocracy to lose most of its power, and today the House of Lords has gradually become nearly powerless. True to the British desire to accommodate tradition, it remains as yet another reminder of the United Kingdom's predemocratic past.

The House of Lords is composed of over 800 members, or peers, who have traditionally been appointed in several ways. **Life peers** are distinguished citizens appointed for life by the Crown upon the recommendation of the prime minister. About a dozen top officials of the Church of England are also members of the House of Lords. Another dozen, known as *law lords*, are top legal experts, appointed for life, who played an important role in legal appeals until recent reforms transferred their judicial responsibilities out of the upper chamber. The most controversial component of the House of Lords is composed of **hereditary peers**, members of the aristocracy (dukes, earls, barons, and so on), who until recently had been able to bequeath their seats to their offspring. In 1999, the Labour government eliminated all but 92 of the hereditary peerages as part of a reform of the upper chamber.

The House of Lords has no actual veto power over legislation, but it can delay some legislation for up to one year and occasionally persuades governments to amend legislation. Historically, the most important role of the lords was their service as the United Kingdom's court of last appeal, and the legal expertise of some members of the lords is often called upon to improve legislation. However, Parliament passed legislation in 2009 creating an independent Supreme Court, depriving the lords of most of their judicial influence.

Currently, there is considerable debate in the House of Commons and among the broader British citizenry about the future of the upper house and whether it should be directly elected and given greater powers. Over the past decade, various commissions and cross-party parliamentary groups have recommended reforms designed, alternatively, to either weaken the ability of the current body to slow legislation or substantially restructure the chamber to increase its authority and relevance. Advisory votes held in the House of Commons have been inconclusive, but clearly seem to favor a directly elected upper house, perhaps with fixed terms of 12 to 15 years. Not surprisingly, the House of Lords has rejected any such reform, voting instead for a fully appointed chamber. Equally unsurprising may be the hesitance of the House of Commons to enact any actual reforms that would strengthen the legislative power of a second chamber at the expense of its own.[11]

Compared with the United States and even with other parliamentary democracies, the judiciary in the United Kingdom plays a relatively minor role. Until recently, there was no tradition of judicial review (the right of courts to strike down legislation that contradicts the constitution), because the British parliament was always supreme: any law passed by the legislature was, by definition, constitutional. Thus, the role of the courts in the United Kingdom has been mainly to ensure that parliamentary statutes have been followed.

Formerly the responsibility of law lords in the House of Lords, since 2009 a separate Supreme Court of the United Kingdom has served as the highest court of appeal on most legal matters. Reflecting their former jurisdiction, all current Supreme Court justices are also law lords from the House of Lords, selected from among distinguished jurists by the Lord Chancellor (the minister who heads the judiciary) and serving until retirement. Their replacements, however, will no longer be members of the House of Lords, but will be appointed by a commission.

Though politically weak, over the past couple of decades a slow move toward greater political involvement of the courts has occurred. In part, this is because British governments have sought legal interpretations that would support their actions. A second factor in this development has been the embrace of international laws, such as the adoption of the European Convention on Human Rights in 1998, which codified for the first time in the United Kingdom a set of basic civil rights. These laws have given the courts new authority to strike down legislation as unconstitutional, though these powers have so far been used sparingly and may be further weakened with Brexit. Still, the days when we could speak of the United Kingdom as lacking judicial review may be slowly coming to an end.

The broader legal system, based on common law and developed in the twelfth century, contrasts starkly with the stricter code law practiced in the rest of Europe, which is less focused on precedent and interpretation. Like most democracies, the United Kingdom has an elaborate hierarchy of civil and criminal courts as well as a complex system of appeals.

The Electoral System

Like the United States, the United Kingdom uses the single-member district (SMD) system based on plurality voting, or what is often known as "first past the post." Each of the 650 constituencies elects one MP, and that member needs to win only a plurality of votes (more than any other candidate), not a majority.

Electoral constituencies are based mostly on population, and they average about 68,000 voters. Constituencies are revised every five to seven years by a government commission.

The implications of the plurality SMD system are fairly clear. First, as shown in the table "Consequences of the British Electoral System, 2010–2017," p. 59, the system favors and helps maintain the dominance of the two main political parties, Labour and Conservative. Second, and related, the system consistently penalizes smaller parties. The Liberal Democrats, whose support is spread relatively evenly across the country, regularly garner between one-fifth and one-quarter of votes in many districts, but they can rarely muster enough votes to edge out the larger parties. In fact, in 2015, support for the Liberal Democrats fell precipitously, matched by big vote gains for both the **United Kingdom Independence Party (UKIP)** and the **Scottish National Party (SNP)**. Like the Liberal Democrats, UKIP's nearly 13 percent of the popular vote was widely dispersed, yielding only one parliamentary seat. On the other hand, in the wake of the failed 2014 Scottish independence referendum, the regionally concentrated SNP swept 56 of Scotland's 59 seats in Parliament on less than 5 percent of the vote. In the 2017 election, however, the SMD system in turn punished both UKIP and the SNP, with the former party losing nearly all of its support and its single seat and the latter losing over a third of its seats.

Third, with the 2010 and 2017 elections as significant exceptions, the British electoral system has generally produced clear majorities in the House of Commons, even when there was no clear majority in the electorate. Indeed, in the elections of 1951 and 1974, the party with the smaller percentage of the vote won the most seats thanks to the nature of the electoral system. Even in 1997, Labour won a huge (179-seat) majority in the Commons with only 43 percent of the vote. These distortions occur when more than two parties contest a seat, so that a majority of votes are wasted—that is, the votes are not counted toward the winning party. Since World War II, more than 60 percent of all seats have been won with a minority of votes.

In a system that gives virtually unchecked power to the party with the majority of seats, an electoral process artificially producing majorities could be considered a serious distortion of democratic rule. It is no wonder that the parties most hurt by the electoral system, especially the Liberal Democrats, have long called for electoral reform. The Labour government elected in 1997 appointed an independent commission to consider a more proportional electoral system, but as the party in government and the chief beneficiary of the current system, Labour had little incentive to act on the recommendations.

The 2010 election, which departed from the single-party-majority outcome predicted by political scientists and confirmed by most UK general elections, afforded the Liberal Democrats the opportunity to press their demand for electoral reform. For the first time since 1974, no party managed to obtain a majority of seats in the election, resulting in a hung parliament. Among other consequences (examined later in this chapter), the successful effort by the Conservatives to draw the Liberal Democrats into a majority coalition included the promise to hold a referendum on electoral reform. In 2011, the referendum was held, allowing voters to choose between retaining the existing plurality SMD system and instituting a majority SMD system known as *alternative vote* (AV). Whereas in the current arrangement the candidate with a plurality of votes is elected, the proposed AV system would have allowed voters to rank candidates by preference. If no candidate obtained an outright majority based on first preferences, then the candidate with the fewest first-choice votes would be eliminated and the second-choice candidate on those ballots received those votes. This process of elimination and reallocation would be repeated until a top candidate obtained a majority of votes.

Ultimately, the 2011 referendum failed resoundingly—over two-thirds of voters rejected the AV system. Despite agreeing to bring the referendum forward, the Conservatives were clear in their preferences to retain the existing plurality system. Labour took no position on the referendum, and even the Liberal Democrats would not have been fully satisfied with a yes vote. They far preferred a more radical reform: the adoption of a proportional representation (PR) system in which each party is allotted seats in the legislature in direct proportion to its percentage of the popular vote.

Devolution has permitted greater electoral experimentation in regional legislatures. Scotland and Wales have adopted a mixed PR-SMD electoral system, and Northern Ireland uses a system known as *single-transferable vote*, similar to the AV system just discussed. Ironically, the governing Labour Party that authorized these regional parliaments in the 1990s—and benefited greatly from plurality SMD—favored a mixed system for the regional legislatures because it feared that plurality SMD would produce large majorities for the local nationalist parties.

Local Government

Unlike the United States with its federal form of government and despite the devolution of some authority to regional bodies, the United Kingdom may be considered a unitary state in which no formal powers are constitutionally reserved for regional or local government. Indeed, during the Conservative governments of Margaret Thatcher, the autonomy of municipal governments was sharply

Consequences of the British Electoral System, 2010–2017

ELECTION YEAR	% OF VOTES	% OF SEATS	SEATS WON
Labour			
2010	29	40	258
2015	30	36	232
2017	40	40	262
Conservative			
2010	36	47	306
2015	37	51	331
2017	42	49	318
Liberal Democrat			
2010	23	9	57
2015	8	1	8
2017	7	2	12
Others			
2010	10	4	29
2015	25	12	79
2017	10	9	58

Note: Due to rounding, percentages do not always equal 100.

curtailed. The Labour government elected in 1997 took bold steps to restore some political power to the distinct nations that compose the United Kingdom as well as to local governments, and Conservative governments since 2010 have continued to grant more authority to local governments and communities. However, Parliament remains fully sovereign and can enact laws at any time to limit or even eliminate this devolved authority. In addition, unlike other federal systems, Britain's upper chamber is unelected and therefore not accountable to states or other regional bodies.

Although there has never been a constitutional provision for local autonomy, British localities have enjoyed a long tradition of powerful local government. Concerned that local governments (or "councils" as they are known in the United Kingdom), especially left-leaning ones in large urban areas, were taxing and spending beyond their means, Thatcher's Conservative government passed a law sharply limiting the ability of these councils to raise revenue. The struggle between the central government and the councils came to a head in 1986 when, in a move deeply resented by urban British citizens, Thatcher abolished the Labour-dominated Greater London Council and several other urban governments. London was left with councils in each of its 32 boroughs, but it had no single city government or mayor. In 1989, Thatcher further threatened local governments by replacing the local property tax with a poll tax—that is, a flat tax levied on every urban citizen. The new policy shifted the tax burden from business and property owners to individuals (rich and poor alike) and was among the most unpopular policies of Thatcher's 11 years in power. In response, rioting broke out in London.

After 1997, Tony Blair restored considerable autonomy to municipal government, enacting reforms that allowed Londoners to directly elect a mayor with significant powers and to choose representatives to a Greater London Assembly. Since restoring the office of mayor, Londoners have elected strong and colorful leaders, including Ken Livingstone (nicknamed "Red Ken" because of his identification with the radical left of the Labour Party) and Boris Johnson, an equally controversial and flamboyant Conservative. London's current leader, Sadiq Khan, is the city's first nonwhite mayor and the first Muslim mayor of any major Western capital.

More recently, under the promise of creating a "big society," Conservative governments have sought to continue this process of devolution, requiring greater transparency in local government and giving local citizens more decision-making power regarding local taxation and public services. Since 2012, 16 additional major municipalities have been granted authority to hold mayoral elections.

Representation at the regional level has historically been very limited. Of the four nations that constitute the United Kingdom (England, Scotland, Wales, and Northern Ireland), only Northern Ireland had its own legislature, until political violence there caused the central government to disband it in 1972. Each of the four nations has a cabinet minister in the central government, called a secretary of state, who is responsible for setting policies in each region.

As it did with local government, the Labour Party promoted devolution, or the decentralization of power, to the United Kingdom's regions. In 1997, Scotland and Wales voted in referenda to create their own legislatures to address local issues, though their powers are not uniform: Scotland's Parliament is substantially more powerful and autonomous than Wales's Assembly, a reflection of the much stronger nationalist tendencies in Scotland as manifested in the 2014 vote for Scottish independence (see "Scotland's Bid for Independence," p. 81). Meanwhile, the 1998 **Good Friday Agreement** between Catholics and Protestants in

Northern Ireland has allowed for the reestablishment of the Northern Ireland Assembly. Some observers view the development of these bodies as the first step toward a federal United Kingdom.[12] Ironically, England, which is the seat of British national government, is the only part of the United Kingdom without its own regional government.

Despite devolution measures and talk of a decentralized "big society," the United Kingdom remains a centralized, unitary state. Regional and local authorities clearly enjoy greater legitimacy and far more powers than in the past—a trend that is likely to continue—but the central government still controls defense policy, most taxation power, and national economic policy, among other aspects of government. The central government also retains the power to limit (or even eliminate) local government if and when it so chooses.

Political Conflict and Competition

The Party System

In the United Kingdom's majoritarian parliamentary system, political parties are extremely important. The majority party controls government and can generally implement its policy goals, which are spelled out in the party manifesto.

From the end of World War II to 1970, the United Kingdom had a two-party system. The Conservative Party and the Labour Party together garnered more than 90 percent of the popular vote. The two large parties were equally successful during that period—each won four elections. After 1974, a multiparty system emerged, which included the birth of a stronger centrist **Liberal Democratic Party** and more recently the UK Independence party as well as a surge of support for nationalist parties in Scotland, Wales, and Northern Ireland. But since the Conservatives and Labour continue to prevail, the current system is often called a *two-and-a-half-party system*, in which the Liberal Democratic Party trails far behind the other two parties.

The United Kingdom's party system differs regionally, even for national elections. In England, the three major parties (Labour, Conservative, and Liberal Democrat) compete with one another. In Scotland, Wales, and Northern Ireland, important regional parties compete with the three national political parties. Before turning to party politics today, let's look more closely at each of the United Kingdom's major parties.

THE LABOUR PARTY

We have discussed the democratization of the United Kingdom as a gradual process that incorporated previously excluded groups into the political system. A clear example of this is the Labour Party, which was formed in 1900 as an outgrowth of the trade union movement. Initially, it sought to give the British working class a voice in Parliament. Only after the mobilizing effect of World War I and the expansion of suffrage in 1918 was the Labour Party able to make significant progress at the polls. By 1918, it had garnered almost one-quarter of the vote. Labour's turning point and its emergence as one of the United Kingdom's two dominant parties came with its landslide victory in 1945, just after the end of World War II.

Like virtually all working-class parties of the world, the British Labour Party considered socialism its dominant ideological characteristic. British socialists, however, were influenced by Fabianism, a moderate ideology that advocated working within the parliamentary order to bring about social-democratic change. While Labour championed a strong welfare state and some state ownership of industry, the party's moderate politics never threatened to replace capitalism.

For most of its history, the Labour Party depended heavily on working-class votes, winning the support of about two-thirds of the United Kingdom's manual laborers. Starting in the 1970s, however, the composition of the class structure began to change as fewer Britons engaged in blue-collar jobs. At that point, the solid identification of workers with Labour began to erode, creating a serious challenge for the party.

By the mid-1970s, the Labour Party was badly divided between radical socialists who wanted the party to move to the left to shore up its working-class credentials and moderates who wanted it to move toward the political center. These divisions involved the party's relationship with the trade unions and its stand on economic and foreign policy. This internal division caused the party's more conservative elements to bolt in 1981. Most serious, the internal bickering led to the defeat of Labour in every election from 1979 to 1997.

In the 1980s and 1990s, the Labour Party began a process of ideological and organizational moderation. The party's constitution was rewritten to weaken severely the ability of trade unions to control party policy. Labour also abandoned its commitment to socialism and advocated a cross-class appeal. Tony Blair, who became party leader in 1994, consolidated these changes and advocated moderate free-market policies with ambitious constitutional reform, policies that were eventually known as the Third Way.[13] Blair's landslide victory in the 1997 elections marked the beginning of a period of party unity and electoral success that has been termed *New Labour,* and the election results of 2001 and 2005 confirmed this success.

Labour's victory in the 2005 elections marked the first time in history that the party had been elected to office three consecutive times. However, those elections reduced Labour's majority by 47 seats, and two years later Blair handed power over to his chancellor of the exchequer, Gordon Brown. Brown's Labour government fared even worse in the 2010 elections, dropping 91 additional seats and losing its majority in Parliament. Brown stepped down as prime minister and resigned as leader of his party, replaced by Ed Miliband, who became leader of the party and leader of the opposition in Parliament for the next five years. Miliband took the blame for Labour's defeat in the 2015 election and was replaced by the left-leaning **Jeremy Corbyn**, a divisive figure initially well-loved by many of the party's rank and file, but highly unpopular among Labour's more moderate leadership. Despite qualms among party leaders who feared he was taking Labour outside of the political mainstream, Corbyn led the party to a strong finish in the 2017 election, denying Conservatives the majority they had anticipated.

THE CONSERVATIVE PARTY

If the Labour Party was never as leftist as some of its counterparts on the continent, the Conservatives (Tories) similarly have made for a rather moderate right. The Conservatives emerged in the late eighteenth century and have come to be identified not only with the democratization of the United Kingdom but also with the origins of the British welfare state through the post–World War II collectivist consensus. Because the Tories have usually been pragmatic conservatives, and because they have always embraced democratic rule, the party has garnered widespread respect and even electoral support among a wide range of voters. In 1997, about one-third of the British working-class vote went to the Conservatives.

Just as the Labour Party developed severe internal ideological divisions beginning in the 1970s, at about the same time, the Tories became divided among advocates of traditional conservative pragmatism, of a limited welfare state, and of radical or neoliberal free-market reforms. The rise to power of Margaret Thatcher in the late 1970s marked the dominance of the neoliberal faction and the Tories' abandonment of support for the collectivist consensus. The party further split over policy regarding the European Union, with so-called Euroskeptics facing off against supporters of integration with Europe.[14]

The Tories struggled in opposition after their defeat in the 1997 elections. A series of ineffective leaders attempted unsuccessfully to lead the Conservative Party back to power. Following the 2005 elections, the Tories chose the young and charismatic David Cameron as party leader. Under Cameron's energetic leadership, and much like Labour under Blair, the Tories forged a more coherent and more centrist ideological position, captured in Cameron's call for a "big society" and more socially liberal policies regarding abortion and gay rights. In the 2010 elections, Conservatives obtained a solid plurality of seats in the House of Commons, but not the majority of seats necessary to govern alone. The Conservatives entered into a coalition government with the Liberal Democrats, forming an unlikely alliance that required ideological and political compromises from both parties.

The party fared better in the 2015 election, winning an outright majority of seats, which allowed the Tories to form a single-party government with Cameron continuing as prime minister.

Despite these gains, the Conservative Party continues to be plagued by fault lines that have persisted within the party since the 1970s. In the wake of the 2008–2009 financial crisis, Cameron's push for austerity measures and a call for leaner government cheered some but angered others. Even more divisive has been the issue of the European Union. Faced with growing disenchantment and fears inside his own party and among the broader British public about increased immigration and threats to British sovereignty, Cameron renegotiated some terms of Britain's EU membership and brought this new arrangement to the British people in 2016 in an "in" or "out" referendum. Although Cameron and EU advocates

British workers and students protest austerity measures imposed by the Conservative-Liberal Democratic coalition.

within the party hoped these efforts would both restore party unity and salvage Britain's membership in the Union, the measure failed on both counts. A number of Conservative MPs, including some party leaders, openly campaigned in favor of Brexit, and several members even defected to the United Kingdom Independence Party (UKIP; see upcoming discussion). Likewise, British voters chose to exit the EU, leading Cameron to take responsibility for the vote and step down as prime minister. Cameron's successor Theresa May sought, like Cameron before her, to restore party unity and obtain a strong mandate to negotiate a favorable Brexit deal by calling a snap election in 2017. But like Cameron's Brexit referendum gamble, her effort backfired. Instead of gaining seats as polls had anticipated, the Tories lost seats and lost their parliamentary majority, forcing a weakened and divided Conservative party to lead a minority government.

THE LIBERAL DEMOCRATS

A third-party refuge for voters embracing a range of values and political positions, the Liberal Democratic Party was formed in 1988 through the merger of the Liberal Party and defectors from the Labour Party. Despite its left-of-center origins, the party's 2010 alliance with the Conservatives was not as unlikely as it may have seemed. And while the "Tory-LibDem" coalition proved less harmonious than its architects hoped, it nonetheless held together for a full five-year term, indicating at least a degree of pragmatic cooperation if not a great deal of ideological common ground.

The Liberal Democratic Party's ideology is a mixture of classical liberalism's emphasis on both individual freedom and a weak state and social democracy's emphasis on collective equality. The Liberals (Whigs) were displaced by the rise of the Labour Party in the early twentieth century, and the current Liberal Democratic Party has been unable to recover the power and influence of the early Whigs. The Liberal Democrats have been consistent supporters of European integration and were staunch opponents of the war in Iraq. Though viewed as a centrist party, the Liberal Democrats have often attacked New Labour's policies as too timid and have frequently called for increased taxation and social spending. Though generally viewed as closer to Labour than to the Conservatives, as early as 2004 the party adopted a policy of strict neutrality vis-à-vis the two major parties, indicating its willingness to consider forming a coalition with either party in the event of a hung parliament. In 2007, Nick Clegg was elected Liberal Democratic leader and became the United Kingdom's youngest party leader.

In the 2010 elections, Clegg and the Liberal Democrats obtained the party's highest-ever share of the popular vote (23 percent), but they were still unable to break through the barriers imposed by the SMD electoral system and actually lost seats in Parliament. The Liberal Democrats have consistently called for electoral reform that would give Britain a system rewarding parties with seats in proportion to their votes. Finding themselves for the first time in the position of deal-maker in Britain's 2010 hung parliament, they were able to demand a 2011 referendum on electoral reform. But because both major parties feared they would not be able to win an outright majority in a proportional representation (PR) system, the Liberal Democrats were able to persuade their Tory coalition partner to agree only to a much more modest proposal which predictably failed. Similarly, Liberal Democrats also secured a promise from Conservatives that the coalition government would put forward a bill reforming the House of Lords. Although the bill was proposed in 2012, Conservative backbenchers derailed it before it ever came to a vote, thus indicating the limitations of coalition cooperation.

The greatest victim of these coalition conflicts turned out to be the Liberal Democrats, whose supporters felt that the party (and particularly its leader and Deputy Prime Minister Nick Clegg) conceded too much ground to the Conservatives in an effort to keep the coalition together. What appeared in 2010 as a great opportunity for this third party to break the Labour/Conservative lock on government ultimately proved to be the party's weakening. In 2015 the party obtained less than 8 percent of the vote and captured only 8 seats in the House of Commons. Although the LibDems picked up four seats in the 2017 election, its percentage of the popular vote declined. Clegg stepped down as party leader after the 2015 election and his successor did the same following the 2017 poll.

OTHER PARTIES

The apparent weakening of the Liberal Democrats as a third contender in British politics does not mean that smaller parties play no role in British politics. However, while a variety of small parties vie for seats in British elections, few of them are successful. The main impediment to the success of small parties remains the structure of the electoral system, since plurality SMD systems tend to work against small parties that fail to win a plurality of votes. Other than the Liberal Democratic Party and the Green Party (which elected its first MP in 2010 after decades of political activity), historically regionally based parties—such as the Scottish National Party (SNP), the Welsh Plaid Cymru, and several Northern Irish parties (for example,

Sinn Féin)—have been most successful in concentrating enough votes in some districts to win seats in the legislature. As noted earlier, the SNP fared particularly well in the 2015 election, securing all but 3 of the 59 seats representing Scotland in Parliament while winning less than 5 percent of the overall vote.

Finally, though it obtained only one seat in the 2015 election and lost that seat in the 2017 election, in recent years the United Kingdom Independence Party (UKIP) garnered significant support for its anti-EU, anti-immigration platform. Such support was particularly pronounced in local elections and, ironically, in elections to the European Parliament (even though the party firmly opposes the European Union). In fact, in the 2014 European Parliamentary elections, UKIP received more votes and seated more members than any other party—the first time in over a century that a political party other than the Conservatives or Labour had won a national election.

How do we account for this success? The party has capitalized on growing "Europhobia" in Britain and rising unease with immigration in general. In addition, the party's outspoken populist leader (and member of the European Parliament), **Nigel Farage**, brought a great deal of publicity and popular support to the party. Finally, British Members of the European Parliament (MEPs) are elected using a proportional representation system, which rewarded UKIP as the top vote-getter. This final point highlights the significance of electoral systems. Although UKIP garnered nearly 13 percent of the popular vote in the 2015 House of Commons election, voters had little reason to remain loyal to this single-issue party following the successful Brexit referendum in 2016. UKIP obtained less than 2 percent of the popular vote in the 2017 election and lost its only MP.

PARTY POLITICS TODAY

In the 2015 elections, although voters ended the hung parliament by awarding a majority of seats to the Conservatives, the two leading parties together won only two-thirds of the vote, with the remaining third divided among a variety of parties. In total, 12 parties won seats in the House of Commons, up from 10 in 2010.[15] But just two years later, voters returned to the major parties, which together secured over 90 percent of the vote. However, no party obtained either a majority of votes or seats, giving Britain its second hung parliament in three elections.

These two near-consecutive hung parliaments point to the challenges facing the two leading parties just as the precipitous drop in support for the Liberal

Democrats demonstrates the difficulties facing a third party seeking significant influence in this majoritarian parliamentary system. If British politics are supposed to be about staid traditions and predictable continuity, trends in the past three elections and disputes and divisions in all three major parties seem to be challenging these conventions. Until 2010, every government since 1945 was run by either the Conservatives or Labour, and only once (1974–79) did either party fail to have a majority in the House of Commons. Until 2010, it had been nearly 70 years since the United Kingdom was governed by a peacetime coalition. (Britain was led during both world wars by coalition governments.) And following the 2017 election, the Conservatives have been forced to form a minority government with promised support on key votes from Northern Ireland's Democratic Unionist Party.

In 2015, support for regional and single-issue parties surged at the expense of the larger parties. Moreover, since the 2015 election all three major parties have swapped out their party leaders: Labour is led by Jeremy Corbyn, a left-wing socialist loved by party loyalists but unsupported by many MPs from his own party. Theresa May now leads a Conservative Party deeply divided by the issue of the UK's exit from the EU and as prime minister must now negotiate Britain's exit from the EU even though she campaigned for her country to remain a part of the body. Meanwhile, the Liberal Democrats, who also favored the losing side of the 2016 Brexit referendum, are licking their wounds from losses in the past two elections. Certainly party politics—and democracy—remain alive and well in contemporary Britain.

Elections

British voters select all 650 members of the House of Commons during a general election. With the passage of the Fixed-term Parliaments Act in 2011, the date for these elections was set on a five-year term beginning with the 2015 election (barring a vote of no confidence, a supermajority override—as happened to allow the 2017 election—or a change in this law). Usually about 60 to 70 percent of the electorate votes in British general elections, below the European average but far above the U.S. turnout.

British campaigns are short affairs, usually lasting less than a month. The voter has a relatively simple choice: which party should govern? British parties are for the most part well disciplined and have clear, published policy manifestos. Compared with voters in the United States, voters in the United Kingdom are far more

Seats in the House of Commons, 2017

PARTY	SEATS
Conservative	318
Labour	262
Scottish National Party	35
Liberal Democrat	12
Democratic Unionist Party	10
Sinn Féin	7
Plaid Cymru	4
Green Party	1
Independent Unionist Party	1
Total Seats	650

Source: www.parliament.uk/mps-lords-and-offices/mps/current-state-of-the-parties (accessed 6/23/17).

likely to know what each party stands for and how the parties differ. UK voters tend to focus on differences between parties rather than on differences between candidates. Candidates may not even reside in the district where they run for office. The notion of a candidate serving local (rather than party) interests first—that is, concentrating on bringing benefits (or pork) to local constituents to secure reelection—is of much less concern than it is in the United States.

Civil Society

As in virtually all democracies, the United Kingdom houses various groups articulating special interests (interests that benefit specific segments of the population instead of the nation as a whole). British interest groups influence public policy and public opinion, but interest-group lobbying of MPs is far less prevalent than such lobbying is in the U.S. Congress, because British parties are more highly disciplined. Interest groups must focus their attention on the party leadership (since parties, not individual MPs, make key policy decisions) and on the government bureaucracies, which often interpret and apply policies.

Perhaps the greatest influence of British interest groups comes through their participation in **quangos** (quasi-autonomous nongovernmental organizations). Quangos are policy advisory boards or other entities appointed or approved by the government that bring government officials and affected interest groups together to help develop policy. First established in the 1960s and 1970s, quangos represent a move toward a neocorporatist model of public policy making, in which government and interest groups work together to develop policy. Although Conservative governments have attacked the quangos (seeing them as costly, empowering special interests and weakening government) and have trimmed the number of quangos as a means of shrinking the size of the public sector and reducing public debt, more than a thousand of these organizations remain, working in different policy areas.

In sheer numbers, the **Trades Union Congress (TUC)**, a confederation of the United Kingdom's largest trade unions, is the most important British interest group. For much of the postwar period, the TUC dominated the Labour Party and was thus extremely influential during periods of Labour government. Yet a variety of factors have weakened the TUC over the past two decades. First, as is the case in all industrial democracies, the number of blue-collar workers is shrinking quickly, and the TUC has seen its membership plummet. Only 20 years ago, about one-half of British workers belonged to trade unions; today, only about one-quarter of workers are union members. Second, the Conservative governments of Margaret Thatcher sharply reduced the political power of the TUC by passing laws designed to restrict union activity. Third, reforms within the Labour Party since the 1990s severely eroded the TUC's control of that party. The TUC is still an important source of funding and electoral support, but the TUC–Labour link has been seriously weakened. The TUC can no longer dominate the selection of the Labour Party leader and no longer dominates the formation of Labour policy.

The most important business organization in the United Kingdom, and the main counterweight to the TUC, is the **Confederation of British Industry (CBI)**. Unlike the TUC, which has formal links to the Labour Party, the CBI has no direct link to the Tories. The main industrial and financial interests in the

United Kingdom usually favor Conservative policy, however, and top business leaders have exercised considerable influence in past Conservative governments. In recent decades, the Labour Party has also been careful to cultivate good relations with the CBI.

Society

The United Kingdom's social makeup is divided in many significant ways. The British state is both multinational and multiethnic; British society reveals class, religious, and even linguistic divisions. But while these divisions may appear rather sharp when viewed from the outside, compared with the social divisiveness in most other states, they have been relatively benign. Over the centuries, the United Kingdom has demonstrated remarkable national unity and enviable social and political stability.

Class Identity

Class identity remains perhaps the most salient of all social divisions in the United Kingdom and the one most noticed by outside observers. Historically, political parties and many key policy debates have reflected class differences, not differences of ethnicity, region, or religion, as is often the case in other states. Certainly the social reforms of the twentieth century did much to ease the huge income disparities and rigid occupation-based class lines of nineteenth-century England that preoccupied both Karl Marx and Charles Dickens. But increased social mobility has not yet erased the perception of a two-tier society divided between an upper class and a working class.

Chief among the legacies of the class system has been the education system, which has long channeled a minority of the British elite into so-called public schools (which are, in fact, private schools originally designed to train British boys for public service). Graduates of these elite schools go on to Oxford or Cambridge University before pursuing white-collar careers in government or industry, careers enhanced by elitist old-boy networks. For example, former prime minister David Cameron graduated from the public school Eton and then Oxford. Likewise, current prime minister Theresa May is also a product of Oxford. Class differences are also perpetuated by continued self-identification with either the upper class or the working class, as manifested in preferred tastes and leisure activities—sherry versus warm beer, cricket versus football, opera versus pub—and variations in speech and accent. Some argue that under the neoliberal reforms of recent decades, class differences have finally begun to break down. However, with a more prosperous and vibrant white-collar southern England and a struggling blue-collar north, regional disparities in income remain a source of social division.[16]

Ethnic and National Identity

Although we have noted that the United Kingdom is relatively homogeneous, religious, linguistic, and cultural divisions do exist and in some cases are becoming more significant, and even volatile. Observers point to the 2005 London bombings by Islamic extremists and racially charged riots across England in 2011 as evidence of continuing ethnic tensions. Nevertheless, the United Kingdom settled most of its religious differences early on, and its politics are more secular than those in the rest of Europe. Even today, however, Scots are mainly Catholic or Presbyterian, and the English mostly identify with the Church of England. Compared with the United States, however, religiously oriented social issues in the United Kingdom, such as gay rights and abortion, have generally not become politicized.[17]

Religion remains a source of conflict in **Northern Ireland**, though, where roughly 48 percent of the citizens are Protestant (of Scottish or English origin) but some 45 percent of the population is Catholic. Northern Ireland, also known as Ulster, comprises the northeastern portion of the island of Ireland (about 17 percent of the island's territory) that remained part of the United Kingdom following the creation of an independent Republic of Ireland in 1921. This religious divide was compounded by both national and class differences, and Catholics were discriminated against in employment and education. Starting in the 1960s, members of the Irish Republican Army (IRA) turned to violence against British targets in the hope of unifying the region with the Republic of Ireland, and the British army and illegal Protestant paramilitary organizations fought back. Known as **The Troubles**, this three-decades-long period of conflict claimed nearly 4,000 casualties on both sides, many of them civilian.

In the 1990s, the British government and the IRA began talks with the aim of establishing peace. Years of negotiation resulted in the 1998 Good Friday Agreement, which bound the IRA to renounce its armed struggle in return for political reforms that would give the Catholic population greater say in local government. Both the British and the Irish governments supported the decision, as did important Northern Irish political groups, including Catholic republicans, who favor Northern Ireland's unification with the Republic of Ireland, and Protestant unionists, who favor maintaining Northern Ireland's inclusion in the United Kingdom. Among other provisions, the Good Friday Agreement authorized the creation of a Northern Irish legislature and a voting system ensuring proportional representation ("first past the post" had effectively marginalized the Catholic minority). With this agreement, violence by both republican and unionist paramilitary organizations virtually came to an end, although the IRA initially refused to give up its formidable arsenal. As a result, the British government suspended Northern Ireland's legislature in 2002. In 2005, the IRA finally renounced the use of armed conflict altogether, and self-rule was restored to Ulster in 2007. The first leader of the restored Northern Ireland government was the Protestant minister Ian Paisley, leader of the only mainstream Ulster party to oppose the agreement. His deputy leader was Martin McGuinness, leader of Sinn Féin and a former IRA militant.[18] Since 1998, the region has been relatively peaceful for the first time in decades, although occasional acts of political violence, including several killings in 2009, are a reminder that the region's political future remains uncertain.

Elsewhere, however, new divisions are emerging. Since the 1960s, former colonial subjects (primarily from Africa, the West Indies, India, and Pakistan) have immigrated to the United Kingdom in increasing numbers, giving British society a degree of racial diversity. For the most part, British society has not coped particularly well with this influx. Racial tension between the overwhelming majority of whites and the non-European minorities (totaling some 13 percent of the population) has sparked conflict and anti-immigrant sentiment, both of which nonetheless remain moderate by American and continental standards. Lacking proportional representation, the British electoral system has limited the impact of both the nonwhite and the far-right vote in most elections. Parliament has also sought to limit the nonwhite population by imposing quotas that restrict the entrance of nonwhite dependents of persons already residing in the United Kingdom. Even so, the country continues to face growing rates of immigration. Some predict that another 2 million immigrants will enter the United Kingdom over the next decade. This has already changed the social dynamics and increased xenophobic sentiment, strengthening parties such as the UKIP and bolstering the successful Brexit vote. Also, the integration (or lack thereof) of the United Kingdom's Muslim population has been a growing concern since the 2005 terrorist attacks on London's transit system.

In addition to ethnic groups, the United Kingdom also comprises a number of national groups, a fact outsiders tend to overlook. The United Kingdom of Britain

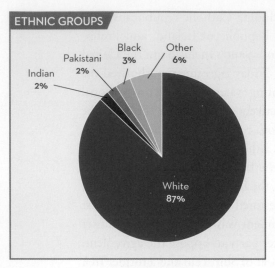

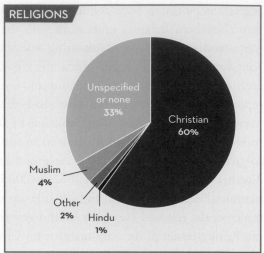

and Northern Ireland is made up of four nations—England, Scotland, Wales, and Northern Ireland—with substantial cultural and political differences among them. Most UK citizens first identify themselves not as British but as belonging to one of these four nationalities.[19] (The U.S. equivalent to this would be a resident of Los Angeles identifying herself first as a Californian, not as an American.)

Long-standing yearning for greater national autonomy has gained increasing political significance since the 1960s. Local nationalist parties including the Scottish National Party and the Welsh Plaid Cymru, with Labour Party support, successfully advocated for devolution: turning over some central-governmental powers to the regions. Tony Blair's Labour government delivered on its campaign promise of devolution in 1999 with the establishment of local legislatures for Northern Ireland, Scotland, and Wales. Some feared that rather than pacify nationalist tendencies, devolution would contribute to the eventual breakup of the country, most notably with an independent Scotland (see the discussion "Scotland's Bid for Independence," p. 81).

While persistent regional loyalties and the localization of government have challenged the British national identity, so, too, have the United Kingdom's growing economic and cultural integration with Europe over the past few decades and, at the same time, its growing ambivalence about this dependence and decision to weaken those ties by exiting the EU. Although nearly half of British voters called for retaining membership in the Union, it is safe to say that virtually all Britons remain generally very loyal to the Crown and to the notion of a sovereign British people (see "Brexit," p. 84).

Ideology and Political Culture

Regarding the goals of politics, British political values have been strongly influenced by the development of classical liberalism and the conviction that government's influence over individuals ought to be limited. However, the postwar goals of an expanded franchise, full employment, and the creation of a welfare state led to a new consensus as many Britons embraced the social-democratic values of increased state intervention and less individual freedom in exchange for increased social equality. Economic decline during the 1970s swung the pendulum back toward personal freedom, which spurned consensus politics, rejected socialist redistributive policies, and advocated privatization.

The electoral success of the Labour Party in 1997 came on the heels of its new policy to reconcile social-democratic and liberal ideologies—the so-called Third Way. While this may indicate that British voters did not fully embrace the stark individualism of the Thatcher revolution, much of Labour's subsequent success came from embracing a kinder, gentler version of her neoliberal program. Calls by subsequent Conservative governments for a "big society" can also be seen in this light—a shift of governance and stewardship from national to local, public to private. Still, most British—like their continental neighbors—tend to be more socially and morally liberal than citizens of the United States. The United Kingdom outlawed capital punishment and legalized abortion and homosexuality, all in the mid-1960s. Handguns were banned outright in 1998 and same-sex marriage has been legal in England since 2013 and Scotland since 2014 (though not yet in Northern Ireland). Also, there is far less emphasis on religion and traditional family values.

British political culture is typically described as pragmatic and tolerant. Compared with other societies, British society is thought to be less concerned with adhering to overarching ideological principles and more willing to tinker gradually with a particular political problem. Scholars often account for this pragmatism by pointing to the incremental and ad hoc historical development of British political institutions, noting that there was no defining political moment in British history when founders or revolutionaries sat down and envisioned or established a political system or a set of rules based on abstract ideals or theoretical principles. Political radicalism, on either the left or the right, is rare in the United Kingdom. Virtually all political actors embrace the willingness to seek evolutionary, not revolutionary, change. This pragmatism is bolstered by a classical liberal tolerance for opposing viewpoints, a strong sense of fair play, and a generally high level of consensus on the political rules of the game.

Although such general characterizations have some utility in accounting for British politics, British political culture in reality comprises multiple subcultures, as is the case in any complex modern or postmodern society. It is certainly still possible to see evidence of an aristocratic culture among the political elite, who share a sense of superiority and noblesse oblige toward those they deem less able to rule, as well as a mass or working-class culture of deference to those in authority. But in addition, policies of devolution, immigration, and multiculturalism, combined with the blurring of class lines, have challenged and complicated these dominant subcultures. And with economic recession, growing social inequality, and increased immigration over the past decade, simmering tensions within some of these groups have boiled over. Several days of violent and destructive riots in the summer of 2011 in London and other cities across England pitted angry inner-city youth against the police and served as a sober reminder that elements among these subcultures were fully prepared to reject deference toward authority. In that same year, labor unions and university students launched widespread anti-austerity demonstrations against deep public-sector spending cuts, protests that also spoke to significant divisions within the political culture.

Political Economy

The United Kingdom is noteworthy for its contribution to the liberal economic model. Indeed, most political analysts would trace classical liberalism itself to the United Kingdom, where philosophers such as John Locke spoke of the inalienable rights of "life, liberty and estate," setting the stage for such political innovations as the U.S. Declaration of Independence.[20] Yet liberalism in the United Kingdom has undergone a number of shifts over the past decades, from the greater emphasis on social-democratic values after World War II to the neoliberalism under Margaret Thatcher, which has been softened but largely continued in subsequent governments.

If there is a common theme in the UK economy in the decades following the end of World War II, it is decline. As we recall, during the Industrial Revolution, the United Kingdom was "the workshop to the world," and the British Empire was led by the richest country on the planet. Yet over time, this position of dominance deteriorated. As of 2016, the country's per capita GDP at purchasing power parity (PPP) ranked 38th in the world, behind once far-poorer colonies such as Ireland and Australia (though the UK economy remains one of the 10 largest in the world).

Why the decline? There is no single explanation, but one of the basic causes is the downside of early industrialization, which made the country the world's first industrial power but later allowed it to be the first country to face the obsolescence of its technology and the difficulty of shifting to a new economic environment (a challenge Japan currently faces). A second factor is the burden of empire. Although industrialization helped fuel imperialism (and vice versa), the British Empire soon became a financial drain on the country rather than a benefit to it. Related to this is the argument that the United Kingdom's orientation toward its empire meant that it was slow to pursue economic opportunities with the rest of Europe when the continent moved toward greater integration after World War II. Finally, many

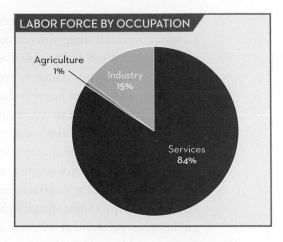

LABOR FORCE BY OCCUPATION

Agriculture 1%

Industry 15%

Services 84%

political analysts have argued that the collectivist consensus not only blocked meaningful economic reform in the United Kingdom for much of the postwar era but also focused the country on social expenditures while causing it to ignore the simultaneous need to modernize its economy.

Where does this leave the UK economy in the new century? Like other advanced democracies, the United Kingdom is a postindustrial economy. Although such industries as steel, oil, and gas still play an important role, nearly three-quarters of the country's wealth is generated by the service sector, in particular financial services and tourism. Privatization has significantly shrunk the role of the state in the economy, including the sale of a range of assets, among them public utilities and housing, British Airways, Rolls-Royce, and Jaguar. Recent governments have sought to extend privatization to railroads, health care, and even the Underground (London's famous subway system). The welfare state also has undergone substantial changes, moving from a system that provided direct benefits to the unemployed to one that sponsors "welfare-to-work" programs emphasizing training to find employment. Even though Labour governments have tended to spend more on social welfare than do their Tory counterparts, even Labour has ended its traditional call for a greater role for the state in the economy—nationalization of industry was enshrined in the Labour Party constitution until 1995—and has distanced itself from its formerly close ties with organized labor.

To some observers, the Thatcher revolution, and its preservation under subsequent governments, helped the United Kingdom finally turn a corner. Until the global recession hit in 2008, the country enjoyed a decade of strong economic growth. And both before the global economic downturn as well as now in a period of recovery, the UK economy has outperformed the economies of Europe and

Japan. However, as in many other countries, neoliberal economic policies have increased financial inequality throughout the United Kingdom, which has one of the highest levels of inequality in Europe. This inequality also has a regional element: the country's south is growing much faster than the north, which is the traditional home of heavy industry. Recognizing this growing inequality and sounding more like a Labour than a Conservative government, Prime Minister May has called for building an economy that works for all citizens, not just the wealthy. Her government has introduced programs designed to help the poor and disadvantaged, who have suffered disproportionately during the global financial crisis of the last decade and the more recent economic downturn caused by Brexit.

Moreover, this public spending has exacerbated the United Kingdom's growing gap between government revenues and government spending, a malady that Britain shares with the United States and most other industrialized countries. Britain's budget deficit became acute following the 2008 global financial crisis and was exacerbated by an inflated housing bubble and an economy largely dependent on financial services—the industry hardest hit by the financial crisis. In response, the Labour government partially nationalized a number of private banks, increased income taxes for the wealthy, and stepped up both public borrowing and public spending in an effort to stimulate the economy. After coming to office in 2010, the Conservative–Liberal Democrat coalition government shifted to a more liberal tack, cutting public spending and pursuing deregulation in an effort to reduce the government's growing deficit. The government faced great resistance from public-sector unions, university students, and others as it pursued these tough austerity measures, which have since been softened by the May government. The success or failure of these measures remains a subject of great debate.[21]

Finally, there is the issue of the United Kingdom's economic relationship with the outside world. Historic ties notwithstanding, over the past half century the country has become closely tied to the rest of Europe; half of its trade goes to other EU member states. However, the United Kingdom never accepted the euro, the common currency of the European Union, and in 2016 elected to end its membership in the body. While the decision pleased Euroskeptics and relieved Britain of some of the political obligations of this decades-long association, it also proved economically costly in terms of investor confidence and concerns that the UK would suffer from the loss of full membership in Europe's single market. However, disentangling Britain from the EU has proven a slow and cautious process, and the May government has done all it can to retain the benefits of European integration while freeing itself from unwanted burdens (see "Brexit," p. 84).

In the end, these issues tie into a much broader question: What is the United Kingdom's place in the contemporary international system?

Early euphoria among the majority of British voters who supported Brexit soon gave way to the sober challenges of disentangling Britain from the European Union.

Foreign Relations and the World

The United Kingdom's political future does not rest on domestic politics alone. Although the country is no longer a superpower, it retains a relatively large army, has its own nuclear weapons, and boasts one of the largest economies in the world. It remains a major player in world affairs but struggles to define its place and role in a post-imperial and post–Cold War world. The central difficulty lies in the United Kingdom's self-identity. As citizens of an island nation and a former imperial power, the British have long seen themselves as separate from continental Europe, which was slower to adopt democracy and remains much more skeptical of the liberal values that first emerged in the United Kingdom. Rather than identifying itself with the continent, the United Kingdom built its identity around its empire, orienting itself toward the Atlantic. When the empire eventually declined, the emergence of the United States gave the United Kingdom the sense that its power had in a way been resurrected in a former colony, whose citizens were imbued with the same liberal values and spoke a common language. Since the end of World War II, the United States has counted on the United Kingdom as its most dependable ally.[22]

The United Kingdom also remains willing to defend its interests militarily. In 1982, Argentina seized the Falkland Islands—a remote British territory of about 2,000 residents some 300 miles off the coast of Argentina—after a long-running dispute over ownership of the islands. The United Kingdom dispatched its military to retake the colony and succeeded in driving out the Argentine forces. In the process, more than 200 British soldiers and more than 600 Argentine soldiers were killed. Many observers may find the deaths of so many soldiers over two small, sparsely populated islands illogical, but the conflict reflects the United Kingdom's post-imperial identity and its desire not to surrender its international power. Both Labour- and Tory-led governments strongly supported the U.S.-led wars in Afghanistan and Iraq, and the United Kingdom was the only other country to contribute a significant military force to the Iraq conflict. But despite the government's support of U.S. foreign policies, the United Kingdom's Atlantic orientation is uncertain. Even as the United Kingdom continues to resist European integration, its relationship with the United States remains a powerful, if problematic, alternative. As we noted, the United Kingdom shares a strong historical affinity with this former colony and current superpower across the Atlantic. Even though the disparity in power between the two countries is enormous, British supporters of the Atlantic alliance argue that limited influence over the only superpower is superior to a more equal standing in a body such as the European Union, whose international authority remains rather limited.

However, particularly in the aftermath of September 11 and the Iraq War, many Britons have come to the disappointing conclusion that the United States sees the United Kingdom not as a critical ally but rather as a junior partner duly expected to follow U.S. foreign policy and provide a veneer of multilateralism no matter what the United States wants to do. This perception has fueled British anti-Americanism much like that seen elsewhere in Europe today. A 2016 poll showed that just over 60 percent of Britons had a favorable view of the United States, down from more than 66 percent in 2014 and more than 80 percent in 2000. Nearly half of those surveyed in 2014 also believed that the United Kingdom should act more independently of the United States.[23]

Despite stepping away from the European Union, the United Kingdom finds itself in greater agreement with its European partners on the question of resolving the Palestinian-Israeli conflict to effect lasting peace in the Middle East. This conflict between European and U.S. foreign policies has left the United Kingdom in the middle with diffuse and uneasy ties to both centers of power.

In 2011, Britain joined France in leading a military intervention in Libya that involved a coalition of 19 countries, including the United States. Although leadership of the limited intervention ultimately shifted to NATO, some observers have pointed to this example of French and British cooperative leadership and American followership as an indication both of declining American hegemony and of growing British security collaboration with at least some of its European neighbors.[24] In 2013, Prime Minister Cameron sought to follow America's lead by introducing a bill to the House of Commons to intervene militarily in the Syrian civil war. A majority of MPs, including a significant number of members of Cameron's own ruling coalition, rejected the motion.

The United Kingdom, then, remains unique, as it was centuries ago. Its economic and political systems gave rise to liberalism but remain shaped by centuries-old institutions that have never been fully swept away. Its industrial strength once propelled it to empire status, though now it is overshadowed by its former colony across the Atlantic and an ever-converging Europe. In recent years, the United Kingdom has grappled with these issues, hoping to modernize old institutions yet retain its distinct identity—and hoping, too, to retain its international stature while reevaluating its relationship to the United States and the rest of Europe. Will the United Kingdom break from its past, creating a new identity to meet its domestic and international challenges? And if so, what might this identity look like? These will be critical issues in its immediate future.

CURRENT ISSUES IN THE UNITED KINGDOM

Scotland's Bid for Independence

Northern Ireland is not the only region where a sector of the population has sought to leave the United Kingdom. Scotland was an independent state until the 1707 Act of Union—passed by the Scottish legislature despite widespread popular protest—fused it with England to form Great Britain. Scotland preserved its own legal system, its own church, and many of its own traditions. The Scottish National Party (SNP), formed in the 1930s, advocated Scottish independence but was relatively unsuccessful until fairly recently. In 1974, the SNP won about a third of all votes in Scotland and sent a record 11 representatives to the House of Commons in London. Both the discovery of oil in the North Sea in the 1960s and dissatisfaction with Thatcher's neoliberal economic policies in the 1980s led to increasingly loud calls for devolution and bolstered the independence movement.

Coming to office on a mandate of devolution in 1997, Labour responded to the calls, granting Scotland its own legislature and government as well as broad powers over regional issues. Scotland has long had its own legal system, but it increasingly differs from the rest of the United Kingdom on a variety of policies. For example, citizens of Scotland pay no tuition to attend university, unlike other UK citizens, and Scots pay less for health care and prescription drugs than do other UK citizens. Scotland's football federation rejected plans by the British Olympic Association to field all-Britain men's and women's soccer teams for the 2012 London Olympic Games, preferring, like Wales and Northern Ireland, to field its own Scottish national team (though Scotland did join "Team GB" for the 2016 Summer Olympics).[25]

The Labour government anticipated that its policy of devolution would satisfy Scottish demands for greater autonomy and weaken, if not silence, the movement for independence. The Labour Party, in coalition with the Liberal Democrats, controlled the devolved Scottish government from 1998 until 2007, but the SNP capitalized on an economic revival in Scotland and widespread Scottish opposition to Blair's Iraq War policy to win the 2007 regional elections. Alex Salmond, the SNP leader, became first minister (leader) of an SNP minority government, pledging to hold a referendum on independence from the United Kingdom in the future. Four years later, the 2011 general elections returned an increasingly popular Salmond and the SNP to government, giving the Scottish National Party its first-ever majority government. The SNP's capturing of an absolute majority is even more remarkable because of the mixed PR-SMD electoral system in place in Scotland, established in part to prevent the dominance of a single party. With majority control of the Scottish parliament, Salmond and the SNP scheduled a referendum on "home rule" for September 18, 2014, the 700-year anniversary of the Battle of Bannockburn, in which the Scots prevailed over English forces.[26] After some wrangling, London (the national government) and Edinburgh (the devolved regional government) came to terms on the vote: Cameron demanded that the referendum consist of a straight up-or-down vote for independence rather than a three-option plan put forward by the SNP featuring a middle ground option of "devo max" that assured even greater devolution of authority to the Scottish parliament. Salmond conceded this point, but secured in return an expanded franchise that would include 16- and 17-year-old Scots (who strongly favored independence).

Despite a strong surge in the "Yes" campaign in the months leading up to the referendum, Scottish voters rejected the proposal by a clear margin of 56 percent no and 44 percent yes. A majority of Scottish voters ultimately doubted whether Scotland could viably function as an independent state. Scotland lacks a military to defend its sovereignty and is integrally linked to the United Kingdom. Because countless Scots live and work in the rest of the United Kingdom and vice versa, creating distinct citizenship would have been extremely complex. Scotland would have lost its economic support from London and its military protection. It sends 59 members to the House of Commons in London; moreover, many prominent UK politicians, including former Labour prime ministers Tony Blair and Gordon Brown, are Scots. Moreover, although the "devo-max" option did not appear on the referendum ballot, apparent growing support for the "Yes" campaign in the weeks preceding the vote prompted the leaders of Britain's three largest parties to agree to hand over substantially more authority to Scotland's devolved government if voters elected to remain within the Union. Although at the time this compromise seemed to satisfy a significant majority of Scots, British voters' decision two years later to exit the European Union may turn the tables.

A majority of Scottish voters rejected the 2014 referendum calling for independence. However, two years later two-thirds of these same voters unsuccessfully opposed the United Kingdom's exit from the European Union, raising the possibility of a new referendum on Scottish independence.

While a majority of British voters elected to leave the EU, nearly two-thirds of Scots who went to the polls voted to remain. Many of these same voters, led by Scotland's devolved SNP government, subsequently called for a new referendum on independence.

Brexit

In recent years, many Scots have grumbled about their "democratic deficit" and other constraints imposed on them as Britons. During this same period, a growing number of British citizens complained that membership in the European Union threatened key aspects of British sovereignty, subjecting them to the dictates of distant Eurocrats.

The integration of Europe began in the 1950s, has progressed in fits and starts, and has involved a variety of institutional efforts. By 1993, a dozen European countries had formed the European Union, a community that now encompasses nearly 30 sovereign states that have struggled to forge ever-closer political, economic, and social ties among its members. As noted earlier, the United Kingdom was late in warming to the idea of the European Union, initially skeptical of membership and then later kept out by the French (who saw British membership as a Trojan horse through which the United States could influence Europe). Even as the United Kingdom joined the European project, it continued to be less than enthusiastic about many aspects of the Union, especially with respect to the latter's ambitions for taking on more power and responsibilities, such as effecting monetary union or promoting unified foreign policy. During the 1970s and 1980s, this attitude was less of a problem because the European Union had entered a period of relative stagnation. Beginning in the 1990s, however, many European leaders moved forward to strengthen the European Union, enabling it to ensure regional stability and act as a counterweight to the "hyperpower" of the United States.

To many Britons, the notion of participating in a stronger European Union was simply unacceptable, fearing the regional economic union would become an unwieldy superstate, undermining national sovereignty, draining the domestic budget, and imposing continental values.[27] The fact that half of the European Union's budget is spent on agricultural subsidies, of which the United Kingdom received relatively little, only underscored this suspicion. In 2014, only 22 percent of those surveyed in the United Kingdom felt they could trust the European Union, the lowest level of any member state (see "In Comparison: European

Union," p. 86). The United Kingdom's unwillingness to adopt the euro provided further evidence of this skepticism, which increased in the wake of the 2011 euro crisis and ongoing economic challenges facing the Continent. The European migrant crisis beginning in 2015, combined with the EU policy of free movement of people throughout the single market, only compounded this sense of Europessimism among British citizens who felt Polish migrants were taking local jobs and migrants from Africa and the Middle East were destabilizing British society. On the other hand, proponents of the EU pointed to the huge trade and investment benefits of membership and the fears that the United Kingdom would lose even more economic and diplomatic power and marginalize itself, becoming a peripheral player in the emergence of a single European power.

In short, Britain's position vis-à-vis Europe over the past few decades remained controversial and ambivalent. Blair and his Labour government promised a referendum on adoption of the euro, but never followed through on the pledge, and Labour also backed away from its initial commitment to the euro. Conservatives and Liberal Democrats agreed at the formation of their 2010 coalition that their government would not adopt the euro while the coalition was in effect but would remain a positive force in the European Union. But as popular British sentiment toward the European Union continued to sour and divisions on the issue within the Conservative Party and among Tory MPs began to widen, Prime Minister Cameron sought to shore up support within his own party by promising in 2013 that if the Tories were to win an outright majority in the 2015 parliamentary elections, the government would hold a national referendum on British membership in the European Union. With the Tories' clear victory in the 2015 election, voters held him to that promise.

In what came to be known as a "Brexit" vote, Cameron promised that his government would first negotiate new agreements with the European Union and then hold a simple "in-or-out" referendum on Britain's EU membership by the end of 2017. In 2016, Cameron negotiated concessions from the EU that exempted Britain from obligations for member countries to pursue greater political integration and limited welfare and employment benefits to migrants. The referendum was held in June of the same year. Those campaigning for the "Leave" side, including several leading MPs and other members of Cameron's Conservative Party, argued that leaving the union would restore British sovereignty, protect British jobs, shield Britain from unmanageable levels of immigration, and free Britain from obligations to bail out struggling European economies. They argued that Britain would then be free to establish unilateral trade agreements with the United States and other countries and could still negotiate free-trade agreements

Do you think things are going in the right direction in the European Union? Percentage saying yes:

COUNTRY	PERCENTAGE
Germany	33
France	21
United Kingdom	20

Do you trust the European Union? Percentage saying yes:

COUNTRY	PERCENTAGE
France	31
Germany	28
United Kingdom	22

Source: "Europeans in 2014," Special Eurobarometer 415, July 2014, http://ec.europa.eu /public_opinion/archives/ebs/ebs_415_data_en.pdf (accessed 7/24/16).

with its European partners.[28] Those stumping for the "Remain" side, including Cameron, contended that the United Kingdom and its citizens were far wealthier as part of the European single market and that a seat at the European table gave Britain significant influence in Europe and beyond.[29] Most polls leading up to the vote gave the "Remain" side a bit of an edge, and most of these pollsters, as well as politicians and the British populace, were surprised by the outcome: nearly 52 percent of voters chose to leave while just over 48 percent elected to remain.

It is difficult to exaggerate the significance of this outcome. Within a day, Prime Minister David Cameron, who called for the referendum bargaining his country's future in an effort to shore up support within his own party, took responsibility for the loss and announced his resignation. Within a month, Theresa May, who actually campaigned for remaining in the EU, had replaced Cameron as leader of the Tories and prime minister. She quickly formed her cabinet, appointing outspoken "Leave" proponents to the posts of both foreign secretary and trade secretary. Another Euroskeptic was given the post of a newly formed ministry responsible for overseeing the complicated process of Brexit. Meanwhile, all major political parties (other than the divided Tories) had joined Cameron in supporting the failed "Remain" campaign, most vocally the majority SNP in Scotland and Sinn Féin in Northern Ireland. Both parties called for referenda of their own that would permit continued membership in the EU; Scotland to again consider full independence and Northern Ireland to unite Northern Ireland with the Republic of Ireland. Both Labour and the Liberal Democrats also favored the "Remain" side, but in many cases kept a low profile during the campaign in recognition that a growing number of their constituents were increasingly Euroskeptic. The United Kingdom Independence Party, long the most outspoken advocate of British withdrawal from the European Union, led the successful "Leave" campaign, and having achieved its long-held goal, seems to have outlived its usefulness. The torch passed to a weak and divided Conservative minority government to negotiate Britain's withdrawal from the European Union.

NOTES

1. R. C. van Caenegem, *The Birth of the English Common Law* (Cambridge: Cambridge University Press, 1989).
2. Jeremy Black, *Walpole in Power* (Stroud, UK: Sutton, 2001).
3. For a discussion of the link between economic and democratic development, see Barrington Moore Jr., *Social Origins of Dictatorship and Democracy* (Boston: Beacon Press, 1966).
4. For a discussion of Thatcherism and its effects, see Earl Reitan, *The Thatcher Revolution: Margaret Thatcher, John Major, and Tony Blair, 1979–2001* (Lanham, MD: Rowman & Littlefield, 2003); for her own perspective, see Margaret Thatcher, *The Downing Street Years* (New York: HarperCollins, 1993).
5. For a discussion of the constitution in practice, see Peter Hennessy, *The Hidden Wiring: Unearthing the British Constitution* (London: Victor Gollancz, 1995).
6. Philip Johnston, "Would a Constitution Save Britain from the EU?" *Telegraph*, July 8, 2014.
7. Vernon Bogdanor, "An Era of Constitutional Reform," *Political Quarterly* (September 2011): S53–S64.
8. Roger Mortimore, "Monarchy as Popular as Ever Ahead of Queen's 90th Birthday Celebrations," *Ipsos MORI*, April 15, 2016. www.ipsos-mori.com/researchpublications/researcharchive /3720/Monarchy-popular-as-ever-ahead-of-Queens-90th-Birthday-celebrations.aspx (accessed 7/27/16). For a useful discussion of the value of the British monarchy to political life, see Vernon Bogdanor, *The Monarchy and the Constitution* (Oxford: Clarendon Press, 1996).
9. British question time can be seen regularly on the public affairs channel C-SPAN and can be accessed online at www.cspan.org.
10. "Captain Malaprop," *Economist*, June 26, 2008.
11. Meg Russell, *The Contemporary House of Lords: Westminster Bicameralism Revived* (Oxford: Oxford University Press, 2014).
12. "Breaking the Old Place Up," *Economist*, November 4, 1999.

13. Anthony Giddens, *The Third Way: The Renewal of Social Democracy* (Malden, MA: Blackwell, 1998).

14. Mark Garnett and Philip Lynch, *The Conservatives in Crisis* (Manchester, UK: Manchester University Press, 2003).

15. Philip Lynch and Robert Garner, "The Changing Party System," *Parliamentary Affairs* 58, no. 3 (June 2005): 533–54.

16. An interesting discussion of the changing nature of class and civil society in Britain can be found in Peter A. Hall, "Great Britain: The Role of Government and the Distribution of Social Capital," in Robert D. Putnam, ed., *Democracies in Flux: The Evolution of Social Change in Contemporary Society* (New York: Oxford University Press, 2002), pp. 21–57.

17. Martin Durham, "Abortion, Gay Rights, and Politics in Britain and America," *Parliamentary Affairs* 58, no. 1 (January 2005): 89–103.

18. For an excellent overview of the success of and challenges facing the Good Friday Agreement, see "The Hand of History Revealed," *Economist*, April 3, 2008.

19. For further discussion, see James Ball, "How British Are the British," *Guardian*, October 6, 2011.

20. John Locke, *Two Treatises on Government: Of Civil Government Book II*, ch. 7 (1689; Online Library of Liberty, 2014), http://oll.libertyfund.org/titles/222 (accessed 11/14/14).

21. John Cassidy, "By George, Britain's Austerity Program Didn't Work," *New Yorker*, December 5, 2013.

22. Lawrence D. Freedman, "The Special Relationship: Then and Now," *Foreign Affairs* 85, no. 3 (May/June 2006): 61–73.

23. Pew Research Center for the People and the Press, www.pewglobal.org/2012/06/13/chapter-1-views-of-the-u-s-and-american-foreign-policy-4/ (accessed 11/14/14).

24. "NATO Libya Coalition Shows Cracks," *Washington Post*, April 14, 2011.

25. Jeré Longman and Sarah Lyall, "A British Soccer Team? What's That? Say Scots, Welsh and Irish," *New York Times*, September 19, 2011.

26. Jonathan Freedland, "Will Scotland Go Independent?" *New York Review of Books*, February 20, 2014. See also W. Elliot Bulmer, "An Analysis of the Scottish National Party's Draft Constitution for Scotland," *Parliamentary Affairs* 64, no. 4 (October 2011): 674–93.

27. David Baker and Philippa Sherrington, "Britain and Europe: The Dog That Didn't Bark," *Parliamentary Affairs* 58, no. 2 (April 2005): 303–17.

28. James Bennett, "After the Brexit," *New Criterion* 32:5 (January 2014): 40–46.

29. Matthijs Matthias, "David Cameron's Dangerous Game: The Folly of Flirting with an EU Exit," *Foreign Affairs* 92 (September/October 2013): 10–16.

KEY TERMS

Blair, Tony Labour prime minister from 1997 to 2007

Brexit British exit from the European Union realized in a 2016 referendum

cabinet Top members of the UK government who assist the prime minister and run the major ministries

Cameron, David Conservative prime minister from 2010 to 2016; resigned following the Brexit referendum, which he campaigned against

Celtic fringe Refers to Scotland and Wales, which were not conquered by the Angles and Saxons

collective responsibility Tradition that requires all members of the cabinet either to support government policy or to resign

collectivist consensus Postwar consensus between the United Kingdom's major parties to build and sustain a welfare state

common law Legal system based on custom and precedent rather than formal legal codes

Commonwealth Organization that includes the United Kingdom and most of its former colonies

Confederation of British Industry (CBI) The United Kingdom's most important group representing the private sector

Conservatives (Tories) One of the United Kingdom's two largest parties; in government since 2010

Corbyn, Jeremy Leader of the opposition Labour Party beginning in 2015

Crown Refers to the British monarchy and sometimes to the British state

English Civil War Seventeenth-century conflict between Parliament and the monarch that temporarily eliminated and permanently weakened the monarchy

Farage, Nigel Outspoken leader of the United Kingdom Independence Party (UKIP) until 2016 and member of the European parliament

Good Friday Agreement Historic 1998 accord between Protestants and Catholics in Northern Ireland that ended decades of violence

hereditary peers Seats in the House of Lords that were granted to aristocratic families in perpetuity but were largely eliminated by recent legislation

House of Commons Lower house of the UK legislature

House of Lords Upper house of the UK legislature, whose reform is currently being debated

hung parliament An election result in which no party wins a majority of parliamentary seats, such as the 2010 and 2017 parliamentary elections

Labour Party One of the United Kingdom's two largest parties; since 2010, it has been the party in opposition

Liberal Democratic Party Centrist third party in the United Kingdom and junior member of a coalition government from 2010 to 2015

Liberals (Whigs) The United Kingdom's historic first opposition party; one of its two major political parties until the early twentieth century

life peers Distinguished members of society who are given lifetime appointments to the House of Lords

Magna Carta The 1215 document signed by King John that set the precedent for limited monarchical powers

majoritarian Term describing the virtually unchecked power of a parliamentary majority in the UK political system

May, Theresa Leader of the Conservatives; prime minister and head of government since 2016

Member of Parliament (MP) An individual legislator in the House of Commons

neoliberalism A set of policies championed by Thatcher's Conservative government in the 1980s aimed at diminishing the role of the state in the economy

Northern Ireland Northeastern portion of Ireland that is part of the United Kingdom; also known as Ulster

Parliament Name of the UK legislature

prime minister Head of government

quangos Quasi-autonomous nongovernmental organizations that assist the government in making policy

Scottish National Party (SNP) Nationalist political party promoting Scottish independence, and currently in control of the Scottish regional government

Thatcher, Margaret Conservative prime minister from 1979 to 1990

The Troubles Name given to the three decades of extreme ethnic conflict (late 1960s to late 1990s) between Northern Ireland's nationalists or republicans, who are mostly Catholic, and unionists or loyalists, who are mostly Protestant

Third Way Term describing recent policies of the Labour Party that embrace the free market

Trades Union Congress (TUC) The United Kingdom's largest trade union confederation

United Kingdom Independence Party (UKIP) Populist and Euroskeptic political party favoring British exit from the European Union

United Kingdom of Great Britain and Northern Ireland Official name of the British state

vote of no confidence Legislative check on government whereby a government deems a measure to be of high importance; if that measure fails to pass the legislature, either the government must resign in favor of another leader or new parliamentary elections must be called

WEB LINKS

- BritainUSA, website of the British government in the United States (www.gov.uk/government/world/usa)
- British Broadcasting Corporation (www.bbc.com)
- British Politics Group (http://britishpoliticsgroup.blogspot.com)
- British Prime Minister (www.gov.uk/government/organisations/prime-ministers-office-10-downing-street)
- Conflict Archive on the Internet, on conflict and politics in Northern Ireland, 1968 to the present (www.cain.ulst.ac.uk)
- Foreign and Commonwealth Office (www.fco.gov.uk)
- London University, on constitutional reform (www.ucl.ac.uk/constitution-unit)
- Parliament (www.parliament.uk)
- Scottish Parliament (www.scottish.parliament.uk)
- Welsh Assembly (www.wales.gov.uk)

3

U.S. citizens are generally patriotic but also skeptical of government. This combination is on display when the legislature or courts debate major policies. This rally, outside the U.S. Supreme Court, protests President Barack Obama's health care reform.

UNITED STATES

Why Study This Case?

Some readers may believe that the United States is the standard to use in measuring advanced industrial democracies. After all, the United States is governed by the oldest written constitution still in effect, and it is the world's greatest military and economic power. Nevertheless, compared with other advanced capitalist democracies, the United States is best viewed as an anomaly filled with paradoxes. It is a large and wealthy nation with a relatively weak state. The United States has a highly legitimate political regime and enjoys widespread adherence to the rule of law despite having a political system deliberately designed to prevent decisive and coherent policy making. U.S. citizens are deeply proud of their state but distrust it and its bureaucracy in far greater numbers than the citizens of other industrialized democracies distrust theirs. Its political system has long been dominated by two political parties, but those parties are themselves relatively weak and at times undisciplined. It has a vibrant civil society but very low voter turnout. The United States is a secular democracy in which religion continues to play a comparatively large role in politics and society. It began as a society of immigrants, and national and regional identities are still in flux because of migration and geographic mobility. The United States has more wealth than any other democracy but is plagued by persistent inequality and the presence of an impoverished underclass more characteristic of developing countries. Americans cherish their freedom and individual liberty, yet 2.4 million American citizens are behind bars—an incarceration rate many times higher than in other advanced democracies. The United States leads the world in medical technology but has more citizens without medical insurance than any other advanced democracy. Blessed with peaceful borders and isolation from major world conflicts, the United States initially favored an isolationist foreign policy but has in recent decades intervened militarily in numerous global conflicts.

UNITED STATES

It is especially vital to understand the unusual workings of the U.S. political system given the country's tremendous power in today's world. The importance of U.S. technology, culture, military power, and economic might is undeniable, and the projection of those strengths is often a source of both admiration and resentment by citizens of other countries.

The twenty-first century has posed new challenges and new questions to the U.S. political system. A bitter dispute over a closely contested presidential election in 2000 raised serious doubts about the integrity of the electoral system and the fairness of the political system. A nation that had become assured of its military might and sovereignty in a post–Cold War world suddenly felt vulnerable after the terrorist attacks of September 11, 2001. The U.S.-led invasion of Iraq in 2003 deeply polarized politics in the United States, and the conflicts there and in Afghanistan have been costly in both lives and wealth. Economic and international concerns have led many Americans to believe that their country's political and economic systems must undergo major changes in order to respond to future challenges. That sentiment was reflected in the 2008 election of Barack Obama. But despite his reelection in 2012, Obama saw much of his reform agenda fall victim to a deeply polarized legislature as America struggled to emerge from a major economic recession. Donald Trump, the Republican Party candidate elected president in 2016, vowed to overturn many of Obama's reforms. One prominent political scientist has argued that U.S. democracy is suffering political decay, calling it a "vetocracy," a system designed to stop government from acting.[1] Here is a central question for this case: Can the oldest constitutional democracy in the world, designed to prevent rapid change, deliver the necessary reforms to meet the challenges of the present and future?

Major Geographic and Demographic Features

By 2016, the population of the United States exceeded 320 million, third in the world after China and India. The United States also ranks third in the world in land size; it is slightly larger than Brazil and China but about half the size of Russia and slightly smaller than Canada. The U.S. population has become increasingly diverse; by 2016 over a third of Americans identified themselves as being part of ethnic minorities (Latinos constituted the largest minority group, followed by African Americans). The United States occupies the central portion of the North American continent, sandwiched between Canada and Mexico and ranging from the Pacific to the Atlantic Ocean. It comprises 48 contiguous states (and the District of Columbia), Alaska (at the extreme northwest of the continent), and the island state of Hawaii, located about 2,100 miles west of the California coast. The United States also possesses numerous overseas territories in the Caribbean and the Pacific. U.S. states are extremely diverse in area, population, geography, climate, and culture.

The United States is blessed with stunning geographic and climatic diversity. Almost half its territory is made up of agriculturally rich lowlands that have become the world's breadbasket. Its climatic diversity allows for the production of food year-round. Several major mountain ranges divide the continental United States, but its extensive coastline and navigable river systems facilitate trade and commerce. The United States is richly endowed with natural resources, including minerals, gas, and oil.

For an industrial democracy, its population is unusual in some ways. Continually replenished by immigration, the population has continued to grow more than that of other industrialized democracies, and the U.S. birth rate is currently higher than both China's and Brazil's. As a result, unlike Japan and some European countries, the United States does not face a labor shortage in the foreseeable future. But immigration has also dramatically changed the country's ethnic and racial composition, prompting political divisions and social strains.

The U.S. population is also more geographically mobile than is common in most industrialized democracies. Despite a very high level of home ownership, approximately one in seven Americans moves from one house to another in a given year. In recent decades, this mobility has hurt the old industrial core of the Northeast and the Midwest, whose cities have lost both population and wealth, and favored the Southwest and the West.

Historical Development of the State

America and the Arrival of the European Colonizers

The origins of the U.S. state can be found in the geographic expansion of European states in the early sixteenth century. A number of European countries began to explore and establish trading missions in the eastern part of the future United States. The French, the Dutch, the Spanish, and the English all attempted to form permanent settlements there.

English citizens migrated to America in search of land, which was becoming scarce in England, and religious freedom. **Puritans**, radical Protestants, constituted a large portion of the early English settlers in North America. English colonists began to establish permanent settlements in the early seventeenth century in present-day Virginia and Massachusetts on the Eastern Seaboard. The Virginia colony began as a business venture and developed into a slave-based plantation society geared toward the production of tobacco and dominated by white landowners. The Massachusetts colony was settled largely by Puritans and developed into a society of small family farmers. Although Massachusetts was established by settlers who had been persecuted for their religious beliefs in England, these colonies themselves were characterized by religious intolerance and repression.

By 1640, England had established 6 of the 13 colonies that would later form the United States. By the 1680s, the English had established 6 additional colonies, including New York, which was taken from the Dutch, and Pennsylvania. The early colonists faced numerous challenges, including food shortages, disease, isolation from England, and understandable resistance by Native Americans. Though it is convenient to begin our discussion of the origins of the American political system with the establishment of the English colonies, more than 100 indigenous tribes inhabited what is now the United States, each with its own political regime. With the arrival of Europeans, many Native American societies collaborated with or tolerated the colonists, while others violently resisted. The chief cause of the declining indigenous population after the arrival of Europeans was disease, against which Native Americans lacked resistance. But Native American societies were also subject to military repression, murder, and forced relocation.

By the late seventeenth century, the British had begun to assert more control over their remote North American colonies. The British government, with the Navigation Act of 1651, sought to force the colonies to conduct their trade using only English ships, thereby creating colonial dependency. By the early eighteenth century, the British government had allowed elected legislatures to be established in the colonies, transplanting its own embryonic democratic institutions, and had imposed royally appointed colonial governors.

The colonies grew rapidly, fueled by a high birth rate, the importation of enslaved Africans, mostly to the southern colonies, and continued emigration from England and other European countries. For Europeans, the lure of a seemingly endless supply of land was irresistible. Indeed, since colonial days, America has been viewed by immigrants worldwide as a land of opportunity and promise.

Between the 1680s and 1760s, the English colonists faced numerous foes. They fought indigenous tribes whose land they had taken. They also fought with

TIMELINE OF POLITICAL DEVELOPMENT

YEAR	EVENT
1607	First permanent English settlement in America is established.
1754–63	French and Indian War ends the French Empire in America.
1775–83	American Revolution is fought.
1776	Declaration of Independence is signed.
1781	Articles of Confederation ratified.
1788	U.S. Constitution ratified.
1803	Louisiana Purchase expands the U.S. frontier westward.
1846–48	Mexican War is fought, further expanding U.S. territory.
1861–65	Civil War takes place.
1865	Thirteenth Amendment to the Constitution, abolishing slavery, is ratified.
1903–20	Progressive era.
1933–38	Era of the New Deal.
1955–65	Civil rights movement takes place.
2008	Barack Obama elected president.
2016	Donald Trump elected president.

the growing Spanish and French empires in America, who often allied themselves with Native American tribes and threatened to limit the English settlers' prospects for colonial expansion. In the French and Indian War (1754–63), the British effectively defeated the French Empire in North America and weakened the Spanish Empire (Spain gave up claims to Florida in 1763). At the end of the French and Indian War, Britain inherited a vast empire in America that would prove both costly and difficult to control.

The Revolution and the Birth of a New State

The United States was the first major colony to rebel successfully against European colonial rule, leading one scholar to call it "the first new nation."[2] At its core, the American Revolution was caused by a conflict between two sovereignties: the sovereignty of the English king and Parliament, and the sovereignty of the colonial legislatures that had been established in America. Both believed that they had the exclusive right to raise the taxes paid by colonists. In the 1760s, the British Parliament unilaterally passed a number of taxes on colonists that sparked a spiral of colonial petitions, protests, boycotts, and acts of civil disobedience. The British responded by disbanding the colonial legislatures and repressing protest with military force. In the Boston Massacre (1770), British soldiers attacked a mob of colonists, further fueling the colonists' opposition to British intervention in colonial affairs. Colonial militias clashed with British military forces, a precursor to the impending revolution.

In 1774, in response to British repression, anti-British colonial elites convened in Philadelphia for the First Continental Congress. The assembly, composed of delegates from each of the 13 colonies, asserted the exclusive right of the colonial legislatures to raise taxes. The Second Continental Congress, meeting in 1775, created a Continental Army and named **George Washington** as its commander. In 1776, the Congress appointed a committee to draft a constitution and approve the **Declaration of Independence**.

The declaration of a new state and a new regime evoked an attack by a large and powerful British army. In the **American Revolution** (1775–83), the colonists were greatly outnumbered but were aided by their knowledge of the terrain and an alliance with France, an enemy of England. After its defeat at Yorktown, Virginia, in 1783, Britain granted independence to the 13 rebellious American colonies.

Consolidation of a Democratic Republic and Debate over the Role of the State

A unique theme of the American Revolution was its opposition to a British state perceived as overbearing. Distrust of a strong state is still a feature of U.S. politics, but it presented special challenges during the Revolution. Fighting a war against the British required a central authority transcending the 13 colonial governments, each of which had begun functioning under new constitutions. The **Articles of Confederation**, approved in 1781, created a loose alliance of sovereign states. It featured a unicameral legislature with a single vote for each state. The Confederation Congress assumed important powers regarding conflicts between states and the regulation of settlement to the west, but it required unanimity for the passage of all legislation, lacked a national executive, did not have the ability to raise taxes or create a national currency, and struggled to create and maintain a national army. This weak central state made it difficult for the country to conduct foreign relations, ensure national security, control inflation, or carry out international trade.

In response to those problems, a Constitutional Convention of state delegates was held in 1787 to consider a stronger national state. The resulting constitutional document was a compromise between advocates of a strong federal state and supporters of sovereignty for the individual states. After a series of compromises, the states ratified the new constitution in 1788, effectively creating a new national state and a new political regime.

The first U.S. Congress met in 1789. It passed legislation that strengthened the state, built a federal judiciary, and imposed a tariff on imports to fund federal expenditures. It also attempted to address the concerns of those who feared the power of a strong central state by passing 12 amendments to the Constitution. The states ratified 10 of these amendments, which became known collectively as the **Bill of Rights**. The 10 constitutional amendments that compose the Bill of Rights aim largely to protect the rights of individuals against the federal government. Over time, most provisions of the Bill of Rights were gradually incorporated into state law, thus protecting individuals from state government as well.

A major political division in the young American republic was between **Federalists**, led by President Washington's secretary of the treasury, Alexander Hamilton, and **Democratic-Republicans**, led by the future president Thomas Jefferson. Hamilton, who advocated a strong central state, was responsible for consolidating the Revolutionary War debt incurred by the states, imposing a federal excise tax, and creating a federal bank to print and regulate currency. Jefferson was a strong advocate of the principles of Republicanism: above all, he believed in individual freedom, popular sovereignty, and a distrust of oligarchic privilege and a too-powerful state. When he became president in 1801, Jefferson moved to reduce the power of the U.S. federal government by paying off the national debt, repealing the excise tax, and reducing the size of the federal bureaucracy and the military. At the same time, Jefferson was responsible for a massive increase in the territory of the United States when he acquired much of France's remaining North American territory in the **Louisiana Purchase** (1803). The Louisiana Territory extended America's westward borders to the Rocky Mountains and expedited future westward migration.

The Move West and Expansion of the State

With the Louisiana Purchase in 1803, the acquisition of Florida from Spain in 1819, and the end of the War of 1812 with Britain in 1815, Americans were free to move westward. Like the original European settlements, this migration came at the expense of Native Americans. As Americans moved westward in search of land to be used for agriculture, the United States used legislation and military force to contain, relocate, or exterminate Native American populations. A particularly egregious example was the 1830 Indian Removal Act, initiated by President Andrew Jackson, which evicted the Cherokee and other tribes from their homelands in the southeastern United States and forced them to relocate to reservations in distant Oklahoma. The forced removal resulted in the deaths of thousands of Native Americans.

The westward expansion continued with the 1845 annexation of Texas, which was a Mexican territory until non-Hispanic Americans led a successful separatist movement there. The United States declared war on Mexico in 1846 (the Mexican War, also known as the **Mexican-American War**) to protect its acquisition of Texas and lay claim to vast Mexican territories in present-day Arizona, California, Colorado, Nevada, New Mexico, Utah, and Wyoming. In all, the rapidly expanding United States gained one-third of Mexico's territory through military conquest, thus further encouraging the flood of migrants westward.

Even as the territorial boundaries of the state expanded, so too did the franchise and popular democracy. Jeffersonian democracy was replaced by what came to be known as Jacksonian democracy, named for President Jackson, whose supporters shared the Jeffersonian distrust of central government and reverence for individual liberty. But Jacksonian democrats placed even greater emphasis on the common man, and by 1830 the right to vote had been extended to virtually all white males. African Americans, Native Americans, and women remained excluded.

Civil War and the Threat to Unity

The American Revolution had temporarily united the English colonies, and under George Washington's leadership and the work of Federalist leaders, the foundations of a strong central state were constructed. But the Federalist project was always controversial, and the creation of a unified United States could not eliminate simmering regional differences that threatened to destroy the Union. These differences culminated in the **Civil War** (1861–65). At its roots were not just slavery but also the divergent paths of socioeconomic development in the southern and northern regions of the country. While the North experienced an industrial boom based on its prosperous cities, southern agriculture was still based on slave labor and export-oriented plantations.

To gain agreement on a federal constitution, the founders of the Republic had largely sidestepped the issue of slavery. Slavery had been abolished in the North after the Revolution, but the Constitution tolerated it. A number of factors brought the issue of slavery to center stage by the mid-nineteenth century. First, the westward expansion of the United States raised the contentious issue of whether new territories would be "slave" states or "free" states. Then, in the first half of the nineteenth century, slavery was banned by England and most of Latin America, and the northern states increasingly viewed the South as an anachronistic threat to free-market capitalism based on individual liberty and a free labor market. Finally, the early nineteenth century saw the emergence of a rapidly growing abolition movement, largely in the North, that viewed slavery as both undemocratic and anathema to Christian values.

The 1860 election of Abraham Lincoln and the rise to power of the new anti-slavery Republican Party provoked the secession of 11 southern states and the commencement of the Civil War. The southern states formed a rebel state, called the Confederate States of America, and enacted their own constitution, which guaranteed the institution of slavery.

During the war, the North held important advantages over the South in terms of population (it was more than twice as large), wealth, and industry. Nevertheless, the South had the advantage of playing defense on difficult terrain, and it hoped to prolong the war long enough to wear down the Northern invaders. The long and bloody conflict cost an estimated three-quarters of a million lives before the South was defeated in 1865 and the Union was preserved. Over the course of the next five years, three key constitutional amendments known as the **Civil War Amendments** were ratified in an effort to guarantee the freedom and civil rights of former slaves and all citizens. These included the Thirteenth Amendment (1865) abolishing slavery, the Fourteenth Amendment (1868) guaranteeing to all citizens due process and equal protection under the law, and the Fifteenth Amendment (1870) prohibiting voter discrimination on the basis of race (though not yet gender).

The importance of the Civil War in the development of the U.S. state was immense. The federal government had increased spending and built a huge army to subdue the South. It also gained enormous power through its role in reforming the South and reintegrating the southern states into the Union. And the use of state power to end race-based slavery and promote democratic values established an important precedent, although it would not be used again to advance civil rights until the 1950s and 1960s.

The Progressive Era and the Growth of State Power

The three decades following the Civil War (known as the Gilded Age) were marked by rapid industrialization, the growing wealth and influence of private business, and a large influx of immigrants. In response to these changes, the U.S. state employed its newfound clout to promote democratic reform during the **Progressive era** (1903–20). Progressives sought to use the federal state to restrict the power of big business, attack corruption, and address inequality.

Under President Theodore Roosevelt (1901–09), the federal government attacked monopolistic businesses and enhanced the ability of the Interstate Commerce Commission to regulate trade among the states. To protect public land from private development, Roosevelt created a vast system of national parks. Under President Woodrow Wilson (1913–21), laws were passed to curb further the power of large monopolies and to establish the centralized Federal Reserve System as a national lender of last resort. Perhaps the single greatest impetus for the growth of a centralized state was the adoption of the Sixteenth Amendment in 1913, which gave Congress authority to levy a national income tax. In addition, Wilson took the United States into World War I. Despite considerable popular opposition, it was an act that dramatically increased the size and power of the state.

The Great Depression and the New Deal

The stock market crash of 1929 and the ensuing Great Depression devastated the U.S. economy. One-quarter of the workforce lost jobs, the gross domestic product (GDP) dropped by about one-third, and there were massive bankruptcies and bank failures. The economic crisis was a pivotal factor in the 1932 election of Democratic Party candidate Franklin D. Roosevelt and the implementation of a set of social democratic welfare policies known collectively as the **New Deal**.

The New Deal policies were aimed at ameliorating the economic crisis and preserving the American capitalist system, but their long-term impact was to increase dramatically the power of the U.S. state. Despite opposition from conservatives and the Supreme Court, Roosevelt, with a Democratic majority in both houses of Congress, passed a series of unprecedented measures. Some of the most controversial pieces of legislation guaranteed workers the right to bargain collectively with employers, created state agencies to generate electric power, provided state subsidies to farmers who agreed to limit production, and heavily regulated the stock market. To carry out these policies, a massive extension of the state bureaucracy and the creation of numerous state agencies, such as the Securities and Exchange Commission and the National Labor Relations Board, were needed. Many of those agencies still exist today. The Social Security Act (1935) established the foundation for the U.S. welfare state (though much later and much less comprehensively than in many northern European countries), creating unemployment insurance, retiree pensions, and other social welfare measures.

Although these New Deal policies increased the role of the state, the entry of the United States into World War II enhanced state power even further. The military grew rapidly, the state set wages and prices, and it directly intervened in private enterprise to serve the war effort. In wartime, the state trampled on civil liberties, censoring the press and sending thousands of citizens of Japanese ancestry to prison camps. The United States emerged from World War II a global power, and the state apparatus expanded to meet the perceived needs and demands of this rising hegemon. In the context of the Cold War with the Soviet Union, the state took domestic measures to persecute suspected Communists, firing them from government positions. Internationally, the United States maintained a large standing army in peacetime, extended its international commitments, and intervened in the domestic affairs of other states.

The Civil Rights Movement and the War on Poverty

Despite constitutional protections and the defeat of the South in the Civil War, U.S. democracy suffered from the legacy of slavery. Widespread discrimination against African Americans continued, most notably in the South but also in the North. After World War II (in which African Americans served and made valuable contributions), a growing **civil rights movement**, often backed by the federal government and the federal judiciary, advocated an end to all forms of racial discrimination.

The struggle for civil rights was only one of the popular reform movements that crystallized in the 1960s. During that decade, many U.S. citizens began to view economic inequality, gender discrimination, and environmental degradation by private business as impediments to democracy. In the mid-1960s, popular movements focused on those concerns combined with growing popular opposition to the **Vietnam War**, contributing to an atmosphere of unrest and rebellion.

Partly in response to popular pressure, the U.S. government attempted to address a number of socioeconomic problems. Under President John F. Kennedy (1961–63), the federal government played a crucial role in imposing civil rights legislation on recalcitrant southern states. President Lyndon Johnson (1963–69) announced a **War on Poverty** and proposed a dramatic increase in federal spending to combat economic inequality. Johnson launched new programs and founded new state institutions to protect the environment, build low-income housing, fund the arts, and redress racial discrimination. The growing state role in the economy and society continued under the Republican president Richard Nixon (1969–74), who imposed wage and price controls to stem inflation and signed into law a measure that provided food stamps to the poorest Americans.

Like Margaret Thatcher, his neoliberal counterpart in Britain, President Ronald Reagan (1981–89) was elected on a platform of reversing the trend toward increased state involvement in the economy. Reagan viewed government as "the problem, not the solution," and rode to power on a wave of conservatism critical of the preceding decades of state-led social activism. Reagan cut social spending and reduced taxes while dramatically increasing defense spending. The reform of a welfare state widely viewed as bloated and inefficient continued under the Democratic president Bill Clinton (1993–2001) and the Republican president **George W. Bush** (2001–09). However, these Bush presidency reforms occurred alongside massive increases in spending on both defense and domestic policies. The 2008 election of **Barack Obama**, the first African American president, took place amid a major economic crisis. Obama campaigned on a platform that included health care reform and the gradual withdrawal of U.S. troops from Iraq. By Obama's second term, he had delivered on both of those campaign promises, but not without significant opposition and controversy. The 2016 election of **Donald Trump** as president delivered a shock to the U.S. political establishment, as the real-estate tycoon and reality television star won the nomination in opposition to the Republican Party's leadership, and then beat the heavily favored Democratic candidate, Hillary Clinton, in the general election.

In retrospect, it is clear that the United States was fortunate to build and consolidate its state under extremely favorable conditions. It did not have to contend with hostile neighbors and, after its founding, faced no appreciable external threats to its sovereignty. The development of the U.S. state during its first two centuries also coincided with the generally steady success of the economy and the steady expansion of U.S. power abroad.

Political Regime

Because of their fresh experience with, and deep distrust of, authoritarian colonial rule, the Founders of the United States established a democratic regime governed by the **rule of law**. This means that government can act and citizens can be punished only as authorized by legal statute, all citizens are equal before the law, and no one is above the law, not even political leaders. Those concepts were framed in a written constitution establishing a democratic regime grounded in rational-legal legitimacy.

But the rule of law by itself was judged insufficient. The power of legitimate government in the hands of a misguided minority or even a well-intentioned majority could still lead to tyranny. Wariness about this possibility led the Founders to establish a liberal democratic political system with institutions intentionally designed to weaken the power and authority of the state. Those institutions included federalism, the separation of powers with checks and balances, and the Bill of Rights. In a sense, the legitimacy of the state was based on its inherent weakness. But this raised a dilemma: How could a state and its elected government manage from a position of weakness the tasks of leading a new and growing nation facing a host of increasingly complex challenges?

As discussed at the beginning of this chapter, the ongoing effort to resolve that dilemma required two regimes in the eighteenth century, a civil war in the nineteenth century, and a dramatic strengthening of central government authority in the twentieth century. In 1777, the Continental Congress established the new nation's first regime under the Articles of Confederation. The Articles called for a decentralized confederation of highly autonomous states that vested most authority in the individual states. The ineffectiveness and insufficiency of this confederal regime grew increasingly apparent as the new republic faced potential threats of internal rebellion and costly foreign trade disputes. By 1787, the Articles of Confederation had been jettisoned, replaced by an entirely new constitution that became the codified embodiment of U.S. rule of law. Inaugurated in

1789, the Constitution established a representative democratic regime governed by a presidential system. This section examines the institutional components of this regime, including its guiding principles of federalism and the separation of powers.

Political Institutions

THE CONSTITUTION

In a nation governed by the rule of law, this 1789 document constituting the regime became all-important. The Constitution of the United States of America was passed largely as a compromise between less and more populous states, between northern merchants and southern planters, between slaveholders and those not holding slaves, and between Federalists (who supported a strong central government) and Antifederalists (who advocated states' rights and preferred the decentralized confederal status quo). But the Constitution's framers and citizens on both sides of the debate shared two characteristics: fear of too much government in the form of an overbearing central authority, and recognition that the Articles of Confederation had provided too little government. The constitutional compromise was one of strengthened but nonetheless limited government checked by **federalism**, which divides governing authority between the national and state governments; the **separation of powers**, which prevents any one branch or office of government from dominating through a system of checks and balances; and the Bill of Rights, which protects the freedoms of individual citizens. In an unprecedented way, the U.S. Constitution created, tempered, and buffered three sovereign spheres—national, state, and individual—within a single political system.

The U.S. Constitution also stands out as the oldest written constitution still in force. Although it has been regularly interpreted by judicial action and occasionally amended (27 times in total), it has been remarkably durable—indeed, it has proven difficult even to amend. Most of it remains fully in effect after more than two centuries, guiding U.S. politics and policy making under circumstances that its framers could hardly have imagined. For better or worse, it has served as the model for constituting the regimes of many newly established countries, and its guiding principles of federalism and separation of powers have become standards for numerous democracies.

The Branches of Government

At the national level, the power of government is shared by three institutions: a president; a bicameral legislature (Congress); and a judiciary, led by the Supreme Court, that has the power to interpret the Constitution. The framers put in place several institutions designed to check and balance the powers of each respective branch of government. For example, the upper chamber of the legislature (the **Senate**) is given the authority to approve or disapprove executive appointments and to ratify or not ratify treaties. Both the Senate and the **House of Representatives** (the House) can refuse to pass legislation. The House can impeach, and the Senate can convict and remove from office, a president or a federal judge (for grievous offenses). The executive (the president) can veto legislation passed by the legislature and appoint judges to the federal judiciary. The judges, once appointed, have lifetime tenure and serve without political oversight. Most significantly, they have the power to interpret the Constitution and void any act of the other two branches or any of the individual states that they deem unconstitutional, if that act is brought before them in a court case. Ultimately, the framers sought to give Congress the upper hand, allowing it to override a presidential veto of legislation (with a two-thirds majority) and to overturn a constitutional decision of the Supreme Court by amending the Constitution (statutory interpretations can be overturned by a simple majority).

The Constitution's framers also intentionally gave each branch sources of legitimacy. Unlike a parliamentary system, which fuses executive authority and legislative authority and makes only members of parliament directly accountable to voters, the U.S. system seats its president and members of the legislative chambers in separate elections. Separate branches and separate elections can also allow a third possible check on power: divided government, in which different parties control the executive and legislative branches. Although a single party has often dominated both, the United States has experienced divided government over 40 percent of the time since 1830 and nearly 60 percent of the time since the end of World War II. Thus, what politicians and analysts often criticize as the tendency for American policy-making "gridlock" is an intended consequence of the system of checks and balances. It fosters a state with weak autonomy and a relatively fragmented policy-making process.

Historically, this formula has generally worked well; and at least until recently, there has been little evidence that divided governments in the United States have been any less able to produce major legislation than have unified party

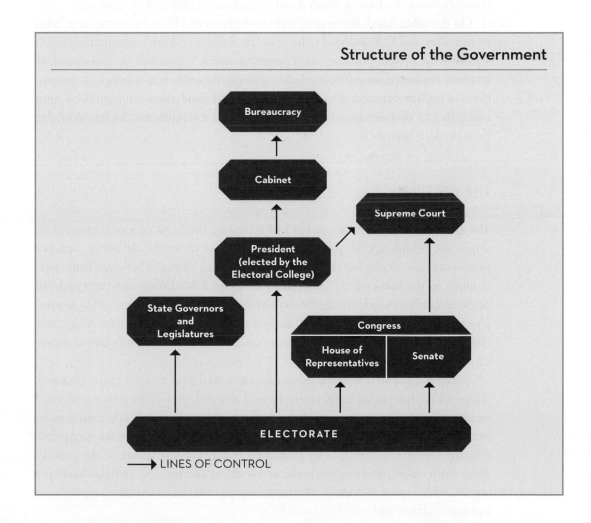

Structure of the Government

Bureaucracy

Cabinet

Supreme Court

President
(elected by the
Electoral College)

State Governors
and
Legislatures

Congress

House of
Representatives

Senate

ELECTORATE

→ LINES OF CONTROL

governments.[3] In recent years, increasingly polarized and unified parties (what might be called parliamentary-style party discipline in a divided government situation) have strained the constitutional order and created gridlock. This issue has led some observers to argue that the United States (and other presidential systems) would be better served by a parliamentary system, which can change the executive quickly when it has lost the support of the legislature.[4] This propensity for gridlock was evident in 2013 when the executive and legislative branches stalemated as the Republican-controlled House of Representatives sought to delay or defund the Obama administration's health care act. The resulting inability to pass the necessary appropriations bill led to a two-week federal government shutdown that required the laying off of all federal employees except emergency personnel and raised the possibility that the United States could default on its financial obligations.

On the other hand, this system reflects the powerful liberal sentiments of both its founders and U.S. political culture today. For many Americans, inefficiency is a price worth paying to keep state power in check. Moreover, in parliamentary systems, coalitions are often needed to form a majority, and a minority government in parliament must deal with its own sort of divided government. Coalition and minority governments, it is argued, can be far less stable and far less workable than the U.S. system.

THE PRESIDENCY

The U.S. president is both the head of state and the head of government. As a result, the presidency is invested with a great deal of formal authority, and key presidents have expanded the power and influence of the office over time, particularly in the past century. The president serves a fixed four-year term and can be elected only twice. Until the election of President Barack Obama, all U.S. presidents had been white men, and all but one have been Protestant Christians (John F. Kennedy was Catholic). Obama's election was clearly a substantial departure from the norm in this regard.

As the head of state and the only leader elected to represent the entire citizenry, the president has traditionally taken the lead role in U.S. foreign policy (although treaties are subject to approval of the Senate). The president is also commander in chief of the military. As head of government, the president—similar to a prime minister—is also responsible for managing the day-to-day affairs of the government and makes senior appointments to the executive and judicial branches (again, with Senate approval). Moreover, the president can initiate proposals for legislative action and veto legislative bills.

The president also manages an enormous bureaucracy, which has mushroomed over the years so that its civilian workforce now approaches 3 million employees. The workforce is overseen by a **cabinet** composed mostly of the heads of key departments, offices, and agencies. Although the degree to which a president comes to rely on cabinet officers and other key advisors has varied over time, all presidents have increasingly relied on a presidential bureaucracy to both manage and control this huge administrative staff of civil servants. The U.S. bureaucracy is technically accountable to the executive branch and is further constrained by the legislature's control of its many budgets. In some respects, U.S. bureaucrats lack both the autonomy and the respect historically accorded to their counterparts in countries such as France, Germany, and Japan. Indeed, *bureaucrat* and *bureaucracy* remain derogatory terms to many Americans.

With a few exceptions (such as Andrew Jackson in the 1830s and Abraham Lincoln in the 1860s), presidents in office before the twentieth century were relatively weak leaders who exerted little political influence. The White House and the Executive Office of the President strengthened considerably over the course of the twentieth century, something seen in executive institutions in other advanced democracies. In recent years, the public has expected, and presidents have sought to deliver, a strong executive offering genuine if not dominant leadership. Predictably, both the legislative and the judicial branches have sought to challenge and check this growing influence.

THE LEGISLATURE

The framers of the Constitution intended Congress to be the dominant branch of the U.S. government. In many ways, despite the growing influence of the presidency and the substantial clout of the Supreme Court, this remains the case. Scholars have argued that the U.S. Congress is "the only national representative assembly that can actually be said to govern."[5] They note that although most countries today have some form of national legislature, the legislatures in authoritarian systems do little more than affirm and legitimate the decisions of the political leadership. And although parliamentary democracies possess the authority to say no to the executive (at the risk, in many cases, of having the parliament dissolved), those assemblies have less power to modify or initiate legislation. Among the world's legislatures, only the U.S. Congress has this much authority.

The Constitution reserves the supreme power—the power to legislate—for Congress. It also gives Congress the power of the purse: sole authority to appropriate funds and thus to control the way its laws are implemented. Whereas the U.S. Congress never accepts the president's annual budget without making its own significant adjustments, governments in Britain and Japan can anticipate their parliaments' acceptance of their budgets without changes.

Another indication of the framers' appreciation for congressional power was their decision to divide the legislature against itself by making it bicameral. The House of Representatives consists of 435 members (a number unchanged since 1910), who are elected to two-year terms in single-member plurality districts. The number of seats and districts allotted to each state is determined by and distributed according to each state's population. For example, following the 2010 national census, Texas saw an increase in its allotment of House seats from 34 to 38, and New York's seat allotment dropped from 29 to 27 based on changes in population; Wyoming retained its single seat. In 1789, there was an average of one representative for every 30,000 people; in 1910, the average was one representative for more than 200,000; and since 2010, each member of Congress has represented more than 700,000 citizens on average.

The Senate is composed of 100 members, each serving staggered terms of six years; one-third of the body is elected every two years. Since 1913, senators have also been elected in statewide single-member plurality districts; before then, they were elected indirectly by the state legislatures. Each state is allotted two seats regardless of its population, which in most cases gives each pair of senators a substantially larger constituency than their counterparts in the House of Representatives. In California, for example, two senators represent approximately 28 million eligible voters, whereas North Dakota's pair of senators represents just under 500,000 eligible voters.

Given the differences in size, tenure, and assigned responsibilities, it is not surprising that the two chambers of Congress play different roles. The Senate is authorized to ratify treaties and approve presidential appointments, whereas the House is given exclusive power to originate tax and revenue bills. The Senate tends to be more deliberative, providing a forum for wide-ranging opinions and topics, and a minority of 41 senators can stop most business through delaying tactics known as filibusters. The House, on the other hand, is more centralized, places strict limits on debate, and conducts business on the basis of majority rules. Because senators serve a larger and more diverse constituency, they tend to be less specialized, less partisan, and more hesitant than representatives to take a position that might offend any major portion of their broad base of voters. House representatives, in contrast, stand for election every two years and are by necessity more attuned to the needs and interests of their more narrowly defined constituencies. House members tend to be more specialized in their expertise and less reliant on a staff. The House is generally more politicized and partisan. And whereas senators are more likely to cross the aisle to form an alliance or vote with members of the opposing party on an important issue, representatives are generally more likely to vote along partisan lines. However, since the election of Barack Obama in 2008, both houses have been extremely polarized.

THE JUDICIARY

The third branch of the U.S. government, the judiciary, was the least defined by the Constitution and initially quite weak. But given the trust and legitimacy vested in the Constitution and the rule of law, it should not be surprising that the U.S. judiciary has come to play a prominent role in the American political system. Over time, the federal court system devised new tools of judicial authority and significantly broadened the scope of its jurisdiction. In 1789, Congress created the federal court system authorized by the Constitution, endowing it with the power to resolve conflicts between state and federal laws and between citizens of different states.

In the landmark decision of *Marbury v. Madison*, the Supreme Court in 1803 established its right of judicial review: the authority to judge unconstitutional or invalid an act of the legislative or executive branch or of a state court or legislature. Although this power of judicial review can be exercised by federal and state courts, the Supreme Court is the court of last resort and has the final word on the interpretation of the U.S. Constitution. This kind of judicial power is uncommon but not exclusive to the United States; Australian and Canadian courts also have such authority.

Federal judges are given lifetime appointments, which afford them substantial autonomy from both partisan politics and the executive and legislative branches of government. But the Court's power is checked by its reliance on presidential nomination and Senate approval of nominees to the federal bench, and by legislative or executive enforcement of its decisions. Nonetheless, the federal courts have played an increasingly influential role, particularly since the second half of the twentieth century. They were involved in determining important policy outcomes in such areas as school desegregation and abortion, and even in determining the winner of the 2000 presidential election. In that case, the Court overturned the decision of a state supreme court (Florida's), and in so doing invalidated a partial recount of ballots in that hotly contested election. Currently, the Court is divided 5–4 between conservatives and liberals. It is little wonder that appointments to the Supreme Court have become bitter political struggles as partisan forces seek to project their influence on this now-prominent third branch of the U.S. government.

This partisanship was in evidence in 2016 when the Republican-controlled Senate took the unprecedented step of refusing to vote on the confirmation of President Obama's nominee to fill a vacancy on the Supreme Court.

The Electoral System

Nearly all elections in the United States are conducted according to a single-member district plurality system. There is one representative per district, and the seat is awarded to the candidate with the most votes (but not necessarily with a majority). This system has favored the emergence of two broadly defined parties and has effectively discouraged the survival of smaller and single-issue parties. Unlike a system of proportional representation, the plurality system in effect "wastes" votes for all but the dominant candidate, forcing coalitions to emerge to compete in the winner-take-all contests.

One process that parties have used to enhance their prospects for electoral success has been to establish electoral districts and thus determine constituencies for the House of Representatives and many state and local offices. States are required to adjust voting districts every 10 years to reflect changes in population, and the dominant party in the state legislature is often able to control the process. Parties seek to influence electoral outcomes by redrawing the districts in ways that will favor their candidates and voting blocs. Political architects often employ **gerrymandering**, the manipulation of district boundaries by one political party to favor the candidates of that party (nowadays achieved through sophisticated computer analyses of demographic data).

Although members of both chambers of Congress are elected directly by a popular vote, the president and the vice president are elected indirectly by the electoral college. The Founders established the electoral college as a means of tempering the particular interests (and feared ignorance) of voters. In this system, voters technically do not vote for a presidential candidate; instead, each party from each state chooses or appoints a slate of electors. Each state receives a total of electoral votes equal to its combined number of senators and representatives. In addition, the federal District of Columbia has three votes, for a sum of 538 electoral votes (100 plus 435 plus 3). But unlike in a plurality system, in the electoral college, a candidate requires a majority of votes (270) to claim victory. If no candidate obtains a majority, the contest is determined by the House of Representatives (this happened twice in the early nineteenth century).

Because all but two states use a winner-take-all formula for awarding electoral votes, winning a plurality of the popular vote in a state earns a candidate all of the

National Election Results, 1992–2016

YEAR	HOUSE OF REPRESENTATIVES* TOTAL SEATS: 435†		SENATE* TOTAL SEATS: 100†		PRESIDENT* (PARTY)
	DEMOCRATS	REPUBLICANS	DEMOCRATS	REPUBLICANS	
1992	258	176	57	43	Clinton (Democrat)
1994	204	230	48	52	—
1996	206	228	45	55	Clinton (Democrat)
1998	211	223	45	55	—
2000	212	221	50	50	Bush (Republican)
2002	204	229	51	48	—
2004	202	232	44	55	Bush (Republican)
2006	233	202	49	49	—
2008	257	178	57	41	Obama (Democrat)
2010	193	242	51	47	—
2012	201	234	53	45	Obama (Democrat)
2014	188	247	44	54	—
2016	194	241	46	52	Trump (Republican)

*House terms of office are fixed at two years, and all seats are elected every two years. Senate terms are fixed at six years, and one-third of the seats are elected every two years. Presidential terms are fixed at four years, and elections are held every four years.

†When Democrats and Republicans together comprise less than the total number of seats, the independent representatives account for the difference.

state's electoral votes. Thus, winning many states by large margins but losing key electoral-rich battleground states by narrow margins can lead to a popular victory but a loss in the electoral college. This has happened five times in U.S. history, most recently in the controversial 2000 election between George W. Bush and Al Gore, and in 2016, when Donald Trump won a majority in the electoral college despite losing the popular vote by almost three million votes.

Even before the 2000 election, many observers had called for the elimination of the electoral college, to match the elimination of the similarly indirect election of senators nearly a century ago. Critics charge that this "quasi-democratic" vestige of the eighteenth century "undermines both respect for and the legitimacy of electoral results."[6] Nor is this the only electoral reform effort being proposed. Long-standing efforts to reform campaign finance are now being joined by bipartisan calls for changes in the logistics of voter registration, the actual mechanics of voting, and the process of conducting presidential primaries, along with a number of smaller issues.

One response to the frustration with the existing electoral and political systems has been the proliferation of state initiatives and referenda. Twenty-seven of the 50 states allow citizen-sponsored statewide ballots called *initiatives* and legislature-proposed statewide ballots called *referenda* (the ballots themselves often are called *propositions*) that enable voters to make direct decisions about policy. For example, in 2008, California Republicans supported a measure to allocate electoral college delegates according to legislative district (to replace the single, statewide, winner-take-all system currently employed) but failed to get the measure on the ballot. The Constitution also authorizes a national ballot in the form of a national convention as one means of amending federal law, though that method has never been employed.

Local Government

The United States has a federal political system dividing authority between self-governing states and the national government that unites the states (hence the name United States of America). The Constitution authorizes the national, or federal, government to manage both national commerce and foreign policy. Although the granting of those federal powers marked a substantial centralization compared with the earlier Articles of Confederation, the states have retained significant powers, including responsibility for many direct social services (such as health, education, and welfare) and authority over internal commerce.

Over time, however, the national government has managed to increase its influence in many of the areas traditionally subject to state sovereignty. The federal government can review the constitutionality of state legislation, impose federal mandates, and make federal grants to states for such services as education and transportation, contingent upon the states' abiding by federal standards. States have given up their sovereignty only reluctantly, however, and in recent years groups advocating states' rights have called for limitations on federal power and for returning or devolving greater political power to the states.

This federal structure of national and state authority has allowed states to experiment with a variety of policies in areas such as welfare restructuring, vehicle emissions standards, legalization of marijuana, and educational reforms. But it has also resulted in a lack of standardization in those areas and varying levels of benefits and enforcement across the states. Not surprisingly, the greatest tension comes in areas of conflicting or overlapping authority. A tragic example was the government's response to the devastation caused by Hurricane Katrina on the southern Gulf Coast in 2005. Although state and local governments have first responsibility to respond to such a disaster, a state governor can invite the federal government to assist—something that, as one observer noted, the Louisiana governor initially refused to do "out of pride or mistrust or a desire to maintain some degree of control."[7] The lack of a timely response by the federal government added to the frustration and confusion. These problems persist: years later, tens of thousands of homes remain uninhabitable in New Orleans, public transportation is limited, and the population remains well below its pre-storm level.

A second example is the Affordable Care Act, or "Obamacare." In 2010, Congress passed this controversial health care reform act, which imposed mandatory health insurance requirements on all citizens. Health care is another area in which the United States is unusual among industrialized democracies.[8] Like other wealthy democracies, the federal government provides public health care, doing so through two national programs (Medicare and Medicaid), which cover roughly one-third of Americans and account for approximately half of total health care spending in the United States. But unlike most other advanced democracies, these programs do not cover all citizens. Before the passage of Obamacare, over 50 million Americans lacked health insurance. Most Americans who do have insurance are covered by private insurance, often provided through employers. Overall, the United States spends about twice as much per capita on health care compared with other advanced democracies, but these expenditures deliver no better overall health outcomes than those in other countries.[9]

Although other presidents had failed in their attempt to reform health care (most notably Clinton in the early 1990s), Obama was elected in 2008 on a platform promising health care reform. Obama's Democratic Party held a majority in both houses of Congress, but lacked enough votes in the Senate to guarantee passage for his proposed health care legislation. As a result, the act that passed in 2010 was a compromise between Democrats and Republicans. It called for the gradual creation of a system of mostly private health insurance that would cover the vast majority of Americans and would require most Americans to purchase insurance. The resulting compromise reform act fell short of the hopes of Democrats, and the feature of the law mandating the purchase of insurance led 28 states and other opposing organizations to file legal actions against the legislation, declaring it an unconstitutional violation of both state and individual rights. In 2012, the Supreme Court ruled that the individual mandate represented a constitutional use of Congress's taxing powers, but struck down other parts of the act. A number of states chose not to implement some "optional" parts of Obama's health care reform. Despite a great deal of technical problems associated with online enrollment when the program was rolled out in 2013, by the end of 2015, over 17 million Americans had gained access to health care through the program.

Political Conflict and Competition

Federalism and the separation of powers have had another important consequence: the multiple levels and branches of elected office in the U.S. political system mean that voters in the United States go to the polls far more often than do their counterparts in other democracies. Whereas a typical British or German voter might cast on average four or five votes in as many years, a U.S. voter may go to the polls two or three times as often and cast dozens of votes in local, state, and national primary and general elections involving hundreds of candidates as well as casting votes on additional issues presented as initiatives and referenda.

Although this surplus of contests and contestants may be an indication of the health of democracy in the United States, some critics have pointed to it as a cause of "voter fatigue" and one of several reasons for the strikingly lower levels of voter turnout compared with those in other democracies. Levels of voter turnout are on average lower in the United States than in all other advanced democracies considered in this volume. Although voter turnout has actually increased in recent presidential elections—62 percent in 2008, the highest level since 1968, and 57 percent in 2016—only about 40 percent of eligible Americans vote regularly. (The turnout rate was only 36 percent in the 2014 midterm elections, the worst turnout for a general election since 1942.)

Suffrage in the United States, as in other democracies, has expanded over time. Limited originally to white male landholders, the franchise was extended first to

President Obama confronted myriad groups with significant (and often competing) vested interests in the outcome of the health care reform efforts.

nonpropertied white males. By the end of the Civil War, African American men gained the right to vote (though African Americans' full participation was not possible until Congress passed the **Voting Rights Act** in 1965), and women first voted in 1920, as a result of the Nineteenth Amendment to the Constitution. Most recently, in 1971, the voting age was lowered from 21 to 18.

The Party System

Another factor sometimes blamed for declining rates of voter turnout is the weakness of political parties. Formerly bottom-up organizations linking party members tightly together in purposive grassroots campaigns, political parties in the United States have evolved over time into top-down, candidate-driven national organizations with much looser ties to voters and citizens. American political parties today tend to be weaker and more fragmented than their counterparts in many other countries. This weakness has resulted from the gradual democratization of the candidate nomination process (primary elections are now used to select candidates) and unintended consequences of campaign finance reform (which has restricted spending by political parties, but not by other private groups).

But with much talk recently about the ideological and even geographic polarization of American voters into "red" (Republican) states and "blue" (Democratic) states, it is clear that the U.S. two-party system has certainly endured even as it has evolved. The U.S. plurality system has fostered a two-party system in which the Democratic and Republican parties have won virtually all votes and political offices since their rivalry began over 150 years ago. In the 2016 presidential election, where candidates of the two major parties were very unpopular, those candidates nevertheless together won about 95 percent of the popular vote.

THE DEMOCRATIC PARTY

The Democratic Party has its roots in the Democratic-Republican Party, which formed in the 1790s with southern agrarian interests as its base. Andrew Jackson led a splinter group to presidential victory in 1828, calling it the Democratic Party and portraying it as the party of the common man. The Democrats dominated the political scene until 1860 and for most of the years between 1932 and 1968. Throughout the nineteenth century, the party embraced the namesake legacies of both Jeffersonian and Jacksonian democracy, championing agrarian society and liberty for the common man. But by the 1930s and with the onset of the Great Depression, the "liberalism" embraced by the Democratic Party had become Franklin Roosevelt's New Deal liberalism, which promoted social welfare, labor unions, and civil rights and was far more concerned with equality than individual freedom.

As a coalition party, like its Republican rival, the contemporary Democratic Party is difficult to characterize fully in terms of a set of philosophical principles or even policy preferences. It may be said, however, that the party tends to embrace policies that support minorities, urban dwellers, organized labor, and working women. Although less so than European social democrats, Democrats in the United States generally perceive state intervention designed to temper the market and enhance equality as both legitimate and necessary. As has been the case with social democratic parties in Britain and elsewhere, however, neoliberal trends since the 1980s have weakened the Democratic coalition, causing conflict over traditional New Deal–type social welfare programs providing such benefits as affirmative action. However, in recent elections healthy majorities of both minority and young voters have consistently favored the Democratic Party. The bitterly contested 2016 Democratic Party presidential primary pitted the more centrist former senator and secretary of state Hillary Clinton against the more leftist Vermont Senator Bernie Sanders. Clinton won the nomination with the support of most of the Party establishment, but Sanders drew strong support from young Democrats.

THE REPUBLICAN PARTY

The Republican Party, nicknamed the Grand Old Party (GOP), is in fact not as old as its rival. It first contested elections in 1856 on an antislavery platform that also appealed to northern commercial interests. With Lincoln's presidential victory in 1860, the party dominated national politics until the 1930s, when the Great Depression brought that era of its supremacy to an end. By the late 1960s, the GOP had regained the presidency, and by the 1990s it regularly obtained congressional majorities as well.

The Republican Party currently brings together a coalition that includes both economic and moral conservatives. It draws support disproportionately from rural dwellers, upper-income voters, evangelical Christians, and voters favoring individual freedom over collective equality, such as libertarians and owners of small businesses. Although there are fewer registered Republican voters than Democratic voters, registered Republicans have tended to vote more regularly than their rivals. Americans identify themselves with both parties in roughly equal numbers: approximately one-third of adults express a preference for one of the two parties, and most of the remaining one-third identify themselves as some sort of independent or unaffiliated voter. As with Democrats, Republicans are often divided between those who favor greater liberalism in economic and moral issues and those whose cultural or religious preferences call for a greater state role in social issues. These divisions were apparent in the 2016 Republican Party presidential primary, which pitted libertarians who favored free trade and states' rights (like Senator Rand Paul) against social conservatives advocating federal restrictions on abortion and opposing free trade agreements (like Senator Ted Cruz).

The most significant movement within the Republican Party in recent years has been the emergence of the **Tea Party**. Taking its name from the 1773 protest by colonists against the British imposition of taxes on tea, the modern-day movement emerged in 2009 as a reactionary group within the GOP. Although members of the movement share a strong opposition to any increase in taxation, they are divided between small-government libertarians and social conservatives.[10] The movement gained strength in opposition to the perceived increase in federal government power and spending, including federal stimulus spending in response to the recent recession, and to passage of President Obama's Affordable Care Act in 2010. The movement's opposition to Obamacare culminated in demands that Congress defund the health care program. Majority Republicans in the House of Representatives were sympathetic to these demands and attached measures to the 2013 government appropriations bill that the majority Democrats in the Senate refused to pass. This deadlock resulted in the 2013 government shutdown discussed previously in this chapter. Polls regularly indicate that more than 10 percent of Americans consider themselves part of the movement, and more than a fourth of Americans consider themselves supporters.[11] However, since the Tea Party's role in the government shutdown, unfavorable views of the movement have risen significantly among both Democrats and even many Republicans. Moreover, the Tea Party's embrace of economic nationalism (opposition to free trade agreements) and white nativism (opposition to immigration) threatens the Republicans' chances of winning the presidency, as the electorate becomes less white and ever more dependent on foreign trade.[12]

The 2016 presidential campaign threatened to destroy the Republican Party, as Donald Trump, a blustery business tycoon and political outsider (with few ties to the Republican Party) easily defeated 16 aspirants competing for the Republican nomination for president. Some of Trump's views, such as his opposition to free trade deals and his stance on immigration, appealed to Tea Party radicals. However, many of his views (especially on foreign policy) clashed with conventional Republican ideas (he was particularly critical of the Iraq War). His views on immigration and his inflammatory statements on race were seen by Party leaders as endangering support from the country's increasingly diverse electorate. After Trump won the nomination, some leading Republicans refused to endorse him. His upset victory over Hillary Clinton thus presents new opportunities and challenges for the Republican Party. After the 2016 elections the Republican Party occupied the presidency, had majorities in both houses of Congress, and controlled both the governorship and legislature in half of the states.

THIRD PARTIES

If fully one-third of Americans do not regularly identify themselves with either party, is there political space for a third party? Certainly single-member plurality systems in other countries, such as the United Kingdom, have yielded more than two parties. But in the United States, establishing the kind of presence essential for national viability has proved difficult, if not prohibitive, for smaller parties. Moreover, the dominant parties have all the advantages of incumbency, such as the ability to establish and preserve laws discouraging the financing of third-party candidates and including them on the ballot.

Still, third parties occasionally have emerged on the U.S. political scene as protest voices. In that sense, third parties and their candidates can claim to have had an impact on the political process even if few of them have had any prospect of national electoral success. Among the third-party movements, the Populists of the late nineteenth century and the Progressives of the early twentieth have been the most successful. More recently, protest voices have emerged from across the political spectrum: George Wallace, a former (and subsequent) Democratic governor of the state of Alabama, ran a populist and segregationist campaign in 1968 under the banner of the American Independent Party and won 14 percent of the vote. Ross Perot's populist United We Stand Party earned nearly 20 percent of the presidential vote in 1992, and Ralph Nader's pro-environment Green Party garnered nearly 3 percent in 2000. In the latter two cases, it can be argued that the third-party candidates took crucial votes from the losing candidate. Nader, for example, garnered nearly 100,000 votes in Florida in the 2000 election. If only 1 percent of his supporters had voted for Gore instead, Gore would have won Florida and the national election. This result had the effect of suppressing third-party candidates in subsequent presidential elections, though they are likely to reemerge in the future. In 2016, only about 5 percent of U.S. voters selected a third party, with the Libertarian and Green Party candidates attracting most of those votes.

One factor contributing to the lack of third-party success in the United States is that the dominant parties have routinely embraced key elements of the more successful third-party movements, bringing at least some of the disaffected voters back into the two-party fold even as they weaken the third parties.

Elections

In the United States, in contrast to countries governed by parliamentary systems, terms for all elected offices—and therefore the sequencing of elections—are fixed. Each state determines the conduct of its elections, including the rules for any primary elections (preliminary direct elections held in many states and designed to narrow the field of candidates). Since the 1950s, electioneering in the United States has shifted from campaigning done almost exclusively by party leaders and grassroots party workers to highly centralized and professionalized media campaigns. Election contests today are hugely expensive and marked by media sound bites, talk show interviews, televised debates, targeted tweets, incessant fundraising, and advertising blitzes, all guided by polls and sophisticated demographic studies.

Campaigns for the presidency epitomize U.S.-style electioneering. These campaigns cost billions of dollars and include social media outreach strategies to get voters to the polls on Election Day. In his successful presidential campaign, Donald Trump made extensive use of Twitter to communicate directly with his followers.

No campaigns are more illustrative of this American-style electioneering than those for the U.S. presidency. As voters have apparently become less loyal to either party, and in many cases less interested in voting or participating at all, the parties and their candidates have redoubled their efforts (and expenditures) to attract support. In total, the 2016 presidential and congressional candidates spent almost $7 billion, far more than that spent on campaigns in any other country.[13] Campaigns begin early, with an extensive season of primaries, and involve an all-out effort both to promote the candidate and to denigrate the opponents, all in an attempt to mobilize new voters and persuade the undecided.

Civil Society

Since nineteenth-century French political philosopher Alexis de Tocqueville, observers have marveled at the vibrancy of U.S. civil society and the willingness of its citizens to become civically engaged. Recently, however, analysts have pointed to an apparent weakening of that civic commitment, noting low voter turnout and other signs of growing political apathy among U.S. citizens as evidence of a broader, generational decline in social capital (the web of relationships connecting individuals in society that can help individual citizens influence political outcomes).[14] Others argue, however, that the participation of individuals and the organized groups that represent their interests have perhaps not declined as much as simply changed: individual citizens associate with one another and seek to influence politics and policy in a variety of new and nontraditional ways.

However, precisely because the U.S. policy-making process is so complex and allows so many points of access—including individual officeholders at the national, state, and local level; legislative committees; regulatory agencies; and the initiative process—it has been difficult for individual citizens to influence the political process. As U.S. political parties have grown weaker and less cohesive, various special-interest groups have emerged and expanded their influence. The remarkable proliferation and enormous influence of these groups in the United States set this case apart from that of other democracies.

Interest groups are often organized around a single issue or a cluster of issues (from gun rights to workers' issues) and therefore typically do not officially affiliate with a particular party or candidate. These organized interests can include a single corporation or business association, public interest groups, and even state or local governments. Perhaps most well known are the political action committees (PACs), political fund-raising organizations that allow corporations and trade unions to support individual candidates. Although a 2002 campaign finance law banned so-called soft money, or unregulated donations to political parties, organized interests were undeterred. Interest groups quickly discovered a loophole in the law in a new type of tax-exempt organization (known as a 527 for the section of the federal tax code governing its behavior) that could raise unlimited campaign funds as long as the funds were spent on voter mobilization and issue advocacy rather than specifically promoting a candidate or party. Then, in 2010, the Supreme Court ruled the 2002 campaign finance law unconstitutional in its restrictions on the ability of companies, unions, and other groups to pay directly for political advertisements during election campaigns. This ruling substantially increased special-interest spending in the 2010 midterm legislative elections. In the 2012 presidential election, it paved the way for "super PACs," which were freed from any restrictions on donations, spending, or public disclosure.

These super PACs, along with all other contributing groups and individuals not directly connected to a candidate's election committee, make up what is called outside money—a segment of campaign finance that has exploded in recent years. These donations totaled over $1 billion in the 2012 election cycle, a tripling from the previous election. In the 2012 Republican primary campaign in Iowa, for example, a super PAC supporting Mitt Romney (though not "officially" linked to him) spent more than the candidate himself. During the 2016 elections, super PACs raised almost $1.8 billion. The effects of such outside money on American democracy remain in dispute. In addition to financing political campaigns, these interest groups, along with business corporations and wealthy individuals, exercise their influence through various lobbying techniques to promote the interests of their constituencies.

Society

Ethnic and National Identity

The first European colonists in America were largely English-speaking Protestants, but early in the country's history the importation of enslaved Africans and a steady stream of emigration from Europe quickly diversified American society. In the mid-nineteenth century, the California gold rush spurred a wave of Asian immigration, and another major migration from southern and eastern Europe began in the 1880s.

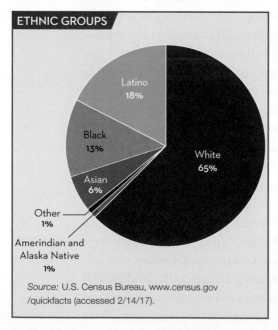

ETHNIC GROUPS

Latino 18%

Black 13%

White 65%

Asian 6%

Other 1%

Amerindian and Alaska Native 1%

Source: U.S. Census Bureau, www.census.gov /quickfacts (accessed 2/14/17).

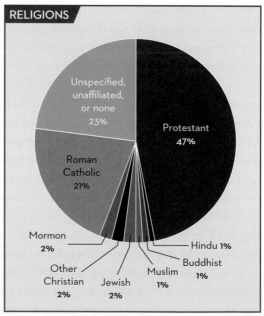

RELIGIONS

Unspecified, unaffiliated, or none 23%

Protestant 47%

Roman Catholic 21%

Mormon 2%

Hindu 1%

Buddhist 1%

Other Christian 2%

Jewish 2%

Muslim 1%

In the 1920s, Congress reacted to the new immigrants by imposing a series of restrictive immigration quotas favoring immigrants from northern Europe. With the amended Immigration and Nationality Act of 1965, Congress abandoned those quotas. As a result, immigration surged again, this time with the bulk of the new immigrants arriving from Latin America and Asia. The influx of non-European immigrants, especially **Latinos**, has become an important issue in U.S. politics (see "Immigration, Cultural Diversity, and U.S. National Identity," p. 140). As of 2011, about 13 percent of U.S. citizens were born abroad. (In Canada, the figure is 20 percent.)

Contrary to the common perception of the United States as a peaceful **melting pot** of cultures, immigrants have always faced resentment and discrimination. The debate about the impact of immigrants on U.S. society has deep roots in American history, and it changes depending on which group of immigrants predominates at the time (Catholics, Asians, Latinos). The debate continues today and is centered largely on the rapidly growing presence of immigrants from Latin America (many of whom reside in the United States illegally).

Ideology and Political Culture

The United States' melting pot image has led to much debate about the distinctiveness of U.S. ideology and political culture. There is broad consensus, however, that the attributes discussed next characterize dominant aspects of U.S. ideology.

INDIVIDUALISM AND FREEDOM

Although citizens of other industrial democracies are more likely to view freedom as resulting from government policy, Americans typically view their individual freedom in terms of what the state cannot do to them. As a result, whereas many other democracies attempt to specify in their constitutions what the state should provide its citizens, the U.S. Constitution emphasizes citizens' protections from the state. Like classic liberal thinkers, Americans tend to eschew collective or societal goals in favor of personal or individual goals. Consequently, the role of private property in U.S. society is especially important, and taxes, which some citizens view as the state's appropriation of private property, are highly unpopular. This individualism may be one factor that has weakened political parties in the United States and limited their ideological coherence.

An often-observed feature of U.S. political culture is Americans' participation in a plethora of voluntary groups that can be referred to collectively as *civil society*. Even in the nineteenth century, Tocqueville noted that Americans were "forever forming associations."[15] The rich web of civic organizations in the United States exemplifies the notion of self-government and political equality and performs a host of tasks that in other societies might be carried out by the state. The large number of protests following the election of Donald Trump might be evidence in support of that view. In their classic work *The Civic Culture Revisited*, Gabriel Almond and Sidney Verba found that American citizens, far more than citizens in other democracies, believe that participation in community affairs is part of good citizenship.[16]

Some leading scholars have expressed alarm about what they see as a rapid decline in the amount of participation in traditional civic groups. Moreover, scholars have noted that the nature of civil society is changing in the United States. This change is manifested in less participation in local grassroots organizations and the emergence of national, professionally managed lobbies (such as the National Rifle Association and the Sierra Club). Others note that the terrorist

Black Lives Matter, formed in 2013 to protest institutionalized racism against African Americans, is an example of the plethora of groups that compose the vibrant civil society in the United States.

attacks of September 11, 2001, and concerns about environmental issues and economic recession may be reviving civic participation, especially among younger Americans. The large number of protests following the election of President Donald Trump might be evidence in support of that view. Clearly, disagreement remains about whether civil society is in danger.

POPULISM

Populism, the idea that the masses should dominate elites and that the popular will should trump professional expertise, is a key feature of the U.S. creed. As a result, Americans believe in electing public officials at virtually all levels of society, including some law-enforcement officials and judges. Increasingly, Americans are expressing the desire to "unelect" government officials as well; in recent years, citizens have demanded recall elections for judges in Iowa, a governor in California, and legislators in a number of states. Many states have also seen an explosion of public initiatives giving the electorate a direct say in a growing variety of policy issues. In the 2016 presidential primary campaigns, Donald Trump and Bernie Sanders, candidates from both major parties, embraced populist themes. One growing manifestation of the populist strain in U.S. political culture is the widespread popular disdain for professional politicians. Recent public opinion research found that a growing number of Americans (especially on the political right) would favor a presidential candidate who did not have prior experience in national politics.[17] Despite the fact that Donald Trump is clearly part of the wealthy elite in the United States, his 2016 election is perhaps best explained by a surge in populist rejection of professional politicians.

EQUALITY OF OPPORTUNITY, NOT OUTCOME

A deep-seated aspect of U.S. political culture, rooted in the frontier mentality of early America, is the belief that all Americans have, and should have, an equal opportunity to become prosperous and successful. In the nineteenth century, Tocqueville observed that the United States had a far more egalitarian class structure than did Europe. Although assessments of economic equality and social mobility were certainly exaggerated even in early America—women were second-class citizens, and many others, such as African Americans, were excluded altogether—the notions of equality of opportunity and social mobility have endured as part of a fundamental ethos.

Opinion research confirms that Americans today hold true to the notion of equality of opportunity but place less value on equality of actual economic outcomes. They are likely to believe that success is a function of individual effort. Today, the reverse of what Tocqueville observed in the nineteenth century is true: disparities of income are greater in the United States than in most of Europe, and they are growing quickly. Indeed, Americans tend to oppose state policies aimed at redistributing income to benefit the poor, and compared with their counterparts in other advanced democracies, Americans are more likely to blame the poor for not taking advantage of opportunities open to them. For example, Americans far more than Europeans believe that hard work is likely to lead to success.

Despite growing inequality and persistent poverty, and although recent studies show that U.S. citizens have less social mobility than the citizens in many other advanced democracies, Americans evince confidence about their future.[18] Most believe they are better off than their parents, two-thirds think they will achieve the American dream of self-improvement at some point in their lifetime, and 80 percent think they can start out poor and become rich through their own labors.[19]

ANTI-STATISM

Although the U.S. public has historically viewed its federal state with relatively high levels of trust and pride, a paradoxical, deep-seated liberal distrust of "excessive" central state power is also a prominent feature of the political culture. The American Revolution began as a rebellion against a powerful British state that was seen as abusing its authority through the unjust taxation of its citizens. The United States is unique in that anti-statism became a founding principle of the new regime.

As already discussed, the founders of the U.S. regime consciously sought to embed in the system myriad checks on the power of the central state through the devolution of much power to state and local governments, the establishment of a powerful and independent judiciary, and the separation of powers. As a result, Americans remain skeptical of state efforts to promote social welfare, an outlook that largely explains the relatively small size of the U.S. welfare state. Compared with citizens in other advanced democracies, far fewer Americans hold the state responsible for providing food and housing for every citizen.

THE IMPORTANCE OF RELIGIOUS VALUES

The United States also stands out among advanced democracies in the importance it continues to place on religion. A far higher percentage of its citizens belong to a church or other religious organization than do the citizens of other advanced democracies, and Americans are more likely to believe that clear guidelines differentiate good and evil.

Some scholars have argued that the high levels of religiosity in the United States stem from the early separation of church and state, which in effect turned religious organizations into voluntary civic groups that competed for membership in a religious marketplace.[20] In the United States, new religious groups (most recently, evangelical denominations) constantly emerge to attract congregants who might be disillusioned with more established denominations. Indeed, it could be argued that the absence of a state religion has led Americans to associate religion with democracy, whereas in other countries, state religions have been viewed as inimical to democracy.

The importance of religion in the United States has been linked to what has been called **utopian moralism**, the tendency of Americans to view the world in terms of good versus evil. At the same time, the "free market" for religion and anti-statism often complicates the quest for moral clarity. On many moral issues, such as abortion, Americans are uncomfortable both with sanctioning behavior they may see as immoral and with restricting personal behavior.

Finally, it is interesting to observe how these values have tracked over time in surveys, the findings of which may run counter to our perceptions of conservative American political culture. Surveys on American values over the past 20 years have shown that the public has grown much more tolerant of homosexuality and gender and racial equality and has become slightly less religious, particularly among the young. Americans (unlike most Europeans) continue to believe that personal success is determined by individual actions (rather than events beyond their control), reflecting the central tenet of American individualism.[21] Moreover, opinion research has shown that the percentage of Americans who are atheists, agnostics, or do not identify with any religion has grown rapidly and now comprises about a quarter of U.S. adults.[22] And despite the dramatic success of conservative Tea Party candidates in recent elections, public opinion research suggests that the long-term success of that movement is likely to be very limited. While many Americans embrace the small-government approach of the Tea Party, polls show they are wary about the movement's socially conservative and evangelical Christian orientation.[23]

Political Economy

Although China surpassed the United States in 2014 as the world's largest national economy, the United States remains the most prosperous and technologically powerful country in the world. With just over 4 percent of the world's population, the United States produces as much of the world's economic output as China, which has nearly 20 percent of the world's population.[24] In the 1990s, while many of the world's economies struggled, the United States enjoyed the longest period of sustained economic growth in its history. For most of the three decades since the 1970s, inflation and unemployment also remained relatively low. However, the global financial crisis and subsequent economic recession that originated with a banking crisis in the United States in 2008 have had long-term negative consequences for the American economy and profoundly influenced its politics as well.

In general, the U.S. state plays a smaller role in the market than do the governments of most other industrialized democracies. The proportion of GDP spent by the state has hovered around 35 percent, less than in most European countries (for example, Sweden's state consumes over 50 percent of GDP), a figure that has not varied much over time.[25] Studies of global economic freedom rank the U.S. economy in the top 15 globally (the United States ranked 11th in 2016, behind Australia and Canada but ahead of Britain and Germany).[26] The United States also has some of the lowest tax rates among the industrialized democracies (see "In Comparison: Taxes as a Percentage of GDP," p. 134). However, what the United States does not provide by way of direct state expenditures is often less visible or "submerged," such as various tax breaks for home ownership, children, or student loans and subsidies for employer-provided health care, to name a few. As a result, some observe that the notion of a weak U.S. welfare system is misleading; rather, benefits are often supplied through the private sector and supported by a complicated system of tax breaks targeting specific groups of Americans. Such a system, however, tends to benefit the middle class much more than the poor, who lack the resources to take advantage of tax exemptions and might more easily benefit from public goods, such as nationalized health care.[27]

Although private enterprise is the main engine of the U.S. economy, the state does play a significant role. At the country's founding, Alexander Hamilton proposed ambitious plans for active state involvement in the marketplace, including providing infrastructure, creating a national bank, and channeling capital to strategic sectors of the economy. Such policies were controversial at the time but were largely implemented over the course of the nineteenth century.

Starting with the New Deal reforms of the 1930s, the state's role in the economy increased significantly to prevent a market collapse, promote equity, and shield the American political-economic system from fascism on the right and communism on the left. Since the 1980s, governments have attempted at times to scale back the role of the state in the economy. The Reagan administration, for example, deregulated many sectors of the economy (including telecommunications and the airlines) to make them more competitive; under the Clinton administration in the 1990s, reforms also devolved many welfare responsibilities to the states. The 2008 financial crisis once again brought the state into the marketplace on a dramatic scale in the form of fiscal stimuli, corporate bailouts, direct government ownership, and tougher government financial regulations. Over the course of the 2000s, an enormous boom took place in the U.S. housing market, facilitated by low interest rates backed by the Federal Reserve and large inflows of foreign funds seeking to profit from the boom. This easy money made cheap loans available to American consumers and fueled a housing construction frenzy and, ultimately, a housing bubble. Unrestrained by government regulators, financial institutions issued increasingly risky loans to increasingly indebted consumers and then bundled these mortgages together into complex securities and sold them to investors at great profit.

For a season, this bubble kept everyone aloft and happy. Americans were living the American dream of home ownership, jobs were plentiful, and banks were extremely profitable. But when the inflated housing bubble popped and housing prices declined, so too did the value of these mortgage-backed securities. The Wall Street financial institutions that had invested heavily in these securities began to suffer huge losses, prompting investors to flee. As interest rates climbed and property values plummeted, more and more Americans found themselves unable to make mortgage payments and were forced into foreclosure. The federal government stepped in to bail out banks, shore up key businesses, calm troubled financial markets, and jump-start the economy. These steps were designed to increase employment, stimulate investment, lift the economy out of recession, and prevent the kinds of market failures that had led to the crisis in the first place.

Additionally, the U.S. state's intervention in the economy has been aimed at improving the business climate. Over the past 40 years, the tax burden has shifted from corporations to individuals, and the state has granted huge subsidies to agribusiness and given generous tax breaks to corporations. At the same time, in contrast to many European countries, the state has done little to support trade unions. Even during a Republican administration, under George W. Bush, the size of the state grew faster than at any time since the 1970s, though this growth largely involved military and national security spending.[28] State expansion in the form of military spending and recession relief efforts has also raised government debt to dangerous levels, complicating efforts to fund government programs and sharpening political debate, calls for austerity, and pursuit of a balanced budget. In 2011, Standard & Poor's downgraded the U.S. credit rating for the first time

Taxes as a Percentage of GDP

COUNTRY	PERCENTAGE
France	45.2
Germany	36.1
Russia	35.3
Brazil	32.8
United Kingdom	32.6
Japan	30.3
United States	26.0
South Africa	22.6
Mexico	19.7
China	18.7
India	16.6
Iran	6.4
Nigeria	2.8

Source: Heritage Foundation Index of Economic Freedom (www.heritage.org). Most recent data available for each country (accessed 8/22/17).

in the country's history, citing concern about both the growing debt and the protracted political struggle over raising the debt ceiling.

Despite its wealth and generally impressive record of economic growth, the United States faces numerous political and economic challenges in the twenty-first century. Compounding the problems of the national recession has been the challenge of persistent and growing income inequality. Since the Social Security Act of 1935, the U.S. state has provided a safety net of welfare measures, but the provisions have been less extensive than those of other advanced democracies. The United States spends about 15 percent of its GDP on social expenditures, a lower share than that of almost any other advanced democracy (only Ireland's is lower). Legislation in the 1960s expanded welfare measures to include some health care coverage for the poor and the elderly, but it stopped short of providing universal health care for all citizens. During the Reagan administration, welfare spending per poor recipient fell by one-fifth. Under President Clinton, there was bipartisan support for measures aimed at cutting welfare expenditures, and with some notable exceptions (such as prescription benefits for the elderly), social expenditures remained flat or declined. The economic downturn in 2008 caused a spike in welfare expenditures, which rose to nearly 5 percent of GDP by 2010, nearly double the proportion of just three years previous. As the economy has regained its footing, welfare expenditures have returned to less than 3 percent of GDP in subsequent years.

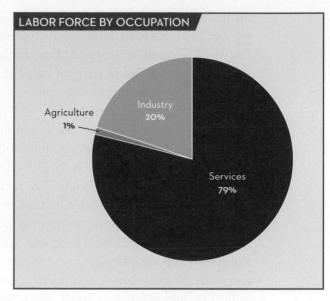

LABOR FORCE BY OCCUPATION

Agriculture 1%

Industry 20%

Services 79%

As a result, income inequality in the United States has become a serious and growing problem. While the main measure of inequality, the Gini index, has remained relatively flat in many countries around the world, the United States has seen a dramatic increase over the past two decades. In 1980, the U.S. Gini index stood at 30, where it had been since the late 1960s. This figure is comparable to the European Union's Gini index in 2007. Since the 1980s, the U.S. Gini number has risen to 41, similar to that of China and many countries in Africa.[29] The United States has the largest number of millionaires in the world, but it also has a disproportionately large number of poor for a country of its wealth (hence the high degree of inequality). About 15 percent of the country's citizens live below the poverty line, including approximately 22 percent of its children (the highest percentage among the advanced democracies). This poverty is particularly concentrated among African Americans and Latinos, indicating how immigration and racism can compound the likelihood of poverty in the United States. Persistent racial divisions in the United States remain one of the greatest challenges to reducing inequality.

Some scholars believe that growing inequality has a corrosive effect on American society. A recent book by political scientist Robert Putnam illustrates the growing social consequences of economic inequality, which he argues threatens the American Dream of social mobility.[30] Other scholars have argued that the United States' political system is increasingly dominated by large economic interests, at the expense of the majority of the population.[31] These concerns dovetail with alarm over the role of money in politics and the weakness of U.S. campaign finance laws. Concern over growing inequality, not usually central to U.S. politics, became a central theme in the 2016 presidential campaign. In the Democratic Party primary campaign, Senator Bernie Sanders mounted a serious challenge to the former senator and secretary of state Hillary Clinton, focused almost entirely on the need to stem the growing economic divide. In the Republican Party primary campaign, real-estate mogul Donald Trump defeated his more mainstream competition by embracing economic nationalism and attacking free-trade deals that he claimed led to the impoverishment of the U.S. working class.

Related to the problems of inequality and poverty is the growing national debt over the past two decades. While U.S. social expenditures are small compared with those of other advanced democracies, the low and declining levels of taxation (see "In Comparison: Taxes as a Percentage of GDP," p. 134), growing numbers of elderly, expanding entitlement programs, inability to control health care expenses, and costs of defense and waging wars in Iraq and Afghanistan have translated into far greater expenses than state revenues can support. This budget deficit has been funded by borrowing. As a result, the United States has an enormous national debt of over $19 trillion; the figure now exceeds the country's annual GDP and has reached a level not seen since World War II. If at some point the United States is no longer able to sustain this debt through borrowing (often from foreign sources such as China), the result could be economic decline and the inability to sustain military commitments and other obligations abroad. Global recession has compounded this problem, making government stimulus spending difficult in the face of declining economic growth, employment, and tax revenues. Predictably, Democrats and Republicans have quite effectively "checked" each other in efforts to resolve this dilemma, finding little common policy ground.

Finally, the U.S. economy also faces the challenges of globalization common to the other cases in this book. Both Democrats and Republicans have pushed for freer world trade, though there has been pressure in the other direction. President Clinton signed the North American Free Trade Agreement (NAFTA), which has further integrated the U.S. economy with the economies of its largest trading partners, Canada and Mexico. Subsequent administrations have pushed for expanding free-trade agreements with much of Latin America and more recently with over a dozen Asian and Pacific countries. In recent years, however, Democrats in particular have singled out NAFTA as a cause of job losses and economic decline, and both parties have frequently pointed to China as a cause of American economic woes. Opposition to free-trade deals emerged as a major theme in the 2016 presidential campaigns within both major political parties. Global economic difficulties and recession currently confront most countries. How will this affect personal and government debt, growth, inequality, and poverty in the United States? How will it affect economic relations between the United States and the rest of the world? We will get a better sense of this as events unfold in the near future.

Foreign Relations and the World

Despite its recent economic challenges, the United States remains the most powerful actor in world politics by virtue of its expansive economy and outsized military. The United States exercises influence beyond its borders in a variety of ways, including military and humanitarian intervention, extensive trade and investment, and active participation in a number of multilateral institutions such as the International Monetary Fund, the World Bank, and the United Nations.

The United States spent its first century after independence relatively removed from world affairs. Governing a country blessed with geographic remoteness from most of the world's major conflicts, U.S. presidents generally sought to avoid what President Thomas Jefferson called "entangling alliances." By the early nineteenth century, the rapid growth of the population and the economy drove the projection of U.S. power beyond its borders, however, in what some Americans came to view as the nation's **manifest destiny**. In the early nineteenth century, President James Monroe (1821–25) warned European powers to stay out of the entire Western Hemisphere (this policy became known as the Monroe Doctrine). Later in the century, the United States extended its borders and its power through economic and military means that included victories in the Mexican War (1846–48) and the Spanish-American War (1898) as well as the annexation of Hawaii (1898).

By the early twentieth century, the United States was the dominant foreign power in Latin America and expanded its influence there under President Theodore Roosevelt. Roosevelt, who bragged that he "took" Panama from Colombia in 1903 to build the canal there, preferred economic domination and the threat of U.S. military action (what he called the Big Stick) as a means of influence, rather than officially acquiring territory. Roosevelt's visit to Panama in 1906, the first-ever foreign trip by a U.S. president, boldly ended the era of isolation.

The long-held preference for avoiding entanglements in Europe was forsaken when the United States belatedly entered World War I. The creation of a national military draft enabled a significant increase in military capability, and the Allied victory resulted in a national sense of pride and confidence. At the same time, revulsion at the deaths of more than 100,000 Americans created a strong popular desire to return to isolationism and avoid future wars. The United States entered

World War II only after the Japanese attack on Pearl Harbor, Hawaii, in December 1941. Involvement in World War II was a major turning point in the nation's foreign policy. The United States created a massive army, and its participation was a decisive factor in the Allied victory against the Axis powers. The controversial decision by the United States to deploy its nuclear arsenal against Japan in 1945 heralded its new status as a global superpower.

Almost immediately after World War II, the United States moved to counter the influence of its wartime ally the Soviet Union; the growing conflict came to be known as the Cold War. Under the Marshall Plan (1947–52), the United States invested heavily in the rebuilding of Western Europe, largely to immunize the region against communism. The United States also formed an alliance of industrialized democracies, the North Atlantic Treaty Organization (NATO), in 1949 to ensure the provision of mutual defense in the event of a Soviet attack. In the second half of the twentieth century, the United States acted frequently through direct invasion or covert action to deter Communist threats (real or perceived) in Asia, Latin America, and Africa.

The record of the United States in its quest to contain the global spread of communism is mixed. In the Korean War (1950–53), it succeeded in protecting South Korea from Communist invasion, and it later helped topple numerous democratically elected governments it viewed as dangerous (such as Guatemala's in 1954 and Chile's in 1973). The United States was unable to prevent a Communist victory in China in 1949, however, though it intervened to preserve the government of Taiwan. It also failed in the Vietnam War (1961–73), a protracted, costly, and politically unpopular conflict that did not prevent a Communist takeover of Vietnam. Similarly, despite an attempted invasion and decades of covert action and economic pressure, the United States failed to overthrow the Communist regime of Fidel Castro in neighboring Cuba.

The fall of the Berlin Wall in 1989 and the subsequent collapse of the Soviet Union effectively brought the Cold War to an end and left the United States as the sole global superpower. This post-Soviet era nonetheless produced serious new challenges. As the undisputed global leader, the United States was called upon to help resolve ethnic violence that erupted in the Balkans and elsewhere. However, America's Cold War involvement in global conflicts and its enhanced power in the post–Cold War era created considerable global resentment. In the 1990s, the United States intervened militarily in the Persian Gulf (to repel the Iraqi invasion of Kuwait) and in the Balkans (to stem ethnic violence), both times taking part in international peacekeeping efforts.

After the terrorist attacks on the United States of September 11, 2001, President George W. Bush declared a "war" against global terrorism and announced that the United States would use unilateral preemptive force against all possible terrorist threats to the United States. Many countries, including some U.S. allies, viewed this **Bush Doctrine** as a rejection of international law and the prerogatives of the United Nations. Some critics viewed it as a dangerous projection of U.S. nationalism and a reassertion of the nineteenth-century view of manifest destiny.[32] As a result, anti-Americanism, a long-standing sentiment extending back to the era of isolationism, rose dramatically around the world.

In October 2001, in the first manifestation of the Bush Doctrine, the United States led a coalition of forces that invaded Afghanistan and toppled the regime that had harbored Al Qaeda, the terrorist organization responsible for the September 11 attacks. The Bush Doctrine was again invoked in March 2003 with the U.S.-led invasion of Iraq. The Bush administration claimed that Iraq was a threat to the United States and the world because of its possession of weapons of mass destruction and because it, too, harbored terrorists (neither of which proved correct). Obama was elected in 2008 on the promise to draw down forces in both theaters and was reelected in 2012 with the assurance that his government would end all combat operations in the region.

In short, despite—or perhaps because of—the United States' failure to obtain the objectives of the invasions, American voters and political leaders had grown tired of and disillusioned with the wars. By 2014, the conflicts in Iraq and Afghanistan had cost more than 100,000 civilian lives and the deaths of nearly 7,000 U.S. troops. The actual government expenditures for war- and security-related costs through 2013 have been estimated at well over $1 trillion. However, a 2014 study estimated that the long-term costs of the war, including the care and compensation for returning veterans of both conflicts, would reach $4 to $6 trillion, making this by far the most expensive war in U.S. history.[33] Although some political analysts hope that the troop withdrawal will improve frayed relations with much of the world, which has grown critical of many of the United States' unilateralist policies, the United States leaves the region and states within the region, including Afghanistan and Iraq, more conflict ridden and less stable than it found them more than a decade ago. The United States' departure does not mean it will end its strategic interest or engagement in the region, nor will it likely retreat from its interests in other areas of the world, including often tense relations with North Korea, Iran, and, at times, China and Russia. Simply put, the United States will continue to face challenges in the international system.

The election of Donald Trump in 2016 created new uncertainty over the direction of U.S. foreign policy. During the presidential campaign, Trump departed from traditional Republican Party stances by opposing existing and future free-trade deals, criticizing President George W. Bush's invasion of Iraq, questioning the U.S. commitment to the North Atlantic Treaty Organization, and by appearing to embrace anti-U.S. autocrats like Russia's president Vladimir Putin.

CURRENT ISSUES IN THE UNITED STATES

Immigration, Cultural Diversity, and U.S. National Identity

From the outset, the United States has been a nation of immigrants. Nonetheless, the current wave of immigration has once again proven to be a hot political issue. In recent years, several states have passed increasingly stringent anti-immigration laws, increased penalties for employers who hire undocumented immigrants, required schools to determine the immigration status of students' parents, forbidden illegal immigrants from working or asking for work, and forbidden anyone from renting apartments or even giving rides to illegal immigrants.

Some observers have gone so far as to warn that the volume of immigration, particularly coming from Mexico and elsewhere in Latin America, will undermine the fundamental values of the United States; they claim that this group will resist assimilation because it is so large and distinct.[34] These fears, combined with concerns about cross-border drug trade and violent crime, led to the construction of hundreds of miles of security fences along the U.S.-Mexico border (nearly one-third of the 2,000-mile boundary is fenced). Others are more optimistic about prospects for integration, noting that since the founding of the United States, successive waves of immigrants have been viewed as a threat to American political culture but over time have been assimilated.

Even those observers who agree that the current flow of immigration differs in many important respects from those of the past generally disagree with the assessment that Latin American immigration poses a threat to U.S. society.[35] There is much evidence that Latino immigrants are speaking English and otherwise assimilating into U.S. culture: more than 90 percent of second-generation Latinos are either bilingual or mainly English speakers, and many intermarry with non-Latino partners. As one scholar has concluded, "Hispanic immigration is part and parcel of broader American patterns of assimilation and integration. Their story, like that of the Irish, Jews, and Italians before them, is an American story."[36]

Similarly, the broader public reflects these same mixed views regarding immigration. After the September 11, 2001 attacks, support for restricting immigration increased significantly, but this support has steadily declined in recent years.[37] More generally, several scholarly studies indicate that the relatively weak level of social expenditures in the United States has much to do with the country's cultural diversity. In short, citizens may be willing to support immigration, but they also appear much less willing to redistribute wealth to those they feel are not like them.[38] Indeed, the rise of the welfare state in the United States coincided with heavy restrictions on immigration following World Wars I and II. Likewise, the rapid increase in immigration starting in the 1980s corresponded with a marked rollback of the welfare state. The United States continues to be a melting pot of cultures fed by a steady stream of immigrants, but Americans remain ambivalent and deeply divided about this aspect of their society. If economic difficulties persist over the long term, this situation may increase pressure for restrictions on immigration and make immigrants the flashpoint for anxieties about economic security. At the same time, population analysts are projecting that by 2042, minorities in the United States will in fact become the majority population.

Immigration was front and center in the 2016 presidential campaign. Republican nominee Donald Trump called for a temporary ban on immigration from Muslim countries (as a response to the threat of terrorism), and he proposed to build a wall on the U.S.-Mexico border (to stop illegal immigration). His opponent, Hillary Clinton, attacked those proposals as racist, unfeasible, and counterproductive. Trump's election will almost certainly mean that immigration will remain a central issue in U.S. politics.

A Dysfunctional Democracy? Political Polarization in the United States

Even before the 2008 election of Barack Obama, scholars of U.S. politics pointed to the rapidly growing level of **political polarization**, or degree of political partisanship among members of the two major political parties. Recent presidential elections seemed to highlight a growing divide between "red states" (conservative, religious, and Republican) and "blue states" (more socially liberal, more secular, and Democratic). A number of high-profile events during Obama's first term seemed to underscore this polarization.

Obama took power vowing to end the partisan bickering in Washington, D.C., but soon found his agenda under fierce attack from the Republican opposition. Obama's massive economic stimulus package, introduced in February 2010 in response to the recession, passed without a single Republican vote in the House and with only three Republican votes in the Senate. Not a single Democrat in the Senate and only seven in the House opposed it. Obama's 2010 Affordable Care Act, a centerpiece of his electoral campaign, faced even more partisan opposition: not a single Republican in either the House or the Senate voted for it.

In 2011 and again in 2013, Republicans in the House of Representatives refused to approve an increase in the U.S. debt ceiling, thus effectively limiting the amount of money that the United States could borrow. Failure to raise the debt limit likely would have resulted in the United States defaulting on its debt and easily could have triggered a global economic crisis. In both cases, House Republicans eventually relented; but following the 2011 deadlock, Standard & Poor's, a leading debt rating agency, downgraded U.S. debt for the first time in the country's history, concluding that "the effectiveness, stability, and predictability of American policymaking and political institutions have weakened at a time of ongoing fiscal and economic challenges."[39] As discussed earlier in this chapter, the 2013 partisan brinksmanship resulted in a three-week government shutdown. In 2016 Senate Republicans took the unprecedented step of refusing to consider President Obama's nominee for the Supreme Court, another example of how partisan polarization has threatened the basic operation of the U.S. political system.

Public opinion research suggests that Americans are increasingly frustrated by the partisan bickering in U.S. politics. A 2011 poll found that 72 percent of the U.S. public described that year's debt ceiling negotiations as "ridiculous," "disgusting," and/ or "stupid."[40] A 2014 poll found that 63 percent of likely American voters were very disappointed with the performance of Congress, an improvement from the high of 75 percent negative assessment reported following the 2013 government shutdown.[41] The 2013–14 Congress passed fewer bills and enacted fewer laws than any other Congress in recent history. Not surprisingly, whether this lack of productivity is viewed as a bad thing (governments are elected to take action on behalf of the public) or a good thing (the government that legislates least, governs best, particularly when the president is a Democrat) depends on which party you belong to.

Scholars note that U.S. politics has become increasingly polarized since the 1970s, although earlier historical periods (during the Civil War, for example) have certainly been marked by high levels of polarization. Evidence of this polarization is strongest among political elites.[42] Since the 1970s, strict party-line votes have dramatically increased in Congress. Party unity scores, measuring the percentage of legislators voting with their party majority, have increased from about 70 percent in the 1970s to about 90 percent at present. Measures of the ideology and voting records of members of Congress point to a growing divide between Democratic and Republican legislators. In 1970, moderates constituted 41 percent of Senators, but today they account for only 5 percent.[43] In the words of two leading scholars of U.S. politics, "Conservative Democrats and liberal Republicans, who were common in American politics during the 1950s and 1960s, are now extremely rare."[44]

Scholars have pointed to a number of potentially corrosive consequences of this polarization among political elites.[45] They have argued, most obviously, that growing polarization makes it difficult to create legislative coalitions, leading to public policy gridlock. The workings of the federal bureaucracy and the judiciary have been hampered because what were once routine legislative approvals of presidential appointees have become long and drawn-out confirmation battles. One scholar has argued that the polarization has made it harder to pass laws to address economic crises, and that the gridlock in Congress has contributed to growing inequality in the United States because the legislature can't pass measures to protect the poorest Americans.[46] Many observers have lamented that the political discourse among political elites has become less civil.

A lively and ongoing scholarly debate questions whether there has been a similar political polarization among the U.S. public. Some scholars have argued that there is little evidence to suggest that mass polarization has increased with elite polarization.[47] Others contend that mass public opinion increasingly mirrors the polarization of political elites. Ticket splitting, in which voters might support a Democratic candidate for one office and a Republican for another, has declined sharply since the 1970s. A recent poll suggested an astonishingly high degree of partisan polarization after presenting respondents with two opposing statements. Eighty-three percent of Republicans, versus only 22 percent of Democrats, agreed with the statement that "government is doing too many things better left to businesses and individuals." In turn, 72 percent of Democrats, and only 15 percent of Republicans, agreed with the statement that "government should do more to solve problems."[48] Partisan views on major issues have become increasingly polarized. In 2000, about half of all Democrats and Republicans believed that immigrants made the United States stronger, but by 2016, 82 percent of Democrats and only 39 percent of Republicans held that view. In 2000, 38 percent of Republicans and 20 percent of Democrats agreed that the right to own guns was more important than efforts to control gun ownership. By 2016, 81 percent of Republicans and only 27 percent of Democrats took that stand.[49] According to one recent study:

Since the 1970s, ideological polarization has increased dramatically among the mass public in the United States as well as among political elites. There are now large differences in outlook between Democrats and Republicans, between red state voters and blue state voters, and between religious voters and secular voters. These divisions are not confined to a small minority of activists—they involve a large segment of the public and the deepest divisions are found among the most interested, informed, and active citizens.[50]

Scholars are even more divided about the causes of political polarization in the United States. Some have attributed it to the "democratization" and consequent weakening of U.S. political parties in the 1960s and 1970s (and especially the creation of party primaries to select presidential candidates) that allowed political activists to enter mainstream politics. Others place the blame on lax campaign finance laws and the explosion of special interest groups aimed at mobilizing citizens around single issues. Still others point to laws that give the media access to almost all political deliberations, together with the emergence of commercial media outlets fostering and even amplifying highly partisan positions.[51]

Can polarization be reversed? Many scholars have suggested political reforms aimed at reducing political polarization in the United States. For example, two experts on Latin American politics have suggested that the United States consider adopting a proportional representation electoral system, a feature of most Latin American presidential systems that they argue has fostered compromise among political parties.[52] Others have suggested reforming the rules of Congress and revising political party primaries to better reflect views in the political center.[53] With a political regime intentionally designed to "check" and "balance" political power, these kinds of reforms may not come easily. Looming challenges, however, may compel the kind of cooperation required to bring about the necessary institutional changes.

NOTES

1. Francis Fukuyama, "American Political Decay or Renewal? The Meaning of the 2016 Election," *Foreign Affairs*, July/August 2016, pp. 58–68.
2. Seymour Martin Lipset, *The First New Nation: The United States in Historical and Comparative Perspective* (New York: W. W. Norton, 1979), p. 2.
3. David R. Mayhew, *Divided We Govern: Party Control, Lawmaking, and Investigations, 1946–2002*, 2nd ed. (New Haven, CT: Yale University Press, 2005).

4. See, for example, Juan Linz, "The Perils of Presidentialism," *Journal of Democracy* 1 (Winter 1990): 51–69.

5. This quotation and its subsequent elaboration are drawn from Theodore J. Lowi, Benjamin Ginsberg, and Kenneth A Shepsle, *American Government: Power and Purpose*, 7th ed. (New York: W. W. Norton, 2002), p. 162.

6. Lowi et al., *American Government*, p. 454.

7. Nicholas Lehman, "Insurrection," *New Yorker*, September 26, 2005, pp. 66–67.

8. See Sven Steinmo, *The Evolution of Modern States: Sweden, Japan and the United States* (Cambridge: Cambridge University Press, 2010), pp. 156–59.

9. See T. R. Reid. *The Healing of America: A Global Quest for Better, Cheaper, and Fairer Health Care* (New York: Penguin, 2010).

10. On the Tea Party movement, see Vanessa Williamson, Theda Skocpol, and John Coggin, "The Tea Party and the Remaking of Republican Conservatism," *Perspectives on Politics* 9 (March 2011): 25–43.

11. NORC Center for Public Affairs Research, "The People's Agenda: America's Priorities and Outlook for 2014," *AP/GfK Polls*, January 2, 2014, http://surveys.ap.org/data/NORC/AP _NORC_2014_PeoplesAgenda_Poll_Topline_Final.pdf (accessed 8/9/14). For a survey of recent polls, see Karlyn Bowman and Jennifer Marsico, "As the Tea Party Turns Five, It Looks a Lot Like the Conservative Base," *Forbes,* February 24, 2014, www.forbes.com/sites /realspin/2014/02/24/as-the-tea-party-turns-five-it-looks-a-lot-like-the-conservative-base (accessed 8/11/14)

12. Peter Beinart, "The White Strategy," *Atlantic*, July/August 2016, pp. 81–86.

13. As reported by the Center for Responsive Politics, https://www.opensecrets.org/overview/cost .php?display=T&infl=Y (accessed 1/14/17).

14. Robert Putnam, *Bowling Alone: The Collapse and Revival of American Community* (New York: Simon and Schuster, 2000).

15. Quoted in "Degrees of Separation, Survey: America," *Economist*, July 14, 2005.

16. Alan Abramowitz, "The United States: Political Culture under Stress," in Gabriel Almond and Sidney Verba, eds., *The Civic Culture Revisited* (Boston: Little, Brown, 1980), p. 179.

17. Jonathan Rauch, "What's Ailing American Politics?" *Atlantic*, July/August 2016, pp. 51–63.

18. Isabel Sawhill and John E. Morton, "Economic Mobility: Is the American Dream Alive and Well?" Brookings Institution, www.brookings.edu/~/media/Files/rc/papers/2007/05use conomics_morton/05useconomics_morton.pdf (accessed 8/17/11).

19. "Degrees of Separation."

20. Lipset, *The First New Nation*, pp. 180–81.

21. Pew Center for the People and the Press, "Trends in Core Values and Political Attitudes 1987– 2007," http://people-press.org (accessed 8/2/08).

22. Michael Dimock, "How America Changed During Barack Obama's Presidency," Pew Research Center, January 10, 2017, www.pewresearch.org/2017/01/10/how-america-changed-during -barack-obamas-presidency (accessed 2/11/17).

23. David Campbell and Robert Putnam, "Crashing the Tea Party," *New York Times*, August 17, 2011, p. A21.

24. See CIA, The World Factbook, 2014, www.cia.gov/library/publications/the-world-factbook (accessed 8/11/14).

25. Graham K. Wilson, *Only in America? The Politics of the United States in Comparative Perspective* (Chatham, NJ: Chatham House, 1998), p. 61.

26. Heritage Foundation, "Index of Economic Freedom 2016," www.heritage.org (accessed 2/11/17).

27. See Sven Steinmo, *The Evolution of Modern States: Sweden, Japan, and the United States* (Cambridge: Cambridge University Press, 2010). For the "submerged state," see Suzanne Mettler, *The Submerged State: How Invisible Government Policies Undermine American Democracy* (Chicago: University of Chicago Press, 2011).

28. Richard Kogan, "Federal Spending, 2001 through 2008," Center on Budget and Policy Priorities, March 2008, www.cbpp.org/3-5-08bud.htm (accessed 8/2/08).

29. For details, see the World Bank, http://data.worldbank.org/indicator/SI.POV.GINI (accessed 7/28/17).

30. Robert Putnam, *Our Kids: The American Dream in Crisis* (New York: Simon and Schuster, 2015).

31. See Martin Gilens and Benjamin Page, "Testing Theories of American Politics: Elites, Interest Groups, and Average Citizens," *Perspectives on Politics* 12, no. 3 (September 2014): 564–81.

32. This is the argument of Anatole Lieven, *America, Right or Wrong: An Anatomy of American Nationalism* (New York: Oxford University Press, 2005).

33. Linda J. Bilmes, "The Financial Legacy of Iraq and Afghanistan: How Wartime Spending Decisions Will Constrain Future National Security Budgets." *HKS Faculty Research Working Paper Series* RWP13-006, March 2013.

34. Samuel P. Huntington, *Who Are We? The Challenges to America's National Identity* (New York: Simon and Schuster, 2004).

35. Tamar Jacoby, ed., *Reinventing the Melting Pot: The New Immigrants and What It Means to Be American* (New York: Basic Books, 2004).

36. Robert A. Levine, "Assimilation, Past and Present," *Public Interest* (Spring 2005): 108.

37. "Fewer Americans Favor Cutting Back Immigration," Gallup, July 10, 2008, www.gallup.com (accessed 2/19/09).

38. Alberto Alesina and Edward Glaeser, *Fighting Poverty in the US and Europe: A World of Difference* (Oxford: Oxford University Press, 2006).

39. The report can be found at www.standardandpoors.com/ratings/articles/en/us/?assetID =1245316529563 (accessed 1/3/12).

40. Cited in R. Pildes, "Why the Center Does Not Hold: The Causes of Hyperpolarized Democracy in America," *California Law Review* 99, no. 2 (April 2011): 203. Available from http://scholarship.law.berkeley.edu/cgi/viewcontent.cgi?article=1039&context=californialawreview (accessed 10/18/14).

41. "Congressional Performance," *Rasmussen Reports*, www.rasmussenreports.com/public_content /politics/mood_of_america/congressional_performance (accessed 8/13/14).

42. A good overview of this evidence can be found in Robin Stryker, National Institute of Civil Discourse Research Brief 6: "Political Polarization," University of Arizona, prepared September 1, 2011, http://nicd.arizona.edu/sites/default/files/research_briefs/NICD_research _brief6.pdf (accessed 11/18/14).

43. R. Pildes, "Why the Center Does Not Hold," p. 277.

44. Alan Abramovitz and Kyle Saunders, "Is Polarization a Myth?" www.csupomona.edu /~smemerson/business318/AbramCulWarMythVSFIORINA.pdf (accessed 11/18/14).

45. See, for example, Ronald Brownstein, *The Second Civil War: How Extreme Partisanship Has Paralyzed Washington and Polarized America* (New York: Penguin Press, 2007), and Nolan McCarty, Keith Poole, and Howard Rosenthal, *Polarized America: The Dance of Ideology and Unequal Riches* (Cambridge, MA: MIT Press, 2006).

46. Nolan McCarty, "The Policy Consequences of Partisan Polarization in the United States," http://bcep.haas.berkeley.edu/papers/McCarty.doc (accessed 1/2/11).

47. See, for example, Morris P. Fiorina and Samuel J. Abrams, "Political Polarization in the American Public," *Annual Review of Political Science*, 11 (2008): 563–88.

48. R. Pildes, "Why the Center Does Not Hold," p. 278.
49. Michael Dimock, "How America Changed During Barack Obama's Presidency."
50. Abramovitz and Saunders, "Is Polarization a Myth?"
51. An excellent discussion of the causes of political dysfunction in the United States is Jonathan Rauch, "What's Ailing American Politics?" *Atlantic*, July/August 2016, pp. 51–63. On the fragmentation and politicization of the U.S. media, see Susan Glasser, "Covering Politics in a Post-Truth America," Brookings Institution,www.brookings.edu/essay/covering -politics-in-a-post-truth-america/?utm_medium=partner&utm_source=politico&utm _campaign=essay17 (accessed 12/7/16).
52. Carlos Pereira and Carlos Aramayo, "Political Polarization: What the U.S. Can Learn from Latin America," www.brookings.edu/opinions/2011/0301_polarization_pereira_aramayo.aspx (accessed 1/3/12).
53. See, for example, R. Pildes, "Why the Center Does Not Hold," pp. 273–333.

KEY TERMS

American Revolution The conflict between Britain and the American colonists that resulted in U.S. independence (1775–83)

Articles of Confederation The weak confederal regime that governed the colonies after 1781; it was replaced by the U.S. Constitution after 1790

Bill of Rights Ten amendments to the Constitution passed by the first U.S. Congress in 1789

Bush, George W. The president of the United States from 2001 to 2009

Bush Doctrine Declaration by President George W. Bush that the United States would use military force to preempt potential terrorist threats to U.S. security

cabinet The appointed officials who serve the executive in overseeing the various state bureaucracies

civil rights movement A movement (1955–65) designed to address the legacy of slavery by ending various forms of racial discrimination

Civil War The conflict between the southern, slaveholding states and the North, or the Union; the victory of the North preserved the unity of the United States and resulted in the abolition of slavery

Civil War Amendments The constitutional amendments that abolished slavery (Thirteenth Amendment), guaranteed all citizens due process and equal protection under the law (Fourteenth Amendment), and prohibited race-based voter discrimination (Fifteenth Amendment).

Declaration of Independence The document declaring the 13 colonies' independence from Britain; issued by the Continental Congress in 1776

Democratic-Republicans Early opponents of a strong federal state; led by
Thomas Jefferson

federalism A system in which significant state powers, such as taxation, law-
making, and security, are devolved to regional or local bodies

Federalists Early advocates of a strong federal state in the United States; led by
Alexander Hamilton

gerrymandering The process of apportioning electoral districts to favor one
political party or marginalize certain groups

House of Representatives The lower house of the U.S. Congress (legislature)

Latinos Residents of the United States who trace their ancestry to Spanish-
speaking countries in Latin America

Louisiana Purchase The 1803 purchase of territory from France that greatly
expanded U.S. territory westward

manifest destiny A view held by many Americans throughout U.S. history
that the United States was destined to expand its power and territory

melting pot The diversity of cultures that has historically characterized
U.S. society

Mexican-American War The 1846 conflict between Mexico and the United
States that resulted in U.S. acquisition of much of the current Southwest of
the United States

New Deal A set of policies implemented between 1933 and 1938 that used
state intervention to stimulate the economy and counter the effects of the
Great Depression

Obama, Barack Two-term president of the United States, 2008–2016

political polarization The degree of political partisanship

populism A key feature of U.S. ideology; the idea that the masses should dominate elites and that the popular will should trump those with professional
expertise

Progressive era The period from 1903 to 1920 when progressives sought to
use the state to limit the power of private business

Puritans Radical Protestant group that comprised a large portion of the original American colonists

rule of law A principle that holds that all citizens are equal before the law and
no one is above the law, including political leaders

Senate The upper house of the U.S. Congress (legislature)

separation of powers A system in which the executive, legislative, and judicial
systems are significant and independent sources of power

Tea Party A reactionary, but diffuse, group within the Republican Party that emerged in 2009; its adherents generally favor low taxes, small government, and socially conservative policies

Trump, Donald The current president of the United States, elected in 2016

utopian moralism The principle describing the tendency of Americans to view the world in terms of good versus evil

Vietnam War The protracted, costly, and ultimately unsuccessful attempt by the United States and its allies to defeat communism in Indochina (1959–75)

Voting Rights Act Legislation (1965) that eliminated barriers that had been imposed by some states to prevent African Americans from voting; seen as a major victory in the struggle for civil rights

War on Poverty President Lyndon Johnson's use of state spending to combat inequality

Washington, George Commander of the Continental Army during the Revolutionary War and first president of the United States

WEB LINKS

- C-SPAN, public-service media outlet focused on U.S. politics (www.c-span.org)
- Library of Congress (www.loc.gov)
- National Archives, repository for government documents (www.archives.gov)
- Project Vote Smart, website on elections, elected officials, and candidates (www.votesmart.org)
- Real Clear Politics, an aggregator of political news and blogs (www.realclearpolitics.com)
- Roll Call, website focused on Congress (www.rollcall.com)

4

Soldiers on guard at the Eiffel Tower after a coordinated set of terrorist attacks in Paris killed 130 people and wounded over 350 others. In 2015 and 2016, Islamic terrorists claimed responsibility for the deadliest acts of violence on French soil since World War II. In response, the French government declared a 16-month state of emergency, intended to last through the May 2017 presidential elections.

FRANCE

Why Study This Case?

In a fundamental sense, comparative politics is the comparative study of political **regimes**. The term *regime*, fittingly, comes from the French word for "rule" or "order" and refers to the norms and rules that govern politics. These norms and rules are institutionalized—often embodied in a constitution—but can and do change as a result of dramatic social events or national crises. Regimes express fundamental ideals about where authority should reside and to what end this authority should be employed.

The French case offers a fascinating study of regimes. In little more than two centuries, France has experienced a wide variety of regimes, ranging from authoritarianism (absolute monarchy, revolutionary dictatorship, and empires) to democracy (parliamentary and semi-presidential). During this period, France has been governed by no fewer than three monarchies, two empires, five republics, a fascist regime, and two provisional governments and has promulgated 15 separate constitutions. A popular nineteenth-century joke had a Parisian bookseller refusing to sell a copy of the French constitution to a would-be customer, claiming he did not sell periodicals.[1] The most dramatic transition was, of course, the **French Revolution** (1789–99), in which French citizens overthrew the **ancien régime** (the European old order of absolute monarchy buttressed by religious authority) and replaced it, albeit briefly, with a democratic republic guided by the Declaration of the Rights of Man and of the Citizen.

France can claim title to the birthplace of modern democracy on the European continent, but democracy has not come easily. The French Revolution embraced a set of universal rights for all people and redefined French subjects as citizens. But French revolutionaries concluded

FRANCE

UNITED KINGDOM

North Sea

THE NETHERLANDS

GERMANY

Dunkerque

BELGIUM

Lille

LUX.

English Channel

Cherbourg

Le Havre
Rouen

Seine R.

Marne R.

Strasbourg
Nancy

CHANNEL ISLANDS (U.K.)

PARIS

Rhine R.

Brest

Orleans

Loire R.

Nantes

Tours

Dijon

SWITZERLAND

ATLANTIC OCEAN

Bay of Biscay

Lyon
Saint-Étienne

Grenoble

ITALY

Bordeaux

Garonne R.

Rhône R.

Nice

MONACO

Toulouse

Montpellier

Marseille

Toulon

ANDORRA

N

SPAIN

Mediterranean Sea

0   50   100 mi
0   50   100 km

that the state had to be strong enough to destroy the old regime, impose the new order, and forge a strong national identity. French republicanism established a short-lived revolutionary dictatorship that was followed by Napoleon Bonaparte's **coup d'état**—a French word that describes a forceful and sudden overthrow of government. Over the next seven decades, French reactionaries battled radicals, and France oscillated between empires, monarchies, and republics while experiencing two more revolutions as well.

Not until the present **Fifth Republic** (established in 1958) has France seemed able to break this alternating cycle of stern authoritarian rule and chaotic, or at least dysfunctional, democracy. Although revolution is no longer politics as usual and today's French citizens are more centrist, French political life is far from mundane. French citizens remain skeptical, if not cynical, about politics and politicians and vigorously divided on issues such as immigration, unemployment, European integration, and the proper role of the state. Whereas most established democracies have vested their constitutions with a certain sanctity and have only cautiously amended them, France's willingness to write and rewrite the rules of the political game offers us a fascinating study in comparative politics and gives us insights into French politics and its political culture.[2]

The French case poses several important questions for students of comparative politics. First, French history has given the state a prominent role in its economic development. Today, French citizens enjoy a variety of state-provided benefits and protections that are absent in many other advanced democracies. However, France currently suffers from the highest levels of unemployment since the birth of its current regime in 1958 and is challenged by rapidly escalating public debt. Is France's statist political-economic model compatible with its role in an increasingly globalized society, and can the French government reform that model to protect France's economic competitiveness?

Second, as a legacy of the French Revolution, the French have a powerful sense of citizenship and equality. It has long been a sacrosanct pillar of French political culture that national identity trumps religious or ethnic identity. Indeed, French law has prohibited the census (or public opinion surveys) from identifying its citizens by ethnicity or race since 1978, since doing so is seen as violating the principle of equality. But over the last few decades, France has become more ethnically diverse and now has a growing Muslim minority. This development has ignited a fierce debate about how the French secular state should deal with this population, and mainstream French politicians have supported policies aimed at limiting the expression of ethnic (as opposed to "French") identity. The most controversial policies were laws passed in 2004 (prohibiting the wearing of religious symbols in public schools, but essentially aimed at the Islamic head scarf) and 2011 (prohibiting French citizens from wearing face veils in public places). In response to these controversies, a right-wing nationalist (some would say racist) movement advocated taking a hard line against any accommodation of ethnic or religious minorities, while France's Islamic minority protested that the French state was disrespecting its customs and beliefs. The debate, and attacks by Islamic terrorists that killed over 230 French citizens (and that wounded hundreds more) in Paris and Nice in 2015 and 2016, have shaken up the French political environment and have moved the previously peripheral issues of religion and ethnicity to center stage. Can France protect its commitment to a secular and multiethnic state while integrating its growing Muslim minority?

Finally, the central tenet of France's post–World War II foreign policy has been its unwavering commitment to a politically and economically unified Europe. The Franco-German alliance has been central to the formation and expansion of the European Union, and the European Union has led to spectacular growth in both countries. However, in recent decades France's economy has lagged behind that of its German partner, and France has proven less adept at reforming its political economy to sustain its competitiveness within the European Union. In the last decade, there have been growing concerns within the European Union about the French economy and a steady rise in domestic French opposition to the European Union. A recent Pew Research study concluded that the once unshakable French support for the European Union had plummeted more than in any other EU country.[3] The stunning performance of the National Front—an anti-EU, right-wing nationalist party—in the 2014 French elections to the European Parliament, and the emergence of that party as a serious contender in the 2017 presidential campaign, have raised serious questions about France's ability to play a leading role in the European Union.

Major Geographic and Demographic Features

France is a large country, roughly the size of Texas. By European standards, it is substantial—twice the area of Great Britain; in Europe, it is third in size only to Russia and Ukraine. France seems even larger than it is because it spans much of western Europe; it shares borders with six countries and is at once an Atlantic, a continental, and a Mediterranean country.

Although this geography has facilitated foreign commerce, it has also exacerbated French feelings of vulnerability. Protected by mountains to the southwest (the Pyrenees) and the southeast (the Alps), France enjoys no such natural barriers on its border with Belgium and Germany, to the north and northeast. Through the centuries, this corridor has been the locus of repeated invasions and confrontations. Abundant mineral resources (in the Saar region) and productive farmland (in Alsace-Lorraine) have raised the stakes and aggravated the conflicts. Vulnerability has also motivated France's preoccupation with establishing a formidable standing army and a strong centralized state (unlike England, which had a strong navy but a weak army). The French solution to its geographic vulnerability after World War I was the construction of the Maginot Line, a series of concrete fortifications along the Franco-German border designed to prevent the next war. Nazi forces, however, simply skirted these defenses and invaded France through Belgium. The French solution after World War II—integration with its long-standing German nemesis in the form of the European Union—has proved much more effective.

Within France, there are no significant geographic obstacles to transportation or communication. A number of navigable rivers have, over the centuries, been supplemented by canals and a highly developed rail system. This ease of internal travel and communication, combined with France's natural mountain and ocean boundaries, has given the French a strong sense of national identity and has facilitated France's economic and political integration.

At the hub of this national integration, both literally and organizationally, lies the capital, Paris. For centuries, Paris has served as the administrative, commercial, and cultural nucleus of France. Generations of Parisian bureaucrats have imposed taxes, *corvée* (mandatory labor assessments), and even the Parisian dialect on all regions of the country. In addition to this linguistic homogeneity, more than 80 percent of all French are at least nominally Catholic.

This national unity should not be exaggerated, however. Although metropolitan Paris is home to roughly one-sixth (10 million) of France's 60 million citizens, the cultural ideal of "provincial" life, with its more rustic and relaxed lifestyle, is mythologized by many French people in preference to the hustle and bustle of urban life. One enduring effect of this view is that while the number of farmers has shrunk in France, they have a disproportionate amount of power and have strongly influenced not only domestic politics but also the politics of the European Union. The preservation of rural life as a symbol of French identity has led to conflicts over agricultural subsidies and globalization as well as complicated domestic and international politics. Similarly, although French citizens are proud of their national heritage, many are likewise proud of their regional differences. Generally speaking, southern France is more rural, conservative, religious, and agrarian—and relatively less prosperous—than northern France, which is more urban, politically liberal, secular, and industrial.

Historical Development of the State

Whereas French history offers us valuable insights into the study of regimes, this same history is also an essential primer on the rise of the modern nation-state. From Louis XIV's declaration of *L'état, c'est moi* ("I am the state") to Napoleon's establishment of bureaucratic legal codes and the rule of law, the development of the French state offers an archetype for the emergence of a powerful state. Yet it exists alongside a society that views mass demonstrations against authority as an important tool of political change.

Absolutism and the Consolidation of the Modern French State

In carving out the Holy Roman Empire in the early ninth century, Charlemagne, leader of a Germanic tribe known as the Franks, established a realm encompassing much of western Europe. In doing so, he unified the area we know as France earlier than would occur in any of the other European states, including Britain. But with Charlemagne's death, Frankish control was reduced to an assortment of small feudal kingdoms and principalities within the confines of what is now France. As with feudal kings elsewhere, the Frankish rulers sought to increase their holdings, stature, and security by squeezing wealth from their subjects. In the United Kingdom, struggles among the aristocracy led to a gradual decentralization of power, as signified by the Magna Carta. In France, however, feudalism led to absolute monarchs, who centralized authority and developed bureaucracies capable of taxing the subjects and administering the affairs of state.

Absolute monarchy, the stage in the evolutionary development of Europe between the more decentralized feudal monarchies of the Middle Ages and the constitutional governments of the modern era, made several important contributions to the modern French state.[4] Though many of the responsibilities we associate with a modern state, such as education, welfare, and transportation, were at that time handled by the family, the church, an assortment of local authorities, or simply not at all, three primary duties—making and executing laws, waging war and providing defense, and raising money to defend the state—became the responsibility of the French kings.

In carrying out these responsibilities, the monarchs did not ignore the social classes outside the court. In fact, the Crown initially allied itself with and—as its autonomy grew—ultimately employed each relevant class, or "estate," in carrying out its duties. The Catholic clergy, or First Estate, had primary responsibility for administering the legal system; the landed aristocracy, or Second Estate, prosecuted the king's wars; and financiers from the commoners who made up the commercial class, or Third Estate, gathered the taxes that paid for the military, the luxuries of the court, and the rest of the state apparatus. To co-opt these groups initially, in the fourteenth century the monarchy established an assembly known as the **Estates General**, which included representatives from each of the three estates.

By the fifteenth century, Louis XI had sufficiently centralized his authority such that he could wage expansive wars. In this way, he doubled the size of his kingdom to roughly the current borders of France. He was also able to weaken the influence of the nobility and largely ignore the Estates General. His successors over the next three centuries reinforced these trends, forging a centralized state with a reputation for administrative efficiency that has largely persisted to this day. The pinnacle of this absolutist authority came during the rule of Louis XIV, who dubbed himself the Sun King and famously declared that he alone *was* the state. Although this was an overstatement, the absolutist French state of the seventeenth century was the envy of all Europe. France had a standing professional army, a mercantilist state-run economy, an efficient (though deeply regressive) tax system, and the extravagant palace of Versailles. In fact, the Sun King never even convened the Estates General.

Neither war nor court life came cheap, however; the drains on the royal coffers, combined with the system of taxation, had by the eighteenth century reduced the French commoners to famine and bankrupted the state. In a desperate attempt to shore up support and seek essential funding, the Sun King's grandson, Louis XVI, convened the long-dormant Estates General in 1789. Although each estate was to have one vote (allowing the more conservative clergy and nobility to override the commoners), the more numerous representatives of the Third Estate argued that all three houses should meet as one assembly (allowing the commoners to prevail). The king resisted, stirring the anger and protests of the commoners. In this revolutionary environment, rising bread prices in Paris prompted Parisians to storm the Bastille, the old Paris jailhouse. They did so on July 14, 1789, thus launching the French Revolution.

TIMELINE OF POLITICAL DEVELOPMENT

YEAR	EVENT
800 C.E.	"France" first emerges as an independent power under Charlemagne.
1661–1715	Absolute monarchy culminates in rule of Louis XIV.
1789	French Revolution is launched with storming of the Bastille in Paris.
1799	Napoleon Bonaparte seizes power and brings revolution to an end.
1848, 1871	Popular uprisings lead to the Second and Third Republics.
1940	Third Republic is replaced by Vichy (German puppet) regime.
1946	The weak Fourth Republic is established.
1954	The French leave Vietnam in defeat.
1958	Threat of civil war over Algeria returns Charles de Gaulle to office, leading to the ratification of his presidency and the Fifth Republic by referendum.
1968	The Events of May rioters in Paris demand social and educational reforms.
1969	De Gaulle resigns.
1981	François Mitterrand and the Socialists are elected.
1986	First period of "cohabitation" between Socialist president Mitterrand and neo-Gaullist prime minister Jacques Chirac takes place.
1992	Slim majority of French voters approve Maastricht Treaty, establishing the Economic and Monetary Union (within the European Union) and the euro.
2005	In a referendum, French voters reject proposed European Union constitution.
2017	Emmanuel Macron elected president.

The French Revolution, Destruction of the Aristocracy, and Extension of State Power

In the early days of the revolution, the Third Estate established the **National Assembly**, and that body issued the Declaration of the Rights of Man and of the Citizen. Inspired by the French political thinkers Jean-Jacques Rousseau and Baron de Montesquieu as well as the example of the American Revolution, this document was a powerful and influential statement on liberty that proclaimed the natural rights of the individual in opposition to the tyranny of monarchy. The revolutionaries concluded that the ancien régime, with its hereditary and religious privileges, must be destroyed and replaced. No longer should birth or faith determine justice, public office, or taxation. "Liberty, Equality, Fraternity!" became the rallying cry of the revolution.

In the new French republic, sovereignty was to rest with the people and their elected representatives, church and state were to maintain a strict separation, and all male citizens could claim the natural and universal rights of both freedom and equality before the law. These revolutionary pronouncements have obviously had a profound effect on French politics and the constitutions of nearly all modern nation-states since then. In addition, the revolution fostered nationalism and patriotism as an expression of the natural right of the French nation-state to exist on terms established by its own citizens. A rational, "scientific" state would be the revolutionaries' goal. But unlike their American counterparts, who feared the tyranny of any centralized authority, French revolutionaries never questioned the need for a powerful centralized state, nor did they fear what might happen were that state to fall into the wrong hands.

Indeed, the new republic embraced what we might now call a technocratic form of rule—it drew from the Enlightenment and the early stages of the scientific revolution to modernize and transform French society and swept away old institutions. The ancien régime, like most absolutist states of that period, inhibited trade and development by its lack of a number of basic standards. In response, the French Revolution became a catalyst for standardization and reform. This development is perhaps best captured in the metric system, introduced in France in 1795 and soon adopted by most of the world (the United States and the United Kingdom are notable exceptions). Calendar and monetary reforms were similarly embraced by the French revolutionaries. These reforms and standardizations were important not only because they changed France and much of the rest of the world but also because they institutionalized the idea that the state could play an important role in directing expertise, science, and technology toward the good of the country as a whole. As we shall see, this idea continues to be an important part of French politics and political culture.

In 1791, French moderates wrote a new constitution limiting the monarchy and setting up a representative assembly that in many ways resembled Britain's constitutional monarchy. But this middle-ground effort was undermined both by monarchists on the right (conservative nobles and clerics) and by radical anticlerical republicans on the left. Led by a militant faction known as the Jacobins, the radicals seized power and launched a class war, known as the **Reign of Terror**, in which many who stood in the way of this radical vision of republicanism were executed (including the monarch). As in other, later revolutions, such as in the Soviet Union and China, terror bred turmoil and paranoia such that the very perpetrators of the revolution were themselves devoured by the violence. The Jacobins' ruthless leader, Robespierre, became the guillotine's final victim as the Reign of Terror came to an end in 1794. Although the violence ceased, the ideological and cultural division between two poles—conservative, Catholic, and rural versus progressive, secular, and urban—would resonate in French politics for centuries and in some ways persists today.

In the wake of the Reign of Terror, moderates established a weak and ineffectual government that limped along for five more years and two more constitutions. In 1799, General Napoleon Bonaparte seized power in a coup d'état that brought the decade of revolutionary turmoil to an end. Unlike the revolution that had swept away the former social and political institutions, Napoleon's coup retained and indeed codified key elements of the revolutionary order. The Napoleonic Code documented the principles that all men are equal before the law; that the people, not a monarch, are sovereign; and that the church and state are separate domains. Further enhancing France's long bureaucratic tradition, Napoleon established a meritocratic civil service that was open to all citizens and a system of elite schools to train these functionaries.[5]

The Return to Absolutism in Postrevolutionary France

Napoleon's strong state became even stronger when he was proclaimed emperor for life in a national referendum in 1804, and the First Republic gave way to the First Empire. Clearly, French citizens preferred the domestic peace, stability, and order of Napoleonic France to the republican chaos that had preceded it, though they also valued their civil and property rights. Yet, over time, Napoleon's rule increasingly resembled the tyranny of the absolute monarchy that had justified the revolution. He ruled for another 10 years and then abdicated the throne for a year in the wake of a series of military defeats at the hands of the hostile conservative monarchies that surrounded France. After a brief return, he was permanently defeated in 1815 by the British at the Battle of Waterloo. He died in exile, remembered by most French people as a national hero.

With military support from the victorious European powers, absolute monarchy, not democracy, replaced Napoleon's empire, and the bitter ideological divisions of the revolutionary era reemerged. The Church and the aristocracy reasserted their privileges until a popular revolt in 1830 forced the Crown to establish a constitutional monarchy and promise to pay more respect to the interests of the rising urban middle class. A third revolution, in 1848, ended monarchical rule, established universal male suffrage, and constituted the short-lived Second Republic. The new republic had a directly elected president—the first such office in Europe. Elsewhere in Europe, executive power was held by monarchs and prime ministers. This development reflects the ongoing French preference for a strong executive, albeit one directly chosen by the people; it also reflects an amalgam of monarchical and revolutionary values. In 1848, the people elected as their first president Napoleon's nephew. Louis-Napoleon, who quickly followed in his uncle's footsteps, used a national referendum to proclaim himself emperor. In 1852, Louis-Napoleon (now called Napoleon III) replaced the Second Republic with the Second Empire. He ruled for nearly two decades, presiding over a period of peace and rapid industrial growth.

Both peace and prosperity halted with France's defeat in the Franco-Prussian War of 1870–71, in which Napoleon III was captured and the Second Empire came to an end. Not surprisingly, the absence of central authority once again led to violent conflict between conservative monarchists and radical republicans. Although conservatives came to dominate the National Assembly, radicals in Paris established a short-lived rival government known as the Paris Commune, until French troops crushed the uprising. While unsuccessful, the Commune would continue to inspire Communists and anarchists worldwide for decades to come; it was in reference to the Commune that Marx and Engels first spoke of a dictatorship of the proletariat that could serve as a model for future revolutions. Interestingly, then, France contributed to the emergence of not only liberal-democratic ideas but also Communist ones, though in both cases the regimes themselves foundered in France.

Democratization and the Weak Regimes of the Third and Fourth Republics

From the ashes of the Second Empire emerged France's Third Republic, which survived for 70 years—until the outbreak of World War II. Its endurance should not be mistaken, however, for either strength or legitimacy. The Third Republic was weakened by the persistent and seemingly irreconcilable splits among various ideological factions, ranging from monarchists to anarchists. These divisions made stable government almost impossible, and successive governments often lasted less than a year. Despite weak government, the powerful bureaucracy remained. And allied with French business interests, it continued to promote economic development.

Political divisions were further polarized by the devastation of World War I, during which more than 1.5 million French people died, and by the economic depression that followed. These crises provided fertile ground for both communism and fascism, as political extremists of the left and the right proffered Stalinist Russia and Nazi Germany, respectively, as preferable alternatives to France's weak and immobilized democratic republic.

This debate was preempted by France's swift defeat at the hands of the overwhelming Nazi military force in the opening weeks of World War II. The Nazi victors collaborated with the French right in setting up the puppet Vichy regime, named after the town in central France where the government was based. Even many French moderates ended up supporting this fascist government, reasoning that the Nazis were better than the threat of a Communist government.[6] Other French citizens, however, including Communists and members of religious groups, resisted the Nazi occupation (both from within France and outside the country). Although the resistance effort was diverse and at best only loosely linked, General Charles de Gaulle, who led French forces in England following his retreat from France in 1940, ultimately came to embody the French anti-Nazi movement.

After World War II, de Gaulle's heroic stature as leader of the resistance effort and his role in France's provisional government positioned him to play an important political role in the new Fourth Republic. However, de Gaulle believed that a major weakness of the previous regime was that too little power had been vested in the presidency—a view not shared by other political leaders. As a result, de Gaulle withdrew from politics. After the war, the new Fourth Republic, based on an electoral system of proportional representation and parliamentary government with a weak prime minister, was frequently as paralyzed as the Third Republic had been. No single party or even a stable coalition of parties was able to form a government for long—20 governments were formed in just 12 years—and thus no political leader was in a position to make difficult choices.

During this period, significant progress took place in such areas as postwar reconstruction and the creation of the European Union. The regime, however, could not effectively deal with France's colonial legacy, as independence movements in many colonies grew powerful. The situation was particularly acute in Algeria, a North African and Muslim country that had been under French control for over a century. It was also home to some 1 million French and European settlers. Growing Algerian resistance to French rule had led to significant violence between Algerians, settlers, and the French military. By 1958, French generals in Algeria responded by establishing a provisional government and threatening military action against France itself if Algeria did not remain French. Under these dire circumstances, the government called on de Gaulle to return to politics and seek a way out of the crisis.[7]

The Recovery of State Power and Democratic Stability under the Fifth Republic

As he had a decade earlier, de Gaulle insisted that he would serve only if the French people authorized and accepted a new constitution that established a strong executive and addressed the other ills of the Third and Fourth Republics. The new constitution was put to a referendum and accepted. De Gaulle, who had served briefly as the last **prime minister** of the Fourth Republic, became the first president of the new Fifth Republic, in 1959.

We conclude this discussion of the historical development of the French state by noting de Gaulle's significant impact on the republic and his 10-year tenure as its leader. Using his sweeping executive authority, from 1959 to 1968 he granted Algeria independence, established France as an independent nuclear power, withdrew it from the military command structure of the North Atlantic Treaty Organization (NATO), promoted European integration, nationalized a number of key industries and private firms, and established a substantial welfare state.

Although he averted civil war, revitalized the French economy, and restored French national pride, de Gaulle was also criticized (particularly by the left) as an authoritarian demagogue. He failed to command the loyalty of a new generation that had no memories of World War II or de Gaulle's role in it. In 1968, many young Parisians took to the streets in what came to be known as **the Events of May**. Students erected barricades and demanded educational changes, and workers seized factories and called for sweeping social reforms. De Gaulle was able to weather these protests, but in the end he lost his mandate. He turned to the public to galvanize support by presenting a referendum in 1969 on various constitutional reforms. When the referendum failed, he resigned from office.

It might seem that de Gaulle's departure would have signaled the end of the Fifth Republic, so tightly connected was it to de Gaulle himself. But rather than prompting a new round of polarized debate, revolution, and yet another constitution, the regime held, and it remains the current regime of France. Although the French had rejected a leader, they chose not to reject his vision of a republic led by a strong national executive. Since de Gaulle, a series of powerful presidents have each contributed to the image of France as a country with a strong bureaucracy, an independent foreign policy, and an economic system tightly connected to the state.

However, over the past decade some French citizens have experienced a growing sense that the country is in crisis, or at least adrift, thanks to low economic growth and a burgeoning, yet marginalized, immigrant population. The 2007 election of President **Nicolas Sarkozy** strongly reflected these concerns, as his supporters and detractors alike focused on issues of reform, immigration, and law and order. The 2012 election of President **François Hollande** reflected public unease over the country's broad direction. Hollande had a deeply unpopular presidency and was challenged by economic decline and security threats. After deciding not to run for a second term he was succeeded in May 2017 by **Emmanuel Macron**, a young, centrist non-party technocrat who had briefly been a minister in Hollande's government. Macron's victory, and the majority of legislative seats won by his recently created political party, were an earthquake that shook up France's political system.

Political Regime

Domestic issues, combined with the European Union's economic crisis, have raised questions within France over the country's role in Europe and the global community. We shall consider these questions as we look at the institutions and policies of this important European state.

Political Institutions

THE CONSTITUTION

As noted earlier, France has experienced different types of authoritarian regimes (from absolute monarchy to revolutionary dictatorship) and a broad range of democratic regimes (both parliamentary and semi-presidential). The French Third (1875–1940) and Fourth (1946–58) republics were purely parliamentary regimes. Many French viewed those regimes as weak and ineffective because fractious legislatures often resulted in a revolving door of prime ministers (France had 20 cabinets in fewer than 12 years during the Fourth Republic). When fragmented legislatures disagreed with government policies, governments collapsed.

France's current regime, the Fifth Republic (1958–present), is codified in the constitution of 1958, the sixteenth constitution since the French Revolution.

That document was very much the product of Charles de Gaulle's reaction to the perceived instability of the previous two regimes. The central goal of de Gaulle's 1958 constitution was to eliminate the pure parliamentary system and enhance the power of the executive vis-à-vis France's traditionally powerful and fractious legislature. France thus developed a semi-presidential executive system that was innovative at the time. The system was subsequently adopted in over 20 countries including Russia, Taiwan, Portugal, and the Ukraine. The Fifth Republic created a system whereby political power is shared by the legislature, a directly elected president, and a prime minister who reports to both the president and the legislature.

The French left saw the Fifth Republic as a regime that very much favored the right and favored a return to a parliamentary system. However, with the first election of a socialist president, François Mitterrand, in 1981, the legitimacy of the regime was no longer challenged. The French constitution has proved durable and has seen relatively few significant amendments over the past 50 years. Most notable changes have involved the presidency: in 1962, the constitution was modified to allow direct election of the president; and in 2000, the president's term was reduced from seven to five years to limit divided government.

The Branches of Government

THE PRESIDENCY

Unlike a presidential system, the French **semi-presidential** system includes a dual executive: the president is head of state, and the prime minister is head of the government. However, the constitution of 1958 is ambiguous in differentiating the powers of the president and the prime minister. Indeed, the French president has relatively few formal powers, but during the course of the Fifth Republic the president has, by precedent, acquired powers somewhat beyond those specified by the constitution.[8] The ability of French presidents to assume powers that are not explicitly delineated in the constitution was facilitated when, from 1958 to 1981, President de Gaulle (and his political heirs, after 1969) controlled both the legislature and the presidency. Subsequently, from 1981 to 1986, the Socialists enjoyed the same control of the legislature and the executive.

The constitution envisions the French president as a head of state above the parties. But unlike the United Kingdom's merely symbolic head of state, French presidents hold important political powers—though they are far less explicit powers than those held by their U.S. counterparts. Much of the authority of the French presidents results from the prestige and precedent of de Gaulle and from the fact that the president is the only directly elected political figure with a national mandate.[9] Moreover, French presidents are elected for long terms (five years), and, since 2008, they are limited to two terms in office.

According to the constitution of the Fifth Republic, presidents do not directly govern. Rather, they appoint a prime minister, who must be approved by a majority of the lower house of the legislature. The prime minister is supposed to select a cabinet (called the **Council of Ministers**) and preside over the day-to-day affairs of the government. In practice, when French presidents enjoy a majority in the legislature, they select (and can dismiss) both the prime minister and the members of the cabinet.

The 1958 constitution appears to create a potential conflict between a directly elected president and a legislature dominated by the opposition. This is because the constitution requires the legislature to approve the president's choice of prime minister. At the time, many observers predicted that this feature would lead to political paralysis. The French system has worked rather smoothly, however, in part because the same conservative coalition dominated the presidency and the legislature from 1958 to 1986, thus reducing the possibility of intra-executive conflict. Yet, as noted in the next section on the prime minister, even when presidents have lacked a majority in the legislature, they have compromised by appointing prime ministers from the opposition. The French have dubbed this situation "cohabitation." What might happen should a president refuse to compromise is not entirely clear, but to date predictions of a constitutional stalemate have not materialized.

The constitution of the Fifth Republic does give the president some formal tools in addition to those that have become institutionalized over time through precedent. Presidents direct the armed forces. They cannot veto legislation, but they can ask the lower house to reconsider it. They can submit referenda directly

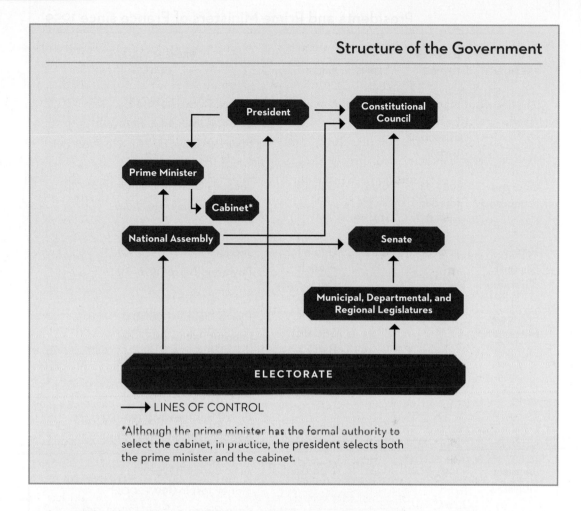

Structure of the Government

President → Constitutional Council

President → Prime Minister

Prime Minister → Cabinet*

Cabinet* → National Assembly

National Assembly → Prime Minister

National Assembly → Senate

Municipal, Departmental, and Regional Legislatures → Senate

Municipal, Departmental, and Regional Legislatures → Constitutional Council

ELECTORATE

→ LINES OF CONTROL

*Although the prime minister has the formal authority to select the cabinet, in practice, the president selects both the prime minister and the cabinet.

to the people. They must sign all laws and decrees. Presidents also have the power to dissolve the legislature and call new elections, a power that has been employed on five occasions, usually to obtain or reinforce legislative majorities to the president's liking. The president also enjoys a powerful staff, whose members help develop and initiate policy and work with the prime minister and the cabinet. The power of the French presidency was underscored in May 2016 when President Hollande used constitutional decree powers to impose a reform of French labor laws, thereby avoiding a vote in the legislature. Opponents of the measure in the lower house failed to win a no confidence vote to remove Hollande's prime minister, Manuel Valls, and the decree stood despite widespread opposition.

Moreover, although the constitution does not specify this authority, presidents have simply asserted the power to remove prime ministers and cabinet members

Presidents and Prime Ministers of France since 1959

PRESIDENT	DATES IN OFFICE	TERMS	PARTY	PRIME MINISTERS (DATES)
Charles de Gaulle	1959–69 (resigned in second term)	Two	N/A	Michel Debré (1959–62) Georges Pompidou (1962–68) Maurice Couve de Murville (1968–69)
Georges Pompidou	1969–74 (died in office)	One	Gaullist	Jacques Chaban-Delmas (1969–72) Pierre Messmer (1972–74)
Valéry Giscard d'Estaing	1974–81	One	Union for French Democracy	Jacques Chirac (1974–76) Raymond Barre (1976–81)
François Mitterrand	1981–95	Two	French Socialist Party	Pierre Mauroy (1981–84) Laurent Fabius (1984–86) Jacques Chirac (1986–88) Michel Rocard (1988–91) Édith Cresson (1991–92) Pierre Bérégovoy (1992–93) Édouard Balladur (1993–95)
Jacques Chirac	1995–2007	Two	Neo-Gaullist	Alain Juppé (1995–97) Lionel Jospin (1997–2002) Jean-Pierre Raffarin (2002–05) Dominique de Villepin (2005–07)
Nicolas Sarkozy	2007–12	One	Union for a Popular Movement	François Fillon (2007–12)
François Hollande	2012–2017	One	French Socialist Party	Jean-Marc Ayrault (2012–14) Manuel Valls (2014–16) Bernard Cazeneuve (2016–17)
Emmanuel Macron	2017–present		La République en Marche! (Republic Onward!)	Édouard Philippe (2017–present)

even if those officials have support in the legislature. In short, the prime minister has become a sort of chief aide whose goal is to carry out the president's political agenda. Consequently, the president—not the prime minister—chairs the weekly meetings of the Council of Ministers.

In the early years of the Fifth Republic, it was often argued that because of the power and prestige of the president, France was developing a republican monarchy.[10] Even during de Gaulle's time, however, the presidency was hardly omnipotent; recall that de Gaulle resigned after the electorate rejected his 1969 referendum. President **François Mitterrand**, despite serving for 14 years, was twice forced into cohabitating with an opposition prime minister; this divided government severely limited Mitterrand's power. President **Jacques Chirac** was similarly stymied when the opposition controlled the lower house and prime minister's office from 1997 to 2002. This divided government led to the change in the president's term of office, which involved synchronizing presidential and legislative elections in the hope that voters would support a single party for both institutions. So far, this has been the case, and it may promise a more consistently powerful presidency in the future.

THE PRIME MINISTER

French prime ministers are appointed by the president but must have the support of both the president and the legislature. As opposed to many parliamentary systems in which the prime minister is drawn from the members of parliament, Article 23 of the French constitution prevents members of the legislature from serving simultaneously as prime minister. This creates a disconnect between the legislature and the prime minister, and it ties the prime minister more strongly to the president. On paper, the constitution appears to make the prime minister the most powerful politician in France. In practice, though, when presidents enjoy a majority in the legislature, French prime ministers are chiefly responsible for cultivating support for presidential policies from within the legislature rather than setting policy themselves. Prime ministers may be removed with a **motion of censure** (effectively a vote of no confidence), though this requires an absolute majority of the 577 members of the lower house. Though not specified by the constitution, presidents have asserted the right to remove prime ministers even when they are supported by a majority of the legislature (though their replacement must have majority support in the legislature).

When presidents lack a majority in the legislature, which leads to the appointment of a prime minister from an opposing party (**cohabitation**), the prime minister assumes a much greater degree of power, since she or he does not feel bound to subordinate policy matters to a president from another party. Under these conditions, the explicit powers of the prime minister as laid out in the constitution become prominent, effectively creating a parliamentary system with a more ceremonial president. However, the 2000 constitutional amendment that modified presidential terms attempted to bring cohabitation to an end, since presidential and parliamentary elections now occur at roughly the same time. In the future, voters might be able to split their ticket, favoring one party for the legislature and the candidate of another party for the president, which would lead again to cohabitation and a strong prime minister.

THE LEGISLATURE

France has a bicameral legislature, known as the **parlement**. In fact, it is from France that we get the term *parliament*, which is based on the French word *parler*, meaning "to speak." France's bicameral legislature is composed of the 577-member Assemblée nationale (National Assembly) and a 348-member upper house, the **Sénat** (Senate). Deputies in the National Assembly are elected for five-year renewable terms, and senators are elected for six-year terms. The constitution of the Fifth Republic clearly weakened the legislature vis-à-vis the executive. As a result, the French legislature is weaker than its counterparts in most advanced democracies, but it still plays an important role.[11]

The constitution gives the legislature the right to propose legislation, but most bills (about 80 percent) originate with the executive. The constitution gives the government considerable control over the workings of the legislature, including control of the agenda and the schedule of parliamentary activity. One particularly important instrument that limits the legislature's ability to amend legislation is the **blocked vote**, which forces the legislature to accept bills in their entirety and allows amendments only if they are approved by the government. French legislators also have no power to introduce bills or amendments that affect public spending; only the government may introduce such legislation. Moreover, if the National Assembly does not approve finance bills and the annual budget within 70 days, those items automatically become law.

Another unique feature of the constitution allows governments to submit legislation as motions of confidence. In such cases, the proposed laws are passed unless the legislature can muster a motion of censure against the government.

This is not an easy task (it requires an absolute majority), and it may trigger new elections. This feature was used frequently during the 1980s and 1990s as a way of passing important legislation without legislative debate. The constitution's Article 38 also grants the legislature the right to enable the government to legislate via decrees, known as ordinances, though this power has been used sparingly. Finally, the constitution limits the number and power of the legislative committees that once served as powerful legislative tools of previous regimes.

Yet with all of these limitations, the legislature has gradually asserted itself more forcefully. Since the 1970s, it has conducted a weekly questioning of government ministers (though not the president) that is somewhat similar to the British practice known as question time. The French National Assembly now regularly amends legislation, and the executive no longer asserts its right to reject all amendments. In 1995, the legislative session was extended from six months to nine months, and extended special sessions have become fairly common. Legislative committees have become more important in proposing and amending legislation, and motions of censure, while unlikely to pass, are used by the opposition as a way to bring controversial issues to the floor for debate. In April 2008, the government faced a motion of censure over sending more troops to Afghanistan, which the opposition Socialists used as a way to criticize President Sarkozy's call for stronger military ties to the United States and NATO.[12]

A major constitutional reform passed in 2008 has strengthened the National Assembly. This reform made it easier for individual members to introduce legislation, reduced the government's ability to set the legislative agenda, and strengthened the National Assembly's government oversight powers.

The French upper house, the Sénat, is clearly the weaker of the two legislative chambers. It is elected indirectly by an electoral college of local government officials and members of the lower house. This indirect election helps deprive the Sénat of popular legitimacy, and its legislative powers are limited to delaying legislation passed by the lower house. Important legislation has been passed over the objection of the Sénat, most notably during the Socialist governments in power from 1981 to 1986, when the more conservative Sénat opposed much of the legislation enacted by the leftist government. The Sénat's main power resides in its ability to reject constitutional amendments, which require the consent of both houses. In 2016, the Sénat rejected a constitutional amendment proposed by the government that would have stripped French citizenship from dual nationals convicted of committing terrorist acts. Still, the Sénat is widely seen as somewhat obsolete and unrepresentative, composed of elderly conservatives (three-quarters of the representatives are over 65). As with the British House of Lords, the French

Sénat has been the subject of regular calls for constitutional reform. But since de Gaulle's failed attempt in 1969, and unlike in the United Kingdom, in France the upper house has undergone few constitutional changes. In perhaps the biggest shift, in 2011 candidates on the left won the majority of Sénat seats. This election result reflected the citizens' unhappiness over local government reform that put many council members out of jobs.

THE JUDICIARY

As in most democracies, the French judiciary is divided into several branches, including civil, criminal, and administrative. The French judicial system is based on continental European **code law**, in which laws are derived from detailed legal codes rather than from precedent (as in common law used in the United States, Canada, and the United Kingdom). During Napoleon's rule, French laws were systematically codified, and much of that original code remains in place today. The role of judges is simply to interpret and apply those codes. Consequently, judges in France have less discretion and autonomy than those in the common law systems.

The French court system also operates very differently from that in the United States or Canada. Judges play a much greater role in determining whether charges should be brought, and they assume many of the roles of prosecuting attorneys. In France, judges, not lawyers, question and cross-examine witnesses.

Because the 1958 constitution created a semi-presidential system with built-in potential for deadlock of the legislature and the executive, the Fifth Republic also created a **Constitutional Council** to settle constitutional disputes.[13] The Constitutional Council is composed of nine members who are appointed for a single nine-year term by the president and heads of the National Assembly and Sénat. Former presidents of France also serve as lifetime members of the council. The council is empowered to rule on any constitutional matter, so long as there is a request from the government, the president, or at least 60 members of either house of the legislature.

In its early years, the Constitutional Council tended to act rarely, and usually backed presidential actions. Buoyed by very high approval ratings in recent decades, however, it has shown more independence. For example, in 2008, it rejected legislation that would have allowed for the indefinite imprisonment of dangerous criminals even after their terms had been served. While citizens now have the right to appeal directly to the Constitutional Council to defend their constitutional rights, the vast majority of appeals to the council have come from groups of legislators. One role that the Constitutional Council does not serve is that of a court of last appeal for cases from lower courts—that function is held by other judicial bodies, including the Council of State, France's top administrative court. In 2016, the Council of State struck down laws passed by numerous local governments that would have banned the wearing of the "burkini" (a swimsuit designed to cover virtually the entire body) on beaches (see "Challenges to French National Identity and the Rise of the Nationalist Right," p. 204).

The Electoral System

France's electoral system is majoritarian rather than proportional. Thus it resembles systems in the United States, Canada, and the United Kingdom more than those in continental Europe. However, the use of a two-round runoff between candidates distinguishes it from the plurality-based system found in those countries. French presidents are directly elected in two rounds of voting every five years. Unless a candidate gets over 50 percent of the vote in the first round (which has never happened in the Fifth Republic), a second round of balloting two weeks later pits the top two candidates against each other.

France also employs a two-round electoral system for its single-member district (SMD) elections of members of the National Assembly. In each district, candidates with over 12.5 percent of the vote face off in a second round of balloting (again, unless a candidate gains over 50 percent of the votes in the first round). During the Socialist administration of François Mitterrand, France experimented with proportional representation for lower house elections, as it had in the Fourth Republic, but then returned to SMDs two years later.[14] Using two rounds of voting does ensure that winning candidates have a majority of the vote in each district, but it still delivers disproportionate outcomes common in SMD elections. In 2017, for example, President Macron's party won 53 percent of the lower house seats with only 43 percent of the nationwide vote.

By using two rounds of voting for presidential and lower house elections, the French system encourages more parties and candidates than do SMD systems in Canada, the United Kingdom, or the United States. At the same time, the second round of elections still uses a winner-take-all format, and the 12.5 percent threshold for entry into the second round of legislative elections severely limits the number of parties that actually win. The National Front, for example, won nearly 5 percent of the vote in the first round of the 2007 elections, but not a single seat. The complexity of a two-round system can create a rather confusing electoral landscape, because parties and individuals compete for seats while not necessarily expecting that they can win, but rather that a good showing in the first round can translate into leverage to be used against more powerful parties. Small parties, coalitions, or candidates may throw their support behind a stronger rival as part of a political deal. Still, these calculations can backfire, as they did in the 2002 presidential elections, when candidates on the left fragmented their vote—with a disastrous outcome. We shall speak more about this in "The Party System and Elections" (see p. 176). Although France's electoral system penalizes small parties, it has clearly produced the type of legislative majorities and political stability that were absent during the Fourth Republic.

Referenda

The constitution of the Fifth Republic also allows the president to call national referenda. President de Gaulle held five referenda, staking his reputation and political capital on each one. Referenda were used to approve controversial policies, such as independence for Algeria, and to approve the direct election of the president. When de Gaulle lost a 1969 referendum aimed at reforming the upper house of the legislature, he resigned.

Since then, referenda have been used less frequently, though often regarding changes to the European Union. In 1972, President Pompidou used a referendum to approve the enlargement of the European Union, and in 1992, President Mitterrand asked voters to approve the European Union's Maastricht Treaty. More recently, in 2005, President Chirac submitted a proposed European constitution to a referendum. Voters delivered a resounding rejection of the document despite Chirac's support for it. The defeat weakened Chirac, and since that time, the government has not been willing to submit further EU treaty reforms to a national vote (it is not required by the constitution). France has suggested, however, that it might require a public referendum on Turkish membership in the European Union, if it is offered. Because such a referendum would surely fail, this suggestion has engendered consternation among other EU members as well as Turkey.

Local Government

France is usually considered a prototypical unitary state—all power is concentrated in Paris, the capital and largest city. Furthermore, compared with most of its neighbors, it has experienced relatively little separatism or demands for greater regional autonomy (an independence movement on the island of Corsica is a rare exception). Whereas this is a generally accurate picture, France also has a long history of localism and regionalism that should not be discounted, and three levels of local government—region, department, and commune—that have enjoyed increasing power over time.[15]

France has 18 regions, five of which are overseas. The regions' primary responsibilities are regional planning and economic development. The regions are led by a council that is elected every six years. One level below, 96 departments (plus five overseas territories) have responsibility for such areas as health services and infrastructure. For nearly two centuries, power in the departments resided with a **prefect** appointed by the central government, but a series of reforms in 1982 transferred a great deal of power to directly elected departmental councils, representing over two thousand constituencies called *cantons*. Since 2013, each canton elects a pair of representatives to the department councils, and the pair must consist of a male and female. Finally, at the municipal level there are communes made up of directly elected councils and mayors who handle the main tasks of these communities.

Since the 1982 reforms, local governments have been given some control over taxes and revenues, and as a result their powers have slowly grown. However, their share of the budgetary pie remains very small. A reform passed in 2010 will gradually streamline and reduce the layers and size of French local government. Local governments have decried this project as an attempt to recentralize the country, but the national government has retorted that the current system is too cumbersome and costly.

Local elections in France often serve as a midterm bellwether of sitting governments. The March 2015 local elections, in which the governing Socialists finished third behind the conservatives and the far right National Front, were viewed as a strong rebuke to President Hollande's government.

Other Institutions

THE FRENCH BUREAUCRACY

The development of the French state is associated with the creation of one of the world's earliest and most efficient bureaucracies, the legacy of which can be seen in contemporary French politics. Compared with that of most other democracies, where the notion of bureaucracy conjures up the image of inefficiency and red tape, the civil service in France retains a high profile and considerable prestige and serves as an important springboard to elected office.

One gateway to the bureaucracy is the **École Nationale d'Administration (ENA)**, a state educational institution whose primary mission is to train civil servants. Indeed, the ENA and several other elite state institutions usually recruit the highest category of civil servants. This specialized training, combined with few barriers between civil service and politics, means that the links between the bureaucracy and elected office are strong and considered normal. In the Fifth Republic, four presidents (including former president Hollande and current president Macron) and seven prime ministers have been graduates of the ENA. The *énarques*, as graduates of the ENA are known, commonly move between the civil service and elected or appointed political office. Former president Chirac graduated from the ENA in 1959 and was a civil servant for nearly a decade before running for office; his last prime minister, Dominique de Villepin, also was an *énarque* with a long career within the state—indeed, Villepin had never held any elected office before becoming prime minister.

This blurry line between state and politics extends to the economy, which has long been subject to state guidance and partial state control. Career bureaucrats often move from the civil service to positions within business through a transition known as *pantouflage*—literally, "putting on slippers." The largest private companies in France remain dominated by *énarques*, though this phenomenon has declined of late.

The impact of the civil service on French life thus is hard to overstate. By one estimate, over half the population either works for—or has a parent, child, or spouse who works for—the public sector. Of course, such a large state comes with a cost, in the form of wages and benefits. And as the French population ages, supporting the civil service and its retirees will be an increasingly costly proposition.

Political Conflict and Competition

The Party System and Elections

As a political leader, de Gaulle was deeply suspicious of political parties; he blamed them for much of the political turmoil of the Third and Fourth republics. The single-member district electoral system helped narrow the field of parties and often produced stable majority governments.

By the 1960s, the badly fragmented party system of the Fourth Republic had been replaced by a less fragmented multiparty system that featured a bipolar alternation of coalitions of the center right and the center left. The political bloc of the right was composed mainly of the **Rally for the Republic (RPR)** and the **Union for a Popular Movement (UMP)**. The political bloc of the left was composed mainly of the **French Communist Party (PCF)** and the **French Socialist Party (PS)**. By the late 1970s, each coalition earned about half the vote in French elections. The four major parties together won over 90 percent of the vote. The electoral system helped to ensure this dominance of the two major blocs, because the SMD system, with its two rounds of voting, required coalition building in the second round.

Since the 1980s, the **four-party, two-bloc system** has been in transition. One important ideological change has been the spectacular demise of the PCF on the left and the emergence of the **National Front (FN)** on the right. This development is changing the prospects for electoral coalitions. In addition, constitutional changes may have brought cohabitation to an effective end, also transforming the power of political parties to act as a counterweight to the president. The 2017 presidential elections may portend the demise of the two-bloc system that has been in place for almost forty years. Neither of the two finalists for the French presidency represented a major party. Emmanuel Macron, a centrist running under the banner of the new centrist *La République en Marche!* (Republic Onward!, REM) party, handily defeated Marine Le Pen, from the far right National Front. The Socialists and the Republicans both performed very poorly. As an additional shock to France's political party system, Macron's REM won an absolute majority in the National Assembly, and France's major parties of the right and left suffered serious losses. Next, we discuss the main ideological groups in the party system.

THE FRENCH LEFT

Since the 1970s the Socialist Party (PS) has been the dominant party of the French left, but its dominance was challenged by the presidential elections of 2017.[16] Formed in 1905, the PS was also long divided into social democratic and Marxist camps. In the 1930s, the Socialists were elected to power and led a brief and ill-fated government. After World War II, the Socialist Party reemerged, though it regularly gained fewer votes than the Communists. In the early years of the Fifth Republic, the Socialist Party essentially disappeared until being refounded in 1969.

François Mitterrand became the Socialist Party leader in 1969. He forged an electoral alliance with the stronger Communists and eventually eclipsed them with a more moderate social democratic ideology. This strategy was vindicated by the 1981 election of Mitterrand to the presidency; he was the first leftist president of the Fifth Republic. Mitterrand's long presidency (1981–95) was marred by allegations of corruption, his party's loss of its legislative majority in 1986, and his need to cohabit with a conservative prime minister during most of his two terms

French Presidential Elections, 2017

FIRST ROUND: APRIL 22–23, 2017

CANDIDATE	PARTY	VOTES (%)
Emmanuel Macron	Republic Onward! (center)	24.0
Marine Le Pen	National Front (right)	21.3
François Fillon	Republicans (center-right)	20.0
Jean-Luc Mélenchon	Indomitable France (left)	19.5
Benoît Hamon	Socialist Party (center-left)	6.4
Nicolas Dupont-Aignan	Republic Arise (center-right)	4.7
Others		4.1
Total		100

SECOND ROUND: MAY 6–7, 2017

CANDIDATE	PARTY	VOTES (%)
Emmanuel Macron	Republic Onward! (center)	66.1
Marine Le Pen	National Front (right)	33.9
Total		100

Source: French Ministry of the Interior, www.interieur.gouv.fr (accessed 5/8/17).

in office. Some of Mitterrand's policies, such as support for the 1992 Maastricht Treaty (which greatly enhanced European integration and called for adoption of the euro), alienated much of the Socialist electorate. The Socialists lost the presidency in 1996, and though they won the legislative election of 1997, they were defeated in the 2002 and 2007 legislative and presidential elections. The 2012 election of President François Hollande and the Socialists' absolute majority in the legislature proved to be a short-lived victory. By 2017 the PS had lost the presidency and its majority in the legislature, losing all but 30 of its seats in the lower house in the June legislative elections.

The son of upper-middle-class parents, Hollande was a graduate of the prestigious National Administrative School (ENA) that produces much of the country's bureaucratic and political elite. After graduation, he entered France's *Cour de Comptes* ("Court of Auditors"), a prestigious branch of government that audits both public and private institutions. In the following years, he served in local government, then as a National Assembly deputy, and finally as the leader of the Socialist Party. In 2011, Hollande won the Socialist Party's first-ever open-party primary election, after the PS's front-runner, Dominique Strauss-Kahn (a former head of the International Monetary Fund), withdrew from the race.

Hollande and the PS campaigned on a traditionally leftist platform that included a major tax increase on the wealthy, stricter regulations on the financial sector, reduction of the retirement age that had been raised by his conservative predecessor, and legalization of gay marriage.

Hollande had a difficult presidency.[17] He took office at a time of rising unemployment and growing budget deficits, and he was further damaged by scandals within his cabinet. In March 2014, the Socialists were trounced in local elections and lost control of over 150 localities, including some traditional PS strongholds. Hollande fired his prime minister, Jean-Marc Ayrault, and replaced him with the young and popular Manuel Valls. Valls had been Hollande's interior minister, and was best known for his defense of the 2013 arrest (during a school field trip) and deportation of a 15-year-old Roma girl and her family who were living in France illegally. Valls was criticized by the PS left, but his hard-line stance on immigration was widely popular. Valls was a political centrist who once suggested that the PS should drop the word *socialist* from its label, and he has advocated limits to immigration, the ban on the face veil, and the types of economic reform that are deeply unpopular among the PS left.

The terrorist attacks in Paris and Nice in 2015 and 2016 strengthened the conservative and far right opposition to the Socialists. The government's response to those attacks, and a very unpopular reform of French labor laws that was decreed by the government in 2016, further weakened and divided the Socialists. By March 2016, Hollande's approval rating had fallen to 17 percent, the lowest percentage since the start of the Fifth Republic.[18] In late 2016, Hollande announced that he would not seek reelection in 2017, and Prime Minister Valls resigned in order to run for the Socialist Party presidential nomination. In a shocking upset, and a repudiation of Hollande's record in office, Valls lost the primary to Benoît Hamon, representing the far left of the Socialist Party, and was trounced in the first round of elections, winning just over 6 percent of the vote, 22 percent less than Hollande had won in 2012.

The Communist Party (PCF), another influential party of the French left, played a major role in the French resistance to the Nazi occupation and was rewarded at the polls after World War II. The Communists, for years staunchly loyal to Moscow, supported the Soviet Union's invasion of Czechoslovakia in 1968 (though it had drifted away from its allegiance by the 1970s). Historically, the PCF had a strong base of support among French workers and in France's trade union movement. For much of the post–World War II period, the party did well in local and national elections, usually winning about 20 percent of the vote. It was also the French political party with the largest membership.

However, its success did not translate into significant national power, even though the PCF participated in government coalitions led by the rival Socialist Party and briefly held cabinet positions in Socialist governments. Rather than giving the PCF credibility, government experience only tarnished its image as a principled party of the opposition. The collapse of the Soviet Union further undermined the appeal of its ideology. By 2017, the PCF polled under 3 percent of the votes in

Former president Hollande, lamenting his record-low popularity ratings (due largely to France's economic woes), notes that he still has a private life. In fact, widely publicized scandals concerning his private life also plagued his presidency.

the first round of parliamentary elections, winning only 10 out of 577 seats in the legislature. In recent presidential elections, the PCF was too weak to field its own presidential candidate, and instead backed leftist Jean-Luc Mélenchon, (in 2017 he placed fourth, behind the center-right Republicans).

Although other leftist parties exist in France, none of them has much clout. France's environmental party, Europe Ecology–The Greens (EELV), has only recently enjoyed much electoral success and has been far weaker than the German Green Party. The EELV performed well in the 2009 European elections, finishing in third place just behind the Socialists, and then did well in the 2011 local elections. In the 2012 elections, the EELV agreed to back the Socialists in the second round in those constituencies where the EELV was eliminated. In exchange, the Socialists backed the EELV in constituencies where the PS was eliminated, and the Socialists committed to a gradual 25 percent reduction in nuclear energy's share of total energy production. The EELV won 5.5 percent of the vote and was awarded two cabinet posts in the Socialist government but lost ground in 2017, winning only one legislative seat.

The Radical Party of the Left (PRG) is a center-left ally of the PS and an heir to the long tradition of non-Marxist French radicalism. Historically, radicals were opponents of the monarchy who promoted individual freedoms and the separation of church and state. They differed from Socialists and Communists in their strong support for private property and the free market. The PRG won 12 seats in 2012, as part of an electoral alliance with the PS, but it was only able to win three seats in 2017.

THE FRENCH RIGHT

For much of the history of the Fifth Republic, the most important force on the right consisted of those who considered themselves the political heirs of General Charles de Gaulle and were often called Gaullists or neo-Gaullists. De Gaulle and his supporters dominated the politics of the Fifth Republic from 1958 to 1981 under presidents de Gaulle, Pompidou, and Giscard d'Estaing. But since de Gaulle never associated himself with any party, his heirs created various competing parties of the right that were frequently divided by personality and presidential ambitions. The two most important forces were the Rally for the Republic, created by Jacques Chirac, and the **Union for French Democracy (UDF)**, an alliance of five center-right parties founded by Chirac's rival, former president Valéry Giscard d'Estaing. These parties differed in part over the role of the state and their view of the European Union, but over the years, the differences mostly disappeared.

In 2002, President Chirac encouraged most of the center right to cohere as a single party, the Union for a Popular Movement (UMP).[19] The UDF continues to run separately in elections, but its importance has steadily declined (it won less than 3 percent of the vote in 2012). Compared with de Gaulle's eclectic blend of populism and nationalism, the UMP behaves much more like a classical conservative party with its pro-business, pro–free market, and socially conservative outlook.

During the presidency of Nicolas Sarkozy, the UMP continued to move in the direction of a free market, though it still supported a relatively strong role for the state.[20] Sarkozy's earliest reforms included a virtual elimination of the inheritance tax and a reduction in taxes on businesses, steps that the president viewed as necessary to stimulate economic growth and employment (but the French left viewed the reforms as favoring the well-off). His administration's proposals to reform the French university and health systems were also controversial and provoked widespread protests. Sarkozy raised the retirement age from 60 to 62, made it easier for firms to employ workers beyond the 35-hour work week, and slashed employment in the public sector. Sarkozy also sought to improve relations with the United States and sent additional French forces to support the U.S.-led war in Afghanistan.

Sarkozy's administration coincided with the global economic crisis. Despite his pledges to reduce unemployment, it doubled during his presidency, reaching almost 10 percent by 2012. Sarkozy was hurt by a cascade of scandals, especially charges of nepotism when he appointed his son Jean to a government position he seemed unqualified for. By the end of Sarkozy's first and only term in office, his popularity rating had plummeted to about 30 percent. Sarkozy weakened his UMP support base when he appointed a number of outsiders (including some leftists) to his first cabinet, and many within his party disliked his flamboyance and his attempt to court voters on the far right by cracking down on immigration and launching an ill-fated public debate on French national identity.

Following Sarkozy's dramatic loss in the 2012 presidential election (no president had been turned out of office after one term since 1981), the UMP experienced a period of internal fragmentation. Sarkozy announced his return to politics in 2014 and was elected UMP chairman. Under his leadership, the UMP was renamed, and his party won a majority of regional offices in the March 2015 elections. In the 2016 **Republican** presidential primary, François Fillon, a former prime minister under Sarkozy, defeated his former boss and a more moderate former prime minister for the nomination. Despite his upset victory in the conservative primary, Fillon's candidacy was soon damaged by allegations of nepotism and corruption. Fillon won only 20 percent of the vote and failed to make it into the second round of the 2017 elections. The Republicans also fared poorly in the 2017 legislative elections, losing 82 seats, but still remained the largest opposition force in the legislature.

Unity among France's two main conservative parties was partly spurred by the emergence and surprising success of the National Front (FN) on the far right. Until the early 1980s, the FN was a tiny fringe party that never attracted more than 1 percent of the vote. Its emergence as a serious political contender, initially at the local level, was rooted in its advocacy of a reduction in immigration and the expulsion of illegal immigrants. Led by the fiery Jean-Marie Le Pen, the FN made its first real mark in national politics when proportional representation was briefly introduced in 1986—it won about 10 percent of the vote, outpolled the French Communist Party, and won its first seats in the lower house (it won 35 seats). The party reached its peak with 15 percent of the vote in the 1997 legislative elections. But under the SMD system, which was readopted in part to stifle the FN, it has never won more than two seats in the lower house. Nevertheless, in the 2002 presidential elections, Le Pen benefited from the divided votes among various leftist candidates and made it into a runoff with President Chirac. In the second round, he won less than 20 percent of the vote as voters recoiled from the possibility of a Le Pen presidency. But the factors that make the National Front a success, particularly fears over immigration, remain.

To a large extent, these fears have been successfully co-opted by mainstream conservatives like Sarkozy, who emphasized law and order and greater controls over immigration and immigrants (and, who, as part of his campaign for the presidency in 2017, has promised to take a hard line on immigration and outward displays of religious affiliation). Indeed, it could be argued that the main impact of the FN to date has been to push parties to its left to take a harder line on immigration and law and order. The National Front leadership has been revived with the election of Le Pen's daughter, **Marine Le Pen**, to the top leadership position of the party in 2011. She has reemphasized antiglobalization and Euroskepticism as central values of the party while distancing the FN from the more xenophobic and provocative statements of her less temperate father (see "Challenges to French National Identity and the Rise of the Nationalist Right," p. 204).[21]

Under Marine Le Pen, the FN remains a rightist, nationalist, and socially conservative political party, but she has had some success in moving the party closer to the mainstream of French politics. In the 2012 electoral campaign, she advocated for France to abandon the euro as well as restore the retirement age of 60 (Sarkozy had raised it to 62). At the same time, she pledged to slash legal immigration and deport foreigners convicted of crimes while dramatically beefing up law enforcement (she promised a referendum on instituting the death penalty). In the 2012 presidential elections, Marine Le Pen won about 18 percent of the vote in the first round of elections. It was a historic high for the FN, and in legislative elections the FN established itself as the third largest political force after the PS and the UMP. In May 2014, the unthinkable occurred: the FN won the European elections with 25 percent of the vote, defeating both the UMP and the PS and quadrupling its share of the votes compared with its 2009 European Parliament result. The FN took advantage of widespread frustration with the European Union, historically low approval ratings of President Hollande, and disarray within the conservative UMP. In recent elections, the FN has taken most of its votes away from parties of the right, but it also attracts disaffected leftists (notably former Communist Party voters). Indeed, the FN attracted the highest percentage of manual workers (almost 30 percent) of any French political party.[22]

As part of her plan to make the FN more acceptable to mainstream French voters, Marine Le Pen expelled her father from the party in August 2015 after he made a series of comments that were viewed as racist and xenophobic. This move, and the 2015 and 2016 terrorist attacks, appear to have bolstered popular support for the FN. In the most recent local elections, the FN placed second to the Republicans, handily beating the governing Socialists. Le Pen placed second in the first round of the 2017 presidential elections, winning just over 21 percent of the vote. Facing opposition from most of the parties in the first round, she was able to win just under 34 percent of the vote in the second round. In the 2017 legislative elections the National Front won only eight seats, a gain of six from previous election, but an outcome that was far below expectations.

THE FRENCH CENTER

By 2017 both the Socialists and mainstream conservatives had been discredited. Hollande's Socialist government was deeply unpopular, and the Socialist Party selected a member of the party's far left as its standard bearer. The candidate for the conservative Republicans was mired in corruption scandals. The election of Emmanuel Macron could portend the emergence of a new political center in France, and perhaps a broader realignment of French politics.

Like most French presidents, Macron was trained as a civil servant at the prestigious National Administrative School and worked in the French Ministry of Economy. After leaving the government to work as an investment banker, he returned to politics to work as an advisor to Socialist president Hollande. In 2014 Hollande appointed him economics minister, and he was responsible for the passage of a series of labor reforms that were bitterly opposed by French trade unions. Macron was briefly a member the Socialist Party, but by 2015 identified himself as an independent. In 2016 Macron quit the government and founded *La République en Marche!*

(Republic Onward!, REM) as a centrist political party to support his presidential bid. The party declared itself to be free-market friendly, socially progressive, and pro–European Union.

During the 2017 presidential campaign Macron was attacked by much of the French left as unsympathetic to workers and beholden to the corporate world. Rightists attacked his strong support for the European Union, his advocacy of free trade, and his progressive stance on social positions. At the same time, his campaign attracted support from more centrist Socialists and conservatives. His youth (at 39 he was the youngest French president ever elected), his relative inexperience, and his vague campaign platform make Macron and his REM party unknown quantities in the context of the previously stable French political party system. Macron was able to quickly recruit members to run for legislative office, drawing on a core of young supporters. Half of REM's candidates had never run for elective office, and half were women. Despite predictions to the contrary, REM won a majority in the National Assembly, shocking the political establishment.

The 2017 election of centrist Emmanuel Macron (right) was a shock to the established parties to his right and left. Although Macron had briefly been a member of the Socialist Party, he selected a member of the Conservative opposition, Édouard Philippe (left) to be his prime minister.

Macron appointed Édouard Philippe, a member of the conservative Republican Party, as his prime minister. Like Macron, Philippe was trained at France's elite administrative schools, spent time in the business sector, briefly held membership in the Socialist Party, and had relatively little experience in government. Half the members of Macron's first cabinet were women, and the new president appointed members from both the center-right and center-left.

Civil Society

As early as the 1830s, the French scholar Alexis de Tocqueville noted the weakness of French civil associations. Most scholars argue that French interest groups and associations remain weaker than those in most advanced democracies, a function of the powerful state and the emphasis on so-called mass action over organized lobbying. Nevertheless, trade unions and organizations representing private

French National Assembly Elections, 2012 and 2017

PARTY	2012			2017		
	% VOTE (FIRST ROUND)	% SEATS (SECOND ROUND)	# SEATS (SECOND ROUND)	% VOTE (FIRST ROUND)	% SEATS (SECOND ROUND)	# SEATS (SECOND ROUND)
Republic Onward!	—	—	—	28.2	53.0	306
Republicans (previously the Union for Popular Movement)	26.2	33.6	194	15.8	19.4	112
Socialist Party	29.2	48.5	280	7.4	5.2	30
Other parties of the left	9.6	10.6	61	20.9	12.8	45
Other parties of the right	2.4	6.1	35	7.3	1.4	8
National Front	13.8	0.4	2	13.2	1.4	8
Others	18.8	0.8	5	7.2	6.8	68
Total	100	100	577	100	100	577

Source: French Ministry of the Interior, www.interieur.gouv.fr (accessed 6/26/17).

enterprise are two important elements of civil society that are worth discussing in detail.

LABOR UNIONS

Observers of French politics, particularly its numerous strikes, commonly speak of how powerful the French labor unions are. This view is misleading. In fact, French labor unions have a long history of being weak and fractious. Less than 8 percent of the French workforce belongs to a union. This rate is one of the lowest in Europe and has decreased from a high of about a third of the workforce after World War II.[23] Union membership has especially plummeted among younger workers. And unlike the powerful trade unions found elsewhere on the continent, French labor unions usually have been divided along partisan lines.

Among the most powerful French union confederations is the **General Confederation of Labor (CGT)**, historically linked to the PCF. Its leadership includes many Communist Party members, but many non-Communists are part of the general membership. The CGT was long France's most powerful union, but its power and membership have dwindled, much as the French Communist Party has become a shadow of its former self. Today, the confederation members represent about a quarter of the unionized workforce (and only about 3 percent of all workers are CGT members).

In contrast, the **French Democratic Labor Confederation (CFDT)** and Force Ouvrire (FO) have tended to have more centrist or anticommunist orientations. The CFDT is roughly equal in strength to the CGT, and the FO is slightly smaller. A number of other independent unions exist outside of these larger confederations, and some of them, like the national teachers' union, have waged fierce battles against government reform efforts. In France, more than one trade union can represent workers in French firms, pitting competing unions against each other (in many countries, workers select a single union to represent them).

Paradoxically, the weakness and fragmentation of French unions partially explains the large number of strikes that occur in France. More powerful unions could effectively engage in productive bargaining with employers or the government, but French unions lack this authority. Instead, they resort to public demonstrations and work stoppages as a vital tool to express discontent, a tactic that capitalizes on the French tendency toward mass action and public protest. This was the case in the spring of 2016, when French unions, led by the CGT, staged a wave of strikes to protest the Socialist government's labor law reform, which would make it easier for French firms to fire workers and weaken the power of unions. The CFDT backed the Socialist government and its proposed reforms, highlighting the fragmentation of the French labor movement.

But despite their weakness, unions continue to play a key role in French society and in the management of the country's major welfare organizations (health care, retirement, and social security). French law gives unions the right to represent all workers in firms that employ over 50 employees, whether or not the workers are union members. They are also strongly represented in France's public-sector

French students demonstrate against the government's proposed labour law reform on March 24, 2016, in Strasbourg, eastern France. Students were at the forefront of protests over the reforms aimed at freeing up the job market and reining in France's high unemployment rate.

workforce and are a power to reckon with when any French government attempts to reform welfare benefits.

PRIVATE ENTERPRISE

Compared with French labor, the business sector is well organized. Large firms are represented by the Movement of French Businesses (MEDEF), and smaller firms are represented by the General Confederation of Small- and Medium-size Businesses (CGPME). Both have tended to support lower taxes on business, more flexible laws to regulate the hiring and firing of workers, and a reduced role for government in the economy. Business has generally supported parties on the right, such as the UMP. Since large numbers of France's business leaders are *énarques*, French business often has privileged access to the state bureaucracy. Not surprisingly, MEDEF has been a strong supporter of economic reforms; CGPME has been less enthusiastic, fearing that deregulation will remove many of the barriers that currently protect small businesses from competition.

Unlike labor unions and private business firms, organized religious institutions have had less of a role in French civil society. France is formally a Catholic nation, and despite minorities of Muslims, Protestants, and Jews, well over half of the French are nominally Catholics. Yet even with the predominance of a single religion, France has long been an anticlerical society. This trait dates back to the revolution, when people saw the church as a tool of monarchical power.[24]

Church and state have been formally separate since 1905 under what is known as *laïcité* (roughly translated as "secularism"). Under *laïcité*, no religion can receive state support, and religious education is restricted. The church continues to play a role in important social rituals (marriages, births, funerals), but not in the daily lives of most French citizens. The church lacks an important or central role in French politics, which has no Christian democratic party as found in other Catholic countries such as Italy or Germany. The church can, however, rally to the defense of its own institutional issues: in the 1980s, church opposition forced the Socialist government to back away from plans to impose stricter government control over religious schools.

As the Catholic Church has waned in power, other religions, particularly Islam, have grown. France has thus seen a rapid growth in mosques and Islamic educational and cultural institutions, something that has made many French citizens nervous. For many of these institutions, the Union of Islamic Organizations acts as an umbrella group. In 2002, the government created the French Council of the Muslim Faith to act as an intermediary between the government and Muslim leaders. This council has had limited success in building state-faith relations, and tensions remain, some of which we discuss next.

Society

Ethnic and National Identity

In modern times, the French have tended to view themselves as ethnically homogeneous. However, historically this was not the case, and recent trends have challenged that notion. In centuries past, many parts of France maintained distinct ethnic identities that included their own languages and cultures: Gascon, Savoyard, Occitan, Basque, and Breton are just a few. Over time, these unique communities were largely assimilated into a single French identity, though certain

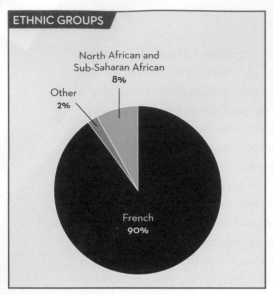

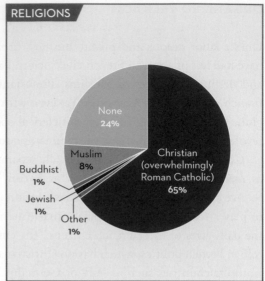

ethnic groups, particularly Basques and Corsicans, have retained stronger language and cultural ties.

Assimilation was in part connected to the particular role the French state played in the development of national identity. An important facet of the French Revolution was the idea of a set of universal rights that identified people as citizens rather than subjects of the state. This form of republicanism was unlike that of the American Revolution, where democracy was predicated on an individualism that demanded federalism and a state with lower autonomy and capacity. French revolutionaries believed in the necessity of a powerful state to destroy the institutions of the past (including ethnic identity) and to serve the people's general interests in building the future. A powerful state thus became a key instrument in solidifying and expressing French national identity and patriotism in a way that did not occur in the United States.[25] In contrast to U.S. policy, in France, rivals for public loyalty were eradicated or brought under the control of the state.

This relationship between state and nation is now being challenged by changes in both religious and ethnic identity. In the past, *laïcité* served to subordinate religious identity to the state, and ethnic identities were downgraded through assimilation and nationalism. In fact, French identity is so primary that the national census and opinion surveys cannot, by law, record such basic information as ethnicity and religion (the data on religion and ethnic identity are therefore inexact estimates). This became a point of debate in the 2007 presidential campaign, during which the candidates and the public were divided over whether recording such information would help address social issues or exacerbate division.

This question emerged because these ethnic and religious identities are becoming more salient. In the past few decades, France has seen an influx of people from outside Europe, notably from Africa, the Middle East, and Southeast Asia. French citizens of immigrant origin today make up perhaps as much as a fifth to a quarter of the population.[26] As in many countries, immigrants to France and their children often find themselves marginalized due to persistent discrimination, language barriers, and/or a lack of education. French citizens of immigrant origin have virtually no representation in the country's political class, and according to one recent study, France lags far behind its European counterparts in this area.[27] The appointment of Manuel Valls as prime minister in March 2014 and the recent election of Anne Hidalgo as mayor of Paris are exceptions to the rule, for both were born in Spain. Many immigrants are concentrated in housing projects on the outskirts of Paris and other large cities, where they have poor social services, limited employment

---

IN COMPARISON — Religion and Morality

Is it necessary to believe in God in order to be moral and have good values? Percentage saying yes:

COUNTRY	PERCENTAGE
Nigeria	91
Brazil	86
South Africa	75
India	70
United States	53
Mexico	52
Japan	42
Russia	38
Germany	33
United Kingdom	20
France	15

Note: Data on Iran and China not available.
Source: Pew Center for the People and the Press, 2011 and 2013.

opportunities, and little access to transportation. This ghettoization compounds the sense of disconnect from French life and has led to violence. In 2005, France saw a month of heavy rioting across its immigrant suburbs, culminating in a state of emergency and approximately $200 million in damages. A second set of riots, not as large though more violent, occurred in 2007.

In the debate over immigration, the future of the Muslim community takes center stage. Currently, France has the largest Muslim population in Europe outside Turkey; it is estimated at 5 to 6 million people (approximately 10 percent of the population, including foreign born and those born in France). The growth of a large Muslim population has been disconcerting for a country that historically has been overwhelmingly Catholic, if now only nominally so. This situation, not unlike that of other Western countries, is compounded by the particular position of the French state. *Laïcité* means that Muslims are expected to place their faith below that of national and patriotic identity as part of the assimilation process. Yet many Muslims believe that the French state should be more accommodating to their needs, rather than vice versa. Furthermore, in the face of persistent marginalization, many Muslims turn to their faith as a source of identity and meaning.[28]

In the past few years, one prominent example of this conflict has been over the head scarf. Growing expressions of Muslim identity have been a challenge to *laïcité*—in particular, whether girls can wear a head scarf in public schools. Many French on both the left and right have argued that educational institutions, as part of the state, cannot allow the wearing of the head scarf without violating the principle of *laïcité*. After a long discussion, France passed a law in 2004 that forbade the wearing of any "conspicuous religious symbol" in schools, whatever the faith. In 2011, the French government went further, banning full-face veils in public and arguing that such coverings promote separatism. While the law generated protest, it has not been much enforced. Whether such steps will help bring minorities into the mainstream or further marginalize them is open to debate. Many French point out that the United Kingdom's much more multicultural approach—for example, female Muslims in the British police force

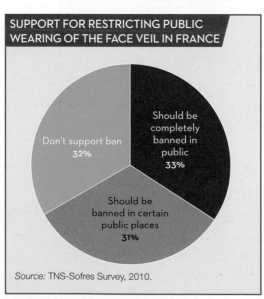

SUPPORT FOR RESTRICTING PUBLIC WEARING OF THE FACE VEIL IN FRANCE

Should be completely banned in public
33%

Don't support ban
32%

Should be banned in certain public places
31%

Source: TNS-Sofres Survey, 2010.

A woman wearing a burkini walks in the water on a beach in Marseille, France, on August 27, 2016, the day after the country's highest administrative court suspended a ban on full-body burkini swimsuits that has outraged many Muslims.

may wear head scarves—has not prevented similar problems of marginalization, and that the Muslim community in the United Kingdom is much more radicalized than it is in France.

How is France resolving these conflicts over immigration and religion? Under President Sarkozy, the government emphasized the need for increased restrictions on immigration, greater emphasis on integrating immigrant populations, and increased emphasis on so-called law and order (which is widely understood to mean a focus on crime committed by immigrants and their offspring and is, to many observers, a not particularly subtle expression of racism). In 2009, Sarkozy proposed a national debate on "what it means to be French." But the debate led to an outpouring of anti-immigrant sentiment, and the government put a stop to the initiative.[29] Sarkozy continued to highlight the challenges of immigration during the 2012 election campaign, partly in an attempt to defend the UMP against the rising National Front. Socialist president Hollande supported the ban on head scarves, and proposed other anti-immigration measures more traditionally advocated by the right. The January 2015 attacks in Paris by French Islamist terrorists on the satirical weekly Charlie Hebdo, the November 2015 bombings in Paris, and the July 2016 terrorist attack in Nice heightened the tension between the French commitment to *laïcité* and its growing Muslim minority. In response to those attacks, millions of French citizens took to the streets to protest Islamist terrorism.

Ideology and Political Culture

The role of the state in shaping French national identity can be seen in the country's ideological landscape and political culture. Ideological divisions in France are much more fragmented than are those in other European countries, where a few coherent and persistent parties tend to dominate the political scene. Divisive historical events, the weakness of civil society, the importance of the state, de Gaulle's hostility toward political parties, the two-round electoral system, and semi-presidentialism have all played a part in creating a system in which individual political leaders, rather than ideological groupings, have been central.

As a result, although we can speak generally of left and right, social democratic or liberal, in fact, the ideological divisions are much more diverse and reflect a range of experiences, such as the battles over the French Revolution and the role of the Catholic Church in French life. In many cases, these values cannot be classified as an ideology at all but rather fall under the term **populism**, or a set of ideas including faith in the common man and suspicion of organized power. From the revolution to Napoleon to de Gaulle, French leaders have often appealed to the masses by seeking to transcend ideology and speak for the people. This populism has helped keep civil society and ideology weak by fostering an ongoing mistrust of such institutions as political parties.

The residual strength of populist ideas explains not only why ideological divisions in France are as much within groups as between them but also why one of the most notable elements of French political culture is the tendency toward mass protests. With civic organizations being too weak to articulate public concerns and with individuals being faithful to the populist notion that the people must struggle against those in power, one of the most common forms of political activity in France is mass protest: marches, demonstrations, and strikes. For example, France regularly averages more than 1,000 workers' strikes per year, compared with fewer than 200 in the United Kingdom, and massive strikes in 2010 paralyzed much of the country for several weeks. Still, French respondents to political surveys tend to put themselves more on the left of the political spectrum than do those in the United States, the United Kingdom, or Canada.

At the same time, France's populism and faith in the power of mass action is combined with a strong sense of national and patriotic identity and pride in the French state as well as a belief that France is exceptional among countries. This perspective has led to frequent conflict with the United States, a rival with a similar notion of its own exceptionalism but whose ideology of individualism runs counter to the French vision.

Political Economy

Like its continental neighbors, France provides for a strong state role in the political economy. Part of this is a function of modern social democratic policies, whereas other elements can be traced over the course of several centuries. As far back as the sixteenth century, the absolute monarchy levied heavy taxes on the populace to support a large bureaucracy. At the same time, the French economy was highly mercantilist domestically. It was divided into a number of smaller markets, each subject to internal tariffs and nontariff barriers. Exports constituted a relatively small portion of the economy.[30] Although the French Revolution and the reign of Napoleon nationalized many of these structures, by the twentieth century, France was lagging behind many of its neighbors in terms of economic development. The country retained a large agricultural sector, had few large firms, and had experienced a relatively low level of urbanization. As one scholar described Paris in 1948, it was "empty of vehicles, needed neither traffic lights nor one-way streets"; electrical services and major consumer goods such as refrigerators were little known. He concluded, "France had not really entered the twentieth century."[31]

In the aftermath of World War II, the French government set out to rapidly transform the economy. This took the form of what the French

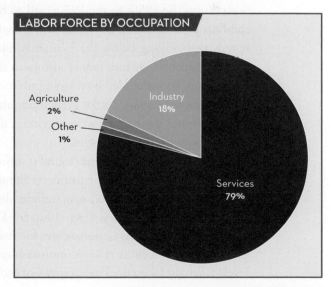

LABOR FORCE BY OCCUPATION

Agriculture 2%

Other 1%

Industry 18%

Services 79%

termed **dirigisme**, which can be explained as an emphasis on state authority in economic development—a combination of both social-democratic and mercantilist ideas. Dirigisme involved the nationalization of several sectors of the economy (such as utilities), the promotion of a limited number of "national champion" industries to compete internationally (such as Airbus), the creation of a national planning ministry, and the establishment of the ENA and similar schools to ensure the education of bureaucrats who would be able to direct the economy.

True to its objectives, the dirigiste system helped bring about a transformation of the French economy. Economic wealth grew rapidly, along with increased urbanization. Through the help of economic subsidies from the European Union, France was also able to change its agricultural sector from one of small farms to one of large-scale production. Whereas in the 1950s, France's per capita gross domestic product (GDP) was approximately half that of the United States, within 20 years it had surpassed its historical rivals, the United Kingdom and Germany.[32] Dirigisme, however, came with costs, including a large public sector, an expansive welfare system, and a heavy tax burden.

In an era when most capitalist democracies, including those with social-democratic political economies, are privatizing state-owned firms, the French state has continued to play a very large role in its economy.

As with many other economic systems around the world, in the past 20 years this model has been put to the test. By the mid-1980s, unemployment had risen to over 10 percent, a rate that has persisted and is disproportionately concentrated among the young. Economic growth, which had been double that of the United States from the 1950s to the 1970s, fell to below 2 percent, among the lowest in the European Union. Due to this slow growth, France's per capita GDP has stagnated, again falling below the United Kingdom and Germany and once-poorer countries such as Ireland. France also faces the Europe-wide dilemma of an aging population, compounded by a large public-sector workforce that can retire early with generous benefits. As the French population has grown older, it is thus using an ever-greater share of the welfare system, though fewer young workers are available to fund those expenditures.

The French government has found it difficult to respond to these challenges, in part because of its political culture. As the dirigiste model faces internal stresses, the French economy is also being buffeted by international competition from the United States and Asia as well as within the European Union itself. Increasing globalization presents new opportunities for France's economy, but for many French, globalization is seen as risky economic liberalism extended to the international level. Tellingly, when the French speak of economic liberalization or globalization, they speak of an Anglo-Saxon model, by which they mean the United Kingdom and the United States. Many French thus are worried that domestic economic reforms will essentially Americanize France, undermining their core identity. France is awash in discussions that the country is in decline and must carry out radical change if it is to survive in a changing world. It was Sarkozy's very call for a rupture with the past that helped him win the presidential election.

During his presidency, President Sarkozy proposed a number of changes, including pension reform, expanding the work week, lowering taxes, raising the retirement age, deregulating business, liberalizing the labor market, and cutting government payrolls (see "The Future of the French Welfare State," p. 207). These were easier said than done. Sarkozy faced numerous protests, including the massive 2010 strikes mentioned earlier, and his emphasis on reform no doubt contributed to his defeat.

In the long term, however, some elements may be working in favor of reform. First is a growing consensus that reform is necessary, even if there is less appetite for the reforms themselves. Second is that despite the structural problems of the French economy, in many ways it is highly competitive and thus amenable to reform. The United States may have a higher GDP per capita, for example, but that is partly because Americans work much longer hours than the French. But French workers produce more, per hour of labor, than Germans, British, or Canadians (and only a bit less than Americans).[33] The question is whether France will be able to seize upon the recent EU crisis to turn the country in a new direction.

Another interesting facet of the debate about the future of the French economy can be seen in the struggle over agriculture. Though the percentage of the French population engaged in agriculture has shrunk dramatically in the past 50 years, agriculture still plays a central role in French identity. French culture is strongly tied to the concept of rural and agricultural life, and this is also bound up with national identity: locally or nationally produced food is central to the French self-image and to international prestige (think of French wines and cheeses). This French identity has been sustained in part, however, by large subsidies from the European Union, through what is known as the Common Agricultural Policy (CAP). Created in part to satisfy French conditions for joining the European Union, this policy became one of the European Union's main expenditures. The CAP consumes over 40 percent of the EU budget, and France is the largest single recipient. Whereas countries with large agricultural sectors have done well under the CAP, member states with smaller or more efficient farms have resented the costs of the CAP. Outside the European Union, the United States and less-developed countries have long opposed the CAP's tariff barriers

French Government's Share in Selected Industrial Firms, 2014

COMPANY	INDUSTRY	PERCENTAGE SHARE
SNCF	Rail services	100
RFF	Rail infrastructure	100
La Poste	Mail	100
Nexter	Defense equipment	100
Areva	Nuclear reactors	86.7*
EDF	Electricity	84.5
ADP	Airports	50.6
GDF	Gas and electricity	33.6
Thales	Aerospace/trainmaking	26.6
Safran	Aerospace	22.4
Alstom	Power/trainmaking	20.0**
Air France–KLM	Airline	15.9
Renault	Carmaking	15.0
Peugeot Citroën	Carmaking	14.1
Orange	Telecoms	13.4
Airbus	Aircraft	11.0

*Includes stakes held by EDF and BPI.

**Proposal.

Source: Economics Ministry; company reports; adapted from the *Economist*, June 28, 2014, www.economist.com /news/business/21605921-other-countries-are-selling-state-owned-industries-france-trading-up-raison-d-tat?zid=307&ah =5e80419d1bc9821ebe173f4f0f060a07 (accessed 6/29/14).

and import quotas, which limit non-EU agricultural products. The cost of the CAP (especially with enlargement), combined with pressure from non-EU countries, has intensified this conflict in recent years. But in spite of the pressure, the French government has resisted restructuring the CAP. French farmers have also turned the issue into one of antiglobalization, arguing that reduced support and open trade will lead to the "McDonaldization" of French food.[34] In a country where agriculture is central to national identity, such arguments carry weight. They may also have significant consequences. Struggles over benefits such as the CAP, combined with several national economic crises, raise the danger of greater acrimony between EU members that may hinder efforts at reform and economic growth across the continent. In the following section, we turn to the challenge of reconciling national and international policy in France.

The return of the Socialist Party to government under François Hollande in 2012 raised new concerns about France's ability to reform its economy. Hollande campaigned on a pledge to raise taxes on the wealthiest French to a 75 percent rate, to rein in the excesses of the financial sector, and to increase social spending. During the first two years of his presidency, the French economy performed very poorly while other European economies were rebounding. Growth was flat, investment was stagnant, and unemployment remained high. In March 2014, after Hollande's Socialists were drubbed in local elections, the president appointed a new prime minister, Manuel Valls, and a new non-Socialist economy minister, (now President) Emmanuel Macron, who implemented spending cuts and rolled back some tax increases (including the 75 percent tax rate on the wealthiest). In 2016, the Hollande government reformed France's antiquated labor laws that made it difficult to fire workers (and therefore discouraged the creation of full-time jobs), leading to a nationwide wave of strikes and protests. Among other measures, the new law weakened the 35-hour work week, allowing workers to work longer hours in exchange for overtime pay. Macron, the reform's main author, resigned from the cabinet to run for president as the candidate of Republic Onward!, a new centrist party.

Foreign Relations and the World

Our discussion has already touched on the idea that France views itself as a product of a revolution with universal application, like the American Revolution before it or the Russian Revolution after. With such a view, France has long seen itself as having a special mission in the international system: to export its revolution's core ideas. Such thinking was part of the legitimizing force of the French Empire in the eighteenth century, when the concepts of egalitarianism and the importance of the nation-state spread from France across Europe. Modern nationalism as we understand it, in the form of mass volunteer armies and patriotic fervor, was first associated with the French Revolution and Napoleon Bonaparte. Today, the historical struggles for national identity across Europe are often traced to the Napoleonic Wars.

France's unique view of its place in the world has persisted to the present, and this role was brought into sharp focus with the rise of two rivals to universal authority: the United States and the Soviet Union. With the onset of the Cold War, France saw itself as caught between two superpowers, both claiming that their ideological mission represented the ultimate political destiny for the rest of the world, including France. During the Cold War, France played an important role in two Western European institutions: the European Union and NATO. France was a founding member of the European Union, along with Belgium, Germany, Italy, Luxembourg, and the Netherlands, in 1951. This proposal was incredibly radical at the time, since France and Germany had concluded a bitter war only a few years earlier. But France's motivation was not driven by a sense that its role in the international system had passed, requiring it to subsume its powers into a larger, supranational organization. Rather, it saw in the European Union the potential to extend its authority, as a counterweight to the United States and the Soviet Union. With a Franco-German motor at its core, the European Union could be a superpower in its own right, changing a bipolar international system into a multipolar one.

Thus, the French have always viewed the European Union somewhat differently than have other member states, particularly Germany and the United Kingdom. For Germany, the European Union has been a necessary instrument for preventing another major war by openly refuting the primacy of nationalism and patriotism. For the United Kingdom, the European Union is an ongoing threat for precisely the same reason. But for France, the European Union has always been an instrument for pursuing the French ideals. Indeed, under de Gaulle, France consistently blocked the United Kingdom's membership in the European Union, viewing it as a Trojan horse for American interests.

Even NATO, explicitly created to counter Soviet power, was viewed by the French in these terms. For de Gaulle, America's domination of NATO reduced the likelihood that the organization could function as an expression of French policies and values. As a result, the French relationship to NATO was much more distant. Seeking to enhance a European position that would be more independent of the United States, France withdrew from the central military command of NATO in 1966 and developed its own independent nuclear capacity. It failed to achieve its objective of developing Europe as a superpower independent of the United States, but it continued to seek its own path and authority in the international system, both independently and through the European Union.

The end of the Cold War and the emergence of the United States as the sole superpower brought a new set of issues and concerns to French foreign policy. Even before 2001, French officials worried about what they termed the United States' "hyperpower." This hyperpower was no longer fettered by the Cold War, and in the absence of any restrictions, the United States would be free to act unilaterally, attempting to remake the world in its own image. Moreover, American military hyperpower would be further enhanced by globalization, which at its core was seen as an internationalization of Anglo-Saxon values and institutions. As a French foreign minister put it, the United States was like a fish in the sea of globalization that was uniquely suited to swim in its waters. For some French observers, then, the end of the Cold War and the rise of U.S. hyperpower not only challenged France's international role but also represented an existential crisis undermining France's place in the world order.[35]

This tension has been evident since September 11, 2001. Although France expressed strong support for the United States after the terrorist attacks, relations between the two countries were strained, especially over the United States' decision to go to war with Iraq. The debate over the war related to a number of factors important to French foreign policy. First, France saw the war as a clear expression of U.S. hyperpower, a unilateralism that rejected international institutions and thus marginalized other countries. Opposition to the war was therefore driven by a desire to have a say as well as by the belief that U.S. force should be part of a multilateral process. The administration of George W. Bush rejected such calls, seeing France's arguments as an attempt simply to stymie U.S. power. Second, France has traditionally cultivated a strong relationship with the Middle East, establishing far friendlier relations with many Arab states than the United States had. Not surprisingly, then, as the United States moved closer to war, France became one of the strongest voices of protest, opposing a UN resolution authorizing force.

During Sarkozy's presidency, these rifts largely were mended. Unlike his predecessors, Sarkozy was unabashedly pro-American, and he sought to identify the country more strongly with the United States. In 2009, France reintegrated into the NATO military command, despite criticisms that doing so would make it subordinate to the United States and other European countries. The United States, weakened by its wars in Iraq and Afghanistan, welcomed France's increased participation as part of a broader move to increase European responsibility for international security. Not long thereafter, this responsibility was tested. When rebels rose up against Muammar Gaddafi in Libya, NATO entered the conflict—first to protect rebels from being overrun by government forces and then, in an offensive manner, to destroy the Libyan military. While the United States played a critical role in this war, by some estimates France flew the largest number of attack sorties (sudden deployments of military units) against Libyan targets (perhaps twice as many as the United States). France also deployed an aircraft carrier and a large number of attack helicopters to the fight. In the end, Sarkozy's rapprochement with NATO appears to have paid off. France was widely praised for its role in the conflict (especially by Libyans), and its profile as a major international actor has risen. The security arrangements between the United States and Europe appear to be developing into ones in which Europe will take on greater responsibilities.

President Hollande continued the activist foreign policy of Sarkozy. He sent French troops to Mali to push back Islamist rebels, played a major role in opposing Iran's development of nuclear weapons, and favored a military response to Syria's use of chemical weapons against anti-Assad rebels. His foreign policy, in stark contrast to his record on the domestic economy, generally drew support from across the political spectrum.

While France seems to be increasingly assertive in global affairs, its relationship with the European Union has become increasingly difficult. One obvious issue, which we have already discussed, is economic. As the European Union moves painfully through the economic crises that have plagued many member states, questions about the long-term viability of its economic institutions, such as the euro, have surfaced. These crises may play themselves out in a number of ways; some heavily indebted countries, such as Greece, may pull themselves out of their situation through austerity measures and support from other EU states. More generally speaking, however, there is the question of what impact these crises will have on the future of the European Union itself. Many are concerned that the shortcomings of the European Union are now painfully clear—a collection of sovereign states, many of them bound by a single currency but not by a single fiscal system. In other words, EU members may share one currency, but they remain independent in how they raise and spend their wealth. A common currency among numerous states raises questions about taxes, budgets, inflation, unemployment, and economic prosperity.

More seriously, the Eurozone economic crisis has created new tensions in the Franco-German relationship and has severely dampened French citizens' enthusiasm for the European Union. Germany's insistence that the Eurozone's troubled economies (which now include France) adopt austerity measures as a way to overcome the crisis has increasingly angered the French, and this irritation has grown since the 2012 election of President Hollande. From the German perspective, Hollande initially backed away from Sarkozy's commitment to painful economic reforms. The shocking victory of the rightist National Front in the 2014 European elections has underscored French frustration with the European Union. The National Front has called for France's abandonment of the euro, an outcome that seems unimaginable for a country that has staked its post–World War II foreign policy on increasing European integration. Only about 40 percent of French respondents have a positive view of the European Union, a figure lower than that in Germany and even the United Kingdom, and a large majority believes that EU integration has damaged the French economy.[36]

There is a growing debate in France about how best to address the European Union's economic crisis. Mainstream parties in France have long suggested that the solution is "more Europe." Specifically, it has been suggested that the only way to deal with the difficulty of monetary union is for the European Union to move toward true federalism, vesting greater economic powers with the European Union itself. However, it is not clear what this proposal means—would all states, including France, give up more power to the various bodies of the European Union? The recent electoral surge of the National Front (and anti-EU parties throughout Europe) makes such an outcome unrealistic. Rather, this vision of a federal European Union could mean greater coordination between the member state leaders to hammer out common economic policies and objectives. And this vision implies that the most powerful member states—such as France and Germany—would be the main leaders of this more federalist Europe.

Predictably, this argument has raised the hackles of many. Few member states disagree with the notion that the long-term success of the euro and the European Union requires greater integration. But for many, France's call for a more federal Europe is little more than a gambit to reassert authority over a body that over the past decade has grown far past the reach of any one state. France was ambivalent about the enlargement of the European Union eastward in 2004, fearing that this shift would dilute its own authority and weaken its historical tie to Germany. Since that time, France has been unsupportive of further enlargement—particularly regarding Turkey, which for several years has been engaged in the formal application process for membership. As the European Union has grown, it has also developed a more clearly pronounced difference between those countries that use the euro (like France and Germany) and those that do not (such as the United Kingdom and some newer members). As tensions grow over economic policies and political institutions, a "two-tier" European Union may emerge, where one tier embraces monetary union, deep economic integration, and the leadership of France and Germany, while the other member states participate (and have say over) much less. While such an outcome might in fact strengthen France within the European Union, the danger is that this step will in fact undermine the European Union as a whole, leaving all member states worse off in the long run. France has long sought to reconcile its concerns over its national power with its support for the European Union, which by definition is meant to erode sovereignty. The proposed plan for federalism may be the ticket to square this difference, but it could also destroy the very body that France sees as a way to assert its power in Europe. The victory of the strongly pro–European Union Emmanuel Macron over the anti-EU Marine Le Pen in the 2017 presidential election would appear to strengthen France's commitment to European unity, and may stem the tide of anti-EU sentiment both within France and throughout Europe.

CURRENT ISSUES IN FRANCE

Challenges to French National Identity and the Rise of the Nationalist Right

The economic downturn across Europe and the surge of high-profile terrorist attacks in France in 2015 and 2016 have raised fears among many Europeans and outside observers that these difficulties will not just undermine the European Union but also lead to the emergence of populist, nationalist, and xenophobic forces across the continent.

The National Front (FN) was founded in 1972, but its pedigree can be traced back much further. Many observers look back to an earlier movement known as Poujadism, based on the ideas and leadership of Pierre Poujade. In 1953, Poujade, a small business owner and representative in local government in southern France, first took up political action in the form of a protest against what was seen as a confusing and heavy array of taxes against small businesses. On the surface, this kind of antitax revolt may be seen as similar to the kinds of protests on the left and right in the United States of late. Poujade's protest was not simply a stand against an unfair tax code, however, but a response to a series of rapid changes occurring in postwar France as the country moved away from small-scale business and agriculture to a greater focus on industrialization and urbanization directed by the state. Farmers, businesses, and small towns saw their way of life under threat as the country underwent a period of rapid modernization. Poujade's protest thus resonated with many who felt dislocated by the changes around them. By the mid-1950s, the Poujadist movement had spread across the country. In 1955, a mass rally in Paris attracted 100,000 people, and by 1956, the Poujadists had founded a political party—the Union et Fraternité Française (UFF)—and won nearly 12 percent of the votes and 52 seats in the National Assembly. The Poujadists drew supporters from both the left and right, in their criticism of state power as well as in their hostility toward large-scale capitalism.

When comparing the recent success of the National Front and the earlier Poujadists, we find parallels but also differences. Like the Poujadists, the FN has gained support because many French citizens feel threatened by social and economic changes that have accelerated over the last decade. The two most important changes are the rapid growth in immigration and the presence of a large Muslim minority, and France's integration into a more powerful European Union. A central platform of FN founder Jean-Marie Le Pen was opposition to immigration, which the party linked to crime, disorder, and the decline of a French identity and French values. Le Pen also exploited the tension over multiculturalism, asserting that the central problem with immigrants (especially Muslims) was that unlike past immigrants, they were unwilling to assimilate fully into the French nation. At times, Le Pen's arguments were unabashedly racist and anti-Semitic, claiming that such hostility was justified toward those who refused to be "truly" French. Under the leadership of his daughter, Marine Le Pen, the FN has adopted a hostile attitude to the European Union—the FN charges the European Union with being overly bureaucratic, views bureaucracy as a sign of all that is wrong with globalization, and blames it for the wave of immigration. Thus, the FN is calling for France to abandon the euro.

The FN has struggled to win seats in the National Assembly, mainly because of France's electoral system. But as we have seen, support for the party has grown steadily, and it placed first in the 2014 European elections (winning almost a quarter of the vote). It won 20 percent of the vote in the first round of the 2017 presidential elections and an FN-record high 33.9 percent in the second round.

For now, France's electoral system will likely continue to limit the FN from becoming a major force in the legislature. However, the continued and perhaps growing power of the party will mean that to win elections, the major parties on the left and right will need to contend with their views and even co-opt them. We can already see ample evidence that the FN has changed France's political landscape. During Sarkozy's presidency, legislation was passed banning the public wearing of the face veil, the full-face covering worn by some Muslim women (this policy was supported by and continued under President Hollande). In 2016, a number of local governments passed laws banning the "burkini" bathing suit (which covers almost the entire body) on public beaches, until the law was ruled unconstitutional by the courts.

In March 2014, after his Socialist party suffered serious losses to the UMP and FN in local elections, Hollande replaced his prime minister with Manuel Valls, known best for his vigorous enforcement of immigration laws during his stint as Hollande's interior minister. Valls supported the laws passed in 2016 to restrict the public wearing of the burkini swimsuit on French beaches, denouncing that swimsuit as a symbol of "fatal, retrograde Islamism."[37]

French president of the far right party Front National (FN) and candidate for the 2017 presidential election, Marine Le Pen speaks during her campaign rally on September 3, 2016, in Brachay, France. She won about a third of the vote in the second round of the 2017 presidential elections.

After the January and November 2015 terrorist attacks in Paris, most French politicians were careful to point out that the acts were not a representation of mainstream Islam. However, Le Pen, who has compared the Muslim presence in France to the Nazi occupation of the country in the 1940s, stated that the attack was carried out "in the name of radical Islam."

The rise of the FN exposes a deep contradiction in French society. On the one hand are France's republican ideals, rooted in the French Revolution and calling for political freedom, equality of all citizens, a strong national identity, and a strict separation of church and state (*laïcité*). On the other hand is a growing uneasiness about France's growing ethnic diversity, its integration into the European Union, and the need to adapt the "French model" to pressures of globalization. The fact that Marine Le Pen was able to make it to the second round of the 2017 presidential election is a sign that the FN has tapped into a deep well of discontent in France. But the FN's drubbing in the 2017 legislative elections shows that a strong majority of French voters continue to reject the FN's message.

The Future of the French Welfare State

What's wrong with France's welfare state? After all, other wealthy European social democracies like Germany, Sweden, and Norway have high taxes and high rates of social spending but have been able to sustain economic growth, high levels of employment, and international competitiveness.[38] France, in contrast, has suffered high unemployment rates (hovering around 10 percent since the 1980s) and has gone from having the world's 8th largest per capita GDP in 1980 down to number 19 by 2008. Private sector growth during that time averaged only 0.8 percent, the second lowest rate among the affluent capitalist democracies that are members of the Organisation for Economic Co-operation and Development (OECD), and the national debt almost tripled. Despite a steady increase in social spending during that period, France faced growing unrest among its poor, immigrant, and underemployed citizens. France's economic stagnation has led to widespread pessimism. In the words of one political scientist, France's "social and economic problems were shared by a handful of other rich European nations, but in no other was the gap between political ideals and social realities so pronounced."[39]

France's European social democratic peers all implemented major reforms of their welfare states in the 1980s and 1990s. They restructured pension and taxation systems, made it easier for employers to hire and fire workers, and trimmed their welfare bureaucracies. Why haven't such reforms prospered in France?

Part of the answer lies in the peculiar nature and rigidity of France's welfare state. Unlike its social democratic counterparts, France has some of the strongest legal protections for its employed workers. These laws make it difficult to lay off workers, in turn making French employers wary of hiring new ones. France's social spending has increased more rapidly than in other social democracies—and, more important, most of that spending went to the already employed middle class. France had one of the world's costliest welfare states that benefited the two-thirds of the population that least needed social benefits. While depriving the poorest French of needed social spending, this system created a solid majority of French citizens who benefit from, and who have opposed any attempt to roll back, France's welfare state.

French political culture became another obstacle to reform. Advocates of implementing the types of welfare reforms that were successful in Scandinavia, Germany, and elsewhere were often portrayed as advocates of globalization and enemies of "the French model." This criticism has come from both the French left and rising French right.

In an attempt to revive France's sclerotic economy, Nicolas Sarkozy campaigned for the presidency in 2007 on a platform of major reform to France's welfare state. He called for a smaller and more efficient public sector, an increase in the retirement age, a reform of French labor laws, and a reduction in taxes. Armed with a strong electoral mandate and a majority in the legislature, Sarkozy might have been expected to implement a significant modernization of France's welfare state. Instead, and despite some relatively minor successes, the reform project stalled. By the end of Sarkozy's term, an additional 1 million people were unemployed, the national debt had skyrocketed, and the poverty rate had increased significantly. What happened?

While it is tempting to blame Sarkozy's failure on the global economic crisis that coincided with his term in office, a better explanation can be found in French politics, the strength of vested interest groups, and the way that French politics reflected French political culture.

A good example was Sarkozy's proposal to raise the retirement age (and receipt of a pension) from 60 to 62—still well below the OECD average (Germany and Denmark had raised their retirement age from 65 to 67). The proposal provoked widespread opposition from a broad cross section of French society, including the trade union movement and even sectors of Sarkozy's own party. Polls showed that 73 percent of voters on the left, but also almost half of voters on the right, wanted to keep the retirement age at 60.

In short, the French public supported the *idea* of welfare state reform by electing Sarkozy in 2007, but it vigorously resisted attempts to implement reforms.

Although France's welfare state was clearly too costly and inefficient (not to mention insufficiently directed toward France's poor), too many French citizens stood to lose from welfare state reform. Frustrated by societal resistance to his proposed reform, under attack from both the left and the right, and eager to win reelection, Sarkozy soon abandoned much of his reform agenda.

Nevertheless, at some point France will need to undertake a reform of its welfare state. Even François Hollande, who campaigned in 2012 against the Sarkozy reforms and advocated instead a series of tax hikes on the wealthy and an increase in social spending, realized that the current model is unsustainable. And, as we have seen, in May 2016 Hollande's government proposed a major overhaul of the country's restrictive labor laws. President Hollande employed a rarely used decree power to impose the law and avoid a vote in the lower house, provoking outrage from within his own party and strikes and protests throughout the country. Emmanuel Macron, elected president in May 2017, was an economics minister under President Hollande, and was responsible for designing the law. Macron's appointment of Édouard Philippe, a center-right politician with experience in the private sector, as well as Macron's ability to win a majority in the legislature, suggest that efforts to reform France's welfare state are likely to continue.

NOTES

1. Rolf H. W. Theen and Frank L. Wilson, *Comparative Politics: An Introduction to Seven Countries* (Upper Saddle River, NJ: Prentice-Hall, 2001), 101.

2. Britain has no single document defining its democratic regime but has a constitutional order dating at least to the seventeenth century. The United States has had only one constitution, which it has amended only 26 times in more than two centuries. Japan has never changed its postwar constitution.

3. Pew Research Center for the People and the Press, www.pewglobal.org/2013/05/13/the-new -sick-man-of-europe-the-european-union/ (accessed 2/17/15).

4. For a useful discussion of these contributions, see James B. Collins, *The State in Early Modern France* (Cambridge, UK: Cambridge University Press, 1995).

5. Malcolm Crook and John Dunne, "Napoléon's France: History and Heritage," *Modern and Contemporary France* 8 (2000): 429–31.

6. John Hellman, "Memory, History, and National Identity in Vichy France," *Modern and Contemporary France* 9 (2001): 37–42.

7. For more, see Serge Bernstein, *The Republic of de Gaulle, 1958–1969* (Cambridge, UK: Cambridge University Press, 1993).

8. Robert Elgie, "The French Presidency," in *Developments in French Politics*, 5th ed., ed. Alistair Cole, Sophie Meunier, and Vincent Tiberj (London: Palgrave MacMillan, 2013), 19–34.

9. From 1958 to 1962, presidents were indirectly elected by an electoral college composed of elected officials. De Gaulle sought direct election of the presidency to enhance both his power and that of the institution of the presidency.

10. Robert Elgie, *The Role of the Prime Minister in France, 1981–1991* (New York: St. Martin's Press, 1993).

11. On the French legislature, see Sylvain Brouard, Olivier Costa, and Eric Kerrouche, "The 'New' French Parliament: Changes and Continuities," in Cole et al., *Developments in French Politics*, 35–52.

12. John Lichfield, "Sarkozy's Military Plans 'Put Independence at Risk,'" *Independent*, April 9, 2008, www.independent.co.uk (accessed 1/19/09).

13. Alec Stone, *The Birth of Judicial Politics in France* (New York: Oxford University Press, 1992).

14. Ironically, one reason France returned to single-member districts was that proportional representation gave the far right National Front its first representation in the legislature, a result that dismayed the mainstream parties.

15. On French local government, see Alistair Cole and Romain Pasquier, "Local and Regional Governance," in Cole et al., *Developments in French Politics*, 69–87.

16. An excellent overview of the PS is by Frédéric Sawicki, "Political Parties: The Socialists and the Left," in Cole et al., *Developments in French Politics*, 104–19.

17. Raymond Kuhn, "Mister Unpopular: François Hollande and the Exercise of Presidential Leadership, 2012–2014," *Modern and Contemporary France* 22, no. 4 (2014): 435–57.

18. James McAuley, "France's Hollande Is So Unpopular That His Own Party May Not Support Him," *Washington Post*, April 16, 2016, www.washingtonpost.com/world/europe/frances-hollande-so-unpopular-that-maybe-his-own-party-wont-support-him/2016/04/15/264bcf66-018d-11e6-8bb1-f124a43f84dc_story.html (accessed 5/30/16).

19. On the UMP, see Florence Haegel, "Political Parties: The UMP and the Right," in Cole et al., *Developments in French Politics*, 88–103.

20. On Sarkozy's presidency, see Andrew Knapp, "A Paradoxical Presidency: Nicolas Sarkozy, 2007–2012," *Parliamentary Affairs* 66 (2013): 33–51.

21. Aurelien Mondon, "The National Front in the Twenty-First Century: From Pariah to Republican Contender?" *Modern and Contemporary France* 22, no. 3 (2014): 301–320.

22. James Shields, "Marine Le Pen and the 'New' FN: A Change of Style or of Substance," *Parliamentary Affairs* 66, no. 1 (January 2013): 186.

23. At http://stats.oecd.org/Index.aspx?DataSetCode=UN_DEN (accessed 6/27/14). For some comparative perspective, the figures for Germany and the United Kingdom are 18 percent and 26 percent, respectively.

24. A good overview of church-state relations in France is Herman Salton, "Unholy Union: History, Politics and the Relationship between Church and State in Modern France," in *Review of European Studies* 4, no. 5 (2012): 135–47.

25. For a discussion of the differences between the United States and France, see Robert A. Levine, "Assimilating Immigrants: Why America Can and France Cannot," Rand Occasional Paper (Santa Monica, CA: Rand Corporation, 2004).

26. Michèle Tribalat, "An Estimation of the Foreign-Origin Population of France in 1999," *Population* 59, no. 1 (2004): 49–79.

27. Vincent Tiberj and Laure Michon, "Two-tier Pluralism in 'Colour-blind' France," *West European Politics* 36, no. 3 (2013): 580–96.

28. Rahsaan Maxwell and Erik Bleich, "What Makes Muslims Feel French?" *Social Forces*, 93, no. 1 (September 2015): 155–79.

29. Robert Marquand, "France President Sarkozy Drops National Identity Debate," *Christian Science Monitor*, February 9, 2010, www.csmonitor.com/World/Europe/2010/0209/France-President-Sarkozy-drops-national-identity-debate (accessed 6/27/14).

30. Douglass C. North and Robert Paul Thomas, *The Rise of the Western World: A New Economic History* (Cambridge, UK: Cambridge University Press, 1973), ch. 10.
31. David S. Landes, *The Wealth and Poverty of Nations: Why Some Are So Rich and Some So Poor* (New York: W. W. Norton, 1998), 468.
32. Angus Maddison, *The World Economy: A Millennial Perspective* (Paris: OECD, 2001), 132, 185.
33. *International Comparisons of GDP per Capita and per Employed Person, 17 Countries, 1960–2008*, report prepared by Division of International Labor Comparisons, U.S. Bureau of Labor Statistics, July 28, 2009, www.bls.gov/fls/flsgdp.pdf (accessed 11/17/11).
34. José Bové and François Dufour, *The World Is Not for Sale: Farmers against Junk Food* (London: Verso, 2001).
35. See Hubert Vedrine, *France in an Age of Globalization* (Washington, DC: Brookings Institution, 2000); see also Philip Gordon and Sophie Meunier, *The French Challenge: Adapting to Globalization* (Washington, DC: Brookings Institution, 2001).
36. "Désillusion," *Economist*, November 16, 2013, www.economist.com/node/21589895/print (accessed 6/26/14).
37. At www.apnewsarchive.com/2016/National-Front-leader-Marine-Le-Pen-says-the-overturning-of-a-ban-on-burkinis-in-a-French-Mediterranean-town-is-not-surprising-but-the-battle-is-not-over/id-dd465614837349caa0686ea0a0065f6c (accessed 8/27/16).
38. This discussion draws heavily on the analysis of Timothy B. Smith, "France in Crisis? Economic and Welfare Policy Reform," in Cole et al., *Developments in French Politics*, 186–202.
39. Smith, "Welfare Policy Reform," 186.

KEY TERMS

absolute monarchy The stage in the evolutionary development of Europe between the more decentralized feudal monarchies of the Middle Ages and the constitutional governments of the modern era

ancien régime European "old order" of absolute monarchy buttressed by religious authority

blocked vote A vote that forces the legislature to accept bills in their entirety and allows amendments only if approved by the government

Chirac, Jacques President of France from 1995 to 2007

code law Law derived from detailed legal codes rather than from precedent

cohabitation An arrangement in which presidents lacking a majority of legislative power appoint an opposition prime minister who can gain a majority of support in the legislature

Constitutional Council Body empowered to rule on any constitutional matter at the request of the government, the heads of each house of the legislature, or a group of at least 60 members of either house

Council of Ministers The cabinet selected by the prime minister

coup d'état Forceful and sudden overthrow of a government

dirigisme An emphasis on state authority in economic development; a combination of social-democratic and mercantilist ideas

École Nationale d'Administration (ENA) National Administrative School; a state educational institution whose primary mission is to train civil servants

Estates General Weak French assembly before the French Revolution, representing the clergy, nobles, and commoners

the Events of May Parisian riots of 1968 in which students and workers called for educational and social reforms

Fifth Republic France's current regime (1958–present)

four-party, two-bloc system A system requiring coalition building in the second round of the two-round single-member district system

French Communist Party (PCF) One of the dominant parties of the French left since the end of World War II

French Democratic Labor Confederation (CFDT) A smaller confederation backed by the Socialist Party

French Revolution Overthrow in 1789–99 of French absolute monarchy and establishment of the First Republic

French Socialist Party (PS) Dominant party of the French left

General Confederation of Labor (CGT) Most powerful French union confederation; linked to the French Communist Party

Hollande, François Socialist president of France from 2012 to 2017

laïcité The subordination of religious identity to state and national identity—state over church

Le Pen, Marine Daughter of Jean-Marie Le Pen and leader of the National Front since 2011

Macron, Emmanuel A young and relatively inexperienced centrist economist, elected president in 2017

Mitterrand, François Leader of the French Socialist Party starting in 1971; president of France from 1981 to 1995

motion of censure An act of legislature against the government, requiring new elections when proposed legislation submitted as matters of confidence are not passed

National Assembly Lower house of the French parliament

National Front (FN) A political party on the far right that was created by Jean-Marie Le Pen in 1972

pantouflage Literally "putting on of the slippers"; refers to the move of the administrative elite from the bureaucracy to the top echelons of the private sector

parlement France's bicameral legislature

populism A political view that does not have a consistent ideological foundation, but that emphasizes hostility toward elites and established state and economic institutions and favors greater power in the hands of the public

prefect Government-appointed local official

prime minister Leader appointed by the French president and approved by the majority of the lower house of the legislature to select a cabinet and preside over the day-to-day affairs of government

Rally for the Republic (RPR) Party formed by Jacques Chirac as the more nationalist, socially conservative, Euroskeptic force of the French right

regime Norms and rules that govern politics

Reign of Terror Seizure of power and class war launched by radical Jacobins in revolutionary France (1793–94)

Republicans The main party of the French right, and a renaming of the Union for a Popular Movement

Sarkozy, Nicolas President of France from 2007 to 2012

semi-presidential A legislative–executive system that shares political power among the legislature, a directly elected president, and a prime minister responsible to *both* the president and the legislature

Sénat France's 348 member upper house of the legislature

Union for a Popular Movement (UMP) A single cohesive party of the center right formed in 2002 with Chirac's encouragement, which has since been renamed the Republicans.

Union for French Democracy (UDF) An alliance of five center-right parties founded in 1978 by Chirac's rival and former president Valéry Giscard d'Estaing as a more neoliberal force of the French right

WEB LINKS

- Assemblée nationale (www.assemblee-nat.fr)
- Constitutional Council (www.conseil-constitutionnel.fr)
- *Le Monde diplomatique* (www.mondediplo.com)
- Ministry of Foreign Affairs (www.diplomatie.gouv.fr/en)
- President's website (www.elysee.fr/)
- Prime minister's website (premier-ministre.gouv.fr/en)

5

Deutschland ist stark.
Und soll es bleiben.

CDU
Gemeinsam

A 2013 CDU campaign poster featuring Chancellor Angela Merkel. It reads: "CDU: Successful Together" and "Germany is strong. And shall remain so." After the September 2017 general elections, Merkel was preparing to begin her fourth term as German chancellor.

GERMANY

Why Study This Case?

Germany commands a prominent position in the world and a pivotal position in Europe. It is Europe's largest and the world's third-largest exporting nation, Europe's biggest economy, the European Union's most populous country, and an integral member of Europe's economic, political, and security organizations. Situated in the heart of the Continent, Germany today in many ways typifies the political, social, and cultural values and institutions of Europe and offers a useful window into the political institutions and public policies shared broadly by many of its European neighbors. By and large, Germans embrace social-democratic political and economic values, champion postmaterialist concerns for the environment, the pursuit of leisure, and human rights, and vigorously promote European integration even as they seek to enhance the competitiveness of Germany's capitalist economy and to strengthen Germany's national security. But in other fundamental ways, Germany sits apart from its European neighbors and poses interesting puzzles for the comparative political scientist.

Unlike many of its western and northern European counterparts, the German state is federal; sovereignty and nationhood came very late to Germany. The modern institution of the nation-state finds its origin in Europe, in no small part with the 1648 Peace of Westphalia, which affirmed the principle of national sovereignty at the end of Europe's bloody Thirty Years' War. But even though this treaty was inked on German soil, it would take another 220 years before a German nation-state was established. Once forged in the nineteenth century, German nationalism took on powerful and ultimately virulent and destructive force in the twentieth century at the hands of Nazi fascists. The disastrous consequences of this hypernationalism led the allies who defeated Germany to divide the nation in 1945, a division perpetuated for over three decades by the Cold War. Despite reunification of East and West Germany in 1990, many Germans today remain hesitant to promote nationalism and

GERMANY

are among Europe's strongest advocates of greater European integration and of the European Union. Although it can claim a thoroughly Western and European heritage, German modernization in many ways better resembles the experience of Japan than that of Britain, France, or the United States. Germany is a latecomer to both modern capitalism and democracy, both of them imposed externally.

The very successes of German industrialization, democratization after World War II, and peaceful reunification have left the country uncertain about its future. Globalization poses new challenges to Germany's vaunted welfare state. Immigration has raised old questions about race and national identity; the end of the Cold War changed Germany's role as a linchpin of East-West relations; and the expansion of the European Union eastward has weakened the central role that the country historically played in that organization. Germany remains a major power, but its role in the post–Cold War international system seems muted, a reflection of a country still troubled by its past and uncertain what future responsibilities it must shoulder.

Major Geographic and Demographic Features

With an area slightly smaller than that of Montana or Japan, even reunified Germany cannot be considered large on a global scale. But its substantial population (more than 80 million), economic vitality, and location in the heart of Europe have placed it at the center of European affairs for many centuries.

German topography has enhanced this centrality. Situated on the plains of northern Europe, Germany shares contiguous borders with nine European countries. Except for the Alps to the south and the Baltic and North seas to the north, Germany possesses no natural boundaries. Unlike England, Japan, and even France, which historically have relied upon natural barriers to offer them protection from foreign predators and to create a strong sense of national identity, Germany traditionally found itself externally vulnerable and internally divided. Its central location, accessibility, and internal incoherence meant that many of Europe's conflicts over the centuries were carried out on German soil and that Germans, unlike the British or Americans, did not have the luxury to remain aloof from the military and political affairs that surrounded and too often engulfed them. This predation by foreign armies only perpetuated Germany's continued political disunity, its sense of vulnerability, and its propensity for military preparedness.

Often the victim of foreign affairs, the German state, once it finally achieved political unity and military capacity in the nineteenth century, took its defense into its own hands and at times engaged in aggressive expansion. A lack of natural resources—much of Germany's coal, iron, and some of its most productive farmland is located in disputed border regions—also inspired German imperialism and military aggression as a means of obtaining resources. The German empire's role in the late nineteenth-century "scramble for Africa" and Nazi Germany's call for Lebensraum ("living space") were justified in these terms. This same sense of vulnerability and the bitter lessons learned from nearly a century of aggression have also propelled postwar German overtures for European integration. Just as Germans in the nineteenth century recognized that German safety and interests were well served by unification, Germans in the postwar era have concluded that German and European security and prosperity are well served by the peaceful integration of Europe.

The absence of geographical barriers also encouraged the migration of Germans and the diffusion of German culture into surrounding regions over time. These German migrants spread the German language and culture well beyond the boundaries of what now constitutes Germany. What at times became bitter conflicts over disputed territories with France (Alsace-Lorraine), Denmark (Schleswig), Czechoslovakia (Sudetenland), and Poland (Silesia) stemmed in no small part from the diffusion of ethnic groups and rival claims to these border regions.[1] The absence of natural borders has also meant that language, physical characteristics, and shared cultural values have been more important national markers in Germany than elsewhere, a cultural theme enhanced and elaborated by German intellectuals over the centuries. Germany's population is aging rapidly, a challenge that has been only partially mitigated by a recent surge in immigration. Although it now hosts Europe's largest immigrant population, Germany today remains quite homogeneous. Over 90 percent of the population is ethnically German, ethnic Turks make up 2.4 percent, and various other European nationalities the remaining 6 percent.

Historical Development of the State

The economic, social, and political forces that swept modernization through much of Western Europe trickled far more slowly into the region we now know as Germany. National unity, industrialization, and democracy all came later to Germany than to its western European neighbors.

Scholars agree that this relative backwardness profoundly shaped the German state. In France and England, feudalism gave way to states centralized by absolute monarchies that established standardized legal and administrative systems and fostered a coherent sense of nationalism. By contrast, national sovereignty and a centralized state eluded Germany until the nineteenth century. Although the German state was long in coming, once established, it loomed very large in Germany's rush to modernize.[2] As the idea of a German nation became institutionalized in a sovereign state, this unity born of national identity gained powerful force. Centuries of decentralization and disunity gave way to intense periods of authoritarian militarism and mercantilism, first under the leadership of the state of Prussia in the late nineteenth century and again under Nazi direction in the 1930s and 1940s. This relatively late unification and catch-up economic development meant that development of the state preceded industrialization, which fostered this state-led mercantilist development and authoritarianism.

Relative backwardness also placed Germany behind in the race for colonies and raw materials to feed industrialization. That status fostered a voracious and aggressive imperialism that led ultimately to the **Third Reich** (empire), fascist Nazi expansionism, and military defeat. As a democratic and decentralized federal state no longer plagued by disunity, postwar Germany vigorously promoted European integration and pursued a costly program of complete German unification. As the original German and French architects of integration hoped, the success of the European Union has largely tempered fears that a reunified Germany would pursue militarist expansionism or any undue unilateral political influence.

The Absence of a Strong Central State during the Holy Roman Empire, 800–1806

In 800 C.E., Charlemagne founded in western and central Europe what came to be known as the Holy Roman Empire. By the middle of the ninth century, a collection of German, Austrian, and Czech princes acquired nominal control of this loosely constituted empire, or **reich**. As a feudal empire, it encompassed an odd assortment of hundreds of principalities, city-states, and other local political entities with varying degrees of autonomy and legitimacy, but there was virtually no allegiance to the center. This weak confederation waxed and waned in size and influence over the next 1,000 years, persisting until the time of Napoleon in the nineteenth century. Whereas comparable feudalism gave way to centralized states in England and France, the Holy Roman Empire remained politically fragmented.

TIMELINE OF POLITICAL DEVELOPMENT

YEAR	EVENT
800–900 C.E.	Loose confederation of German principalities forms Holy Roman Empire; later known as the First Reich.
1871	Otto von Bismarck unifies Germany; later dubbed Second Reich.
1918	Germany defeated in World War I.
1919	Weimar Republic formed under difficult conditions.
1933	Hitler and Nazis rise to power, establishing the Third Reich.
1945	Hitler and Nazis defeated in World War II.
1945–49	Germany divided among Allies into four occupied zones.
1948	Berlin blockade and airlift takes place.
1949	Federal Republic of Germany (FRG) founded in the west and German Democratic Republic (GDR) in the east.
1952	FRG joins European Coal and Steel Community.
1955	FRG joins NATO, and GDR joins Warsaw Pact.
1957	FRG participates in founding of European Economic Community.
1961	Berlin Wall constructed.
1969	FRG Chancellor Willy Brandt launches policy of *Ostpolitik*.
1989	Berlin Wall falls.
1990	Germany unified as GDR is incorporated into FRG.
1993	Germany becomes a founding member of the European Union.
2005	Angela Merkel elected to first of four terms as chancellor.

The empire took political form with the office of a weak emperor, which rotated among princes, and the imperial Reichstag, or "Congress." This precursor to the contemporary German parliament began as a royal court composed of prominent princes and dukes who met irregularly to elect the emperor. By the fifteenth century, the Reichstag had become slightly more representative, and lesser princes and free cities also were seated. However, the dominant princes, lesser princes, and urban representatives met in separate bodies, which made the Reichstag more divided, weaker, and less representative than its British counterpart. Indeterminate boundaries, centuries of entrenched localism, and mutual suspicions and prejudices among these localities hampered any efforts at unification.

Although religion had earlier served an important role in unifying much of Europe under the banner of Christianity, by the sixteenth century it, too, had become a divisive force within the Holy Roman Empire in the form of the Protestant Reformation. In 1517, the German monk and professor Martin Luther publicly displayed his writ of complaints about certain Catholic practices and doctrines. Among many other significant outcomes, this revolt split the previously religiously unified Holy Roman Empire and its German core. This religious divide took on political significance. It led to separate and often competing state churches in German locales, giving new sources of legitimacy to the local chieftains and additional justification for resisting unification. The Reformation also touched off the Thirty Years' War (1618–48), a religious conflict between Catholics and Protestants that was fought largely on German soil. For reasons beyond religion, the protracted war came to envelop most of Europe before ending with the Peace of Westphalia in 1648. This settlement affirmed the sovereignty of local political entities, thereby preserving decentralized German authority and further weakening the Holy Roman Empire.

Unification of the German State, the Rise of Prussia, and the Second Reich, 1806–1918

Napoleon's invasion of Germany in 1806 effectively destroyed the empire, inadvertently began the process of German unification, and unleashed the forces of German nationalism that would ultimately lead to the rise of Nazi fascism. Napoleon's offensive wiped out many of the empire's sovereign principalities (there were some 300 at the time) and compelled others to merge with their larger neighbors for protection. Ultimately, only **Prussia** to the east and Austria to the south were strong enough to resist Napoleon's onslaught and avoid inclusion in the confederation of defeated territories he formed. After Napoleon's defeat in 1815, German allies under Prussian leadership set up a loose confederation of some 40 sovereign mini-states that created for the first time the semblance of a German state.

Over the course of the eighteenth and nineteenth centuries, the kingdom of Prussia in eastern Germany gradually acquired the autonomy, capacity, and legitimacy that allowed it to emerge as a viable core for a modern German state.

A series of generally enlightened monarchs established an authoritarian state administered by an efficient and loyal bureaucratic staff, supported by a conservative and wealthy landed aristocracy known as the **Junkers**, and defended by a large and well-trained standing army. (Voltaire once commented that "while some states have an army, the Prussian army has a state.") Just as important as the state's monopoly on violence was its mercantilist promotion of economic growth through the development of national infrastructure, the expansion of education among its subjects, and the enhancement of trade. Prussia established a customs union with neighboring German states that by 1834 included all but Austria. This highly capable and autonomous state managed to defend itself from aggressors, expand its territory, grow its economy, and thereby enhance its legitimacy beyond Prussia as it successfully competed with Austria for ascendancy in unifying Germany.

That this unification was not accompanied by greater liberalization in the political regime can be explained in part by the relative weakness of Germany's commercial and industrial middle class. Much as in China during the early twenty-first century, the educated and intellectual elite of nineteenth-century German society comprised fewer merchants and entrepreneurs and more bureaucrats, judges, and professors, most of them employed by the state. Though modern in its thinking and in many ways even liberal in its outlook, this portion of society saw the state (in its hands) as a positive and essential instrument in building German national unity, wealth, and power. German intellectuals argued that individual freedom was a luxury or indeed a weakness not fit for the forging of German national identity. It would be militarist and mercantilist "blood and iron," not liberal elections, that would unify Germany.

By the 1860s, Prussia had forceful and capable leadership, a powerful military, and a growing industrial economy. Impressive war victories over Denmark, Austria, and ultimately France drew other German states into the cause and led, in 1871, to the establishment of a national German empire, or what came to be known as the Second Reich. Although the Prussian king was crowned emperor of all Germany, the key figure in the process of expansion and unification was Count Otto von Bismarck, prime minister, or chancellor, of Prussia. A politician, military officer, and member of the Junker landed class, he led a so-called revolution from above in which regime change came not from the lower, disenfranchised classes, but rather from an alliance of "iron and rye"—meaning the industrialists and the landed aristocracy. Through the savvy use of diplomacy, war, and political machinations, the Iron Chancellor, as Bismarck came to be known, dominated German politics for two decades and brought about the first unified modern German state.

Not surprisingly, unified Germany's first national constitution established an authoritarian monarchy with only the trappings of liberal democracy. Sovereignty remained vested in the emperor, or kaiser (derived from the Latin *Caesar*), and political power flowed from him. Although the constitution established a federal structure in which all the states were to have equal influence (a nod to the long-standing regional autonomy of the German states), it ensured the dominance of Prussia by mandating that the Prussian prime minister always become imperial chancellor. Similarly, although the constitution gave nominal deference to the notion of political equality (thus addressing the demands of the small but growing liberal middle class) by granting universal male suffrage for elections to the Reichstag, it retained aristocratic privilege in Prussian state elections. In addition, the imperial chancellor, the bureaucracy, and the military answered only to the emperor as head of state, not to the constitution. The emperor appointed the imperial chancellor, and the Reichstag could not dismiss the government. The emperor, chancellor, and their unelected administrators controlled foreign affairs and the military.

The Iron Chancellor took no chances that the constitution's nominal democratic allowances would get in the way of his forced-draft modernization drive. Bismarck bullied or circumvented the Reichstag in those few areas where it did have some authority (such as the budget). He encouraged the creation of multiple political parties and then skillfully played them off one another. Through the promotion of patriotism and German culture and the expansion of national wealth and empire, Bismarck enhanced the popularity and legitimacy of his authoritarian rule. The core of this support remained the landed gentry, military, and industrial elite, but the middle and lower classes were "largely swept along" by growing prosperity and appeals to national pride as Germany's international stature grew.[3] Groups opposing Bismarck's authoritarian rule (including Catholics, liberals, social democrats, and Marxists) were met at times with coercion and other times co-optation. This policy of an "iron fist in a velvet glove" kept the peace through the deft use of both violence and the granting of social welfare benefits such as health insurance and old-age pensions.

But if democracy found infertile ground in modernizing Prussia, catch-up industrialization proved much more successful. In 1890, Bismarck was eased out of office, and Emperor Kaiser Wilhelm II assumed personal control, continuing the policy of rapid industrialization and imperialist expansion. By the early twentieth century, Germany had surpassed Britain in iron production and become a leading industrial power. Society became more complex as both the middle and working classes grew in size and political strength, and the socialist movement captured one-third of German votes by 1912. As socialist opposition grew, some traditional sectors of German society, such as small-scale capitalists and landed aristocrats, embraced nationalism and anti-Semitism.

German patriotism, however, prevailed over these social divisions and differences. Frustrations associated with Germany's efforts to expand its empire and suspicions about the intentions of its neighbors stoked feelings of nationalism and unfulfilled destiny and contributed to German willingness to bring about World War I (1914–18). But as the war pressed on and took a particularly heavy toll on Germany, the social differences once again rose to the surface. Political liberals, Catholics, and others began to question openly why they had lent their support to an authoritarian government waging war against countries that provided their citizens democratic rights. Workers wondered why they could fight and die but not have an equal vote in the parliament. As the war ground to its bitter conclusion, the emperor made assurances of reform, but these promises offered too little and came too late. German defeat in 1918, combined with urban uprisings, prompted the emperor to abdicate and proclaim Germany a republic.

Political Polarization and the Breakdown of Democracy during the Weimar Republic, 1919–33

The political vacuum that followed the collapse of the Second Reich proved to be particularly infertile ground for the establishment of Germany's first republic. One scholar concluded that with radical Communists on the left, reactionary monarchists and militarists on the right, and no historical experience with liberal democracy, German society could claim "virtually no republicans."[4] No one was prepared for the sudden departure of the emperor, and few had considered how Germany ought to be constituted as a republic with no monarchy. The seeds of cynicism and elitism sown in this era would grow into the extremism and fascist totalitarianism that spelled the republic's doom in less than two decades.

In the face of these and other difficulties, an elected assembly met in the city of Weimar in 1918 to draft a constitution. Promisingly, most of the socialists retreated from their revolutionary goals and participated in the process. The **Weimar Republic** featured a remarkably democratic constitution that offered universal suffrage for all adults (ahead of both Britain and the United States), universal health insurance and pensions, and the right to employment or to unemployment compensation. Drafters of the constitution looked to the British parliamentary system as a model, retaining a bicameral parliament with a strong, popularly elected lower house (Reichstag) and a weaker upper chamber (Reichsrat) representing the states. But, in a measure that ultimately doomed the republic, they mistakenly saw the British monarch as the key to that system's stability and replaced the German kaiser with a strong president. This choice resulted in a dual executive, semi-presidential system (similar to the current Russian and French systems) in which the president as head of state was directly and popularly elected, could nominate the chancellor as head of government, and could rule through emergency decree under threatening circumstances.

The Weimar Republic also adopted a proportional representation (PR) electoral system for the Reichstag that specified no minimum threshold of votes and thus fostered a proliferation of parties, many of them small and representing narrow interests. This meant that no party ever won an outright majority in the Reichstag, and increasingly, weak and short-lived coalitions became the norm. Between 1919 and 1933, Germany had more than 20 governments, often functioning as minority coalitions unable to cobble together a majority of seats.

By the mid-1920s, Weimar Germany had achieved some stability. Moderate parties in the center managed to counterbalance the more radical and reactionary fringes (including a failed coup attempt in 1923 by a young firebrand reactionary named Adolf Hitler). The Weimar Republic faced anything but ordinary circumstances, however, and struggled with internal and external challenges that might have doomed even the most stable and resilient regime.[5] These challenges included the humiliation and burden of the Treaty of Versailles concluding World War I, which imposed upon Germany billions of dollars in reparations, military demobilization, the forfeiting of portions of German territory to France, and the loss of Germany's overseas colonies. Moreover, the Weimar Republic faced devastating hyperinflation brought on by war reparations and postwar economic turmoil (the inflation rate at one point in 1923 was 26 billion percent) as well as the consequences of the Great Depression, which caused widespread unemployment in Germany (nearly a third of German workers were unemployed by 1932).

Those opposed to the Weimar regime were able to blame for all these ills the democratic parties that had authored the constitution. A threatened middle class, defeated soldiers, and unemployed workers all proved ripe for recruitment into extreme nationalist and radical Communist movements as the Weimar Republic began to unravel. By 1930, moderate center parties favoring liberal democracy had lost their majority in parliament. Germany's Communist Party, which received only 2 percent of the popular vote in the 1920 Reichstag election, had by 1932 garnered 17 percent. In 1928, the **National Socialist (Nazi) Party**, led by **Adolf Hitler** and running on a platform of militarism and anti-Semitism, commanded less than 3 percent of the vote, but by 1932 it had obtained 37 percent, the highest total for any party during the Weimar period.

Under conditions of increasing instability, German state capacity weakened as violence replaced legislative politics and Communist and Nazi militias fought regularly in the streets. Following the 1932 election, conservative president Paul von Hindenburg and his nationalist supporters faced the difficult choice of forming a coalition government in alliance with moderate parties against the Nazis, declaring martial law and attempting to forcibly shut down the Nazis, or allying with Hitler and the Nazis in an effort to tame them. Hindenburg chose the latter option. In 1933, Hitler used this alliance and mounting disorder first to secure the office of chancellor and then to gain passage of the Enabling Act. The act yielded the Reichstag's powers to the chancellor, effectively dissolving the constitution and bringing the Weimar Republic to an end.

Fascist Totalitarianism under the Third Reich, 1933–45

Unfettered by constitutional restrictions, Hitler moved swiftly to establish the Third Reich, replacing the democratic institutions of the Weimar Republic with those of a Nazi-led fascist totalitarian regime. Although the term *fascism* is often misused to describe the ideologies or motives underpinning various authoritarian regimes and political movements, the term accurately describes the corporatist (rejecting individual freedom), hierarchical (rejecting social equality), and hypernationalist values driving Hitler's Nazi Party. The Nazis imprisoned political opponents, required a loyalty oath of all civil servants, banned opposition political parties, and placed all social organizations, including clubs and churches, under restrictions or direct party control. Hitler employed state terror and a state-supervised mercantilist economy to achieve the regime's ideological goals of restoring German national power, expanding the German empire, and destroying those political ideologies and ethnic groups that threatened his vision of Aryan supremacy.

In hindsight, it is difficult to understand how a totalitarian political regime with such reprehensible means and ends could be successful, popular, and even legitimate. For many Germans facing social chaos and economic collapse, the stability, order, and national wealth and pride Hitler promised were far more important values than either freedom or equality. Hitler identified and vilified scapegoats for Germany's ills, resurrected the depressed economy, and united the divided country. With extraordinary charisma, he delivered heroically and almost miraculously on his promises to rearm the nation, reclaim lost territories, and restore Germany's pride, power, and prestige. The Nazi propaganda machine effectively used pageantry and propaganda to amplify Hitler's inherent magnetism. As with other totalitarian regimes, such as Stalin's Russia and Mao's China, in Germany Hitler did not hesitate to use terror at the hands of an extensive security apparatus to intimidate opponents and destabilize and atomize society. In increasingly bold and aggressive measures, he rearmed Germany (in violation of the Treaty of Versailles), annexed Austria, occupied Czechoslovakia, and in 1939 invaded Poland, provoking World War II.

But by invading Russia in 1941, Hitler attempted one too many miracles and pushed Nazi aggression, racism, and ultimately genocide beyond the bounds that the world and, increasingly, Germans themselves would tolerate. As with Napoleon before him, Hitler's vaunted war machine proved no match for the harsh Russian winter or the bravery of the Russian people. But before the Nazi machine was ultimately defeated in 1945, it had exterminated some 6 million Jews and millions of other noncombatants on racial and ethnic grounds. The war killed more than 50 million people in Europe alone. Among those casualties was Hitler himself, who committed suicide in a Berlin bunker in 1945, a week before Russian, American, British, and French allies overran and occupied a defeated Germany.

Foreign Occupation and the Division of the German State, 1945–49

In 1945, Germany found itself utterly defeated. Its industry, infrastructure, society, and polity were completely in ruins. Germans often describe this complete institutional vacuum from which they would begin to rebuild as zero hour (*Stunde Null*), a starting from scratch. The German state surrendered sovereignty to the four Allied powers (Britain, France, Russia, and the United States), each of which occupied a portion of the country. The capital, Berlin, was similarly quartered. Territories that had been seized and annexed by the Nazis were carved off and returned to neighboring countries, and Poland annexed parts of Germany.

Although initial plans called for cooperation among the four occupying forces in moving toward the reestablishment of German sovereignty, the Cold War intervened, leading to a de facto division between the Soviet-occupied eastern zone and the regions in the west occupied by the other three powers. In an obvious step toward establishing a separate West German state, the three Western allies established a common currency for their three zones in 1948. The Soviet Union reacted by blocking land access from the West German sector into West Berlin (located in the eastern sector) that same year. Western allies in turn responded to this blockade with the Berlin Airlift, which delivered vital supplies to West Berlin by air for nearly a year. The Western allies also ordered the West Germans to convene a separate constitutional assembly, something the Germans were reluctant to do for fear such a move would permanently institutionalize a divided German state. This convention led not to a constitution (deemed too permanent) but to the **Basic Law**, which established the **Federal Republic of Germany (FRG)**—also called West Germany—in 1949 as a democratic and demilitarized state. The Soviets quickly responded by setting up the **German Democratic Republic (GDR)**—also called East Germany—in the same year. "Independence" for both German states did not, however, bring complete sovereignty; each Germany remained beholden to its Cold War patron, exercising what one scholar has labeled semi-sovereignty.[6] Both the United States and the Soviet Union reserved the right to control much of their respective client's foreign policy and even to intervene in domestic matters as deemed necessary, and neither patron fully relinquished that authority until the reunification of the German states in 1990.

In West Germany, as in defeated Japan, Western allies and German reformers took steps to weaken those institutions seen as responsible for Nazi militarism, including sweeping denazification. Reformers also devolved authority from the central state to Germany's federal regions and strengthened democratic institutions. The authors of the Basic Law reformed and broadened the party system to create fewer, larger parties and to encourage coalitions in an effort to prevent the emergence of narrowly defined interests and ideologies. These measures included uniting Catholics and Protestants in separate but like-minded wings of the newly established **Christian Democratic Union (CDU)**, healing a political divide that had persisted since the time of the Reformation in the sixteenth century.

In the context of the Cold War, the United States sought to rebuild the West German economy as an engine of economic revitalization for Western Europe. Like Japan, Germany took up this task of capitalist economic development with seemingly miraculous success, growing rapidly to become one of the wealthiest countries in the world. At the same time, strong democratic leadership brought stable constitutional democracy and a prosperous social democratic political economy to the Federal Republic. Effective chancellors included Konrad Adenauer (1949–63), who sought to integrate Germany into the Western alliance and bind it to its former military foes in Europe by joining the Coal and Steel Community and the North Atlantic Treaty Organization (NATO), and Willy Brandt (1969–74), who introduced a pragmatic policy of reconciliation with East Germany known as *Ostpolitik* ("eastern policy"). Despite political competition among thriving democratic parties, general consensus prevailed across the political spectrum, favoring domestic policies of comprehensive social welfare programs and a state-regulated marketplace as well as a foreign policy that promoted growing European integration and pragmatic measures to ease tensions with East Germany and ultimately embrace unification.

In the GDR, Stalinist totalitarianism replaced fascist totalitarianism. Because the Soviets blamed the capitalist system both in Germany and more globally as responsible for the Third Reich and both world wars, their first step was to eliminate East Germany's capitalist economy and replace it with a new socialist system presided over by a totalitarian Communist Party state. By the end of the 1940s, the eastern portion of Germany possessed political and economic systems almost identical to those of its Soviet mentor. With economic growth rates over the first two postwar decades nearly as impressive as those of its western counterpart, East Germany became the economic showcase of the Communist bloc. But like its Soviet mentor, the East German socialist economy ultimately could not keep pace with the capitalist West. Its failure to do so was demonstrated by the grim reality of life in the GDR. The East German state retained power by force and terror, manifested in its reliance on the *Stasi* ("secret police") to squelch dissent, the construction of the fortified Berlin Wall surrounding West Berlin in 1961, and the summary execution of those caught trying to flee to the West from East Berlin.[7]

Soviet leader Mikhail Gorbachev's efforts to revitalize Communist rule and the economy in the Soviet Union through his 1980s reforms had their more immediate effects not on the Soviet Union but on its central European allies, including East Germany. These political and economic reforms threatened to undermine the Stalinist foundation on which the East German system was built. In early 1989, Hungary opened its borders with Austria, and East Germans vacationing in Hungary quickly took advantage of this breach in the Iron Curtain to leave for the West. Over the next six months, some 2 percent of the East German population immigrated to West Germany. This movement led to a rapid weakening of the GDR's legitimacy and its capacity to control events. Gorbachev urged the East German leadership to follow the Soviet reforms, further threatening the regime as the entire Communist system seemed to be crumbling around them. As public protests in East Germany grew and the pace of the exodus to the West picked up, the economy ground to a halt and the party-state lost its capacity to govern. The East German leaders stepped down and on November 9, 1989, announced the opening of the border between East and West Berlin. Crowds swarmed both sides of the Berlin Wall as the gates were opened, and this tangible and iconic image of the beginning of the end of Germany's division and the collapse of the Iron Curtain was televised across the world.

Reunification of the German State, 1990–Present

The collapse of the East German state and the euphoria shared by all Germans propelled events much more rapidly than anyone could have anticipated. East and West German leaders prepared for a gradual process of thawing and increasing contacts, but it quickly became apparent that the only source of stability would be a quick process of unification. The flood of Germans migrating from East to West prompted hurried negotiations leading to full reunification in 1990, less than one year after the wall fell. In effect, **reunification** meant the incorporation of East Germany into the FRG, the adoption of the West German Basic Law as the constitution of a unified Germany, and the imposition of West Germany's capitalist economic system on East Germany. Although the Basic Law called for a new constitution and national referendum upon reunification, thus far no such action has been taken.

The 1990 merger probably averted a much more disastrous political implosion of East Germany, but the long-sought reunification proved much more difficult and costly than the early optimists had predicted. The initial euphoria of national unification gave way to the cold, hard reality of bringing together two sovereign nation-states that shared a language and a pre–World War II history and culture, but little else. The huge inequality in living standards, infrastructure, and income between the western and eastern portions of Germany has been tempered in the two decades since unification, but despite huge transfers of wealth, these inequalities are still not resolved. Since reunification, the government has spent nearly $2 trillion on eastern Germany in an effort to modernize its infrastructure and stabilize its economy. Following reunification, inefficient and bloated state-owned enterprises collapsed and shrank, leading to massive layoffs. Unemployment in the former East Germany remains higher than in the former West Germany. Likewise, while the gap in per capita wealth has narrowed since 1990, Germans living in the former West Germany are, on average, about 30 percent wealthier. Twenty-five years later, the vast majority of all Germans view reunification favorably.[8]

Political Regime

For students of political science, Germany's political regime since 1949 (often called the **Bonn Republic** because Bonn was West Germany's capital from 1949 to 1990) is a fascinating example of constitutional engineering. The republic's founders wanted to prevent the breakdown of democracy that doomed the Weimar Republic. Thus the Bonn Republic's architects sought a better balance between local and national power, between the legislature and the executive, between political stability and representative democracy, and between the power of the state and the rights of individuals. They created an innovative political system that also contained some elements of continuity with Germany's institutional past. The German political system has more checks and balances, and is thus less efficient and decisive than the British model, but to date it has proved remarkably stable and effective.[9]

Political Institutions

THE CONSTITUTION

The Basic Law (intended to serve as West Germany's temporary constitution until its unification with East Germany) was amended in 1990 to incorporate East German states and has become Germany's permanent constitution. The Basic Law is founded on five principles, designed to avoid both the chaos of the Weimar Republic and the authoritarianism of the Third Reich.[10] First, where Hitler destroyed the power of German states, the Bonn Republic Basic Law created a system of cooperative federalism, in which the federal government and state governments share power. Second, the Basic Law guaranteed an elaborate set of basic political, social, and economic rights. Third, to counter the powerful Weimar president, the Bonn Republic established a weak, indirectly elected head of state. Fourth, political power is concentrated in the head of government, the chancellor, elected by and directly responsible to the legislature. Fifth, the Bonn Republic established a powerful and independent judiciary to check the

---

ESSENTIAL POLITICAL FEATURES

- **Legislative–executive system:** Parliamentary

- **Legislature**: Parliament

  - **Lower house**: Bundestag (Federal Diet)

  - **Upper house**: Bundesrat (Federal Council)

- **Unitary or federal division of power**: Federal

- **Main geographic subunits**: *Länder* (states)

- **Electoral system for lower house**: Mixed single-member districts and proportional representation

- **Chief judicial body**: Federal Constitutional Court and Federal Court of Justice

government. Each of these constitutional features will be discussed in more depth in the following sections.

The Basic Law can be amended by a two-thirds majority in both houses. To prevent excessive concentration of state power, however, some constitutional features, such as Germany's federal system and individual rights, cannot be altered.

The Branches of Government

THE HEAD OF GOVERNMENT AND THE CABINET

German democracy is often referred to as chancellor democracy because the **federal chancellor**, or prime minister, is the most powerful political figure and the chief executive authority in Germany. The Basic Law made the office of the chancellor far more powerful vis-à-vis the head of state to create a stronger, more stable, and more democratic regime than the Weimar Republic.

As is typical in a parliamentary system, the lower house of the legislature (the Bundestag) elects the head of government, who has always been the leader of the largest party in the legislature. As the leader of the largest party or coalition, chancellors expect to see most of their government's policy proposals approved by the legislature. Chancellors appoint and oversee the cabinet, the group of ministers (currently 15) who head government departments. Cabinet ministers need not be members of the legislature (though most are). Chancellors may create or eliminate cabinet posts at will. Chancellor Helmut Kohl, for example, created a minister for the environment, conservation, and nuclear safety; his successor, Gerhard Schroeder, combined the ministries of economics and labor. Chancellors may fire cabinet ministers at any time, although chancellors who preside over coalition governments may threaten the stability of the government when dismissing a cabinet member from a party that is a coalition partner. Indeed, all German cabinets since 1949 have been coalitions of at least two parties, and coalition partners often designate their preferred candidates to occupy the cabinet posts allotted to them.

The actual power of German chancellors has varied over time, depending in part on their ability to dominate their own parties. Two recent German chancellors, Helmut Kohl and Gerhard Schroeder, were especially dominant political figures. Kohl was the unquestioned leader of his party, had few powerful rivals, and oversaw German reunification. Schroeder also came to dominate his party and his coalition partner, the Greens. Chancellors have at their disposal considerable

German Chancellors and Their Coalitions, 1949–2017

BUNDESTAG ELECTION YEAR	GOVERNING COALITION	CHANCELLOR (PARTY)
1949	CDU/CSU–FDP, DP	Konrad Adenauer (CDU)
1953	CDU/CSU–FDP, DP	Konrad Adenauer (CDU)
1957	CDU/CSU, DP	Konrad Adenauer (CDU)
1961	CDU/CSU–FDP	Konrad Adenauer (CDU) (to 1963) Ludwig Erhard (CDU)
1965	CDU/CSU–FDP (to 1966) CDU/CSU–SPD (1966–69)	Ludwig Erhard (CDU, 1965–66) Kurt Kiesinger (CDU, 1966–69)
1969	SPD–FDP	Willy Brandt (SPD)
1972	SPD–FDP	Willy Brandt (SPD, to 1974) Helmut Schmidt (SPD, to 1976)
1976	SPD–FDP	Helmut Schmidt (SPD)
1980	SPD–FDP (1980–82) CDU/CSU–FDP (1982–83)	Helmut Schmidt (SPD, 1980–82) Helmut Kohl (CDU)
1983	CDU/CSU–FDP	Helmut Kohl (CDU)
1987	CDU/CSU–FDP	Helmut Kohl (CDU)
1990	CDU/CSU–FDP	Helmut Kohl (CDU)
1994	CDU/CSU–FDP	Helmut Kohl (CDU)
1998	SPD–Greens	Gerhard Schroeder (SPD)
2002	SPD–Greens	Gerhard Schroeder (SPD)
2005	CDU/CSU–SPD	Angela Merkel (CDU)
2009	CDU/CSU–FDP	Angela Merkel (CDU)
2013	CDU/CSU–SPD	Angela Merkel (CDU)

Key to party acronyms:
CDU/CSU: Christian Democratic Union/Christian Social Union
DP: Deutsche Partei, conservatives
FDP: Free Democratic Party
SPD: Social Democratic Party

Note: As this text went to press in September 2017, the composition of Angela Merkel's coalition government was being negotiated.

resources, including the chief of the chancellery, a chief of staff with broad powers over the government. In addition to naming the cabinet, the chancellor makes numerous political appointments to government posts.

THE HEAD OF STATE

As in most parliamentary systems, in Germany the head of state (the **federal president**) is separate from the head of government. In contrast to the Weimar Republic, in which the substantial powers of a directly elected president were abused to facilitate Hitler's rise to power, the Basic Law makes the president an indirectly elected and mostly ceremonial figure who performs mainly symbolic tasks. The president may formally sign bills into law, must sign treaties, and can pardon convicted criminals—but usually takes such actions only at the behest of the chancellor. Presidents can, however, refuse to sign laws they believe contravene the constitution. (President Horst Köhler did so twice in 2006.) They formally nominate candidates to become chancellor but are expected to select the head of the majority party in the legislature or, absent a majority, the head of the largest party in the legislature. Those candidates, moreover, must receive a majority of votes in the lower house of the legislature. In the case of a badly fragmented legislature, the president could conceivably exercise some significant discretion in deciding on a nominee, but to date this situation has not occurred. Presidents also decide whether to dissolve the legislature and call new elections when there is no majority.

German presidents are elected for a maximum of two 5-year terms by a special Federal Convention that includes all members of the lower house of the legislature and an equal number of individuals selected by Germany's state legislatures. Presidents are intended to be consensus choices who are highly respected elder statesmen, and they are expected to behave in scrupulously nonpartisan fashion once in office.

The president from 2004 to 2010, Horst Köhler, was a highly respected conservative economist and former head of the International Monetary Fund. Köhler was a somewhat controversial president.[11] In 2006, he refused to sign a consumer information law passed by the legislature because he viewed the legislation as violating states' rights as enshrined in the Basic Law. He was narrowly reelected in May 2009, but resigned in May 2010 after he made controversial statements about Germany's overseas military deployments. He was replaced by another conservative, Christian Wulff, a former premier of the state of Lower Saxony and a close ally of Chancellor Merkel. Wulff became Germany's youngest president (he was 51 at the time) and was the first Catholic president in more than 40 years. In 2011, Wulff was forced to resign in response to allegations that he failed to disclose the receipt of a home loan from a businessman while he was a state premier and then attempted to intimidate the newspaper that broke the story. Joachim Gauck, an East German anti-communist opposition leader best known for his role of heading the agency that gave Germans access to files kept by the East German secret police, was elected president in 2012. In February 2017, Frank-Walter Steinmeier, a Social Democrat and former minister of foreign affairs, was elected president with the support of both major political parties.

THE LEGISLATURE

In parliamentary systems, the legislature is normally the center of political power. Germany's bicameral legislature, Parliament, is a powerful institution, but the Basic Law weakened the legislature's power vis-à-vis the chancellor to avoid the problems that had undermined the Weimar Republic. The lower house, the **Bundestag** (Federal Diet), represents the population; the upper house, the **Bundesrat** (Federal Council), represents Germany's 16 states.

The Bundestag is the more powerful of the two houses. It currently has 709 deputies, who are Germany's only directly elected public officials at the federal level. Deputies are elected for a maximum of four years, though elections can occur before the four-year term is complete. The Bundestag's chief power is its capacity to elect the chancellor. Because no German party has ever won a majority of seats in the legislature, members of the lower house select a chancellor (normally the head of the party with the most seats) who can form a majority coalition among the parties in the legislature. The current chancellor, **Angela Merkel**, was first elected after the 2005 elections, when her conservatives were able to form a majority legislative coalition with the Social Democrats. After the 2009 elections, she began a second term, this time in coalition with the centrist Free Democrats. The Free Democrats failed to win seats in the legislature in the 2013 general election, forcing Merkel to seek a new coalition. After protracted negotiations, Merkel formed a coalition with the Social Democrats.

The Bundestag can remove the chancellor, but only through a "constructive" vote of no confidence. During the Weimar Republic, chancellors were often removed from power by the legislature, usually with votes from extreme parties of the right and left who were unable to agree on a new chancellor. The result was a succession of weak chancellors, political paralysis, and the imposition of presidential rule that facilitated the rise of Hitler. As a result, the Basic Law allows the Bundestag to remove a chancellor only if a majority of its members can (constructively) approve a replacement. There have been only two constructive votes of no confidence since 1949, and only one of those (in 1982) was successful. Chancellors may also call for a motion of confidence, and if that motion fails to win a majority, the legislature can be dissolved and new elections can be convened. (This occurred most recently in 2005.)

While the Bundestag must approve all federal laws, the government (not the legislature) initiates most legislation. The lower house can amend and debate legislation submitted by the government. In addition, the lower house can question members of the government during weekly question hours that are similar to question periods in the United Kingdom. Members submit written questions to ministers ahead of time but can ask supplementary questions during the debate. Much of the work of the Bundestag is performed by powerful legislative committees that have the ability to question government ministers and investigate government activities; they also have the expertise to challenge bills submitted by the government.

The upper house, the Bundesrat, is made up of 69 members who are delegates of the governments of Germany's *Länder* ("states"). Each state appoints between three and six members, depending on its population, and the minister-president (state prime minister or governor) is usually the head of the state delegation. Within the Bundesrat, delegations of representatives cast their ballots as a bloc, following the instructions of the state government.

All legislation is submitted to the upper house before being sent to the lower house. The Bundesrat must approve all laws that affect the states (including laws that require states to implement policies of the federal government), giving it an effective veto power over about one-third of all legislation. For all other legislation, the Bundesrat's opposition can be overridden by the lower house. When the two houses disagree, joint committees often convene to negotiate a compromise. The Bundesrat must also approve all constitutional amendments.

The Bundesrat has traditionally served as an important check on the federal government because it has very often been controlled by the opposition. Since state elections do not coincide with federal ones, the outcome of state elections can alter the balance of power in the upper house. In 2003, a nine-month battle took place over the **Social Democratic Party (SPD)** Agenda 2010 legislative program, a controversial package of economic reforms that eventually was approved. The SPD–Greens coalition in the lower house locked horns with the

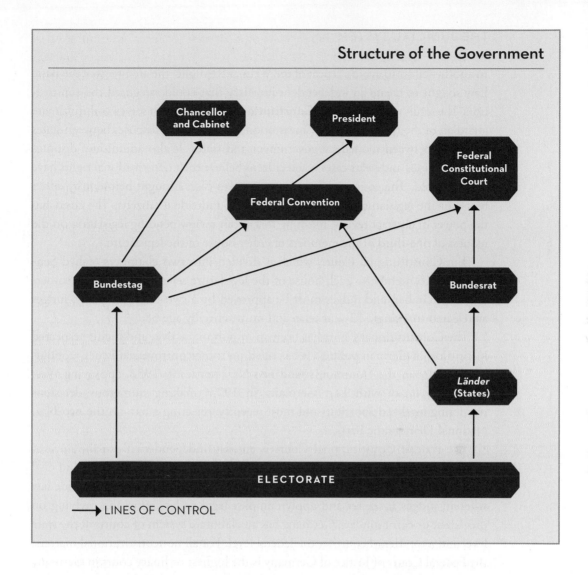

Structure of the Government

Chancellor and Cabinet

President

Federal Constitutional Court

Federal Convention

Bundestag

Bundesrat

Länder (States)

ELECTORATE

→ LINES OF CONTROL

Conservative-dominated Bundesrat. When in 2005 the SPD lost power in Germany's most populous state, thus further eroding its position in the upper house, the SPD government pushed for early elections in order to obtain a renewed national mandate. This pattern was repeated after the 2009 elections. A series of electoral setbacks for the governing coalition in state elections strengthened the opposition in the upper house. A package of reforms passed in 2006 limited somewhat the growing tendency of the upper house to assert its right to block legislation.

In another effort to avoid a repeat of the Weimar Republic, the architects of the Basic Law sought to create an independent judiciary that could safeguard the constitution. The result was the **Federal Constitutional Court**, which serves as the ultimate guardian of the Basic Law. The Constitutional Court settles disputes between states as well as between the federal government and states. It also adjudicates disputes about elections and hears cases when citizens believe their constitutional rights have been violated. The court acts only in response to cases brought before it by either house of the legislature, by lower courts, or by individual citizens. The court has the power of abstract review, meaning that it can review pending legislation on the request of one-third of the members of either house of the legislature.

The Constitutional Court, which is divided into two chambers (called Senates), has 16 members. Each house of the legislature selects half of the members of each chamber, and judges must be approved by a two-thirds majority. Judges are elected to a single 12-year term and must retire by age 68.

The Constitutional Court has been an important, active, and highly respected institution in German politics. It has ruled on some controversial issues, upholding the ban on the Communist and neo-Nazi parties in 1952, approving West Germany's treaty with East Germany in 1973, making numerous decisions restricting legalized abortion, and most recently, rejecting a ban on the neo-Nazi National Democratic Party.

The Federal Constitutional Court is entirely independent from the government and from the rest of Germany's legal system that handles criminal and civil matters. For all nonconstitutional issues, Germany employs a system of code law wherein judges interpret and apply complex legal codes rather than relying on precedent or common law. Germany has an elaborate system of courts at the state level and a top tier of courts at the federal level. For all nonconstitutional matters, the Federal Court of Justice of Germany is the highest ordinary court in Germany and the highest appeals court.

The Electoral System

The Basic Law created an innovative mixed electoral system that has since been emulated by other democracies, including three of the cases in this volume (Japan, Mexico, and Russia). Its authors sought a system that would combine the fairness of Proportional Representation (PR) with the voter-representative link that is a feature of single-member district (SMD) systems. In addition, the framers of the Basic Law envisioned a system that would represent diverse political interests but avoid the legislative fragmentation and instability that characterized the Weimar Republic.

Using SMDs, where seats are allocated according to first-past-the-post criteria (the candidate with the most votes wins the seat), 299 seats are elected. The remaining seats are awarded to parties from their party lists in each state, according to the proportion of the vote won by each party nationally. Thus, when voting for the Bundestag, Germans vote once for a representative in their district and once for a list of party candidates. The PR seats are subject to a 5 percent threshold; to win seats from PR lists, a party must win at least 5 percent of the vote nationally or win three SMD seats. For decades that threshold successfully limited the number of parties in the Bundestag, including small extremist parties, and has prevented the kind of fragmentation and polarization that plagued the Weimar Republic.

The German electoral system contains one additional feature that is often confusing for German citizens and students of German politics alike. If results from the SMDs produce a Bundestag with a membership that does not accurately reflect each party's national support (as determined by the PR list vote), additional seats must be awarded to parties that are underrepresented. In short, Germany has a "corrective" measure to ensure that any party exceeding the 5 percent threshold is entitled to a Bundestag share of seats equivalent to its percentage of party list votes. In the 2017 election, the two largest parties (the CDU/CSU and the SPD) did particularly well in the SMDs, giving them more seats in the Bundesrat than their national percentage of the vote would indicate. The German system allowed these parties to keep their "overhang" seats, and the list system was used to award additional seats to parties whose percentage of the national vote merited greater representation in the lower house. Consequently, the number of seats in the Bundestag can change from election to election. The minimum number of seats is 598; after the 2013 elections there were 631 members of the lower house, and after the 2017 elections there were 709 members.

The implications of Germany's electoral system are profound. Political parties are strengthened because the national party lists are drawn up by party leaders. Parties are thus directly responsible for selecting at least half of the lower house, and they can more easily enforce internal discipline. PR means that parties (at least those large enough to win 5 percent of the vote or three SMDs) can have a voice in the legislature. Only once since 1949 have the centrist Free Democrats been able to win an SMD seat, but they won PR seats in every election until 2013. Because of the electoral system, a small party such as the Free Democrats has had far more influence in Germany than the United Kingdom's Liberal Democrats, even though the Liberal Democrats consistently win a higher percentage of the vote. The presence of more parties in Germany has also meant that no German political party has ever won a legislative majority. Whether this is a positive or negative feature can be debated. The absence of a clear majority can sometimes lead to prolonged negotiations after elections (as was the case after the 2013 elections, when it took two months to form a new government). The German political system, however, represents a wide range of political views, and the need to form coalitions means that political compromise is a built-in feature. The German electoral system is certainly complex, but it has produced stable and effective governments; turnout for elections, moreover, has been consistently high.

Local Government

The Basic Law provides for a system of federalism that is a rarity among Western Europe's mostly unitary systems, although state and local governments in Germany have fewer powers than more robust federal systems like that of the United States.[12] Germany's 16 states share power with the federal government, which controls some areas, such as defense and foreign policy; the states have exclusive power over education, administration of justice at the state level, culture, and law enforcement. For all remaining areas not covered by the Basic Law, power is given to the states. German states implement the vast majority of the legislation passed by the federal government. States also have a direct check on the federal government via their representation in the upper house. Unlike U.S. states, German *Länder* and municipal governments have no power to raise taxes, and they are dependent on revenues allocated by the federal government. States are responsible for about two-thirds of German government spending.

Each German state has its own unicameral legislature (elected for four years), which in turn selects a **minister-president** (governor). Minister-presidents are often powerful figures in German politics, and German chancellors have often built their political careers in state politics.

Germany does not allow referenda or initiatives at the national level, but state and local governments have used them and have experimented with other forms of direct democracy.[13] Some states have eliminated the 5 percent threshold for local elections, most localities now directly elect their mayors (rather than having the mayor elected by the council), and some states allow for votes to recall elected officials.

Seats in the Bundestag after the 2013 and 2017 General Elections

PARTY	2013			2017		
	% VOTE*	% SEATS	# SEATS	% VOTE*	% SEATS	# SEATS
CDU/CSU	41.5	49.2	311	33.0	34.8	246
SPD	25.7	30.5	193	20.5	21.7	153
AfD	4.7	0	0	12.6	13.2	94
FDP	4.8	0	0	10.7	11.2	80
The Left	8.6	10.1	64	9.2	9.7	69
The Greens	8.4	10.0	63	8.9	9.4	67
Others	6.3	0	0	11.3	0	0
Total	100	100	631**	100	100	709**

*Based on the national aggregate of the party list vote.

**Of this total, 299 seats were awarded in single-member constituencies. The remaining seats were awarded via the national party PR list. The extra seats (32 in 2013 and 110 in 2017) were awarded to parties to make their percentage of legislative seats more equivalent to their proportion of the national vote.

Key to party acronyms:
   AfD: Alternative for Germany, far right
   CDU/CSU: Conservatives
   FDP: Free Democratic Party
   SPD: Social Democratic Party

Source: Preliminary Results, https://bundeswahlleiter.de/en/bundestagswahlen/2017/ergebnisse/bund-99.html (accessed 9/25/17).

Political Conflict and Competition

The Party System

As in most parliamentary systems, political parties are the central political actors in German politics. Founders of the Basic Law believed that a highly structured party system could prevent the kind of charismatic authoritarian leadership that doomed the Weimar Republic. The Basic Law thus envisions representation of the people through political parties, rather than through direct elections for a head of government or head of state, or referenda (which are not permitted at the federal level). As a result, the German state provides about one-third of the budget of the major political parties, in addition to free advertising on public television and radio during campaigns.

Since 1949, Germany has had a remarkably stable system of political parties, even taking into account reunification and the emergence of new political forces in the 1980s and 1990s.[14] From 1957 to 1983, the party system was dominated by two large forces (the center-right CDU/CSU and the center-left SPD) and one smaller party (the liberal FDP). During that period, those three parties won all the seats in the Bundestag. In the early 1980s, the Greens were able to break into the legislature and occupy political space to the left of the SPD. Reunification in 1990 led to a fifth political force, composed mainly of former East German Communists (currently named the Left).

The two German political parties that have provided every chancellor since 1949 (the CDU/CSU and the SPD) have been characterized as **catchall parties**. During the Weimar Republic, parties aimed their appeals at narrow constituencies based most often on social class or religion. Aided by the climate of the Cold War, the dramatic postwar economic recovery, and the advent of television, catchall parties represented a more modern, mass party that appealed more broadly to voters of all types. Such parties therefore presented a more centrist image.

In recent years, Germany's political party system has seen major changes. Chief among them is the decline of Germany's two main parties, described by one author as "shrinking elephants."[15] In the mid-1970s, the two main parties captured over 90 percent of the vote, but in 2017 that percentage declined to about 54 percent. Likewise, in the 1970s well over half of Germans reported a strong attachment to a political party, but that figure had dropped to 30 percent by 2009. The emergence of new political parties (the Greens, the Left, and most recently the rightist Alternative for Germany) has shifted Germany from a two-and-a-half party system to a six-party system. Small, upstart parties (such as the Pirate Party, a libertarian group advocating Internet freedom, which won 2 percent of the vote in 2009 and 2013) have further eroded the dominance of the major parties. An increasing number of Germans (now about a quarter of voters) split their ticket, voting for different parties with their SMD and list ballots. Voter turnout, while still high, has been on the decline (it was 76.2 percent in 2017). In the 2017 general elections, Alternative for Germany won over 12 percent of the vote and over 90 seats in the lower house, the first time a far right party had gained seats since the restoration of democracy after World War II. All these trends explain why political scientists now describe Germany's political system as undergoing a process of "de-alignment."

THE CHRISTIAN DEMOCRATS

The notion of a modern catchall party was best illustrated by the creation in 1945 of the Christian Democratic Union (CDU).[16] Together with its Bavarian component, the Christian Social Union (CSU), the CDU emerged as a pro-business, antisocialist, Christian political party that for the first time in German history appealed to both Catholics and Protestants. The CDU established itself both as a strongly pro-West party with close ties to the United States and as a staunch supporter of a European union.

Two CDU chancellors, Konrad Adenauer and Helmut Kohl, were dominant figures in the history of the CDU/CSU. Under Konrad Adenauer's long chancellorship (1949–63), the CDU/CSU was able to steer the German right in a modern, market-oriented, and pro-European direction.

Helmut Kohl, who was chancellor from 1982 to 1998, was responsible for Germany's rapid reunification after the fall of the Berlin Wall in 1989. Voters initially rewarded the CDU/CSU under Kohl for its support of reunification. By 1994, however, they punished it for the consequent economic and social costs of Kohl's policies. Kohl's political comeback was derailed in the late 1990s when he admitted to accepting illegal campaign contributions. Although the CDU/CSU is a pro-business party, it has broadly accepted Germany's welfare state, and some of its members even opposed market-oriented reforms proposed by the Social Democrats in recent years.

The CDU/CSU has been led since 2005 by Angela Merkel. Merkel has won four elections, and in 2013 her conservatives won their highest percentage of the vote in almost three decades as well as the second highest percentage of legislative seats in the party's history.

Germany's chancellor since 2005, Angela Merkel is the first woman to hold that position and the first to be raised in the former GDR. She is the daughter of a Protestant pastor and was trained as a scientist (she has a doctorate in chemistry and physics) and managed to avoid membership in the Communist Socialist Unity Party. She was elected to the Bundestag in 1990, during the first elections that included East Germany. She gained a series of ministerial posts under Helmut Kohl's chancellorship in the 1990s. In 2002, the CDU passed her over for the nomination to oppose SPD chancellor Gerhard Schroeder.

After being elected head of the CDU in 2000, Merkel pushed hard to change the CDU's traditional policy orientation. On the one hand, she moved the party toward the center on such social issues as immigration and the environment. On the other hand, she encouraged the party to adopt free-market policies more similar to those of Britain's Conservatives. Under her leadership, the CDU has promoted tax cuts and reforms to the health care system and has been closer to the United States in foreign policy.

While Merkel is hardly a charismatic leader, as she begins her fourth term as chancellor, she remains Germany's most popular politician. She has maintained a high profile in international affairs, has enacted economic reforms to address Germany's economic challenges, and has promoted policies that seek to improve the lives of women. The CDU's 2009 campaign portrayed her as a *Superfrau* ("superwoman"). Germany's central role in the Eurozone economic crisis, and the more recent Syrian refugee crisis, damaged Merkel's popularity, but has not substantially weakened the chancellor. On the eve of the 2017 general election her approval rating had rebounded to an impressive 74 percent. Nevertheless, her party lost 65 seats in the election.[17]

THE SOCIAL DEMOCRATS

Unlike the CDU, the Social Democratic Party (SPD) is Germany's oldest party (it was founded in 1863) and was a major actor during the Weimar Republic.[18] The SPD originally had a Marxist orientation and defined itself as a party of the working class. In part because of its radical orientation, the SPD won less than 30 percent of the vote in the first two elections of the new democracy.

Party leaders realized they needed to broaden the SPD's appeal. At its 1959 party convention, the SPD renounced Marxism and adopted a strategy to market the party to Germans of all social classes, as a classic catchall party. This approach paid immediate electoral dividends. The SPD's vote grew steadily through the 1950s and 1960s; by 1966, the SPD had gained enough respectability to be included in a grand coalition government with the CDU/CSU. In 1969, the SPD finally formed the first coalition government of the left under SPD leader Willy Brandt. Brandt promoted better relations with the Communist bloc and increased worker participation in the management of private enterprise. The SPD continued its success between 1974 and 1982, under the chancellorship of Helmut Schmidt.

Hurt by its ambivalent support for reunification, the SPD found itself out of power until the election of Gerhard Schroeder in 1998. Schroeder formed a coalition with the Greens and backed some controversial environmental policies, such as a phasing out of nuclear power, a proposed speed limit on Germany's expressways, and new taxes on carbon emissions. On economic matters,

Schroeder represented the more conservative wing of the SPD, and his call for fundamental reforms to Germany's welfare state and his foreign policy alienated the SPD left, led by Oskar Lafontaine, who would eventually take his supporters out of the SPD to form a party called the Left. The SPD–Greens alliance narrowly won the 2002 elections, but Schroeder's gamble of calling early elections in 2005 backfired: the SPD narrowly lost the election, and although his party entered government as a junior coalition member, Schroeder lost the chancellorship.

In 2008, the Social Democrats selected the popular foreign minister Frank-Walter Steinmeier, a longtime aide to Schroeder, to lead the party in the 2009 general elections. The SPD was the biggest loser in those elections and suffered its worst results since 1949. After 11 years in government, the SPD found itself in opposition. At its November 2009 Party Congress, the SPD elected Sigmar Gabriel, a former environment minister, as its leader. In 2013, the SPD selected Peer Steinbrück, a former minister of finance in the 2005–09 CDU–SPD coalition government, as its candidate for chancellor. Although the SPD was able to

After the 2013 general elections, Germany's two major parties formed a "grand coalition." This cartoon portrays the coalition's main leaders (conservative Chancellor Angela Merkel and Social Democratic Party Vice Chancellor Sigmar Gabriel) as odd bedfellows.

increase its vote slightly (winning 46 more seats than in 2009), the party was trounced by the conservatives and its level of support was stuck at about a quarter of the electorate. The SPD leadership, worried that the party could be damaged electorally if it entered a coalition government as a junior partner (as was the case after its 2005–09 coalition with the conservatives), formed a "grand coalition" government with the CDU, but only after gaining approval for the move in a referendum among SPD members. In exchange for entering the coalition, the CDU promised that it would support a package of reforms (implementation of Germany's first-ever national minimum wage, a reduction in the retirement age, and a reform of Germany's citizenship policy for immigrants). The SPD was awarded some top cabinet positions, including the vice-chancellorship and the foreign affairs, justice, labor, and environment ministries. Chancellor Merkel's popularity and her willingness to embrace some SPD policies have posed a severe challenge to the Social Democrats. Its leader for the 2017 campaign was Martin Schulz, a former president of the European Union. In 2017, the SPD had its worst electoral result since World War II, and after the election announced that it would leave the governing coalition and return to the opposition.

THE FREE DEMOCRATS

By one measure, the **Free Democratic Party (FDP)** has been Germany's most successful party; it has been a member (always as a junior coalition partner) of more post–World War II governments than any other German party. But on another measure, the party has been a colossal failure; it has never led a German government and currently has no seats in the Bundestag. The FDP has been a staunch defender of free-market economic and civil liberties and has consistently drawn support from professionals and upper-middle-class Germans. Since 1949, support for the FDP has ranged from a low of 4.9 percent (2013) to a high of about 15 percent (2009). Nevertheless, from 1949 to 2008, the FDP was a junior coalition partner in 13 of 18 German governments, making it a crucial "hinge" party that could determine the nature of coalition governments.

In the early years of German democracy, the FDP was a natural ally of the conservatives, given its support of free-market policies. In the late 1960s, the FDP found common cause with the Social Democrats over social reforms and foreign policy. In general, the FDP has been less socially conservative than the CDU/CSU but less supportive of the welfare state than the SPD, and it has consistently supported tax and social spending cuts.

In the past decade, the FDP has faced new challenges. It has suffered internal divisions, and the rise of the Greens has to some extent supplanted its advocacy of civil liberties, personal freedoms, and a less cumbersome bureaucracy. The FDP was the biggest winner of the 2009 elections, capturing its largest percentage of the vote ever (almost 15 percent) and entering into a coalition government with the CDU/CSU. Party leader Guido Westerwelle became Germany's foreign minister. However, the party's disastrous performance in the 2013 elections, in which its vote dropped 10 percent, to just below the 5 percent threshold for receiving legislative seats, eliminated the FDP from the Bundestag for the first time in its history. The FDP staged a political comeback at the national level under its young new leader, Christian Lindner, the FDP leader from the state of North Rhine-Westphalia, winning over 10 percent of the votes and 80 seats in the lower house in the 2017 general election.

THE GREENS

In the 1970s, some Germans became disenchanted with the three main parties, all of whom shared a broad consensus on promoting rapid industrial growth via the market economy. While coalescing around environmental policies (especially opposition to nuclear energy), **the Greens** represented a host of postmodern issues, such as women's rights, gay rights, pacifism, and grassroots democracy.[19] The Green Party initially viewed itself as an "anti-party party" that would not behave like the established parties and would not compromise its principles in pursuit of power.

The Greens won their first Bundestag seats in 1983, bringing with them a fresh style of politics. Green members of the Bundestag wore blue jeans, sported long hair, and boasted a less hierarchical internal party structure. From the start, the Green movement was divided between moderates (known as *realos*) and radicals (known as fundamentalists, or *fundis*). The moderates sought to achieve Green goals by entering into coalition governments and exercising political power. The radicals feared that such tactics would compromise Green values and destroy the distinctive identity of the movement.

Electoral realities tipped the balance of power within the Greens toward the moderates: in 1990, the West German Greens failed to reach the 5 percent threshold and were shut out of the lower house (although the East German Greens, known as *Alliance 90*, were able to win seats). The Greens reevaluated their previous opposition to electoral alliances, and in the 1994 and 1998 elections a new alliance of East and West Greens (known as *Alliance 90/The Greens*) increased its share of the vote and won Bundestag seats. In a controversial decision, the Greens entered a coalition government as junior partners of the SPD in 1998 and again in 2002, gaining control of three cabinet seats.

By entering government, the Green Party and its leader, Joschka Fischer (who became vice chancellor and foreign minister), gained new respectability and a high profile but also became subject to new political contradictions and pressures. The Greens' traditional pacifism clashed with the SPD–Greens government's policy of German intervention in Kosovo and Afghanistan, leading some members to abandon the party. Even a policy to phase out nuclear power by 2020, spearheaded by a Green environment minister, disappointed radicals within the party, who sought a more immediate end to nuclear power.

The 2005 elections failed to deliver a victory for the SPD–Greens coalition, and the Greens left the government, even though they lost only one seat in the Bundestag. In 2008, the Greens entered a first-ever coalition with the conservative CDU in the Hamburg state government, demonstrating a further willingness to compromise to advance some of their policy goals. The Greens won almost 11 percent of the vote in the 2009 elections and made further gains in state legislative elections during 2011, buoyed by popular angst over the nuclear disaster in Japan. The most dramatic victory occurred in March 2011, in the prosperous state of Baden-Württemberg, which had been governed by the conservative CDU for 58 years. The elections produced the first-ever Green Party minister-president, in a government coalition with the Social Democrats.

The Greens were dealt a minor setback in the 2013 elections, in part due to Chancellor Merkel's decision to abandon nuclear energy. The party's steady rise in votes since 1998 was halted as the Greens vote declined by 2 percent, and the party lost five seats in the Bundestag. The Greens have distanced themselves from their more radical beginnings. The party has abandoned its early anti-capitalist and even anarchist outlook in favor of a more pragmatic emphasis on sustainability that is more palatable to its mostly affluent, educated, and urban supporters. Nevertheless, the Greens still retain some aspects of their old radicalism, such as the requirement that party lists alternate male and female candidates, and the tradition of having two individuals lead the party (of which one is required to be female). In the 2013 campaign, the Greens proposed income and inheritance tax increases as well as a special wealth tax on incomes over $1.3 million.

THE LEFT

The Left (*Die Linke*) was founded in 2007 through a merger of the heirs of the former East German Communists and some leftists who abandoned the SPD.[20] After reunification, the remnants of East Germany's Communist Party reformed into the renamed Party of Democratic Socialism (PDS). The party performed poorly in the 1990 elections and struggled to surpass the 5 percent threshold in subsequent elections, winning only two SMD seats in the 2002 elections. After the merger with disgruntled Social Democratic defectors, led by the charismatic Oskar Lafontaine (a former SPD party chairman), the Left's political fortunes increased, as did its appeal in the west of Germany. Since 2005 the Left has regularly won about 10 percent of the vote, and in 2017 it won just over 9 percent of the vote and 69 seats in the lower house.

Although the platform of the Left Party is still evolving, it opposes the policies of privatization and tax cuts that recent German governments have pursued, and it has fiercely opposed both the SPD and CDU/CSU foreign policy. The party opposes Germany's membership in NATO (and views the alliance as a tool for U.S. hegemony). In a posture reminiscent of the early Greens, the Left has called itself Germany's only real opposition party (and so was dubbed "the party of no") and vowed not to enter into coalitions with any of the major political parties. However, the Left has entered into coalitions with the SPD at the state level.

OTHER PARTIES

Because of Germany's history with totalitarianism, the Basic Law was designed to prevent the emergence of extremist parties on the left or right. Thus Germany has been less tolerant than other European democracies of parties that are deemed to be anti-system. Far right parties—for example, the National Democratic Party (NPD)—are tolerated in Germany, and they have won seats in state legislatures. But until 2017 they had never surpassed the 5 percent threshold at the federal level. The Constitutional Court banned the Communist left in the 1950s, and until reunification, no party of the extreme left was able to win seats in the legislature. Recent efforts, unsuccessful to date, have tried to get the Court to ban the NPD, a party viewed by some as anti-Semitic. The aforementioned Pirate Party, which advocates Internet freedom

Frauke Petry, co-leader of the anti-immigration Alternative for Germany party, at the 2016 AfD federal conference. In the September 2017 general elections the AfD won over 12 percent of the vote and was the first German party of the far right to win seats in the lower house since World War II.

and privacy, has fared poorly in federal elections but was able to gain seats in four state legislatures.

The fastest growing and most alarming newcomer to German politics is the Alternative for Germany (AfD). This right-wing populist party, founded in 2013, ran on a platform calling for Germany to abandon the euro (though not the European Union). In the September 2017 general election it won over 12 percent of the vote and 94 lower house seats. A wave of anti-immigrant and anti-Muslim marches and protests in response to the Syrian refugee crisis that began in 2015 appears to have strengthened the AfD, which began to call for limits to immigration. Many of those rallies were organized by Patriotic Europeans against the Islamization of the West (PEGIDA), and the AfD has incorporated PEGIDA's platform. At its 2016 Party Congress, the AfD called for a ban of all Islamic symbols, adopting the slogan "Islam Is Not Part of Germany." The party has done remarkably well in state elections over the last few years, and the AfD became the second-largest party in Saxony-Anhalt, taking votes away from the major national parties. In September 2016, the AfD defeated Merkel's party in elections in her home state, winning 21 percent of the vote and finishing second behind the SPD. At the time, Vice Chancellor Sigmar Gabriel had warned that the AfD's rhetoric is dangerously similar to the popular appeal used by the Nazis in the 1920s and 1930s. In April 2016, German authorities arrested some leaders of the anti-immigrant movement, charging them with inciting attacks on refugees.[21] The AfD's surprisingly strong performance in the 2017 general election shocked the German political establishment and led to widespread anti-AfD demonstrations throughout Germany. The AfD is unlikely to enter a governing coalition in the near future, as all other major parties refuse to work with the far right, but its electoral success may have opened the door for further electoral gains.

Elections

The 17 German federal elections since 1949 have enjoyed consistently high voter turnout, although numbers have been decreasing since the 1970s. Germany recorded its highest voter turnout in 1972 (91.1 percent) and its lowest in 2009 (70.8 percent). German campaigns have traditionally centered on parties and their platforms, but in recent elections they have become more Americanized— more about personalities and slick advertising.

Owing to the dominance of the CDU and SPD, German campaigns inevitably become a battle between titans. For example, in the 1998 electoral campaign, the SPD attacked CDU Chancellor Kohl for having underestimated the costs of reunification, labeling Kohl the "unemployment chancellor." In 2002, the SPD played up Chancellor Schroeder's popular opposition to the Iraq War, while the CDU attacked rising fuel taxes under the SPD–Greens coalition government. In the 2005 campaign, the focus became the economy: the CDU's Merkel called for tax cuts and faster reform of the economy, and the SPD proposed a tax on wealthy Germans. Despite its potentially divisive political issues (the war in Afghanistan, the economic crisis, and immigration), the 2009 campaign was considered among the dullest ever, chiefly because the two largest parties were coalition partners. The 2017 campaign was widely criticized as lackluster, as both major parties appeared to agree on most issues, and their leaders were not charismatic campaigners. The CDU and SPD lost votes to smaller parties with younger and more energetic leadership.

Civil Society

German citizens did not greet the return of democracy with much civic enthusiasm. The experience of Nazism and Germany's defeat in World War II rendered most Germans apathetic about politics. In the early years of the Bonn Republic, opinion polls showed lingering support for authoritarian ideas. Germany's only real experience with democracy during the Weimar Republic had been short-lived, unsuccessful, and traumatic.

Nevertheless, we have seen that Germans after 1949 regularly turned out in large numbers to vote and that they overwhelmingly rejected parties on the political extremes. With Germany's spectacular economic recovery, Germans came to support democratic politics, and a democratic German civil society began to germinate. Recent opinion surveys reported that more than half of all Germans were interested in politics, over half had signed a petition, over a third had attended a lawful demonstration, and almost 10 percent had joined in some type of boycott. Survey research has shown that Germany has the second-highest level of protest activity in Western Europe, and the vibrancy of Germany civil society was on display in 2016 as both supporters and opponents of the massive influx of Syrian refugees took to the streets.[22]

LABOR UNIONS AND BUSINESS ORGANIZATIONS

Compared with most advanced democracies, trade unions in postwar Germany have been both strong and influential. The Federation of German Labor (DGB) represents most of Germany's trade unions, and during the postwar period about two-thirds of workers were unionized. The DGB has enjoyed a close relationship with the SPD and played a key role in German policy making.

German trade unions, however, have experienced a rapid decline in membership since the 1990s. Between 1991 and 2006, the DGB lost almost half its membership for a variety of reasons, and today only under a quarter of the labor force is unionized. Reunification flooded the labor market, unemployment soared, and economic growth rates declined. Over half of German workers are presently covered by collective bargaining agreements between unions and employers, but that percentage has dropped considerably and rapidly over the past two decades.

German business is also highly organized. The Federal Association of German Employers (BDA) and the Federation of German Industry (BDI) are powerful groups with close ties to the CDU. The BDI is a powerful interest group that

Antinuclear protesters outside a German nuclear power plant in March 2011. The protesters created a human chain that was almost 30 miles long.

often weighs in on major political-economic issues. In 2011, the BDI raised concerns that Angela Merkel's decision to expedite the phasing out of nuclear power could seriously damage Germany's economy by raising energy prices for industry.

OTHER GROUPS

As in many Western democracies, German society experienced the growth of a variety of political groups in the 1960s and 1970s. These groups challenged various aspects of the German model of economic growth, including pollution, the status of women, its reliance on nuclear energy, and the dominance of the major political parties. Some of the groups were later integrated into the Greens, thus reflecting the centrality of political parties in the German system; other groups remained autonomous from the party system.

The German women's movement has been particularly influential. Since the founding of the Bonn Republic, women have organized regarding issues of unequal pay, access to legal abortion, and other political rights. In the 1980s, the Greens established a quota for female candidates, thus spurring most other political parties to adopt similar policies.

German churches have also been an important interest group since 1949. Before reunification, over 90 percent of West Germans belonged to either the Catholic or Protestant Church, and the German state provided those churches with generous economic support. Of the two churches, the Catholic Church has been more outspoken on social issues and has a closer relationship to the CDU/CSU. In Communist East Germany, the Protestant Church was an important political actor as one of the few autonomous organizations permitted there. The influence of organized religion is likely to decline, because religiosity and church attendance have declined. Moreover, the inclusion of East Germans, over half of whom are nonreligious, has weakened the power of organized religion. In Germany, the churches, mosques, and synagogues are funded by a portion of the income tax collected and allocated by the government.

Society

Ethnic and National Identity

As with many other European countries, Germany is relatively homogeneous in terms of its ethnic identity. Although unification came late to Germany, a strong shared cultural and even national identity has bound Germans together for a much longer period. Important cultural figures, such as Beethoven, Wagner, and Goethe, helped generate the idea of a single German people, even if what bound these individuals together was not territory, constitutions, or regimes. Interestingly, then, a shared German identity developed long before there was a single German state; indeed, a single state, encompassing all Germans, has never existed (except under the Nazi regime). Austria, Switzerland, Liechtenstein, and Luxembourg are also countries where German is a state language. One result of this gap between national identity and a single state has been a weak German attachment to the state and state symbols. Such attachments were further weakened by the effects of World War II, wherein nationalism became the fuel for war and genocide. That war also destroyed the Jewish population of Germany, further reducing the country's ethnic and cultural diversity, and large portions of eastern Germany were annexed by Poland.

At the level of national identity, there remain important distinctions across the country, again a reflection of late unification. Recall that Germany can be seen as a fusion of two different systems: the Prussian empire in the north and a series of "free states" and kingdoms in the south. This distinction remains particularly important in the state of Bavaria, which still calls itself a *Freistaat* ("free state"), indicating both its historical role as an independent state before unification and a sense that the region remains separate from (and superior to) much of the rest of Germany.

Bavaria is noted for its high level of economic development and the still-strong role played by Catholicism. Indeed, the former pope, Benedict XVI, hails from Bavaria and was noted for his religious conservatism (a source of pride for many Bavarians). In contrast, northern and eastern Germany are overwhelmingly Protestant, though religious affiliation or identity is much weaker there. It may be a stretch to think of Bavarians (or any other German cultural subgroup) as having a distinct ethnic identity, but these groups do identify themselves by custom, dialect, and even particular stereotypes regarding attitudes and behavior.

These distinct, if relatively weak, identities have become more diverse over the past 50 years, through immigration and unification. First, unification with East Germany brought into the country a new population whose historical experiences were quite different. For West Germans, the aftermath of World War II brought denazification, a deep suspicion of national pride, and an emphasis on democratic institutions. In contrast, East Germans did not undergo the type of denazification experienced in the west; the Communist government instead redirected public identity toward the East German state and gave little attention to such events as the Holocaust. At the time of unification, Germany's population in the east embodied an identity that had been shaped by 50 years of socialism—that is, strongly secular and having a complicated relationship to nationalism. Germans as a result often speak of the differences between *Ossi und Wessi* ("east and west"); how distinct these differences are, or will remain, we shall discuss in greater detail later.

Another factor that has transformed national and ethnic identity has been the role of immigration. Germany's postwar economic growth created a demand for labor that the country could not meet; as a result, Germany turned to **Gastarbeiter** ("guest workers") to fill this role. Guest workers from Mediterranean Europe, including especially large numbers from Turkey, were expected to stay only temporarily in Germany and thus were not part of any formal plan for naturalization. Far fewer guest workers returned home than were expected, and eventually entire families and children became part of the German population. By 2010, immigrants constituted about 8 percent of the German population, and about a quarter of these were of Turkish origin.

This growing immigrant population, the largest (in sheer numbers) in Europe, has created significant challenges for the German state and nation. In the past, German identity, including citizenship, centered on notions of race. As such, descendants of ancient German communities in Russia, for example, could gain citizenship, but Turkish children born and raised in Germany were not German citizens. Since 2000, the citizenship laws in Germany have been reformed to recognize and integrate non-German immigrants (though the law forces immigrants to renounce citizenship from their country of origin), but their social integration is far more difficult. Many Germans still have difficulty imagining nonethnic Germans as so-called true Germans, and concerns about political Islam have added a new tension to the situation. Some Germans worry that the country's failure to integrate its Muslim population is leading to the development of a "parallel society" disconnected from democratic institutions and susceptible to fundamentalism (see "Germany's Immigration Dilemma," p. 266).[23]

Ideology and Political Culture

We have already alluded to many of the central facets of German ideology and political culture. German political identity is complicated both by the legacies of late unification and by the rise of fascism. The war and denazification led to a strong undercurrent of national shame and the conclusion that nationalism and even patriotism were values that, at least for Germany, were dangerous and unacceptable. For most of the postwar period, then, the emphasis on democratic institutions was less an expression of national or patriotic identity than a belief that such institutions were a necessary bulwark against extremism and a recurrence of past policies. German political culture emphasized a greater pride in the country's economic achievements than in the state or nation, both of which had taken on negative connotations.

Over the past 30 years, a significant percentage of the German population (30 to 40 percent) has consistently stated not being proud of their country; compare this with France and the United Kingdom, where under 10 percent of the population responds with this answer. Germans show overwhelming support for democracy, and most Germans express pride in their political institutions and constitution. Indeed, Germans are prouder of their political system than any other aspect of their society, including the economy.[24] Former citizens of East Germany still show lower levels of support for democratic institutions (compared with West Germans) and a weaker awareness that they have particular democratic rights (such as free speech).[25] Some of this behavior is understandably generational, for these differences between westerners and easterners are much smaller among people under 25. The concern about a lingering *Mauer im Kopf* ("Berlin Wall of the mind") that still separates the two peoples seems to be fading. Ideologically, there

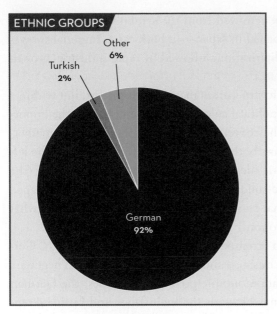

ETHNIC GROUPS

Other 6%

Turkish 2%

German 92%

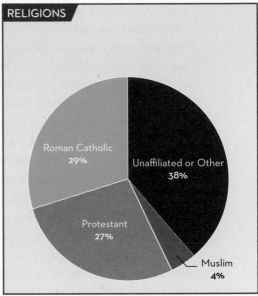

RELIGIONS

Roman Catholic 29%

Unaffiliated or Other 38%

Protestant 27%

Muslim 4%

is similarly strong support among eastern and western Germans for a political regime that emphasizes collective well-being over individual rights and favors a system that combines capitalism with consensus.

One dramatic shift in Germany's political culture was the rise in post-materialist values (such as political participation, feminism, the environment, and other quality-of-life issues) and a decline in bread-and-butter materialist concerns (such as economic growth, jobs, and order). In 1973, only 13 percent of Germans felt that postmaterialist concerns were a priority, but 43 percent took that position in 1995.[76] Postmaterialist values have become more pronounced in all advanced democracies, but they are by far the strongest in Germany—which perhaps explains why Germany has had one of the world's most successful Green parties.

Political Economy

Although the legacy of Nazism and war still casts a shadow over its national identity, Germany can be rightly proud of its economy. Many observers would assert that the *Wirtschaftswunder* ("economic miracle") of the 1950s and 1960s was in part a way for Germany to reinvest national energy and identity around institutions and projects that were removed from the symbols of its fascist past. This result is similar to what happened in Japan—in both cases, imperialism was replaced by occupation and demilitarization, followed by rapid industrial growth with the support of the United States.

The German political-economic structure is manifestly capitalist, but within a social-democratic mold. German political culture strongly emphasizes the importance of collective rights within the context of private property and the marketplace. This view can be found across both the left and the right: those on the left are influenced by social-democratic ideas of the state role in the economy (the SPD emphasizes social justice and solidarity), and those on the right are shaped by Christian-democratic values that similarly favor a "moral" marketplace (what the CDU calls a "social market economy").

Beginning in the 1960s, in an attempt to stimulate economic growth, German governments sought to bring business and labor groups together to negotiate labor agreements and to coordinate economic policy. For decades, the German state regularly coordinated meetings between the main labor and business representatives. Beyond the call for regular meetings, one particularly controversial aspect of German political economy is **codetermination**, a policy advocated by the Social Democrats that requires Germany's largest private firms to give unions half of all seats on their board of directors. A 2014 revision to the codetermination law requires that 30 percent of all board of directors seats be filled by women.

The German political-economic model has been credited with fostering rapid growth rates and with limiting conflict between labor and business. However, the model has its critics. German business resisted codetermination and unsuccessfully fought it in the courts. German unions became extremely powerful, often at the expense of other civil society groups that were not part of the system. Critics on the left also argued that workers still have limited power over major economic decisions.

These concerns have been negligible for most of the postwar period, during which Germany developed a sophisticated economy (the fifth largest in the world) and one of the world's most prosperous societies. German

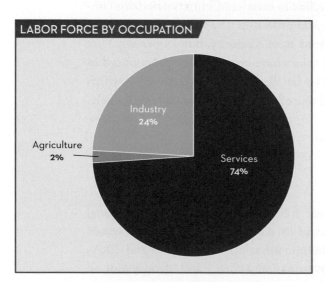

LABOR FORCE BY OCCUPATION

Industry 24%

Agriculture 2%

Services 74%

industry is famous for its advanced industrial and consumer products, such as automobiles and chemicals, and built much of its economic structure around exports. However, by the 1990s, the economic miracle began to show signs of strain, for several reasons. First, a high level of social expenditures has led to a growing cost of labor. Over time, the German workforce has become less competitive as costs have risen. Second, thanks to globalization, other regional economies have rivaled German exports with their lower costs and increasing technical sophistication. German firms, too, have in many cases chosen to invest outside of Germany, especially in eastern Europe, where German capital could find an inexpensive yet relatively productive workforce close to home. The expansion of the European Union eastward has only increased this investment, thus raising concerns among Germans. Finally, although Germany has spent enormous amounts of money revitalizing eastern Germany (over $100 billion per year since 1990), productivity, entrepreneurialism, and investment in that region remain much weaker. Assumptions that massive government spending on infrastructure and new technologies would lead to significant private investment and growth in the east have not been borne out.

Growing concerns about the potential decline in German competitiveness in the global economy, a potential shortage of labor that could result from Germany's low birthrate, and rigid rules governing hiring and firing workers have led to reforms, although not without resistance. In 2003, the Social Democratic government proposed what was known as Agenda 2010, a series of measures meant to liberalize the economy. Agenda 2010 met with fierce resistance from labor unions in particular, which limited its implementation. However, changes that did occur included restructuring unemployment benefits, the generosity of which had led to a large number of permanently unemployed recipients. In addition, the increased pressures of the global economy have forced many labor unions to recognize that increased flexibility may be the only way to compete in the global market. What's more, Germany's reputation of having one of the world's most transparent economies was damaged by the discovery that Volkswagen, the country's largest automobile company (and one of its biggest employers) had intentionally designed some of its engines to circumvent emissions testing, and that those cars polluted far more than it claimed.

To be sure, Germany's economy faces myriad challenges, including a graying population and a shortage of skilled labor. But despite recent problems and looming challenges, the German economy continues to be among the world's strongest. In 2010, the economy grew at the fastest rate since unification in 1990, and unemployment dropped to its lowest level since 1992. Today, Germany has a budget surplus, low unemployment, and a competitive economy that is growing steadily, if not spectacularly. Reflecting on the first six decades of the German Federal Republic, two scholars conclude:

> The German social market economy remains . . . remarkably resilient, regularly vying for the title of the world's most important exporting country with China. Welfare provision remains broadly available and very comprehensive in scope. . . . Standards of living [remain high] (no matter how they are measured) and social dislocation nowhere near as obvious or deeply rooted as in many of Germany's closest allies.[27]

Foreign Relations and the World

As in many other areas of German politics, the country's position in the international system is complicated and freighted with history. For the past half century, the legacy of Germany's role in World War II and subsequent denazification has been a strong sentiment of pacifism in the country and a wariness of national pride or patriotism. Even though Germany regained its sovereignty and rebuilt its military after World War II, it consciously decided to bind its foreign policy to larger international institutions and objectives. Germany became a NATO member and a strong partner of the United States, which saw Germany as the front line in the Cold War and in a possible war with the Soviet Union. As a result, the United States could rely on Germany even in controversial decisions, such as the deployment of American nuclear missiles on German soil. In addition to NATO, Germany became one of the central actors within the European Union. Indeed, many viewed the European Union as driven by a Franco-German "axis" that provided much of the impetus for integration. Resolving age-old animosities between France and Germany, and binding Germany to international military commitments, was seen as a way to solve "the German problem" once and for all. At the same time, Germany developed a strong pacifist streak that contributed to the emergence of the Green Party (which was as much antiwar as environmentally focused) and remained literally divided into East and West Germany.

The collapse of the Soviet Union and the East German regime placed "the German question" back on the table for the first time in decades. There were widespread fears that German reunification, combined with the dramatic changes in East-West politics, would set the stage for a resurgent and potentially dangerous Germany. In retrospect, these concerns were unfounded. If anything, a great deal of energy and effort was directed inward to integrate East Germany into the country as a whole and modify institutions to accommodate these dramatic changes. In fact, Germany's defense budget has shrunk from 3 percent of GDP during the Cold War to 1.2 percent today, and the country's military has been reduced from about a half million soldiers to under 200,000.

Although Germany has remained a central actor in NATO and the European Union, it has also sought to play a more independent role in foreign affairs. This has led to mixed results. In the 1990s, Germany was an important player in brokering the breakup of Yugoslavia, providing support for Croatia and Slovenia in their quest for independence. This move raised concerns that Germany was siding with its former wartime allies and that this support contributed to the brutal wars that followed. In 1999, violence between Kosovar Albanians and the Serb-controlled Yugoslav government led NATO to carry out air strikes against Yugoslavia, with German participation—its first military action since World War II. Germany has several thousand troops in Kosovo and Bosnia and, since 2001, has also contributed to the NATO mission in Afghanistan. In all these situations, however, the German military has avoided a direct combat role—even in Afghanistan, where its troops are not in the front lines of battle against the Taliban. Indeed, all Germany's international deployments to date have required constitutional review. Even within Europe, Germany's military power is dwarfed by that of Britain and France. An excellent example of Germany's reticence in asserting itself militarily was the 2010 resignation of German president Horst Köhler. After returning from Afghanistan, he commented that a country of Germany's size and with its export orientation must sometimes deploy troops to protect its interests, a statement that was seen as contradicting the German constitution (which prohibits Germany from waging war unilaterally).

Since the formation of the European Union, Germany has been one of the central engines of integration, working in partnership with France to expand the European Union. Germany was also an important actor in securing EU membership for many of the former Communist countries of Eastern Europe, where Germany has long had strong ties. Much of the impetus driving Germany forward within the European Union was the desire to solidify relations with France and build a strong Europe that would avert war. This is one of the European Union's greatest accomplishments; the notion that EU members would wage war against one another now seems absurd, even though the last such conflict occurred just over 70 years ago.

With these accomplishments has come increased uncertainty about Germany's future role in the international system. Most notably, while German foreign policy has become increasingly independent of the United States, this shift has not translated into a greater, or certainly more unchallenged, leadership role in the

European Union. France and Germany's traditional partnership inside the European Union has, in fact, lately become more strained, affected in part by France's increased focus on the Mediterranean and Middle East while Germany's attention has been directed eastward—each reflecting their traditional spheres of influence. Germany continues to maintain a very close relationship with the United States, but U.S.-German relations were severely strained when documents released by a former employee of the U.S. National Security Agency revealed that the United States had been snooping on e-mails and phone calls of top German leaders, including Chancellor Merkel. These revelations, and allegations by opposition politicians that the government had known about and had tolerated the spying, were particularly controversial in a country whose citizens are deeply protective of their privacy (citizens of the former East Germany remember the ubiquitous spying of the communist secret police).

Germany and the Eurozone Debt Crisis

As we have seen in this chapter, Germany's post–World War II economic recovery, the consolidation of its democracy, and its successful reunification were closely linked to its steadfast promotion of European integration. Germany was a founding member of what is today the 28-member European Union and is a chief promoter of the euro (€), the currency adopted in 1999 and now used by 19 EU members. Virtually all scholars believe that Germany has been a main beneficiary of European integration. As a major export power, Germany has profited from access to a large and affluent single market. In the decade after the 1999 introduction of the euro, Germany's balance of trade surplus with Eurozone countries almost quadrupled.[28]

The European **sovereign debt** crisis (*sovereign debt* refers to debts of sovereign states) that began in the fall of 2009 posed a serious challenge to Germany as the European Union's wealthiest and most powerful state. In the first decade after the introduction of the euro, European economies experienced rapid growth. The worldwide economic downturn that began in the United States in 2008 burst the bubble of economic growth in some European countries and led some countries to incur large sovereign debts. Worries that the most indebted European countries (especially Greece, but also Italy and Portugal) might be unable to repay their sovereign debt led to a rapid increase in interest rates for a number of countries suffering economic downturns, thus making it costlier for those countries to borrow and further endangering their economies. By 2011, there was widespread fear that several countries in the Eurozone could default on their debts, and the future of the euro was called into question.

Angela Merkel's Germany was at the center of the controversy over Europe's attempt to respond to the crisis. In May 2010, Europe's finance ministers approved a €750-billion bailout package that was widely viewed as too timid to calm financial markets. In October 2011, that package was increased significantly. But financial markets did not respond positively, and the most seriously indebted European countries continued to face very high interest rates. Merkel approved and was able to gain legislative approval for both bailout packages, but only after winning commitments to painful economic austerity measures in the indebted countries. The chancellor refused to consider solutions that were favored by many other Eurozone governments and by the European Commission in Brussels. Most important, she vetoed plans to have the European Central Bank issue "Euro-bonds" that would in effect pool debt from strong and weak European economies (and would reduce interest rates for struggling economies, but raise the rate some-what for stronger economies like Germany).

Merkel's tough stance brought widespread global criticism. Some critics viewed Germany's refusal to endorse stronger short-term measures in response to the crisis as self-centered, myopic, and dangerous.[29] The editor of the weekly *Die Zeit* asked, "In the European currency war, Germany has the biggest arsenal and the strongest interest in forestalling the collapse of the euro. So why is it playing Hamlet: 'To lead or not to lead?'" Germany's reluctance to respond more force-fully to the crisis has several possible explanations. Germany's historical aversion to excessive debt is partly rooted in its traumatic pre–World War II experience, when hyperinflation helped undermine democracy and facilitated Hitler's rise to power. Germany fears that bailing out indebted countries will only reward their profligacy and will lead to inflation. Many German politicians, and much of the German public, believe that countries like Italy and Greece need to live within their means and should not be supported by German taxpayers. German domes-tic politics may also be partly responsible. By 2011, Germany's coalition govern-ment was in trouble and had lost a number of key state elections. Some members of Merkel's coalition strongly opposed further bailouts. Opinion polls showed that two-thirds of Germans opposed any more bailouts to indebted countries.[30] In this context, Merkel was eager to address the immediate euro crisis, but she also needed to demonstrate her toughness in order to placate public opinion and her own political base.

In December 2011, as the crisis continued to escalate, Merkel was able to gain approval of an EU agreement that further increased bailout funds in exchange for political changes that will limit the ability of Eurozone members to run up future deficits and will impose strict penalties for countries that do not adhere to the rules. While the agreement was mostly viewed favorably within Germany,

many in Europe questioned whether it was sufficient to stop the short-term threat to the euro. Merkel's hard-line approach during the crisis was unpopular within Europe and has led to declining support for European integration, but it played well at home. The chancellor's party made significant gains in the 2013 elections, and she was able to promote her record of stemming the crisis while protecting German taxpayers.

Germany, Russia, and the European Union

A lack of clarity about Germany's international role has become particularly evident within the European Union and in Europe's relationship to Russia. In response to the Russian invasion of part of Georgia in 2008, and the Russian invasion and annexation of the Crimean region of Ukraine in 2013, Germany adopted an ambiguous stance. It might be expected that given its own history and ties to countries subjected to Soviet domination, Germany would have supported a strong EU position against Russian aggression in both cases. Chancellor Merkel did support EU economic sanctions on Russia in response to the Russian invasion of Ukraine. Her decision ignited a vigorous debate within Germany—a surprising number of politicians across the political spectrum backed Russia, or at the very least opposed tough sanctions on Russia. Opinion research revealed that Germans were evenly split on sanctions against Russia.[31]

According to one analysis, the reluctance of many Germans to take a hard line against Russia can be explained by multiple factors. These include the fear of igniting a new Cold War, widespread anti-Americanism (according to a 2013 study, Germans view the United States more unfavorably than any other Western European country), and a tendency to romanticize Russia.[32] But the economic argument may best explain Germany's Russia policy. Germany is highly dependent on imported oil and gas, and Russia provides over a third of those imports. Trade relations between Germany and Russia—and German foreign investments in Russia—are substantial, and German business leaders have been critical of EU sanctions on Russia. Some 300,000 German jobs depend on exports to Russia. Many Germans fear that poor relations with Russia could have a disastrous effect should the latter ever choose to turn off the energy supply, especially given Germany's recent decision to phase out nuclear power (see "The Politics of Germany's Energy Future," p. 265).

Thus, while Germany urged a more cautious approach, the European Union found itself divided over how to respond to Russia.[33] Since the creation of a CDU–SPD coalition government in 2013, after which SPD leader Frank-Walter

Steinmeier became minister for foreign affairs, these tensions have grown. Merkel's Social Democratic coalition partners have generally been less willing to criticize Russia. Perhaps as a legacy of the SPD-led rapprochement with the USSR during the Cold War, the SPD favors diplomacy and cooperation over a potentially dangerous and counterproductive confrontation with Russia. In the future, relations between Russia and Europe as a whole are likely to remain strained, even as German dependence on Russian energy is likely to increase. This situation raises the possibility of an increasingly fractured policy toward Russia from within the European Union as well as the potential for Germany to lose its ability to act as a leader in this area.

German foreign policy remains uncertain and unclear. At one level, the country emerged from the Cold War unified and with a strong belief in the importance of democracy, peace, and international institutions. Germany supported the transitions away from authoritarianism during the Arab Spring but did not participate in the NATO mission to remove Libya's Muammar Gaddafi. Germany has supported the EU arms embargo on Assad's Syria but has strongly opposed British and French efforts to arm opposition militias. At another level, however, Germany seems to lack a clear sense of its mission both in Europe and in the world as a whole. Further, it seems unable to gauge the extent to which it *should* take the lead and bear the possible repercussions of such a leadership role. Top members of the coalition government that took office in 2013 vowed to raise Germany's foreign policy leadership profile, but opinion polls show that most Germans oppose such a change. It may take another generation before Germany can clearly articulate its role in Europe and the world.

CURRENT ISSUES IN GERMANY

The Politics of Germany's Energy Future

About a quarter of Germany's energy is provided by nuclear power. The Social Democrat–Greens coalition government of Gerhard Schroeder (1998–2005) decided that nuclear power would be phased out by 2020. In 2010, Merkel's Conservative-Liberal government, whose top leaders supported nuclear power, extended the deadline by 12 years, spurring antinuclear protests throughout Germany. After the 2011 nuclear disaster in Fukushima, Japan, and in advance of state elections in which the antinuclear Green Party was poised to make big gains, Chancellor Merkel, who has a doctorate in nuclear physics, suddenly reversed course. She temporarily shut down eight of Germany's 17 nuclear plants and suspended the extension of the nuclear phase-out date. However, opponents of nuclear power viewed Merkel's about-face as too little, too late: her party was trounced in the March 2011 Baden-Württemberg state elections, where it had governed since 1953. The antinuclear Green Party was able to lead a coalition government after winning a quarter of the vote. In May 2011, Merkel announced that Germany would completely abandon nuclear power by 2022, stating that Germany "believes we can show those countries who decide to abandon nuclear power—or not to start using it—how it is possible to achieve growth, creating jobs and economic prosperity while shifting the energy supply toward renewable energies."[34]

Germany is already a leader in renewable energy production, thanks in part to policies enacted under Schroeder's government, and it is the world's third-largest producer of solar panels.[35] By 2010, Germany got about 17 percent of its electricity from renewable sources (hydro, solar, wind, biomass, and biogas), but that figure is slated to increase to almost 40 percent by 2020. If Germany is going to shy away from nuclear energy in the post-Fukushima era, it will have to accelerate its already impressive pursuit of renewable energy.

The political risks of abandoning nuclear power are formidable. German households already pay energy bills that are 40 percent higher than the European Union average, and these costs are likely to rise as nuclear power goes off-line.

Germany's Immigration Dilemma

In August 2010, Thilo Sarrazin, a prominent banker, member of the SPD, and board member of Germany's Central Bank, published *Deutschland schafft sich ab* (*Germany Does Away with Itself*). The book, which became an instant best seller, argued that immigration was destroying Germany because most Arab and Turkish immigrants were unwilling to integrate into German society.[36] Sarrazin was expelled from the SPD for his book and subsequent statements, and Chancellor Merkel denounced the book. In denouncing Sarrazin, however, Merkel admitted that immigration was a serious concern and claimed that multiculturalism had been a "total failure." Other politicians vigorously defended Sarrazin. Indeed,

Renewable Energy

Renewable energy as percentage of total energy production:

COUNTRY	PERCENTAGE
Brazil	84
Germany	33
China	24
United Kingdom	22
Nigeria	21
India	19
France	17
Russia	17
Mexico	16
Japan	16
United States	14
Iran	6
South Africa	1

Source: "International Energy Statistics," Report, EIA—International Energy Statistics, May 25, 2010, www.eia.gov (accessed 1/25/17).

the controversy over Sarrazin's book revealed a major division among Germany's political class and German society. For example, a poll taken in September 2010 found that 36 percent of Germans agreed that the country was being "overrun by foreigners," and 58 percent thought that Germany's Muslim population should have their religious practices "seriously curbed."

However, the debate about immigration and the growing resentment of immigrants may hamper Germany's ability to deal with a severe shortage of skilled labor. Since 2005, Germany has enacted legislation that requires immigrants to learn German and make an effort to integrate into German culture. Such policies are politically popular, but they may discourage skilled laborers from immigrating to Germany. Given Germany's low birthrate, a skilled worker shortage threatens to derail the growth of the German economy and drive up labor costs.

Germany's immigrant population has its origins in the wave of *Gastarbeiter* ("guest workers") invited to Germany in the 1950s and 1960s. These people, at first mainly from Southern Europe, were needed to help fuel Germany's rapid postwar economic recovery. Turkish citizens, most of whom are Muslim, soon became the largest group of immigrants, and today Germans of Turkish origin number about 4 million. Initially, most Germans viewed the immigrants as temporary workers and were reluctant to grant them rights as citizens, even when it became apparent that most immigrants wanted to remain in Germany. While the term *Gastarbeiter* is no longer applied, Germans of foreign origin, even those who have lived in Germany for decades, are still often viewed as *Ausländer* ("foreigners"). In the early 1990s, an outbreak of anti-immigrant attacks heightened tensions and caused alarm among German politicians.[37] The shocking discovery in 2011 of the National Socialist Underground (NSU), a far-right terrorist group that had murdered immigrants over a 13-year period, led to a parliamentary inquiry, caused the resignation of some top Germany security officials, and prompted Chancellor Merkel to call for the banning of far-right anti-immigrant parties like the NPD.

Members of PEGIDA (Patriotic Europeans against the Islamization of the West) protest government immigration policies in Dresden, in November 2016. The banner reads "Islamization, No Thanks."

Partly in response to such violence, Germany has made some progress in recognizing the need to better integrate immigrants into German society.[38] Legislation passed in 2000 gives children of immigrants the right to gain citizenship, and a recent reform pushed by the Social Democrats within the governing coalition will allow more immigrants to have dual citizenship. A national office of immigration and integration was opened in 2005 and now offers a variety of free courses aimed at providing immigrants with skills that can facilitate their integration into society. Still, German schools have worked poorly for children of immigrants. High school students of Turkish background attend university at far lower rates than the German population at large.

Chancellor Merkel's controversial decision to welcome a large number of refugees from war-torn Syria in 2015 significantly damaged her normally high approval ratings. Over a million refugees settled in Germany in 2015, and another 280,000 arrived in 2016, forcing Germany to impose border controls (usually there are no such controls between EU members). Anti-immigrant violence rose sharply in 2015, especially in eastern Germany. A 2016 survey showed that 81 percent of Germans disapproved of Merkel's handling of the refugee crisis.[39] As a result, in April 2016 Merkel brokered a European Union deal with Turkey aimed at stemming the flow of refugees into Europe. In 2016, Germany's interior minister and some conservative state leaders proposed a ban on face veils in schools, while driving, and in some public offices, a move that was likely to inflame relations with Germany's growing Muslim minority. Chancellor Merkel, perhaps with an eye toward her 2017 reelection campaign, announced her support for a ban on face veils. The anti-immigrant right-wing AfD performed surprisingly well in the 2017 legislative elections, making it the third largest party in the lower house. Germany's reputation as a tolerant country with almost no organized far right is clearly being put to the test by the immigration challenge.

NOTES

1. These disputes in many cases continue to simmer. See, for example, Mark Landler, "Lawsuit Reopens Old Wounds in Polish-German Dispute," *New York Times*, December 25, 2006, A1.
2. See Michael Hughes, *Nationalism and Society: Germany, 1800–1945* (London: Edward Arnold Press, 1988).
3. Monte Palmer, *Comparative Politics: Political Economy, Political Culture, and Political Interdependence* (New York: Wadsworth, 2005), 139.

4. Arnold J. Heidenheimer, *The Government of Germany* (New York: Crowell, 1967), 15. Or, as Dahrendorf describes the Weimar Republic: "a democracy without democrats." See Ralf Dahrendorf, *Society and Democracy in Germany* (New York: Doubleday, 1967).

5. On the Weimar Republic, see M. Rainer Lepsius, "From Fragmented Party Democracy to Government by Emergency Decree and National Socialist Takeover: Germany," in *The Breakdown of Democratic Regimes: Europe*, ed. Juan Linz and Alfred Stepan (Baltimore, MD: Johns Hopkins University Press, 1978), 34–79.

6. See Peter Katzenstein's discussion of West Germany's "semi-sovereignty," in Peter Katzenstein, *Policy and Politics in West Germany: The Growth of a Semi-Sovereign State* (Philadelphia: Temple University Press, 1987).

7. For an excellent discussion of the Stasi, see Timothy Garton Ash, *The File* (New York: Vintage, 1998).

8. Pew 2009 Pulse of Europe Survey, www.pewglobal.org/files/2009/11/Pew-Global-Attitudes-2009-Pulse-of-Europe-Report-Nov-2-1030am-NOT-EMBARGOED.pdf (accessed 12/9/14).

9. Dan Hough and Emil Kirchner, "Germany at 60: Stability and Success, Problems and Challenges," *German Politics* 19, no. 1 (March 2010): 1–8.

10. Adapted from M. Donald Hancock and Henry Krish, *Politics in Germany* (Washington, DC: CQ Press, 2009), 80–103.

11. On the German presidency and the controversy surrounding Köhler, see Gerd Strohmeier and Ruth Wittlinger, "Parliamentary Heads of State: Players or Figureheads? The Case of Horst Köhler," *West European Politics* 33, no. 2 (March 2010): 237–57.

12. On German federalism, see Carolyn Moore and Wade Jacoby, eds., *German Federalism in Transition: Reform in a Consensual State* (London: Routledge, 2010).

13. Brigitte Geissel, "How to Improve the Quality of Democracy? Experiences with Participatory Innovations at the Local Level in Germany," *German Politics and Society* 27, no. 4 (Winter 2009): 51–71.

14. On the German party system, see Steven Weldon and Andrea Nusser, "Bundestag Election 2009: Solidifying the Five Party System," in *Between Left and Right: The 2009 Bundestag Elections and the Transformation of the German Party System*, ed. Eric Langenbacher (New York: Berghahn Books, 2010), 69–85.

15. David Conradt, "The Shrinking Elephants: The 2009 Election and the Changing Party System," in Langenbacher, ed., *Between Left and Right*, 48–68.

16. A good historical treatment of the CDU is Ulrich Lappenküper, "Between Concentration Movement and People's Party: The Christian Democratic Union in Germany," in *Christian Democracy in Europe since 1945*, vol. 2, eds. Michael Gehler and Wolfram Kaiser (New York: Routledge, 2004), 25–37. An excellent analysis of recent changes in the party is Clayton Marc Clemens, "Beyond Christian Democracy? Welfare State Politics and Policy in a Changing CDU," *German Politics* 22, nos. 1–2 (2013): 191–211.

17. "Germany's Social Democrats pick Martin Schulz as leader," *The Economist*, January 28, 2017, www.economist.com/news/europe/21715589-they-will-probably-still-lose-angela-merkel-germanys-social-democrats-pick-martin-schulz (accessed 2/8/17).

18. On the SPD, see Jonathan Olsen, "Past Imperfect, Future Tense: The SPD before and after the 2013 Federal Election," *German Politics and Society* 32, no. 3 (Autumn 2014): 46–58.

19. Wolfgang Rüdig, "The Perennial Success of the German Greens," *Environmental Politics* 21, no. 1 (2012): 108–30.

20. On the Left Party, see Dan Hough and Michael Kob, "Populism Personified or Reinvigorated Reformers? The German Left Party in 2009 and Beyond," *German Politics and Society* 27, no. 2 (Summer 2009): 77–91.

21. On the AfD, see Thomas Meaney, "Germany's New Nationalists," *New Yorker*, October 3, 2016, 54–62.

22. Taehyun Nam, "Rough Days in Democracies: Comparing Protests in Democracies," *European Journal of Political Research* 46, no. 1 (January 2007): 97–120.

23. "Paving the Way for a Muslim Parallel Society," *Der Speigel*, March 29, 2007.

24. David Conradt, *The German Polity*, 9th ed. (New York: Houghton Mifflin Harcourt, 2009), 77.

25. See, for example, the World Values Survey 1981–1999, "Views of a Changing World 2003," Pew Center for the People and the Press, www.people-press.org/2003/06/03/views-of-a -changing-world-2003 (accessed 3/8/17).

26. Russell J. Dalton, *Citizen Politics* (New York: Chatham House, 2002), 84.

27. Dan Hough and Emil Kirchner, "Germany at 60: Stability and Success, Problems and Challenges," *German Politics* 19, no. 1 (March 2010): 1–8, and "Germany's Reunification 25 Years On," *Economist*, October 2, 2015, www.economist.com/node/21677622/print (accessed 5/11/16).

28. Hans Kundnani, "Germany as a Geo-economic Power," *Washington Quarterly* 34, no. 3 (2011): 37.

29. See, for example, Joe Nocera, "Germany Cuts Off Its Nose," *New York Times,* November 28, 2011, www.nytimes.com/2011/11/29/opinion/nocera-germany-cuts-off-its-nose.html?scp=7 &sq=Germany&st=cse (accessed 3/8/17).

30. M. Petrou, "Merkel under Siege," in *Maclean's* [serial online] 124, no. 39 (October 10, 2011): 32 34. Available from Academic Search Premier, Ipswich, MA (accessed 2/8/17).

31. "How Very Understanding," *Economist*, May 10, 2014, www.economist.com/news/europe 21601897-germanys-ambivalence-towards-russia-reflects-its-conflicted-identity-how -very-understanding?zid=307&ah=5e80419d1bc9821ebe173f4f0f060a07 (accessed 5/26/14).

32. Ralf Neukirch, "The Sympathy Problem: Is Germany a Country of Russia Apologists?" *Spiegel Online International*, www.spiegel.de/international/germany/prominent-germans-have -understanding-for-russian-annexation-of-crimea-a-961711.html (accessed 5/24/14); and data from the Pew Research Global Attitudes Project, www.pcwglobal.org/database/indicator/1 /group/3/response/Unfavorable (accessed 5/24/14).

33. A good overview of Germany's role in the Ukraine crisis is Elizabeth Pond, "Germany's Real Role in the Ukraine Crisis," *Foreign Affairs* 94, no. 2 (March 2015): 173–76.

34. Juergen Baetz, "Germany Decides to Abandon Nuclear Power by 2022," *Seattle Times*, May 30, 2011, http://seattletimes.nwsource.com/html/businesstechnology/2015187458_apeugermany nuclearpower.html (accessed 3/8/17).

35. "Renewable Energy Policy in Germany: An Overview and Assessment," Joint Global Change Research Institute, 2009, www.globalchange.umd.edu/energytrends/germany/6 (accessed 3/8/17); and "German Lessons," *Economist*, April 3, 2008, www.economist.com/node/10961 890?story_id=10961890 (accessed 3/8/17).

36. An excellent overview of this controversy and the immigration issue in Germany is Tamar Jacoby, "Germany's Immigration Dilemma," *Foreign Affairs* 90, no. 2 (March/April 2011): 8–14.

37. J. Mushaben, "From Ausländer to Inlander: The Changing Faces of Citizenship in Post-Wall Germany," *German Politics & Society* [serial online] 28, no. 1 (March 30, 2010): 141–64. Available from Academic Search Premier, Ipswich, MA (accessed 2/8/17).

38. Marc Morjé Howard, "Germany's Citizenship Policy in Comparative Perspective," in *German Politics and Society* 30, no. 1 (Spring 2012): 39–51.

39. Anna Sauerbrev, "The End of the Merkel Era," *New York Times*, February 10, 2016, www .nytimes.com/2016/02/11/opinion/the-end-of-the-merkel-era.html (accessed 5/12/16).

KEY TERMS

Basic Law Germany's current constitution

Bonn Republic The nickname for the Federal Republic of Germany from 1945 to 1990 during Germany's postwar division into East and West; named after West Germany's capital city

Bundesrat The upper house of Germany's legislature

Bundestag The lower house of Germany's legislature

catchall parties Parties that attempt to attract voters of all classes and are, therefore, generally centrist in their platforms

Christian Democratic Union (CDU) Germany's largest conservative party

codetermination The system requiring that unions occupy half of all seats on the boards of directors of Germany's largest private firms

federal chancellor Germany's prime minister and head of government

Federal Constitutional Court The powerful court that interprets Germany's Basic Law

federal president The indirectly elected and largely ceremonial head of state

Federal Republic of Germany (FRG) The official name of democratic West Germany during the postwar division of Germany

Free Democratic Party (FDP) A small centrist party that has often formed part of governing coalitions

Gastarbeiter The German term for "guest workers," or foreign workers allowed to reside temporarily in Germany to provide much-needed labor

German Democratic Republic (GDR) The official name of Communist East Germany during the postwar division of Germany

the Greens Germany's environmental party

Hitler, Adolf The Nazi leader during the Third Reich who led Germany to defeat in World War II

Junkers Politically powerful Prussian landed aristocrats

Länder German states

the Left The party farthest to the left of all Germany's major parties; an alliance of leftist Social Democrats and remnants of former East German Communists

Merkel, Angela Germany's current conservative chancellor, as of 2017

minister-president The governor of a German state

National Socialist (Nazi) Party Hitler's fascist party

Prussia The most powerful German state before Germany's unification

reich The German term for "empire"

reunification The 1990 integration of East and West Germany

Social Democratic Party (SPD) Germany's oldest party, located on the center left

sovereign debt Debts of sovereign states

Third Reich The name Hitler gave to his fascist totalitarian regime (1933–45)

Weimar Republic Germany's first democratic republic (1919–33), the collapse of which led to Hitler's totalitarian regime

WEB LINKS

- Germany's Basic Law, online version (www.constitution.org/cons /germany.txt)
- Germany's Christian Democratic Party (www.cducsu.de)
- Germany's Free Democratic Party (www.fdp-fraktion.de)
- Germany's Green Party (www.gruene-bundestag.de)
- Germany's Left Party (www.linksfraktion.de)
- Germany's legislature (www.bundestag.de)
- Germany's Social Democratic Party (www.spd.de/)
- Information about Germany, a one-stop portal (www.deutschland.de/)
- Spiegel Online International (www.spiegel.de/international/)

6

Japanese demonstrators protest the ruling Liberal Democratic Party government's efforts to reinterpret Japan's pacifist constitution.

JAPAN

Why Study This Case?

Japan offers an important case for the study of contemporary politics, perhaps foremost to educate a Western audience about what Japan is *not*. Too much of our understanding of Japan is shaped or at least shadowed by dangerously misleading stereotypes. For example, Japan is *not*

- *small*. It has a landmass greater than that of Germany or Great Britain; a population larger than that of all non-Asian countries other than the United States, Brazil, Nigeria, and Russia; and an economy fourth in size only to those of the United States, China, and India.
- *defenseless*. Despite the constitution's famous **Article 9**, which renounces war, Japan possesses a **Self-Defense Force** second only to the U.S. military in technical sophistication, and boasts defense expenditures comparable to or greater than those of all member countries of the North Atlantic Treaty Organization (NATO) except the United States.
- *unique, or at least no more so than any other country*. In its political stability, state involvement in the economy, cultural conformity, and even ethnic homogeneity, Japan may be quite different from the United States, but in these and other ways, it is more often the United States that is exceptional, not Japan.

If Japan is more "normal" than we might have assumed, it nonetheless remains an intriguing case that defies generalization and begs further investigation.

Politically, an authoritarian vanguard of low-ranking nobles launched a sweeping revolution from above in the latter half of the nineteenth century, modernizing Japan under the mercantilist slogan "**rich country,**

JAPAN

RUSSIA

Sea
of
Okhotsk

Kurile Islands occupied
by the Soviet Union
since 1945, today
administered by Russia,
but southern islands
claimed by Japan

Kurile Islands

CHINA

Sapporo

HOKKAIDO

NORTH
KOREA

Sea
of
Japan

Akita

Sendai
Fukushima

Takeshima

HONSHU

SOUTH
KOREA

Yellow
Sea

TOKYO

Yokohama
Nagoya

Hiroshima   Kobe
Kitakyushu   Osaka

Fukuoka

SHIKOKU

KYUSHU

East
China
Sea

Ryukyu Islands

PACIFIC

OCEAN

*Bonin
Islands
(Japan)*

*Senkaku
Islands*

Okinawa

*Minami Daito
Jima
(Japan)*

N

*Iwo Jima
(Japan)*

*Sakishima
Islands*

0   100   200 mi
0   100   200 km

Philippine Sea

strong military." As in Germany during the same period, the aristocracy and its militarist successors waged wars of imperialist expansion in the name of the Japanese emperor during the first half of the twentieth century, which led ultimately to stunning defeat at the hands of the United States in 1945. U.S. occupiers then launched a second revolution from above, replacing authoritarian rule with a remarkably liberal and democratic constitution written entirely by the Americans (in just six days) and unamended by the Japanese in more than seven decades.

For nearly six of these past seven decades, the conservative **Liberal Democratic Party (LDP)** governed Japan. Moreover, elected politicians have historically deferred to Japan's nonelected career civil servants, who for much of this period have written most of Japan's laws. But in watershed elections in 1993 and again in 2009, opposition parties unseated LDP governments and took measures to break up this long-standing conservative alliance between nonelected bureaucrats and the LDP. Over the past two decades, significant reforms have been implemented, yet political change has not come readily to Japan. This situation raises several important questions: Where does political authority reside in Japan? How has Japan's externally imposed democracy evolved over the years? And does Japanese democracy differ in substantial ways from other advanced industrial democracies?

Economically, under conditions of state-directed industrialization, imperialism, and war, Japan's authoritarian leaders forged a highly centralized economy over the course of the first half of the twentieth century. Concerned about Japan's economic stability in a heightening Cold War, the United States allowed the wartorn nation to retain many aspects of its state-led economic structure, even as it promoted sweeping political reforms. Japan therefore extended into peacetime its wartime mercantilist economy, which linked career bureaucrats, conservative politicians, and big-business elite and was spectacularly successful for several decades.[1] By the 1980s, Japan had achieved and in many cases surpassed the levels of technological prowess, commercial competitiveness, and economic prosperity of the advanced Western industrialized nations.

By the early 1990s, however, this seemingly invincible economy began a dramatic and persistent decline. If Japan's state-led expansion draws comparisons with Prussian modernization or French *dirigisme* (planned economy), Japan's more recent economic downturn invites comparisons with Great Britain's earlier postwar economic slide. Japan has experienced nearly three decades of stagnant or slow economic growth and lagging industrial production. For much of this period, banks have been in crisis and unemployment has climbed as the stock market has languished. Japan's workforce is graying even as its population rapidly shrinks. In 2010, China surpassed Japan as the world's second-largest economy, and in 2014 India pushed it out of third place. Adding tragic and unprecedented insult to these decades of economic stagnation, in 2011 a devastating 9.0 earthquake and tsunami struck northeast Japan, killing tens of thousands and damaging several nuclear power plants. This catastrophe further hobbled the country's economy, threatened its energy infrastructure, exacerbated political instability, and severely strained state capacity to deal with the humanitarian disaster. Although Japan remains wealthy and most of its citizens relatively prosperous, few countries have faced such a striking peacetime turnaround in economic fortune. How does one account for this dynamic of rapid growth followed by precipitous decline and long-term stagnation? What have been the causes of Japan's economic success and its more recent failures? If its mercantilist policies persisted throughout the past century, can they be held responsible for both the rise and the decline of the nation's economy? Must Japan change, and if so, how and when?

Finally, Japan may not be unique, but its particular balancing of freedom and equality certainly differentiates it to some degree from many other countries. Although income inequality is rising in Japan, historically its citizens have enjoyed high levels of equality. However, this relative equity has been managed with low levels of taxation, social services, and other state measures designed to redistribute income (what one political scientist described as "equality without effort"[2]). By the same token, the civil and personal freedoms enshrined in Japan's postwar constitution are unrivaled by all but the most liberal Western regimes, yet Japanese politics remains elitist, Japan's society conformist, and its economy mercantilist.

Even the less stereotypical and more nuanced generalized features of Japan's economy and polity now face the prospect of unprecedented, if not revolutionary, change. In the wake of the country's prolonged economic downturn, long-standing corporate practices, such as lifetime employment for white-collar workers, are fading. In the face of persistent government scandal and a growing popular sense of political inefficacy, policy making in a previously harmonious Japan is becoming far more fractious and perhaps even more pluralist. Is Japan facing a third revolution, this time from below? Only by understanding this country and where it has come from will we be able to make sense of where it may be going.

Major Geographic and Demographic Features

Even though Japan may not be a particularly small country, its topography and demography certainly make it seem small and have given the Japanese a keen sense of vulnerability and dependency. Although the Japanese archipelago includes nearly 7,000 islands (including several of disputed sovereignty), few are inhabited, and nearly all Japanese citizens reside on one of the four main islands: Hokkaido, Honshu, Kyushu, and Shikoku. Even on the main islands, mountainous terrain renders only about one-fourth of the land habitable and a little more than 10 percent arable. More than 80 percent of all Japanese live in an urban setting, and half the population is crowded into three megametropolises located on Japan's eastern seaboard: Tokyo, Osaka, and Nagoya. This means that most of Japan's 126 million inhabitants are crammed into an area about twice the size of New Jersey, thus making Japan one of the most densely populated countries in the world.

Land (both habitable and arable) is not the only scarce natural resource in Japan. Although it has maintained rice self-sufficiency through heroic levels of subsidies for inefficient domestic producers and trade restrictions on foreign rice (imported rice faces a nearly 800 percent tariff, and Japanese consumers pay twice the world market price for the homegrown variety), Japan remains dependent on imports for nearly three-fourths of its food. This critical dependence extends to most of the crucial inputs of an advanced industrial economy, including virtually all of Japan's oil and most of its iron ore, thus compelling modern Japan to rely on external trade relations and making it particularly sensitive to the vagaries of such trade.

Japan's external focus has sharpened at important historical junctures because of its relative proximity to the Asian mainland. The Korean Peninsula in particular served as a ready conduit to ancient and medieval Japan for importing language, technology, religion, and even the popular cultures of Korea, China, and places beyond. Over time, Japan adopted (and adapted) from its mainland mentors traditions as varied as Buddhism and bowing, chopsticks and Chinese written characters. At the same time, Japan feared vulnerability at the hands of its powerful neighbors to the west (particularly China and, later, Russia), and Japanese cartographers and rulers identified the Korean Peninsula as a dagger poised at the heart of Japan.

Japan's fears of vulnerability were not unfounded. In the thirteenth century, a formidable force of Mongols and Koreans mounted two separate attacks on Japan, both of which were repulsed in part by typhoons (named *kamikaze*, or "divine wind," by the Japanese) that blew the attacking ships off course. These incursions and the subsequent arrival of both religion and guns brought by Western imperialists led rulers first to practice for several hundred years and then to impose for two and a half centuries a formal policy of *sakoku* ("closed country"), or xenophobic isolation. This ended only when Western imperialists forcibly opened Japan in the nineteenth century, reaffirming Japanese fears of external threats.

Japan's insular status has certainly contributed to its racial, ethnic, and linguistic homogeneity and its cohesive national identity. This cultural uniformity, however, should not be overstated. Although today virtually all citizens of Japan identify themselves as Japanese, this image masks the earlier assimilation of the indigenous Ainu (now found almost exclusively on Hokkaido) and the Okinawans. In recent decades, Japan has witnessed an influx of Asian migrant workers (predominantly from Southeast Asia, China, and South Asia) who continue to face varying degrees of political discrimination and social marginalization.

Historical Development of the State

Despite the many cultural oddities that European traders and missionaries discovered when they first arrived in sixteenth-century Japan, they had actually stumbled upon a nation and society whose historical development bore striking similarities to that of their own countries. As in Europe, isolated tribal anarchy had gradually given way to growing national identity and the emergence of a primitive state. Aided by clearly defined natural borders and imperial and bureaucratic institutions borrowed from neighboring China, the Japanese state grew in both capacity and legitimacy, particularly after the seventh century C.E. Imperial rule was first usurped and then utilized by a feudal military aristocracy that came to *rule* over an increasingly centralized and sophisticated bureaucratic state for many centuries, even as it allowed the emperors to continue to *reign* symbolically.

Whereas in Europe gradually weakening feudalism gave way to powerful modernizing monarchs and ultimately middle-class democracy, Japan's version of centralized feudalism persisted until Western imperialism provided the catalyst for change in the nineteenth century. Faced with external threats to their nation's sovereignty, forward-looking authoritarian oligarchs further centralized state power and consciously retained the emperor as a puppet to legitimize their forced-draft efforts to catch up with the West. During this Meiji era, the oligarchs, borrowing this time not from China but from the institutions of modern European states, established a modern Japanese state that grew in autonomy and capacity as it became a formidable military and industrial power. In further emulating the Western imperial powers, Japan also began to establish its own empire (what it would come to benignly label as the "Greater East Asian Co-Prosperity Sphere"), obtaining colonies in Taiwan (after defeating imperial China in 1895) and Korea (after defeating tsarist Russia in 1905). In the 1930s, Japan continued its expansion on the Asian mainland, capturing Manchuria (1931), invading China proper (1937), and sweeping through Southeast Asia at the same time that it launched its attack on Pearl Harbor and the United States (1941). However, this course of imperial expansion and military conquest ended with defeat at the hands of the Americans in 1945, who defanged Japan's militarist state but allowed its mercantilist bureaucracy to remain intact.

Although modernization brought dramatic changes to Japan, several themes or continuities emerged from this process that are relevant to the development of Japan's modern state and its contemporary politics. First, at critical junctures in its history, outside influence or foreign pressure (what the Japanese call *gaiatsu*) has brought change to Japan. Second, in the face of this pressure, the Japanese have often chosen not to reject or even resist the external influence but rather to adopt and then adapt it, deftly assimilating what they perceive as valuable foreign innovations and achieving modernization without all of the trappings of Westernization. Third, for many centuries and arguably to the present, Japan's ruling elite has maintained a persistent division of labor between those who rule, holding substantive power and authority, and those who symbolically reign. This division of responsibility has preserved the autonomy and strengthened the political capacity of those rulers controlling power while enhancing the continuity of the regime and the legitimacy of the state by retaining symbolic reigning authority. Fourth, Japan early on established a highly effective and respected bureaucratic leadership that has guided the state and pursued economic development as a means of achieving national sovereignty and state legitimacy. Scholars have argued that the resulting institutional arrangements facilitated a close working relationship between national bureaucrats and private business and propelled Japan's rapid modernization throughout the twentieth century. Japan's recent economic malaise and the apparent incapacity of the Japanese state to address this challenge,

TIMELINE OF POLITICAL DEVELOPMENT

YEAR	EVENT
645 C.E.	China-inspired Taika political reforms introduced.
1192	Minamoto Yoritomo declared first shogun.
1603	Tokugawa Shogunate established.
1853–54	Japan forcibly opened by U.S. Commodore Matthew C. Perry.
1867–68	Meiji Restoration takes place.
1894–95	First Sino-Japanese War is fought.
1904–05	Russo-Japanese War is fought.
1918–31	Era of Taishō democracy.
1937–45	Second Sino-Japanese War takes place.
1941	Pacific War begins.
1945	Japan is defeated and surrenders in World War II.
1945–52	The United States occupies Japan.
1955	Liberal Democratic Party (LDP) is formed.
1993–94	LDP briefly loses majority in Diet's House of Representatives to an opposition coalition.
2007	LDP loses majority in Diet's House of Councillors.
2009	Democratic Party of Japan (DPJ) gains majority in House of Representatives and forms a coalition government.
2011	Tōhoku earthquake, tsunami, and nuclear disasters take place.
2012	LDP regains a majority in the House of Representatives and forms a coalition government with Shinzō Abe as prime minister.
2014	LDP coalition obtains a super majority in the House of Representatives.
2016	LDP coalition obtains a super majority in the House of Councillors.

however, have called into question this developmental model and remind us how difficult it can be to dismantle entrenched institutions that may no longer be beneficial.

Premodern Japan: Adapting Chinese Institutions

As early as the third century C.E., shifting coalitions of tribal hunters and early rice cultivators formed a primitive state in southern Honshu under the leadership of a tribal chieftain whose legitimacy rested on a claim of divine lineage descending from the sun goddess. By the seventh century, Japan had come under the powerful cultural influence of Tang dynasty China, whose influence cannot be overstated. Among the most significant and lasting of the dynasty's cultural exports were Buddhism, Confucianism, the Chinese written language (which by that time had become the dominant script throughout Asia), and the trappings of material culture (including modes of dress, architectural styles, and even the use of chopsticks).

Tang China also had a profound influence on political reforms in seventh century Japan, inspiring the country's leaders to establish an administrative system modeled on the Tang imperial state. To finance this new bureaucracy, the state introduced sweeping land reform, purchasing all land and redistributing it among peasants so that it could be taxed. Although Buddhist religious doctrines and Confucian social values thrived, the Tang-inspired Taika administrative and land reforms did not take hold as well as the other borrowings. The meritocratic civil bureaucracy soon evolved into a hereditary, self-perpetuating ruling elite supported by a declining tax base. Squeezed mercilessly, the peasants, either for survival or for protection, were forced to sell out to local wealthy officials who had managed to arrange tax immunity for their own lands.

From the eighth to the twelfth centuries, political power and wealth steadily shifted from the central government to independent rural landowners, and the urban-centered imperial system gradually disintegrated into a formalistic body concerned only with the trappings and rituals of state. These emerging decentralized hierarchies included territorial nobles or lords, known as *daimyo*, who governed the lands they occupied; former peasants, who had become their serfs; and the lords' warrior retainers, or **samurai**.

As their power grew, the landed aristocrats became increasingly dissatisfied with the ineffectual rule of the court. Over the course of the next 400 years, from the thirteenth through the sixteenth centuries, power completely shifted to this military aristocracy. Different clans vied for supremacy, and ascendant clans established a government known as the *bakufu* (literally, "tent government," referencing its martial origins). This was a period of continual warfare based on attempts at establishing a line of succession and a semblance of unity through military conquest, during which the emperor was largely disregarded. But in Japan, unlike in Europe, the imperial household was neither absolutely empowered nor completely displaced. The emperor had become not so much a person as a reigning symbol; whoever spoke in the name of the imperial chrysanthemum crest spoke with legitimate authority. The best comparison to a Western arrangement is perhaps that of powerful European kings who sought claim to spiritual authority through papal anointing. The emperor became a puppet in the hands of aspiring daimyo, who never destroyed the head of state but forced him to anoint the strongest among them **shogun**, or dominant lord.

Tokugawa Shogunate: Centralized Feudalism

By the end of the sixteenth century, the feudal wars had come to a head, and Japan was slowly but surely unified by the **Tokugawa** shogunate, which imposed an enforced peace for the next two and a half centuries. Successive shoguns from the Tokugawa clan ruled over this feudal hierarchy in the name of the emperor, successfully shoring up the shogunate's authority and keeping the daimyo in check through an effective strategy of divide and rule at home and *sakoku*, or closed-country isolation, abroad.

The power of a local daimyo rested, in turn, on the size and productivity of the hereditary fief or feudal domain he controlled, the peasants who tilled the land, and, most important, the number of samurai the domain could support. The warrior retainers lived with their lords in the castle towns that served as the fortresses and administrative centers from which the lords governed their domains. But as the Tokugawa-enforced peace settled over the countryside, the samurai were gradually converted from warriors to civil officials with fiscal, legal, and other administrative responsibilities. These samurai-turned-bureaucrats tackled civilian tasks in the same devoted, selfless manner in which they had been trained to carry out their martial responsibilities. It is difficult to overstate the value of this cadre of efficient, skilled, disciplined, and highly respected bureaucrats as the country faced the challenges of abrupt modernization in the nineteenth and twentieth centuries.

Although Tokugawa Japan's political system was remarkably stable, its social organization and economy developed what proved to be volatile contradictions. Tokugawa society was strictly hereditary and rigidly hierarchical; individuals were born into a particular station and could neither move between classes nor, for the most part, even advance within their own class. The samurai class was at the top of the hierarchy, but not all samurai were equal. This diverse warrior class ranged from the wealthy and powerful shogun and daimyo to the lowly retainers barely getting by on a subsistence stipend of rice. Next down on the social rung were the peasants, who formed the bulk of the remaining subjects, followed by artisans and craftsmen, and finally, at (or near) the bottom of the social hierarchy, the merchants.[3] As in other Confucian societies, commercial activities, including moneylending, and those people who participated in them were viewed with great disdain. Despite being socially despised, however, by the nineteenth century these merchants had established sophisticated and lucrative trading networks throughout Japan. Moreover, they had established themselves as the financiers of the lifestyles of the upper ranks of the samurai, who over time grew increasingly indebted to the merchants.

When Commodore Matthew C. Perry steamed into Edo Bay with his fleet of U.S. warships in 1853 seeking coaling stations and trading opportunities for American ships, he unsuspectingly came upon this system, which was apparently stable but internally ripe for change. The ruling class had status and privilege but was heavily indebted and, in the case of many low-ranking samurai, even impoverished. The merchants were wealthy but socially disdained, lacking both political power and social status. Many Japanese, particularly among the lower ranks of the samurai, had become dissatisfied with what they saw as an increasingly ineffectual and redundant Tokugawa government and were ready for revolt. Perry did not cause this revolt, but he certainly facilitated it.

The forceful entry of American and (subsequently) European powers into Japan and the pressure they placed on the shogunate created a crisis of legitimacy for Tokugawa rule. Virtually free from foreign military threats and isolated from external innovations during the centuries of *sakoku*, the Tokugawa government lacked the military capacity to resist the unfair trade demands of the Americans and Europeans. The regional daimyo, however, judged these demands as unacceptable and thus revolted.

A decade of political chaos ensued, prompting a revolution launched not from below, by restive peasants or even aspiring merchants, but from above, by a handful of junior samurai officials. Much like Germany's nineteenth-century modernizers, this aristocratic vanguard was committed to sweeping change cloaked in traditional trappings. They recognized that the maintenance of Japanese independence required the end of the feudal regime and the swift creation of a modern economic, political, social, and, perhaps most important, military system capable of holding its own against the Western powers. But rather than deposing the symbolic leader of the old regime, the modernizers launched their reforms in the name of the 16-year-old emperor Meiji, ostensibly "restoring" him to his rightful ruling position.

Meiji Restoration: Revolution from Above

The group of junior samurai who led the **Meiji Restoration** in 1867 and 1868 came to be known as the **Meiji oligarchs**. What began as a spontaneous rejection of the Western threat by xenophobic nationalists quickly gave way to regime change led by a handful of low-ranking samurai promoting positive reform that involved emulation of and catching up with the West. These oligarchs served as a vanguard in establishing the foundations of the modern Japanese state.

Their first priority was to make Japan a strong and wealthy state capable of renegotiating the inequitable treaties the West had imposed on the country. Under the slogan "rich country, strong military," they promoted their mercantilist view of a strong relationship between economic development and industrialization on the one hand, and military and political power in the international arena on the other. They dismantled the feudal state, deposing the shogun and converting the decentralized feudal domains to centrally controlled political units. They jettisoned the feudal economy, eliminated hereditary fiefs, returned land to the peasants and introduced a land tax that provided steady revenues to the state, and converted samurai stipends to investment bonds. Perhaps most surprisingly, they destroyed their own class, ending samurai privileges.

In 1889, the oligarchs adopted an imperial constitution (patterned after the German constitution) that was presented as a "gift" from the emperor to his subjects. It specified not the rights and liberties of the citizens but the duties and obligations that the subjects owed the emperor and the state. The constitution created some of the formal institutions found in Western democracies, including a bicameral parliament, known as the **Diet**, though its members were chosen by a limited franchise and exercised little real authority. The constitution vested all executive power in the emperor, who appointed the cabinet ministers (just as reigning emperors had previously appointed the ruling shogun) and retained supreme command over the military. The oligarchs further legitimized this power structure by promoting an emperor-centered form of Shintoism as the mandatory state religion and by inculcating both national patriotism and emperor worship in the education system.

Buttressed by the traditional and charismatic legitimacy of a reigning emperor and the rational-legal legitimacy of an equally symbolic (and largely powerless) parliament, the oligarchs had obtained both the authority and the autonomy to promote painfully rapid development and to create a modern military. The highly capable agents for carrying out these goals were threefold:

1. *Bureaucracy*: This revolution from above was envisioned by a handful of elites, but it was carried out by a modern, centralized bureaucracy recruited on the basis of merit. Although the civil service was open to all, it was staffed almost entirely by former samurai who were literate, respected, and had served their feudal lords in similar administrative capacities for generations.

2. *Zaibatsu*: Believing they did not have the luxury to wait for the emergence of an entrepreneurial class, the oligarchs established state-owned industries in key sectors and then sold them off to former rice merchants. These state-nurtured but privately owned industrial conglomerates, known as *zaibatsu* or financial cliques, forged the first of the enduring ties between big business and the state that have persisted to the present.

3. *Military*: Although the military was created initially for defense, the country's resource dependency, the voracious appetite of the zaibatsu, and the example of Western imperialism soon launched Japan on its own successful path of imperial warfare.

By the end of World War I, the Meiji oligarchs had realized many of their initial goals. In foreign policy, they had successfully renegotiated the inequitable treaties with the West, which now recognized Japan as a rising world power. Japan had not only defeated both imperial China (1894–95) and tsarist Russia (1904–05) but had also acquired colonies in Taiwan (1895) and Korea (1910). Furthermore, by this time Japan had established a fragile but rapidly growing economy.

However, Japan's foreign policy and economic successes were not matched in the domestic political realm. By the 1920s, Japan was becoming a nation of diverse economic and political interests no longer easily subsumed under a single banner or slogan, and pressure to change the highly authoritarian system was building. The desire for change became increasingly apparent during the reign of the Taishō emperor (1912–26), particularly in the era of Wilsonian democracy after World War I. By that time, the original Meiji oligarchs had passed from the scene, and efforts by their bureaucratic and military successors to maintain the state autonomy of the Meiji political system faced challenges from a middle class demanding democratic rights, laborers organizing for better working conditions, and peasants rioting against onerous taxes.

In an era that came to be known as **Taishō democracy** (1918–31), efforts by these groups and their liberal political proponents to institute democracy were significant but short-lived and ultimately unsuccessful. Different groups increasingly sought to exercise influence in the political realm, and with some success, including the establishment and flourishing of competitive political parties by the early years of the century, election of the first commoner as prime minister in 1918, the alternation of elected governments during the 1920s, and the granting of universal male suffrage by 1925.

The Militarist Era: Imperial Expansion and Defeat

By the end of the 1920s, a number of events had stymied Japan's first genuine but short-lived effort to establish liberal democracy. The Great Depression and the rising global protectionism of the 1930s dealt trade-dependent Japan harsh blows, bringing about increased labor agitation and political unrest as the economy weakened. This domestic instability, combined with anti-Japanese sentiment in China, spurred rising nationalist and fascist sentiments at home and reemerging militarism and adventurism abroad. As in Europe and elsewhere, the emergence of such forces led in the early 1930s to a period of political polarization and increased political violence in which democracy became the chief victim. One Western observer labeled this period an era of "government by assassination."[4]

The era of Taishō democracy ended with the Japanese army's seizure of Manchuria in 1931 and the assassination of the last elected head of government by naval cadets in 1932. Over the next decade, the military steadily expanded its control of the state, ruling in an often uneasy alliance with the bureaucracy and the zaibatsu. Although most historians are not comfortable labeling the Japanese militarist state fascist, the emperor-based system lent itself to the establishment of a near-totalitarian state, one with many similarities to the European fascist states. The state sought to bring under its auspices or otherwise eliminate virtually all pluralist groups and autonomous organizations; that process entailed censoring the press, repressing all forms of political dissent, crushing political parties and other forms of free association, and gaining almost complete control over industrial production.

Also, like its fascist allies in Europe, Japan promoted an ultranationalist ideology and expansionist foreign policy, with the intent of extending its empire. At the height of its power, Japan's so-called Greater East Asian Co-Prosperity Sphere of conquered lands included most of the eastern half of China, Sakhalin and some of the Aleutian Islands, Korea, Taiwan, the Philippines, Indochina, Thailand, Malaya, Burma, Indonesia, and portions of the South Pacific. But as in Europe, Allied forces met, stemmed, and turned back Japanese aggression by 1944. Costly and stunning defeats at sea and on land, followed by the destructive U.S. firebombing of Japanese cities in early 1945 and the atomic bombing of Hiroshima and Nagasaki in August of that year, prompted Japan's unconditional surrender on September 2, 1945.

U.S. Occupation: Reinventing Japan

Japan's defeat and destruction were devastatingly complete: militarily, industrially, even psychologically. One historian estimates that the war cost Japan some 2.7 million lives (nearly 4 percent of its population), and that by war's end many more millions were injured, sick, or seriously malnourished.[5] Under these conditions, it was once again foreign (specifically, American) pressure that provided the impetus for revolutionary change in Japan. Although the seven-year occupation of Japan was technically an Allied operation, it remained overwhelmingly a U.S. enterprise managed by a single individual: the Supreme Commander of the Allied Powers in Japan, General **Douglas MacArthur**.

Like the arrival of Commodore Perry's ships nearly a century earlier, the American occupation of Japan following World War II is significant both for what it changed and for what it did not. The initial plan called for demilitarization to exorcise Japan's militant feudal past and then for democratization to establish American-style democratic values and institutions. Demilitarization proceeded swiftly and included not only the purging of all professional military officers, key wartime politicians, and zaibatsu leaders but also the disbanding of the ultranationalist associations and political parties. These thorough purges destroyed the military class and replaced entrenched politicians with technocrats (in most cases, former bureaucrats) and zaibatsu families with professional managers. Most dramatically, the new "Japanese" constitution (quickly drafted by MacArthur's staff and adopted by the Diet in 1947 almost unaltered) included Article 9, the so-called peace clause. The clause stipulated that Japan would "forever renounce war as a sovereign right" and never maintain "land, sea, and air forces, as well as other war potential."

Changing the status of the emperor—constitutionally and in the eyes of the Japanese citizens—to no longer be a political force was key to MacArthur's democratization efforts. The constitution reduced the emperor's stature from godlike and inviolable to simply symbolic, and it transferred sovereignty to the Japanese people. Other measures of this regime change included extending suffrage to women; clarifying relations among the prime minister, the cabinet, and the two houses of the Diet; guaranteeing civil rights and freedoms; breaking up the zaibatsu and imposing antitrust measures; encouraging labor unions and other interest groups; redistributing land to the peasants; and reforming the education system.

The two-stage approach of demilitarization and democratization remained largely in place for the first two years of the occupation. But continued economic hardship (due in part to war reparations and an American policy of little economic aid), combined with the newfound freedom of socialist and Communist activists, pushed Japan rapidly toward the left. This political shift and the onset of the Cold War (compounded by the Communist victory in China in 1949 and the outbreak of the Korean War in 1950) led to a "reverse course" in occupation policies.

The earlier desire to fully demilitarize and democratize Japan in the manner of an Asian Switzerland gave way to a plan that would make Japan a full, albeit still unarmed, ally of the West. In an effort to rebuild the economy, occupation authorities scaled back the deconcentration of industry and prohibited labor strikes. They purged and in some cases (re)jailed leftist labor activists even as they released and rehabilitated numerous conservative politicians. Notably, in all the twists and turns of occupation policy, the wartime bureaucracy of technocratic planners was left intact, in part because the American occupiers needed it and in part because the United States saw the bureaucracy as simply civil servants compelled to carry out the orders of the military government.

Today, some occupation reforms are universally considered to have been both successful and beneficial. Others largely failed, whereas still others remain highly controversial and even contradictory. For instance, on paper, Japan has one of the most liberal political systems in the world. But by default and design, its postwar state featured a core elite of

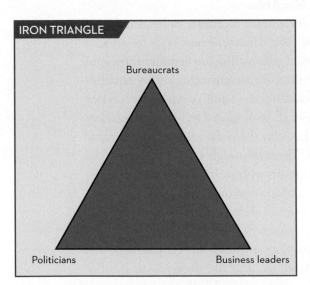

IRON TRIANGLE

Bureaucrats

Politicians

Business leaders

Japan's postwar corporatist and elitist state structure is often referred to as an iron triangle, and has limited the political influence of Japanese citizens and other pluralist interests.

experienced bureaucrats closely allied with conservative politicians (many of them former bureaucrats) and big-business executives. Many aspects of this ruling triad, or **iron triangle**, have persisted throughout the past seven decades and have been credited for Japan's remarkable postwar development as well as blamed for its more recent economic troubles. We now turn to an examination of this contemporary political structure.

Political Regime

Is Japan a democracy? The persistent relevance of Japan's ruling triad of bureaucrats, politicians, and business leaders has led to much controversy on this issue. In important ways, Japan's political structures and procedures are democratic. The rights and liberties enshrined in Japan's 1947 constitution certainly exceed those of the U.S. Constitution and are perhaps globally unrivaled. Its citizens are well protected by the rule of law, and its electoral system is probably no more corrupt than that of other advanced liberal democracies. Unlike its American counterpart, Japan's political arena hosts both socialist and Communist parties, arguably resulting in a greater range of political debate and choice than in the United States.

Yet these formal institutions and procedural safeguards of democracy do not tell the whole story. Although democratic practices seldom live up to the ideals of political pluralism in any democratic regime, the initial dominance and persistent influence of the postwar bureaucracy and its conservative political and corporate allies have led some analysts to conclude that Japan's democracy is dysfunctional, if not an outright mockery. For nearly six decades, the conservative LDP has dominated the legislature, and both LDP and opposition governments have in

---

ESSENTIAL POLITICAL FEATURES

- **Legislative–executive system:** Parliamentary

- **Legislature:** Diet
  - **Lower house:** House of Representatives
  - **Upper house:** House of Councillors

- **Unitary or federal division of power:** Unitary

- **Main geographic subunits:** Prefectures

- **Electoral system for lower house:** Mixed single-member district and proportional representation

- **Chief judicial body:** Supreme Court

---

many cases been overshadowed in policy making by nonelected career civil servants. Long-standing political practices and informal levers and linkages of power have constrained the full functioning of this imported democracy. This dualism becomes more apparent upon examination of the formal institutions and substantive practices of Japanese democracy.

Political Institutions

THE CONSTITUTION

"We, the Japanese people . . ." The opening phrase of Japan's unamended 1947 constitution reveals what are perhaps the document's two most significant aspects: its American imprint and the transfer of sovereignty from the emperor to the Japanese people. Although America's allies called for the prosecution of Emperor Hirohito as a war criminal, General Douglas MacArthur insisted that the emperor renounce his divinity but be allowed to retain his throne to offer continuity and legitimacy to both the occupation government and the new democratic regime. The constitution reduces the emperor's godlike stature to that of a "symbol of the State and of the unity of the people with whom resides sovereign power." To empower Japanese citizens, the American framers of the Japanese constitution constructed an elaborate system of representative institutions, including universal suffrage, a parliamentary legislature in which the cabinet is responsible to the Diet (rather than to the emperor), and an independent judiciary. The constitution also introduced a greater measure of local autonomy by increasing the role of local elected officials.

Although the constitution has never been amended, a growing number of conservative politicians have advocated rewriting Article 9, the peace clause, in an effort to make Japan, in their words, a "normal" country. And in 2015, the LDP-led coalition government managed to pass legislation that effectively reinterprets the clause, permitting Japan for the first time to engage in "collective defense" with its allies, chiefly the United States. However, this legislation faced widespread opposition, and popular support for the pacifist constitution remains generally strong. Nonetheless, the growing military strength and regional ambitions of neighboring China as well as heightened threats from an unpredictable and nuclear-weapons-capable North Korea are strengthening the resolve of conservatives and softening the resistance of pacifists to formally amend the constitution.

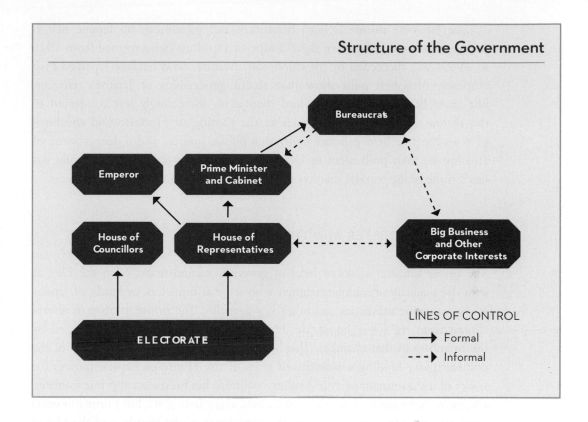

Structure of the Government

Bureaucrats

Emperor

Prime Minister and Cabinet

House of Councillors

House of Representatives

Big Business and Other Corporate Interests

ELECTORATE

LINES OF CONTROL

→ Formal

--→ Informal

The Branches of Government

THE HEAD OF STATE

Although invested by the Meiji Constitution with total authority, the imperial institution was always controlled by de facto rulers. The 1947 constitution eliminated even this derivative authority, making the role of the emperor wholly symbolic. Unlike the British monarch, the Japanese emperor is technically just a symbol of the Japanese state, not the head of state. Like the British queen, however, this standard bearer of the world's oldest imperial dynasty continues to play a significant role in symbolizing the unity and continuity of contemporary Japan. The emperor also performs purely ceremonial tasks, such as appointing both the prime minister (once elected by the Diet) and the chief justice of the Supreme Court (once designated by the government), and he receives foreign ambassadors and represents the nation on many important ceremonial occasions at home and abroad.

The Japanese throne is both hereditary and patrilineal; no female heir is permitted to rule in her own right. Emperor Hirohito (who reigned from 1926 to 1989) was succeeded by his eldest son, Akihito, who became Japan's 125th emperor. Although polls show that recent generations of Japanese citizens, like their British counterparts, find themselves increasingly less connected to the throne, significant events, such as the passing of Hirohito and the birth of a prospective heir, generate enormous public interest and a deeper sense of attachment than polls seem to indicate. Furthermore, Japan's royal family has faced none of the scandal that has challenged the British royals in recent years.

THE PRIME MINISTER AND THE CABINET

The prime minister serves as head of government and draws from the Diet at least the majority of cabinet members who serve as ministers, or heads, of Japan's 17 bureaucratic ministries and other key agencies. The prime minister is always chosen from the lower house, the House of Representatives, and is elected by the members of that chamber. This has meant that the leader (president) of the political party holding a majority of seats in the House of Representatives (or leader of the dominant party in a ruling coalition) has been elected prime minister. Elections in the lower chamber must be held every four years, but prime ministers serve only as long as they maintain the confidence of the members of the House of Representatives as well as the members of their own party. This process has enhanced the role of internal factional party politics and required that successful candidates to the office of prime minister not just belong to the right party but also curry sufficient favor and rise high enough in a dominant faction within that party.

As the dominant party for nearly six decades since its formation in 1955, the LDP fostered prospective party leaders who were more concerned with factional ties, personal connections, and backroom bargaining than with promoting a particular ideological or policy agenda. Faction leaders typically brokered this selection process and rotated the office of LDP president (and prime minister) among various factions somewhat frequently. Therefore, although Japanese prime ministers have been experienced and savvy politicians, they tend to be older, have less policy expertise, and, with notable exceptions, serve for far shorter tenures than do their counterparts abroad. The recent exceptions to this rule have been the tenures of LDP Prime Minister **Junichiro Koizumi** (2001–06) and current LDP Prime Minister **Shinzō Abe** (2006–07; 2012–). But during the intervening decade, prime ministers averaged little more than a year in office; overall, a total of 38 heads of government have led the country since 1945 (compared with 14

Serving for only one year in his first term (2006-07), Prime Minister Abe was reelected to lead the LDP ruling coalition in 2012, making him one of Japan's longest-serving heads of government.

for the United Kingdom and 9 for Germany). Following Koizumi's departure in 2006, three successive LDP prime ministers came and went in just three years before the LDP lost lower house elections in 2009 to the opposition **Democratic Party of Japan (DPJ)**.

Although elected by a landslide with a mandate to reform politics as usual, the DPJ government followed the same pattern as the LDP. The DPJ put up three prime ministers in three years before losing elections in equally dramatic fashion in 2012 and returning the LDP to government. These short-lived governments were further weakened by what the Japanese call a **twisted Diet**, in which no ruling party or coalition controlled both chambers of parliament. That condition persisted from 2007 (when the governing LDP coalition first lost its majority in the upper house) until 2013 (when the LDP coalition regained control of the upper house). In addition to divided government, scholars also point to disgruntled voters (particularly following the government's handling of the 2011 tsunami, earthquake, and nuclear disaster), weak political leaders, and the rise of new media as possible reasons for the frequent brief tenure of Japan's prime ministers.[6] But whatever the cause, this rapid turnover of elected heads of government has made these political leaders very dependent on the expertise, experience, and connections of the unelected bureaucrats within the ministries over which they ostensibly preside.

THE LEGISLATURE

The 1947 constitution establishes Japan's legislature, or Diet (from the Latin *dieta*, meaning both "assembly" and "daily food allowance"), as the "highest organ of state power" and claims exclusive law-making authority for the bicameral parliament. The Japanese Diet has two directly elected chambers: the House of Representatives and the House of Councillors.

The **House of Representatives**, the lower house, has 475 members elected for a four-year term. As in other parliamentary systems, the government typically dissolves the lower house before the term has expired to call elections from a position of strength. Alternatively, a vote of no confidence can force dissolution, as it did most recently in 1993 (one of only four successful postwar no-confidence votes). General elections have taken place on average every two to three years since 1947. The upper chamber, the **House of Councillors**, comprises 242 members, elected for fixed six-year terms (staggered so that half the chamber stands for election every three years). Unlike the lower house, the upper house cannot be dissolved. However, in recent years the House of Councillors has passed several symbolic but influential votes expressing no confidence in the party controlling the lower house while control of the upper house has shifted hands between coalitions led by the LDP and DPJ.

In fact, for most of the six years between 2007 and 2013, parliament faced a "twisted Diet." As in other parliamentary systems, Japan's constitution grants the lower house far more power than the upper; the House of Representatives can override any House of Councillors decision on significant legislation with a two-thirds majority vote. However, recent elections in both houses have permitted first the opposition DPJ and then the opposition LDP to use their position in the upper house to obstruct or at least slow the policies and embarrass the leadership of the party in government. Significantly, any effort to amend the constitution's Article 9, the peace clause, would require two-thirds majority support in both chambers in addition to majority support in a national referendum.

The Diet convenes for 80 days each year and on additional days permitted for special sessions, a schedule roughly half the duration of that of the British Parliament. The brevity of the session has enhanced the role and responsibility of standing committees and party policy committees in the House of Representatives. Many veteran politicians have established expertise in particular policy areas as well as close ties to bureaucrats and interest groups having jurisdiction over or interest in those policy areas. This position has given individual legislators a substantial degree of influence over policy formerly reserved for bureaucratic experts and simultaneously has somewhat weakened party discipline in voting. The importance of pursuing **pork-barrel projects** for home-district constituencies has also weakened allegiance to the government. Therefore, even though the LDP maintained single-party rule for decades and confronted growing demands for change in the face of persistent economic decline, LDP governments hesitated to promote reforms over the objections of these experienced and entrenched politicians bound to networks of bureaucrats, businesses, and local constituencies. Over the years, these institutional relationships have yielded both LDP and DPJ governments hesitant to promote change, despite being elected on platforms promising dramatic reforms to address Japan's economic woes.

THE JUDICIAL SYSTEM

The 1947 constitution established for Japan a court system with a high degree of judicial independence from the other branches of government. In practice, however, the LDP over the years has used its political dominance, appointment powers, and other administrative mechanisms to manipulate the courts and ensure judicial decisions in accordance with its political interests. This process was made easier because, unlike the dual system of federal and state courts in the United States, the Japanese system is unitary—all civil, criminal, and administrative matters are under the jurisdiction of a single hierarchy. At the top is the constitutional court, or Supreme Court, whose 15 members are appointed by the cabinet and subject to a retention referendum every ten years.

Although politicians in all democracies seek to influence the courts, this combination—of a unitary judicial system dominated for many decades by a single conservative party—has rendered Japan's courts particularly subservient and, like the political party that served as its political patron, distinctly conservative. Perhaps not surprisingly, even though the Supreme Court is invested with the constitutional power of judicial review, it has seldom used this authority and has been extremely hesitant to declare policies or statutes unconstitutional. Since its creation in 1947, the Court has struck down only nine laws on constitutional grounds and has steadfastly refused to rule on matters relating to what is arguably postwar Japan's most significant constitutional issue: challenges to Japan's military and security activities under Article 9.[7] In another recent case, the court ruled in 2013 that while malapportionment of electoral districts placed lower house elections the previous year "in a state of unconstitutionality" (in effect concluding that the elected government was illegitimate), no remedial action was necessary because the Diet was already taking measures to address the problem.

The Electoral System

As with other political institutions in Japan, the electoral system is both a cause and consequence of the LDP's long-standing reign. As noted earlier, postwar LDP governments maintained grossly disproportionate voting districts favoring rural, conservative voters who kept the LDP in power and established additional electoral rules that clearly favored the party's interests.[8] Only in recent decades have reforms enacted by a short-lived opposition coalition government in the mid-1990s begun to chip away at these LDP advantages and shift the landscape of electoral institutions and outcomes in Japan.

Representatives in the two chambers of the Diet are elected according to different rules. Although the membership of the weaker House of Councillors varied slightly during the postwar period, its electoral rules were not affected by the 1990s reforms and have remained largely unchanged. The 242 councillors serve fixed six-year terms, and half of them face election every three years. Councillors are elected according to a mixed system: 96 are chosen from party lists using proportional representation (PR) in a nationwide election, and the remaining 146 are elected from 47 multimember districts (MMDs) that coincide with Japan's 47 prefectures. Each district returns between one and five members, but rather than drawing from a party list, voters have a single, nontransferable vote that they cast for an individual candidate. In other words, rather than first-past-the-post in a single-member district (SMD), as in legislative elections in Great Britain and the United States, each district elects the top several-past-the-post (ranging from one to five members).

Before 1994, the electoral system used to determine membership in the House of Representatives resembled the second part of the system used for the upper house.[9] In 1993, a series of notorious scandals, unpopular tax measures, and precipitous economic decline led numerous LDP members of parliament to defect from the party and form or join opposition parties. These defections brought into government an opposition coalition that lost no time in reforming the rules governing lower house elections. These reforms established a new mixed electoral system similar to those of Germany and Mexico. Under this system, the lower chamber was reduced from 512 to 480 seats, and 300 of the seats were elected from SMDs. Further reforms in 2013 reduced the total number of SMD seats from 300 to 295 with the elimination of five rural electoral districts.[10] The remaining 180 seats are chosen by PR from 11 regional constituencies, in which seats are assigned to the parties according to their share of the total bloc-wide votes. As in the German system, candidates may run in their own districts and be included in a regional party list, to safeguard their seats in case of defeat in the home SMD.

The architects of these reforms sought to shift electoral competition away from local and individual candidate-based campaign organizations known as *koenkai* and highly personalized factional politics within the LDP to national party politics between two dominant parties offering genuine policy alternatives. Although the PR portion of the ballot provides some seats for smaller parties able to garner the minimal threshold of votes, nearly two-thirds of the seats are chosen from SMDs. That system favors well-organized and well-established parties, as in the United States and Great Britain. The 1994 reforms also began a process (still far from complete) of reapportioning districts to reflect demographics more accurately, giving more equitable clout to the much more numerous (and typically less conservative) urban voters. This process has begun to weaken the disproportionate clout of rural voters, who historically were among the LDP's most loyal supporters. As a testament to the importance of these kinds of formal political institutions, scholars attribute the recent tectonic political shifts that consolidated opposition forces in the DPJ and brought the party to power in 2009 at least in part to these electoral reforms. Reflecting the continued elitism of Japanese politics, the reforms were less successful in dealing with (and in fact were less concerned about) political corruption, which the Japanese call "money politics"—precisely the issue that the public and foreign observers most hoped would be addressed. Although anticorruption measures were implemented, as in other capitalist democracies, individual candidates and the corporations and other interest groups that woo them have discovered plenty of loopholes to keep campaign funds flowing, and campaign finance scandals continue to plague politicians from both the LDP and the DPJ (in a 2016 merger, the DPJ changed its name to simply the **Democratic Party**, or **DP**.)

Because the government automatically registers voters, virtually all eligible voters in Japan are registered. Accordingly, voter turnout in national elections has been relatively high, usually between 60 and 75 percent. But significantly, even as the system has become more competitive and politicians have increased their clout vis-à-vis the bureaucracy, voter turnout has declined. Although there are a number of reasons for the decline, popular distrust of politicians across the party spectrum as well as disillusionment with the political process and with government's seeming incapacity to bring about genuine reforms are paramount.

Local Government

Japan is divided into 47 administrative divisions, known as prefectures, each with its own elected governor and legislature. Japan is nonetheless a unitary (not a federal) system in which most political power is invested in the central government.

The prefectural governments decide many local issues and are able to raise sufficient taxes to cover about one-third of their expenditures (what the Japanese call 30 percent autonomy). These subnational governments depend on the central government, however, for the remainder of their budget. Central authorities delegate all local authority (at the prefectural and municipal levels) and can, and sometimes do, retract that authority. The national government can override the decision of any local governor and has done so most notably in the case of Okinawa, whose elected local officials have attitudes toward the overwhelming U.S. military presence there that differ significantly from those of

A common sight during Japan's election season—a white-gloved campaign worker advocates for her candidate from a loudspeaker-equipped van.

national leaders. Okinawans are not alone, however, in wishing for the devolution of more authority and increased local autonomy.

Recognizing the political value of this issue, the DPJ/DP and regionally based parties have garnered electoral support by promising to devolve greater authority to prefectural governments. Similarly, some regional politicians have called for the merger of city and prefectural governments in an effort to strengthen the hand of local authorities vis-à-vis Tokyo. In a nod to the American neoliberal and populist "Tea Party" movement, one recent movement labeled its successful political campaign a "sake" party similarly focused on cutting taxes, slashing salaries for elected officials, and wresting power from the central government. Populist parties have also capitalized on issues such as rising conflict with China to promote Japanese nationalism and concern with nuclear power following the 2011 nuclear disaster in Fukushima.

Other Institutions

BUREAUCRACY AND THE IRON TRIANGLE

Arguably, the Japanese state's most influential—yet entirely extra-constitutional— institution of policy-making authority remains the bureaucracy. As in other liberal democracies, the Japanese bureaucracy staffs the dozen or so ministries comprising the Japanese state, but it is at once smaller in size and greater in influence than any of its Western counterparts.

Ministers appointed to head these ministries are often not experts in their assignments, but rather elected politicians who obtain their appointments based on political criteria. Therefore, these ministers rely almost entirely on the career civil servants within their ministries to formulate, facilitate, and ultimately implement and enforce laws and policies. In each ministry, an administrative vice minister with some 30 to 35 years of experience in that particular ministry heads these efforts, presiding over a staff of Japan's brightest, who willingly subject themselves to grueling workweeks for relatively meager compensation.

Enduring linkages among senior bureaucrats, conservative politicians, and corporate executives form what has been referred to as an iron triangle, in which the determination and implementation of policies are often facilitated not by formal negotiations, hearings, or parliamentary votes but by extra-legal directives from government officials to the private sector. Known as **administrative guidance**, these policy directives are often communicated over the phone between former colleagues or during after-work drinking sessions among friends. This web of informal connections within the Japanese state actually consists of hundreds of triangles involving veteran politicians with particular policy expertise, bureaucrats in a particular ministry or division, and the private-sector representatives of interest groups in the given policy area. In the past, ruling bureaucrats traditionally dominated these associations while reigning LDP governments made sure that the party's most important constituents, including corporations (from which the party received massive campaign funds) and rice farmers (on whose overrepresented vote the party depended), were well taken care of with producer-oriented industrial and financial policies and protectionist trade barriers. Representatives of Japan's large corporations in turn offered firsthand policy advice to the bureaucrats and generally accepted the business-friendly policies and guidance they received in return.

Why are Japan's unelected civil servants so powerful? First, the Japanese state has a long-standing tradition whereby leaders who have formal authority do not necessarily exercise power. Rulers and ruled alike are accustomed to legitimate governance by those who may not be vested with formal authority. Nonelected administrators have long exercised such power in Japan. Second, whereas U.S. occupation authorities jailed wartime politicians, purged the military, and broke up the zaibatsu, the experienced bureaucrats continued to administer Japan uninterrupted and unscathed. Third, this political vacuum prompted many veteran bureaucrats to move into leadership positions in Japan's conservative postwar political parties, which gave them significant political influence. Fourth, the legitimacy and prestige of this dominance have been enhanced by the strictly meritocratic nature of hiring and advancement within the bureaucracy. As these bureaucrats advance, only the very best are promoted to senior leadership positions; the bureaucrats who have been passed over are expected to resign from the ministry, thus maintaining a hierarchy of seniority. Senior civil servants exercise extensive policy authority in potent ministries, such as the Ministry of Finance and the Ministry of Economy, Trade, and Industry (formerly and famously known as the Ministry of International Trade and Industry, or MITI).

This orderly promotion-and-retirement policy also helps explain the willingness of the bureaucrats to work so hard for apparently so little and offers a final reason for the remarkable reach and power of the Japanese bureaucracy. Each year, a contingent of retiring but nonetheless highly qualified bureaucrats in their 40s and 50s undergo *amakudari* ("descent from heaven"), either to try their hand in politics or, more commonly, to take senior positions in the very corporations they previously regulated. In turn, the corporations that employ retired civil servants gain not just their skills but also their connections, giving the private sector substantial clout in the policy-making process. At any given time, Japan's policy elite comprise people who not only share a common outlook but also often attended the same prestigious schools and may have worked for decades in the same ministry.

Long credited with leading the postwar economic miracle, Japan's elite bureaucracy is now understandably a logical culprit for the country's more recent decades of economic malaise and growing political dysfunction. The bureaucracy's reputation has been badly tarnished not just by the economy's poor performance but also by a series of scandals and gaffes. These include revelations of kickbacks from politicians and corporations, a series of costly cover-ups involving HIV-infected blood transfusions, lost pension records, and nuclear accidents as well as the mishandling of natural disaster recovery efforts following the 1995 earthquake in Kobe and the triple tragedy of the **2011 earthquake**, tsunami, and Fukushima nuclear catastrophe. Declining confidence in the bureaucracy and in Japan's iron triangle has led many to conclude that this "well-oiled, conservative machine" is undergoing a "regime shift," in which parliament, interest groups, and even Japanese citizens are gaining political influence. Elected politicians have pursued administrative reforms that have given the prime minister increased leverage over the bureaucracy and electoral reforms that permitted the election of non-LDP governments. Politicians have also gained increasing policy expertise in their own right, which has made them less dependent on their bureaucratic counterparts in policy making.

Where, then, does power reside in the Japanese state? Although Japan, unlike the United States, lacks the formal separation of powers between federal and subnational government and between the executive and legislative branches, it is fair to say that there is no single locus of power in the Japanese state. Even during the era of the bureaucracy's greatest strength, from the 1950s through the 1970s, powerful prime ministers still often held sway over the bureaucracy.[11] Some of Japan's most famous and successful corporations, such as Sony and Honda, achieved their status in part because they defied bureaucratic dictates. And while each bureaucratic ministry may have substantial authority within its own domain, these independent fiefdoms are subject to no overriding direction or guidance.

Scholars critical of the Japanese state have described it as headless and susceptible to the kind of uncoordinated drift that led to a quixotic war against the United States in the twentieth century, followed by unsustainable trade surpluses with virtually every industrialized country and an inability to reform sufficiently its twentieth-century mercantilist economy to cope with the challenges of a twenty-first-century globalized economy.[12] Will Japan be able to change, and if so, what will be the impetus? Because elements within the iron triangle have demonstrated little willingness or incentive to change, many observers argue that it is necessary to look beyond this ruling triad and perhaps even beyond Japan to locate the forces and pressures capable of bringing about change.

Political Conflict and Competition

The Party System and Elections

Like postwar Italy or Sweden, Japan until recent years has offered an example of an advanced industrial democracy governed by a predominant party system. The LDP dominated all other parties from the time of its formation as the merger of conservative parties in 1955 until its defeat at the hands of the DPJ in upper house elections in 2007 and lower house elections in 2009. For most of this period, the Japan Socialist Party (JSP; renamed the Social Democratic Party, or SDP, in 1996), formed as a merger of leftist parties in 1955, served as its perennial loyal opposition. The JSP regularly garnered fewer than half as many votes as the LDP in parliamentary elections and, thanks to LDP gerrymandering, obtained even fewer seats. During this period of LDP dominance, several other parties joined the JSP in opposition by taking advantage of Japan's former electoral system to carve out niches in the Japanese electorate among voters who felt excluded by both the larger parties. These included the Japan Communist Party (JCP), which consistently embraced policies to the left of the JSP, and the more moderate Democratic Socialist Party (DSP) and New Komei Party (NKP), which occupied a middle ground between conservative, pro-business LDP politics and the socialist (and pacifist) platform of the JSP. These three and a couple of other short-lived parties typically accounted for roughly 20 percent of the popular vote.

This remarkably stable one-and-a-half-party system, an important component of the equally stable iron triangle, remained intact for nearly four decades. However, the bursting of Japan's economic bubble in the early 1990s, combined with the LDP government's inept and unpopular efforts to address the structural economic problems that prolonged the economy's slide, led in 1993 to a historic vote of no confidence in LDP rule and the defection of LDP parliamentarians to an opposition coalition. Two successive short-lived opposition coalitions held power long enough (just under a year) to implement electoral reforms that fostered the emergence of the DPJ, a party strong enough to legitimately and consistently challenge LDP rule. To understand the causes and the nature of this revolt and why it was so long in coming, it is necessary to examine both the long-dominant LDP and the DPJ/DP that has emerged to challenge this dominance.

THE LIBERAL DEMOCRATIC PARTY

Although the LDP no longer has a guaranteed lock on Japan's parliament, the party has managed to control government for nearly six decades since its founding in 1955. The nature of this rule has led some observers to conclude that the LDP has been woefully misnamed: It is conservative, not liberal. Its internal politics have been highly authoritarian, not democratic. And its factional divisions have made it more a collection of mini-parties than a single party.

The LDP can perhaps best be understood as a collection of politicians acting as independent political entrepreneurs bound together in a highly pragmatic electoral machine in which ideological consistency has never taken priority over winning. Over the years, the party established electoral rules and engaged in campaigns and elections with the express purpose of staying in power by maintaining a majority (or at least a healthy plurality) of seats in the parliament. But the LDP became more than just a political machine for members of parliament. The party's persistent control of the government meant that the competition for the LDP presidency was in almost all cases a contest for the office of prime minister.

These contests fostered the emergence of factions, or mini-parties, within the LDP and a clientelist system in which candidates had to vie for the support of patrons within the party who could provide loyal faction members with campaign funds, official party endorsements, appointed positions within the party and the government, and other favors. These faction leaders in turn could count on the support of their faction members in the party's all-important presidential elections. At the local level, to help individual candidates obtain sufficient votes in their home districts, each candidate also constructed a local support group or *koenkai*, made up of local elites or members of a particular professional or other special-interest group within the district. In the same way that the LDP candidates promised allegiance to their factional patron in exchange for support from above, so they promised policy favors, contracts, and other pork-barrel enticements in exchange for the votes and campaign donations delivered by their *koenkai*. And just as the party factions outlived individual leaders, so have the *koenkai* been multigenerational. It is not uncommon for an entire *koenkai* to throw its full support behind the son, grandson, or other descendant of a retiring member of parliament.

Although factions have become less significant in recent years thanks to electoral reforms that have fostered the emergence of a more competitive two-party system, patron-client relations and informal personal relationships remain important institutions in the LDP and in all of Japan's political parties. Both campaign contributions and votes are secured through expanding circles of co-optation of businesses and other large interest groups as well as through clientelist currying of favor among local communities and individuals by means of pork-barrel projects, favors, and gifts. As in any democracy, projects in the home district, such as bridges and schools, create jobs and deliver votes, and the lucrative contracts and licenses awarded to corporations to build these projects bring campaign donations. One scholar notes that while residents of other democracies are certainly familiar with pork-barrel politics in their own political systems, Japan's extensive clientelist arrangements are more like an "industrial hog farm."[13] In addition, politicians and their supporters are also expected to attend the funerals, weddings, graduations, and other important family events of their loyal constituents (on average more than 30 each month), honoring them with their presence and an appropriate (monetary) gift. As a result, the huge expenses of politicking in Japan have plagued the LDP with campaign finance scandals throughout its history.

Persistent—indeed, mounting—corruption scandals, combined with growing dissatisfaction with LDP governance, prompted the defection of a number of LDP members of parliament to an opposition coalition that wrested power briefly from the LDP in the 1990s. But after a year in exile, the less than popular LDP nonetheless returned to office as part of a series of coalition governments. As Japan entered its second decade of economic malaise, the LDP received a boost in support when voters pinned their hopes for economic recovery and political reform on the promises of maverick politician Junichiro Koizumi, who served as LDP prime minister from 2001 to 2006. With his raffish hairdo and populist style, Koizumi represented in many ways the antithesis of the traditional LDP politician. He secured the LDP presidency without the explicit backing of any major LDP faction and won three consecutive elections with promises to halt Japan's economic malaise and take on the country's conservative bureaucratic and political elite (including his own LDP) and their deeply entrenched constituencies. In 2005, he led the LDP to a dramatic (and short-lived) victory in lower house elections in which the party won an outright majority of seats for the first time since 1990 (see "House of Representatives Election Results by Major Political Party, 2000–2014," p. 307).

House of Representatives Election Results by Major Political Party, 2000–2014

| | PARTY (IDEOLOGY) | | | | | |
YEAR	LDP (RIGHT)	DPJ (CENTER)	NKP (CENTER)	SDP (LEFT)	OTHERS	TOTAL SEATS
2000	239	129	29	19	64	480
2003	237	177	34	6	26	480
2005	296	113	31	7	33	480
2009	119	300	21	7	33	480
2012	294	57	31	2	96	480
2014	291	73	35	2	74	475[*]

*Total seats reduced from 480 to 475 beginning with the 2014 election.

Although LDP party rules required the popular prime minister to step down in 2006 after five years as party president, his government managed to implement a number of modest reforms, including the privatization of Japan's postal savings system. But Koizumi's successor, Shinzō Abe, an ardent Japanese nationalist supported by the LDP's more conservative wing, returned Japan to LDP politics as usual, including factional infighting, cozy arrangements with bureaucrats, and corruption scandals. Abe presided over a stunning defeat in the 2007 upper house elections that denied the LDP a majority in the chamber and "twisted" Japan's parliament. Following this embarrassing loss and suffering from poor health, Abe stepped down after only one year and was followed by two equally unsuccessful LDP prime ministers over the next two years. The LDP next lost control of the lower house and government in an even more dramatic drubbing in the 2009 House of Representatives election that brought the DPJ to power for the first time. For reasons discussed later, the DPJ also cycled just as quickly through three prime ministers in three years and lost even more dramatically in the 2012 election than had the LDP in 2009. The surprising agent of this LDP turnaround was none other than a rejuvenated Shinzō Abe. Abe led the LDP in an election that more than doubled the LDP's seats in the lower house while promising both to revive the economy through a three-pronged strategy that has come to be known as **Abenomics** and to stand up to China in an increasingly dangerous dispute over islands claimed by both countries (see "Territorial Tempests," p. 329). In a bid to strengthen his party's hand in carrying out controversial reforms, Abe called for elections in 2014, held on to nearly all of the LDP's seats, and, with its coalition partner, maintained the two-thirds majority of seats necessary to override any potential veto in the upper house.

Toning down his personal nationalist sentiments and making genuine progress with his economic revitalization strategy, Abe and the LDP followed the 2009 and 2014 lower house victories with solid wins in both the 2013 and 2016 upper house elections. These electoral results gave the LDP, with its NKP coalition partner, two-thirds majorities in both chambers of the Diet. This mandate gave the government confidence to push forward with some of the more painful measures of economic reform, including passing a controversial tax increase and negotiating trade deals that threaten the protection of rice farmers.

The string of electoral victories has also given Abe sufficient confidence to act more boldly on the nationalist front. In 2013, he paid a visit to the controversial **Yasukuni Shrine**, which honors Japan's war dead, including those executed as war criminals at the end of World War II. In 2015, in the face of widespread popular

Elected with a mandate to reform Japan's economy, Prime Minister Abe's LDP government has secured supermajorities in both chambers of the Diet. Many believe Abe intends to use this dominant position to push for constitutional reform.

protest, his government forced through the Diet divisive legislation reinterpreting Article 9 that authorizes Japanese troops to fight (defensively) overseas for the first time since 1945. The super majorities in both chambers have also given Abe and his governing coalition the ability to initiate outright revision of the constitution, should they choose to do so. Such a measure would also require ratification by a majority of voters in a national referendum, something polls indicate Japan's citizenry is not yet prepared to do.

DEMOCRATIC PARTY OF JAPAN/DEMOCRATIC PARTY

Capitalizing on mounting public frustration with LDP rule during the 1990s and anticipating the intended consequences of the electoral reforms to favor large, organized political parties, the DPJ formed in 1998 as a merger of several reform-minded opposition parties. Led early on by future prime ministers Yukio Hatoyama and Naoto Kan, the DPJ received a significant boost in 2003, when former LDP kingpin and political mastermind Ichirō Ozawa joined his opposition Liberal Party with the DPJ. Despite (or perhaps because of) his questionable reputation as a backroom "shadow shogun," Ozawa helped the DPJ to upper house electoral victories in 2004 and 2007. In 2009, after being implicated in a fund-raising scandal, Ozawa was forced to resign as DPJ president before the party's victory in the 2009 House of Representatives elections that swept the LDP from power.

Despite this decisive and unprecedented victory, the DPJ fell just short of winning the two-thirds majority of seats in the lower house required to override a veto from the upper chamber, where it held a substantial plurality of seats but not a majority. To ensure a majority in this weaker House of Councillors, the DPJ formed a coalition with two smaller parties. Elected into office on a platform of bold promises and with a significant mandate for carrying out political, economic, and social reforms, the DPJ nonetheless struggled both to realize its campaign pledges and to retain the support of voters. The DPJ's first prime minister, **Yukio Hatoyama** (2009–10), came to office vowing to weaken the iron triangle by shifting political authority from bureaucrats to elected politicians and to devolve central political authority to local communities and citizens. The Hatoyama government promised to jump-start the economy by spurring consumption and reducing growing income inequality through subsidies for children and farmers. The new government also pledged to strengthen cooperation with China and reduce the American military footprint in Japan's island prefecture of Okinawa.

This last promise proved Hatoyama's demise: U.S. pressure and growing regional security concerns led him to break his campaign promise to close an American military base in Okinawa and forced him to resign after less than a year in office.

In the hope of strengthening the party's prospects in the 2010 upper house elections, the party replaced Hatoyama with Naoto Kan, who had a reputation for taking decisive action, implementing bold reforms, and standing up to bureaucrats. But the DPJ and its coalition partners fared poorly in the elections, losing their upper house majority and once again giving Japan a twisted parliament in which the DPJ held a majority in the lower chamber but the LDP-led opposition dominated the upper house. Following that election, the DPJ government struggled to keep together its coalition, carry out reforms, or even maintain a consistent policy position. The tragic earthquake, tsunami, and nuclear disaster of 2011 further stalled hope of progress and prompted Kan's resignation later that year and the party election of Yoshihiko Noda to replace him. An increasingly vocal public and invigorated media voiced criticism of the DPJ government's inept handling of the crisis (see "3/11: Japan's Triple Tragedy," p. 327) and its inability to revive Japan's economy. Voters echoed these concerns in the 2012 election that brought the LDP back to government, and the 2014 election that retained LDP rule, sending not so much a message of confidence in the capacity of the LDP as a resounding rejection of this maiden effort of the DPJ to govern effectively. Despite a 2016 merger with another party and a name change, the new "Democratic Party" continues to struggle at the polls. Some have concluded that the solutions to Japan's continued persistent malaise and frequent political intransigence may in fact need to come from this newly invigorated civil society.

THE EMERGENCE OF LOCAL PARTIES

Japan's unitary political system, the LDP's half-century lock on both party politics and government, and successive electoral systems that favored first a one-party dominant system and now a two-party dominant system have all conspired to restrict the emergence of regional and local political parties in Japan. But the tectonic shifts that permitted the DPJ to unseat the LDP from government in 2009 also began to weaken the grip that national party organizations have held over local politics. In particular, populist local political leaders—including Tokyo's prefectural governor and the mayors of Japan's third (Osaka) and fourth (Nagoya) largest cities—all established local political parties in recent years that garnered significant electoral success in both local and national competitions. Regional parties also emerged in Aichi and Shiga prefectures, but were less successful. All of these local leaders ran campaigns based on platforms reminiscent in some ways of populist movements taking place in the United States and Europe: devolving authority from the national to local levels, promoting nationalism, and in some cases lowering taxes, tightening budgets, and liberalizing trade.[14]

Not surprisingly, both the LDP and DPJ observed the popularity of many of these ideas and brought elements of them into their own party platforms. For Abenomics, the LDP's ambitious economic recovery program, they explicitly lifted several elements from the local parties' playbooks, including participating in multilateral free-trade negotiations, devolving authority to local "special economic zones," and loosening government regulations that have stifled entrepreneurship. While these efforts of co-optation may weaken the power of local parties, democracy appears to be working. Many objectives of these local political movements may still be realized, even if they are ultimately enacted by the national parties.

Civil Society

Because the reforms that brought about Westernization and democracy were imposed from above (and, in many cases, from *outside*), Japan's political system historically fostered a tradition of "top down" bureaucratic society rather than a "bottom-up" civil society whose citizens independently organized and participated in political, economic, and social affairs. Like other authoritarian systems, the Meiji and militarist states fostered corporatist and mercantilist institutions to harness Japan's industrial society in the service of modernization and imperialism. Although the U.S. occupiers destroyed many aspects of Japanese authoritarianism and carried out sweeping political, social, and economic reforms, they retained the bureaucracy and, out of fear of communism, squelched many of the nascent civic groups they had initially fostered.

In pursuing economic development and political stability, the postwar Japanese state organized or co-opted interest groups that were important to these goals, such as business and agricultural associations, and formed associations for facilitating their political participation. In exchange for their support, these groups have had their interests well represented (and protected), and they have prospered. During the postwar decades of economic growth, this symbiotic relationship expanded to include many other smaller groups and constituencies in a system of distributional welfare. These corporatist arrangements prolonged LDP bureaucratic rule, but they did so at the increasing expense of economic health and political flexibility. In addition, labor unions, consumers, and other groups that often are prominent in the politics of industrialized countries have been notably absent from these arrangements, and in many ways, they bore the burden of the corporatist system, which was sometimes referred to as Japan, Inc. On occasion, students, environmentalists, and other groups excluded from Japan, Inc., resorted to extra-parliamentary protests in order to be heard. Some of these protests, particularly in the 1950s, were quite violent and at times successful.

The third point of the iron triangle in addition to politicians and bureaucrats is made up of Japan's large corporations and the large industrial groupings (**keiretsu**) to which they belong. These players have been proponents of and participants in Japan's postwar development. Big business exercises political influence through the business association Nippon Keidanren (Japanese Federation of Economic Organizations), which voices the concerns of large corporations and offers policy recommendations to the government. Keidanren is the conduit through which substantial campaign contributions have been channeled from large businesses to political campaigns and therefore has inclined LDP (and more recently, DPJ) governments to champion business-friendly policies, such as cheap access to capital, investment incentives, and various forms of market protection. During economic hard times, businesses have bridled at having to make these campaign contributions and have complained about the use of growing corporate taxes to subsidize inefficient farmers and pork-barrel projects. Analysts point to this divergence of interests as yet another sign of the weakening of the iron triangle.

Another key pillar of political support has been the agricultural sector, whose highly organized political interests are channeled through local agricultural cooperatives to the national "peak organization" known as JA (Japan Agriculture) or Nokyo (Central Union of Agricultural Cooperatives). Agriculture's key political contribution has been its capacity to provide a dependable and geographically concentrated bloc of votes. In exchange, both the LDP and DPJ governments have enacted policies that favor farmers, including price supports, relatively low taxes, and protection from agricultural imports. Although urbanization and electoral redistricting have somewhat weakened the significance of the rural farm vote, Japanese farmers remain an important political force that has fervently resisted initiatives to liberalize agricultural trade.

Big business and agriculture are not the only interest groups to have offered their campaign contributions and votes in exchange for favorable policies and a share of the benefits of Japan's postwar economic boom. Small and midsize businesses comprise the lion's share of the Japanese economy, despite their unsung status when compared with such high-profile large firms as Toyota and Sony. The smaller manufacturers and retailers have been very well organized and have parlayed their electoral support into tax breaks, subsidies, and protection from larger firms. For example, Japan's ubiquitous mom-and-pop corner grocery stores effectively kept large retailers out of local neighborhoods for many years. Another group worth mentioning comprises the half million construction firms in Japan, most of which are small, unproductive, and well cared for by an inefficient and corrupt government bidding system for public works.

Japan's faltering economy and growing corruption scandals involving both the LDP and DPJ/DP and their supporters have cast new light on the economic and political costs of the country's corporate welfare system. Critics argue that the LDP's varied and growing host of constituencies led to distributional tyranny, fueled Japan's economic crisis, and stifled political change. Corporatist arrangements have also long excluded interests deemed potentially harmful to the goals of either rapid industrialization or corporate welfare, including trade unions, consumers, environmentalists, and women's groups. Consequently, Japan's major labor organizations—including RENGO (Japanese Trade Union Confederation) and the teachers' and public employees' unions—have had long-standing adversarial relationships with the LDP and have traditionally supported the more left-leaning political parties, such as the Socialists and Communists. More recently, these unions and other groups consistently excluded from the iron triangle have thrown their support to the DPJ/DP, confirming the influence of electoral reforms designed to produce a two-party system and enhancing the prospects of weakening and transforming the corporatist arrangements of the iron triangle.

As Japan's postindustrial and postmaterialist society grows more complex and the political marketplace more competitive, and in the wake of natural disasters such as the Kobe earthquake in 1995 and the 2011 earthquake, tsunami, and nuclear disaster in Fukushima, a host of nongovernmental and nonprofit organizations have emerged and are strengthening Japan's civil society. These civic associations include groups representing pacifists, nationalists, environmentalists, antinuclear advocates, AIDS activists, religious organizations, and many other interests that are broadening and deepening Japan's civil society and enhancing pluralism in this advanced industrial democracy.[15]

Society

Ethnic and National Identity

Few national populations view themselves as racially and ethnically homogeneous as do the Japanese. Because immigrants constitute only 1 percent of the population and foreign nationals comprise only 2 percent, this perception is grounded in demographic reality. Nonetheless, those of foreign ancestry in Japan make up some 5 percent of the population. The notion of a racially pure and monoethnic Japan was fostered largely by the Japanese state from the Meiji period onward as it sought to forge a Japanese nation from the culturally and even linguistically diverse feudal domains of nineteenth-century Japan and to establish Japanese racial superiority over the peoples of its far-flung empire in the first half of the twentieth century.

Japan's strong ethnic and national identity has come at the expense of several minority groups, who have been prevented from developing a Japanese identity and enjoying the full privileges of citizenship as Japanese nationals with a separate ethnic heritage. These minorities include the indigenous Ainu in the north and Okinawans in the south; descendants of Koreans, Chinese, and Southeast Asians; and the children of mixed ancestry and foreigners. Although not racially separate, the 2 to 4 million *burakumin* ("social outcasts") whose ancestors worked in the "unclean" occupations such as grave digging, butchery, and tanning are also seen as a minority group and have faced intense prejudice. Discrimination in areas such as employment and marriage against these minority groups has been widespread and persistent. While members of some of these minorities have chosen to remain resident noncitizens (chiefly Korean-Japanese), those individuals who have sought to assimilate by taking on Japanese names, mastering the Japanese language, and adopting Japanese cultural mores have generally nonetheless remained socially marginalized and culturally scorned.

If cultural assimilation is difficult, the naturalization process is nearly as arduous. Being born in Japan does not automatically confer citizenship or voting rights. Non-Japanese can become citizens only after adopting a Japanese name and enduring a process that includes a series of interviews, home visits, and consultations with neighbors to ensure that the candidate has sufficiently assimilated Japanese culture—a process that many find invasive and humiliating. In addition, permanent residents who do not choose citizenship are fingerprinted and required to carry alien registration identification.

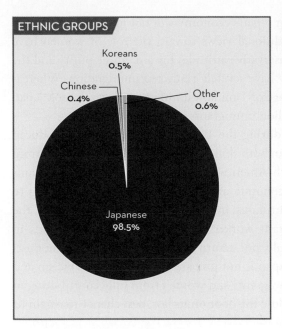

ETHNIC GROUPS

Koreans
0.5%

Chinese
0.4%

Other
0.6%

Japanese
98.5%

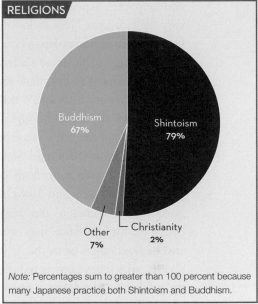

RELIGIONS

Buddhism
67%

Shintoism
79%

Other
7%

Christianity
2%

Note: Percentages sum to greater than 100 percent because many Japanese practice both Shintoism and Buddhism.

However, scholars note that demographic and economic necessity may eventually compel the social integration and mobility that cultural obstacles and state policy have prevented. Japan finds itself at the forefront of a problem confronting many advanced industrial societies: the convergence of an aging population and dwindling fertility rates. The ratio of Japanese senior citizens to the total population was only 12 percent in 1990, but it is expected to climb to nearly 40 percent by 2050. By midcentury, demographers predict, Japan will have 1 million centenarians and 30 percent fewer people overall, and nearly 1 million more people will die each year than are born.

The graying of Japan's population brings economic challenges that other countries certainly face as well, including health and financial care. But the most acute problem Japan faces, far more so than other advanced countries, is that of a declining workforce. The size of Japan's workforce peaked in 1998 and will continue to decline rapidly as fewer and fewer Japanese reach maturity each year to replace retiring and dying workers. But whereas most advanced societies have expanded their labor pools by more fully integrating women and immigrants into the workplace, Japan has been unwilling to embrace either group. And even if Japanese women were fully empowered, economists argue that the only long-term hope for stabilizing Japan's population and workforce is to increase and sustain immigration over many years. Absent this source of workers, consumers, and taxpayers, experts predict that Japan's economy will not just decline but may very well collapse. Just as its traditional views toward the role of women have kept women at home, Japan's conservative attitudes toward ethnic purity and the insular nature of Japanese society have severely restricted immigration. Whereas the United States accepts an average of 1 million immigrants a year, it took Japan a quarter century to absorb 1 million immigrants into its society.

Upon facing labor shortages during the 1980s, the government introduced policies designed to attract to Japan both skilled and unskilled migrant labor from China, Southeast Asia, and South America. But more recently, these programs faced local resistance on both economic and cultural grounds. Responding to popular discontent and labor surpluses in Japan's recessionary economy, the government offered to pay migrant workers to return to their homelands in exchange for assurance they would not return to Japan. However, economists and demographers warn that if Japan is not prepared to overcome its racism and sexism, which have prevented immigrants and women from fully contributing to the workforce, the country may close the door on its last, best chance to regain its status as an economic powerhouse.[16]

Ideology and Political Culture

Japan's historical experiences with Shintoism, Buddhism, Confucianism, feudalism, militarism, and bureaucratism have certainly shaped the norms and values that guide Japanese political behavior. So have its experiences with the West, from imposed inequitable treaties and democratic institutions to military defeat and the embrace of Western popular culture. In efforts to attribute political behavior to culture, scholars often point to the group conformity and social hierarchy that pervade most aspects of Japanese life. The basic unit of Japanese society is not the individual but the group, as manifested in such institutions as the family, the company, the political faction, and the nation. Japanese are socialized to defer to the needs of the group and to make decisions through consensus rather than majority vote. Similarly, hierarchy governs most social relationships in Japan, and Japanese are most comfortable in settings where their social standing in relation to that of others is clear. Inferiors yield to their superiors' authority, and superiors are obliged to care for their subordinates' needs. Promotion in firms, bureaucratic ministries, and political party factions is more often based on seniority and personalized patron-client relationships than on merit.

Japan has undergone political and economic modernization, but on its own (not fully Western) terms. Individual freedom and social equality remain less important than being accepted by the group and holding a rightful position in that group's hierarchical division of labor. Japan's relatively equitable distribution of wealth (until recently, on par with that of the European social democracies) has had little to do with cultural norms of egalitarianism or explicit government policy. In fact, Japan has had a weak labor movement, and its conservative governments promoted the low taxation and public spending policies that typically foster inequality (though policies of agricultural protectionism have effectively redistributed wealth from consumers to farmers). Rather, Japan's relative economic and social equality can be attributed largely to three factors.

First, World War II reduced all of Japanese society to poverty levels. Second, postwar occupation reforms—including land reform; the breakup of the huge zaibatsu conglomerates; purges of the political, military, economic, and aristocratic elite; and empowerment of labor unions to bargain collectively for improved working conditions—fostered equality. Third, Japan's rapid and sustained postwar economic growth showered unprecedented prosperity on virtually all social groups in Japan. These factors have consistently weakened the salience of class and issues of redistribution of wealth as an ideological cleavage in Japan, contributing to the weakness of the Japanese left and shoring up support for the LDP and its pro-growth policies. In a recent poll, nearly three-fourths of respondents identified themselves as having a political stance ranging from conservative to neutral, whereas less than one-fourth saw themselves as progressive or close to progressive.

Japan's persistently weak economy (combined with the forces of globalization and an ongoing generational change in values) has led to greater income inequality and economic insecurity, and it may lead to greater diversity of political attitudes and perhaps even to a shift in political culture in Japan. The fading of guaranteed permanent employment (so-called lifetime employment) for Japan's corporate *sarariman* (white-collar "salaryman") and rising unemployment among college graduates (and indeed, an increasing number of college and even high school dropouts) have led to disillusionment with business and politics as usual and to mounting calls for change. Such disillusionment is particularly strong among Japanese youth, who have no memory of wartime hardship or postwar poverty and who place more value on individual fulfillment through leisure diversions and risky entrepreneurial opportunities than through long hours and long years of work for the sake of a company. Younger Japanese have less incentive to remain loyal to a company that can no longer promise them job security, and they have little patience for the corruption and authority of long-in-the-tooth

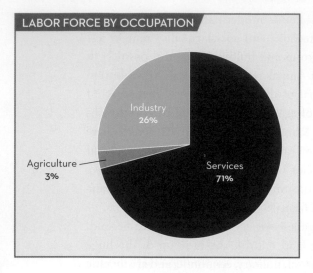

LABOR FORCE BY OCCUPATION

Industry
26%

Agriculture
3%

Services
71%

bureaucratic rule. In short, change may be initiated by a younger generation far more willing and likely to switch both their jobs and their political loyalties.

But as this chapter has indicated, change does not come easily to entrenched Japanese institutions, no matter how dysfunctional. Unwilling to conform and unable to bring about change, a growing minority of Japanese are choosing to "exit" Japan's "straitjacket" society through more or less extreme measures. A growing number of youth, labeled "parasite singles," are electing to opt out of the career track of university education leading to full-time employment, marriage, and family. Instead, they happily choose to live at home, work part-time, and pursue leisure activities, creating a lifestyle decidedly foreign (and troubling) to Japan's older generations. More troubling, homelessness has risen sharply since the early 1990s, particularly among middle-aged men. Japan has regularly ranked first among industrialized countries for suicides, and suicide is the leading cause of death in Japan among men ages 20 to 44. Hundreds of thousands of Japanese youth and young adults (mostly male) have elected to drop out of society, shutting themselves in their rooms or apartments for years at a time. The antisocial behavior of the homeless, reclusive "shut-ins," and those who take their own lives speaks to the powerful institutional inertia of groupism in Japan and the drastic measures some nonconformists feel compelled to take to escape the system.

Political Economy

Japan's sudden introduction to the global political economy in the nineteenth century fostered the development of a mercantilist political-economic system concerned with neither liberal freedom nor Communist equality. Compelled by U.S. gunships to open the country's borders to "free" trade with the West, the Meiji oligarchs recognized that Japan must either modernize quickly or, like China, be overrun by Western imperialism. State-led economic development became not a way of serving the public but rather a means of preserving national sovereignty. The oligarchs' national slogan, "rich country, strong military," reflected Meiji modernizers' awareness from the outset of the strong relationship between economic development and industrialization on the one hand, and military and political power in the international arena on the other.

Despite the tumultuous change that Japan experienced in the late 1800s and early 1900s, the basic structure of its catch-up mercantilist political economy continued through much of the twentieth century, and key elements persist to the present. Forged under conditions of military rigor, refined during the U.S. occupation, and perfected under the aegis of American military and economic protection, this developmental model propelled Japan from the ashes of devastating military defeat to become the second-largest economy in the world. Not surprisingly, scholars and policy makers alike have sought to understand this developmental "miracle," and the investigation of the model of Japan's **capitalist developmental state** has become an important field of academic study and policy analysis.[17] Japan's capitalist developmental state differed significantly from the liberal capitalist system that Americans often presume to be the only "true" form of capitalism. Like Germany's coordinated market economy, Japan's political-economic system has permitted a far higher level of state guidance of competitive markets and cooperation with private firms than do the liberal systems in the United Kingdom and the United States. This guidance has included a host of formal and informal economic measures often grouped under the term **industrial policy**. Industrial policies are formulated and implemented by Japan's elite economic bureaucracy after consultation and coordination with the private sector. Measures have included imposing protective tariffs and nontariff barriers on imports, encouraging cooperation and limiting "excessive" competition in strategic export sectors, and offering low-interest loans and tax breaks to firms willing to invest in targeted industries and technologies.

Government guidance has not always worked well or as planned. But for many decades, state-led developmental capitalism kept Japan's economy strong, prosperous, and internationally competitive while keeping its iron triangle of bureaucrats, politicians, and business leaders closely linked. The prewar family zaibatsu were replaced by professionally managed keiretsu business groups with ready access to cheap capital. Workers agreed to forgo disruptive labor strikes in exchange for promises of permanent employment, ensuring management a skilled and disciplined workforce. As early heavy-handed policies of protectionism and explicit control proved unwieldy, bureaucrats came to rely more on informal directives known as *administrative guidance* and on subtle incentives more suitable for the increasingly internationalized Japanese economy. After growing at an average rate of over 10 percent per year during the 1950s and 1960s, Japan's economy still managed to grow over 5 percent per year during the 1970s and 1980s. In fact, from the early 1950s to 1990, Japan's gross domestic product

(GDP) grew at twice the rate of those in the other advanced industrial economies. The flagship automotive and consumer electronics companies within Japan's large conglomerates became multinational giants and household names, and the fruits of Japan's rapid growth lifted incomes and opportunities for nearly all Japanese.

By the 1980s, Japan's very prosperity was masking what now, in hindsight, is much easier to detect as serious structural problems within the model. Even as the international political economy grew ever more integrated and hypercompetitive, the costs of doing business in Japan were mounting. Japan's multinational automotive and electronics exporters felt this competitive pressure first, but kept their heads above water by shifting production overseas and drastically cutting costs at home. Most of Japan's companies were not able to react so nimbly, however; nor was the government prepared to tolerate the kind of unemployment that would have resulted from the wholesale transfer of production abroad. Rather than face global competition, inefficient industries used their influence within the iron triangle to seek protection. They obtained it from a government that had become accustomed to looking after not just economically strategic industries but also politically and socially important ones. This government assistance maintained employment and social stability but also led to waste, overcapacity, and overpricing.

These corporate welfare measures, combined with a rapid jump in the value of Japan's currency, propelled the country's stock and real estate markets skyward in the latter half of the 1980s. This led to dangerous overvaluation of both securities and land. At one point in the early 1990s, Japan's stock market was valued at fully half of all the world's stock markets combined. At its peak value, the less than 400 acres of land under the emperor's palace grounds in central Tokyo was worth (at least nominally) as much as the land of the entire state of California. Japan was awash in overinflated assets and easy money, which led companies, banks, the Japanese Mafia, and even the government to invest in grossly overpriced assets and risky (even foolish) business ventures. When this asset bubble burst in 1992, the value of stock and property plummeted, growth slowed, and already uncompetitive companies were left with huge debts (and dwindling assets and production with which to repay them). The Japanese labeled these firms **zombies**—essentially dead but propped up by banks and a political system unwilling to force them into bankruptcy and face the social costs of closed businesses and spiraling unemployment.

The government slid deeper into debt as it sustained not just these insolvent firms but also the banks that carried their debts (valued in the trillions of dollars), even as it attempted to stimulate consumer spending. Although a combination of government stimulus measures and liberalizing reforms have breathed some life back into the economy, Japan is now mired in its third consecutive decade of no or slow growth. The economy remains plagued by the three Ds of deflation (declining prices), government debt (more than twice Japan's annual GDP and the largest in the world), and budget deficits (running annually at about 10 percent of GDP).

Over the course of two decades, Japan experienced a reversal of fortune unprecedented in a peacetime economy. It has slipped from its position as one of the richest and most powerful countries in the world to one that seems increasingly overshadowed by its neighbors. In 2010, China surpassed Japan as the second-largest economy in the world, and in 2014, India bumped Japan to number four. It is predicted that by 2050, Brazil, Indonesia, Mexico, and Turkey will also overtake Japan. While government-business cooperation and a targeted focus on economic development promoted rapid postwar economic growth, this mercantilist political-economic structure proved far less successful once it had caught up and found itself pursuing cutting-edge technologies and competing in unpredictable and rapidly changing markets. Moreover, as the economy struggled, politicians and bureaucrats boosted the funding of public works and provided generous subsidies to inefficient and uncompetitive firms to prop up employment and preserve voter support. Although these destructive inefficiencies were tolerable during the boom years, they became a significant drag on the Japanese economy and a political albatross for the long-ruling LDP.

The DPJ came to government in 2009 promising to weaken the iron triangle, curtail public works, and end corporate welfare, but soon backed away from its early campaign pledge to shift funding "from concrete to people." Like its LDP predecessor, the DPJ recognized that swiftly ending corporate welfare in a weak economy would be political suicide. At the same time, it fostered its own "pork constituencies" among organized labor, agriculture, and urban consumers.[18] Hampered by the 2011 earthquake and its aftermath, the DPJ also failed to deliver on its promises of stimulating economic recovery. In elections for both the lower (2012) and upper (2013) chambers of the Diet, voters—perhaps grudgingly—offered Abe and the LDP another chance. Promising to lift Japan's struggling economy, the government launched a three-pronged recovery program that came to be labeled Abenomics. The first of the program's three "arrows," as Abe called his economic stimulus measures, sought to increase demand in the economy, and the second took aim at boosting inflation. These fiscal and monetary stimulus policies did spur Japan's economic growth rate and raise prices, but thus far have had less impact on job creation and wage increases.

The third arrow of Abenomics provides for a broad array of structural reforms intended to raise the economy's growth potential and put Japan on track for long-term recovery and growth. But this arrow has proven more difficult to launch, and skeptics fear it may never hit its target. These reforms include proposals for deregulated economic zones, reduced protectionism in agriculture, and more open immigration policies. None of these proposed measures are new, but because each threatens to harm particular interests, both former and present governments have struggled to deliver on these kinds of bold promises of structural reform in the face of conservative bureaucratic, political, and corporate resistance. This resistance has led many observers to conclude that the key to substantial economic liberalization remains political reform.

Foreign Relations and the World

Despite the vicissitudes of Japan's external relations, its foreign affairs have been marked by several continuities worth noting. First, though insular, the Japanese have been inveterate adopters and adapters of things foreign. From Chinese ideograms to American popular culture, the Japanese have at key periods in their history pragmatically embraced foreign elements that they deemed beneficial. Second, historically the Japanese have maintained a hierarchical perception of the world, one in which international entities (countries, empires, races), like internal entities (family members, classes, companies), are seen and ranked in hierarchical terms. Third, Japan's island status and catch-up strategy of mercantilist development have given the Japanese a very strong and sharply delineated sense of nationalism, which has made Japanese citizens highly responsive to calls for sacrifice on behalf of the nation when faced with a foreign challenge.[19]

Japan and Asia

Given these continuities, it should not surprise us that some frustrated advocates of political and economic reform in Japan are calling for *gaiatsu* ("foreign pressure") or even a "third opening" of Japan (after Perry and MacArthur) as the impetus for change. Although Japan's external dealings over the past century and a half have been the source of understandable anxiety and much military disaster, they have also been the impetus for beneficial change. By the same token, Japan's substantial international stature has meant that both its earlier economic success and its more recent problems have been spilling over into the rest of the world, and with a variety of consequences.

If Japan's international relations were viewed as a series of concentric circles, the most immediate and significant circle would include Japan and its Asian neighbors. These neighbors have felt most acutely both the cost and the benefit of Japan's military, economic, and cultural expansion. Under the promise (or guise) of a Greater East Asian Co-Prosperity Sphere, modern Japan in the first half of the twentieth century expanded its empire first to Taiwan and Korea and then to the Chinese mainland, Southeast Asia, and the Pacific Islands. Japan brought oppressive colonial rule, imperial exploitation, and military destruction wherever it went. But it also built economic infrastructure, transferred technology and training, and exported its version of developmental capitalism to several of its longer-held colonies. Moreover, it brought much of Asia into what it termed in the 1930s a **flying geese** pattern of economic development that positioned Japan at the head of a flock of dependent Asian economies. Japan offered leadership by exploiting its comparative advantage in advanced industries and then passing its skills on to the next tier as newer technologies became available. The second tier would do the same for the third, providing a ladder of industrial progress for (and Japanese dominance of) all Asia.

Since Japan's World War II defeat and its embrace of American-directed pacifist prosperity, the rest of Asia has viewed Japan with understandable ambivalence. On the one hand, though its constitution renounces war, Japan has never been required to atone for or even acknowledge its colonial and wartime legacies in the way that Germany has faced and frequently reexamined its Nazi past. The Japanese Imperial Army forced thousands of Korean and other Asian so-called comfort women to serve as sexual slaves for its troops in the field, and (like most conquering armies) the military committed a host of other war-related atrocities. Koreans, Chinese, and other Asians are troubled that Japanese textbooks have largely glossed over these events and that many of Japan's conservative politicians and prime ministers have made regular pilgrimages to Yasukuni Shrine, a controversial Shinto shrine honoring Japan's war dead. Prime Minister Abe's 2013 visit caused particular consternation, aggravating the already tense relations between China and Japan over competing territorial claims (see "Territorial Tempests," p. 329). Chinese and Korean patriots regularly take to the streets, demanding Japanese apologies and threatening boycotts of Japanese products.

On the other hand, the past benefits and future fruits of investment from and trade with Asia's most-advanced and second-largest economy make it difficult for the rest of the region to turn its back on Japan. Despite memories of war, many

Japanese paying their respects at the controversial Yasukuni Shrine. Yasukuni is revered by Japanese nationalists but criticized by Japan's Asian neighbors, who think the shrine honors the spirit of people who have been convicted of war crimes.

Asians are more interested in high-tech imports from Japan or employment in a Japanese factory than they are in an apology for past offenses. Despite historical tensions, its own economic woes, and the growth of China, South Korea, and other economies in the region, Japan remains the region's largest provider of technology and investment capital and is an essential link in regional trade networks. At the same time, resource-poor Japan finds itself increasingly competing with and confronting resource-hungry China and other neighboring nations seeking to exploit regional sources of fossil fuels and other natural resources.

Japan and the United States

Japan's very real economic clout in Asia must be placed in the broader context of growing security concerns in the region and Japan's continued economic (and, particularly, military) dependence on the United States. In the context of Japan's overwhelming defeat in World War II and America's decades-long struggle with the Soviet Union, this patron-client relationship made good sense and good foreign policy for both the United States and Japan. The United States sponsored Japan's return as a member in good standing of the U.S.-sponsored world trade system and Cold War alliance. In turn, Japan kept its full attention on rebuilding its economy, employing what came to be known as the Yoshida Doctrine—the government's postwar foreign policy strategy of singular focus on domestic economic recovery and reliance on American military protection. But by the 1970s, its very success as dutiful client had led to a divergence in Japan's economic and security relations with its American patron. Whereas both the United States and Japan were willing to retain a relationship of military protection and dependence, Japan's rapid economic growth made it a full-fledged economic competitor. Over the next few decades, the United States and Europe engaged in trade wars with Japan and increased their demands that Japan end its economic protectionism and shoulder the burdens of a full-fledged economic partner. Japan has acceded to those demands, albeit at times reluctantly.

Many contend that Japan, the rest of Asia, and the rest of the world have changed too much to allow Japan's status quo to persist. Critics both inside and outside Japan express frustration over the country's split personality as economic giant and political pygmy and call for it to become a "normal" or "ordinary" country. These terms mean different things to different advocates, but they typically entail liberalizing Japan's economy and society; opening the country's borders to trade, investment, immigrants, and students; and militarizing Japan, developing its ability to defend itself as well as contribute to regional and global security. We have already discussed the obstacles to and prospects for economic and social change in Japan. Now, we turn finally to Japan's security and its political role in the world.

Japan and the World

Despite a constitution that prohibits the use or threat of war in resolving conflicts (Article 9) and the presence of nearly 50,000 U.S. troops on its soil, Japan has its own means of defense. It currently has a Self-Defense Force (SDF) of nearly 250,000 personnel and an annual military budget of over $40 billion, which ranks it eighth in the world in military expenditures.

Although sentiment in Japan since World War II has been decidedly pacifist, neighboring North Korea's pursuit of nuclear weapons, the growing capacity of China's military (which ranks second only to the United States in expenditures and spends four times as much as its Japanese counterpart), and growing tensions between China and Japan over competing territorial claims have shifted public opinion in Japan quite dramatically. Only 38 percent of Japanese respondents in a 2016 opinion poll favored changing Article 9 of the constitution, but this result marks a doubling of support from the previous decade.

The Abe government capitalized on its parliamentary majority and this growing (albeit still minority) support by passing controversial legislation in 2015 reinterpreting Article 9 and permitting Japan to engage in collective self-defense. This authorization permits the SDF to respond beyond its own borders to an attack on the United States or other ally if the government determines that the attack threatens Japan's security. While Japanese citizens are increasingly nervous about China's regional ambitions and North Korea's unpredictable belligerence, they remain much less enthusiastic about Abe's ambitions to lift the military restraints of Japan's constitution than they are about his promises and plans to revive the economy.

At the same time, however, the United States has also urged Japan to bear more of the burdens of its own defense and participate more fully in regional and global peacekeeping operations. Japan was widely criticized for its so-called checkbook diplomacy, by which it largely limited its participation in the Gulf, Afghan, and Iraq wars to financial contributions. Not surprisingly, the Abe government has used this convergence of *gaiatsu* ("foreign pressure") with its own political and ideological interests to bolster the technological sophistication of Japan's military and the capacity to project force beyond its borders. The SDF has built three flat-decked "helicopter destroyers" (other countries call them aircraft carriers) and maintains hundreds of highly sophisticated fighter jets and amphibious landing craft.

Nowhere is Japan's ambivalence about pacifism, militarism, and its alliance with the United States more apparent than in the controversy over American military bases on the Japanese island of **Okinawa**. Occupied and administered by the United States from the end of World War II to the time of its reversion to Japan in 1972, the small island continues to host over half of all U.S. military personnel in Japan on some 14 bases. Widespread local opposition to this American presence has garnered national support in recent years, leading the former DPJ government to make a campaign promise to relocate U.S. troops from Okinawa. The inability of the government to deliver on this promise in the face of U.S. pressure and growing regional security concerns forced the DPJ's Hatoyama to resign after less than a year in office in 2010 and weakened the government. While Abe and his LDP government were able to resolve a long-standing conflict over the moving of an air base from a more to a less congested area within Okinawa, local resistance remains strong.

Although a growing minority of Japanese citizens are willing to accept a greater role for Japan's armed forces, most Japanese—and certainly most Asians—remain highly wary of Japanese militarism. Advocates of a nonmilitarized Japan argue that the country can project and indeed has projected its power and influence abroad in a host of beneficial ways, and they view striving for militarized "normalcy" as contrary both to the intent of Japan's pacifist constitution and to the interests of Japan and the world. They argue that Japan need not be a military power to be a global power, and they point to numerous areas in which Japan has already shown global leadership. They note that Japan has been among the world's top donors of international aid, giving over $10 billion in foreign development assistance annually. They contend that Japan ought to focus its efforts on areas of global benefit, such as humanitarian relief, technology transfers to developing countries, and meeting the challenges of climate change, rather than engage in a dangerous and costly arms race with China or other countries.

Can Japan use its unique constitutional restrictions to create a new kind of nonmilitary global influence? More fundamentally, can it implement the economic and political reforms necessary to right its economic ship in time to maintain this international presence? Will these reforms come from above, from below, from the outside, or perhaps not at all (or not in time)? In this, as in other areas, Japan's capacity and willingness to change in the twenty-first century will prove crucial to its future security as well as its economic prosperity and political stability.

CURRENT ISSUES IN JAPAN

3/11: Japan's Triple Tragedy

Japan is no stranger to earthquakes or other natural disasters—it has experienced 17 significant earthquakes since 1995 and gave us the word *tsunami*. But this island nation was wholly unprepared for the disastrous Tōhoku earthquake and tsunami that struck the northeast region of Honshu, Japan's largest island, on March 11, 2011. The biggest (of many) tremors registered 9.0 in magnitude on the Richter scale, making it the largest recorded earthquake ever to strike Japan and one of the five most powerful anywhere. With its epicenter 40 miles off the coast and 20 miles under the ocean's surface, the quake generated tidal waves up to 133 feet high that wreaked havoc on the coastline and traveled as far as 6 miles inland. The entire island of Honshu shifted some 8 feet to the east. The earthquake and tsunami caused an estimated 25,000 casualties and hundreds of billions of dollars in damage, and it shaved roughly 5 percent off Japan's annual GDP.

Perhaps, though, a greater long-term danger posed by this disaster has come from the destruction and meltdown of nuclear reactors at the Fukushima Daiichi plant and the associated nuclear accidents and radioactive fallout. Experts have judged this to be the worst nuclear catastrophe since the meltdown in Chernobyl in the former Soviet Union some 25 years earlier. They estimate that the process of cooling and dismantling the three damaged reactors and decontaminating the area could take decades. This ongoing threat of radiation is particularly poignant for Japan, the only country to have experienced widespread radioactive contamination following the atomic bombing at the end of World War II.

This most recent nuclear fallout has led growing numbers of Japanese citizens and political leaders to question the safety and wisdom of relying on nuclear energy. Before the crisis, Japan met nearly one-third of its energy needs through nuclear power and had plans to boost this figure to fully half its power generation.

Scene of the extensive destruction resulting from Japan's Tōhoku earthquake and tsunami.

But the disaster prompted increasing calls for reducing nuclear energy dependency and at one point led the DPJ government to shut down or suspend operations at all of Japan's reactors and promise to phase out atomic energy entirely.

Despite continued popular concern about the safety of nuclear power, ongoing contamination of the Fukushima site, and delays in the promised cleanup of surrounding communities, Abe's LDP government moved forward with a new energy strategy that called for restarting many of Japan's current reactors and increasing reliance on nuclear energy in an effort to increase energy independence.

The political fallout from the disaster has been significant as well. The crisis initially provided a boost to the flailing DPJ government, but its slow and inadequate response to the disaster prompted growing frustration and activism among Japanese citizens. The iron triangle of Japan, Inc., became a particular target of this popular dissatisfaction when it became apparent that the bureaucratic ministry charged with ensuring the safe operation of the private utility corporation's nuclear plants had in fact served as its chief promoter. As often happens in these kinds of disasters, the real heroes were its victims. The region experienced virtually no looting or other crimes in the days and weeks following the earthquake and tsunami, and the Japanese people demonstrated a remarkable degree of patience, cooperation, and national purpose. Today, as the government's cleanup efforts fall hopelessly behind schedule and stretch from months to years, and now perhaps decades, this patience has in many cases turned to bitterness and hopelessness.

Territorial Tempests

An additional thorny challenge lies beyond the shores of Japan's main islands and concerns territorial disputes with each of the country's largest continental neighbors. Although the total landmass of these contested islands could easily fit within the area of metropolitan Tokyo, conflicts with Russia, South Korea, and China over these mostly uninhabited (and in many cases uninhabitable) territories has been rancorous, persistent, and seemingly intractable. Ironically, the conflicts are not so much about the islands themselves, but rather a convergence of bitter historical memories, expressions of national sovereignty, and competition for access to lucrative fisheries and seabed petroleum resources.

The largest of these territories and the source of the most long-standing dispute are what the Russians call the Kurile Islands and the Japanese refer to as the "Northern Territories." Control of this chain of islands stringing northward from Hokkaido (the most northern of Japan's four largest islands) has shifted back and forth between Japan and China since the nineteenth century. However, since Japan's defeat in World War II, the entire archipelago has been occupied by the Russians. Because each country forfeited control over the islands as a result of war defeat (Russia in 1905 and Japan in 1945), neither side is willing to legitimize the claims of the other. In fact, this dispute has prevented Japan and Russia from ever concluding a peace treaty ending World War II. Although Japan currently lays claim to only the four southernmost islands in the chain, the two countries appear as far away as ever from resolving this issue that has festered for nearly seven decades. In 2010, Russian president Dimitri Medvedev became the first Russian political leader to visit the islands, an area valued for its highly productive fishing grounds. Choosing to tour the islet closest to Japan, he posted photos to his Twitter account, noting "how many beautiful places there are in Russia!"

Moving southward, Japan's island dispute with South Korea concerns two tiny islets whose sizes belie the degree of bitter acrimony between the two countries. The two jagged outcroppings of rock known as the Dokdo (Korea) or Takeshima (Japan) islands are located almost equidistant (just over 100 miles) from both the Korean mainland and Japan's main island of Honshu. Although each country claims sovereignty over the territory, South Korea administers the 46 acres of volcanic rock on which an octopus fisherman and his wife (both Korean citizens) comprise the entire permanent residents (guarded by 37 South Korean police officers also stationed on the island). South Korea, in particular, remains highly sensitive to this issue, since Japan's claim to the territory is founded chiefly on its harsh colonization of Korea in the early twentieth century. When the Japanese prefecture laying claim to the islets launched a "Takeshima Festival" in 2005, an angry Korean mother responded in protest by severing her own finger and that of her son. Another Korean protester set himself on fire.

Likewise, Japan's dispute with China over the Diaoyu Islands (China) or **Senkaku Islands** (Japan) finds its roots in Japan's imperial past. However, rising tensions between these two East Asian powers over the barren outcroppings threaten to escalate this quarrel into outright military conflict. Although each country cites centuries-old historical records to justify its respective claims of sovereignty, Japan formally annexed the five islets in 1895 after its military victory against China that year. The same treaty awarded the far larger island of Taiwan (which lies some 100 miles to the south) to Japan as its first colony. The uninhabited outcroppings lie almost equidistant (approximately 200 miles) from the Chinese mainland and Japan's Okinawa.

Although abundant fishing in the area has led to numerous incidents between Chinese fishing boats and Japanese patrol boats (involving at times water cannons, ramming, and even the impounding of boats and personnel), the greater stake in this dispute has been the oil and gas fields discovered in this region. Both countries agreed in 2008 to make the East China Sea a "sea of peace, cooperation and prosperity" and to jointly exploit the seabed petroleum fields; however, bitter accusations and rising nationalist protests on both sides have been common. In 2012, Tokyo's right-wing nationalist governor threatened to use government funds to purchase three of the five islands from their private Japanese owner. Seeking to preempt the governor's provocative move and deescalate the conflict, Japan's national government purchased the islands. But this step, too, was seen by the Chinese as inflammatory and led to diplomatic protests and public outcry. Nor is it just the seabeds, islands, and fisheries that are being contested. In 2013, the Chinese unilaterally declared an "air defense identification zone" that would require any foreign aircraft flying through the zone to identify itself to Chinese authorities and comply with Chinese regulations. Naturally, the new zone encompassed the islands, and just as predictably, Japanese aircraft have ignored the Chinese requirement (as has the United States, Japan's military ally). Dangerous near misses between Japanese and Chinese military aircraft now compete with sea-based clashes.

These multinational island (and sea and air) disputes are ostensibly foreign policy issues, but they remain salient largely because of conservative nationalist groups in each country. Those groups see any show of flexibility or compromise on the parts of their own governments as a sign of weakness against the imperial designs of their neighbors. This dynamic dangerously demonstrates the compelling power of nationalism and proves in the case of Japan, as illustrated elsewhere in this textbook on comparative politics, that perhaps all politics in the end are domestic politics. But this tempest between Japan and rising China also demonstrates that domestic politics can have profound and potentially deadly international consequences.

NOTES

1. T. J. Pempel and Keiichi Tsunekawa, "Corporatism without Labor: The Japanese Anomaly," in *Trends toward Corporatist Intermediation,* eds. Philippe Schmitter and Gerhard Lehmbruch (New York: Sage, 1990).
2. Margaret A. McKean, "Equality," in *Democracy in Japan,* ed. Takeshi Ishida and Ellis S. Krauss (Pittsburgh: University of Pittsburgh Press, 1989), 203.
3. There was also an underclass or outcast segment of society known as the *eta* or *burakumin,* who were discriminated against for their work in the ritually impure trades, such as tanning and butchering.

4. Hugh Byas, *Government by Assassination* (New York: Alfred A. Knopf, 1942).

5. John Dower, *Embracing Defeat: Japan in the Wake of World War II* (New York: W. W. Norton, 1999), 45.

6. "Experts Ponder Reasons for Japan's Rash of Short-Term Prime Ministers," *Japan Times*, January 1, 2012.

7. David S. Law, "The Anatomy of a Conservative Court: Judicial Review in Japan," *Texas Law Review* 87 (June 2009): 1545–93.

8. Although the population of voting districts was relatively balanced when districts were originally set up after the war, the LDP never reapportioned them even as the countryside became depopulated. In exchange for their voting loyalty, farmers were assured high prices for their rice and were given voting clout as much as five times greater than that of urban voters, who were less likely to vote for the LDP. In the 1990 lower house elections, for example, opposition parties won nearly 54 percent of the popular vote but garnered only 44 percent of the seats. Likewise, even though the DPJ outpolled the LDP in the 2010 upper house elections, it garnered fewer seats.

9. Under the old system, all representatives were elected from multimember districts (MMDs) in which voters had a single nontransferable vote (SNTV), which they cast for a specific candidate instead of a party list. This unusual MMD/SNTV system created a variety of incentives and consequences both for the LDP, which benefited immensely from the rules, and for opposition parties struggling to compete.

10. Under 2013 changes to the electoral law designed to reduce malapportionment, district boundaries in 17 prefectures have been redrawn and five districts have been eliminated without replacement (one each in Fukui, Yamanashi, Tokushima, Kōchi, and Saga). The number of first-past-the-post seats has reduced to 295, and the total number of seats decreased to 475.

11. Kakuei Tanaka, who served as prime minister during the early 1970s, was the consummate Japanese politician and likely Japan's most influential. He presided over a powerful LDP faction but was forced to resign and ultimately was convicted of financial misdeeds involving huge sums of money.

12. See, for example, Karel van Wolferen, *The Enigma of Japanese Power* (New York: Alfred A. Knopf, 1989).

13. See Andrew DeWit, "Dry Rot: The Corruption of General Subsidies in Japan," *Journal of the Asia Pacific Economy* 7 (2002): 355–78.

14. Ken Victor Leonard Hijino, "Delinking National and Local Party Systems: New Parties in Japanese Local Elections," *Journal of East Asian Studies* 13 (2013): 107–35.

15. See Simon Andrew Avenell, "Civil Society and the New Civic Movements in Contemporary Japan: Convergence, Collaboration and Transformation," *Journal of Japanese Studies* 25 (2009): 247–83.

16. For immigration, see Deborah J. Milly, *New Policies for New Residents: Immigrants, Advocacy, and Governance in Japan and Beyond* (Ithaca, NY: Cornell University Press, 2014). For challenges facing women in the workforce, see Junko Nishimura, *Motherhood and Work in Contemporary Japan* (New York: Routledge, 2015).

17. The seminal study in this field is Chalmers Johnson, *MITI and the Japanese Miracle: The Growth of Industrial Policy, 1925–1975* (Stanford, CA: Stanford University Press, 1982).

18. T. J. Pempel, "Between Pork and Productivity: The Collapse of the Liberal Democratic Party," *Journal of Japanese Studies* 36 (2010): 227–54.

19. Clyde Prestowitz, *Trading Places* (New York: Basic Books, 1988), 82–94.

KEY TERMS

2011 earthquake Disastrous 9.0 earthquake that struck the northeast region of Honshu, Japan's largest island, causing a destructive tsunami that resulted in the meltdown of several nuclear reactors

Abe, Shinzō Conservative nationalist Liberal Democratic Party politician and two-time prime minister (2006–07; 2012–)

Abenomics Prime Minister Abe's three-pronged plan for economic recovery, including monetary easing (raising inflation), fiscal stimulus (budget increases), and structural reform

administrative guidance Extra-legal policy directives from government officials to the private sector

amakudari Literally "descent from heaven," in which retiring Japanese senior bureaucrats take up positions in corporations or run for political office

Article 9 The clause in Japan's postwar constitution that requires Japan to renounce the right to wage war; also known as the *peace clause*

capitalist developmental state Japan's modern neomercantilist state, which has embraced both private property and state economic intervention

Democratic Party of Japan (DPJ)/Democratic Party (DP) Social democratic party in government from 2009–12; formed from the merger of reform-minded opposition parties in 1998 and re-formed as "Democratic Party" after a subsequent 2016 merger

Diet Japan's bicameral parliament

flying geese A model of regional economic development imposed on Asia in the 1930s; positions Japan at the head of a flock of dependent Asian economies

Hatoyama, Yukio Democratic Party of Japan's first prime minister (2009–10)

House of Councillors The upper and weaker chamber of Japan's parliament

House of Representatives The lower and more powerful chamber of Japan's parliament

industrial policy Government measures designed to promote economic and industrial development

iron triangle A term describing the conservative alliances among Japan's elite bureaucrats, conservative politicians, and big-business executives

keiretsu Japan's large business groupings

koenkai Japan's local campaign organizations; designed to support an individual candidate rather than a particular political party

Koizumi, Junichiro A populist Japanese Liberal Democratic Party prime minister (2001–06)

Liberal Democratic Party (LDP) Japan's conservative political party, which governed Japan for over five decades since the party's inception in 1955

MacArthur, Douglas The U.S. general who presided over the seven-year occupation of Japan (1945–52)

Meiji oligarchs The vanguard of junior samurai who led Japan's nineteenth-century modernization drive

Meiji Restoration Japan's 1867–68 "revolution from above," which launched Japan's modernization in the name of the Meiji emperor

Okinawa Japanese prefecture composed of several island archipelagoes located southwest of Japan's four major islands and host to several controversial U.S. military bases

pork-barrel projects Government appropriation or other policy supplying funds for local improvements to ingratiate legislators with their constituents

rich country, strong military The mercantilist slogan promoting Japan's nineteenth-century modernization efforts

***sakoku* ("closed country")** Tokugawa Japan's policy of enforced isolation, which lasted from the seventeenth to the nineteenth centuries

samurai Japan's feudal-era warrior retainers

Self-Defense Force Japan's military, ostensibly permitted only defensive capacity

Senkaku Islands A collection of five uninhabited islands and rock outcroppings located in the East China Sea and contentiously claimed by both Japan and China

shogun A dominant lord in feudal Japan

Taishō democracy The era of tentative democratization in Japan (1918–31)

Tokugawa The military clan that unified and ruled Japan from the seventeenth to the nineteenth centuries

twisted Diet Situation in which no party or coalition of parties controls both chambers of the Japanese parliament; common since 2007

Yasukuni Shrine The controversial Shinto shrine honoring Japan's war dead

zombies Japanese firms rendered essentially bankrupt during Japan's recession but propped up by banks and politicians

WEB LINKS

- Japanese constitution (http://japan.kantei.go.jp/constitution_and _government_of_japan/constitution_e.html)
- Japanese prime minister and cabinet (http://japan.kantei.go.jp/index.html)
- Japanese Statistical Data; provides regularly updated statistical information in 19 different categories, including demographic, geographic, and economic data (http://www.stat.go.jp/english/)
- National Diet of Japan; links to House of Councillors and House of Representatives that provide extensive information on membership, relative strength of parties, and electoral and legislative procedures (http://www .sangiin.go.jp/eng/; http://www.shugiin.go.jp/internet/index.nsf/html /index_e.htm)

7

In response to international sanctions, a Russian supporter of Vladimir Putin shows off a T-shirt that reads, "Our nuclear missiles are not afraid of sanctions."

RUSSIA

Why Study This Case?

For decades, Russia stood out from all other countries in the world. Established in 1917, the Soviet Union (which included present-day Russia and many of its neighbors) was the world's first Communist state. The Soviet Union served as a beacon for Communists everywhere, a symbol of how freedom and equality could be transformed if the working class could truly gain power. It provoked equally strong responses among its opponents, who saw it as a violent, dangerous, and power-hungry dictatorship. The rapid growth of Soviet power from the 1930s onward only exacerbated this tension, which eventually culminated in a Cold War between the United States and the Soviet Union following World War II. Armed with thousands of nuclear weapons, these two ideologically hostile states struggled to maintain a balance of power and to avoid a nuclear holocaust. Until the 1980s, many observers believed that humanity would eventually face a final, violent conflict between these two systems.

Yet when the Soviet Union's end finally came, it was not with a bang but with a whimper. In the 1980s, the Soviet Union saw the rise of a new generation of leaders who realized that their system was no longer primed to overtake the West, economically or otherwise. The general secretary of the Soviet Union's Communist Party, Mikhail Gorbachev, attempted to inject limited political and economic reforms into the system. His reforms, however, seemed only to exacerbate domestic problems and polarize the leadership and the public. Gorbachev's actions resulted in the actual dissolution of the Soviet Union and the formation of 15 independent countries, one of which is Russia.

How would Russia be reconstructed from the ruins? Like many of the other postcommunist countries, it had to confront the twin tasks of forging democracy and establishing capitalism in a land that had little

RUSSIA

Provideniya

Anadyr

Petropavlovsk-Kamchatskiy

Magadan

Bering Sea

Sea of Okhotsk

Khabarovsk

Sea of Japan

JAPAN

NORTH KOREA

SOUTH KOREA

Yellow Sea

Vladivostok

S I B E R I A

Lena R.

Yakutsk

Lake Baikal

MONGOLIA

C H I N A

Irkutsk

ARCTIC OCEAN

Norilsk

Krasnoyarsk

Yenisey R.

Novosibirsk

Ob R.

Omsk

KAZAKHSTAN

N

Barents Sea

Yekaterinburg

Chelyabinsk

KYRGYZSTAN

TAJIKISTAN

Norwegian Sea

GREENLAND (DENMARK)

ICELAND

Murmansk

Arkhangelsk

Petrozavodsk

UZBEKISTAN

AFGHANISTAN

NORWAY

SWEDEN

FINLAND

ESTONIA

Vyborg

St. Petersburg

LATVIA

LITHUANIA

BELARUS

Nizhniy Novgorod

Kazan

MOSCOW

Volgograd

Astrakhan

CHECHNYA

Caspian Sea

TURKMENISTAN

IRAN

GERMANY

POLAND

MOLDOVA

Kiev

UKRAINE

CRIMEA (controlled by Russia)

Rostov

Novorossiysk

Sochi

GEORGIA

ARMENIA

AZERBAIJAN

TURKEY

Black Sea

500 mi

250

0

500 km

250

0

366

historical experience with either process. How does a nation go about creating a market economy after communism? How does it go about building democracy? Russia proves a fascinating study of the quest to build new institutions that reconcile freedom and equality in a manner far different from that of the previous regime. We can learn a lot from Russia's attempt at meeting this awesome challenge.

A quarter century on, the prospects for Russian democracy and development appear to be poor. After an initial decade of incomplete and chaotic political and economic reform, the country began moving away from a liberal economic system and liberal democracy. Under the leadership of President **Vladimir Putin**, Russia has seen the effective end to democratic institutions, as ever-greater authority is concentrated in the hands of the president and those around him. Limitations on federalism, elections, and other changes have all been directed at reducing political power beyond the presidency. Additionally, steps have been taken to restrict civil society: the state has brought the mass media under federal control and increasingly is preventing independent political parties and nongovernmental organizations (NGOs) from functioning. Today, an incipient democratic ideology has been replaced by a focus on Russian nationalism and militarism, reflecting a sense of humiliation that the country has lost its authoritative role in the international system. Russia's seizure of the Crimea from Ukraine in 2014 and accusations of Russian meddling in American and European elections have only further increased hostility. Relations between Russia and the West are now at their worst since the Cold War.

Similarly, the economy, which in the 1990s experienced a drastic and incomplete shift to private property and market forces, has seen both increasingly curtailed. Powerful economic leaders whose fortunes rose during that period, the **oligarchs**, have now been largely divested of their wealth, driven from the country, or imprisoned. Assets, particularly natural resources, have been renationalized or transferred to individuals close to Putin. Economic growth has been inconsistent and largely propelled by oil and gas prices. In economics and politics, the country has fallen under the control of the *siloviki* ("men of power"), individuals who, like Putin, have their origins in the security agencies. And yet Putin's consolidation of power and his limitations on democracy and the market have garnered public support. Tired of the chaos of market reforms, cynical about postcommunist politics, and angry about Russia's loss of power in the world, most Russians have appreciated Putin's promise to restore order and Russian pride. To a large extent, he has succeeded.

In 2008, President Putin stepped down from power, having served the two-term limit on the office. His handpicked successor, Dimitri Medvedev, easily won the presidential election and promptly appointed Putin to be his prime minister. Given Medvedev's non-*siloviki* background and the power inherent in the presidential office, some expected that this transfer of power could represent a break with the Putin era. Instead, as prime minister, Putin still called the shots; then he returned to the presidency in 2012, appointing Medvedev as prime minister. Because he is able to serve another two 6-year terms, it appears that Putin will remain in office until 2024. At that point, he will have governed Russia for a quarter of a century.

In many ways, Russia has become as opaque and resistant to change as it was under communism—a worrying sign for that country and the rest of the world. In this chapter, we will look at the past, the promise, and the present of Russian politics and political change, with an eye to where this country may be headed.

Major Geographic and Demographic Features

As we study Russia's geography, the first thing we notice is the country's vast size. Even when viewed separately from the various republics that made up the Soviet Union, Russia is nearly four times the size of the United States and covers 11 time zones. Yet much of this land is relatively unpopulated. With some 144 million people, Russia's population is far smaller than that of either the United States or the European Union (total populations around 300 million and 500 million, respectively). Much of the Russian population is concentrated in the western, geographically European part of the country.

Russia's east, Siberia, is a flat region largely uninhabited because of its bitterly cold climate. Siberia represents an interesting comparison to the American frontier experience. While Americans moved westward toward the Pacific Ocean in the nineteenth century to find new lands to settle, Russians moved eastward toward the same ocean. Alaska was part of the Russian Empire until it was sold to the United States in 1867. But Russian and American experiences of the frontier were quite different. In America, the amenability of the climate and soil helped spread the population across the country and reinforce a sense of pioneer individualism. In contrast, the harsh conditions of Siberia meant that only the state could function effectively in much of the region, where it developed infrastructure and created populated communities. Many of the people who settled Siberia, before and after 1917, were political prisoners sent into exile.

Because of Russia's enormous size and location, the country has many neighbors. Unlike the relative isolation of North America, Russia shares borders with no fewer than 14 countries. Many of these countries were part of the Soviet Union and are considered by Russians to remain in their sphere of influence. But Russia also shares a long border with China, a neighbor with whom it has often had troubled relations. Russia also controls a series of islands in the Pacific that belonged to Japan until 1945, and this situation remains a source of friction between the two countries. Russia has long felt uneasy about its neighborhood. Over the centuries, unable to rely on oceans or mountains as natural defenses, it has been subject to countless invasions from Europe and Asia. Physical isolation has never been an option, and Russian territorial expansion has a long history.

Russia may suffer from some intemperate climates and uneasy borders, but it benefits in other areas. The country is rich in natural resources, among them wood, oil, natural gas, gold, nickel, and diamonds. Many of these resources are concentrated in Siberia and are thus not easy to extract, yet they remain important and have been central to the Russian economy.

Historical Development of the State

Religion, Foreign Invasion, and the Emergence of a Russian State

Any understanding of present-day Russia and its political struggles must begin with an understanding of how the state developed over time. Though ethnically Slavic peoples have lived in European Russia for centuries, these peoples are not credited with founding the first Russian state. Rather, credit is usually given to Scandinavians (Vikings) who expanded into the region in the ninth century C.E., forming a capital in the city of Kiev. Nonetheless, the true origins of the Russian state remain open to debate. This issue is highly politicized, because many Russians reject the notion that foreigners were first responsible for the genesis of the Russian people. The dispute even involves the very name of the country. Scholars who believe in the Viking origin of the Russian state argue that the name Russia (or **Rus**) comes from the Finnish word for the Swedes, *Ruotsi*, which derives from a Swedish word meaning "rowers." Those who dispute this claim argue that the name is of a tribal or geographic origin that can be traced to the native Slav inhabitants.[1]

Whatever its origins, by the late tenth century the Kievan state had emerged as a major force, stretching from Scandinavia to Central Europe. It had also adopted **Orthodox Christianity**, centered in Constantinople (modern-day Istanbul). Orthodoxy developed distinctly from Roman Catholicism in a number of practical and theological ways, among them the perception of the relationship between church and state. Roman Catholics came to see the pope as the central leader of the faith, separate from the political power of Europe's kings. Orthodoxy, however, did not draw such a line between political and religious authority. This situation, some argue, stunted the idea of a society functioning independently of the state.

Another important development was the Mongol invasion of Russia in the thirteenth century. The Mongols, a nomadic Asian people, first united under Genghis Khan and controlled Russia (along with much of China and the Middle East) for over two centuries. During that time, Russians suffered from widespread economic destruction, massacres, enslavement, urban depopulation, and the extraction of resources. Some scholars view this occupation as the central event that set Russia on a historical path separate from that of the West—one leading to greater despotism and isolation. Cut off from European intellectual and economic influences, Russia did not participate in the Renaissance, feel the impact of the Protestant Reformation, or develop a strong middle class.

Not all scholars agree with this assessment, however. For some, the move toward despotism had its impetus not in religion or foreign invasion but in domestic leadership. Specifically, they point to the rule of Ivan the Terrible (1547–84), who came to power in the decades following Russia's final independence from Mongol control. Consolidating power in Moscow rather than Kiev, Ivan began to assert Russia's authority over that of foreign rulers and began to destroy any government institutions that obstructed his consolidation of personal power. In a precursor to the Soviet experience, he created a personal police force that terrorized his political opponents. Though Ivan is viewed in much of Russian history as the unifier of the country, many historians see in him the seeds of repressive and capricious rule.[2] Whatever his legacy, in Ivan's rule we see the emergence of a single Russian emperor, or **tsar** (or *czar*, from the Latin word *Caesar*), who exercised sovereignty over the nation's lands and aristocrats.

We might argue that no one factor led to Russia's unique growth of state power and its dearth of democratic institutions. Religion may have shaped political culture in a way that influenced how Russians viewed the relationship between the individual and the state. Historic catastrophes such as Mongol rule may have stunted economic growth and cut the country off from the developments that

TIMELINE OF POLITICAL DEVELOPMENT

YEAR	EVENT
1552–56	Ivan the Terrible conquers the Tatar khanates of Kazan and Astrakhan; establishes Russian rule over the lower and middle Volga River.
1689–1725	Peter the Great introduces reforms, including the subordination of the church, the creation of a regular conscript army and navy, and new government structures.
1798–1814	Russia intervenes in the French Revolution and the Napoleonic Wars.
1861	Edict of Emancipation ends serfdom.
1917	Monarchy is overthrown and a provisional government established; Bolsheviks in turn overthrow the provisional government.
1918–20	Civil war takes place between the Red Army and the White Russians, or anticommunists.
1938	Joseph Stalin consolidates power; purges begin.
1953	Stalin dies.
1985	Mikhail Gorbachev becomes general secretary and initiates economic and political reforms.
1991	Failed coup against Gorbachev leads to the collapse of the Soviet Union; Boris Yeltsin becomes president of independent Russia.
1993	Yeltsin suspends the parliament and calls for new elections; legislators barricade themselves inside the parliament building, and Yeltsin orders the army to attack parliament; Russians approve a new constitution, which gives the president numerous powers.
1994–96	In a war between Russia and the breakaway republic of Chechnya, Chechnya is invaded, and a cease-fire is declared.
1999	Yeltsin appoints Vladimir Putin prime minister and resigns from office; Putin becomes acting president.
1999	Russia reinvades Chechnya following a series of bomb explosions blamed on Chechen extremists.
2000	Putin is first elected as president.
2008	Dimitri Medvedev becomes president; Putin becomes prime minister.
2012	Putin returns to presidency.
2014	Russian armed conflict with Ukraine and annexation of Crimea.

occurred elsewhere in Europe. Political leadership might also have solidified certain authoritarian institutions. None of these conditions, individually, may have had a defining influence on the country's development. But taken together, they served to pull Russia away from the West. This interpretation of events has been reemphasized of late in Russian politics.

Ivan's death left Russia with an identity crisis. Did it belong to Europe, one of numerous rival states with a common history and culture? Or did differences in history, religion, and location mean that Russia was separate from the West? Even today, Russia continues to confront this question. Some rulers, most notably Peter the Great (1689–1725), saw Westernization as a major goal. This view was typified in the relocation of the country's capital from Moscow to St. Petersburg, to place it closer to Europe (it was moved back to Moscow after the Russian Revolution of 1917). Peter consulted with numerous foreign advisers in his quest to modernize the country (particularly the military) and carry out administrative and educational reforms. In contrast, reactionaries such as Nicholas I (1825–55) were hostile to reforms. In Nicholas's case, this hostility was so great that in the last years of his reign even foreign travel was forbidden. Reforms, such as the emancipation of the serfs in 1861, proceeded over time but lagged behind the pace of changes in Europe. As Russia vacillated between reform and reaction, there was continuity in the growth of a centralized state and a weak middle class. Industrialization came late, emerging in the 1880s and relying heavily on state intervention. This inconsistent modernization caused Russia to fall behind its international rivals.

The Seeds of Revolution

The growing disjunction between a largely agrarian and aristocratic society and a highly autonomous state and traditional monarchy would soon foster revolution. As Russia engaged in the great power struggles of the nineteenth and twentieth centuries, it was battered by the cost of war, and national discontent grew. In 1904, Russia and Japan came into conflict as each sought to gain control over portions of China. To Russia's surprise, Japan asserted its military strength and quickly proved itself the more modern power, defeating Russia. In 1905, Russia experienced a series of domestic shocks in the form of protests by members of the growing working class, who had migrated to the cities during the rapid industrialization of the previous two decades. The Revolution of 1905 forced Nicholas II to institute a series of limited reforms, including the creation of a legislature (the

Duma). Although these reforms did quell the revolt, they were not revolutionary (the changes themselves were limited), nor did they bring stability to Russia. Shortly thereafter, the tsar began to weaken the very rights and institutions to which he had agreed. Meanwhile, many radical political leaders refused to participate in these new institutions and sought the removal of the tsar himself.

World War I was the final straw. The overwhelming financial and human costs of the war exacerbated domestic tensions, weakening rather than strengthening national unity. As the war ground on, Russia faced food shortages, public disturbances, and eventually a widespread military revolt. The tsar was forced to step down in March of 1917, and a noncommunist, republican leadership took control, unwisely choosing to remain in the war. This provisional government had little success asserting its authority. As disorder and public confusion grew, Communist revolutionaries, led by Vladimir Ilyich Lenin (1870–1924), staged a coup d'état. This was no mass rebellion but rather an overthrow of those in power by a small, disciplined force. After a subsequent civil war against anticommunist forces, Lenin began transforming Russia, which was renamed the Soviet Union, the first Communist state in world history.[3]

The Russian Revolution under Lenin

In many aspects, Lenin's takeover was a radical, revolutionary event, but in other ways, the new Communist government fell back on the conservative institutions of traditional Russian rule. Under Lenin, local revolutionary authority (in the form of **soviets**, or workers' councils) was pushed aside, though it was given superficial recognition in the new name of the country: the Union of Soviet Socialist Republics (USSR). Similarly, although the Communist Party embraced Russia's multinational character by creating a federal system around its major ethnic groups, the new republics had little power. Authority was vested solely in the Communist Party, which controlled all government and state activity. Alternative political parties and private media were banned. A secret-police force, the **Cheka**, was formed to root out opposition; it later became the **KGB**, the body that would control domestic dissent and supervise overseas surveillance. The "commanding heights" of industry were nationalized—seized by the state in the name of the people. Managing all of this newfound power was a growing bureaucratic system composed of the *nomenklatura*—the select list or class of Communist Party members to whom politically influential jobs in the state, society, or economy were given. The Communist state took on the enormous task of managing the basic economic and social life of the country. Such tasks necessitated the state's high degree of capacity and autonomy.

Yet even under Lenin's harsh leadership, the Soviet state did not reach its zenith. For the Soviet leadership, 1917 was intended simply as a first step in a worldwide process. One historian writes evocatively of Soviet telephone operators ready to receive the call that revolution had broken out elsewhere in the world in response to their triumph.[4]

As the years passed without other successful revolutions, the Soviet Union had to confront the possibility that it alone might have to serve as the vanguard of world revolution. Its focus had to shift so that domestic politics, not spreading revolution, would be paramount. Yet many old revolutionaries (those who had taken part in the 1917 events) had little interest in the day-to-day affairs of the party and state. One exception was Joseph Stalin (1879–1953), whose power over the party grew after Lenin died. By appointing loyal followers to positions of power and slowly consolidating his control over party and state institutions through increasingly brutal means, Stalin was able to force out other revolutionary leaders. One by one, those who had fought alongside Lenin in the revolution were removed from power, demoted, exiled, imprisoned, and/or executed.

Stalinism, Terror, and the Totalitarian State

By the late 1930s, Stalin had consolidated control over the Soviet party-state and was thus free to construct a totalitarian regime that reached across politics, economics, and society. When a central planning bureaucracy was created to allocate resources and distribute goods, the last vestiges of private property were wiped away. The impact of this change was particularly dramatic in agriculture, which was forcibly collectivized. Farmers often destroyed their livestock and crops rather than surrender them to the state, and many wealthy peasants were executed. Agricultural production collapsed, and as many as 7 million lives were lost in the resulting famine. In industry, the government embarked on a policy of crash industrialization in an attempt to catch up with and overtake the capitalist countries.

Power was thus centralized to a degree unknown before Soviet rule.[5] This growing power of the bureaucratic elite was enforced by the secret police, who turned their attention to anyone suspected of opposing Stalin's rule, whether outside the party or within. Estimates are that more than a million people were imprisoned in the 1930s, and nearly 1 million were executed. Terror became a central feature of control, and the innocence or guilt of those arrested was often largely irrelevant. Finally, Stalin's power was solidified through a cult of personality that portrayed him as godlike, incapable of error, and infinitely wise.

Stability and Stagnation after Stalin

With Stalin's death in 1953, the Soviet leadership moved away from its uses of unbridled terror and centralized power, and Stalin's excesses were publicly criticized to a certain extent. The basic features of the Soviet system, however, remained in place. Power was vested in the **Politburo**, the ruling cabinet of the Communist Party. At its head was the general secretary, the de facto leader of the country. Government positions, such as national legislators, the head of the government, and the head of state, were controlled and staffed by the Communist Party and simply implemented the decisions of the Politburo. The economy also remained under the control of a central planning bureaucracy, and although Russians were no longer terrorized, security forces continued to suppress public dissent through arrest and harassment. All basic aspects of Soviet life were decided by the *nomenklatura*. The party elite became, in essence, a new ruling class.

For a time, this system worked. The state was able to industrialize rapidly by controlling and directing all resources and labor. Moreover, in its infancy, Soviet rule enjoyed a high degree of legitimacy among the public. Even in the darkest years of Stalin's terror, citizens saw the creation of roads, railways, massive factories, homes, and schools, as well as the installation of electricity, where none had existed before. If individual freedom was restricted, the system was more equal than at any time in Russian history. Many people were given education, jobs, health care, and retirement benefits, often for the first time. The Soviet people saw their standard of living increase dramatically.

But by the 1960s, some party leaders had begun to realize that a system so controlled by a central bureaucracy was becoming too institutionalized and conservative to allow for necessary change or innovation. General Secretary Nikita Khrushchev, who took office in 1953 after Stalin's death, made an initial attempt at reform. But Khrushchev was thwarted by the party-state bureaucracy and forced from his position by the Politburo in 1964. He was replaced by Leonid Brezhnev (1964–82), who rejected further reform and placated the *nomenklatura* by assuring them that their power and privileges were protected. Under these conditions, economic growth slowed. Those in power became increasingly corrupt and detached, using their positions to gain access to scarce resources.

Public cynicism grew as economic development declined. In the 1960s, it was still possible to believe that Soviet development might match or even surpass that of the West. But by the 1980s, it was clear that, in many areas, the Soviet Union was in fact stagnating or falling behind.

The Failure of Reform and the Collapse of the Soviet State

Upon Brezhnev's death in 1982, a new generation of political thinkers emerged from the wings seeking to transform the Soviet state. Among its members was Mikhail Gorbachev, who became general secretary in 1985. Unconnected to the Stalinist period, Gorbachev believed that the Soviet state could be revitalized through the dual policies of **glasnost** ("political openness") and **perestroika** ("economic restructuring"). Gorbachev believed that a limited rollback of the state from public life would encourage citizen participation and weaken the *nomenklatura*'s powerful grip. Similarly, it was thought that economic reforms would increase incentives (like better pay) and reduce the role of central planning, thus improving the quality and quantity of goods. Overall, the ruling bodies expected that the Soviet people would be better off and that the legitimacy of the Communist Party would be restored.

In hindsight, we can see that the attack on state power was disastrous for the Soviet system. Gorbachev unleashed forces he could not control, which led to divisive struggles inside and outside the party. Nationalism grew among the many ethnic groups in the various republics, and some went so far as to demand independence. Critics attacked the corruption and incompetence of the party, calling for greater democracy, and others demanded a greater role for market forces and private property. Still others were disoriented by the changes and upset by the implication that the Soviet past had in fact been a historical dead end.[6]

Party leaders became polarized over the pace and scope of reform. Among them was **Boris Yeltsin** (1931–2007), an early protégé of Gorbachev's who was sidelined as his calls for change grew more radical. Though ejected from the Politburo, Yeltsin was elected president of the Russian Soviet Socialist Republic (the largest republic in the ostensibly federal Soviet system). The moderate Gorbachev was now under attack from two sides: by Yeltsin and other reformers who faulted Gorbachev's unwillingness to embrace radical change, and by conservatives and reactionaries who condemned his betrayal of communism. The very institutions of the party-state, unresponsive and unchanged for decades, began to unravel. In some ways, the Soviet Union began to resemble the chaotic Russia of pre-1917, and the tensions eventually came to a head. In August 1991, a group of anti-reform conservatives sought to stop the disintegration of Soviet institutions by mounting a coup d'état against Gorbachev, hoping that the party-state and the military would join their ranks. After the conspirators placed Gorbachev under arrest, Yeltsin led the resistance, famously denouncing the takeover while standing atop a tank. The army refused to back the coup, and it unraveled within two days.

As the coup collapsed, so did Gorbachev's political authority. The public blamed him for the chaos that had led up to the takeover (in fact, the conspirators were members of his cabinet, appointed to solidify his power). Moreover, Gorbachev was eclipsed by Yeltsin, whose authority was bolstered by his heroic stance against the coup. Yeltsin seized the opportunity to ban the Communist Party, effectively destroying what remained of Gorbachev's political base. In December 1991, Yeltsin and the leaders of the various Soviet republics dissolved the Soviet Union, and Yeltsin became president of a new, independent Russia. He held this position until 1999, when he named his prime minister, the otherwise unknown Vladimir Putin, acting president. Putin won the presidential elections in 2000 and again in 2004; he stepped down due to term limits in 2008. However, he retained power as prime minister and was reelected as president in 2012. Much of Russia's post-Soviet regime has thus been under the rule of one man.

Political Regime

Any sense that Russia could be considered a democracy has come to a definitive end. Certainly the country enjoys a much higher degree of individual freedom than did its Soviet predecessor, in such areas as the right to travel or own property. But while a number of ostensibly democratic structures have been built since 1991, under Putin they have been restricted or ignored.

It is hard to speak of Russia as even an illiberal democracy, since it has few elements of democracy that in fact function to any meaningful degree. Whereas in the 1990s, democratic institutions and civic organizations were weak and poorly institutionalized, in the Putin era they have been effectively stifled. An illiberal regime presumes the existence of democratic institutions whose power and legitimacy are uncertain. In Russia now, it is difficult to point to any institutions among state or society that are allowed to contribute to democratic activity in a substantive way. As we consider Russia's political regime, therefore, we need to keep in mind the extent to which any of the powers or responsibilities elucidated by the constitution match politics in reality.

Political Institutions

THE CONSTITUTION

The Russian constitution is a document born of violent conflict. Independent Russia emerged in the aftermath of a failed coup d'état by opponents of radical reform. This history is different from the recent history of most other Eastern European Communist countries, where Communist leaders were removed from power through public protest and elections. Although the Soviet state was dissolved, many elements of the old regime, including its political leaders, remained intact and in power. Boris Yeltsin thus faced a set of political institutions that were largely unchanged from those of the previous era. This carryover led to conflict. Most problematic was the battle between President Yeltsin and the existing parliament. At first, the parliament was a bicameral body consisting of the Congress of People's Deputies and the Supreme Soviet, both of which remained packed with former party members. The parliament initially supported Yeltsin but soon clashed with him over the speed and scope of his economic reforms.

As Yeltsin sought increased reform, the parliament grew so hostile that it sought to block his policies (including constitutional reform) and impeach him. In September 1993, Yeltsin responded by dissolving the parliament. His parliamentary

---

ESSENTIAL POLITICAL FEATURES

- **Legislative–executive system**: Semi-presidential

- **Legislature**: Federal Assembly

  - **Lower house**: State Duma

  - **Upper house**: Federation Council

- **Unitary or federal division of power**: Federal

- **Main geographic subunits**: Republics, provinces, territories, autonomous districts, federal cities (Moscow and St. Petersburg)

- **Electoral system for lower house**: Proportional representation

- **Electoral system for upper house**: Appointed by local executive and legislature

- **Chief judicial body**: Constitutional Court

---

opponents barricaded themselves in their offices, attempted to seize control of the national television station, and called for the army to depose the president. The army sided with Yeltsin, however, containing his opposition and suppressing the uprising with force. This support paved the way for Yeltsin to write a new constitution, which was ratified in 1993. Though the new constitution formally swept away the old legislative order, it could hardly be described as an auspicious beginning for democracy because it facilitated the development of a system that emphasized presidential power.

The Branches of Government

THE KREMLIN: THE PRESIDENT AND THE PRIME MINISTER

For centuries, Russians have referred to executive power, whether in the form of the tsar or the general secretary, as the **Kremlin**. Dating back to the eleventh century, the physical structure known as the Kremlin is a fortress in the heart of Moscow that has historically been the seat of state power. Today, much of the Kremlin's power is vested in the hands of the presidency, as elaborated in the 1993 constitution. That constitution created a powerful office through which the president could press for economic and political changes despite parliamentary opposition. Under Yeltsin and Putin, the result has been a semi-presidential system in which the president served as head of state while a prime minister served as head of government. Power is divided between the two offices, but the president has held an overwhelming amount of executive power. Since 2012, the president is directly elected to serve a six-year term (before then, presidential terms were only four years). The president may serve no more than two consecutive terms and can be removed only through impeachment. Vladimir Putin was elected in 2000 after serving as Boris Yeltsin's last prime minister, and he was reelected in 2004 after facing little serious competition for the office. His successor, Dimitri Medvedev, was similarly selected by Putin to run for the office in 2008. Medvedev won easily, since other candidates were effectively barred from running for the office. Putin returned to the presidency in 2012, following an election against a set of weak opposition candidates. Putin's return came as a surprise to many who hoped that he would remain in a secondary position of power, and it is widely assumed that Medvedev stepped down at Putin's instruction.

On paper, the president's powers are numerous. The president, not parliament, chooses and dismisses the prime minister and other members of the cabinet. The lower house of parliament, the State Duma, may reject the president's nominee, but if it does so three times, the president must dissolve the Duma and call for new elections. The president cannot, however, dissolve the Duma either in the year following parliamentary elections or in the last six months of his term. The president also appoints leaders to eight federal districts that constitute all of Russia, which allows him to oversee the work of local authorities.

The president may propose and veto bills, and, just as important, he can issue decrees—laws that do not require legislative approval, are often not made public, and may not be challenged by citizens in the courts. President Yeltsin frequently relied on decrees to bypass his obstreperous legislature. Even with a more compliant body, Putin has often used the power of the decree to directly conduct foreign or domestic policy, such as withdrawing from the International Criminal Court or to reorganize federal districts (both of which occurred in 2016).[7]

Another source of power lies in the president's control of important segments of the state. The president has direct control over the Foreign Ministry, the Defense Ministry, and the Interior Ministry (which handles the police and domestic security), as well as over the armed forces. He also controls the successor to the KGB, the **Federal Security Service (FSB)**, which manages domestic intelligence and is viewed by many as the main political actor in Russia, alongside Putin. Presidential control over these ministries and services allows the office a great deal of influence in foreign affairs and domestic security, and reinforces the power of Putin's core supporters, the *siloviki*.

As in the United States and other presidential or semi-presidential systems, it is difficult to remove the Russian president; impeachment is possible only on a charge of high treason or another grave crime. The impeachment process must first be approved by the high courts, after which two-thirds of both houses of parliament must vote in support of the president's removal. In 1999, the parliament attempted to impeach President Yeltsin on various charges, including his 1993 conflict with the legislature, economic reform, and the war in **Chechnya**. None of the charges passed.

In contrast to that of the president, the prime minister's role is to supervise those ministries not under presidential control and propose legislation to parliament that upholds the president's policy goals. The prime minister also promulgates the national budget. The Russian prime minister and other members of the cabinet, unlike their counterparts in many other parliamentary systems, are not appointed from and need not reflect the relative powers of the various parties in parliament. Because of the president's ability to choose the prime minister and other members of the cabinet, there is less need to form a government

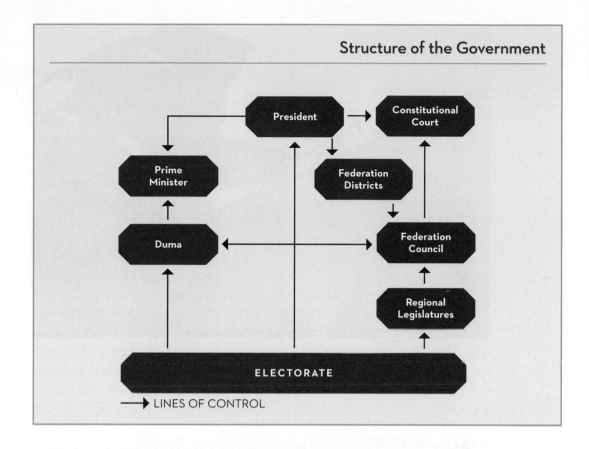

Structure of the Government

President → Constitutional Court

Prime Minister

Federation Districts

Duma

Federation Council

Regional Legislatures

ELECTORATE

→ LINES OF CONTROL

that represents the largest parties in parliament. During Putin's first tenure as president, Russian prime ministers were largely career bureaucrats chosen for their technical expertise or loyalty to the president rather than party leaders who had climbed the ranks in parliament.

The appointment of Putin to be prime minister "under" Medvedev raised many questions about the nature of the semi-presidential system in Russia. In advance of the 2008 presidential elections, Putin made it clear that he expected to become prime minister in return for his selection of Medvedev to run for president, and he continued to dominate politics from what was ostensibly the weaker office. This led to a great deal of confusion about where executive power really lay, and Medvedev's decision to step down after one term only reinforced the sense that power is more vested in an individual than any particular office. Putin's personal authority has trumped institutional authority, rendering problematic our understanding of Russian politics based on formal institutions like the constitution.

A 2012 protest by the Communist Party against Putin's reelection. As the banner suggests, Putin (on the left) will hold office another 12 years, when an elderly Medvedev (right) could again return to the presidency until 2030.

THE LEGISLATURE

Given the power of the Russian presidency, does the national legislature have any real role? Its lack of effectiveness is certainly consistent with the Soviet past. Under Communist rule, the legislature served as little more than a rubber stamp, meeting for a few days each year simply to pass legislation drafted by party leaders. Today, Russia's parliament has little direct influence over the course of government, but it would be an exaggeration to say that nothing has changed since Soviet times.

Russia's bicameral parliament is known officially as the Federal Assembly. It comprises a lower house, the 450-seat State Duma, and an upper house, the 170-seat Federation Council. Members of the Duma, the more powerful of the two houses, serve five-year terms, while members of the Federation Council serve varied terms depending on the rules of federal territory they represent. The Duma has the right to initiate and accept or reject legislation and may override the president's veto with a two-thirds vote. The Duma also approves the appointment of the prime minister, though repeated rejections can lead to its dissolution. As in other legislatures, the Duma can call a vote of no confidence in opposition to the prime minister and his government. Should a no-confidence vote pass, the president may simply ignore the decision. If a second such vote passes within three months, however, the president is obliged to dismiss the prime minister and cabinet or call for new Duma elections.

In the instances of prime ministerial approval and votes of no confidence, then, the Duma wields unpredictable weapons. The Duma's opposition to the prime minister (and, by extension, the president) could lead to its own dissolution. Under the right circumstances, however, this could lead to elections that strengthen the position of parties that oppose the current leadership. Of course, the exact opposite could also occur. Thus far, the Duma has not put this power to use, though in 1998 the Yeltsin administration was forced to withdraw a candidate for prime minister after he was rejected twice. In that case, the president feared new elections would only bring more anti-Yeltsin representatives into the Duma.

Another area in which the Duma can theoretically wield power is in the drafting of legislation. During the Yeltsin administration, the majority of legislation originated in the Duma, much of it dealing with substantial public issues. However, under Putin the legislature's powers have become increasingly theoretical. As the Duma became dominated by a single party loyal to Putin (see "The Electoral System," p. 357), it has receded from any significant political role, to the point where some view it as little more than a rubber stamp to validate the president's rule. Virtually no legislation submitted by the government is opposed by the Duma, and vice versa. This does not mean that the Duma is inactive, however, as it remains a forum for legislators to lobby for their own preferences and also for the government to provide the appearance of democracy. In fact, the Duma has been described as a "mad printer" for the speed at which it produces legislation, much of which is ambiguous and/or focused on limiting personal freedoms.[8]

As the upper house, the **Federation Council** holds even less power than the Duma. The Federation Council primarily serves to represent local interests and act as a guarantor of the constitution. The body represents all of the 85 federal administrative units, and each unit has two representatives. Since 2002, one representative has been selected by the governor of each region and another by the regional legislature (see the discussion of "Local Government," p. 358). Although the Federation Council does not produce legislation, it must approve bills that deal with certain issues, including taxation and the budget. If the Federation Council rejects legislation (which rarely occurs), the Duma may override the upper house with a two-thirds vote. The Federation Council also theoretically has the ability to impeach the president as well as to approve or reject presidential appointments to the Constitutional Court, declarations of war and martial law, and international treaties.

As with the Duma, the Federation Council does not serve as a particularly powerful institution inside the Russian state. Even when legislation goes against the interest of the regions, representatives rarely oppose it.

THE JUDICIARY

One of many tasks Russia faces in the coming decades is the establishment of the rule of law. By this, we mean a system in which the law is applied equally and predictably, and no individual is exempt from its strictures. Before Communist rule, Russia did not develop any real traditions of a law-bound state: the tsar acted above the law, viewing the state, society, and economy as his subjects and property. This situation continued into the Soviet era.

Under Stalin, any legitimate legal structures were undermined by the arbitrary use of terror and the vast secret-police force, which maintained its own courts and jails. While these excesses were curbed after Stalin's death, the legal system remained an important means of blocking opposition to the Communist regime. Moreover, no constitutional court existed until 1991. By definition, the party claimed to represent the true expression of the people's will and therefore could not be accused of unconstitutional acts. In reality, the party was not representative of the people's interests. The lack of legal safeguards served only to undermine public confidence in the political order.

Given the history of weak legal institutions, it has been difficult to generate the rule of law in the postcommunist era. Since 1991, Russia has faced an explosion in corruption. Economic and political change have created opportunities to generate fortunes and have allowed those with political power to gain access to new sources of wealth. Organized crime remains a serious problem. At the same time, surveys show that the public mistrusts law enforcement agencies such as the police.

At the top of the Russian legal structure lies the **Constitutional Court**. First developed under Mikhail Gorbachev's reforms in the late-Soviet era, the court has 19 members, nominated by the president and confirmed by the Federation Council. As in other countries, the court is empowered to rule on such matters as international treaties, relations between branches of government, violations of civil rights, and impeachment of the president. It has the power of both abstract review (the ability to rule on constitutional issues even when a case has not been brought before it) and concrete review (the ability to rule on specific cases). One role the Constitutional Court does *not* play is that of a court of last appeal for criminal cases; this is the responsibility of the Supreme Court. As in the case of the legislature, the court has not played an activist role. In 2014, following Russia's invasion of the Ukrainian region of Crimea, the court quickly recognized Crimea's annexation. It similarly approved legislation that requires nonprofit organizations that engage in influencing public policy (such as environmental and LGBTQ issues) and receive foreign funding to be registered as "foreign agents."[9]

At the start of the Putin administration, the president promised to implement what he called a dictatorship of law, though the result has tended to be more dictatorship than law. The country remains mired in what Prime Minister Medvedev evocatively termed "legal nihilism," wherein legal codes are not respected and the state frequently uses the courts to settle political vendettas or target political opposition. The Rule of Law Index, which looks at such things as constraints on government, regulatory enforcement, and criminal justice, ranked Russia 92nd out of 113 countries surveyed. This is below China (80) and Iran (86).[10]

The Electoral System

Like Russia's other institutions, its electoral structure has changed dramatically over the past 20 years. In the late-Soviet period, the president of Russia was indirectly elected by the republic's Congress of People's Deputies. Just before the 1991 coup, the presidency was made a directly elected office; Yeltsin won the election and retained the office when Russia became an independent country. Since that time, Russians have continued to elect their president directly. Elections as an independent country were first held in 1996, when Yeltsin was reelected; since then, they have been held in 2000, 2004, 2008, and 2012.

Candidates for president must be nominated by a party represented in the Duma. If they are independent candidates, they must collect 2 million signatures in support of their candidacy. This is a formidable task that eliminates many potential contenders. Presidential elections are relatively straightforward: if no candidate wins a majority in the first round, the top two candidates compete against each other in a second round. A president can serve no more than two consecutive terms, though as we've seen in the case of Putin, this can mean simply stepping aside for one term and then running again. In 2000 and 2004, Putin won a majority (over 70 percent in 2004), eliminating the need for a runoff. In 2012, when he returned to office, he won 63 percent of the vote (amid numerous accusations of voter fraud).

The Duma has also held regular elections. Between 1990 and 1993, these were conducted using a plurality system of single-member districts (SMDs), as in the United Kingdom and the United States. With the 1993 constitution, however, Russia adopted a mixed system similar to that found in Japan and Germany. That is, half the seats in the Duma were elected through a plurality system, and the other half were selected in multimember districts (MMDs) using proportional representation (PR), in which the share of the vote given to a party roughly matches the percentage of seats it is allotted.

Under Putin, this system was again changed to consolidate political power. In 2007, Duma elections were held solely under PR to eliminate individual candidates not under party control. Electoral reforms also prevented parties from forming an electoral bloc to compete as a single group to overcome the threshold (a minimum percentage of the vote to gain seats in the legislature). All of these changes had the effect of eliminating independent candidates and small parties. Interestingly, 2016 Duma elections returned to a mixed system. Why? Some suggest that a return to single-member districts was intended to provide to the public a greater sense of direct influence over the Duma (though as we noted, it remains a weak body). Perhaps more importantly, reducing PR limits the ability of rival parties to gain a large foothold in the legislature. These explanations suggest that Putin and his ruling party, United Russia, do not take their hold over the Duma for granted.

Local Government

One of the greatest battles within the institutional framework of Russia over the past 15 years has been between the central government and local authorities. Just as tensions between Soviet central power and the republics contributed to the dissolution of the Soviet Union, so, too, centrifugal tendencies have beset Russia since 1991. Like the Soviet Union that preceded it, Russia is a federal system with a bewildering array of more than 80 different regional bodies: 21 republics (22 if we include Crimea, seized from Ukraine in 2014), 46 *oblasts* ("provinces"), 9 *krays* ("territories"), 4 autonomous *okrugs* ("districts"), and the 2 federal cities of Moscow and St. Petersburg (3 if we include Sevastopol, the capital of Crimea).

Each of these bodies has different rights. The 21 republics, for example, represent particular non-Russian ethnic groups and enjoy greater rights, such as to have their own constitution and a state language alongside Russian. In the early 1990s, several republics went so far as to make claims of sovereignty that amounted to near or complete independence; in Chechnya, the result was outright war against the central authorities, which was brought under control only after years of warfare and terrorism. In contrast, many other federal bodies are much weaker. This difference is commonly termed **asymmetric federalism**—a system in which power is devolved unequally across the country and its constituent regions, often because of specific laws negotiated between a region and the central government. Each of the territories, regardless of its size or power, has its own governor and local Duma; as described earlier, the governor appoints one representative to the Federation Council, and the Duma appoints the other.

As in other areas, the Putin administration took several steps to reduce regional power and make the territories comply with national laws and legislation. First, a number of regional laws and agreements between the central and local governments were changed or annulled, compelling the regions to revise their laws and agreements in accordance with the Putin administration. In some cases, these local laws were clearly unconstitutional, but in many other cases the changes simply aimed to reduce local power. Moreover, in 2000 the government created federal districts (now eight in total) that encompass all of Russia and its constituent territories. Each district is headed by a presidential appointee, who serves to bring the local authorities more directly under presidential control.

Below the federal districts are governors for the different regional bodies. Since 2012, these governors are directly elected, which, as with the electoral reforms for the Duma, was presented as a way for the public to have more direct control over those in power. In reality, as with the Duma the governorships are nominated by the Kremlin and filled by pro-Putin figures who often have little to no connection to the region they rule. The positions can be attractive to candidates since they provide an opportunity for individuals to enrich themselves, while for the Kremlin they allow the government to maintain greater control over the regions and those it has placed in these offices.

These frequent changes have severely curtailed federalism in Russia, though local offices continue to have power. Many local mayors remain directly elected, and in large cities (such as Moscow and St. Petersburg), they can exercise a great deal of political clout. In 2013, prominent opposition figure Alexei Navalny ran for mayor of Moscow and won nearly 30 percent of the vote (perhaps more, depending on the degree of fraud). Navalny was subsequently arrested on charges of embezzlement and was again briefly detained in March 2017 due to his role in promoting anticorruption protests across the country. Clearly, Putin and his allies realize that local authority could reemerge as a significant threat to those in power. This possibility explains recent proposals to eliminate the direct election of most mayors in favor of their appointment by city councils (this has already occurred in some cases). To sum up, there have been numerous changes that have in some cases allowed direct elections to local offices while restricting them in others.

This apparent inconsistency is a function of whether the regime sees that change as a means to co-opt the public and political elites, or as a way to block political opposition. In the end, the role of the Kremlin in directing political elites from the executive down to the local level is indicative of what Putin termed "the power vertical," a centralized, top-down form of political control.[11]

Political Conflict and Competition

The Party System and Elections

Russia has yet to see the formation of political parties with clear ideologies and political platforms. In most democracies, parties serve to articulate and aggregate preferences and hold elected officials accountable. It is hard to say that such a system exists in Russia. For most of the past 25 years, multiple parties have risen and disappeared between elections, for a number of reasons. The relative weakness of ideology among the public (see "Society," p. 367) contributes to some extent. A second factor is the power of the presidency. Largely divorced from the legislature and its party politics and standing alongside a weak prime ministerial office, the presidency has contributed to the creation of parties that largely serve one individual's presidential ambitions. Making clear distinctions between the parties is thus difficult. But given Putin's consolidation of political power, it might be tempting to argue that the country has largely become once again a one-party state, controlled by the pro-Putin United Russia. In fact, following the 2007 Duma elections, the other three parties in parliament (the Communist Party, A Just Russia, and the Liberal Democratic Party of Russia) combined held less than a third of the total seats. However, the 2011 Duma elections proved a surprise. Despite United Russia's overwhelming control over the media and state, the three parties just mentioned captured nearly half of the seats in the Duma. This result challenges the view that United Russia or any one party is impervious, as well as the idea that Russian society is unable or unwilling to challenge those in power.[12]

THE PARTY OF POWER: UNITED RUSSIA

Although so-called **parties of power** have since 1991 consistently represented the largest segment of parties in the Duma, they cannot be described in ideological terms. Russia's parties of power can be defined as those parties created by political elites to support those elites' political aspirations. Typically, these parties are highly personalized, lack specific ideologies or clear organizational qualities, and have been created by political elites during or following their time in office. For example, the Our Home Is Russia Party was created in advance of the 1995 Duma elections as a way to bolster support for Prime Minister Viktor Chernomyrdin and President Yeltsin. Subsequently, in the 1999 elections, two contending parties of power emerged. Fatherland–All Russia was formed to advance the presidential aspirations of former prime minister Yevgeny Primakov and Moscow mayor Yuri Luzhkov. Meanwhile, Unity was created to bolster Putin's campaign. After Unity beat Fatherland–All Russia handily in the Duma elections, Primakov and Luzhkov withdrew from the presidential campaign, and in 2001 the two parties merged to form **United Russia**, essentially climbing on the bandwagon of power. Drawing on Putin's popularity and the government's increased control over the electoral process, United Russia swept the 2003 elections and has won a majority of seats ever since (as well as extending its reach over local government). As of the 2016 elections, United Russia holds 344 of 450 Duma seats—a supermajority that gives it the ability to change the constitution without needing the support of any other party.

United Russia boasts a cult of personality around Putin, a youth wing that advances the cause of the party, and party membership as a means for individual access to important jobs in the state and economy. In that sense, Russia resembles a one-party state like Mexico prior to its democratization in the 1990s.[13] Less clear is United Russia's ideology. Given the tight linkage between Putin and the party, its ideology is less important than its role in reinforcing executive rule as a "transmission belt" for elites into power. United Russia's campaign platforms have emphasized stability and conservatism, economic development (though this has receded as economic difficulties have mounted), and increasingly the restoration of the country as a "great power" in international politics. National pride and stability are the main selling points of United Russia, and Putin is positioned as the individual who can achieve this goal. To contrast the country with what is portrayed as the immorality of the West (such as its support for LGBTQ rights), United Russia has also increasingly positioned itself as the defender of traditional values.

The 2007 Duma elections were widely regarded as evidence that Russia could no longer be considered democratic, even in the most generous definition of the term. The media, largely in the hands of the state, gave overwhelming support to United Russia. Observers concluded that the elections were not fair, did not meet basic standards for democratic procedures, and have become only more fraudulent over time.[14] And yet, in 2011, United Russia suffered a major upset when over half of the popular vote went to several opposition parties (though none represents significant opposition to the Kremlin). In 2016, United Russia managed to reclaim its dominant role in the Duma through a mixture of media control and harassment, but also public disenchantment with elections. Turnout was a record low, at less than 50 percent. Whether this reflects the strength or weakness of United Russia is an open question.

COMMUNIST AND LEFTIST PARTIES

Before the rise of United Russia, the strongest and most institutionalized party was the **Communist Party of the Russian Federation (CPRF)**, successor of the Soviet-era organization. Though banned by Yeltsin in 1991, the party was allowed to reorganize in 1993 and draws support from a portion of the population that is ambivalent about or hostile to the political and economic changes that have taken place since the 1980s. In the 1995 elections, the CPRF reached its peak, becoming the largest single party in the Duma and raising the fear among many that the country would return to Communist rule. However, since that time, its vote share has declined to less than 15 percent. Even at that small level, it remains the second-largest party in the Duma. The CPRF's head, Gennady Zyuganov, has come in second place in every presidential election since 1996 (though in recent years this has meant gaining less than 20 percent of the vote).

The CPRF differs from most other postcommunist parties in Eastern Europe, many of which broke decisively from their Communist past in the 1990s and successfully recast themselves as social-democratic organizations. In contrast, the CPRF remains close to its Communist ideology and rejects Western capitalism and globalization. It also embraces the Stalinist period and has called for the return of the country to Stalinist ideals. The CPRF criticizes the government but is careful not to attack Putin. To some extent, this is a matter of self-preservation, because a direct confrontation with the Kremlin would surely result in the destruction of the party. A more cynical interpretation is that the CPRF serves Putin as a way to maintain a semblance of political diversity and to co-opt opposition forces. As the Russian population ages, the CPRF is losing its traditional base. However, as the second-largest party, it enjoys protest votes from those opposed to United Russia, particularly those who have suffered from the economic changes (especially the high levels of inequality) that have emerged since the end of the Soviet Union. There are some suggestions that the CPRF may find a new base of support among Russians born after 1991, who have struggled economically. If so, the party could reemerge as a real force in the future. For now, it runs a distant second behind United Russia, with just 13 percent of the vote in 2016 and 42 seats.

A much newer party, **A Just Russia**, can also be placed in the leftist camp. Founded in 2006 as a merger of several smaller parties, A Just Russia defines itself as a social-democratic party along European lines. Its platform emphasizes social justice and reducing inequality, and in general its ideological profile is perhaps clearer than any other party in the Duma. Unlike the CPRF, A Just Russia has been considered by many to be little more than a façade, supported (if not created) by the Kremlin to provide a veneer of multiparty democracy. But again, the 2011 Duma elections confounded many assumptions. A Just Russia came in third, with approximately 13 percent of the vote, and its more confrontational tone suggested that it might become a force in its own right. However, the party quickly resumed its loyalty to the Kremlin, expelling party members who had taken part in public demonstrations against Putin during the 2011 elections. In the 2016 elections, A Just Russia slipped to the smallest party in the Duma, with only 6 percent of the vote and 29 seats.

NATIONALIST PARTIES

During the 1990s, one of the most infamous aspects of the Russian party spectrum was the strength of extreme nationalism. That faction is manifested by the ill-named **Liberal Democratic Party of Russia (LDPR)**, headed by Vladimir Zhirinovsky. Neither liberal nor democratic, the LDPR espouses a rhetoric of nationalism, xenophobia, and anti-Semitism, calling for such things as the reconstitution of the Soviet Union (perhaps by force) and exhibiting general hostility toward the West.

In the 1993 elections, many observers were shocked by the LDPR's electoral strength and its gain of 14 percent of the seats in the Duma. Subsequently, the LDPR's fortunes waned to the point where it barely met the 5 percent PR threshold in the 1999 elections. In recent elections, however, it has staged something of a comeback and is now the third-largest party in the Duma, with 39 seats. The survival of the party can be attributed in part to the LDPR's consistent support for Putin and his government: indeed, many observers suspect that the LDPR was created and is supported by the government to serve as a pseudo-opposition that can be controlled.[15] Nevertheless, the LDPR is able to tap into a strong current of Russian nationalism, especially among those lower-class individuals for whom the Putin era has not translated into an improved standard of living.

Despite Russia's move toward capitalism, liberalism has made relatively few inroads into political life, and even these have declined of late. During the 1990s, liberalism's standard bearer in Russia was the party **Yabloko**, whose pro-Western and pro–market economy stance drew support from white-collar workers and urban residents in the major cities. Never a major force, Yabloko has seen its electoral fortunes decline to such an extent that in recent Duma elections, it has failed to gain a single seat in the legislature. In 2016, the party won less than 2 percent of the vote in the proportional representation portion of the ballot. It currently holds only a few seats in regional legislatures.

Why has liberalism found such rocky soil in Russia? Several factors are at work. First, given the historically statist and collectivist nature of Russian politics, a liberal political ideology is not likely to find a wide range of popular support. A large percentage of the population continues to support an active role for the state in the economy, a stance that runs counter to liberal political platforms. A 2011 survey, for example, showed that half of those questioned favored an increased role for government ownership of the economy; such views were not just among older Russians, but also those under age 29 as well as those with a university education (both of whom might be expected to do better in a private economy).[16] Infighting and a lack of strong leadership within liberal parties have not helped. Finally, worsening relations between Russia and the West have also served to tarnish liberalism as a foreign ideology associated with Russian subservience.

Civil Society

As with political parties, civil society in Russia developed in fits and starts. Before the 1917 Russian Revolution, civil society was weak, constrained by authoritarianism, feudalism, and low economic development. With the revolution, what little civil society did exist quickly came under control of the Soviet authorities, who argued that only the party could and should represent the "correct" interests of the population. The state created a wide range of institutions to link the people to the party, through the workplace, media, culture, and even leisure activities. The few remnants of independent organized life, such as religion, were brought under tight control. With the advent of glasnost in the 1980s, however, civil society slowly began to reemerge. The first independent group that resulted from liberalization may have been the fan club of a Moscow soccer team, established in

1987. By late 1989, tens of thousands of groups had appeared and were playing an important role in eroding Soviet rule.

After 1991, civil society grew dramatically in Russia. An array of movements and organizations filled the gaps left in the aftermath of one-party rule. However, during the Putin administration civil society came under state pressure and control, especially those groups that openly criticized the government. Tools to control civil society include the tax code, used to investigate sources of income; the process of registering with authorities, which can be made difficult; and police harassment and arrest on various charges ranging from tax evasion to divulging state secrets. In 2006, the government passed its toughest measures against nongovernmental organizations (NGOs), requiring all of them to be approved by the government, restricting their funding from foreign sources, and making them subject to regular inspections and preapproval for any activity. Russian authorities forcibly closed a number of foreign NGOs. Still, antigovernment protests in Russia in 2011, 2012, and again in 2017 suggested that there remained a current of social activism that could translate into a revived civil society. Not surprisingly, Putin's return to the presidency in 2012 ushered in a new wave of restrictions. As noted earlier, all organizations that receive foreign funding must now be registered as "foreign agents," allowing for a high degree of state oversight and control and the possibility of fines and arrest for failing to follow state regulations. A corresponding new law on treason has further intimidated civic organization.[17]

Another notable effect of the restrictions on civil society is in the area of religion. Historically, Russians have been overwhelmingly, if nominally, Orthodox Christians, and smaller numbers have belonged to other faiths. Although Soviet-imposed atheism seriously weakened the role of religion, in recent years Orthodox Christianity has begun to reclaim a role in public life. Other religious movements, ranging from Islam and Buddhism to evangelical Christianity, also have emerged or reemerged.

As the Russian government has turned more toward nationalism as a source of legitimacy, it has also emphasized Orthodox Christianity as a central part of what makes Russia unique (and distinct from the West and Western liberalism). In turn, the Russian government has increasingly restricted the ability of many religious groups to proselytize, build seminaries, publish their literature, or run educational programs and has relied on anti-extremism legislation to justify these actions. Much of this effort is directed toward Islam, though similar restrictions have been directed toward religious groups such as Jehovah's Witnesses, Mormons, and Christian groups considered foreign imports. The return of Orthodox Christianity as a quasi–state religion has been accompanied by attacks on liberal activism, such as the arrest of members of the punk band Pussy Riot, several of whose members were jailed in 2012 for two years on charges of religious hatred.[18]

Civil society has been restricted in Russia not just through direct government control but also through the means of expressing itself—specifically, the media. The collapse of communism saw the emergence of private Russian media that for the first time were able to speak critically on an array of issues. This is not to say that the media were truly independent; the most powerful segments of the media, such as radio and television, remained in the hands of the state or came under the control of oligarchs with ties to Yeltsin. Indeed, Yeltsin's victory in the 1996 elections was attributed in part to the strong support he received from media outlets whose owners feared the repercussions should the Communist candidate come to power. Similarly, the media came to support Putin during his consolidation of power, viewing him as the successor to Yeltsin who would preserve the power of the oligarchs. Despite this support, Putin soon put strong economic pressure on much of the independent media, employing economic and legal tactics to acquire them and curb their editorial independence.

During the past decade, all of the largest private television stations have come under direct state ownership or have become indirect state-controlled firms. As we noted earlier, these were hardly objective stations to begin with, and most of them served as mouthpieces for their oligarch owners. But with nationalization, the Russian media have become even less diverse and are clearly oriented toward supporting those in power. Although a few open media outlets remain, particularly newspapers, their audience pales in comparison with radio and TV audiences, and the outlets are often under pressure from the Kremlin to provide a pro-government slant or not to cover subjects that the government dislikes. The domestic media have become a consistent purveyor of conspiracy theories that tend to center around the efforts of the United States and the European Union to destroy Russia. Such arguments were especially pronounced during Russia's war with Ukraine. Russia denied the presence of its own troops in Crimea and eastern Ukraine while arguing that U.S. troops were on the ground. Russia even claimed that the Malaysian Airline flight destroyed over Ukraine had been shot down by the CIA.

Those who continue to openly oppose the government find that their livelihoods and even their lives can be at stake. Alexei Navalny, who as we mentioned earlier ran for Moscow mayor, was arrested in 2012 on embezzlement charges and held under house arrest for a year. Boris Nemtsov, a former deputy prime minister under Yeltsin and an outspoken critic of Putin, was assassinated near the Kremlin in 2015. Since 1992, more than 50 journalists have been killed in Russia. In terms of press freedom, Russia is ranked 148 out of 180 countries by the organization Reporters without Borders.[19]

Society

Ethnic and National Identity

The Soviet Union, like the Russian Empire before it, was an ethnically diverse country made up of a number of republics, each representing a particular ethnic group. The dissolution of the Soviet Union, however, eliminated much of this ethnic diversity. Today, Russia is overwhelmingly composed of ethnic Russians, part of a larger family of Slavic peoples in Eastern Europe who are linked by similarities in language (and, to a lesser extent, culture and religion). Inside and outside the borders of the former Soviet Union, there are Slavic peoples, such as Ukrainians and Belarusians. In some areas, there is a strong affinity among the Slavs; in others, animosity is more the norm.

Nearly 80 percent of the Russian population is ethnically Russian, and although there are scores of minority groups, none represents more than 4 percent of the population. These minorities include other Slavic peoples, indigenous Siberians who are related to the Inuit of North America, and many others whose communities were absorbed into Russia as part of its imperial expansion over time. And as we mentioned earlier, Russia is historically dominated by a single religious faith, Orthodox Christianity, a branch of Christianity that is separate from the Roman Catholicism and Protestantism that dominate Europe.

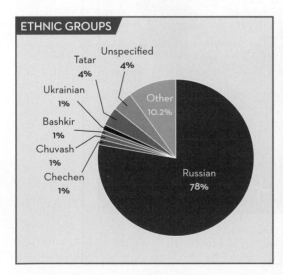

ETHNIC GROUPS

- Unspecified 4%
- Tatar 4%
- Ukrainian 1%
- Bashkir 1%
- Chuvash 1%
- Chechen 1%
- Other 10.2%
- Russian 78%

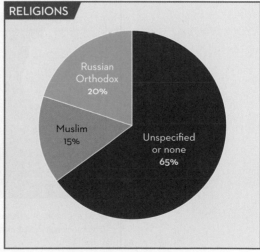

RELIGIONS

- Russian Orthodox 20%
- Muslim 15%
- Unspecified or none 65%

Russia's relative homogeneity has not helped it avoid ethnic conflict. As in many other countries, some of Russia's ethnic groups have developed nationalist aspirations and seek greater autonomy from the central authorities, even to the point of outright independence. Serious ethnic conflicts have been most prominent among non-Russian populations in the mountainous region known as the **Caucasus**, in southwestern Russia, near the Black Sea and Turkey. This area is home to a diverse mixture of non-Slavic peoples with distinct languages, customs, and religious faiths. Whereas only about 15 percent of the Russian population is Muslim, Islam is the dominant faith in many parts of the Caucasus.

Most notable is the case of Chechnya. With the collapse of the Soviet Union in 1991, the various republics broke off to form independent states. Chechnya, however, was not a republic in its own right, but rather part of now-independent Russia. Many Chechens believed that they, too, should have the right of independence and so began to agitate for an independent state. The conflict eventually led to outright war between Russian military forces and Chechen rebels, during which much of the Chechen capital was demolished and tens of thousands of

THE CAUCASUS

Source: University of Texas Austin, www.lib.utexas.edu/maps /commonwealth/chechnya_rev01.jpg (accessed 1/2/09).

civilians were killed or left homeless. During the mid-1990s, an uneasy peace allowed Chechnya to function as a de facto independent country; in 1999, however, Russian forces reinvaded Chechnya in the aftermath of a series of apartment house bombings in Russia attributed to Chechen rebels. Indeed, it was the second invasion of Chechnya, during Putin's tenure as acting president, that helped pave the way for Putin's 2000 presidential victory. Subsequent terror attacks, most notably the hostage taking at an elementary school in Beslan during which more than 300 died, have served as justification for the further centralization of state power. Domestic terrorism has declined over the past five years, facilitated by an extremely repressive rule in Chechnya. The current leader of Chechnya, Ramzan Kadyrov, is thought by many to be connected to the assassination of Boris Nemtsov, a former deputy prime minister under Yeltsin, opposition politician, and outspoken critic of Putin. In the meantime, the government has tacitly encouraged radical Islamists to join jihadist forces in Iraq and Syria, hoping to divert them from fomenting domestic terrorism. There is, however, the threat that these individuals may eventually return and reignite the still simmering conflicts in the Caucasus.

Ideology and Political Culture

As mentioned earlier in our discussion of political parties, ideology is ill-defined in Russia. Following the Russian Revolution, essentially only one ideological viewpoint was legally tolerated: communism. Alternative views on the relationship between freedom and equality were suppressed. People could read Marx but not Jefferson, nor any other political thinker who expounded views differing from the state's. Since 1991, Russia has experienced a much greater diversity of ideas, but in many ways those ideas have not made a deep impact on political life. This is particularly true in the case of democratic values. The World Values Survey finds that a majority of citizens are uninterested in politics, would never attend a peaceful demonstration, and show low levels of social trust.

What values, then, can we speak of in Russia today? During the past decade, we have seen the growing importance of nationalism as a central political value in Russia. This is not surprising; in a number of postcommunist countries, the decline of communism has meant that leaders have attempted to recast political legitimacy around the idea of patriotism and nationalism. In Russia, the government has actively promoted this trend by evoking nostalgia for the country's superpower status and by asserting that Russia is not truly Western but somehow different (and thus not subject to such Western notions as pluralism). This sense of restoring a "great Russia" has found an eager audience among many Russians. Most obvious in this regard was Russian involvement in the Ukrainian crisis in 2014, which led to open warfare in the east along the Russia border and the Russian invasion and annexation of Ukrainian Crimea. Similar motives are at work regarding Russia's involvement in the Syrian civil war. Both actions have led to increased international suspicions of Russia and largely unfavorable views by publics around the world. However, for many Russians these actions are evidence that the country has restored itself to the status of a great world power after the humiliation of the collapse of the Soviet Union. While international sanctions (due to Russia's role in Ukraine) and other economic challenges have weakened the country's standard of living, support for Putin's domestic and foreign policies remains high. Is this a function of a highly institutionalized political culture, or the government's control over the media? Some suggest it is the latter, rather than the former.[20]

Political Economy

How is it possible to build capitalism, with its private property and open markets, in a country that historically has had little of either? This was the challenge Russia faced as it moved away from communism, and as in other areas, the results have been very mixed: the new economic system is no longer communist, nor is it liberal. Russia's economy has improved from the chaos of the 1990s, but what this portends for the future development of the country is uncertain and increasingly worrisome.

Like other former communist countries, Russia undertook a series of dramatic reforms in the 1990s to privatize state assets and free up market forces. Looking to the lessons of Poland and acting on the advice of Western economic advisers, Russia opted for a course of **shock therapy**, rapidly dismantling central planning and freeing up prices with the hope that these actions would stimulate competition and the creation of new businesses. The immediate result was a wave of hyperinflation: in 1992 alone, the inflation rate was over 2,000 percent. Savings were wiped out, the economy sank into recession, and tensions between President Boris Yeltsin and the parliament deepened, helping to foster the violent clash between the two branches of government in 1993. The gross domestic product (GDP) contracted dramatically; only in the late 1990s did it begin to grow again.

The Moscow skyline. In the foreground is the Kremlin. In the background is the Moscow International Business Center, whose growth reflects the influx of oil revenues over the past decades.

During the late 1990s, Russia began the process of privatization, which was equally problematic. Privatization started with the distribution of vouchers to the public so that Russians could purchase shares that would give them ownership in formerly state-owned businesses. In many cases, however, businesses were not sold off to a large number of shareholders but became subject to **insider privatization**, which enabled the former directors of these firms to acquire the largest number of shares. Therefore, wealth was not dispersed but was concentrated in the hands of those who had strong economic and political connections. Despite the power of this old *nomenklatura* elite, however, a small number of new businessmen quickly emerged from various ranks of society. Taking advantage of the economic environment to start new businesses and buy old ones, they amassed an enormous amount of wealth in the process. This group of businessmen, who came to be known as the *oligarchs*, were noted for their control of large amounts of the Russian economy (including the media), their close ties to the Yeltsin administration, and the accusations of corruption surrounding their rise to power.

The problem of the oligarchs was compounded in 1996, when the government instituted the loans-for-shares program. Strapped for cash (and fearful of a

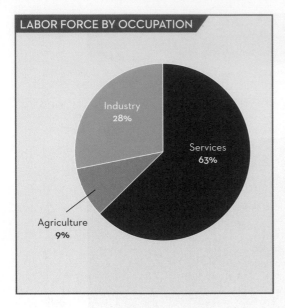

LABOR FORCE BY OCCUPATION

Industry 28%

Services 63%

Agriculture 9%

Communist Party victory in the 1996 presidential elections), the Yeltsin administration chose to borrow funds from the oligarchs in return for shares in those businesses that had not yet been sold off by the state—in particular, the lucrative natural resources industry and the energy sector. Overall, foreign investment played a very small role in the Russian privatization process.

To be fair, Russia's ongoing economic problems are not simply the result of the economic reform policies of the 1990s. Many of these problems are a function and legacy of a Soviet order that had reached a crisis stage, a condition that any set of policies would have had difficulty confronting. Still, the economic reforms of the 1990s left Russia in a tough situation as Putin came to power. The government faced high rates of poverty, a great deal of inequality, the disproportionate power of the oligarchs, widespread corruption and organized crime, and an inefficient state. During the 1990s, the country's GDP declined by around 40 percent.

What has changed in the Russian economy since the 1990s? One of Putin's first steps was to act against the oligarchs and divest them of power. Using a variety of tools, he stripped them of their assets, many of which they had gained under the loans-for-shares scheme. A number of the most prominent oligarchs left the country to avoid imprisonment; others wound up in jail under dubious charges. Best known among these oligarchs is **Mikhail Khodorkovsky**, who grew rich following the opening up of the Soviet economy in the 1980s by investing in such ventures as computer imports. Later, he took advantage of the state sale of natural resources, gaining control over a large portion of the oil and gas sector. However, under the Putin administration, Khodorkovsky came under pressure, in part for his increasingly political activity. In 2003, he was arrested and charged with tax evasion; his firms were liquidated and in many cases nationalized. He was sentenced to prison and was not pardoned until 2013, after which he was sent into exile.

The destruction of the oligarchs was extremely popular among the Russian public, but their elimination did not lead to greater economic transparency. Many assets were renationalized and brought under state control, while in other cases,

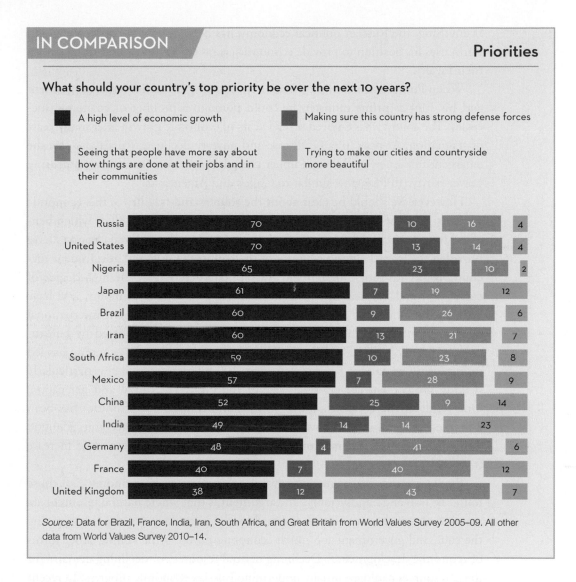

What should your country's top priority be over the next 10 years?

■ A high level of economic growth

■ Seeing that people have more say about how things are done at their jobs and in their communities

■ Making sure this country has strong defense forces

■ Trying to make our cities and countryside more beautiful

Country	Economic growth	More say	Defense forces	More beautiful
Russia	70	10	16	4
United States	70	13	14	4
Nigeria	65	23	10	2
Japan	61	7	19	12
Brazil	60	9	26	6
Iran	60	13	21	7
South Africa	59	10	23	8
Mexico	57	7	28	9
China	52	25	9	14
India	49	14	14	23
Germany	48	4	41	6
France	40	7	40	12
United Kingdom	38	12	43	7

Source: Data for Brazil, France, India, Iran, South Africa, and Great Britain from World Values Survey 2005–09. All other data from World Values Survey 2010–14.

ownership is murky, hidden behind an array of shell corporations, or firms whose owners are unknown. A large portion of state firms have been partly or entirely redistributed among the *siloviki*, forming a new economic elite around the security services. These "state oligarchs," as one scholar calls them, include such individuals as Putin's former judo partner (and now a construction billionaire). The economic system can be viewed as dominated by a set of factions composed of *siloviki* and other elites who support Putin while competing with one another.

If anything, the Russian political economy has become highly patrimonial, and Putin uses his position to provide economic access to his inner circle in return for their loyalty.

When Putin returned to the presidency following his earlier terms as president and his stint as prime minister, he could point to a number of economic successes. The country has enjoyed several years of economic growth after many years of stagnation. As per capita GDP rose and poverty declined, Russia also saw the emergence of a new middle and upper class. Its per capita income at purchasing power parity (PPP) is now similar to Chile's and Argentina's.

However, we should be clear about the sources and fragility of this economic progress: most of the country's exports are oil, gas, and metal, all of which benefited from a dramatic growth in the international markets. These resources have provided the overwhelming majority of the country's GDP and government revenues. Many investors, foreign and Russian, are deterred by the high degree of corruption and political intervention in many areas of the economy, and have been further scared off by the war with Ukraine and subsequent international sanctions. Small and medium-size businesses are similarly hindered by bureaucracy and bribery. Finally, the prominence of the *siloviki* in the economy has led to increasing inequality. Russia boasts over 100 billionaires, which is particularly striking given the relatively small size of the GDP, both total and per capita. One result of the concentration of wealth and limited opportunities has been a marked emigration of the well-educated. According to one account, 350,000 individuals, many of them professionals, left Russia in 2015, a tenfold increase from 2010.[21]

Russia appears to be moving toward a "resource trap" economy like those found in Iran and Saudi Arabia. The argument is that where natural resources are a major part of the economy and owned by the state, they run the risk of giving the state and government too much economic power while stifling other forms of economic development.[22] Declining natural resources or declining demand for those resources could eventually undermine Russia's economic progress. In recent years, a drop in prices for oil and other natural resources, combined with international sanctions, have reversed the country's steady economic rise during Putin's time in power. Weakening exports have led to a declining gross domestic product since 2015. This, in turn, has restricted government spending and reduced the public's standard of living. This, in turn, appears to have increased rivalry among the *siloviki*, who are fighting over a shrinking pie. A series of purges among Putin's long-standing allies suggests that the president questions their loyalty should economic difficulties continue.

Foreign Relations and the World

Like the United Kingdom, Russia has struggled to deal with its position as a former superpower.[23] Yet unlike the United Kingdom, it has been forced to confront this change suddenly and dramatically. Not long ago, the Soviet Union was one of the world's most powerful countries, boasting an impressive military, a nuclear arsenal, and a network of allies around the world. One of Gorbachev's reforms was to reduce hostility between the Soviet Union and the West, to foster greater cooperation between the superpowers. Little did he (or others) suspect that this reconciliation would create such turmoil. The collapse of the Soviet Union has left Russia in an odd situation as it considers its role in the international community. Russian pride was dealt a blow when the Soviet Union splintered and the United States emerged as an unequaled international power. In recent years, this situation has led to international tension and military conflict not seen since the end of the Cold War. Why has reconciliation between Russia and the West failed?

The answer includes several elements. One factor was the eastward expansion of the North Atlantic Treaty Organization (NATO) and the European Union. NATO was founded in 1949 as an international alliance that stood in opposition to the Soviet Union, but since 1989 many postcommunist countries have gained membership in order to cement their relationship with Western Europe and the United States. Russia initially cooperated with NATO to some extent, but under Putin quickly came to view it as an organization opposed to Russian interests. One specific source of tension was the series of wars in the former Yugoslavia in the 1990s, in which Russia expressed greater sympathy with the Serbs, a Slavic people who share the culture and Orthodox Christianity of many Russians. In contrast, NATO eventually intervened on behalf of the Muslims in Bosnia and Kosovo. Russia also saw NATO's eastward expansion, incorporating a number of former Communist countries, as an incursion into its traditional sphere of influence and territory. Despite Russian pressure, from 1999 on, a number of former Soviet satellites and even former republics of the Soviet Union itself have joined NATO, thus bringing the organization to the border of Russia.

Just as Russia has had to confront an ever-larger NATO alliance on its border, it has also had to contend with the enlargement of the European Union. In May 2004, the European Union accepted 10 new countries into its ranks, including three (Estonia, Latvia, and Lithuania) that had once been part of the Soviet Union. As with NATO, its increased membership brings the European Union to the borders of Russia. The expansion of NATO and the European Union has made Russia feel as if its traditional sphere of influence were being chipped away.

The U.S. wars in Afghanistan and Iraq, and intervention in places ranging from the former Yugoslavia to Libya, have also been seen by Russia as examples of the United States' willingness to depose any government it dislikes. This view goes to the heart of the sense of loss Russians feel over the collapse of the Soviet Union and what they perceive as their humiliation by Western countries that once feared their military might.

These complicated and dangerous relations are best seen in the recent war in Ukraine. One of the former republics of the Soviet Union, Ukraine is a mix of Ukrainian and Russian speakers, the latter concentrated along the Russian border in industrial regions that have fared poorly after communism. In contrast, many western Ukrainians strongly identify with western Europe, favoring membership in the European Union and even NATO as a bulwark against Russian influence. Since 1991, presidential elections have shifted power back and forth between western and eastern Ukraine. In 2013, President Viktor Yanukovych, following pressure from Putin, abruptly rejected plans that would have brought Ukraine into a free-trade agreement with the European Union. Thousands protested in the capital, Kiev, leading to violent clashes in which nearly a hundred protesters were killed. As unrest spread, Yanukovych fled to Russia, and then Russia intervened militarily, taking advantage of the chaos to seize and annex Crimea (an act not recognized by the vast majority of countries). Armed militias began to appear in eastern Ukraine as well, seizing control of cities and supported by Russians who claimed to be volunteers but were clearly backed by the Russian government with training and weapons.

Russian territorial expansion raises a danger in Europe that most people thought had disappeared. Resurgent nationalism in Russia has justified the use of force to "correct" the mistakes that resulted from the humiliating collapse of communism, suggesting the danger of future military conflict. Such conflicts in turn reinforce Putin's authoritarianism as a charismatic leader who can confront the West.

Consistent with its role in Ukraine, as Russia's relationship with the West has soured it has sought to rebuild its own sphere of influence. In 1991, it helped create the **Commonwealth of Independent States (CIS)**, a loose integrationist body that incorporated many former Soviet republics. While the CIS has had little formal power, Russia has used it to coordinate its relationship with a number of former Soviet republics, particularly in the Caucasus and Central Asia. Russia has also pursued the goal of more formal integration with other former Soviet republics, a move that would bring them under greater Russian influence. In particular, over the past few years Russia has been deeply

Vladimir Putin (right), Kazakh president Nursultan Nazarbayev (middle), and Belarusian president Alexander Lukashenko (left) shake hands after signing an agreement to establish the Eurasian Economic Union in May 2014.

involved in strengthening its ties to former Soviet republics in Central Asia such as Kazakhstan and Uzbekistan, which by and large remain undemocratic and controlled by former members of the Soviet *nomenklatura*. In one of his first announcements coinciding with his campaign to return to the presidency, Putin called for the creation of a **Eurasian Economic Union (EAEU)** for economic and political integration (see the following section, "Current Issues in Russia"). This goal has developed alongside the increased promotion of the idea that Russia has a distinct national destiny, unconnected to European or liberal cultural and political traditions.

Finally, in addition to formal means to expand or reassert its power, Russia has returned to an array of other tools in pursuit of its foreign policy. Most noteworthy of late has been Russia's use of disinformation and cyberattacks to influence domestic politics in the United States and Europe. Such tactics are not new; propaganda was an important part of the Soviet foreign policy, including disinformation to sow confusion abroad. Globalization has given the Russian government new tools. These include RT, a Russian state broadcasting network that takes an anti-American and often conspiracy theory–based view of international relations; fake news and "troll factories" supported by Russia's security agencies, and direct cyberattacks on various organizations worldwide, from political parties to government infrastructure. How do democratic societies, where news is increasingly decentralized, fight back against policies intended to sow mistrust?

Russia has historically vacillated between the poles of internationalism and nationalism, engagement and isolationism. Russians have long argued about whether their country is somehow separate from Europe and the West: different in culture, religion, and historical traditions. During the 1980s and 1990s, Russia began to move into the European and liberal-democratic orbit, albeit chaotically. Under Putin, the Russian state and government have become less engaged with Europe and other developed democracies. It was once said about the United Kingdom that it had lost an empire and not yet found a role in the international system. The same could be said about Russia—and for now, at least, it seeks to recapture the glory of the past while pressing questions about the future remain unresolved.

CURRENT ISSUES IN RUSSIA

Russia and Central Asia: A New "Silk Road" or the Old "Great Game"?

In the early nineteenth century, both Russia and the United Kingdom expanded their power into the Caucasus and Central Asia. The case of the United Kingdom is more familiar to us, because we recall Britain's control over India and its largely unsuccessful attempt to conquer Afghanistan (in which large numbers of British soldiers died). What fewer people (at least non-Russians) recall is Russia's expanding, and relatively late, role in this region during that same period. The contest between these two powers was called in the West, somewhat glibly, the "Great Game." This conflict intensified further as both Russia and the United Kingdom gained direct and indirect control over the fragmenting Persian empire (the ensuing contest would later come to influence the 1979 Iranian Revolution). Although the Russian Revolution in 1917 and the decline of the British Empire after World War II limited the conflict between these two powers, the notion of a contest between superpowers for this region never really came to an end.

More specifically, the United States usurped Britain's role as a player in the region, and the conflict shifted to one between Russia and the United States. Soviet intervention in Afghanistan in 1979 led to the American arming of anti-Soviet guerrillas and the rise of Al Qaeda. The breakup of the Soviet Union in 1991 fostered conflicts, fueled by ethnic and religious divisions, across the newly independent states in the Caucasus and Central Asia. The September 11, 2001, attacks brought the United States directly into the region through its occupation of Afghanistan and its increased role in Central Asia.

The United States' role in the Great Game, however, is on the wane. Military forces in Afghanistan have drawn down, and the locus of conflict has shifted westward to Iraq and Syria. The constant actor remains Russia, which since 1991 has sought to retain or regain influence over its lost republics in the Caucasus and Central Asia. The new map of the Great Game appears to have moved east, to the countries of Central Asia (such as Kazakhstan, Kyrgyzstan, and Uzbekistan). These countries share a number of similarities. First, they have had little success in democratization since 1991, and power has remained directly in the hands of the Soviet-era leaders. Second, many of them are ethnically diverse, have weak national identities, and have faced serious violent conflict as a result. Most Central Asian states are nominally Islamic, and though religion was suppressed under Soviet rule, Islam—and sometimes, radical variants of it—has surfaced. Finally, the region contains significant deposits of oil and gas.

Now other, new players are entering this game. Since 1991, China has become a major economic actor in the region, in some ways overshadowing the Russian presence. As China has grown, it has looked for energy to fuel this development, and accordingly invested billions of dollars in developing oil, gas, and hydropower across the region, and in transmission and pipelines to carry this energy to China. It has also invested in mining projects to work deposits of gold, uranium, and other metals. China has become a major exporter of finished goods and consumer products to much of Central Asia. Some speak of a "New Silk Road," with the historical analogy of pathways between East and West.

One of the first statements of Putin's new administration articulated Russia's ambitions in the struggle over Central Asia. Putin called for a "Eurasian union" that would remove all barriers to trade, capital, and labor movements among its members. He asserted that this integration was "not about re-creating the USSR," but rather about seeking "a powerful supranational union that can become one of the poles of today's world."[24] The Eurasian Economic Union (EAEU) came into force in 2015, and its charter members were Belarus, Kazakhstan, and Russia. Armenia and Kyrgyzstan followed shortly thereafter. Ukraine's decision not to join the union in favor of closer ties with the European Union was a central factor in the 2014 war. Given the Ukrainian crisis, the Eurasian Economic Union might seem to be an attempt to project Russian power in competition with Europe. However, its effects may well be felt in Asia instead.

How has the EAEU fared to date? A single tariff barrier has eased trade between members, though this has largely benefited Russia. As Chinese imports have become more expensive, other EAEU members have turned to Russian alternatives. Freedom of movement has increased, allowing members from poorer EAEU states to move to Russia for work. One area where regional integration has been weaker is in the creation of a common EAEU foreign policy. Members continue to pursue their own preferences, with some refusing to back Russia's role in the Ukraine crisis and the annexation of Crimea. Nor do other former Soviet republics appear interested in joining in the near future. For now, Russia's hope to develop a regional bloc, loosely built around the idea of a "Eurasian" identity that is neither Asian nor Western, seems premature. However, future political reforms among its members could provide the opportunity for greater integration, just as in Europe after World War II.

Russia's Demographic Future

One issue that plagues Russia—and worries its leaders—is the country's demographics. This concern is nothing new—it dates back to the Soviet era and takes several forms.

The first worrisome demographic trend is the general level of Russian health: Russian life expectancy at birth is approximately 70 years: 75 for women and 64 for men. This figure is shockingly low, given the overall level of development of the country. Russia's life expectancy ranks 110th out of 193 countries and is worse than that in Egypt or Guatemala. Why? Some of the problem may be due to the erosion of Russia's health care system following the collapse of the Soviet Union and the transition to capitalism, though the erosion in fact began to emerge in the 1960s. It is not a function of a high infant mortality rate, which in Russia is roughly similar to rates in other countries within the same economic range. Rather, Russia shows an unusually high level of *adult* mortality, especially among men, whose life expectancy is about that of men in India. The primary explanation appears to be a relatively simple one: alcohol. Russian alcohol consumption, particularly among men, is extremely high, by some estimates among the top five in the world. Russia is also by far the highest consumer of hard liquor as opposed to beer or wine. This pattern leads to two results: first, a high level of death by circulatory diseases, and second (and perhaps more striking), a very high level of death by accidents, suicides, and homicides—three times higher than in advanced democracies. The abuse of alcohol in Russia has a long history, and it could be argued that it is ingrained in Russian culture, something not easily dislodged. In fact, one of Gorbachev's first reform policies in the 1980s was an anti-alcohol campaign, which provoked public discontent (though brief, the campaign appeared to have a positive health effect).

Two young men drinking beer in Moscow. The high level of alcohol consumption in Russia, especially among men, is a major factor in the country's demographic and health concerns.

A second demographic trend worrying Russian leaders is the country's low birth rate. Just as Russia has a low life expectancy rate, it also has an extremely low rate of fertility, even when compared with other European countries where such rates also tend to be low. Again, this issue dates back to the 1960s and is marked by the high rate of abortion, a result of limited access to birth control (Russia's abortion rates are double the European average). The high participation of women in the workforce, as well as economic stresses, creates disincentives to having larger families. When combined with low life expectancy, the result is a shrinking population. By 2050, Russia may lose more than 20 million people. Ongoing migration from Central Asia may mitigate this decline, but it will also increase the Muslim share of the population, which has a tense relationship with the government.

Russia is struggling with how to respond to its demographic troubles. In recent years, the government has sought to crack down on alcohol abuse by relying in part on increased taxes on alcohol as a way to deter consumption. It has also offered cash bonuses for women who have more than two children. Consistent public health and pro-family policies could certainly alleviate many of these demographic concerns, and some suggest that Russian fertility will soon show steady improvement as a result of economic growth. An aging, unhealthy population is not a positive sign for the future.[25]

NOTES

1. Håkon Stang, *The Naming of Russia* (Oslo: University of Oslo, Slavic and Baltic Division, 1996). See also Nicholas Riasanovsky, *A History of Russia* (New York: Oxford University Press, 1963).

2. For a fascinating Soviet-era interpretation of Ivan's leadership, see the Sergei Eisenstein film *Ivan the Terrible* (1945).

3. For a discussion of this period, see Richard Pipes, *Three "Whys" of the Russian Revolution* (New York: Vintage, 1995).

4. Mary McAuley, *Soviet Politics: 1917–1991* (New York: Oxford University Press, 1992), 26–27.

5. See Robert Conquest, *The Great Terror: A Reassessment* (New York: Oxford University Press, 1991); Anne Applebaum, *Gulag: A History* (New York: Doubleday, 2003).

6. For a discussion of the last days of Soviet rule, see David Remnick, *Lenin's Tomb: The Last Days of the Soviet Empire* (New York: Random House, 1993).

7. Thomas Remington, *Presidential Decrees in Russia: A Comparative Perspective* (New York: Cambridge University Press, 2014).

8. Alexander Podrabinek, "Useless Parliament," Institute for Modern Russia, May 20, 2014. https://imrussia.org/en/politics/747-useless-parliament (accessed 3/16/17).

9. "Russia: Government vs. Rights Groups," *Human Rights Watch*, January 9, 2017, https://www.hrw.org/russia-government-against-rights-groups-battle-chronicle (accessed 1/10/17).

10. World Justice Project, Rule of Law Index 2016, http://data.worldjusticeproject.org/ (accessed 1/8/17).

11. Elizabeth Teague, "Russia's Return to the Direct Election of Governors: Re-Shaping the Power Vertical?" *Region: Regional Studies of Russia, Eastern Europe, and Central Asia* 3, no. 1 (2014): 37–57.

12. Richard Sakwa, *Putin Redux: Power and Contradiction in Contemporary Russia* (New York: Routledge, 2014).

13. Andrew Konitzer and Stephen Wegren, "Federalism and Political Recentralization in the Russian Federation: United Russia as the Party of Power," *Publius* 36, no. 4 (2006): 503–22.

14. Mikhail Myagkov, Peter Ordeshook, and Dimitri Shakin, *The Forensics of Election Fraud: Russia and Ukraine* (Cambridge, UK: Cambridge University Press, 2009).

15. Sakwa, *Putin Redux*; Luke March, "Managing Opposition in a Hybrid Regime: Just Russia and Parastatal Opposition," *Slavic Review* 68, no. 3 (Fall 2009): 504–27.

16. World Values Survey, Wave 6, http://www.worldvaluessurvey.org/ (accessed 1/9/17).

17. "Laws of Attrition: Crackdown on Russia's Civil Society after Putin's Return to the Presidency," *Human Rights Watch,* April 24, 2013, www.hrw.org/reports/2013/04/24/laws-attrition (accessed 10/30/14).

18. Masha Gessen, *Words Will Break Cement: The Passion of Pussy Riot* (New York: Riverhead, 2014).

19. Reporters without Borders, *Press Freedom Index 2016*, http://en.rsf.org/ (accessed 1/10/17).

20. Sergei M. Guriev and Daniel Treisman, "What Makes Governments Popular," https://ssrn.com/abstract=2882915 or http://dx.doi.org/10.2139/ssrn.2882915 (accessed 1/10/17).

21. "Russia Facing Biggest Brain Drain in Two Decades," *Moscow Times*, June 10, 2016, https://themoscowtimes.com/articles/russia-facing-biggest-brain-drain-in-two-decades-53254 (accessed 3/16/17).

22. Some emphasize that "resource traps" are much more complicated than simply asserting that resources lead to authoritarianism or poorly functioning state institutions. See Pauline Jones Luong and Erika Weinthal, *Oil Is Not a Curse: Ownership Structure and Institutions in Soviet Successor States* (Cambridge: Cambridge University Press, 2010).

23. For a good discussion of Russian foreign policy from a Russian perspective, see Alexander Lukin, "What the Kremlin Is Thinking," *Foreign Affairs*, 93, no. 4 (July/August 2014): 85–93.
24. Vladimir Putin, "A New Integration Project for Eurasia: The Future in the Making," *Oriental Review,* October 11, 2011, http://orientalreview.org/2011/10/11/new-integration-project-for-eurasia-making-the-future-today/ (accessed 3/16/17).
25. Kazuhiro Kumo, *Mortality Trends in Russia Revisited: A Survey,* Institute of Economic Research, Hitotsubashi University, 2012, https://ideas.repec.org/p/hst/ghsdps/gd12-239.html (accessed 9/14/14).

KEY TERMS

A Just Russia A small party in the Russian Duma with a social-democratic orientation

asymmetric federalism A system where power is devolved unequally across the country and its constituent regions, often the result of specific laws negotiated between the region and the central government

Caucasus Southwest Russia, near the Black Sea and Turkey, where there is a diverse mixture of non-Slavic peoples with distinct languages and customs as well as a much stronger historical presence of Islam than Orthodox Christianity

Chechnya Russian republic that has been a source of military conflict since 1991

Cheka Soviet secret police created by Lenin; precursor to the KGB

Commonwealth of Independent States (CIS) A loose integrationist body that incorporates many former Soviet republics

Communist Party of the Russian Federation (CPRF) Successor party in Russia to the Communist Party of the Soviet Union

Constitutional Court Highest body in the Russian legal system; responsible for constitutional review

Duma Lower house of the Russian legislature

Eurasian Economic Union (EAEU) Economic and political union among several former Soviet states

Federal Security Service (FSB) Successor to the KGB, the Russian intelligence agency

Federation Council Upper house of the Russian legislature

glasnost Literally, "openness"; the policy of political liberalization implemented in the Soviet Union in the late 1980s

insider privatization A process in Russia whereby the former *nomenklatura* directors of firms were able to acquire the largest share when those firms were privatized

KGB Soviet secret-police agency charged with domestic and foreign intelligence

Khodorkovsky, Mikhail Oligarch arrested and imprisoned for his opposition to the Putin administration

Kremlin Eleventh-century fortress in the heart of Moscow that has been the historical seat of Russian state power

Liberal Democratic Party of Russia (LDPR) Political party in Russia with a nationalist and antidemocratic orientation

nomenklatura Politically sensitive or influential jobs in the state, society, or economy that were staffed by people chosen or approved by the Communist Party

oligarchs Russian people noted for their control of large amounts of the Russian economy (including the media), their close ties to the government, and the accusations of corruption surrounding their rise to power

Orthodox Christianity A variant of Christianity separate from Roman Catholicism and Protestantism; originally centered in Byzantium (now roughly modern-day Turkey)

parties of power Russian parties created by political elites to support their political aspirations; typically lacking any ideological orientation

perestroika Literally, "restructuring"; the policy of economic liberalization implemented in the Soviet Union in the 1980s

Politburo Top policy-making and executive body of the Communist Party

Putin, Vladimir Current president of Russia, as of 2012; also president of Russia from 1999 to 2008; prime minister from 2008 to 2012

Rus Origin of the word *Russia*, thought to refer to Vikings who settled the region in the ninth century C.E.

shock therapy A process of rapid marketization

siloviki "Men of power" who have their origins in the security agencies and are close to President Putin

soviets Name given to workers' councils that sprang up in 1917

tsar Russian word for emperor (also *czar*, from Latin *Caesar*)

United Russia Main political party in Russia and supporter of Vladimir Putin

Yabloko Small party in Russia that advocates democracy and a liberal political-economic system

Yeltsin, Boris President of Russia from 1991 to 1999

WEB LINKS

- Carnegie Endowment for International Peace, Russian and Eurasian Program (www.carnegieendowment.org)
- *Moscow Times* (www.moscowtimes.ru)
- Radio Free Europe/Radio Liberty (www.rferl.org)
- Russia Today (http://rt.com/)
- Transitions Online (www.tol.org)

8

China's economy has grown at an astonishing pace, epitomized by the Shanghai skyline. Will that growth continue? And with what consequences? Will growth keep pace with the increased demands of an expanding middle class? And as growth outpaces capacity, how will China cope with increased pollution and pressure on natural resources?

CHINA

Why Study This Case?

Napoleon Bonaparte is said to have described China as a sleeping giant. Centuries later, that description continues to resonate, though with every passing year, it seems less and less appropriate. Today, China is indeed stirring, after centuries of slumber, with repercussions that are transforming the world. But it is not simply these changes that draw our attention; after all, China is neither the first nor the only country to undergo dramatic change. Rather, it is that these changes are taking place in a country that we tend to speak of in superlatives, as having qualities no other country can easily match.

The first of China's superlatives is its history, which extends back at least 4,000 years. Several millennia before most modern nations and states existed in even rudimentary form, China had taken shape as a relatively unified country and people. Civil strife and external invasion tore it apart innumerable times during this process. Yet despite these difficulties, a continuous Chinese civilization has existed for thousands of years and directly shapes and informs modern Chinese society and politics. The best Western equivalent to this kind of long-lived civilization would be an ancient Greek or Roman Empire that successfully conquered all of Europe and persisted for thousands of years to the present.

Second, China is the most populous country in the world with nearly 1.4 billion people. This is four times the population of the United States. Except for India (whose population also exceeds 1 billion), no other country's population comes close to China's. China has over 175 cities with more than a million inhabitants; the United States has nine. Overpopulation has been both a source of concern for the Chinese government and a lure for foreign businesses that have dreamed for centuries of the profits that could be gained if they somehow tapped into this vast market.

CHINA

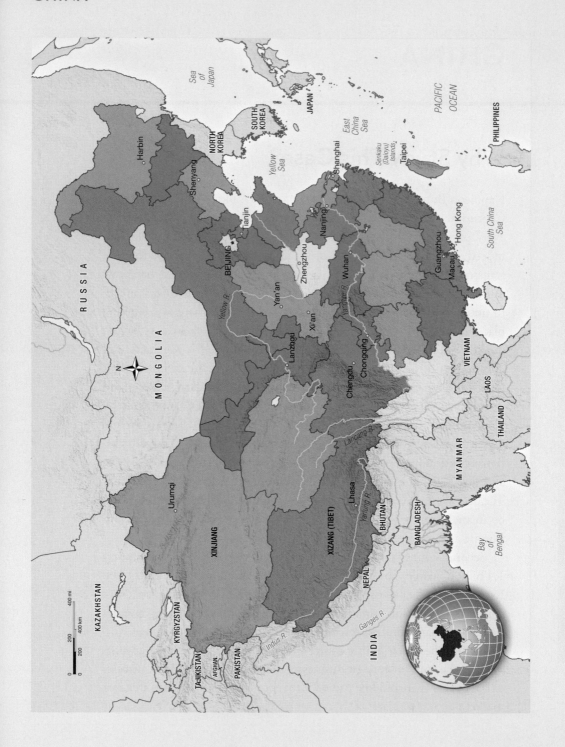

China's recent and rapid development is a third superlative quality. In centuries past, China was one of the most powerful empires in the world, easily dominating its much smaller neighbors. Indeed, it saw itself as the "middle kingdom," the center of the world. Over time, this superiority led to isolation and then stagnation. Foreign imperialism in the nineteenth century forced China open but also led to war and revolution. By the time of the communist takeover in 1949, foreign powers had finally been expelled, and China not only regained its sovereignty but once again enjoyed a period of relative isolation. But starting in the late 1970s, the ruling Chinese Communist Party introduced more liberal economic policies while maintaining its tight control over political power. Known as **reform and opening**, these changes launched a period of extended economic growth unmatched in the world. For more than three decades since reform and opening began in 1978, China's gross domestic product (GDP) grew at an average rate of just under 10 percent a year—double the rate of the other fast-growing "Asian Tigers," such as South Korea and Taiwan, and quadruple the average growth rates of the United States, Japan, and the United Kingdom.

China's rapid economic growth can be measured in many ways, but one of the most obvious has been the country's remarkable building boom. Before the year 2000, China had only six world-class skyscrapers, while the United States had 31. Since 2000, the United States constructed an additional 12 skyscrapers for a total in 2014 of 43. During that same period, China built an additional 66 high rises for a total of 72. Visitors to the city of Shanghai stand awestruck before the towering buildings that line the banks of the Huangpu River. Political reform, however, has been much more limited, and public demands for change, such as the **Tiananmen Square** protests in 1989, have garnered violent reactions from the Communist party-state. In this sense, China stands in contrast to Russia, whose initial transition from communism in the early 1990s made way for greater democracy but came at the cost of economic decline and marginalization from the rest of the world.

The World Bank estimates that reform and opening has raised some 400 million Chinese out of poverty over the past several decades. At the same time, economic reforms have also led to growing income disparities and widespread social disruption. Moreover, growth has slowed in recent years, and observers both in China and abroad are beginning to question the sustainability of this state-led, growth-at-all-costs developmental model. Local governments have run up enormous debts in funding lavish projects, and corruption at all levels of government is widespread. China is thus engaged in a precarious race to reform itself before the shock of these changes overwhelms the country.

Economic modernization is not only transforming the physical and social landscape of the country but also reshaping international finance, trade, politics, and the environment. China, moreover, is becoming a central factor in globalization. Indeed, the flood of cheap Chinese exports into the world market has displaced many workers outside China, heightened concerns in advanced countries about the safety of China's food and toy exports, and substantially lowered rates of global inflation. China's voracious consumption of oil and other raw materials has become a focus of international discussions about global shortages and global climate change. And while China has taken significant steps to address its dangerous levels of air and water pollution, the country faces an environmental crisis of unprecedented proportions that spreads well beyond its borders. Rapid development has also given China increased military might and inspired new confidence to assert territorial claims beyond its traditional borders. These assertions have raised tensions with neighboring countries and prompted concern that a "rising" China may not be a "peaceful" China. Now that the giant is awake, its development and growing international status have profound effects not just internally but also around the world.

Major Geographic and Demographic Features

In addition to boasting the largest population in the world, China, not surprisingly, is also one of the largest countries in terms of landmass—only Russia, Canada, and the United States are larger. China's physical size allows for a range of climates and geographic features. The southwestern portion of the country, including Tibet, is known for its mountain ranges (the Himalayas and the Altai), and most of the northwestern Xinjiang region is desert. The northeastern portion, bordering Mongolia and Russian Siberia, is marked by bitterly cold winter temperatures.

Most of the Chinese population, therefore, lives in the southern and seaboard portions of the country, where the temperate climate and greater rainfall yield most of China's arable land. Intersecting this region are the two lifelines of China: the Yellow (*Huang He*) and Yangtze (*Chang Jiang*) rivers, which flow east toward the Pacific Ocean. The Yangtze has garnered much domestic and international attention due to the Three Gorges Dam project, which was completed in 2008. The largest dam ever constructed, it generates millions of kilowatts of electricity (something desperately needed in China) and helps prevent the flooding that has been a recurrent problem. Critics point out that the dam has destroyed countless historic sites, displaced millions of people, caused major environmental damage, and even increased seismic activity in the region. Moreover, failure of a dam this size would have catastrophic results. Even more ambitiously, China has completed two of three planned projects diverting water from the Yangtze and its tributaries in southern China, where water is more plentiful, to the arid and heavily populated north, a region suffering chronic water shortages. Estimates place the final cost of the completed projects at more than twice that of the Three Gorges Dam—and, critics contend, it could be just as environmentally destructive.

Given the country's large population and landmass, the Chinese are a puzzlingly homogeneous population. Over 90 percent of the population is considered (and considers itself) part of the main ethnic group, known as Han. This quality stands in contrast to the persistence of ethnic diversity in Europe, Africa, and South Asia, even within individual countries. What explains the difference? The answer lies in the geography.

The southern portion of the country is not only more amenable to human habitation but also free of the extreme geographic barriers, such as high mountains and deserts, that impede travel and migration. Historically, the Yellow and Yangtze rivers connected much of the country, allowing knowledge, foods, animals, and culture to spread more easily than in other parts of the world. Such connections helped foster the emergence of a single Han identity, though not always intentionally. The lack of land barriers made it much easier for early empires to develop and bring a large area under their bureaucratic control. China was first unified as early as 221 B.C.E., and with political centralization, the diverse cultures and languages of southern China were slowly—and at least partially—absorbed into the larger Han identity. At this early point in history, we can begin to speak of the emergence of a singular Chinese state.

One political consequence of China's huge population was the government decision in the late 1970s to implement a "one-child policy." Although the measure did curtail population growth, it led to a number of unintended consequences. Supporters of the policy claim that it has averted some 400,000 births and contributed to China's dramatic economic growth. But other scholars note that China's fertility rate was already declining before the policy was enacted and that it spurred sex-selective abortions and a dangerous imbalance between male and female births. It is estimated that by 2020, China will have some 30 million more men than women. Moreover, critics warn that these single offspring, dubbed "little emperors" by the Chinese press, are being overly coddled and insufficiently socialized by doting parents and grandparents. Finally, as these singletons reach maturity and enter the workforce and their parents and grandparents live longer lives, they will have the potentially unsustainable burden of providing the pensions and health care for the much more numerous elder generations. Recognizing this possibility that China will grow old before it grows wealthy, policy makers relaxed the policy in 2016 to permit two children, a measure that many argue offers too little change and comes too late.

Historical Development of the State

China's political development is a paradox. How could a country with such an ancient civilization and such early political centralization become such a weak state by the nineteenth century, lacking both the capacity and autonomy to resist Western imperialism? A closer examination reveals that China's early development and later weakness are closely related.

The country's first political leaders can be traced to the Shang dynasty, which reigned from the eighteenth to the eleventh century B.C.E., two thousand years before European states appeared in their earliest forms. During this time, written Chinese (ideographic, not phonetic, characters) emerged. Power in the country was decentralized, however, and feudal wars among various rivals were commonplace. It was only much later, during the Qin dynasty (221–206 B.C.E.), that a single Chinese empire (and the name China) was born. During this period, China first experienced political centralization through the appointment of nonhereditary officials to govern provinces, the minting of currency, the development of standard weights and measures, and the creation of public works, such as roads, canals, and portions of the famous Great Wall.

Centralization and Dynastic Rule

Sovereign power was centralized and expanded by the Han dynasty (206 B.C.E.–220 C.E.), a reign marked by great cultural flowering and the rise of domestic and international trade, foreign exploration, and conquest. During this period, China far outpaced Europe in its understanding of timekeeping, astronomy, and mathematics. The philosophy of **Confucianism** influenced the imperial leaders with its emphasis on a fixed set of hierarchical roles, meritocracy, and obedience to authority. Confucianism also helped foster the development of the Chinese

TIMELINE OF POLITICAL DEVELOPMENT

YEAR	EVENT
1700 B.C.E.	Chinese civilization under Shang dynasty begins.
221 B.C.E.	China unified under Qin dynasty.
1839–42	First Opium War takes place.
1911	Qing dynasty is overthrown.
1919	May Fourth movement takes place.
1921	Chinese Communist Party (CCP) is founded.
1934–35	Long March takes place.
1937–45	Sino-Japanese War is fought.
1949	People's Republic of China (PRC) is founded.
1958–60	Great Leap Forward takes place.
1966–76	Cultural Revolution takes place.
1976	Mao Zedong dies.
1978	Deng Xiaoping comes to power and launches economic reform and opening.
1989	Chinese government cracks down on protesters in Tiananmen Square Massacre.
2001	China joins the World Trade Organization.
2008	China hosts the Beijing Summer Olympics.
2013	Xi Jinping declared president of China.

civil service, a corps of educated men chosen on the basis of a rigorous series of competitive examinations testing their familiarity with Confucian thought. The notion of a meritocratic, professional bureaucracy did not emerge elsewhere in the world for centuries.

With the collapse of the Han dynasty, China was divided for nearly four centuries, until the Sui and Tang dynasties (591–907 C.E.). These periods of imperial rule restored the unity of the empire; resurrected the bureaucratic institutions of the Han period; and fostered flourishing economic and cultural life. The institutionalization of the bureaucracy also helped promote the development of a gentry class made up of landowners and their children, who were groomed from birth to join the bureaucracy. This bureaucratic class became the glue that held China together. Subsequent dynasties continued to rely upon the bureaucracy to maintain Chinese unity, even when new dynasties were established by foreign conquerors, as under the Yuan (Mongols) and the Qing (Manchus) dynasties. Such continuity helped foster economic development and innovation, which continued to advance faster than in Europe and other parts of the world.

Affluence without Industrialization— and the Foreign Challenge

At the advent of the Ming dynasty (1368–1644), China still led the world in science, economics, communication, technological innovation, and public works. Although such knowledge offered the foundation for Chinese modernization and industrialization, these processes did not take place. During these three centuries, as Europe experienced the Renaissance, international exploration, and the beginnings of the Industrial Revolution, Chinese innovation and economic development began to stagnate. By the mid-1400s, the Chinese Empire had banned long-distance sea travel and showed little interest in developing many of the technological innovations it had created. Why did this occur?

There are several possible reasons. One argument is cultural. Confucian thought helped establish political continuity and a meritocratic system in China, but over the centuries these ideas became inflexible and outdated. During the early twentieth century, bureaucratic examinations were still based on 2,000-year-old Confucian dogma. Rigidly conservative, Confucian ideology placed China at the center of the world (and universe), viewing any new or outside knowledge as unimportant and rejecting changes that might disrupt the imperial system.

A second argument is economic. During the early centuries of the Chinese Empire, entrepreneurialism offered the main path to wealth. But the rise of the bureaucratic elite usurped entrepreneurialism's role and became a more powerful means of personal enrichment, particularly through rent seeking and corruption. The financial rewards of public employment led many in the upper classes to divert their most talented children to the civil service. It also concentrated economic power in the hands of the state, while business activity was stunted by a Confucian disdain for commerce and by steep, arbitrary taxation. Naturally, the bureaucracy opposed any reforms that might threaten its privileges. Historians have also argued that the very success of China's pre-industrial economy, with its relatively efficient trade and production networks and plentiful cheap labor, offered little incentive to pursue additional scientific and technical innovations. These conditions created in China a "high-level equilibrium trap" that thwarted entrepreneurial and technological impulses. Its circumstances thus differed substantially from those in Europe that would give rise to the Industrial Revolution, where labor was more expensive, trade and production less efficient, and enlightenment thought was promoting scientific and technical exploration.[1]

A third argument is geographic and furthers the points just made. The geographic factors that facilitated early unification and continuity also limited competition, since there was less danger that a lack of innovation might lead to destruction by outside forces. In Europe, by contrast, innumerable states continuously vied for power, making isolation impossible and conservatism a recipe for economic and military defeat. No single power in Europe could ban seafaring or abolish the clock; states that resisted progress and innovation soon disappeared from the map. China, however, could reject technology and embrace isolation because it faced no rival powers to challenge such policies. In short, a combination of cultural, economic, and geographic forces allowed China's lengthy isolation.

Europe's economic and technological development continued, and its age of exploration and conquest began just as China was closing itself off to the outside world. The Portuguese first reached China by 1514, and during the sixteenth and seventeenth centuries other European traders sought to expand these initial contacts. These remained tightly controlled by the Chinese, however, and attempts to expand connections were futile. In perhaps the most famous example, a British trade mission led by Lord Macartney was rebuffed by the Chinese emperor, whose reply to King George III read in part, "I set no value on objects strange or ingenious, and we have no use for your country's manufactures."[2]

But the Chinese Empire was losing its ability to ignore the outside world, and external forces were beginning to test China's power. The First Opium War (1839–42) with Great Britain resulted in a resounding Chinese defeat, forcing China to cede Hong Kong to the British and pay restitution. Various Western powers quickly demanded similar access, and subsequent wars with the French and the Japanese only further weakened China's sovereignty and extended the control of imperial powers over the country. Foreign pressures in turn contributed to growing domestic instability.

The Erosion of Central Authority: Civil War and Foreign Invasion

By the beginning of the twentieth century, the centralized authority of the Chinese state, developed over 2,000 years, effectively crumbled. In 1911, a public revolt finally swept away the remnants of the Qing dynasty. China was declared a republic, but it soon fell under the control of regional warlords. In the midst of this chaos, two main political organizations formed to compete for power. The Nationalist Party, also known as the **Kuomintang (KMT)**, slowly grew in strength under the leadership of **Sun Yat-sen**. The party was aided by student protests in 1919 that came to be known as the **May Fourth movement**. These nationalist revolts rejected foreign interference in China and called for modernization, radical reform, and a break with traditional values and institutions, including Confucianism.

The second organization was the **Chinese Communist Party (CCP)**, formed in 1921 by leaders of the May Fourth movement. Adhering to the principles of Marx and Lenin, the CCP's founders sought to organize China's nascent working class to resist the exploitation of both foreign imperialists and domestic warlords. Though the KMT's Sun had been educated in the United States, both parties received support from the recently established Soviet Union. In fact, the Soviets saw the KMT as a more likely contender for power than the much smaller CCP and hoped to move the KMT into the Soviet orbit. Following Sun's death in 1925, relations between the KMT and the CCP shortly unraveled. Chiang Kai-shek, head of the KMT's armed forces, took control of the party and expelled or eliminated pro-Soviet and pro-CCP elements. Chiang subdued or co-opted key regional warlords and brutally suppressed the CCP in areas under KMT control. By 1928, the KMT had emerged as the nominal leader of much of the country, while the CCP was pushed out of the cities and into the countryside. The KMT quickly shed any pretense of democracy, growing ever more dictatorial and corrupt.

During the repression of the CCP, power within the party began to pass into the hands of **Mao Zedong** (1893–1976). Deviating from the Marxist convention that revolutions be led by the urban proletariat, Mao believed that a communist revolution could be won by building a revolutionary army out of the far more numerous peasant class. He and the CCP established their own independent communist republic within China, but KMT attacks forced the CCP to flee westward in what came to be known as the **Long March** (1934–35). In this circuitous retreat, the CCP and its loyal followers traveled over 6,000 miles and lost many lives. (Indeed, of the 100,000 who set out on the Long March, only

10 percent arrived at their final destination in Yan'an, located in north-central China.) Though heroic, the Long March represented a setback for the CCP. At the same time, it secured Mao's leadership and strengthened his idea that the party should reorient itself toward China's peasant majority. The CCP fostered positive relations with the peasantry during the Long March, engaging in actions that contrasted strongly with the more brutal policies of the KMT. The revolutionary ideology of the CCP and its call for equality drew all classes of Chinese to its ranks.

In 1937, both the KMT and the CCP faced a new threat as Japan launched a full-scale invasion of the country after several years of smaller incursions. The two parties formed a nominal united front against the invading Japanese, though they continued to battle each other even as they resisted the Japanese advance. While the war weakened KMT power, which was based in the cities, it bolstered the CCP's nationalist credentials and reinforced its ideology of a peasant-oriented communism of the masses. The war also forged a strong communist military, the **People's Liberation Army (PLA)**, trained both to fight the enemy and to win public support. This birth of Chinese communism through peasant guerrilla warfare is quite different from the Soviet experience, in which a small group of urban intellectuals seized control of the state through a coup d'état. In fact, the CCP and PLA comprised a new state and regime in the making.

Establishment and Consolidation of a Communist Regime

Japan's defeat at the end of World War II found the CCP much strengthened and the KMT in disarray. The Communists now commanded the support of much of the countryside, while the KMT's traditional urban base of support was shattered by war and weakened by widespread corruption and rampant inflation. Communist attacks quickly routed the KMT, and in 1949 the communist forces entered Beijing unopposed and established the People's Republic of China (PRC). Chiang and the remnants of the KMT fled to the island of Taiwan, declaring *their* Republic of China as the legitimate government of all of China—which the United States recognized (rather than the PRC) until 1979. The island nation continues to claim and maintain its sovereignty, though the PRC has never recognized it and asserts that eventually the province of Taiwan will return to mainland control.

The new communist regime faced the challenge of modernizing a country that was far behind the West and ravaged by a century of imperialism and war. The CCP's assets, forged during the war, were its organizational strength and a hard-earned reservoir of public legitimacy. Forming a close (if prickly) alliance with the Soviet Union, China began a process of modernization modeled after the Soviet experience under Joseph Stalin: nationalization of industry, collectivization of agriculture, and central planning. At the same time, the CCP began to repress ruthlessly those viewed as hostile to the revolution, including landowners, KMT members and sympathizers, and others suspected of opposing the new order. Several million Chinese were killed.

Experimentation and Chaos under Mao

Within a few short years, China had diverged from the typical Soviet-style path of communist development. This difference resulted partly from growing tensions between the Soviet Union and China and partly from the particular ideological facets of Chinese communism that had developed in the wake of the Long March. Stalin died in 1953, bringing to an end his ruthless terrorizing of the Russian people. His successor, Nikita Khrushchev, openly denounced Stalin in 1956, taking tentative steps toward allowing greater personal liberty and bringing an end to the unbridled use of violence against the public.

In China, too, some liberalization took place. Mao's **Hundred Flowers Campaign** of 1956 encouraged public criticism and dissent, though it soon ended, and the most prominent critics were removed from their positions of authority. Mao and other Chinese leaders began to see Soviet de-Stalinization as a retreat from communist ideals and revolutionary change, and they upheld China as the true vanguard of world revolution. China's own experience in constructing peasant-based communism in a largely agrarian country provided its leaders with justification for assuming this leadership role. After all, its experiences were not dissimilar to the many anti-imperial struggles taking place across the less-developed world at the time.

China's first major break from the Soviet model was the **Great Leap Forward** (1958–60). Departing from the model of highly centralized planning, Mao reorganized the Chinese people into a series of communes, which were to serve all basic social and economic functions, from industrial production to health care. Each commune was to set its own policies for economic development within the guidelines of general government policy. In Mao's view, revolutionary change could be achieved by putting responsibility directly into the hands of the masses, which would move the country rapidly into communism. State capacity was thus devolved, albeit within an authoritarian system.

Without clear directives and organization, the Great Leap Forward quickly went awry. For example, a campaign to increase steel production led not to the creation of large foundries staffed by skilled employees, as had happened in the Soviet Union, but to the production of a million backyard furnaces built by unskilled communes that consequently produced worthless metal. Overall economic and agricultural production declined, leading to disorder, famine, and the deaths of tens of millions of Chinese. In the face of this debacle, Mao stepped down as head of state in 1959 (though he remained head of the CCP), and China recentralized production and state control. Poor relations with the Soviet Union compounded these setbacks, which culminated in 1960 with the Soviet withdrawal of technical and financial support.

From these events, Mao drew the conclusion that the problem was not that CCP policies had been too radical but that they had not been radical enough. Soviet history proved, he reasoned, that without an unwavering commitment to radical change, revolution would quickly deteriorate into bureaucratic conservatism (as Mao now saw occurring in China). He thus sought to place himself back at the center of power and reignite revolutionary fervor by constructing a cult of personality. This effort was first captured in the publication of *Quotations from Chairman Mao Zedong*, the "Little Red Book" of Mao's sayings that became standard reading for the public.[3]

In 1966, the cult took shape, as Mao and his supporters accused the CCP itself of having "taken the capitalist road" and encouraged the public (particularly students) to "bomb the headquarters"—meaning, to challenge the party-state bureaucracy at all levels. Schools were closed, and student radicals, called **Red Guards**, took to the streets to act as vanguards of Mao's **Cultural Revolution**. Authority figures (including top party and state leaders, intellectuals, teachers, and even parents) were attacked, imprisoned, tortured, exiled to the countryside, or killed. Historic buildings, writings, and works of art were condemned as "bourgeois" and "reactionary" and then destroyed.

By weakening all social, economic, and political institutions in China, Mao made himself the charismatic center of all authority and wisdom. The result of this new vision was years of chaos and violence as the country slid into near civil war among various factions of the state, society, and the CCP. State capacity and autonomy largely disappeared. The only remaining institution with any authority, the PLA, was finally used to restore order. The excesses of the Cultural Revolution were largely curbed by 1968, though factional struggles within the party persisted until Mao's death in 1976 and beyond.

Youthful Red Guards gather to read aloud from Quotations from Chairman Mao Zedong *during the Cultural Revolution.*

Reform and Opening after Mao

With Mao's death, the incessant campaigns to whip up revolutionary fervor ended. The party gradually came under the control of leaders who had themselves been victims of the Cultural Revolution. Most important was **Deng Xiaoping** (1904–97), a top party leader from the earliest years of the CCP who had been stripped of his post (twice) during the Cultural Revolution. In the race to take control of post-Mao China, Deng initially allied with Mao's successor, Hua Guofeng, who had outmaneuvered Mao's widow, Jiang Qing, and her allies (known as the Gang of Four). Deng then marginalized Hua and, by late 1978, had consolidated his power and set the nation on a very different course.

In contrast to Mao's emphasis on revolutionary action for its own sake, Deng pursued modernization at the expense of communist ideology, in what became known as "reform and opening." The government encouraged the gradual privatization of first agriculture and then business; it also cultivated foreign relations with capitalist countries, continuing a process that began under Mao with U.S. president Richard Nixon's visit to China in 1972. Moreover, the government expanded foreign investment and trade while deemphasizing ideology. To quote Deng, "Whether a cat is black or white makes no difference. As long as it catches mice, it is a good cat." Ironically, the destruction of much of the party-state during Mao's Cultural Revolution made these pragmatic reforms easier. China began to embrace the market economy with all of its benefits and difficulties.

One reform that did not take place, however, was political. Despite the downgrading of communist ideology, the CCP still maintained complete control over political life, and attempts at public debate in the 1970s were quickly silenced. Although reform and opening lifted millions out of poverty, by the 1980s, serious problems had emerged—among them inflation, unemployment, and widespread corruption (particularly within the CCP).

As with the earlier May Fourth movement and the Red Guards of the Cultural Revolution, students once again played a major role in expressing discontent over this situation. In 1989, an estimated 100,000 students and other citizens—rallying for political reform—marched in the streets of Beijing. By May 17, hundreds of thousands of Chinese had joined demonstrations, and a large group of protesters occupied Tiananmen Square. Martial law was declared, but many protesters remained, and on June 4 (now known in China simply as *liusi*, or "6/4," much as Americans refer to 9/11), the party leadership brought in the military. Although those gathered in the square itself were permitted to leave, hundreds of protesters were killed that day in clashes around Beijing and in other major Chinese cities. Over the next few months, thousands of students and others connected to the protests were arrested, and students throughout China were required to attend communist ideology indoctrination courses.

The regime's swift and violent response to the protest and its vigilant suppression of even hints of political unrest in the decades since Tiananmen have been combined with continued economic reform and opening. Deng Xiaoping and, with his passing in 1997, China's successive CCP leaders have in essence offered an unwritten social contract to their citizens: in exchange for accepting the CCP's monopoly over political power, the Chinese public has been permitted an unprecedented degree of economic freedom and the right to pursue prosperity. Most Chinese have accepted this bargain, resulting in two additional decades since 1989 of white-hot growth and relative political stability. But as economic growth has slowed in recent years and the challenges associated with this growth-at-all-costs strategy have multiplied, many predict this social contract must change. Can a conservative, authoritarian state continue to preside successfully over a weakening economy and an increasingly vibrant and restive society?

Political Regime

Despite China's four decades of economic reform and global trends of democratization, the country remains stubbornly authoritarian. In fact, approximately half of the world's population that does not democratically elect its leaders resides in China.[4] Certainly China's historical legacy of more than 2,000 years of centralized authoritarian rule (legitimized by Confucian precepts) has buttressed the current regime. But to understand the nature and resilience of China's communist authoritarianism, we must examine the ways in which political control is organized and exercised in a communist party-state.

In spite of China's economic liberalization, this party-state retains the essential organizational structure that the Chinese Communist Party adopted from the Soviet Union at its founding in the 1920s. Though China's reformist leaders have almost fully rejected Marx in their embrace of market freedoms, their decision to retain a closed political system is very much in accord with Lenin's vision of the communist party-state. Lenin contended that for the communist revolution to succeed in Russia, a self-appointed Communist Party elite, enlightened with wisdom and imbued with revolutionary fervor, would need to serve as a vanguard on behalf of the masses. This group alone would have the organizational capacity and resolve to lead the revolutionary transitions from feudalism and capitalism to state socialism and ultimately communism. The need to guide this revolutionary process, Lenin argued, justified the party in maintaining a political monopoly and serving as a "dictatorship of the proletariat."

This ideological and organizational logic has had several consequences for the exercise of political control in China (as was true in the Soviet Union and other communist party-states) in the period of reform and opening. True to its Leninist heritage, political authority both within the party-state and from the party-state to broader Chinese society still flows largely *from* the party elite *to* those within the party, the state, and society, who are expected to submit to this authority. However, China's rapid economic growth in recent years and its increasingly complex society have compelled the party-state to devolve substantial authority to regional and local officials and to ease its iron grip on society. This strengthening of regional and local authorities has had significant consequences for China's political regime and its state capacity.

Political Institutions

The CCP exercises control over the state, society, and economy through the *nomenklatura* system. Party committees are responsible for the appointment, promotion, transfer, and firing of high-level state, party, and even public-industry personnel. (In China's case, this comprises some 10 million positions.) The party also maintains direct control over the government and bureaucracy through a political structure of "organizational parallelism" in which all government executive, legislative, and administrative agencies are matched or duplicated at every level of organization by a corresponding party organ (see the table "Parallel Organization of the Chinese Communist Party and the Chinese Government," p. 404). These CCP bureaus supervise the work of the state agencies and ensure that party interests prevail. This means that although the Chinese state has a premier, a parliament, and bureaucratic ministries just as we see in democratic regimes, party officials and organizations orchestrate the policy process and direct the votes of the party members who hold elected and appointed government and state offices (typically more than four-fifths of all officeholders). The CCP maintains this same organizational control at the regional and local levels of government and also places party "cadre," or officials, in schools, state-owned businesses, and social organizations to supervise—at least theoretically—all aspects of government, economic, and social activity.

In fact, scholars describe ruling communist parties as "greedy institutions" not satisfied with simply controlling the political process, rather seeking to control all aspects of public and even private life. This description was particularly true during the Maoist era of mass campaigns and totalitarian penetration of society. Mao and the party-state ensured control through the ***danwei*** **(work unit) system**, which gave all urban-dwelling Chinese citizens a lifetime affiliation with a specific industrial, agricultural, or bureaucratic work unit that dictated all aspects of their lives, including family size, housing, daily food rations, health care, and other social benefits. This organizational plan was reinforced by the ***hukou*** **(household registration) system**, which tied all Chinese to a particular geographic location.

Firmly in place for decades, reform and opening has erased most aspects of these hierarchical structures of state control. Today, the day-to-day choices of most Chinese citizens are governed much less by the party-state and much more by the free market. Increasingly, Chinese families live where they can afford to live, workers seek employment wherever they can find a job, and Chinese consumers pay cash for many of life's necessities and pleasures. Among other consequences of the weakening of the party-state's institutions of social control, China today has a **floating population** of over 250 million itinerant workers (more than

Parallel Organization of the Chinese Communist Party and the Chinese Government

PARTY OFFICE OR ORGAN	OFFICEHOLDER OR NUMBER OF MEMBERS OR DEPARTMENTS	CORRESPONDING GOVERNMENT OFFICE OR ORGAN	OFFICEHOLDER OR NUMBER OF MEMBERS OR DEPARTMENTS
Chairman	Office abolished in 1982	President (head of state)	Xi Jinping
General secretary	Xi Jinping (head of party)	Premier (head of government)	Li Keqiang
Politburo Standing Committee (PSC)	7 members	State Council Standing Committee	10 members
Politburo	25 members	State Council	35 members
Central Committee (CC)	205 members	National People's Congress Standing Committee	Approximately 150 members
National Party Congress	2,270 members	National People's Congress (NPC)	2,943 members
Central Military Commission (CMC) of the CCP	11 members	Central Military Commission of the PRC	11 members (same members as CCP's CMC)
CMC chairman	Xi Jinping	CMC chairman	Xi Jinping
Secretariat	Large staff of party officials	State Council General Office	Large staff of civil servants
Party departments	Approximately 25 departments	Bureaucratic ministries	Approximately 25 ministries, bureaus, and commissions
Central Commission for Discipline Inspection	130 members	Ministry of Supervision	Minister and 4 vice ministers

Source: Updated and adapted from Melanie Manion, "Politics in China," in Gabriel Almond et al., *Comparative Politics Today: A World View* (New York: Pearson/Longman, 2004), 428.

the entire population of Brazil) who have abandoned their rural *hukou* designation to seek employment in China's cities. Unhindered in leaving the countryside, these rural migrants are in most cases unable to obtain an urban *hukou* designation. They are therefore deprived of the public goods, such as public health care and education for their children, that the state still provides for city dwellers.

Still, although market reforms have dramatically increased mobility and altered state-society relations, China's twenty-first-century authoritarian party-state has worked diligently to maintain control over society. The state has drawn on the same technologies that have aided China's rapid development and hastened social mobility to maintain and even enhance its efforts of social control through high-tech surveillance and censorship. We should not, however, overestimate the authoritarian grasp of China's political leaders. Despite Herculean efforts at supervision, the opening of the economy and the growing complexity of Chinese society have inevitably weakened China's authoritarian regime. Economic and financial decentralization have given local authorities and private firms the autonomy to resist central policies and develop greater independence. These changes, combined with the long-standing inefficiency of China's enormous bureaucracy and growing problems of corruption and nepotism at all levels of government (and the sheer size, growing complexity, and persistent backwardness of much of China), also call state capacity into question. Before exploring the potential consequences of this diminished central authority, we first examine the political institutions of China's authoritarian rule.

THE CONSTITUTION

China is ostensibly governed by a constitution that is designated "the fundamental law of the state" and that vests formal authority in both party and state executive and legislative offices. However, under the conditions of authoritarian rule in China, political power has not been highly institutionalized.

Just as the party always prevails over the state, Mao Zedong and his successors have been little deterred by checks or balances inherent in the formal institutions of either the party or the state. Political leaders have sought in recent years to formalize rules for policy making and succession and have succeeded in imposing mandatory term limits and age limits for appointments at all levels, including the top leadership posts. China's political elites nonetheless continue to rely on their informal sources of power (including personal connections, age, experience, and patronage) as much as or more than on their formal positions or titles. Although there has been collective agreement among current leaders to avoid a return to the tyranny of the Maoist era, political rule in post-Mao China has remained largely vested in a single "paramount" leader surrounded by a key group of 25 to 35 highly influential political elites. These leaders hold key positions in the party and the state, but their stations for the most part affirm rather than determine their status and authority.

Historically, the personal and particular nature of political rule has meant that the Western notion of the *rule of law* (in which all citizens are equal under the law and are protected from arbitrary state power) has generally not prevailed in China. Most significantly, during the Maoist period (but even during the reform era), the country's legal issues were highly politicized. Most legal institutions have been subject to the ideological priorities of the party-state and the personal motivations of its leaders. But reform and opening has forced the state to seek new means of maintaining control and influence, including increased reliance on legal statutes.

The growing complexity of economic and social life has required the state to adopt new laws governing the environment, contracts, labor relations, trade, and even property. China's reliance on foreign trade, in particular, has had a huge impact on legal reforms, as foreign investors, local entrepreneurs, and international bodies such as the World Trade Organization (WTO) have increased pressure on Chinese authorities to abide by contracts and to respect property rights (though not always successfully). This newfound legal adherence is spilling over into other aspects of policy making and portends an even greater role for some of China's other formal political institutions.

Communist Party Institutions and Organs

The National Party Congress "elects" its Central Committee (CC), which in turn "selects" the Politburo (short for "political bureau"). But in fact, the seven or so members of the Politburo Standing Committee (PSC) make up the top political leadership of China. The PSC convenes in weekly meetings headed by the general secretary of the party, currently Xi Jinping. PSC members are "elected" by the 25 or so Politburo members, but it is the PSC (meaning the Politburo's dominant senior members) that typically determines all key national policy decisions and political appointments. The Politburo effectively serves as China's governing cabinet, and each member is responsible for a particular set of policy areas or issues that roughly correspond to the ministerial portfolios of the government's State Council.

Technically, the Politburo, the PSC, and the general secretary are all "elected" by the CC of the National Party Congress. But in reality, party leaders determine the makeup of both the Politburo and the PSC before the actual casting of ballots. When the 200 or so CC members vote, it is on a ballot on which all candidates run unopposed. The CC typically meets annually and carries out the ongoing approval and endorsement functions of the National Party Congress between its sessions. Despite the largely ceremonial role of the CC, its members constitute the pool of China's party officials who are groomed for top leadership. However, in this system of largely informal power, membership in the CC simply confirms the elite status that these party leaders have already earned through personal connections and patronage ties.

The **National Party Congress** is the party's cumbersome representative body and somewhat akin to an American political party nominating convention. With well over 2,000 delegates, the National Party Congress is far too unwieldy and meets too infrequently (every five years) to conduct any real policy making. Instead, its "plenary," or full, sessions have been used as venues for announcing changes in policies and leadership and formally endorsing the ideological "line" of the party. In recent decades, the Party Congress has regularly convened at five-year intervals. Eighteen party congresses have convened since the founding of the party in 1921; the 18th Party Congress was held in 2012.

This most recent 18th Party Congress marked the start of General Secretary **Xi Jinping**'s first of what is likely to be two 5-year terms. Once confirmed, Xi—like his predecessors—unveiled a policy vision that would become the hallmark of his tenure: the pursuit of the **Chinese Dream**. Xi defined this vision as "the rejuvenation of the great Chinese nation" and obtaining what he called the "two 100s": China's ascendance to a "moderately well-off society" by 2021 (the centennial of the CCP's founding) and becoming a fully developed nation by 2049 (the hundredth anniversary of the PRC's founding). The party-state has since elaborated the Chinese Dream to include four components: strength (economic, political, military, and scientific); civility (equity, fairness, and high morals); harmony (peaceful relations among social classes); and beauty (a healthy environment). This vision replaced and built upon the mission statement of the previous decade announced by Xi's predecessor, **Hu Jintao**, at the 17th Party Congress. Hu called for "scientific development and the creation of a **harmonious society**," party-speak for the continuation of economic growth but with more concern for the rising wealth and welfare gaps between urban and rural China.

Delegates to these Party Congress conventions ostensibly represent the more than 88 million members of the CCP, organized at the provincial and local levels. In both the Party Congress and its CC, delegates are left with few if any choices of candidates for the higher-level bodies, and their senior leaders heavily influence the choices they can make. Since 1982, however, members of the CC have been elected by secret ballot, and since the late 1980s, the CC has actually had more candidates than seats available.

Several other party organs are worth noting. Like the government, the CCP also staffs its own bureaucracy, known as the Secretariat. The Secretariat oversees the implementation of Politburo decisions and, just as important, the distribution of propaganda in support of these decisions through its propaganda department. Given the important political role of China's military, party leaders have used the Central Military Commission (CMC) to retain tight control over the armed forces. The CMC presides over China's military, reports directly to the Politburo, and has always been chaired by China's paramount leader or his designee. A final party organ, the Central Commission for Discipline Inspection, is charged with maintaining party loyalty and discipline and rooting out corruption. In 2014, Xi Jinping also took charge of three new party organizations known as "leading groups" concerned with national security and the Internet.

Each of the institutions just discussed is part of the central party structure located in Beijing. Each province also has a party committee that includes a secretary and a standing committee with departments and commissions following the pattern of the central party apparatus. Below this level, the party is represented by comparable organizations at the county, city, district, township, and village levels. The lower-level party leaders have often exercised a degree of autonomy, which has potentially significant consequences for the devolution of authority and the political liberalization of China.

The Branches of Government

The complex hierarchy of governance of the Chinese party-state becomes even more complicated when we add the state government institutions to those of the CCP just described. Although the national constitution designates China's unicameral legislature, the **National People's Congress (NPC)** (not to be confused with the National *Party* Congress), as the highest organ of the state, all government

President Xi Jinping (left), China's paramount leader, serves as head of party, state, and military. Premier Li Keqiang (right) functions as a much weaker head of government.

organizations and bureaucratic ministries remain subservient to party oversight. Nonetheless, day-to-day responsibilities for managing the country's affairs are largely in the hands of the executive State Council's ministries and commissions.

THE HEAD OF STATE

The president of the PRC is China's head of state, an entirely titular office. During the reform era, the paramount leader or his designee has always held this office.

Deng Xiaoping, preferring to rule behind the scenes, designated **Jiang Zemin** as head of state in 1993. Jiang held that office for two terms until 2003, concurrently with his positions as general secretary of the CCP and head of the CMC. In the early 2000s, Jiang resigned from all three of these positions, handing them one by one to his successor, Hu Jintao (whom Deng had also designated before his death in 1997). And in a move indicating the increasing institutionalization of the leadership succession process, Hu Jintao likewise surrendered all three offices to current leader Xi Jinping, culminating in the transfer of the largely ceremonial office of PRC president in 2013. Like his predecessor, it is anticipated that Xi will serve two consecutive terms as president, from 2013 until 2023.

The State Council, China's executive branch, is the primary organ of daily government activity and is led by the premier (who serves as head of government). The premier is recommended by the party's Central Committee and then formally elected by the NPC, which has always chosen the recommended candidate.

Li Keqiang was named premier in 2013, when Xi Jinping became PRC president, and will likely serve for two 5-year terms in tandem with President Xi. The premier is typically the second- or third-ranking member of the PSC. With the assistance of several vice premiers, the premier and his cabinet of ministers and commissioners (collectively, the State Council) govern China. The council oversees the work of China's 25 or so bureaucratic ministries and commissions, which manage the country's economy, foreign relations, education, science, technology, and other affairs of state. The ministers who lead each ministry or commission may also serve as vice premiers or hold party offices as members of the Politburo

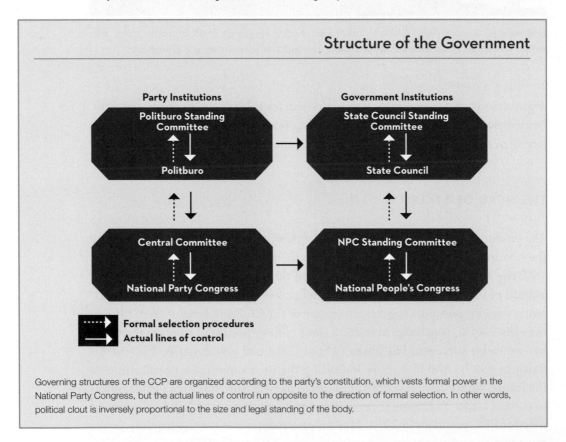

Structure of the Government

Party Institutions

Politburo Standing Committee

Politburo

Central Committee

National Party Congress

Government Institutions

State Council Standing Committee

State Council

NPC Standing Committee

National People's Congress

······▶ Formal selection procedures
───▶ Actual lines of control

Governing structures of the CCP are organized according to the party's constitution, which vests formal power in the National Party Congress, but the actual lines of control run opposite to the direction of formal selection. In other words, political clout is inversely proportional to the size and legal standing of the body.

or even the PSC. Like the CCP's Politburo, the State Council has its own standing committee, which meets twice weekly.

Historically, the State Council's primary responsibility was the management of China's socialist economy, devising the annual and five-year economic plans and managing the state-owned enterprise system. But learning perhaps from the Soviet Union's failed efforts at perestroika, China's State Council has shown more administrative flexibility in adapting to the needs of a more open economy. Under the guidance of its party counterparts, the council's ministries and commissions formulate and implement most of China's laws and regulations.

THE NATIONAL PEOPLE'S CONGRESS

The State Council is formally appointed by China's parliament, the National People's Congress (NPC), which serves as China's unicameral legislative branch. NPC elections are held every five years, a schedule observed faithfully only since Mao's death.

The NPC's nearly 3,000 delegates represent both geographic and functional constituencies (for example, industry and the military). Delegates to the NPC are elected indirectly by provincial people's congresses and typically convene annually for about two weeks to "elect" a standing committee of approximately 150 members. The top leader of the NPC must also be a member of the CCP's Politburo Standing Committee, an arrangement that guarantees party control of legislative affairs and demonstrates, once again, the interlocking nature of the party and state. This NPC Standing Committee then meets regularly as a legislative assembly roughly every two months throughout the year.

Despite having the constitutional authority to pass laws and even amend the constitution, the NPC has never had an independent or influential role in policy making. Rather, it has most often served to ratify policies already determined by central leaders. In more recent years, however, as China's economy and society have become more complex, the NPC and its standing committee have gradually become venues for delegates to offer opinions, express dissatisfaction with government policy, and even occasionally cast dissenting votes. As its constituent committees and specialized policy groups have become more knowledgeable and sophisticated, the NPC has started to shape policies of reform. The full NPC is, of course, still far from a democratic parliament. Like its party counterpart, the institution is too large and meets too seldom and too briefly to exert any substantial influence. And while its standing committee is gaining substance, it, too, remains far weaker than both the executive State Council and (of course) the CCP and its ruling organs.

Under China's system of authoritarian rule, the law is subject to the leaders, not the other way around. In other words, China's leaders practice rule *by* law, rather than submitting to the rule *of* law more common in constitutional democracies.

In fact, for the most part, the PRC's legal system did not function under Mao, and no criminal code existed before 1978. Legal reforms since that time have established a judicial system, but it remains subservient to the party hierarchy, which routinely protects officials from the law. Party leaders have often applied corruption or abuse-of-office statutes selectively and have fabricated or exaggerated crimes to snare political opponents or hold up one deviant as an example to others (or, as the Chinese saying goes, "kill the chicken to scare the monkey").

China has been severely criticized by human rights groups, both for its extensive incarceration of political prisoners and for its eagerness to employ capital punishment for a variety of crimes (including corruption, smuggling, theft, bribery, and rape). Observers estimate that hundreds of thousands of prisoners are being held in labor reeducation camps (ostensibly closed in 2013), "rehabilitation" centers, and other secret jails, with no access to the legal system (roughly 10 percent of them are political prisoners). Recent prominent political detainees have included literary critic and human rights activist Liu Xiaobo, who was awarded the 2010 Nobel Peace Prize while serving his fourth prison term, and artist and outspoken government critic Ai Weiwei, who was detained for two months in 2011, ostensibly for tax evasion.

Amnesty International notes that during one of China's periodic "strike hard" campaigns, Chinese authorities executed more criminals (1,781) in three months than did the rest of the world in the previous three years.[5] Scholars estimate that China annually executes more than 2,500 prisoners—half the annual total of just a few years ago, but still more than the rest of the world combined and at a per capita rate roughly comparable to those of Iran and North Korea. Amnesty International also contends that an estimated 50,000 practitioners of the outlawed **Falun Gong** meditation sect and numerous other religious practitioners and ethnic minority activists have been detained as political prisoners. Many of them, as well as other prisoners of conscience, are subjected to torture, inhumane conditions, and even execution.

Local Government

Unlike both Japan and Europe, which experienced decentralized feudalism in the not so distant past, China has been unified and ruled centrally for over 2,000 years. This system has led successive authoritarian regimes, including the current one, to resist notions of federalism and hold to the belief that unity and stability are possible only under strong central leadership.

Central control over such a huge and diverse nation has been far from complete. But China has managed this regime through the central structure of parallel party and government rule, replicated throughout the descending levels of government. This structure includes 34 provincial-level administrative units (23 provinces, 4 provincial-level cities, 5 autonomous regions, and 2 special administrative regions), almost 3,000 counties, over 40,000 townships, and more than 700,000 villages.[6] Each level is modeled on the central government and has parallel party and government councils, administrative departments, and congresses at the provincial, county, and township levels.

Though China's authoritarian rule has always been somewhat fragmented, increased social complexity and the political and financial demands brought on by reform and opening are making their mark on local politics. In recent years, the central party leadership has devolved substantial economic policy-making authority to regional and local officials. These measures have enhanced efficiency and promoted development, but they have also greatly expanded opportunities for local corruption and abuse of power.

Local officials are given no authority to tax nor provided with other sources of revenue and have therefore used their control of property and licensing within their jurisdictions to seize lands occupied by local residents, offering only meager compensation in return. These local party-state leaders then sell the property and the right to build factories or other projects at huge profits to developers and factory owners. These local officials then share the profits with the developers, leading to the overexpansion of factories and the sprouting of a number of questionable mega-projects across China, including so-called ghost cities filled with currently uninhabited high rises, shopping malls, and office complexes. Too often, the local residents are forced to endure dangerous levels of pollution emitted from these factories or are thrown off the land altogether. Most of the estimated 200,000 annual local protests are related to these kinds of land disputes.

In an effort to address the growing discontent within local communities as well as shore up the legitimacy of communist rule, central political leaders have been experimenting over the past three decades with gradually increasing measures of local democratization. Initial ventures during the 1980s granted rural villages the right to secret ballot elections for county-level people's congresses; later, they were allowed to popularly elect relatively powerless "village committees" and "village heads." By the early 2000s, some 600,000 villages across China had begun conducting local elections. But at the same time, increasingly brazen farmers, workers, and entrepreneurs had begun to call for the right to elect their local party secretaries, who are the real locus of power at the village level. Although this last demand has not yet been granted, and political liberalization has not yet "trickled up" in any formal way, its impact on the nearly half of all Chinese still living in villages ought not to be underestimated.[7]

Other Institutions

THE PEOPLE'S LIBERATION ARMY

Chairman Mao famously stated that "political power grows out of the barrel of a gun." Later, he claimed that he had not meant that military might is the means of obtaining political power, but rather that "the Party commands the gun, and the gun must never be allowed to command the Party."[8] Although the CCP has sought to abide by Mao's admonition, the People's Liberation Army, which comprises China's army, navy, and air force, has played a significant role not just in China's revolutionary history but also in contemporary Chinese politics.

Mao used the prestige and heroic stature the PLA garnered in battle before 1949 to add legitimacy to the communist party-state once the PRC was established. The PLA played a key role in economic reconstruction in the 1950s, brought the Red Guard to heel during the chaotic Cultural Revolution, and smashed the protests at Tiananmen Square in 1989. The crackdown on the Tiananmen Square demonstration left hundreds (some say thousands) of protesters dead and captured the world's attention.

In the reform period, party leaders have sought to narrow both the economic and political roles of the military. Party leaders have forced the military to sell off its extensive industrial and commercial interests, reduce personnel, and upgrade the PLA's professionalism and technological prowess. Even with its new, "leaner" status, the PLA remains the world's largest military force with a standing army of some 2.3 million personnel and an annual military budget in 2016 of nearly $150 billion. These military expenditures comprise nearly 2 percent of China's GDP, compared with 3.5 percent of GDP and a $600 billion military budget for the United States.

Because of the size and historically important role of the PLA, the CCP established the Central Military Commission, first within the party and later as a second government agency, to guarantee party-state control over the gun. Although this control seems more certain now than perhaps at any other time in PRC history, China's increased security needs and its regional and global interests have enhanced the status of the military and led to growing military assertiveness in shaping China's foreign policy.

Political Conflict and Competition

The Party System

Although China's political system includes eight nominally independent political parties, each of these very small parties is entirely subservient to the Chinese Communist Party. The CCP's monopoly of power and the absence of any formal political opposition allow us to consider China an authoritarian regime led by a one-party state.

THE CHINESE COMMUNIST PARTY

The policy of reform and opening has created new avenues of economic and social mobility in China. Still, membership in the Chinese Communist Party remains essential for acquiring political influence and status and has proven extremely beneficial financially.

Because it offers the primary path to political advancement and is an obligatory credential for many careers and appointments, membership in the CCP is both sought after and selective. In 2016, the CCP had more than 88 million registered members, making it by far the largest political party in the world (and larger than the population of Germany). Party members account for roughly 8 percent of China's adult population; every year, the CCP accepts more than 2 million new members, who are drawn from a carefully screened applicant pool of over 20 million aspirants. Significantly, over a quarter of current CCP members are under age 35, over a third of them have college degrees, and millions of these card-carrying Communist Party members are capitalists.

While party membership has always been the chief pathway to elite recruitment, over time, different sectors of society have been gradually targeted for inclusion in the party as the needs and priorities of the party-state have evolved. Mao Zedong's most significant contribution to communist doctrine was his inclusion of peasants as an integral component of communist revolution. Whereas Lenin described the Russian peasants as backward "vermin," Mao glorified their role in the Chinese revolution and recruited them to take political office in the new People's Republic of China. During the 1950s, the CCP sought first to create and then to recruit a sector of industrial workers to establish a more orthodox (Marxist) Communist Party. During the Cultural Revolution, the keys to political advancement were ideological purity and a background untainted by either feudal or bourgeois heritage.

Since Mao's death, China's reformist leaders have successively broadened the definition of political correctness in an effort to co-opt into the ranks of the party those deemed important to the reform program. Deng Xiaoping pragmatically emphasized that an "ability to catch mice" (expertise), and not the "color of the cat" (ideological conformity), was the true measure of contribution to China's progress. He welcomed professionals, scholars, and intellectuals into the party and encouraged all Chinese to "seek truth from facts." And, in a move very much anathema to Marx and Lenin's vision of a communist party, the CCP broadened the definition of the party in a 2001 policy known as the **Three Represents** to include not just workers and peasants but even private entrepreneurs. As of 2011, over 90 percent of China's 1,000 wealthiest individuals were either officials or members of the CCP, and over 200 of China's wealthiest individuals were delegates of the National People's Congress in 2015.[9] This convergence of private financial wealth and political influence, combined with the growing income inequality in Chinese society, has led critics to wonder how long a ruling party founded on the principle of destroying the very social class it has now chosen to embrace and reward can endure.

But even as increasing numbers of scholars and other interested observers inside and outside China predict the collapse of CCP rule, this ruling party that is making plans to celebrate the centennial anniversary of its founding in 2021 has managed thus far to resist both external challenges and internal decay.[10] Although the CCP's original heroic stature and revolutionary legitimacy may have little hold on China's younger generations, recent party leaders have effectively employed a mixture of authoritarian controls, patriotic nationalist appeals, and economic benefits to maintain the CCP's virtual monopoly of political power.

THE SUCCESSION AND CIRCULATION OF ELITES

One of the greatest challenges to perpetuating the CCP's political dominance has been the issue of political succession. As in most authoritarian systems, China faces the problem of having no institutionalized "vice office" to ease the transition to a successor when the top leader dies.

The passing of longtime leader Mao Zedong in 1976 led to a leadership crisis and caused a rancorous struggle among several elite factions. In an effort to avoid repeating this problem, Deng Xiaoping did not assume formal leadership positions in either the party or the government when he came to power two years later and launched his reforms. Although he retained his position on the PSC

China's Paramount Leaders

GENERATION	LEADER AND TENURE	FORMATIVE EXPERIENCE	CAREERS OF POLITICAL ELITE
1st	Mao Zedong (1935–76)	May Fourth movement	Confucian intellectuals and peasants
2nd	Deng Xiaoping (1979–92)	Long March	"Reds": peasants and workers
3rd	Jiang Zemin (1992–2002)	Great Leap Forward	"Experts": engineers and technocrats
4th	Hu Jintao (2002–12)	Cultural Revolution	"Experts": engineers and technocrats
5th	Xi Jinping (2012–22)	Tiananmen Square Massacre	Academics (social science, law) and entrepreneurs

Source: Adapted from Bruce Dickson, "Beijing's Ambivalent Reformers," *Current History* 103 (September 2004): 249–55.

until 1987 and chaired the CMC until 1989, his only other official title, until his death in 1997, was honorary president of the China Bridge Players Society.[11] From behind the scenes, however, he served as the paramount leader of China.

Deng also sought to institutionalize a succession process that would avoid the uncertainty and instability associated with his own ascendance. As paramount leader, he chose not only his own "third-generation" replacement, Jiang Zemin, but also tapped "fourth-generation" successor Hu Jintao. Just as Jiang and Hu each served a decade as head of state, head of party, and head of military, it is anticipated that current "fifth-generation" leader Xi Jinping will likewise complete 10-year terms as CCP general secretary (2012–22), PRC president (2013–23), and CMC chair (2013–23).

In explaining the apparent success of this smooth transition of party leaders and the continued resilience of China's authoritarian rule, scholars point to a number of factors. Significantly, each of these successive leaders came to power possessing less personal authority than his predecessor. Mao's nearly absolute authority as a revolutionary cult leader gave way to Deng's pragmatic reform program, made possible by his seniority and extensive leadership experience going back to the founding of the party. Deng chose the next two leaders, intentionally selecting technocrats and taking into account factional interests among the party elite. Similarly, preeminent leader Xi Jinping and second in seniority Li Keqiang each represent a separate faction within the PSC, reflecting an effort to balance interests and secure the support of a core group of 20 to 30 leaders.

To retain the party's monopoly of power, this core group of party elite has shown its willingness and ability to follow established norms of succession, putting in place term limits and mandatory retirement ages to ensure the circulation of elites. Moreover, the promotion of elites within the party is now based as much on merit as on personal or factional connections.[12] The question remains regarding how long this single-party authoritarian state can balance the co-optation of an increasingly wealthy elite—and the corruption that tends to accompany this co-optation—with the necessary accommodation and repression of a society that is rapidly growing more vocal and varied in its demands. The party-state's careful management of this increasingly complex society is the focus of the next section.

Civil Society

Because the CCP historically claimed to represent all legitimate social interests, civil society did not officially exist in Mao's China. By strict definition, any organized interests outside the party-state were considered illegitimate and potentially harmful. Pains were taken to eliminate any ethnic, religious, labor, or other forms of organized association not fully controlled by the state. Not surprisingly, however, the profound changes associated with reform and opening since Mao's death have not been limited to the economy alone.

In an effort to confine the social and political impact of economic reform, the party-state has created a number of mass organizations to control society and mobilize social groups to fulfill its own national goals. Awkwardly labeled "government-operated nongovernmental organizations" or GONGOs, these legitimate "mass organizations" formed by the CCP include the Women's Federation, the All-China Federation of Trade Unions, and the Youth Development Foundation. Such groups are led by party officials and assist the party-state in disseminating information and implementing policies.

China's political leaders have watched nervously as the interests and demands of China's citizens have expanded in pace with China's modernization. Although the party-state has begun to open space for civil society by authorizing the work of some half a million legally registered nongovernmental organizations (NGOs), these have largely been restricted to nonpolitical arenas such as providing services to the poor, disabled, and elderly and promoting local environmental protection, typically still with government sponsorship or monitoring. But as rapid urbanization and industrialization have placed increased demands on government at all levels, an estimated 1 to 2 million additional unregistered NGOs have emerged with at least the party-state's tolerance. Many of these organizations offer much-needed services in health care, education, disaster relief, and other areas that local governments are unable or unwilling to provide.

Predictably, a number of these NGOs and social activists have moved from simply providing services to advocating for the groups they serve, including displaced peasants, exploited migrants and factory workers, and those seeking legal redress from corrupt government officials. The party-state has not hesitated to harass, detain, and arrest those groups and individuals who have become too vocal or who stray into controversial areas. In 2016, the government enacted a law further restricting the operation of foreign NGOs in China, requiring them to secure an approved local partner and subjecting them to increased government oversight.

As good Communists, the CCP certainly realized the potential influence and threat of China's growing middle class that its economic reforms had created. But in a move of political expediency that would have been incomprehensible to both Marx and Mao, this communist party-state decided in 2001 to welcome private capitalists into the CCP with its "Three Represents" policy. Leaders argued that under the current conditions of "socialism with Chinese characteristics," the CCP ought to represent the interests not just of workers and peasants but also of the private agents of China's "advanced productive forces." This open, if awkward, embrace of what was long considered socialism's class enemy acknowledges the growing economic influence (and political potential) of China's capitalists and the inevitable pressures of the growing middle class to express its interests.

The state's efforts in co-optation have given rise to a growing group of **red capitalists**—private entrepreneurs who belong to the CCP—who have benefited from economic reform, prefer social stability, and therefore have little reason to challenge the state or make new demands on the policy agenda.[13] China's Communist Party leaders have recognized that, one way or another, capitalist interests will be heard. However, their determination that such interests be heard from within the party rather than from without may nonetheless have "revolutionary" consequences.

Although this revolutionary potential was perhaps most vividly manifested in the 1989 demonstrations of students and their supporters at Tiananmen Square, a wide variety of social protests have bubbled up outside the official confines of the party-state, both before and since that event. In fact, the events at Tiananmen Square in 1989 were the site's third such protest during the reform era. To date, all significant attempts to form unauthorized political or social interest groups have been swiftly repressed.

A decade following the crushing of the student movement at Tiananmen Square, the party-state launched a repression campaign against practitioners of the meditative martial arts movement Falun Gong. Founded in 1992, this traditional Chinese martial arts sect was initially promoted by the party-state as a safe domestic alternative to potentially threatening Western social and religious movements. But as the movement rapidly gained adherents and grew in stature and organizational capacity, it caught the attention of the state, which began to impose restrictions.

In response, Falun Gong mounted larger demonstrations and rallies—in 1999, some 10,000 adherents staged a daylong silent protest outside the Beijing residential compound of China's top leaders. This prompted a swift crackdown by the regime, which labeled the sect an evil cult, banned the organization, and arrested some 5,000 practitioners. Human rights groups charged that many of those arrested were tortured and in some cases executed, after which their corpses were rendered for organ harvesting.

Despite the persecution, Falun Gong still claims millions of followers in China. The party-state's determination to squelch this social movement and to restrict the free association of other independent religious groups deemed too large or too influential—but that nonetheless claim no political agenda—demonstrates both the extent of state paranoia and the persistent desire of many Chinese to give organizational expression to their social interests.

The increasing complexity and openness of China's twenty-first-century society—coupled with the inevitable growing pains of its ongoing economic revolution—almost guarantee that this cycle of subversive rebellion, state repression, and renewed social resistance will repeat itself. Scholars point to a growing variety of increasingly motivated and articulate social groups—out-of-work state employees, displaced farmers, migrant workers, internationally connected environmentalists, members of underground Christian "house" churches, and many others—that are no longer easily subsumed under Mao's one-size-fits-all category of the "masses" and that have stepped up their demands, even in the face of state repression. Peasant protests against illegal land seizures, onerous taxes, local corruption, and environmental hazards as well as urban workers' strikes against layoffs and horrific working conditions are both increasingly common and well organized. Scholars estimate more than 500 such protests take place each day

Is the State Too Powerful?

The state controls too much of our daily lives. Percentage of survey respondents who agree:

COUNTRY	PERCENTAGE
Brazil	76
Germany	74
India	71
Mexico	68
France	65
United States	65
United Kingdom	64
South Africa	63
Canada	59
Nigeria	59
China	39
Russia	36
Japan	34

Note: Data on Iran not available

Source: Pew Center for the People and the Press, 2007.

across China. Potentially even more destabilizing is China's floating population of migrant workers, estimated now at over 250 million and growing. These nomadic laborers flock from rural to urban China with little job security, in most cases no legal residency beyond their abandoned villages, and no authorized access to housing, health care, or education. Likewise, China now boasts 700 million "netizens" (active users of the Internet and online communities), 1.2 billion mobile phone subscribers, and more than 300 million bloggers who are increasingly interconnected with one another and the world. These citizens regularly surf and blog, severely testing the regime's capacity to monitor their networking activities and censor their access to politically dangerous resources on the Web.

Although none of these groups is yet an organized social movement like Falun Gong or a political separatist movement like those active in China's western border regions, some observers predict that such grassroots movements could combine with ongoing intellectual dissidence to rekindle demands for democratization and the end of CCP rule. Others counter that the party-state's combination of co-optation, responsiveness, and censorship and the extensive reach of its security apparatus have largely managed to keep a lid on social unrest and thwart the emergence of an autonomous civil society. They note that although Western observers and political leaders have denounced the brutal state repression of Tibetan and Uighur protests in recent years, Chinese authorities have been able not only to control almost completely what its own citizens heard and saw but also to portray these protests to its own people as violent threats to Chinese sovereignty.

MICROBLOGS: A SOCIAL REVOLUTION?

China's Communist Party leaders recognize that the country's capacity to compete in the twenty-first century requires embracing the technology of this digital age. With over 700 million Internet subscribers and a third of a billion bloggers, Chinese netizens are happily obliging. While most of these bloggers and surfers are typically connecting with friends, downloading music, or playing online games, this explosion of social media has also given Chinese activists new means to publicize government corruption and abuse, rally support for social causes, and organize protests (both real and virtual).

Predictably, the authoritarian party-state has also taken up its keyboards and filters, in a concerted effort to control social media and restrict its uses. Labeled "Golden Shield" by the government, and more colloquially known as the "Great Firewall of China," the party-state's huge project of social media control has to date been surprisingly successful. By deploying an army of more than 50,000 human monitors, a raft of harsh censorship laws, and a vast, sophisticated network of filtering software, the government has managed to prevent or quickly remove much of the content it finds politically or morally objectionable.

However, even as the party-state has banned Twitter, Facebook, and Instagram; cowed Yahoo and Google; and taken control of China's domestic private Internet service providers, the CCP's net nannies have not been able to fully tame China's mobile phone–based microblogs. For several years, the popular microblogging service Weibo (literally "microblog") offered a relatively open venue for Chinese to express their opinions and share uncensored news and rumors. Like Twitter, this Chinese social network limited messages to 140 Chinese characters. But also like more sophisticated sites such as Facebook, it accommodated user-friendly layered and threaded discussions and permitted a variety of multimedia attachments. This capacity to disseminate a wide range of content quickly and easily from mobile phones made the service hugely popular and connected people across China in new but, from the party-state's perspective, potentially dangerous ways.

In 2012, the central government cracked down on Weibo by no longer permitting anonymous postings, filtering and censoring sensitive content, flooding the site with pro-government propaganda, and punishing those who violated strict new laws governing the site. But China's Internet activists have shown remarkable

China's governing party-state has thus far employed its "Great Firewall" to good effect in thwarting the free flow of information. However, it is uncertain how long or how effectively the state will be able to outmaneuver the country's growing population of "netizens."

creativity in skirting the censors. Many have now migrated to new, more private social media platforms such as WeChat (the English translation for *weixin*, literally "micromessage"), a mobile text and voice messaging communication service that permits communication among friends. Predictably, the government censors have taken steps to throttle this digital venue as well. But for all the party-state's capacity, silencing these proliferating message apps and social networking platforms would be hugely unpopular and perhaps at this point impossible. In 2013, Chinese netizens daily posted over 250 million microblog messages and over 20 billion WeChat and other instant messages. It remains to be seen how microblogging and micromessaging will continue to change Chinese society and perhaps even its politics.

Can this juxtaposition of an increasingly open economic system and a persistently closed political system endure? Scholars disagree as to whether China's state is "brittle," and therefore unresponsive to societal demands, or "adaptive" and even "consultative" and sufficiently responsive to the country's increasingly complex and vocal civil society to retain its vanguard role.[14] Although these debates persist over whether China's authoritarian political system remains securely intact or is moving toward greater liberalization or inevitable collapse, most observers conclude that this volatile combination is far too contradictory to prevail as is for long.

Society

Ethnic and National Identity

Though the Chinese commonly view themselves as a homogeneous society, China is not without ethnic diversity. The country is populated mostly by Han Chinese (who make up more than 90 percent of the total population), but it recognizes at least 55 minority nationalities.

Even among Han Chinese, there is tremendous linguistic diversity. For thousands of years, Han Chinese have shared a written language, but Han speakers are divided into eight main language groups and hundreds of dialects. Since the twentieth century, Beijing has imposed Mandarin as the official language of government and education. Despite the persistence of local dialects in many rural areas, education, television, and increased mobility have privileged Mandarin and made it the common tongue, especially among younger Chinese.

Although China's minority nationalities comprise only a small percentage of the population, many reside in strategic "autonomous areas" that make up more

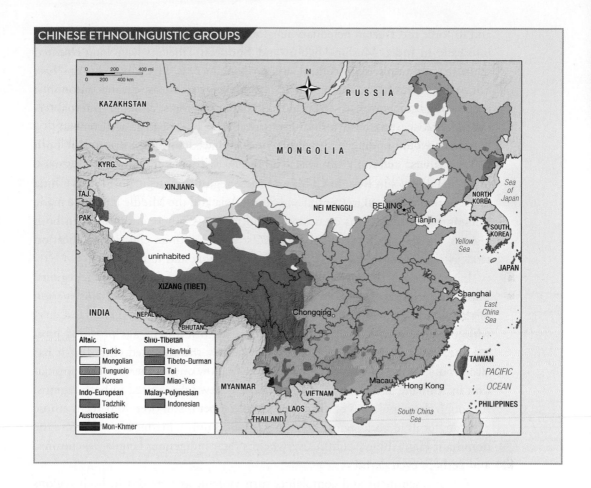

than 60 percent of China's territory and have a long and often violent history of resistance to the Chinese state (see the map above). For millennia, China has struggled to maintain sovereignty over its border regions, particularly its western frontiers.

This struggle continues in the twenty-first century as the country faces demands for increased autonomy from the Turkic Uighur minority in the northwestern province of Xinjiang and from Tibetans in the southwest. Advocates for greater autonomy in both regions can point to periods of independence during the first half of the twentieth century and much longer periods of separation from the Chinese empire in the centuries before. But the Chinese communists moved quickly after 1949 to consolidate control over these two sparsely populated regions. They used an uprising in Tibet in 1959 to eliminate opposition to Chinese sovereignty and to force the Tibetan hereditary religious and political leader, the Dalai Lama, into exile in India. Muslim Uighurs and Buddhist Tibetans have long resented Chinese Communist Party control, and proponents of a "Free Tibet" and an "East Turkestan" continue to champion independence or at least greater autonomy. These voices come primarily from outside China's borders, although internal terrorism, violence, and other forms of resistance have been regular occurrences.

Chinese Communist leaders have always viewed sovereign control of both regions as vital and nonnegotiable. The recent discovery, moreover, of extensive fossil fuel reserves in western China and these regions' strategic position as China looks farther westward to Central and South Asia and the Middle East have made full control of these areas even more important to Chinese authorities. In both regions, the regime has countered separatist efforts with an effective pacification strategy that has combined co-optation, assimilation, and repression.

In recent years, the government has pumped billions of dollars into the regions, improving transport and communication infrastructure, including construction of the world's highest-altitude (and most expensive) railway (to Tibet) and city-wide broadband in Xinjiang's larger cities. This investment has provided jobs, income, and opportunities for locals, particularly the educated elite. But it has also brought waves of ethnic Han Chinese, who now outnumber the local population in Xinjiang and claim the largest share of new jobs created in both regions. Although the population of the less-accessible Tibet is still over 90 percent ethnic Tibetan, locals in both regions complain that it is only a matter of time before the dominant Han Chinese culture overwhelms their indigenous languages, cultures, and perhaps even faiths.

When resentment and complaints turn violent, as they did in both regions most recently in Tibet in 2008 and Xinjiang in 2009, the regime has not hesitated to react with harsh repression. Harsh repression has not, however, quelled ethnic protest. Since 2009, nearly 150 Tibetans have resorted to self-immolation as a means of protest. China's ethnic Uighurs have targeted Han Chinese with increasingly bold acts of terrorism not just in Xinjiang but also in the cities of Beijing (2013) and Kunming (2014).

Ideology and Political Culture

Chinese political culture is in a state of flux, and many of the details will remain unknown until more extensive and reliable public opinion data (banned until very recently) are available. During the rule of Mao Zedong, the party-state attempted to reshape China's traditional political culture through massive propaganda, mobilization, and repression. The importance of communist ideas has waned since the time of Mao's death, especially as a capitalist economy has come to replace state socialism. Communist ideology still has some hold on the countryside, but China's cities reflect a growing diversity of information and ideas. And while Mao violently rejected traditional Confucian cultural norms, China's current leaders have embraced these values as a homegrown source of legitimacy, even as premodern and communist emphasis on the group (whether familial clan or agricultural collective) is giving way to modern cultural values of individualism.

TRADITIONAL CENTRALIZED AUTHORITARIANISM

Mao viewed China's "poor and blank" population as ripe for the party-led makeover of political culture, but traditional Chinese political culture was far more resilient than Mao had imagined. Before the communists took power in 1949, China had a long history of centrally imposed authoritarian politics. Mao's communists moved the capital from Nanjing back to Beijing (which had been the imperial capital for centuries) and in doing so directly connected their rule to traditional Chinese authoritarianism.

In many ways, the communist regime replicated elements of the rigid and hierarchical imperial system. For example, China still administers extremely competitive national examinations that determine university admission, and under communist rule, the tradition of respect for one's elders is still reflected in the elevated average age of party leaders. Despite significant efforts by some to improve the status of Chinese women, the male domination of China's communist leadership continues to expose the traditional paternalism of Chinese politics.

CONFUCIANISM

One significant influence over the political culture and ideology of the Chinese people has been the teachings of the scholar Confucius (551–479 B.C.E.). Mao launched his 1960s Cultural Revolution with the explicit intent of destroying once and for all the institutional legacies of Confucianism. However, in the moral vacuum resulting from the waning influence of communist ideology in recent decades, the post-Mao Chinese Communist leadership has embraced key elements of Confucian philosophy.

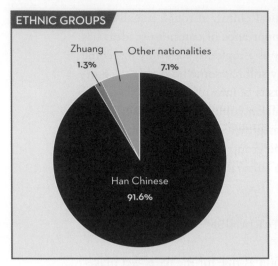

ETHNIC GROUPS

Zhuang
1.3%

Other nationalities
7.1%

Han Chinese
91.6%

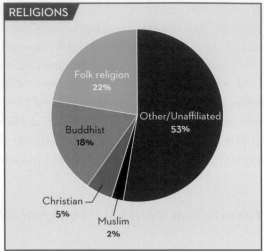

RELIGIONS

Folk religion
22%

Other/Unaffiliated
53%

Buddhist
18%

Christian
5%

Muslim
2%

Under the tenets of Confucianism, the role of government is to impose a strict moral code and foster "correct" behavior. Central to the Confucian worldview are the ideas of hierarchy and social harmony. Peace, order, and stability in both the family and the nation flow from the proper actions of benevolent superiors and obedient inferiors who all know their rightful place in society and act accordingly. Not surprisingly, China's authoritarian leaders have found reason to champion these traditional values bolstering central authority, social harmony, and even "small prosperity," a Confucian precept calling for the acceptance of a moderately well-off society short of full prosperity.

MAOISM

Mao believed that the key to revolutionary success lay in the ability of the Communist Party to create a "new socialist man" and to alter the way people think. While building in important ways on traditional Chinese political culture, Mao introduced some radical concepts. For example, instead of rallying to the traditional Confucian notion of harmony, he promoted constant class struggle. On the other hand, Maoism emphasized the collective over the individual, here drawing on traditional Confucian notions. Where traditional Chinese values favored loyalty to the extended family, Mao sought to transfer that loyalty to the larger community, as embodied by the party, the state, and, locally, the *danwei* (work unit).

The Communists also claimed to promote egalitarianism, and thus an improvement of the lot of the nation's poor, peasants, and women.

In Mao's view, revolutionary thought (as decreed by the party leadership) could replace Chinese values, and the party could promote these ideas through constant propaganda and slogans, mass campaigns, and the education system, which included intensive sessions of "thought reform" and "self-criticism." Likewise, economic development could be "willed" through massive acts of peasant-driven voluntarism. Mao regularly favored political correctness over technical expertise, often at great cost to China's economy and most infamously during the Great Leap Forward and the Cultural Revolution.

Given the dearth of modern opinion research in Communist China, it is impossible to know whether Maoism has changed Chinese political culture or merely reinforced traditional Chinese characteristics. The ease with which the Chinese people have embraced capitalist reforms and increased individualism as well as tolerated the growth of inequality suggests that Mao's ideas were accepted more out of deference to central authority than out of any deep convictions.

Since Mao's death, the importance of Maoism, and indeed of communism, has waned. China's current leaders neither demand nor desire the type of mass mobilization that was a hallmark of Mao's China. The current leadership instead prefers a largely depoliticized public that is more common in the authoritarian regimes of developing countries, as it was in pre-communist Confucian China.

NATIONALISM

Nationalism was a dominant feature of twentieth-century China. It has perhaps become even more important in the twenty-first century as the nominally communist party-state seeks new sources of legitimacy for retaining its monopoly on political power. The country's long and powerful imperial past (and its humiliation at the hands of foreigners in the nineteenth and twentieth centuries) has bred a strong sense of national pride. Mao's Communists capitalized on this sense of nationalism by melding the struggle for communism with the bitter struggle to expel the Japanese occupiers during World War II.

Fierce nationalism, often manifested as xenophobia, has been a cornerstone of Chinese political culture. Communist leaders frequently use nationalism to maintain support for the political system. China's hostile reaction to the inadvertent U.S. bombing of China's embassy in Yugoslavia in 1999 and the downing of a surveillance plane in 2001, widespread anti-Japanese street protests in 2005, and angry Chinese reactions to foreign protests leading up to the 2008 Summer Olympics are all manifestations of this Chinese nationalism. Indeed, China's successful hosting of the Beijing Olympics both expressed and confirmed the key role of patriotism and nationalism in twenty-first-century China. More recently, China has stirred nationalist sentiment in its territorial disputes with Japan and several Southeast Asian countries over contested islands in the East and South China Seas.

CHALLENGES TO CHINA'S COMMUNIST POLITICAL CULTURE

There is growing evidence that the strict party control of Chinese political culture is steadily eroding. The widespread support for the pro-reform student movement in Tiananmen Square in 1989 was the first major sign that the Communist Party no longer had a monopoly on political ideas (even as the party's crushing of the protests demonstrated that the state retained a monopoly of force). Subsequent years have seen steady growth in dissent and protest by China's rural poor, disgruntled industrial workers, and disaffected ethnic minorities. The spiritual success of Falun Gong and China's thousands of illegal Christian "house churches" has frightened the Chinese government, especially these groups' ability to attract and mobilize followers independent of state control. As noted earlier, Internet and social media usage vital to economic growth has exploded in China and created a venue for Chinese social and political activism. For better or worse, booming trade and study and travel abroad have released a flood of Western ideas and values. In sum, it is unclear how long China's leaders can depend on a largely passive and compliant public, especially as rapid economic growth and globalization create new tensions, problems, and opportunities.

Political Economy

From 1949 to 1978, China adopted a Soviet-style communist political-economic model. In choosing this model, Mao Zedong and the CCP leadership consciously opted for equality over freedom. They promised all Chinese an **iron rice bowl** (lifetime employment, health care, and retirement security) and retained state ownership of all property and full control of the economy through central planning. State bureaucrats assigned targets and quotas to producers at all levels of the economy and allocated basic goods to consumers.

As in the Soviet Union, this centrally planned political-economic model favored the development of heavy industry at the expense of consumer goods. It also led to the creation of a massive state economic policy-making bureaucracy not present in capitalist political economies. Between 1949 and 1952, the state gradually nationalized most private industries and mobilized the economy to recover from the eight years of war with Japan and two decades of civil war. By 1952, the communist state had redistributed land to more than 300 million landless peasants. In the mid-1950s, peasants were strongly encouraged to form larger agricultural cooperatives by pooling land, equipment, and labor and sharing profits; such cooperatives gave the state greater political control over the countryside.

Despite the agrarian roots of the Chinese revolution, Mao and the CCP sought to rapidly industrialize China by launching a crash industrialization campaign called the Great Leap Forward (1958–60). Mao believed that China's communist-led masses could be harnessed to carry out rapid industrial growth. To pursue that goal, he favored a policy of **Reds versus experts**—setting politically indoctrinated party cadres (Reds) over those with economic training (experts). Vowing to progress "twenty years in a day" and to catch up with the industrialized West in 15 years, Mao promoted the creation of small-scale, labor-intensive industry (so called backyard industries) in both cities and the countryside. The Great Leap Forward also collectivized agriculture by creating gigantic communes that became party-controlled providers of education, health care, public works, and industrial production. Ultimately, however, the Great Leap Forward was a colossal failure. The diversion of energy from agriculture to inefficient industry and a drop in food production caused by the forced collectivization of farm production were largely responsible for a three-year famine that killed tens of millions of Chinese people.

By the early 1960s, Mao had been marginalized from the realm of economic policy making, and most of his Great Leap Forward policies had been abandoned. Although agricultural communes remained in place, peasant households were permitted to grow small, private plots. Once they met state production quotas, the peasants were permitted to sell their surplus on the free market. Industries began to emphasize expertise over political correctness and material over moral incentives.

In response to his own marginalization, Mao attacked these new policies as "capitalist." In 1966, he launched the Great Proletarian Cultural Revolution. The persecution unleashed during the next decade targeted those with the most expertise, and the impact on the education system and the economy was devastating. Following several years of utter chaos in which schools were closed and many factories shut down, Mao's disastrous policies were once again shelved.

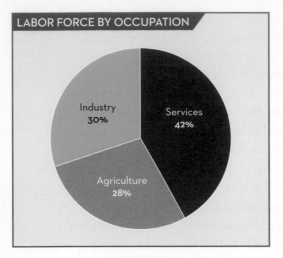

LABOR FORCE BY OCCUPATION

Services 42%

Industry 30%

Agriculture 28%

The chaos of the Cultural Revolution left China a poor and isolated economy. However, things started to improve after the death of Mao in 1976. By late 1978, under the leadership of Deng Xiaoping, economic reform and opening began in fits and starts as the Chinese Communist leadership shifted its focus from the traditional communist goal of equity to creating rapid economic growth.[15] Agricultural communes were disbanded and gradually replaced with the **household responsibility system**—a euphemism for largely private farming. Individual farmers still had to sell a set amount of their produce to the state, but they were free to sell any surplus on the open market. Food production grew dramatically, and the widespread famines that had plagued China for millennia became a thing of the past. Industries were decentralized; in their place, "collective" and "town and village" enterprises were allowed greater economic freedom and encouraged to generate profits. The importance of China's state sector gradually diminished, dropping from about 80 percent in 1980 to under 20 percent by 1996. By the mid-1980s, private industry was permitted (though initially heavily regulated), and the state gradually eliminated price controls. Hoping to end China's economic isolation, the government created **special economic zones** in 1979, offering tax breaks and other incentives to lure foreign investment to a handful of coastal enclaves.

During the 1990s, China's reformers shifted their focus to the urban industrial sector and devolved substantial economic decision-making authority to provincial and local officials and private entrepreneurs. China's socialist command economy had been transformed into what China's communist leaders acknowledged had become a "socialist market economy." These liberal reforms have sparked nearly four decades of astounding economic growth.

Growing at a pace and scope unprecedented in human history, China's economy expanded nearly 10 percent annually for the first three decades of reform and opening, and its GDP has grown some 15-fold. Hundreds of millions of people have been lifted out of poverty, but China remains a poor country. Its per capita GDP at purchasing power parity (PPP) in 2016 was only $14,600; thus China ranked 111th in the world, just ahead of Macedonia but far behind both Mexico (89th at $18,900) and Russia (71st at $26,100).

Prized for their dexterity and docility, single women comprise much of China's increasingly sophisticated assembly-line workforce.

State Capitalism and Foreign Investment

Communist China's twenty-first-century economy is decidedly capitalist. Since the 1990s, party-state reformers have sold off or closed down tens of thousands of inefficient state-owned enterprises (SOEs), putting millions of SOE employees out of work. Since 2002, the private sector's share of industrial output grew from just over half to over three-fourths of total output. But the remaining SOEs are very large, very important, and remain very much favored by China's capitalist system.[16]

In fact, the party-state has tightened its grip on a number of "strategic" industries at the commanding heights of the economy, such as oil and coal, transport, and telecommunication. Of the 98 Chinese firms in the *Fortune* 500 list of the world's largest companies in 2015, the top 12 and all but 22 of them were SOEs. These state firms receive preferential lending, favored market access, and other benefits—privileges that have enhanced their growth and made employment there highly desirable and quite lucrative for Chinese executives. Moreover, the party-state has retained partial or substantial ownership in many of China's ostensibly "private" firms.

Although China's "state capitalism" has permitted the party-state to retain firm control over China's economy and to nurture infant industries in key sectors such as green technology and automobiles, critics note that state-sponsored industrial policies have led to inefficiency, corruption, and surplus labor in the state sector. They have allowed the SOEs to consume the largest share of credit granted by state-owned banks. Despite these drawbacks, China's continued success with its version of state-led capitalism has led some to give this neomercantilist development model the label **Beijing consensus**—an alternative to the long-standing neoliberal free-market developmental model championed by the West and often labeled the "Washington consensus."

In addition, this preferential state treatment for domestic firms has hampered prospects for foreign companies investing or doing business in what has long been coveted as the world's largest potential consumer market. Many observers predicted that China's entry into the World Trade Organization (WTO) in 2001 would spur additional privatization and liberalization. Its WTO membership has required China to take significant market-opening measures; and domestic firms, especially SOEs, face growing competition from foreign enterprises. Still, despite the significant liberalization of the Chinese economy, the country's economic system remains substantially closed. China's economy is freer than Nigeria's and Brazil's but is still more restricted than the economies of Mexico, India, and South Africa.[17]

China's Growth Model Brings Challenges

Reform and opening has created rapid growth as well as huge problems. First, as China's enterprises have become more profit oriented, employers are free to lay off unproductive labor. As a result, Mao's iron rice bowl has given way to labor mobility, job uncertainty, and unemployment. The Chinese leadership is betting that China's growing private sector will be able to absorb the unemployed, but the economy must produce at least 25 million jobs a year just to keep up.

Second, after decades of communist emphasis on equality, the reforms of the past four decades have made China much less equal. Inequality has grown between individuals, between urban and rural Chinese, and between regions. China's Gini index (a measure of economic inequality: a score of 0 equals perfect equality, and 100 equals perfect inequality) rose from 16 in 1978 to 39 in 1988. The number peaked at 49 in 2008, and as of 2014 remains at 47. This figure compares with 48 in Mexico, 45 in the United States, and 42 in Russia for the same year.

Much of China's inequality is regional. Most of the activity in direct foreign investment and industrialization is concentrated along China's eastern coast, especially in Guangdong Province, Shanghai, Beijing, and Tianjin. Although development is creeping westward and inland megacities such as Chongqing are now full participants in China's explosive economic growth, much of China's poorer hinterland has received far less investment.

Thus China is rapidly urbanizing, but nearly half of its population still lives in the countryside. Early economic reforms largely benefited the rural areas, but more recent reforms have focused primarily on China's cities, and much of rural China remains desperately poor and largely neglected. Prices for agricultural goods are low, taxes are high, school is expensive, health care is poor, and the modern consumer amenities that are increasingly available in urban China are mostly absent in rural areas.

This disparity among regions has pushed hundreds of millions of Chinese to migrate to the cities to escape rural poverty, pulled by the lure of factory jobs and employment in the growing service sector. Although this internal migration is not illegal, most rural Chinese who migrate to cities are unable to secure an urban *hukou*, or residency permit, and therefore are excluded from the relatively more generous urban welfare system. This means that benefits provided to urban *hukou* holders, such as state-provided health care, pensions, unemployment insurance, and education, are for the most part denied to these rural migrants. Even with this discrimination, the state has been unable to stem the tide of migration, despite recent promises to redress the imbalance between urban and rural benefits from reform and opening.

Third, rapid industrial development has created huge resource shortages and environmental damage for China. A fourth of the country is desert, and three-fourths of its forests have disappeared. Its rivers are drying up, and the water and air that remain are filling with harmful chemicals. Half a billion Chinese lack access to safe drinking water, and an equal number breathe dangerously unsafe air—the Chinese are literally "choking on their own success."[18] And increasingly, China's problem has become the world's problem: China surpassed the United States in 2008 as the world's largest emitter of greenhouse gases, and its voracious economy is consuming world resources at an unprecedented rate. Last, China's exports, the engine of its growth, are also causing problems as its trade surplus with its trading partners grows and controversy mounts concerning China's violation of intellectual property rights and the safety and quality of its products.

Add to these growing pains of rapid development a final, potentially far more serious problem: China's economic growth engine is slowing. More than three decades of nearly 10 percent annual GDP growth have given way since 2012 to GDP growth that is averaging closer to 7.5 percent. While this pace is still far more rapid than any of the advanced industrialized economies (or even most developing economies), the prospect of declining growth is particularly troublesome to a government that has staked its legitimacy on the ability to continue delivering prosperity to its populace. Many argue that China's reform process finds itself at a crossroads in which China's leaders will have to make difficult choices while pursuing deep structural changes in the near future.

Disagreement about how to proceed with these reforms has led to the emergence of two broad factions within China's core leadership. One faction, known as **populists**, is led by former paramount leader Hu Jintao and includes current premier Li Keqiang. Leaders in this faction worked their way up through the CCP, often beginning in humble circumstances and serving as local and provincial leaders in poor inland provinces. While recognizing the need for continued reform, the populists favor equality and the need to address China's growing economic disparities, unemployment, and the tattered social safety net.

The other faction, known as **elitists**, is led by Hu Jintao's predecessor, Jiang Zemin, and includes current paramount leader Xi Jinping among others. Leaders in this faction, also known as "princelings," are the offspring of former high-ranking officials. They favor economic freedom and efficiency over equality. Xi Jinping has called for measures to ensure continued economic growth and the strengthening of China's integration into the global economy.

How will this factional struggle play out, and what will it mean for China's twenty-first-century economy? Optimists argue that this "team of rivals" will balance each other out, ensuring that the imperatives of economic freedom and equality will be met. Pessimists caution that if growth continues to slow and economic, social, and environmental conditions continue to worsen, factional compromise may turn to feuding with grave consequences for the world's largest economy.[19]

Foreign Relations and the World

During much of their long history, the Chinese viewed themselves as economically and culturally superior to the rest of the world. When nineteenth-century incursions by more economically and militarily advanced powers (both Western and Japanese) shattered that perception, Chinese society entered an extended period of crisis and self-doubt. The defeat of the Japanese at the end of World War II in 1945 ended the humiliation of Japan's brutal occupation of China, and in 1949, the victorious government sought to restore China's past grandeur. China's return to relative isolation reached its zenith during the Cultural Revolution, when Mao Zedong attacked all foreign cultural and economic influences. China was not only isolated from Western capitalist nations and most of its neighbors but also estranged from its erstwhile mentor, the Soviet Union, beginning in the late 1950s—when Soviet and Chinese policies diverged after Stalin's death.

Since Mao's death in 1976, China has steadily emerged from decades of isolation under the policy of reform and opening. U.S. president Richard Nixon's historic visit to China in 1972 marked the beginning of China's opening to the West and reengagement with the rest of the world. By the end of the 1970s, the United States and most other countries had normalized relations with Communist China and had, in effect, ceased to recognize the anticommunist regime in Taiwan. Today, China's position as the world's largest economy, its growing military might and technological prowess, and its status as a permanent member of the UN Security Council make it an important international power. However, the country's long legacy of isolation continues to color its foreign relations and inform its official rhetoric.

Precisely because of its rapidly growing influence, scholars and diplomats have debated whether China's emergence as a key global actor would be the kind of "peaceful rise" Chinese leaders have promised. Skeptics point to frequent outbursts of nationalist rhetoric from government officials and the public. They doubt that economic liberalization and increased trade will moderate Chinese behavior toward its neighbors and make it a more peaceful member of the international community. They point to China's huge and growing demand for natural resources and the territorial disputes and questionable alliances those resource needs have fostered.

Optimists point to these same economic interdependencies and to China's remarkably successful staging of the 2008 Olympics as evidence that the country's growth has given it both the need and the confidence to participate fully as a peaceful leader of the international community. They note that although there has been some friction along the way, as China's regional and global interests and involvement have expanded, China has continued to improve its relations with much of the world over the past two decades, signing major accords with the European Union, Russia, Japan, and the Association of Southeast Asian Nations (ASEAN).

By far the most serious threat to China's peaceful rise is the potential conflict over the future of Taiwan, which is located only 100 miles off the coast of the Chinese mainland. After the victory of the Chinese Communists in 1949, Nationalist (Kuomintang) troops under Chiang Kai-shek retreated to Taiwan, where Chiang established the Republic of China and claimed the island as the temporary location of the legitimate government of all China. Although Taiwan prospered as a capitalist authoritarian state under Nationalist rule and gained the military protection of the United States during the Cold War, at the urging of the PRC, it was forced to surrender its claim to China's UN seat in 1971. The United States (along with most other nations) effectively ceased to recognize Taiwan after formal diplomatic relations were established with China in 1979. By the 1980s, Taiwan appeared increasingly vulnerable to Chinese attack.

The CCP leadership has always regarded Taiwan as a province of China and therefore a "core interest," and has persistently demanded the full reintegration of Taiwan into the PRC.[20] China has historically threatened Taiwan—first with bombardment, and later with harsh rhetoric and military displays—and wooed it with promises of enhanced economic ties. The Chinese have repeatedly claimed that they would view any declaration of independence by Taiwan as an act of war. Tensions have become more volatile since Taiwan democratized in the late 1980s and since Taiwan's citizens have had more freedom to voice their preferences. In the 1990s, the PRC sought to intimidate voters in Taiwan's presidential election by using aggressive military exercises and veiled threats. The United States' unique relationship with Taiwan and the continued promises of military protection and weapons sales have often proved to be a thorn in the side of Sino-U.S. relations. Despite the continued tension between Taiwan and China, however, Taiwan's trade and investment with China have grown rapidly in recent years and were normalized with the signing of a free-trade pact in 2010. China is now Taiwan's largest trading partner and largest investment destination. While this situation inexorably draws the two economies closer together, it also prompts fears among Taiwan nationalists about the dangers of this growing dependency.

The case of Hong Kong may provide a model for peaceful resolution of the Taiwan issue. British gunboats forced imperial China to cede the island of Hong Kong to England in the nineteenth century. The island and surrounding territory were ruled as a British colony for more than 150 years. During that time, the colony became a successful capitalist economic powerhouse and gateway to Communist China.

In the 1980s, China and the United Kingdom agreed to a plan that would return Hong Kong to Chinese sovereignty in 1997 under the principle of **one country, two systems**. The Chinese guaranteed Hong Kong virtual autonomy for a transitional period of 50 years, a pledge that it has thus far respected in most regards. China has argued that a Hong Kong–style reintegration of Taiwan into the PRC would involve little or no disruption for the Taiwanese. However, China's handling of social unrest in Tibet and Xinjiang and its recent meddling in Hong Kong affairs have left many of Taiwan's citizens skeptical.

If ties between China and Taiwan have been warming, relations with neighboring Japan have not. Despite strong economic connections, bitter memories of Japan's brutal occupation of China during World War II have been exacerbated by a tense territorial standoff between the region's two dominant powers. Known as the Diaoyu (China) or Senkaku (Japan) islands, this grouping of uninhabited outcroppings lies almost equidistant (roughly 200 miles) from the Chinese mainland and Japan's Okinawa. Although Japan currently maintains control over the islands, both countries claim sovereignty and assert rights to the region's abundant fishing resources and seabed petroleum reserves. Moreover, vocal nationalist interests in both countries have spurred growing tensions that risk spiraling into military conflict. Even more controversially, China has been stepping up claims of sovereignty over islands and coral reefs in the South China Sea that have strained relations with Vietnam, the Philippines, Malaysia, and Brunei. These unilateral and increasingly strident claims have led many to question the prospects of China's "peaceful rise" as a regional and global power and have contributed to the Obama administration's decision to shift increasing attention to the region in what the United States deemed a "pivot" to Asia.

Farther to the south, rivalry with India, with which China fought a border war in the early 1960s, has given way to recent agreements to resolve outstanding border disputes. China became India's largest trading partner in 2010. These two regional nuclear powers are poor but rapidly developing countries with populations exceeding 1 billion, and the potential for a dangerous confrontation between them has diminished in recent decades. India has recognized Chinese sovereignty over Tibet, but has also provided refuge for the Dalai Lama and the exiled Tibetan government. China once supported Pakistan in its conflict with India but is now officially neutral.

In 2001, China and Russia signed their first friendship treaty in 50 years. In 2008, the two countries resolved their final border disputes, bringing to an end what had been a long-standing Cold War rivalry for world communist leadership.

China has also played an important role in the growing global concern about the nuclear capabilities of North Korea, its neighbor and traditional ally. Despite talk of a Beijing consensus, North Korea shows only vague interest in the Chinese model of gradual economic liberalization. It maintains a closed state and a communist political economy similar to Maoist China's policies. Nevertheless, since the end of the Cold War, China has been North Korea's only reliable ally and its chief source of economic aid. This special relationship has given China a key role in diplomatic efforts to address North Korean threats. China must balance its relationship with this often prickly and unpredictable neighbor with its now-booming trade and investment ties with capitalist South Korea and its strong desire to maintain peace in the region.

Ever since President Nixon's visit, China's volatile relationship with the United States has been characterized by periodic tension and mistrust. When U.S. pilots mistakenly bombed the Chinese embassy in Belgrade in 1999, China's leadership responded with bellicose rhetoric that alarmed U.S. leaders. In 2001, China and the United States faced off over China's capture of a U.S. surveillance plane that was forced to make an emergency landing on Chinese soil; China's leaders responded to the incident by issuing statements explicitly inciting anti-American sentiment reminiscent of the Maoist era.

Since the events of September 11, 2001, however, security relations between China and the United States have generally improved. Although some Chinese intellectuals viewed the attacks on the United States as understandable retaliation for so-called U.S. imperialist behavior, China supported the U.S. invasion of Afghanistan and the broader war on terrorism (though not the U.S. invasion of Iraq in 2003 or the Western intervention in the Libyan civil war in 2011).

China viewed with understandable concern the Obama administration's claimed "pivot" to Asia in 2011. Though this shift was explained as a "rebalancing" of the U.S. economic and security focus from the Atlantic to the Pacific region, the Chinese viewed it as yet another American "encirclement" campaign designed to threaten and thwart legitimate Chinese interests.[21] Ironically, though Obama's presidency did little to make good on the promise of an Asian pivot, the subsequent Trump administration, though elected on an "America First" platform, has found itself increasingly at odds with China on regional issues involving Taiwan, the Korean peninsula, and the South China Sea. And increasingly, China's interests are not just regional but worldwide, as it "goes global," seeking resources, markets, and other interests beyond the Pacific region to include Europe, Africa, and the Middle East.[22] To this end, in

2014 Xi Jinping called for the establishment of a twenty-first-century version of China's ancient "silk road" that first brought silk, ceramics, and tea to the West. China has proposed two separate routes and has begun to finance both overland infrastructure from China's northeast through Central Asia, Turkey, and on to Europe and a second, maritime trade route through the Indian Ocean and the Persian Gulf. Not all of the parties concerned share China's enthusiasm, but few have been able to resist its generous investment offers or the prospects of its huge market.

Likewise, despite the very real tensions between the United States and China, at the heart of their bilateral relationship is the more than $600 billion in two-way trade and the substantial direct investment ties that bind the two countries. China is currently America's largest trading partner (surpassing Canada for the first time in 2015), and the United States is number-one on China's trade list. This huge trade flow is immensely beneficial to both countries' economies, but it has been controversial in the United States. Critics claim that China's currency has been artificially undervalued and its domestic market unfairly shielded from American imports. They charge that these unfair trade practices have given Chinese exports an unfair competitive advantage and have led to the large and growing American trade deficit with China. In the coming years, this bilateral relationship is certain to remain of utmost importance to both countries, to the region, and to the world.

CURRENT ISSUES IN CHINA

Can Polluted China Go Green?

The current state of China's environment is horrific. Air, water, and soil pollution in many areas of the country have reached toxic levels; in recent years, "airpocalypses" in northern Chinese cities have made visibility difficult, breathing dangerous, and respiratory ailments almost inevitable. Water scarcity, desertification, deforestation, the silting of rivers, salinization of soil, and carbon emissions threaten not only China's people and lands but also increasingly China's neighbors and the entire planet. China contains 9 of the 10 most polluted cities in the world, and a 2015 study estimated that air pollution alone led to the premature death of over 1.6 million Chinese in 2014.[23] In recent years, China has become the world's biggest producer of greenhouse gases and the largest consumer of energy. The country showers much of Asia with toxic acid rain; and it discards over 50 billion pairs of disposable chopsticks annually, produced from some 25 million imported trees. Although it is certainly not the first industrializing country to face environmental challenges, China's sheer size and the rapid pace of its development have made the country's pollution problems particularly daunting and their potential consequences dire.

China's acute environmental problems have their roots in the Maoist communist developmental model, which focused on heavy industrialization, wasteful technologies, and pricing policies that undervalued the true cost of inputs such as coal and water and overvalued the economy's industrial outputs.[24] The

The "airpocalypse" that has plagued northern China in recent winters offers graphic evidence of the acute environmental problems facing the country.

policies of reform and opening have only exacerbated the environmental crisis. Lacking other sources of legitimacy, China's reformers have pursued growth at all costs in order to boost employment and thereby maintain social and political stability. The party-state has also devolved the bulk of industrial decision-making authority to local officials who have both autonomy and incentive to promote industrialization with little concern for the negative environmental impact of their choices. China has welcomed foreign investment from countries such as Japan, Korea, Taiwan, and the United States. These nations have been happy to export their polluting industries to China rather than retain them in their own backyards.

Finally, China's growing middle class has anxiously pursued the habits and lifestyles of comfort and conspicuous consumption it has seen elsewhere. Everyone in China aspires to own a car, and many consumers now have the means to attain this dream. China has surpassed the United States as the world's largest auto market, leading critics to warn that China is simply too populated and the world's resources too scarce for its citizens to mimic the lifestyles of the West. If China were to achieve parity with the United States in per capita car ownership, it would possess well over a billion cars—more than the entire global fleet of vehicles in 2011.

What is the solution? Can China "go green"? Although China's environmental situation is bleak, those concerned about pollution point to signs of hope. China's urban middle class has begun to adopt not just modern consumption patterns but also increasingly postmodern and postmaterialist values concerned with health, the environment, and quality of life. More broadly, the swelling numbers of victims of this pollution are becoming increasingly vocal in speaking out and organizing successful protests against local developers and local government officials.

For the first time, the party-state is not only tolerating but also encouraging the efforts of environmental NGOs to address China's many environmental problems. And perhaps most promising, government planners have targeted green energy as a leading growth sector in China's ongoing economic development and have invested heavily in hydroelectric, solar, wind, and clean coal technologies. China has been able to leapfrog to the latest green technologies, using government subsidies and its huge domestic market to obtain a significant share of the global renewable energy market. It has constructed dozens of dams and deployed extensive wind and solar farms domestically. Optimists both inside and outside China argue that the same combination of strong state leadership and entrepreneurial drive that fueled China's remarkable industrialization is now pushing China toward a solution to its huge environmental problems. Time will tell if China can indeed match its industrialization miracle with an environmental one.

China's Developmental Model and the Problem of Corruption

Environmental pollution poses a very real threat to China's continued development; however, many scholars point to political and economic corruption as an even more insidious challenge to China's economic growth and political stability. All political economies are vulnerable to the abuse of public office for private gain, but authoritarian regimes are particularly susceptible due to the absence of transparency and the rule of law.

Corruption is not just a recent problem in the PRC; the protests a quarter century ago at Tiananmen were motivated by broad dissatisfaction with elite privilege and corrupt practices, not demands for democracy. And while some scholars have argued that China's greater reliance on market competition since then would limit corruption, the combination of increased wealth (more spoils for the taking) and the devolution of decision-making authority to local officials (more public offices for the exploiting) have increased incentives to engage in bribery, kickbacks, rent-seeking, patronage, nepotism, and outright theft.

The costs of corruption to China are significant. Estimates place the outright economic costs of political corruption as high as $100 billion annually, but these corrupt practices exact a far higher toll. They exacerbate inequality, further harm the environment, undermine the legitimacy of the party-state, and feed social frustration with elite privilege. Recognizing this, China's leaders from Mao to the present have launched periodic anticorruption campaigns. But the sweeping effort undertaken by current leader Xi Jinping is impressive both in its breadth and in Xi's willingness to take on top-ranking officials.

Promising to go after both "flies and tigers" (both low- and high-ranking officials), Xi's government announced the arrest and punishment of 182,000 officials for corruption and the abuse of power in 2013. Among those arrested in recent years are wealthy red capitalists, top-ranking military officers, government ministers, and even the high-ranking party cadre. Among the latter is Chongqing party chief **Bo Xilai**, who before his highly publicized arrest and trial in 2013 had been on track to join the PSC as one of China's handful of core party leaders.

Ironically, Xi's anticorruption campaign may cost China's economy even more than the corrupt activities it has ostensibly targeted. Wealthy government officials, business elites, and their families have drastically cut back on the gift giving, parties, and under-the-table deals that have lubricated the "connections" or *guanxi* so important to political and economic transactions in today's China. Economists have estimated that this drop in consumption and the dampening effect of these austerity measures could lead to a loss of over $100 billion in economic activity annually. Others have concluded that this calculation of economic loss is beside the point. They argue that the real purpose of these anticorruption campaigns is to enhance political legitimacy in the eyes of the masses and to eliminate political rivals. In short, the deeply institutionalized corruption of China's authoritarian regime presents a dangerous double-edged sword. As former party elder Chen Yun once stated, "Fight corruption too little and destroy the country; fight it too much and destroy the Party."

NOTES

1. Mark Elvin, *The Pattern of the Chinese Past* (Palo Alto, CA: Stanford University Press, 1973).
2. Qianlong, letter to George III, 1793, Internet Modern History Sourcebook, Fordham University, 1998, www.fordham.edu/halsall/mod/1793qianlong.html (accessed 5/18/17).
3. For a list of quotations, see Mao Zedong, *Quotations from Chairman Mao Tse Tung*, Mao Tse Tung Internet Archive, 2000, www.marxists.org/reference/archive/mao/works/red-book (accessed 5/18/17).
4. Bruce Gilley, "The Limits of Authoritarian Resilience," *Journal of Democracy* 14 (2003): 18.
5. See Amnesty International, "China: 'Strike Hard' Anti-Crime Campaign Intensifies," press release, July 23, 2002, web.amnesty.org/library/Index/engASA170292002?Open (accessed 11/17/03).
6. China's 23 provinces include the island of Taiwan, claimed by the PRC. The four provincial-level municipalities refer to the megacities of Beijing, Shanghai, Tianjin, and Chongqing. The five autonomous regions are Inner Mongolia, Xinjiang, Guangxi, Ningxia, and Tibet. Hong Kong and Macao are separately counted as "special administrative regions."
7. Salvatore Babones, "A Rural Incubator for China's Political Reforms?" *Foreign Affairs* (October 14, 2015), www.foreignaffairs.com/articles/china/2015-10-14/country-lessons (accessed 6/22/16).
8. Mao Zedong, "Problems of War and Strategy," in *Selected Works*, vol. 2 (Beijing: Foreign Language Press, 1965), 225.
9. See *Hurun Report*, September 22, 2011, www.hurun.net/usen/NewsShow.aspx?nid=154 (accessed 11/9/11), and October 14, 2015, www.hurun.net/en/ArticleShow.aspx?nid=14678 (accessed 6/22/16).
10. See, for example, Richard McGregor, *The Party: The Secret World of China's Communist Rulers* (New York: HarperCollins, 2010).

11. Like many Chinese, Deng Xiaoping was an avid bridge player.
12. Francis Fukuyama, "China and East Asian Democracy: Patterns of History," *Journal of Democracy* 23 (January 2012): 14–26.
13. Bruce Dickson, *Red Capitalists in China: The Party, Private Entrepreneurs and Prospects for Political Change* (Cambridge, UK: Cambridge University Press, 2003).
14. See, for example, George Gilboy and Eric Heginbotham, "China's Coming Transformation," *Foreign Affairs* (July/August 2001): 26–39, and Jessica Teets, "Let Many Civil Societies Bloom: The Rise of Consultative Authoritarianism in China," *China Quarterly* 213 (March 2013): 19–38.
15. Gordon White, *Riding the Tiger: The Politics of Economic Reform in Post-Mao China* (Palo Alto, CA: Stanford University Press, 1993).
16. Nicholas Lardy, *Markets over Mao: The Rise of Private Business in China*, Washington, DC: Peterson Institute for International Economics, 2014.
17. James Gwartney, et al., "Economic Freedom of the World: 2016 Annual Report," The Fraser Institute (2016), www.fraserinstitute.org/sites/default/files/economic-freedom-of-the-world-2016.pdf (accessed 5/18/17).
18. Joseph Kahn and Jim Yardley, "As China Roars, Pollution Reaches Deadly Extremes," *New York Times*, August 26, 2007.
19. Cheng Li, "China's Team of Rivals," *Foreign Policy* (March/April 2009): 88–93.
20. Scott L. Kastner, *Political Conflict and Economic Interdependence across the Taiwan Strait and Beyond* (Palo Alto, CA: Stanford University Press, 2009).
21. Robert E. Kelly, "The 'Pivot' and Its Problems: American Foreign Policy in Northeast Asia," *Pacific Review* 27, no. 3 (2014): 479–503.
22. David Shambaugh, *China Goes Global: The Partial Power* (Oxford: Oxford University Press, 2013).
23. Dan Levin, "Study Links Polluted Air in China to 1.6 Million Deaths a Year," *New York Times*, August 13, 2015, www.nytimes.com/2015/08/14/world/asia/study-links-polluted-air-in-china-to-1-6-million-deaths-a-year.html (accessed 6/23/16).
24. Kenneth Lieberthal, *Governing China: From Revolution through Reform* (New York: W. W. Norton, 2004), 277–79.

KEY TERMS

Beijing consensus Neomercantilist model of state-led capitalist development adopted by China and proposed as alternative to Western neoliberal model known as the Washington consensus

Bo, Xilai High-ranking CCP official arrested in 2013 on anticorruption charges

Chinese Communist Party (CCP) Authoritarian party that has ruled China from 1949 to the present

Chinese Dream Paramount leader Xi Jinping's policy vision calling for China's national rejuvenation, modernization, and prosperity

Confucianism Philosophy attributed to Chinese sage Confucius (551–479 B.C.E.) emphasizing social harmony

Cultural Revolution Mao's radical movement launched in 1966 to regain political control from rivals and resulting in a decade of social and political chaos

danwei **(work unit) system** Maoist program providing all Chinese citizens lifetime affiliation with a work unit governing all aspects of their lives

Deng, Xiaoping Paramount leader (1978–97) who launched China's policy of economic reform and opening

elitists Faction of CCP officials who are the offspring of former high-ranking cadre and who favor economic growth and market liberalization

Falun Gong Meditative martial arts movement founded in 1992 and banned by the Chinese government in 1999 as an "evil cult"

floating population China's roughly 150 million itinerant peasants who have been leaving the countryside seeking urban employment since the 1990s

Great Leap Forward Mao's disastrous 1958–60 effort to modernize China through localized industrial production and agricultural communes

harmonious society CCP propaganda term for the continuation of economic reform but with more concern for the growing wealth and welfare gap between urban and rural China

household responsibility system Deng's highly successful 1980s rural reform program that lowered production quotas and allowed the sale of surplus agricultural produce on the free market

Hu, Jintao China's paramount leader from 2002 to 2012

hukou **(household registration) system** Maoist program that tied all Chinese to a particular geographic location

Hundred Flowers Campaign Program (1956–57) in which Mao encouraged intellectuals to offer criticism of national policy, followed by crackdown on critics

iron rice bowl Term for Mao's promise of cradle-to-grave health care, work, and retirement security, which has largely disappeared under reform and opening

Jiang, Zemin Deng's successor in the 1990s as China's paramount leader

Kuomintang (KMT) China's Nationalist Party founded by Sun Yat-sen and led by Chiang Kai-shek, who was overthrown by Mao's Communists in 1949 and forced to flee to Taiwan

Li, Keqiang China's premier and head of government (2013–)

Long March The CCP's 6,000-mile heroic retreat (1934–35) to northwestern China during the country's civil war with the Chinese Nationalist Party, KMT

Mao, Zedong Leader of the Chinese Communist revolution who dominated Chinese politics from the founding of the PRC until his death in 1976

May Fourth movement Student-led anti-imperialist cultural and political movement growing out of student demonstrations in Beijing on May 4, 1919

National Party Congress Chinese Communist Party's cumbersome legislative body; more akin to a national political party convention

National People's Congress (NPC) China's national legislature

one country, two systems Term for China's guarantee to Hong Kong of 50 years of domestic autonomy as a "special administrative region" after the British colony was returned to China in 1997

People's Liberation Army (PLA) China's military

populists Faction of CCP officials who have risen from relatively humble backgrounds and who favor decreasing inequality

red capitalists Private entrepreneurs who are also members of the CCP and whose interests generally align with those of the party-state

Red Guard Radicalized youth who served as Mao's shock troops during the Cultural Revolution

Reds versus experts Term describing Mao's policy favoring politically indoctrinated party cadres (Reds) over those people who had economic training (experts)

reform and opening Deng's economic liberalization policy, starting in the late 1970s

special economic zones Enclaves established since 1980 by the Chinese government that have offered tax breaks and other incentives to lure foreign investment

Sun, Yat-sen Founder of China's Nationalist Party (Kuomintang) and considered the father of modern China

Three Represents Jiang Zemin's 2001 policy co-opting private entrepreneurs into the CCP

Tiananmen Square Historic plaza in Beijing where the Chinese party-state crushed the 1989 pro-reform demonstration

Xi, Jinping China's paramount leader, serving simultaneously as head of the party (CCP general secretary), head of the state (PRC president), and head of the military (CMC chair)

WEB LINKS

- China general information: an unofficial site offering useful general information (www.chinatoday.com/general/a.htm)
- China's political system: this official government site describes the political structure, fundamental laws, rules, regulations, and practices of China since its founding (www.china.org.cn/english/Political/25060.htm).
- A Country Study, China: this Library of Congress Country Studies Series presents a description and analysis of the historical setting and the social, economic, political, and national security systems of China (lcweb2.loc.gov/frd/cs/cntoc.html).

9

Despite its incredible diversity, persistent ethnic and religious conflicts, and massive levels of poverty, India maintains a thriving democratic system. Here, a man in Amritsar prepares to cast his vote in the 2014 parliamentary elections. Over 550 million votes were cast in this election.

INDIA

Why Study This Case?

India presents a remarkable and instructive case for the study of comparative politics. This South Asian nation will, by 2022, eclipse China as the world's most populous country and in 2015 also outpaced China's gross domestic product (GDP) growth. Already, it is the world's largest democracy—more people vote in a typical election than the entire population of any other country in the world except China.

Besides being the largest, India is also one of the most improbable of democracies, and herein lies a key puzzle of this case. Scholars most often associate democracy with critical levels of prosperity, mass literacy, urbanization, and national unity. India seemingly disproves this theory with regard to each of these factors, because large, though declining, numbers of the population remain poor and illiterate. Paradoxically, poor and illiterate Indians—most often living in rural areas, not cities—are three times as likely to vote as the national average.

Most puzzling, perhaps, is how democracy can survive and thrive in a country so dangerously divided by history, language, religion, and **caste**. India has thousands of years of history as an authoritarian, hierarchical culture that has stratified, segmented, and compartmentalized its society. Today, more than 1.2 billion Indians speak some 325 distinct languages with more than 1,500 dialects.[1] They worship more than 5,000 gods, and six separate religions have at least 50 million adherents each. Caste divisions still segregate India socially, economically, and culturally. At times, these ethnic and social divisions have erupted into violent conflict and dramatic threats of secession. Given these circumstances, some observers marvel that the country can even stay together, let alone accommodate the cacophony of demands that present themselves.

INDIA

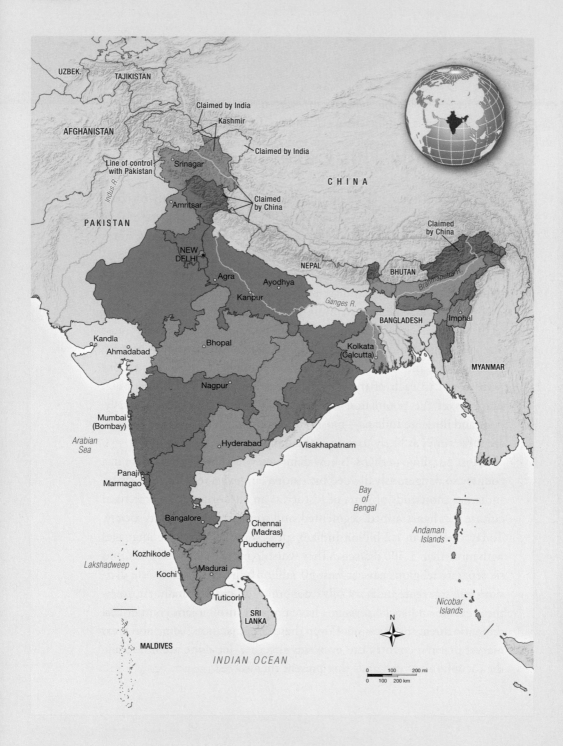

Others argue that democracy may not be so much the puzzle as the solution. A ponderous but flexible democracy may be the only way of holding this patchwork nation together. Before gaining its independence in 1947, India had already been introduced to—if not allowed to participate in—the liberal practices of its British imperial master. As a sovereign nation, it adopted the political institutions of British democracy, including the parliamentary model. This system has taken root and flourished, but it remains distinctly Indian. India thus offers comparative political scientists a useful petri dish for studying the transferability of democratic institutions to a postcolonial setting in a developing country and the challenges facing such a transplant.

In recent years, the greatest challenge to Indian democracy and political stability has come from persistent religious conflict and increasing fundamentalism. As this case will demonstrate, Sikh and Muslim separatism and Hindu chauvinism have threatened the very democratic system that has sought, so far successfully, to accommodate them. India prevailed in its struggle for colonial independence largely because of one devout Indian's ability to combine the Hindu concept of nonviolence with the liberal notions of tolerance and the separation of religion and state. The charismatic leadership of **Mahatma (Mohandas K.) Gandhi** and the political secularism of his followers successfully united an ethnically diverse colony in the common cause of national independence and democratic nation building.

As has been the case in nearly all other postcolonial countries, modernization has come neither quickly nor easily to India. This huge and still impoverished nation must juggle the maintenance of its notable democracy with the challenges of development and increasing globalization. Although India's urban centers can boast a prosperous and technically savvy elite minority that stands very much in the twenty-first century, the country's rapid economic development over the past two decades has left much of the rest of the population behind. So to the many other divisions threatening India's democracy and political integrity, we must add the inequalities of income and opportunity.

To some extent, India shares with most other less developed and newly industrializing countries the multiple and simultaneous threats of ethnic conflict, political instability, and economic inequality. In that regard, it offers insight into the challenges and opportunities that developing countries face. India is important not just because of its relative ability to manage these challenges democratically but also because its sheer size and growing international prominence guarantee it will have increasing influence in the rest of the world.

Major Geographic and Demographic Features

India looms large in both size and population, surpassed only by China as Asia's largest and most populous country. The country can be divided into two "triangles": a northern one pointing up, and a southern one pointing down. The northern triangle is home to territorial disputes that have led to four wars with Pakistan to the west and ongoing tension with China to the east. The northernmost state of Jammu and Kashmir, at the apex of the northern triangle, is claimed by both Pakistan and India and remains a volatile area of ethnic and nationalist dispute. The southern triangle forms a huge peninsula that juts into the Indian Ocean, historically buffering the area from India's neighbors but opening the region to Western trade and, ultimately, imperial conquest.

Both the climate and the politics of India have been profoundly shaped by geography. The Himalayas serve as towering sentinels on the northern border, shielding the subcontinent (comprising India, Pakistan, and Bangladesh) over the millennia from Siberian winds and Central Asian invaders. The Himalayas (Sanskrit for "abode of snow") are also the source of India's two most important river systems: the Indus, long the cradle of Indian civilization; and the Ganges, a river that Hindus value as sacred and worship as a goddess. These rivers and the sheltered climate of India's northern plains have made the north remarkably fertile, sustaining dense levels of civilization.

Crop production in southern India is no less important, but is riskier because of its dependence on the monsoons, the four summer months of heavy rains. A successful monsoon season—neither too little nor too much rain—can make the difference between drought or flood and famine or feast for many Indians. The **Green Revolution** of the 1960s and 1970s, with its technologically enhanced crops and cropping methods, improved production dramatically, particularly in the arid regions of the northwest. Nonetheless, India's rapidly growing population remains highly dependent on an agricultural economy, often called a "gamble in rains."[2]

Although India possesses a wide range of natural resources, its per capita endowment of oil, timber, minerals, and petroleum reserves is relatively low. More than half of all Indians remain dependent on an agrarian livelihood, comprising the world's largest population of peasants. And only China has more people. The United Nations predicts that India will not only soon surpass China as the world's most populous country but will continue to grow until around 2050, when, it is estimated, its population will peak at roughly 1.8 billion, or more than one-fourth of the world's total population.

The product of numerous waves of empire building, India's population is racially, ethnically, and linguistically diverse. The simplest division of Indian society is between the Aryans to the north and the Dravidians to the south, though this division is amplified by linguistic differences. In the north, most Indians speak some variety of Indo-Aryan, which is part of the Indo-European family of languages. Most common among these is **Hindi**, now one of two national languages (the other is English). Most people in the south speak one of four major dialects of the Dravidian language, which is almost completely distinct from Hindi. English has become the only universal language, but one that is spoken largely by the elite. Even so, India has more English-speaking citizens than Canada. The use of English has been a major factor not only in binding the country together but also in prompting many foreign firms to move some of their business transactions, such as call centers, to India. This **outsourcing** has become a growing part of the economy, and we will speak of it later in the section on India's economy.

Historical Development of the State

Civilization on the Indian subcontinent predates a unified Indian state by several thousand years. Three religious traditions and nearly a thousand years of foreign domination mark the contours of the gradual formation of a sovereign Indian state.

Hinduism, Buddhism, and Islam

Over 3,000 years ago, nomadic Indo-Aryans began migrating eastward from Persia into the northern and central plains of present-day India, subduing the darker-skinned Dravidians, many of whom moved southward. From the fusion of the two cultures emerged the customs, philosophical ideas, and religious beliefs associated with **Hinduism**. Like other traditional religions, Hinduism governs not just worship practices but also virtually all aspects of life, including the rituals and norms of birth, death, marriage, eating, and livelihood. For roughly the next 2,000 years, India enjoyed relative freedom from outside influence as Hindu traditions such as polytheism, reincarnation, and the social and political hierarchy of caste infused Indian society.

Because the caste system has so profoundly influenced Indian history, society, and politics, a brief introduction of the institution is in order. Like many other premodern societies, India's was divided and compartmentalized for thousands of years according to such categories as birth, region, occupation, and social obligations. However, its "caste" system (the term derived from the Portuguese *casta*, meaning "species" or "breed") was at once more complex and more flexible than often portrayed.

The term *caste* is typically used for two different but related types of social divisions. The first of these affiliations is known as *jati*, which refers to the thousands of separate but not wholly rigid occupational and regional groups and subgroups that make up Indian society (*Gandhi*, for instance, means "greengrocer"). Each category possessed its own detailed rules for the social behavior and interactions involved in such activities as eating, communicating, and marrying.

More generally, Indian society was also divided into four broader castes, or *varnas*, including Brahmins (priests), Kshatriyas (warriors and rulers), Vaishyas (traders and merchants), and Sudras (peasants and laborers). At the bottom of—technically outside—the hierarchy were the so-called untouchables. These people included two groups: those who performed duties deemed unclean, which involved handling the dead and disposing of human waste; and those aboriginals living outside village life, in the mountains or forests (often referred to as *tribals*). High-caste Hindus traditionally considered the touch or even the shadow of these outcastes as polluting.

In an effort to enhance social order, British colonial bureaucrats painstakingly cataloged these various classifications and hierarchies long sanctioned and legitimized by the Hindu religion, thereby rendering the castes increasingly rigid over time. In independent India, Hindu elites have used these social divisions to establish political patronage networks and to justify and enhance their dominant position in the caste system. Critics of the divisive and exploitative consequences of caste, however, have made efforts to ease the discrimination associated with it and, in particular, its deleterious effects on the untouchables. Mahatma Gandhi worked tirelessly on behalf of untouchables, referring to them as *harijans*, "the children of God." India's 1950 constitution not only banned that status but also legislated special "reservations," or affirmative action, designed to improve the lives of these disadvantaged groups, referred to in the constitution as "scheduled castes and tribes." Calling themselves Dalits ("suppressed groups"), they now number some 170 million people, or about 15 percent of the population.[3]

Under the auspices of Buddhism—a second religious tradition, originating in India in the sixth century B.C.E.—rulers commenced India's first efforts at nation building. Spreading Buddhism's message of peace and benevolence to subjects of all ethnic groups and social ranks, dynastic rulers unified much of what is now

TIMELINE OF POLITICAL DEVELOPMENT

YEAR	EVENT
1857–58	Sepoy Mutiny is put down, and formal British colonial rule is established.
1885	Indian National Congress is created.
1930	Gandhi leads a boycott of British salt.
1947	India gains independence from Britain; India and Pakistan are created with partition.
1948	Mahatma Gandhi is assassinated.
1947–64	Jawaharlal Nehru serves as prime minister until his death.
1971	India-Pakistan War leads to creation of Bangladesh.
1975–77	Indira Gandhi institutes emergency rule.
1984	Indira Gandhi launches military operations at Amritsar and is assassinated by Sikh bodyguards.
1984–86	Rajiv Gandhi serves as prime minister.
1991	Rajiv Gandhi is assassinated.
1992	Ayodhya mosque is destroyed.
1996	Electoral victory of the Bharatiya Janata Party (BJP) leads to the rise of coalition governments.
1998	Nuclear weapons are tested.
2002	Muslim-Hindu violence breaks out in Gujarat.
2004	Congress-led coalition defeats BJP coalition; Manmohan Singh becomes prime minister.
2005	India and United States begin negotiating controversial nuclear agreement.
2007	Pratibha Patil is elected India's first female president.
2008, 2011	Muslim terrorist bombings in Mumbai and other Indian cities.
2009	Congress-led coalition reelected; Singh continues as prime minister.
2014	BJP-led coalition wins election and Narendra Modi becomes prime minister.

India by the fourth century B.C.E. and remained in power for several hundred years. The development of the Silk Road by the first century C.E. spread Buddhism eastward to China and beyond. At home, however, Hinduism gradually reemerged as the dominant religion and has remained India's prevailing faith. Over 80 percent of Indians identify themselves as Hindu. Today, Hinduism is the world's third-largest religious tradition after Christianity and Islam.

India's 2,000 years of relative isolation gave way to more than a millennium of foreign domination that began with marauding Muslim invaders in the eighth century. (Foreign invasion and occupation did not end until India gained its independence from British imperialism and colonialism in 1947.) The arrival of this third religious tradition at the hands of martial Muslim rulers never fostered the kind of tolerance shared by Hindus and Buddhists. But the introduction of Islam to India gave birth to a new religious tradition, **Sikhism**, which shares beliefs and practices with both the Hindu and Muslim faiths. It also sowed persistent seeds of mutual animosity among India's Hindus, Muslims, and Sikhs. A final wave of Muslim invaders, descendants of Genghis Khan known as **Mughals** (Persian for "Mongol"), ruled a relatively unified India for several hundred years beginning in the sixteenth century. But by the eighteenth century, Mughal rule had weakened at the hands of growing internal Hindu and Sikh dissatisfaction and expanding Western imperialism.

British Colonialism

Beginning with the Portuguese and the Spanish in the sixteenth century and followed by the Dutch and the British by the seventeenth century, the lucrative spice trade beckoned European powers to the Indian Ocean. Lacking a strong centralized state, India was vulnerable to foreign encroachment, and the British in particular made significant commercial inroads. In 1600, the British Crown granted a monopoly charter to the private **East India Company**, which over the years perfected an imperial strategy of commercial exploitation. This private merchant company first cultivated trade, then exploited cheap labor, and ultimately succeeded in controlling whole principalities. It did so through a strategy of setting up puppet Mughal governors, known as *nabobs*, with British merchant advisers at their side. This **nabob game**, as the British called it, greatly facilitated the plundering of Indian wealth and resources.

The British introduced both the concept of private property and the English language. With the new language came its science, literature, and—perhaps most revolutionary—liberal political philosophy. Also, as the East India Company lost its monopoly on Indian trade, a growing number of British merchants sought Indian markets for British manufactures, particularly cotton cloth. Because British cotton was selling at less than half the price of local handmade cloth, this "free" trade put millions of Indian cloth makers out of work. Communication and transportation technology—the telegraph, print media, the postal system, and the railroad (the British laid some 50,000 miles of track)—did much to unify India and give its colonial subjects a shared recognition of their frustrations and aspirations. This was particularly true of those native Indians employed in the colonial military and civil service who were beginning to develop and articulate a sense of Indian nationalism.

Growing economic frustration, political awareness, and national identity led to the **Sepoy Mutiny** of 1857–58, a revolt backed by the Indian aristocracy and carried out by sepoys (Indian mercenaries employed by the British). The sepoys were incited to arms by the revelation that their British-issued guns fired bullets greased in either pork lard or beef tallow (offensive to Muslims and Hindus, respectively). The mutinous Indians failed largely because they were too divided, both by British design and by the long tradition of religious animosity that split the Hindu and Muslim conscripts. The failure of the revolt convinced the growing number of Indian nationalists that independence from British colonialism would first require national unity. To British authorities, the mutiny signaled the weakness of nabob rule, the threat of Indian anticolonialism, and the dangers of liberal ideas and institutions in the hands of the locals. In 1858, the British Parliament passed the Government of India Act, which terminated the East India Company's control of India and placed the territory under direct and far harsher colonial rule. Under this British **raj** (rule), civil servants and British troops replaced private merchants and puppet nabobs, and British talk of eventual Indian self-rule gave way to calls for the "permanent subjection of India to the British yoke."[4] The colony of India became the "brightest jewel in the crown of the British empire."[5]

The Independence Movement

By the end of the nineteenth century, calls for self-rule had become louder and more articulate, though they were still not unified. Two local organizations came to embody the anticolonial movement: the **Indian National Congress (INC)**—also referred to simply as Congress or the Congress Party—founded in 1885, and the **Muslim League**, founded in 1906. But hopes for a gradual transfer of power after World War I were instead met with increased colonial repression, culminating in a 1919 massacre in which British troops opened fire on unarmed civilians, murdering hundreds and wounding more than 1,000 innocent Indians.

This massacre galvanized Indian resistance and brought Mahatma (Mohandas K.) Gandhi, a British-trained lawyer, to the leadership of Congress and the broader independence movement. Gandhi, affectionately known by Indians as Mahatma, or "Great Soul," was born in 1869. He first experienced racism while practicing law in South Africa, when he was thrown out of the first-class compartment of a train because of his skin color. This event prompted his tactics of revolutionary nonviolent resistance, first practiced against South African discrimination and then perfected in India after his return there in 1914. In India, he adopted the simple dress, ascetic habits, and devout worship of a Hindu holy man and developed his philosophies of *satyagraha* (holding firmly to truth) and *ahimsa* (nonviolence, or love). He argued that truth and love combined in nonviolent resistance to injustice could "move the world." He also taught that Western industrial civilization must be rejected in favor of a simpler life. He led a charismatic nationalist movement embodied in his example of personal simplicity and campaigns for national self-sufficiency. The movement was punctuated by dramatic instances of nonviolent resistance, hunger strikes, and periods of imprisonment.

Gandhi led successful protests and nationwide boycotts of British commercial imports and employment in British institutions such as the courts, schools, and civil service. Perhaps the most successful of these protests was his 1930 boycott of British salt, which was heavily taxed by the colonial raj. In declaring the boycott, Gandhi led a group of followers on a well-publicized 200-mile march to the sea to gather salt—an act that violated the British monopoly. Upon their arrival, Gandhi and many others were jailed, and the independence movement garnered national and international attention.[6]

Gandhi's integrity and example, the charismatic draw of his remarkable strategy of nonviolence, and the increasingly repressive and arbitrary nature of colonial rule swelled the ranks of the independence movement. Among those who joined was a younger generation of well-educated leaders schooled in the modern ideas of socialism and democracy. Chief among them was **Jawaharlal Nehru**, who succeeded Gandhi as leader of the INC and ultimately became independent India's first prime minister.

Weakened by both economic depression and war, Britain was in no shape to resist Indian independence and entered into serious negotiations toward this end following World War II. The biggest obstacle to independence became not the British but disagreements and divisions among India's many interests, most particularly Hindus and Muslims. Fearful that Muslims, who constituted 25 percent of the population, would be unfairly dominated by the Hindu majority, Muslim leaders demanded a separate Muslim state. Negotiations collapsed as civil war broke out between militant adherents of the two faiths.

Against this background of growing violence, the British opted for **partition**, creating in 1947 the new state of Pakistan from the two regions of the subcontinent most heavily populated by Muslims: West Pakistan in the north-west and East Pakistan (what would become independent Bangladesh in 1971) in the northeast. From the remaining 80 percent of the colony, the British formed independent India. This declaration led to the uprooting and transmigration (in effect, ethnic cleansing) of more than 12 million refugees—Muslims to Pakistan, Hindus and Sikhs to India—across the hurriedly drawn boundaries. Authorities estimated that as many as 1 million Indians and Pakistanis were killed in the resulting chaos and violence.[7] Among the victims of this sectarian violence was Gandhi himself, assassinated in 1948 by a militant Hindu who saw the leader and his message of religious tolerance as threats to Hindu nationalism. Not surprisingly, the ethnic violence that marked partition and the birth of the Indian nation continues to plague Hindu-Muslim relations in contemporary India as well as India's relations with neighboring Pakistan.

Independence

Like many of the other newly minted countries that would become part of the postwar decolonization movement, independent India faced a host of truly daunting challenges. This included settling some 5 million refugees from East and West Pakistan, resolving outstanding territorial disputes, jump-starting an economy torn asunder by partition in an effort to feed the country's impoverished millions, and creating democratic political institutions from whole cloth. This last task, promised by Nehru and his INC, had to be carried out in the absence of the prosperity, literacy, and liberal traditions that allowed democracy to take hold in advanced democracies and seemed to many an unlikely prospect in India. Given India's particular circumstances and its kaleidoscopic social, political, and economic interests—what one author called "a million mutinies now"[8]—such an endeavor seemed particularly foolish.

Unlike many other postcolonial countries, however, India brought to the endeavor of democratization several distinct advantages. First, its lengthy, grad-ual, and inclusive independence movement generated a powerful and widespread sense of national identity. Although the country had not experienced a thorough-going social revolution in the style of Mexico or China, most Indians had come to identify themselves not just by their region, caste, or even religion but also as citizens of the new republic. The legacy of Gandhi's charismatic outreach to all Indians, including outcastes, Muslims, and Sikhs, brought much-needed (if per-haps ultimately tenuous) unity to its disparate population.

Second, although Indians did not control their own destiny under the British raj, the Indian intellectual class was well schooled in both the Western philosophies and the day-to-day practices of liberal democracy. Generations of the Indian elite had been taught in the British liberal tradition, and many of them had served faithfully in the colonial bureaucracy. By the time of independence, Indians for most practical purposes were in fact governing themselves, albeit following the dictates of a colonial power. Indeed, their appreciation of and aptitude for the virtues of democracy made its denial under British imperial rule seem all the more unjust.

Moreover, independent India inherited not just liberal ideas and traditions but also a sophisticated and generally well-functioning central state apparatus that included an extensive civil service and standing army. The comparison between a relatively democratic India and the more authoritarian Pakistan and Bangladesh is significant. Although all three shared a common British colonial heritage, the territories that would come to constitute Pakistan and Bangladesh did not develop India's degree of centralized state administration during the colonial period. In addition, the Muslim League was much less successful than the INC in bringing effective political organization to these regions. When the time came to assert state authority over their respective territories, independent Pakistan and Bangladesh turned more readily to an authoritarian military and bureaucracy. In contrast, India was able to rely, at least more frequently, upon democratic political parties and politicians.[9]

Finally, the long-standing role of the INC as the legitimate embodiment of the independence movement and Nehru as its charismatic and rightful representative gave the new government a powerful mandate. Like Nelson Mandela, whose African National Congress took its name from its Indian predecessor and was swept to power in South Africa's first free election in 1994, Nehru led the INC to a handy victory in India's first general election in 1951. This event gave the INC government the opportunity to implement Nehru's vision of social democracy at home and mercantilist trade policies abroad. The INC would govern India for 45 of its first 50 years of independence and was led for nearly all those years by either Nehru, his daughter, or his grandson.

A Nehru Dynasty

Uncle Nehru, as Jawaharlal Nehru was affectionately called, led the INC to two subsequent victories in 1957 and 1962. But by his third term, he had realized the intractability of many of India's economic and foreign policy challenges and his own inability to transform the nation as quickly as he had hoped. As one scholar observed, "In India, nothing changed fast enough to keep up with the new mouths to be fed."[10] Nehru died in office in 1964; and with his death, the INC began to lose some of its earlier luster and its ability to reach across regional, caste, and religious divisions to garner support.

Within two years, Nehru's daughter, **Indira Gandhi** (no relation to Mahatma), assumed leadership of a more narrowly defined INC and became India's first female prime minister. Far more authoritarian than her father, Gandhi saw her first decade of rule divide the party between her supporters and detractors. When her popularity within the party waned in the 1970s, Gandhi sought support from India's impoverished masses by initiating a populist campaign to abolish poverty. Although the program was highly popular and initially successful, the global oil crisis reversed many of its early economic gains. Riots and strikes spread throughout India, and citizens of all classes complained about the dangerous dictatorship of the "Indira raj."

Facing declining support, charges of corruption, and calls to step down, Gandhi instead chose in 1975 to suspend the constitution by declaring martial law, or **emergency rule**. The Indian constitution authorizes such a measure, and during the two years of emergency rule, riots and unrest ceased and economic efficiency improved. Nonetheless, Gandhi's swift suspension of civil liberties, censorship of the press, banning of opposition parties, and jailing of more than 100,000 political opponents (including many of India's senior statesmen) chilled Indian democracy and prompted widespread (albeit largely silent) opposition to her rule.

When Gandhi unexpectedly lifted emergency rule in 1977 and called for new elections, virtually all politicians and the overwhelming majority of voters rallied to the cause of the new Janata (People's) Party in what was seen as an effort to save Indian democracy. This Janata coalition formed the first non-Congress government in India's 30 years of independence. Although key supporters shared a common interest in rural causes and the party drew its strength largely from rural constituencies, the coalition was unified primarily by its opposition to Gandhi's emergency rule. After two years of factional disputes and indecisive governance, the INC was returned to office—with Gandhi as its leader. Indian voters had spoken, indicating their preference for the order and efficiency of Gandhi's strong hand over the Janata Party's ineptitude.

During Indira Gandhi's second tenure, persistent economic problems were compounded by growing ethnic conflict and increasing state and regional resistance to central control. Demands for the devolution of central authority were sharpest among the Sikh-majority Punjab in northern India, whose leaders had become increasingly forceful in their political and religious demands. Violence escalated, and calls for an independent Sikh state of Khalistan heightened. In 1984, Gandhi declared martial law, or **presidential rule**, in the state of Punjab. This state-level equivalent of declaring emergency rule is also constitutionally authorized, permitting the federal government to oust a state government and assume national control of that state. Gandhi then launched a military operation on the Golden Temple in **Amritsar**, Sikhism's holiest shrine. The Sikh separatists' firebrand leader and some 1,000 of his militant followers ensconced in the temple were killed in the operation, and loyal followers swore vengeance. The vengeance came months later, when Gandhi's Sikh bodyguards assassinated her. In what was to become a motif of communal violence, the assassination sparked violent retribution as angry Hindus murdered thousands of innocent Sikhs throughout India.

Indira Gandhi presided over Indian politics for almost as long as her father had. But whereas Nehru's legacy was one of national inclusion and consensus building among a wide range of regional interests, Gandhi's rule was far more divisive, intolerant, and heavy-handed. The Indian state she bequeathed to her son Rajiv, who replaced her as leader of the INC, was more centralized and its party politics far more divided. This was not, however, necessarily a negative experience for Indian democracy. For the first time, a viable political opposition was emerging, one capable of standing up to the powerful INC.

Widespread sympathy in the wake of Gandhi's assassination made it natural for the INC to select her younger son, Rajiv (her older son and heir apparent in the political dynasty, Sanjay, had died in a plane accident), and it assured the Congress Party its largest (and last) outright majority in the 1984 election. Rajiv Gandhi governed for five years, during which he began to shift India's economic focus away from the social-democratic and mercantilist policies of his mother and grandfather. Coming to government in the wake of Thatcher and Reagan's neoliberal economic reforms in the United Kingdom and United States, Rajiv Gandhi used his mandate to promote more liberal market measures that succeeded in boosting the Indian economy and have been expanded in the decades since. Ethnic violence and political divisiveness persisted, however. Trouble simmered between Hindus and Muslims in the Punjab and in new hot spots in the border region between India and Bangladesh to the east as well as between Hindus and ethnic Tamil separatists to the south. During a 1991 campaign, two years after Rajiv Gandhi had been turned out of office by a weak opposition coalition, he was assassinated by a Tamil suicide bomber. The Nehru dynasty thus ended (at least for the time being), and by the early 1990s coalition governments had become the norm.

Coalition Governments

The decline of the INC's dominance has led to a series of coalition governments typically headed by a national party, such as Congress, but shored up by regional partners. Coalitions of all political stripes have maintained the reforms begun under Rajiv Gandhi and the INC, including economic liberalization and increased political devolution to state governments. The INC's strongest competition has come from the **Bharatiya Janata Party (BJP)**, which had potential for nation-wide scope and appeal. The BJP has been able to articulate a Hindu nationalist vision, an alternative (some would say a dangerous one) to the vision of a secular India established by the INC at the time of India's founding. Drawing its strength initially from upper-caste Hindu groups, by the late 1990s the BJP was attracting Hindus of all castes under the banner of Hindu nationalism.

The event that began to galvanize support for the BJP was yet another incident of sectarian violence at a temple site. The Babri Mosque, located in the northern Indian city of **Ayodhya**, had been built by Mughals on a site alleged to be the birthplace of the Hindu god Ram. Muslims and Hindus alike deem the site sacred, and for decades it has been a point of controversy for local adherents of both faiths. By the 1990s, various Hindu nationalist groups had seized on Ayodhya as both a rallying political issue and a gathering place. In 1992, BJP supporters and other Hindu extremists destroyed the mosque, vowing to rebuild it as a Hindu shrine. This act ignited days of Hindu-Muslim rioting and violence and the killing of many Indians across the country.

Repercussions have persisted. In 2002, on the tenth anniversary of the event, in the city of Godhra in the western state of **Gujarat**, Muslims set fire to railcars carrying Hindu activists back from a ceremony at Ayodhya. They killed 58 people. Hindu retaliatory violence incited by religious militants in the state of Gujarat killed thousands. The issues continued to simmer as extremist elements in both the Muslim and Hindu camps regularly took aim at each other. The year 2008 proved particularly violent: Muslim terrorists carried out bombings in several of India's large urban centers, and a dramatic assault on Mumbai was led by a Pakistani-based terrorist group that targeted wealthy Indians, Westerners, and Jews.

This communal violence has served to harden positions on both sides and polarize political support. A BJP coalition that came to power in 1998 remained in office until 2004, when it was turned out by a surprisingly resurgent INC and assorted coalition partners. Organizations loosely affiliated with the BJP continue to promote divisive Hindu nationalist rhetoric to garner support and sponsor violence and discrimination against various minority religious and ethnic groups. During its six years in office, however, the BJP coalition governed relatively moderately. It did so both to retain its coalition partners and to promote India's national goals of economic growth and stable relations with neighboring countries. These current domestic and international priorities will be taken up in subsequent sections.

Significantly, the president of the INC at the time of its surprise return to office in 2004 and reelection in 2009 was **Sonia Gandhi**, the Italian-born widow of Rajiv Gandhi. Although she would have been the logical choice to assume the office of prime minister (and extend the Nehru dynasty), the BJP made her foreign birth a divisive campaign issue. Thus she stepped aside and allowed **Manmohan Singh** to become the country's first Sikh prime minister. Singh's Congress-led coalition governed for two full terms with a great deal of behind-the-scenes influence from Sonia Gandhi.

In an effort to perpetuate both Congress rule and the Nehru dynasty, the family groomed Sonia Gandhi's son and Jawaharlal Nehru's great-grandson, Rahul Gandhi, as the heir apparent. He gained a Congress seat in parliament in 2004 and led the INC's 2014 parliamentary election campaign. But in a sign of both the declining influence of the Nehru dynasty and the maturation of India's democratic regime, a resurgent BJP led by **Narendra Modi**, the outspoken governor of the state of Gujarat and rising star of the party, swept Congress out of office in the 2014 election. A popular Hindu nationalist, Modi led the BJP to the largest margin of victory and first outright parliamentary majority for any party in three decades. He has formed a government armed with both ardent Hindu sympathies and a strong mandate to carry out bold reforms.

Political Regime

India can easily claim the title of the world's largest democracy. But is this democracy genuine? And does it work? Certainly, it is democratic in form. Its constitution and other political institutions were modeled explicitly on Britain's Westminster parliamentary system, and few changes to the original blueprint have been enacted. Except for Indira Gandhi's authoritarian interlude of the 1970s, the democratic institutions in India seem to function more effectively and legitimately than those in many other former British colonies that share a similar institutional inheritance. Indian democracy nonetheless differs in important ways from that of its colonial mentor and other advanced Western industrialized democracies.

Why has democracy fared better in India than, for example, in neighboring Pakistan, a country that shares with India many cultural and historical legacies? Although a full answer to this question is beyond the scope of this work, the well-established stability and near universal legitimacy of the political institutions discussed in this section provide an important part of that answer. Three generations of Indian politicians and citizens from across the ideological spectrum have been schooled in the lessons of parliamentary democracy. They function and participate in a system that maintains civil parliamentary debate, a politically neutral bureaucracy, an independent judiciary, and firm civilian control over the military.

Political Institutions

THE CONSTITUTION

Perhaps befitting India's size and population, its constitution is one of the world's longest, expressing in writing the fundamental principles of Britain's unwritten constitutional order of parliamentary democracy. It establishes India as a federal republic, reserving significant authority for the state governments. During its nearly 50 years of hegemonic rule, the INC limited the autonomy of these state governments. However, the weakening of the Congress Party and the strengthening of regional political parties have led to growing reliance on coalition governments. This shift in turn has spurred a process of devolution, allowing these regional political parties and the states they represent to wrest significant authority from the **Center** (a term referring to India's national government and its capital in New Delhi). It is too early to tell, but the BJP's decisive electoral victory in

---

ESSENTIAL POLITICAL FEATURES

- **Legislative–executive system:** Parliamentary

- **Legislature:** Parliament
  - **Lower house:** House of the People
  - **Upper house:** Council of States

- **Unitary or federal division of power:** Federal

- **Main geographic subunits:** States

- **Electoral system for lower house:** Single-member district plurality

- **Chief judicial body:** Supreme Court

2014 may mark a reversing of this trend of regional devolution and bring more power back to the Center.

Two controversial tenets of the Indian constitution have certainly enhanced the power of the Center. The first of these authorizes the central government to suspend or limit freedoms during a "grave emergency," when India faces threats of "external aggression or internal disturbance." This "emergency rule" (nationwide martial law) was invoked twice during international conflicts, with China in 1962 and with Pakistan in 1971. More controversially, Indira Gandhi invoked this clause to institute emergency rule from 1975 to 1977, using it as a blunt (but nonetheless effective) tool against her political opponents. After her defeat in the subsequent election, the constitution was amended to limit emergency rule to conditions of external aggression or domestic armed rebellion.

Indira Gandhi was not the only prime minister to invoke the second measure, that of presidential rule, which allows the central government to oust a state government and assert direct rule of that state. National governments have employed this measure on more than 100 occasions, when ethnic unrest, local resistance, or simply a political stalemate rendered a state, in the judgment of the Center, ungovernable. Although these measures may seem unusual and have at times been imposed for purposes of political expediency, the violence, disorder, and corruption often associated with regional Indian politics have made presidential rule an important and generally legitimate tool of the central government.[11]

The Branches of Government

THE PRESIDENT

Because India is a republic, its head of state is a president, not a monarch; as in most other parliamentary systems, the president's role is largely symbolic. The president is authorized to appoint the prime minister, but as with the monarchs of Britain and Japan, this appointment is simply a ceremonial affirmation of the leader of the dominant party or coalition in the parliament.

The constitution does, however, bestow upon the *office* of president several significant responsibilities, even if this authority is largely nominal. As noted earlier, it is technically the president's role to declare emergency rule, temporarily suspending constitutional rule in either a state or the entire country. This formal declaration can be made, however, only on the advice of the prime minister and cabinet. Similarly, the Indian constitution contains a provision authorizing the president under certain circumstances to enact legislation without the consent or participation of parliament. These "ordinances" (in effect, presidential decrees) may be enacted only under limited conditions but have the same weight and effect as parliamentary legislation. Despite limitations, nearly 20 percent of Indian legislation has originated as a presidential ordinance.[12] But as with the declaration of emergency rule, while the formal decree authority is vested in the president, the prime minister and cabinet in fact propose and then draft the ordinances.

The substantive exception to these symbolic presidential tasks has been the president's role following elections that have produced no majority party (which, until the 2014 election, had been the norm for the past quarter century). Under these circumstances, the president seeks to identify and facilitate the formation of a workable governing coalition. If that is not possible, the president dissolves the parliament and calls new elections. An electoral college, made up of the national and state legislators, elects presidents to five-year renewable terms, though many presidents have in effect been appointed by powerful prime ministers.

The current president, Ram Nath Kovind, was elected in 2017 and serves as India's second Dalit president. Nominated by the BJP government, Kovind most recently served as the governor of the state of Bihar (also a largely ceremonial post). Despite the generally ceremonial nature of the presidency, in recent years several significant measures have been taken through the office. These have included a 2013 presidential ordinance instituting the death penalty for rape, which was enacted in the wake of a particularly brutal gang rape (see "The Politics of Rape," p. 498). In 2014, the previous president, Pranab Mukherjee, declared presidential rule in the state of Andhra Pradesh after the chief minister of the state resigned in protest against the decision to divide the state in half and create the new state of Telangana.

THE PRIME MINISTER AND THE CABINET

As in the British system, the Indian prime minister and cabinet constitute the executive branch. The prime minister, as head of the government, manages the day-to-day affairs of government and is the state's most important political figure. The prime minister is typically the leader of the majority party in the lower house of the legislature or, in recent years, a leader from within a coalition of parties that can garner sufficient support to constitute a majority, or even a minority, government. During the tenure of Congress government from 2004 to 2014, Sonia Gandhi retained the position of president of the INC, but because of the controversy surrounding her nonnative status, she did not serve as prime minister. As in other parliamentary systems, to remain in office, the prime minister must retain the confidence of the lower house but also has the power to dissolve the lower house and call elections to solidify support for the government.

The prime minister chooses members of the parliament to serve in a Council of Ministers that presides over all government ministries and departments. From this larger council, a smaller and more manageable group of the 20 to 25 most important ministers meets weekly as a cabinet to formulate and coordinate government policy. The current prime minister, Narendra Modi, is also president of the BJP and began his tenure in 2014 following his party's decisive electoral victory.

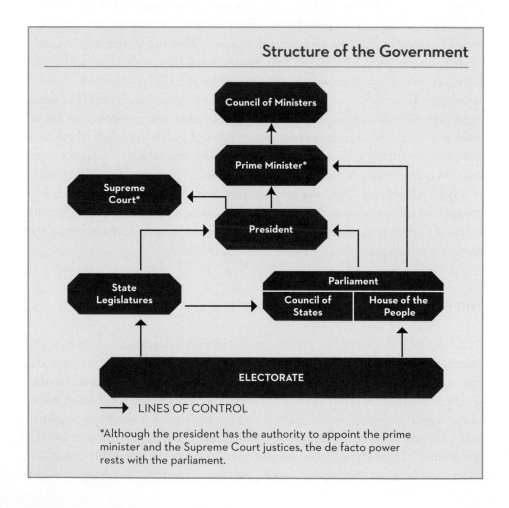

Structure of the Government

Council of Ministers

Prime Minister*

Supreme Court*

President

State Legislatures

Parliament

Council of States | House of the People

ELECTORATE

→ LINES OF CONTROL

*Although the president has the authority to appoint the prime minister and the Supreme Court justices, the de facto power rests with the parliament.

During the years of Congress Party dominance, the three generations of Nehru prime ministers wielded overwhelming executive power. Although this was most apparent during Indira Gandhi's authoritarian tenure, her father and even her son were also dominant prime ministers who left their personal imprints on the office and on Indian politics. Even during the more recent era of coalition governments in which the prime minister's influence has weakened, the office remains the primary source of policy making and political power. Modi's popularity, the BJP's convincing electoral victory in 2014, and the overwhelming majority its coalition holds in parliament give the prime minister the necessary means to likewise exercise decisive executive power.

THE LEGISLATURE

As is true in many parliamentary systems, the lower house, or **House of the People**, dominates India's bicameral legislature. This lower chamber seats 545 members. All but two of them are elected by voters for terms not to exceed five years; the final two seats are reserved for Anglo-Indians appointed by the president. Despite this chamber's enormous size, India's huge population remains relatively underrepresented. Each representative serves nearly 2 million people—nearly three times that of a member of the U.S. House of Representatives and 20 times that of a member of Britain's House of Commons.

Like the British lower house, the House of the People serves primarily as a chamber of debate between the government and the opposition. It has adopted many of the rituals and institutions of its colonial model, including a neutral Speaker of the House who presides over "question hour." Seen during the era of the INC's dominance as little more than window dressing for the party in power and its prime minister, the lower house has had an increasingly important political role since the emergence of multiparty coalition governments and the strengthening of regional parties.

As its name denotes, the upper house, or **Council of States**, represents India's 29 states and seven territories. All but 12 of its 250 members are indirectly elected by state assemblies (the president appoints the remaining 12) to fixed six-year terms. Although the upper chamber technically possesses most of the same powers as its lower counterpart—including the right to introduce legislation—in practice it has been much weaker. Only the House of the People can introduce bills to raise revenue, and any financial measure the Council of States votes down can be enacted with the majority support of the lower house. Any other deadlocked legislation is put to a majority vote of a joint session, which ensures that the more numerous lower chamber has the upper hand. Most significantly, the prime minister and cabinet are responsible only to the lower house, which can force the prime minister from office by a vote of no confidence.

THE JUDICIARY

India has a Supreme Court with a bench of 30 justices (when all vacancies are filled). They are appointed by the president and may serve until age 65. Typically, the most senior judge serves as chief justice.

India's Supreme Court is a constitutional court with the authority of judicial review (the right to rule on the constitutionality of acts of the parliament). This power to interpret the constitution is limited, however, by the comprehensive nature of the Indian constitution. Its power has also been limited by the parliament's ability to reverse court decisions by amending the constitution, as it has done on a number of occasions (the Indian constitution has 98 amendments, making it the longest and most amended in the world). Except during Indira Gandhi's two-year-long emergency rule in the 1970s, when the judiciary was seen as having yielded to the prime minister's political influence both in the appointment of justices and in the suspension of constitutionally guaranteed civil rights, the Supreme Court has enjoyed (and earned) a reputation for fairness and independence.

The Electoral System

As with many of its other political institutions, India's electoral system closely resembles the British model. At the national level, voters use a plurality system to elect representatives to the House of the People, as in Britain and the United States. The country is divided into 543 single-member districts (SMDs), in which the candidate who earns a plurality of votes on the first ballot is elected. The districts are based primarily on geography and population, but some districts are reserved for the scheduled castes and tribes, or so-called **untouchables** (also called the **Dalits**). The state legislatures elect or otherwise appoint members of the Council of States to staggered six-year fixed terms. The legislature uses a complex single transferable voting system, and seats are apportioned according to each state's population.

Whereas the plurality electoral system in the United States and Britain has favored the emergence of few or only two nationally based large parties and has penalized smaller parties, this is increasingly not the case for India's lower house. The INC certainly used the electoral system to its advantage during its period of dominance. The party won clear majorities of seats in the House of the People in most elections, even though it never won a majority of the popular vote (nor has any other party in India's history) and often received little more than a plurality. The largest of the other parties, including the BJP and the Janata Party, have also benefited, winning a higher percentage of seats than votes. The weakening of the INC's hegemony since the 1990s has splintered the national vote, however, and has given new significance to regional parties based on caste or on linguistic or religious identity. This has meant that while two parties tend to dominate each electoral district, these regional and caste-based parties are not nationally dominant.[13]

Recent lower house elections have seated representatives of nearly 40 different political parties, 10 parties with more than 9 seats each. And, until the BJP's decisive win in 2014, no party in recent elections had won a majority of the seats (see "House of the People Election Results, 2004, 2009, and 2014," p. 482).

Local Government

India's extensive regional diversity and the sectarian conflicts troubling the country at the time of its founding led the framers of India's constitution to establish a federal republic that preserved substantial powers for both the various states and the central government. Each of the 29 states has its own elected government consisting of a legislature and a chief minister. Most of the state legislatures are unicameral, though a few—most notably, those in large states such as Uttar Pradesh and Maharashtra—are bicameral. The **chief minister** is elected by the state legislature to serve a five-year term and can be removed from office by a vote of no confidence.

State governments in India have a great deal of power, but as in other federal systems, they have limits. In India, the Center's constitutional powers to declare a national emergency or impose presidential rule on a mismanaged or rebellious state are muscular examples of its authority. The federal government is also authorized to challenge any state legislation that contradicts an act of parliament and can even change the boundaries of states as it sees fit. But like their American counterparts, in the day-to-day management of government affairs, Indian states retain a great deal of jealously guarded autonomy. Public policies concerning health, education, economic and industrial development, and law and order are largely determined at the state level and vary significantly from state to state. The rise of coalition governments and the growing influence of regional parties in national affairs have only strengthened state power.

India's current division into 29 states and 7 territories reflects several territorial permutations since independence. In 1947, India consisted of 12 provinces previously under British control and some 562 princely states that needed to be persuaded (or coerced) to join the newly formed republic. In 1956, boundaries were redrawn along linguistic lines, forming 14 new states and six territories. As various other regions and ethnic groups made more demands, 14 additional states were formed between 1960 and 2000. Most recently, in 2014, the state of Andhra Pradesh in southeastern India was divided to form the new state of Telangana, satisfying the long-standing demand of local residents for statehood. The new state has 35 million people, making it larger than many of India's neighboring countries, including Afghanistan and Nepal. Although the division pleased Telanganese, who complained that their region had long been discriminated against, the new state retained the prosperous high-tech city of Hyderabad as its capital, angering the citizens of the now smaller Andhra Pradesh, which will also retain Hyderabad as its capital for the short run.

Given India's extensive ethnic diversity, it is perhaps no surprise that 21 additional proposals for new states are now pending with the central government. This growing demand for more states and more devolved authority speaks to an important difference between India's federalism and the American model. State borders in India reflect in most cases linguistic or ethno-religious differences, which pit regional interests against the Center. This conflict has been most pronounced in states such as Punjab, which is dominated by the Punjabi-speaking Sikhs, and Jammu and Kashmir, the only Indian state in which Urdu-speaking Muslims constitute a majority. However, other ethnic groups have also wielded the mechanisms of state authority to assert state interests against the federal government. India is a good example of what political scientists call **asymmetric federalism**, where power is devolved unequally across the country and its constituent regions, often as the result of specific laws negotiated between a given region and the central government.[14]

Perhaps the best government to compare with Indian federalism is not the United States, but rather the historically diverse and linguistically distinct European Union.[15] Like the Danes and the Greeks, the Hindi speakers of Bihar in the north and the Tamil speakers of Tamil Nadu in the south converse in mutually unintelligible tongues and share little common history and equally little interaction. Like the citizens of Sweden and Portugal, their customs, cultures, and traditions vary widely, as do their social and economic profiles. Bihar is impoverished and largely illiterate, whereas Tamil Nadu is relatively more prosperous and technologically advanced. There are no similarly intense contrasts in the United States.

Comparison of India with the European Union also points to one of the crowning accomplishments of India's democratic resilience. For all of the local conflict and secessionist violence that India has experienced, the Center has held, and the strife has remained localized. With larger populations and religious, linguistic, and territorial disputes sufficient to rival any of those that led to the numerous wars of Europe (and ultimately prompted the formation of the European Union), India has for the most part managed these disputes peacefully and democratically. This is no small feat.

Political Conflict and Competition

Despite occasional heavy-handed government restrictions on civil rights and periodic demonstrations of communitarian intolerance and even violence, Indian politics remains vibrant, open, and generally inclusive. Voter turnout typically averages around 60 percent for parliamentary elections and reached a record of nearly 67 percent in the 2014 election. The nonpartisan Freedom House in 2017 deemed India "free" and gave it a rating of 2 in its political rights and 3 in civil liberties (on a scale of 1 to 7, where 1 is the most free).

In fact, given India's size and diversity, some might argue that political competition has been too inclusive. As one Indian journalist complained, "Everyone in India gets a veto."[16] The competition and conflict—typically, but not always, healthy—reflect the dualism and diversity of India: a prosperous, cosmopolitan, and highly literate minority voting side by side with roughly two-thirds of the electorate who cannot read, have their roots in rural villages or urban slums, and may survive on less than a dollar a day. Both are important components of Indian democracy.

The Party System

During the first few decades of independence, India's party system was stable and predictable. Like Japan's Liberal Democratic Party or Mexico's Partido Revolucionario Institucional (Institutional Revolutionary Party), the Indian National

Congress presided over a one-party-dominant system that effectively appealed to a broad range of ideological and social groups and co-opted numerous disaffected constituencies, including the poor and minorities. More recently, as national opposition parties and regional and even local interests have gained ground in both state and national elections, this system has become far more fragmented, complex, and unpredictable.

THE CONGRESS PARTY

More than just a political party, the Indian National Congress, from its founding in 1885, became the flagship of national independence, commanding widespread appeal and support across the political and even ethnic spectrums. After independence, Jawaharlal Nehru and the INC pursued a slightly left-of-center political ideology of social democracy. This included social policies of "secularism" (more a program of religious equal opportunity than a separation of religion and state) and social reform, continuing the efforts of Gandhi to eliminate caste discrimination.

The party's economic program was marked by democratic socialism, including national five-year plans, state ownership of key economic sectors, and income redistribution through affirmative action programs. These policies earned the support of workers, peasants, and particularly members of the lower castes. At the same time, the INC retained the support of business by respecting private property and supporting domestic industry with mercantilist policies of import substitution. For decades, Congress remained the only party with national appeal.

The INC's dominance began to weaken after Nehru's death, as disagreements grew between Indira Gandhi and party elders in the late 1960s. These disagreements led to divisions within the party and to Gandhi's capture of the dominant faction, known as Congress Party (I) (for Indira) during the 1970s. Gandhi made populist promises to India's poor, vowing to abolish poverty through government programs, but never delivered on those promises. By the 1980s, the INC had begun to move away from its traditional priorities of democratic socialism and religious neutrality. Indira Gandhi began promoting Hindu nationalism, and her son Rajiv launched neoliberal economic reforms. These legacies have outlived their architects and have been embraced even more enthusiastically by other political parties.

By the late 1980s, the INC had surrendered its position of primacy, and the single-party-dominant system gave way to a regionalized multiparty system and coalition governments. Since then, the INC has alternated rule with various permutations of Hindu nationalist coalitions, controlling the government in the first half of the 1990s and then returning to power for a decade from 2004 to 2014. Although the INC has continued to embrace in principle the neoliberal reform program first launched by Rajiv Gandhi, its most recent stint in government was largely a result of its progressive appeal to India's peasantry, a nod to both Nehru's democratic socialism and Indira Gandhi's populism. In the 2014 general election, voters expressed their displeasure with the party's growing reputation for political corruption and inaction, handing Congress its worst-ever electoral defeat. The Congress-led coalition government lost nearly three-fourths of its seats, while the INC itself lost nearly 80 percent of its total seats (see "House of the People Election Results, 2004, 2009, and 2014," p. 482). With only 44 seats in the lower house, the INC fell short of the 10 percent of total seats necessary even to be designated a parliamentary party or lead the opposition. This lopsided victory handed the BJP an unprecedented mandate for change.

THE BHARATIYA JANATA PARTY

As opposition to the INC grew during Indira Gandhi's 1970s autocratic interlude, a number of contending parties began to emerge or take on new importance. A coalition of some of these opposition parties, under the name Janata (People's) Party, ultimately wrested the government from the INC in the late 1970s. One of the smallest of these coalition partners was Jana Sangh, a Hindu nationalist party that left the Janata coalition in 1980 and changed its name to the Bharatiya Janata Party (BJP), or Indian People's Party.

The BJP's popularity climbed rapidly as support for secularism gave way to increasing sentiment for ethnic and religious parties. The BJP won only two seats in the 1984 House of the People elections, but increasing Hindu nationalist sentiment (manifested most violently in clashes with Sikhs at Amritsar in 1984 as well as with Muslims in Ayodhya in 1992 and in Gujarat in 2002) allowed it to expand its representation to 161 seats by 1996 and form a coalition government, led by Atal Bihari Vajpayee. Although the first BJP coalition lasted only 12 days, by 1998 the BJP had become the largest party in the parliament. Vajpayee and his BJP-led coalition governed from 1998 until being turned out of office in the 2004 elections. Although support for the BJP waxed and waned over the next decade, the party returned to government in 2014 after obtaining a majority of seats in the lower house.

From its founding, the BJP has been an outspoken advocate of Hindu national identity. It is a member of a larger constellation of more than 30 loosely tied Hindu nationalist organizations known collectively as the RSS (the Hindi acronym for "National Association of Volunteers"). These religious, social, and political associations vary widely in their acceptance of violence and militancy in promoting Hindu nationalism, but all embrace **Hindutva**, or "Hindu-ness," as India's primary national identity and ideal. Whereas some of the more moderate RSS member organizations promote benign patriotism, other reactionary or fundamentalist association members teach a Hindu chauvinist version of Indian history and condone and even train their members in violent tactics of religious and racial discrimination.

Similarly, the BJP itself has both moderate and militant elements. Its elected national leaders tend to downplay the party's religious ties, promote it as a more honest alternative to the INC, and emphasize its neoliberal economic policies of privatization, deregulation, and foreign investment. This reputation of honesty and neoliberalism has appealed in particular to India's growing middle class, which is more interested in economic freedom and prosperity than secular equality. This predominantly Hindu middle class has become frustrated with what it perceives as the reverse discrimination of the INC's secular policies of tolerance of minority religion- and caste-based affirmative action.

The extremist and fundamentalist elements in the BJP are more overtly anti-Muslim. They contend that India's Muslims were forced to convert by foreign invaders and would naturally revert to their native Hinduism in an India permitted to promote its true heritage. They are more prone to violence, praising the assassin of Mahatma Gandhi and the combatants of Ayodhya and Gujarat as heroes and protectors of Indian heritage. Their leaders have been more successful politically at the local and state levels (particularly in the region of India's so-called cow belt, in the Hindu-majority north) but also have been important allies in the BJP's efforts to form national ruling coalitions.

The most successful and controversial of these rising regional BJP leaders was current prime minister and former chief minister (governor) of the state of Gujarat, the charismatic and outspoken Narendra Modi. "NaMo" was swept to power as chief minister just before the anti-Muslim violence in Gujarat in 2002 and reelected in 2007, and he has long been viewed as a controversial figure. On the one hand, his policies of fighting corruption and promoting privatization and small and efficient government proved very successful, bringing consistently high economic growth to Gujarat during his tenure. On the other hand, critics charged that Modi and his government did not do enough to prevent the violent attacks against Muslims in the riots of 2002 and in some cases actually condoned and even inflamed the violence. Although Modi was ultimately cleared of all charges against him, he and the BJP recognized that he could not lead the party in a national election contest campaigning on the narrow platform of Hindu

Although criticized both at home and abroad for his long association with Hindu nationalism, Prime Minister Narendra Modi brought his BJP to government in 2014 on promises to promote growth and limit corruption.

nationalism. Instead, the BJP's successful 2014 campaign focused on basic issues that appealed to wide sectors of the population, promising to rein in corruption and inflation, promote education and infrastructure, and boost economic growth. Although Modi's BJP retains a core ideology of Hindu nationalism, both constitutional and electoral constraints have moderated the government's policies.[17]

PARTIES OF THE LEFT

India's so-called Left Front consists of a collection of communist and other left-leaning parties whose popularity for many years seemed unaffected by the declining success of communist parties and countries elsewhere in the world. These parties until the 2014 election together managed to garner on average 7 to 10 percent of the national vote and as many as 50 seats in parliament's lower house. This bloc of seats gave the communist parties a decisive role in the making and breaking of recent coalitions and therefore a degree of leverage in government policy, despite their minority status.

Following the 2004 general elections, the INC-led coalition required the support of four communist parties in order to gain a voting majority in parliament. The fragile nature of this arrangement became apparent in parliamentary wrangling in recent years over a controversial nuclear cooperation treaty between India and the United States. Supported by the Congress Party, the deal was adamantly opposed by its communist allies, who ultimately withdrew their support from the coalition in 2008. This forced the INC in its second term to form ad hoc alliances with other small parties to assemble a majority and avoid a vote of no confidence that would have brought the government down and forced a new election. Like the INC, India's parties of the left did not fare well in the 2014 general election, winning only 11 seats and rendered largely irrelevant to either the ruling BJP-led coalition or the much-diminished opposition INC.

The leftist parties' past success can be attributed largely to their willingness to evolve and seek alliances with other parties. Although the two largest leftist parties—the Communist Party of India and the Communist Party of India (Marxist)—initially supported violent revolution, over the years they both have ultimately embraced peaceful means to achieve communism. More recently, both parties have come to look and act much more like social-democratic parties. They embrace a mixture of state and private ownership and even promote foreign investment. Like nearly all other parties in India, these leftist parties rely upon strong local and regional bases of support. The largest share of party leadership and voting strength has come from the states of **Kerala** in the far south of India and West Bengal in the far east.

Not all political movements on the left, however, have been willing to work within the democratic system. Chief among these radical groups is the Maoist (or guerrilla communist) insurgency known as **Naxalism**. Named for the region in West Bengal where it originated in the late 1960s, the movement has grown in recent decades, particularly in rural, impoverished areas in more than a dozen states of western India. Naxalite recruits—estimates place the number of armed insurgents at more than 20,000—are drawn primarily from the low castes, outcastes, and tribal natives largely excluded from India's recent and dramatic economic growth.

REGIONAL AND OTHER PARTIES

The declining dominance of the INC and the rise of coalition governments have given new prominence to regional and local political parties, which have come to dominate in many states and tip the balance in national elections. Moreover, as INC-supported secularism has waned, ethnic, linguistic, and religious identities have become increasingly important rallying points for political interests that are often concentrated by region. For example, states with predominant ethnic or religious identities, such as the Dravidian Tamils in the southern state of Tamil Nadu and the Punjabi Sikhs, have often been led by these regional and state parties. Other parties draw support from lower-caste Indians in several of India's poorer states. Neither the INC nor the BJP holds a majority in a number of India's state parliaments.

The localized parties also often have sufficient voting strength to control small but influential blocs of seats in the national parliament. In the 2009 election, for example, state and special-interest parties won approximately 40 percent of the seats in the lower house. This reflects in one sense a devolution of central power that could be healthy for Indian democracy. But given the diversity of India's interests, it also speaks to the highly localized interests of Indians and may be a sign of dangerous centrifugal forces. In addition to ethnic-based regional parties, a single-issue party emerged in 2012 in Delhi, the nation's capital, capitalizing on an anti-graft campaign that began a year earlier. Led by a former tax official, Arvind Kejriwal, the Aam Aadmi ("Common Man's") Party (AAP) performed very well in the 2013 local assembly elections, fared poorly in the 2014 general elections, but retains national ambitions (see "Anti-Graft Campaign and the Common Man's Party," p. 500).

Elections

Campaigns and elections are essential procedures in any democracy and are often dramatic theatrical events. Certainly this is true of India, where all aspects of an election must be measured in superlatives. For instance, in the spring of 2014, nearly 540 million of the eligible 815 million voters flocked to the nearly 1 million polling stations to cast votes (a record turnout of nearly 67 percent) using over 1.4 million electronic voting machines. They selected their favored parliamentary candidates from the thousands of choices, representatives of one of six "national" parties or the dozens of regional ones. The task was so huge that polling was spread out over more than a month as election officials and their machines migrated across the country harvesting votes. Indeed, this five-week election process was the longest ever—and longer than the government-limited campaign that preceded it.

Perhaps most surprising was the outcome itself, again testament to the authenticity of Indian democracy. Although even the governing Congress Party all but acknowledged in the weeks leading up to the election that its coalition was likely to be turned out of government, few predicted just how thoroughly the BJP would

House of the People Election Results, 2004, 2009, and 2014

PARTY OR COALITION	2004 SEATS	2009 SEATS	2014 SEATS
UPA			
INC	145	206	44
Other allied parties	72	56	26
NDA			
BJP	138	116	282
Other allied parties	47	43	54
LF	59	24	11
Other Parties	84	100	128
Total	545	545	545

Key to Party Acronyms:
BJP: Bharatiya Janata Party
INC: Indian National Congress
LF: Left Front
NDA: National Democratic Alliance
UPA: United Progressive Alliance
UPA and NDA are party coalitions that include the INC and BJP, respectively.

sweep the election. Winning over 30 percent of the popular vote and over 50 percent of the seats, the BJP became the first party other than Congress to win an outright majority of seats and the first party to do so in 30 years (see "House of the People Election Results, 2004, 2009, and 2014" above). This victory and the severe weakening of the opposition gave the charismatic Modi and his party a mandate to carry out promised reforms, something that heartened his many supporters. His detractors, on the other hand, feared that a victorious Modi would reveal his true stripes—not as a pragmatic economic reformer, but an ardent Hindu nationalist.

Despite some troubling signs to the contrary, the BJP government's Hindu nationalist ideology has been largely tempered by both India's secular constitution and an electorate that remains primarily concerned with the economy.

Civil Society

As the INC's dominance has faded and political authority has become decentralized, more—and more diverse—interests and elements of Indian society have demanded political influence. India has conventional civil organizations representing business, labor, and even peasants, but these groups tend not to be particularly effective in influencing policy. Labor unions are organized by political party and are therefore fragmented and limited in their effectiveness, although they have done much to champion the interests of labor. Business certainly influences both politics and politicians. Corruption is a serious problem among Indian politicians—nearly a third of members of national and state legislatures elected since 2008 face criminal charges—but this influence has been held in check by both traditional Hindu and more modern socialist biases against private business. Peasants are plentiful and at times vocal, but their political demands tend to be episodic and particular.

Communal interests representing ethnic, religious, and caste groups have been far more influential in Indian politics than have other factors. Hindus, Muslims, and Sikhs all have well-organized groups representing their political interests. This is also true of the Dalits, or untouchables, who have their own political party and constitute one of India's largest mass movements. Although there is good reason to be concerned about the destabilizing and divisive potential of these religious- and caste-based groups, evidence indicates that their multiple demands have often been addressed substantially (if not fully met) through the political process, thereby defusing civil discord and strengthening the legitimacy of the system.

Less traditional divisions and demands are also taking shape in contemporary Indian civil society, particularly among India's growing middle class. These include significant anticorruption, environmental, and women's movements. A 2011 anti-graft campaign led by social activist Anna Hazare in the nation's capital prompted nationwide protests in support of the effort. Environmental protests include resistance to development projects, such as deforestation and the Narmada Valley Project dam, and advocacy of redress for industrial accidents, such as the 1980s Union Carbide gas-leak disaster in Bhopal. Women's movements bridging class and ethnic divisions have organized to protest so-called dowry deaths, which claim the lives of as many as 25,000 Indian women annually, and more recently the plight of women who are victims of sexual violence (see "The Politics of Rape," p. 498).

Another important voice of Indian civil society is the media establishment, arguably one of the largest and most active in the world. It comprises 40,000 newspapers and other periodicals, including some 4,000 dailies, all of which enjoy a significant degree of editorial and political freedom and influence, especially as illiteracy recedes. India's extensive radio and television networks are even more important conduits of information and have been subject to more careful government scrutiny and control. This oversight has become increasingly difficult, however, because satellite television has introduced new competition into the market. India's substantial investment in networking the entire country with broadband cable has also expanded avenues for civic communication.

Society

Ethnic and National Identity

Contemporary India is a complicated jigsaw of astounding ethnic and social diversity pieced together by centuries of imperial conquest.[18] Independent India has sought to create from this patchwork imperial raj a unified and secular nation-state or, more accurately, a "state-nation," recognizing that the country contains multiple ethnic groups with distinct cultural and in many cases political identities.[19] This effort has required of India and its citizens a measure of social tolerance that has not always been available, seemingly leaving the country on the edge of disintegration. Yet for all the communitarian conflict and threats of secession, national unity has prevailed. Before noting the political culture that has at least to some degree preserved this unity, we turn first to the ethnic and social divisions that threaten it.

When lighter-skinned Indo-Aryans migrated into what is now northern and central India thousands of years ago, they pushed the native, darker-skinned Dravidians southward. Each culture retained separate linguistic and cultural identities that persist to some extent today. Roughly two-thirds of Indians (virtually all in the north) speak some variation of the Sanskrit-based language brought by the Indo-Aryans, which now forms some 10 distinct languages. The most common of these is Hindi, one of two official national languages, which is spoken by over one-third of all Indians. Approximately one-fourth of all Indians speak one of the four main Dravidian languages, and another 5 percent claim Urdu as their first language. In all, the constitution recognizes 14 languages, but at least another 30 languages claim over 1 million speakers each. The only other national language is English. Although

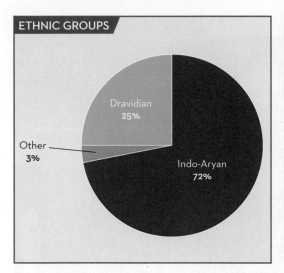

ETHNIC GROUPS

Dravidian
25%

Other
3%

Indo-Aryan
72%

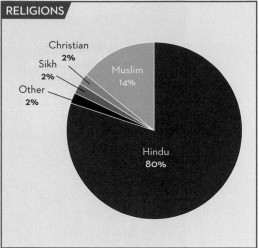

RELIGIONS

Christian
2%

Sikh
2%

Other
2%

Muslim
14%

Hindu
80%

only some 3 percent of the population speaks English fluently, as in other polyglot former colonies it has become an essential medium for national and international politics and commerce and a significant binding force of Indian unity.

These divisions are at once exacerbated and moderated by religious differences. Although just under 80 percent of Indians share a common faith, regional and linguistic groups practice their Hinduism in different ways. The promotion of Hindu nationalism has brought a degree of unity to these groups, but at the expense of some 14 percent of Indians who are Muslim, 2 percent who are adherents of Sikhism (an amalgam of Hindu and Muslim theologies), and a comparable percentage who are Christian. These religious differences have often acquired political significance, leading at times to assassinations and violent pogroms as well as bitter reprisals, secessions, and threats of secession.

The most dramatic flare-ups of sectarian violence have been between Hindus and Muslims. These include the initial partitioning of Muslim Pakistan and Hindu India, their ongoing territorial disputes in Kashmir, and the events at Ayodhya in 1992, Gujarat in 2002, and sporadic violence since then. Many Muslims, including most of the political leadership, moved to Pakistan following partition, leaving behind a weakened community in India whose loyalty is still questioned by Hindu nationalists. However, Muslim and Hindu identities are more blurred than we would imagine, especially in villages and at the lower rungs of society, where Muslims incorporate Hindu rituals and Hindus pray at Muslim shrines. Religious and other identities in India are often sharper among elites than in the population as a whole—a common result of modernization worldwide.

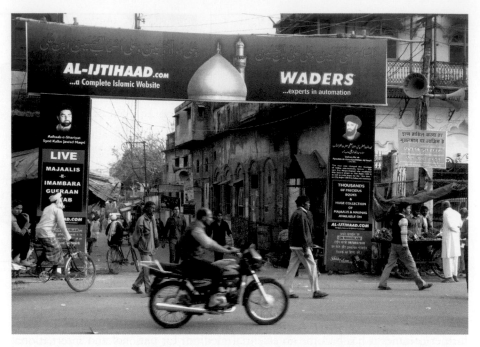

Muslims are a relatively small minority in India, but they have played a powerful role in the country's history. Technology links members of the Muslim community to one another and the wider Islamic world.

As if the linguistic and religious differences were not sufficiently divisive, the hierarchical separation of Indian society into castes remains the most significant of India's social divisions. Although industrialization and urbanization have made the caste system today more permeable and flexible than it once was, the system remains socially, politically, and economically important. Neither class identity nor income inequality is as severe in India as in many other developing countries. But those in the lower ranks of India's caste system are typically also the poorest, and the scheduled castes and hill tribes are the poorest of the poor. In an effort to redress discrimination against these suppressed groups, or Dalits, the government has established affirmative action programs to reserve for them jobs, scholarships, and even seats in the parliament.

In Uttar Pradesh, the largest state in India (nearly 200 million people), the chief minister from 2007 to 2012, Mayawati, is herself a Dalit. She was thus able to draw on a huge reservoir of support among other Dalits, who saw her as a harbinger of change. Her caste also allowed her to build a virtual personality cult, including a number of expensive public monuments, complete with bronze statues of important Dalit figures (including her). For many Dalits, such extravagances, alongside related charges of corruption, were outweighed by the significance of having one of their own in charge of a major Indian state.

In contrast, the rise of Mayawati and affirmative action programs in general have angered many higher-caste Hindus, who see the measures—along with special protections afforded to minority religious groups—as reverse discrimination. The Hindu nationalist BJP has seized on this issue in expanding its constituency among the growing Hindu middle class and stirring the embers of Hindu chauvinism.

Ideology and Political Culture

As with many other aspects of Indian politics, India's political culture defies generalization. Nonetheless, two somewhat contradictory values are worth mentioning. On the one hand, Indians tend to identify themselves and their politics locally. Indians are tied most strongly to family, occupational group, and their immediate regional linguistic and religious associates. These immediate ties tend to segment and even fragment politics in India, which promote political identity, awareness, and cooperation locally but also cause political friction and even violence between groups. Although such localization may limit the scope of conflict, it also constrains the kind of mobilization that could address pressing national needs.

On the other hand, despite their cultural diversity and contentious politics, Indians continue to identify themselves as Indians and generally support—and see themselves as an important part of—Indian national democracy. So while the bonds of national unity are less powerful than local ties, India's "bewilderingly plural population" nonetheless considers itself as "capable of purposeful collective action."[20] Gandhi and Nehru remain national heroes for most Indians, who take their role as citizens seriously and see Indian democracy as legitimate.

Some find in this combined sense of local power and political efficacy a dangerous tendency toward identity politics in Indian democracy. Nehru's secular nationalism has ceded ground to political movements that mobilize supporters in the name of religion or region. Majority Hindus perceive themselves as threatened by minority religions, the prosperous middle class depicts itself as victim of India's poorest outcastes, and Kashmiri Muslims clamor for independence. Globalization has further created a sense that Indian identity as a whole is under threat and must be defended. Yet democracy and unity prevail, which speaks to India's remarkable capacity to adopt and adapt foreign institutions for its own use. An Indian adage claims that "democracy is like cricket—a quintessentially Indian game that just happened to have been invented elsewhere." There is no question that India has made democracy its own.

Fears about Foreign Influence

Our way of life must be protected from foreign influence. Percentage saying yes:

COUNTRY	PERCENTAGE
India	92
Nigeria	85
South Africa	80
Brazil	77
Russia	77
Mexico	75
China	70
Japan	64
Canada	62
United States	62
United Kingdom	54
Germany	53
France	52

Note: Data on Iran not available.
Source: Pew Center for the People and the Press, 2007.

Political Economy

By the time India finally obtained its independence from British imperialism, it had seen quite enough of the West's version of liberal free trade. For nearly four decades, successive (mostly INC) governments adopted a foreign policy of mercantilist economic nationalism, promoting **import substitution industrialization** and restricting foreign investment and trade. Governments also promoted social-democratic policies domestically to limit the private sector, redistribute wealth, and give the state the leading role in guiding the economy. These policies achieved several significant results. By the late 1970s, chiefly through the technological gains of the Green Revolution, India had become one of the largest agricultural producers in the world. For most years since then, it has been a net exporter of food. Import substitution policies established a relatively large—if not broad—middle class and enabled some niches in the economy and some regions of the country to truly prosper.

By the mid-1980s, however, frustration with poverty, corruption, and continued slow growth at home had reached a critical point. In comparing India's relatively slow rate of development with the more rapid pace of India's East Asian neighbors, an Indian economist famously labeled this slower pace the "Hindu rate of growth." Although the phrase seems to implicate India's culture, most observers agree that the greatest obstacle to Indian growth has been (and in important ways remains) India's huge bureaucracy with its associated red tape and corruption. Due to the growing dissatisfaction with persistent economic stagnation at home, coupled with the popularity of export-led growth and structural adjustment programs abroad, India's successive governments adopted neoliberal policies of economic reform. Piecemeal efforts during the 1980s to dismantle nearly four decades of mercantilist protectionism gave way to substantial liberalization by the early 1990s. Although the process was gradual and the results have been less thorough than reforms made in China, measures to liberalize India's foreign trade and privatize the economy have been significant. Restrictions on foreign investment have been eased, and many state-owned companies have been sold to the private sector.

More significantly, successive governments have sought to weaken India's notorious **license raj**, the bureaucratic red tape requiring licensing and approval processes for operating a business or importing and exporting products. The license raj is a legacy of an extensive British colonial civil service, superseded by independent India's far larger state bureaucracy. As part of his social-democratic vision for India, Nehru established an interventionist state that pursued socialist and mercantilist economic policies, including protectionist measures designed to safeguard both workers and consumers and lift India's poorest. The result was a highly bureaucratized and politicized system of licenses, permits, and quotas governing virtually all aspects of the Indian economy. Although some of the most stifling aspects of the license raj have been reduced or eliminated, the country continues to suffer from an array of bureaucratic and other barriers to business. According to the World Bank, India remains one of the world's most difficult places to set up and run a business.[21] Because Indians have found it so difficult to work within this system, most have little choice but to work around it. They do so by paying bribes, which have come to be expected "at almost every point where citizens are governed, at every transaction where they are noted, registered, taxed, stamped, licensed, authorized, or assessed."[22]

Despite the remaining challenges and ongoing resistance to reform in some areas of the economy, the liberalization effort has achieved impressive results. In the decade after launching the reforms, India's economic growth averaged nearly 6 percent per year (twice the rate of the previous 20 years). During the first decade of this century, growth rates averaged over 8 percent a year, in some years nearing the frenzied rates of economic expansion of neighboring China (but with inflation rates to match). Even as the population continued to grow rapidly, the total number of poor Indians declined. Trade and investment grew, and Western outsourcing has brought jobs and growth to some segments of the Indian economy. In recent years, however, economic growth has slowed dramatically, declining to barely half the pace of the previous decade. Inflation remains high, bringing "stagflation" to India. Employment and investment have slowed, even as government deficits and bank debts have ballooned.

There is great hope, and some evidence, that Modi's forceful leadership and the sweeping mandate given to the current BJP government will provide the necessary vision and momentum to reignite rapid and sustained growth in the Indian economy. In fact, India's 2015 growth rate outpaced China's, making India the fastest growing large economy in the world. Yet huge economic problems persist. More than one-fourth of Indians live on less than a dollar per day—though the percentage of Indians living in poverty has been cut nearly in half since 1990. Over 40 percent of Indian children are underweight—a number that has not moved significantly for 20 years. The largest number of the world's undernourished people resides in India, even as India consistently ranks among the top two exporters of rice. Corruption and protectionism persist, and the pollution accompanying India's industrial expansion and urban growth threatens to undermine the development success the country has achieved to date. The World Bank predicts that by 2020, India's water, air, and soil resources will be under greater threat than those of any other nation.

Comparing India's development trajectory with that of neighboring China is instructive. China was poorer than India when both countries were established in the late 1940s, and it remained so through the 1970s. But since then, China has dramatically outperformed India. Its growth rates have hovered near 10 percent for the past 30 years, population growth has slowed, and trade and investment have skyrocketed. The difference in these countries' development rests in two challenges that continue to perplex India: too many people and too little education. Whereas China's population growth has slowed to less than 1 percent per year, India's remains closer to 2 percent. This has meant fewer mouths to feed in China and more wealth to spread around. The World Bank has concluded that extreme poverty has been nearly eradicated there.

In addition, China has done a far better job providing basic education for its citizens. More than 90 percent of Chinese adults are literate, and the difference in literacy between men and women is smaller than in India. (In China, 7 percent more men than women are literate; in India, the difference is 17 percent.) Economists and demographers argue that if India can educate its citizens, particularly its women, population pressures will ease. Women will gain more control over reproductive choices, and families are more likely to deem it rational to limit family size. More important,

Despite the sweeping victory of the BJP in the 2014 parliamentary elections, questions remain as to whether the BJP and new prime minister Narendra Modi will be able to clean up India's many problems.

this demographic liability could become an asset as mouths to feed develop into skilled, competitive workers in the global economy of the twenty-first century.

Like China and many other developing countries that have been drawn into the global economy, India faces an additional problem. Although the economy is growing, it is doing so unevenly. Much has been made of India's recent information technology (IT) boom, and for good reason. Several large Indian computer firms are now globally competitive, and Western companies have flocked to such cities as Bangalore in the south and Hyderabad in the center to take advantage of India's wealth of service workers and English-speaking engineers.

Nevertheless, the IT industry remains largely irrelevant to most Indians. As a whole, it employs little more than 3 million workers out of a labor force of some 500 million and makes up less than 10 percent of India's GDP. Each year, some 12 million Indians enter an economy that produces fewer than 6 million jobs. A handful of India's 29 states receive virtually all of India's foreign investment, and most of the population remains employed in agriculture. This situation has created for India

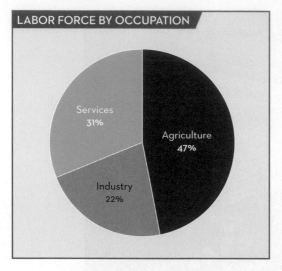

LABOR FORCE BY OCCUPATION

Agriculture 47%

Services 31%

Industry 22%

a dual economy that exacerbates both regional and class tensions. An elite, urban, prosperous, and Westernized middle-class minority sits precariously atop a huge lower class that is largely rural, illiterate, and in many cases unemployed or underemployed.

If India is to eliminate or at least address this persistent poverty and inequality, stay ahead of its rapid population growth, and compete with China and other developing economies, scholars and policy makers agree that it must do several things. Among them are improving conditions for its rural population; improving roads, telecommunication, and other aspects of the infrastructure; increasing foreign investment; and reducing bureaucracy and corruption. Above all, India must provide better education and health care, particularly to Indian girls and women. There is evidence that this can be done. The state of Kerala, in southwestern India, boasts female literacy rates of nearly 90 percent and fertility rates and population growth far lower than the national average. These changes are not the result of neoliberal market reforms, but of several decades of socialist state policies in education, health care, and land reform that have generally emphasized equality over freedom and state intervention over free-market policies. These efforts are not the priorities of the Modi government, which has called for greater market competition and smaller government.

In the digital age, smaller government does not have to mean a less capable state. Among other critical tasks, the Indian state must do more to keep better track of its citizens. A central concern for any developing state is the ability to identify its people. For millennia, states and leaders have relied on the census to tax their population or identify other obligations that the population may have to those in power. With the development of modern states, however, the balance of power began to shift. People also saw their own identity and identification as a way to assert their rights. Citizenship and the documentation that comes with it—birth certificates, passports, and voter cards—are central elements of modern and democratic states. Democracies frequently struggle over privacy rights—who needs to know what about someone else, and why.

For less-developed countries such as India, however, the question of privacy is overwhelmed by the problem of anonymity—in other words, the issue of people without the means to identify themselves to the state and other actors in society. Poor people often lack any fixed means of identification, which weakens many of the rights

Modern shopping malls have sprung up in cities across India, including this one in Lucknow. Filled with Western and Indian stores, the malls serve the growing middle class but are far beyond the reach of most Indians.

or benefits that might follow. For example, without identification, it is hard to lay claim to property or land. It is difficult to start a business or set up a bank account. It is hard to apply for government benefits. India's poor system of personal identification is particularly ironic given the license raj, with its elaborate and stifling degree of regulations, licenses, and paperwork. However, some argue that this is no coincidence in that the disenfranchisement of the population has both justified the license raj (the bureaucracy must function on behalf of the anonymous population) and allowed for its corruption and expansion (since the population cannot take the place of bureaucrats or hold the bureaucracy accountable). But how is it possible to identify the population in a country that is so large and diverse and has such problematic state capacity?

India is attempting to use high technology both to empower the population and to weaken the license raj. Starting in 2010, it began to implement a system known as Aadhaar (or "support"), which would give every citizen a unique 12-digit identification number. To identify the population, workers rely on biometrics. In locations across the country, 20,000 teams were formed to scan the fingerprints and irises of any individual seeking an identification number. These data are in turn added to a growing national database, which will be linked to various state agencies and made accessible by computer, cell phone, and other electronic devices. By 2016, some 93 percent of adult Indians had voluntarily obtained identification numbers.

Although costly to implement, India is reaping the benefits of Aadhaar. Relying on the new identification numbers, government subsidies to the poor can be transferred directly, eliminating corrupt intermediaries and saving the government billions of dollars. Indian banks can connect secure private accounts to smartcards and cellular phones, giving the poor access to banking services (such as government payments and individual deposits) that in the past barely existed. This economic mobility may in turn increase physical mobility, allowing people to move easily and control their economic resources no matter where they are. Aadhaar's proponents argue that by linking all Indians directly to the state and market, this program has become the single most powerful weapon in the ongoing battle to weaken the license raj.[23]

Foreign Relations and the World

Once India gained its independence, Nehru charted for the country a foreign policy of "peaceful coexistence" with its neighbors and "nonalignment" in the superpower Cold War that was just then taking shape in the postwar world. In fact, Nehru became a leader of the nonaligned movement of postcolonial developing countries seeking to create a neutral "third world" separate from the American-led Western nations (the first world) and the Soviet-led Eastern bloc (the second world). Unfortunately, the ethnic politics of partition and the geopolitics of big-power relations derailed this course. In the decades that followed, India fought four wars with neighboring Pakistan and maintained frosty relations with both Communist China and the capitalist United States. With the end of the Cold War, however, and under conditions of much higher stakes (first China, then India, and finally Pakistan joined the United States as nuclear powers), India has sought improved relations with its neighbors and the United States. With growing economic and political clout, India is beginning to command the attention accorded to an emerging global power.

Pakistan and the Kashmir Dispute

No issue has haunted India's foreign relations more than the legacy of partition. The bitter division of India into Muslim Pakistan and Hindu India in 1947 not only soured relations between these erstwhile partners in the independence struggle but also left jagged and festering wounds in the very boundaries between them. At the center of the conflict is the contested region of **Kashmir**.

Situated on the northern portion of the border between the two countries, Kashmir is claimed in whole by both nations. On one side of the conflict is the Indian state of Jammu and Kashmir; on the other is the Pakistani-administered state of Kashmir. At the time of partition, Kashmir was the largest of three principalities that had not committed themselves to joining either India or Pakistan. Most of its subjects were Urdu-speaking Muslims whose ethnic sentiments leaned toward Pakistan, but its prince was a Hindu who hoped Kashmir would remain independent. This ambivalence gave way to armed conflict—the first of three undeclared wars between India and Pakistan—within months of the partition.

A year of armed conflict ground to a halt in 1948, and the line of conflict has remained the de facto border between the two countries (see the map on p. 496). Pakistan launched a second war in 1965, hoping to sever Kashmir from the rest of India. But the Pakistani advantage of surprise was no match for India's superior forces, and the hostilities ended in three weeks. A third war was waged not over Kashmir but over the struggle for independence in Bangladesh, which was then known as East Pakistan. Although the original partition created one Pakistan, its eastern and western halves were linked only by a shared religion and were divided by language, culture, and—most troubling—nearly 1,000 miles of Indian territory. Backed by a recently signed security agreement with the Soviet Union and with newly acquired Soviet armaments, India came to the aid of the secessionist movement in 1971. As a result, Pakistan was forced to accept liberation and Bangladeshi independence.

India and Pakistan fought a fourth, limited war over Kashmir in 1999 (perilously, for by that point both countries possessed nuclear weapons), and Kashmir remains to this day the world's most militarized border dispute. The level of tension has waxed and waned, but as one author notes, the cease-fire line has continued "to serve as a target range" that claims thousands of lives each year. Because both countries can use nuclear weapons as potential ammunition, many political analysts hope that caution will prevail over the "pathological politics" of ethnic hatred.[24] Ongoing violent protests in Kashmir for greater autonomy (or independence or unification with Pakistan), combined with instability in Pakistan, continue to make this area a flashpoint for future conflict.

Some observers feared that Prime Minister Modi, a staunch Hindu nationalist, would take measures in office that would escalate tensions with Pakistan. Instead, Modi invited the Pakistani prime minister to his 2014 swearing-in ceremony and paid a surprise visit to Pakistan on the Pakistani leader's birthday in 2015. Both countries initially agreed to relaunch comprehensive bilateral discussions in 2016,

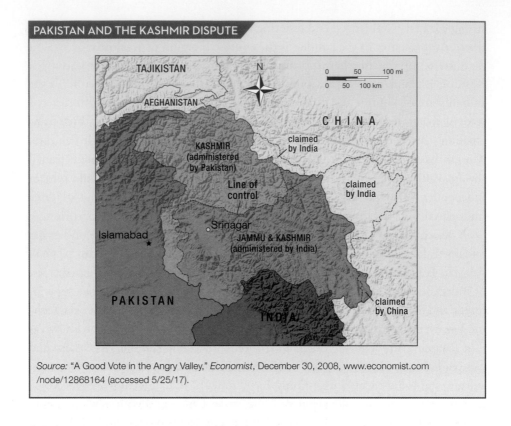

PAKISTAN AND THE KASHMIR DISPUTE

Source: "A Good Vote in the Angry Valley," *Economist*, December 30, 2008, www.economist.com /node/12868164 (accessed 5/25/17).

but negotiations were short-lived as clashes have intensified. Any lasting solution to this thorny conflict remains elusive.

China, Terrorism, and Great Power Relations

India's early hopes for peaceful relations with China, its neighbor to the north, were dashed by Chinese expansion into areas of India's northeastern Himalayan region. Tensions led to a limited Chinese invasion of India in 1962 to resolve what China viewed as "border disputes," but India deemed the move as outright aggression. India claims several territories now held by China—mostly Kashmiri land ceded to China by Pakistan—that are larger in area than Switzerland. China, in turn, claims three times as much real estate that is now in the hands of India.

Efforts since 1998 to settle these disputes finally yielded positive results in 2005, when both sides agreed to allow a cross-national committee to resolve this conflict. In 2006, a Himalayan border crossing reopened between the two countries for the first time since the Sino-Indian Border War of 1962. In 2013, the two signed a bilateral border defense cooperation agreement. Perhaps even more encouraging, bilateral trade between China and India exceeded $71 billion in 2015, with plans to grow the two-way trade to $100 billion in the near future.

Still, despite the recent thawing of border relations and expanding economic ties, the relationship remains fragile and complicated. India acknowledges China's claim to Tibet, but at the same time plays host to the Dalai Lama, his government-in-exile, and some 150,000 Tibetan refugees. China has stepped up military incursions into disputed Indian territory and has participated in the construction of naval facilities in both Bangladesh and Pakistan. It has also helped Pakistan keep pace with India's nuclear capabilities.

India's dealings with China, the United States, and even Pakistan took on a new dynamic after the September 11, 2001, terrorist attacks in the United States and the subsequent war on terror launched by the United States. Historically, India's relationship with the United States has been cool at best. But like China, India saw the benefits of recasting its own struggle with Muslim insurgents as part of a larger global war on terror. The United States responded warmly, lifting sanctions in place since India's nuclear tests in the 1990s, expanding trade, and—to Pakistan's chagrin—increasing military sales. Most significantly, in 2005, the United States negotiated a nuclear cooperation deal that permitted India to purchase nuclear technology for the first time in three decades, despite India's refusal to sign the Nuclear Non-Proliferation Treaty (NPT). The U.S. drawdown of military forces from Afghanistan has also affected India's role in the region. Both India and Pakistan see Afghanistan as a vital asset, but Pakistan especially views that country as important to its own defense against India. Pakistan's fear of India and of its potential influence in Afghanistan are in fact central to understanding how Pakistan could support the Afghan Taliban against the United States even while claiming to be a U.S. ally in the war on terror.

Pakistan's animosity toward India also accounts for its implicit and at times explicit support of acts of political violence carried out by Muslim extremists in India. These include a 2001 attack (just months after 9/11) by Pakistani nationals on the Indian parliament building as well as bombings in New Delhi in 2005, Varanasi in 2006, and Hyderabad in 2007. Over a period of three months in 2008, bombs rocked neighborhoods in Jaipur, Bangalore, and Ahmedabad, killing more than 100 and injuring hundreds more. Perhaps most dramatic was the sophisticated 2008 assault on Mumbai's city center, carried out by a well-trained and well-armed group of Muslim terrorists with clear Pakistani ties. In 2011, bombings in Delhi and Mumbai killed nearly 40 people; these actions were also linked to groups based in Pakistan.

In the coming decade, the likely drawing down of the American presence in Central Asia should create new opportunities for India to extend its power, though not without substantial risks to regional security. At the same time, the United States shares India's concerns about China's spreading influence and ambition in the region. The United States has taken a number of steps to enhance economic and security ties with India, including carrying out joint military operations (annually since 2001), lifting export controls on sensitive technologies, and offering to support India's bid for a permanent seat on the UN Security Council. But despite warming relations with the United States and persistent threats from neighboring countries, India has always valued its independence and sovereignty and strongly emphasizes its strategic autonomy. Whether India can enjoy a "peaceful rise" (as the Chinese like to describe their foreign policy) will become clearer in the next decade.

CURRENT ISSUES IN INDIA

When Indians went to the polls in 2014 to elect a government, most voters saw foreign policy concerns as far less pressing than several of the country's key domestic issues. Among these were the growing outrage at the government's seeming indifference toward violence against women and anger regarding the persistent corruption in government. Neither problem is new, but a growing middle class and increasingly vocal civil society are becoming far less tolerant of these and other public policy problems. It remains to be seen if the Indian government and state have either the capacity or the will to tackle these issues and address the demands of an increasingly impatient Indian electorate.

The Politics of Rape

On a December evening in 2012, a 23-year-old college student and her male friend were abducted on the streets of Delhi by six men in a private bus. The men brutally gang-raped the young woman, who later died from the extensive injuries she incurred in the vicious attack. Tragically, such grisly accounts of sexual assault are all too commonly reported in the Indian press. A month earlier, a 17-year-old

The government's perceived indifference toward rape has angered many Indians. Here, protesters hold a vigil for Nirbhaya, a 23-year-old medical student who died after being attacked on a bus and gang-raped.

village girl in Punjab who had been drugged and gang-raped committed suicide after a police officer tried to persuade her to drop charges and marry one of the rapists. In January of 2014, a woman from West Bengal was gang-raped by 13 men as punishment for her involvement with a man from another community. Three months later, the corpses of two Dalit teenage rape victims were discovered hanging from a tree near their village in Uttar Pradesh. In 2016, a Dalit woman law student from Kerala was savagely tortured, raped, and killed. These and many other reports of sexual violence against women (rape complaints have increased substantially in the past five years even as experts agree that most sexual assaults in India still go unreported) have galvanized India's middle class in protest against both a "culture of complicity" in the discrimination against women and the government's unwillingness or inability to adequately address such violence against women.[25]

Clearly, gender discrimination is not new to India, nor is it limited to sexual violence. Scholars point to social norms and attitudes in India that have traditionally valued sons over daughters, afforded women unequal status in the home and workplace, and tolerated the harassment, molestation, abduction, and in some cases even murder of girls and women. But an increasingly modern, urban, and vocal civil society has expressed outrage at these practices. People have joined sit-ins, protests, and other demonstrations demanding that the government address the problem.

Critics argue that while long-standing social attitudes and cultural practices will not change overnight, much of the problem and therefore the solution rests with the Indian state. They point to India's ponderously slow and overburdened criminal justice system, in which prosecution rates are low, convictions infrequent, and sentences far too lenient. They also note that while India needs a more efficient and effective legal system, the performance of the judges as well as the police is unlikely to improve until elected politicians compel them to do so. Moreover, too many of these officials do not take sexual violence against women seriously. The Mumbai chief of police recently blamed rape on a culture of "promiscuity," and in two separate instances state ministers argued that rape often happens "accidentally" and is "sometimes right, sometimes wrong." The leader of one of India's largest regional parties argued publicly that those convicted of rape are often judged too harshly, concluding that "boys make mistakes."

There is growing awareness among India's citizenry that if politicians are the key to motivating bureaucrats, civil society must in turn hold elected politicians accountable. In the wake of nationwide protests following the rape of the Delhi student in 2012, state and federal governments have passed laws that establish special courts to handle crimes against women; that criminalize voyeurism, stalking, and sexual harassment; and that impose the death penalty for rape attacks leading to the victim's death. The BJP government, after coming to office in 2014, listened to the electorate and pledged "zero tolerance" for violence against women.

Certainly, rape and sexual violence are not exclusively an Indian problem. Three times as many rapes are reported in the United States as in India, although the United States has roughly a fourth of India's population. But no one, least of all India's increasingly agitated and sophisticated citizenry, doubts that India has a rape problem. Or that the government—and the public—must become a larger part of the solution.

Anti-Graft Campaign and the Common Man's Party

Another issue that has stirred anger and frustration among the Indian people is the country's endemic public corruption. Like gender discrimination, political corruption is not a new phenomenon in India. But the recent exposure of a number of particularly egregious political scandals, combined with (and contributing to) a growing public awareness, has spawned a political movement that mobilized Indian civil society, gave birth to a political party, and shook India's political class. Whether the movement will lead to any permanent solutions or lasting political change is yet to be seen.

The decade-long, Congress-led coalition government (2004–14) found itself embroiled in a series of high-profile scandals. The biggest of these involved the auctioning of the 2G wireless spectrum by the government's Telecommunications Ministry in 2008. A subsequent investigation revealed that insider deals involving the issuing of licensing may have cost the government some $40 billion. Delhi's hosting of the Commonwealth Games in 2010 (chaired by a Congress politician) also involved a number of under-the-table, no-bid contracts that resulted in extensive delays and huge cost overruns. A 2012 "Coalgate" scandal concerning the improper distribution of coal resources may have cost taxpayers another $33 billion.[26]

These and other scandals, not to mention the host of petty inconveniences and expenses resulting from the license raj, brought public anger to a boil. The charismatic leader who gave voice and order to this anger was Anna Hazare, a social activist and former Army officer. Employing the nonviolent tactics and even the signature white cap worn by Gandhi, Hazare had decades of experience in leading populist protests against political and social ills. In 2011, he set his sights on government corruption and launched an "indefinite fast," demanding that parliament pass a law establishing an independent watchdog agency to fight official corruption. His hunger strike, conducted from a central square of Delhi near the parliament building, struck a chord not only with India's middle class but also with lower-class workers who felt disenfranchised and ignored by India's political class. Millions rallied to the cause of "Team Anna." Caught off guard, the Congress-led government first ignored, then decried, and after two weeks ultimately capitulated to his demand, agreeing to draft a bill that would set up a powerful new anticorruption body.

By mid-2012, however, little progress had been made on the bill. The situation prompted Arvind Kejriwal, a former civil servant and one of the chief architects of Hazare's political protest, to form a political party. It was called the Aam Aadmi (Common Man's) Party (AAP) and sported a broom as its party symbol (for sweeping away corruption). In 2013, Kejriwal and the AAP obtained 30 percent of the vote and 28 of the 70 seats in the Delhi regional parliamentary elections. Although the BJP won 32 seats, the AAP was able to form a minority government with Kejriwal as chief minister.

True to the Common Man image, Kejriwal refused to move into the chief minister's plush residence and even spent one night sleeping on the sidewalk.

The AAP government lasted only 49 days, however, before Kejriwal resigned in protest after the Delhi assembly failed to pass the AAP's bill to establish a state ombudsman. The AAP next set its sights on the 2014 national parliamentary elections, hoping to deny a majority of seats to either the BJP or the INC and thereby give the party a strong bargaining position to further promote its anti-graft agenda. Ultimately, the AAP fared poorly in the voting, taking only 4 of the 535 seats. Kejriwal campaigned for a seat from a Varanasi precinct, going head-to-head against the BJP's Modi, and was soundly beaten. Although a watered-down version of the independent watchdog bill was finally passed into law in 2013, it fell far short of the measure advocated by civil activists.

Like others before them, both Hazare and Kejriwal learned the difficulty of turning a single-issue protest movement into a political campaign. On the other hand, the AAP fared better in its national debut than the BJP did in its first national elections in 1984. More significantly, in 2015, the AAP swept Delhi state elections, winning 67 of the 70 seats to the BJP's 3 seats. This stunning victory indicates that the Indian electorate has not forgotten the issue that inspired the movement. The Indian political establishment ignores the issue of political corruption at its peril.

NOTES

1. The Indian Constitution identifies 18 official or "scheduled" languages.
2. Stanley Wolpert, *India* (Berkeley: University of California Press, 1991), 14.
3. For a careful and thorough discussion of the caste system, its origins, evolution, and social and political consequences for India, see Susan Bayly, *The New Cambridge History of India: Caste, Society, and Politics in India from the Eighteenth Century to the Modern Age* (Cambridge, UK: Cambridge University Press, 1999).
4. Francis G. Hutchins, *The Illusion of Permanence: British Imperialism in India* (Princeton, NJ: Princeton University Press, 1967), xi.
5. Wolpert, *India*, 55.
6. Though successful in his campaign to end colonialism, even the Great Soul could not prevent either Hindu-Muslim violence or, ultimately, the partition of Pakistan and India, despite his best efforts. For a valuable biography of Gandhi, see Judith M. Brown, *Gandhi: Prisoner of Hope* (New Haven, CT: Yale University Press, 1992).
7. Yasmin Khan, *The Great Partition* (New Haven, CT: Yale University Press, 2007).
8. V. S. Naipaul, *India: A Million Mutinies Now* (New York: Penguin, 1990).
9. For a useful historical comparison of democracy and authoritarianism in India and Pakistan, see Maya Tudor, *The Promise of Power: The Origins of Democracy in India and Autocracy in Pakistan* (Cambridge, UK: Cambridge University Press, 2013).
10. Wolpert, *India*, 212.

11. Bhagwan D. Dua, "Presidential Rule in India: A Study in Crisis Politics," *Asian Survey* 19 (June 1979): 611–26.

12. The limiting conditions for the "promulgation" of a presidential ordinance include (1) at least one of the chambers of parliament must not be in session; (2) the circumstances must necessitate immediate action; and (3) the ordinances must ultimately be approved by parliament or repromulgated. See Shubhankar Dam, "An Institutional Alchemy: India's Two Parliaments in Comparative Context," *Brooklyn Journal of International Law* 39, no. 2 (2014): 613–55.

13. Pradeep Chhibber and Ken Kollman, "Party Aggregation and the Number of Parties in India and the United States," *American Political Science Review* 92 (June 1998): 329–42.

14. See Alfred Stepan, Juan J. Linz, and Yogendra Yadav, "The Rise of 'State-Nations,'" *Journal of Democracy* 21 (July 2010): 50–68.

15. The following comparisons are taken from Susanne Hoeber Rudolph and Lloyd I. Rudolph, "New Dimensions of Indian Democracy," *Journal of Democracy* 13 (2002): 52–66.

16. Arun Shourie, "Two Concepts of Liberty," *Economist*, March 3, 2005.

17. Ashutosh Varshney, "Hindu Nationalism in Power," *Journal of Democracy* 25 (October 2014): 34–45.

18. Mukul Kesavan, "India's Embattled Secularism," *Wilson Quarterly* 27 (Winter 2003): 61.

19. Stepan et al., "The Rise of 'State-Nations.'"

20. Kesavan, "India's Embattled Secularism," 63.

21. World Bank Doing Business website, www.doingbusiness.org (accessed 5/25/17).

22. Edward Luce, *In Spite of the Gods* (New York: Anchor Books, 2007), 78

23. Unique Identification Authority of India, http://uidai.gov.in (accessed 5/25/17).

24. Ishtiaq Ahmed, "The 1947 Partition of India: A Paradigm for Pathological Politics in India and Pakistan," *Asian Ethnicity* 3 (March 2002): 9–28.

25. Beina Xu, "Governance in India: Women's Rights," *Council on Foreign Relations Backgrounder*, June 10, 2014, www.cfr.org/india/governance-india-womens-rights/p30041 (accessed 8/6/14).

26. Sumit Ganguly, "India and Its Neighbors," *Journal of Democracy* 25 (April 2014): 93–104.

KEY TERMS

Amritsar Northern Indian city and location of the Golden Temple, Sikhism's holiest shrine

asymmetric federalism A system where power is devolved unequally across the country and its constituent regions; often the result of specific laws negotiated between the region and the central government

Ayodhya North-central Indian city where the Babri Mosque was destroyed in 1992

Bharatiya Janata Party (BJP) Indian People's Party; Hindu nationalist party in government since the 2014 general election

caste Hindu hereditary social grouping

Center Term referring to India's national government and its capital in New Delhi

chief minister Chief executive of federal states in India; elected by the state legislature to serve a five-year term

Council of States Upper house of Indian parliament, representing India's 29 states and seven territories

Dalits "Suppressed groups"; formal name of India's outcastes

East India Company A firm created to develop trade between the United Kingdom and India

emergency rule Law invoked by Indian national government to suspend the constitution by declaring martial law

Gandhi, Indira Indian prime minister (1966–77; 1979–84) and daughter of Jawaharlal Nehru

Gandhi, Mahatma (Mohandas K.) (1869–1948) Indian nationalist and leader of the Indian independence movement

Gandhi, Sonia Italian-born wife of Rajiv Gandhi and leader of the Indian National Congress Party

Green Revolution Period during the 1960s and 1970s when technologically enhanced crops and cropping methods dramatically improved food production in India

Gujarat Western Indian state in which Hindu-Muslim violence broke out in 2002

Hindi One of two national languages in India

Hinduism India's dominant religious tradition

Hindutva Literally, "Hindu-ness"; Hindu nationalism

House of the People Lower and more powerful house of Indian parliament

import substitution industrialization Mercantilist strategy of development in which local production is protected from imports

Indian National Congress (INC) Major Indian political party; began as leading organization of Indian independence movement

Kashmir Contested region in northern India claimed by both India and Pakistan

Kerala Southwestern Indian state governed by Communists; famous for its high rates of literacy, low rates of fertility, and low population growth

license raj India's highly bureaucratized and politicized mercantilist system of licenses, permits, and quotas governing virtually all aspects of the economy

Modi, Narendra BJP prime minister since 2014 and former successful and controversial chief minister (governor) of the state of Gujarat

Mughals Muslim invaders who ruled India for several hundred years beginning in the sixteenth century

Muslim League Indian Muslim independence organization

nabob game Strategy of British East India Company for controlling India by setting up puppet Mughal governorships, or nabobs

Naxalism Radical Maoist (or guerrilla communist) insurgency in India

Nehru, Jawaharlal India's first prime minister (1947–64) and successor to Mahatma Gandhi as leader of the INC

outsourcing Moving the production of goods and services to another country to take advantage of cheap labor or other savings

partition Creation of the new states of Pakistan and India from the South Asian British colony of India in 1947

presidential rule State-level equivalent of emergency rule in India in which the national government takes temporary control of a state by imposing martial law

raj Hindu word for "rule"

Sepoy Mutiny Failed 1857–58 revolt against the British, sponsored by the Indian aristocracy and carried out by sepoys, who were Indian soldiers employed by the British

Sikhism Indian religious tradition combining elements of Hindu and Muslim beliefs

Singh, Manmohan INC prime minister of India, 2004–14

untouchables India's outcaste groups, including tribal aboriginals and those who traditionally performed "unclean" duties

WEB LINKS

- GOI directory of Indian government websites (http://goidirectory.nic.in)
- Government and politics of South Asia, South and Southeast Asian Studies, Columbia University Libraries (www.columbia.edu/cu/lweb/indiv/southasia/cuvl/govt.html)
- *Outlook*, a popular weekly newsmagazine (http://outlookindia.com)
- Parliament (http://parliamentofindia.nic.in)
- *Times of India* (http://timesofindia.indiatimes.com)

10

Hassan Rouhani speaks at a campaign rally prior to his successful campaign for president in 2013.

IRAN

Why Study This Case?

Like many of the cases in this volume, Iran illustrates important dynamics in comparative politics. Most important, it is associated with what we think of as **Islamism**, or **Islamic fundamentalism**. When we speak of fundamentalism, we mean a view of religion as absolute and inerrant that should be legally enforced by making faith the sovereign authority. Faith becomes ideology.

In 1979, the authoritarian, secular Iranian monarchy fell to revolution, an uprising inspired in part by the charisma of the religious leader **Ayatollah Ruhollah Khomeini**. This Islamic revolution dramatically transformed all aspects of Iranian life, as Khomeini and his followers sought to create a **theocracy** in which a religious elite dominated the regime. In this "Islamic Republic," law and politics are expected to flow from the **Koran**, the main spiritual text of Islam. The Iranian Revolution became a source of inspiration for Islamist movements around the world. As numerous countries struggle with reconciling Islam and the state today, the Iranian Revolution remains an important example of the power of Islam as a political vision.

In looking more deeply, however, we find that Iran is atypical and unrepresentative of the politics of Islam or even the politics of the Middle East. Contrary to what many assume, Iran is not an Arab country—the major ethnicity of Iran's population is Persian. Nor do Iranians speak Arabic, the common language of the Middle East; they speak, instead, **Farsi**, a language closer to English and other European languages. Indeed, Iranians see themselves as a distinct nation; they look upon Arab countries as foreign and often view them with some degree of contempt. Iranians do not necessarily see themselves as part of a broader pan-Islamic or pan-Arabic movement, and that feeling has only intensified since the Arab Spring.

IRAN

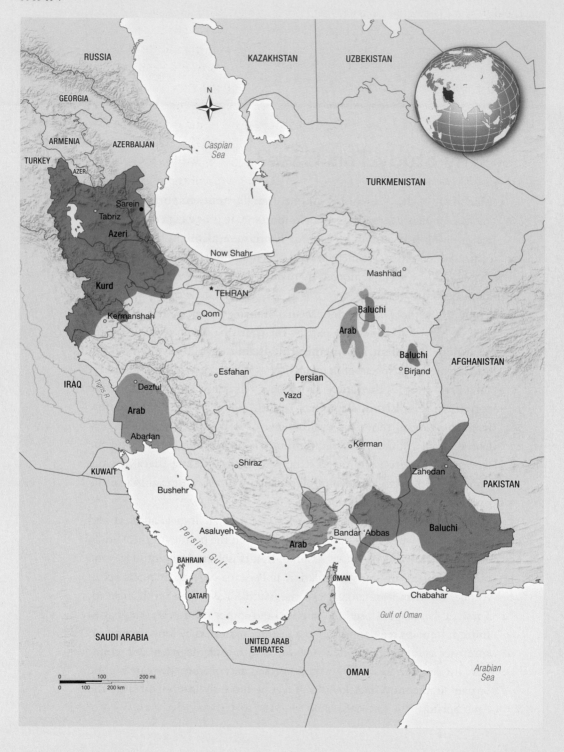

RUSSIA

KAZAKHSTAN

UZBEKISTAN

GEORGIA

ARMENIA

AZERBAIJAN

TURKEY

AZER.

Caspian
Sea

TURKMENISTAN

Sarein

Tabriz

Azeri

Now Shahr

Mashhad

Kurd

★ TEHRAN

Baluchi

Kermanshah

Qom

Arab

Baluchi

IRAQ

Esfahan

Persian

Birjand

AFGHANISTAN

Dezful

Yazd

Arab

Abadan

Kerman

KUWAIT

Shiraz

Zahedan

PAKISTAN

Bushehr

Asaluyeh

Arab

Bandar 'Abbas

Baluchi

BAHRAIN

Persian Gulf

OMAN

QATAR

Chabahar

SAUDI ARABIA

UNITED ARAB
EMIRATES

Gulf of Oman

OMAN

Arabian
Sea

N

| 0 | 100 | 200 mi |
| 0 | 100 | 200 km |

The difference between Iranian ethnicity and Iranian national identity is compounded by religion. Again, at first glance, Iran's revolution might be seen as the first spark in the current wave of Islamist activism and conflict, and there can be no doubt that in its early years the revolution did inspire a new wave of radicalism and political violence across the region. But the international impact of the revolution was tempered because Iranians practice **Shiism**, a minority form of Islam (practiced by about 10 to 15 percent of the global Muslim population) that differs from the rest of Islam in its belief regarding the rightful heir of the prophet **Muhammad**. As a result, many followers of Islam around the world reject the Iranian theocracy for avowing a mistaken, even heretical, form of the faith. Despite these divisions, Iran has certainly influenced modern debates on the relationship between politics and Islam, especially among Shiite groups elsewhere in the region (as in Iraq, Afghanistan, and Lebanon). For some, Iran remains an inspiration for political change; for others, it is an example of how religion and politics should not mix. Such conflicting views can be found not only among average Shiites (both inside and outside Iran) but also among Shiism's top clergy.

These complexities help shape Iran's role in the international system. In recent years, Iran has moved toward developing its own nuclear capacity, creating worries among many states that such weapons would make the country a significant regional threat. While an international agreement reached in 2016 has lessened concerns and improved international relations, ongoing tension remains and there is a significant risk that the agreement could unravel.

Such tensions occur against the backdrop of domestic unease. In the 1990s, reformists sought to liberalize political, economic, and social institutions in Iran. This goal translated into the 1997 election of President **Mohammad Khatami**, who spoke of an expansion of civil society and a "dialogue of civilizations" in place of international conflict. Hopes were high that Khatami's election would pave the way for dramatic political change. Religious conservatives, however, managed to beat back the reformers and limit Khatami's powers.

The June 2005 election of the conservative **Mahmoud Ahmadinejad** as president dealt a serious blow to the reformers and led to a new period of increased conservatism at home and confrontation abroad. This trend resulted in widespread support for reformist candidates in the 2009 presidential election, such that it appears that the top leadership chose to falsify the election results to ensure a second term for Ahmadinejad. The election results, and the subsequent public protests and violent state response, only deepened divisions over the future direction of the country.

In 2013, cleric **Hassan Rouhani** won a surprising landslide victory, following a campaign in which he promised to advance those social reforms lost under

Ahmadinejad as well as improve relations with the West. But like Khatami before him, Rouhani has found challenging conservative institutions and actors, such as the more powerful Supreme Leader **Ali Khamenei**, a formidable task. Many of Rouhani's supporters have been disappointed in the limited changes to date—not unlike Khatami's presidency two decades earlier. In 2017 Rouhani won a strong mandate in the elections for his second term, but this was less a vote of popular confidence than opposition to his hard-line opponent. Rouhani has yet to deliver on many of his promises. Can Iran truly reform and become a more liberal, even democratic regime?

Despite its unique institutions, Iran can give us a glimpse into the potential power of Islamic fundamentalism, its limitations, and the sources of resistance to it.

Major Geographic and Demographic Features

Iran occupies an important position in Middle East politics, yet it is in many ways an outlier. As noted earlier, Iranians do not belong to the wider Arab community of the Middle East; they have different national origins, and their national language is Farsi—related to English and other Indo-European languages—instead of Arabic.

Iran itself is on the eastern periphery of the Middle East, sharing borders with Afghanistan, Pakistan, and several states that were once part of the Soviet Union. But its geographic position does not mean that it is insignificant. It is about the size of Alaska (somewhat smaller than Mexico) and has a population of nearly 80 million, larger than that of the United Kingdom. For both its size and its population, Iran ranks among the world's top 20 nations. Not only is its population large, but it is relatively young in comparison with that of Europe or North America. The median age is 30; compare this with Canada, for example, where the median age is 42.

Demography matters. A large percentage of Iran's population has no memory of the country before the 1979 revolution and has experienced only economic stagnation under the current regime. Moreover, the state must deal with a large influx of young people seeking higher education, employment, and housing, all of which the government has difficulty providing. This segment of the population thus currently represents the greatest challenge to the regime. It was the youth who took to the streets in protests following the contested presidential election of 2009 and backed the election of Rouhani in 2013 and 2017.

Iran's population is also diverse. Only about 60 percent of the population is ethnically Persian. Nearly 20 percent is Azeri, a Turkic-speaking people concentrated in the northwest of the country, near the borders of Armenia and Azerbaijan. The remaining population is made up of several smaller ethnic groups, including Kurds, Arabs, and Baluchis. Some of these ethnic groups follow Sunni rather than Shia Islam. This diversity contributed to ethnic conflict after the 1979 revolution. Although such tensions have largely subsided, there remain sporadic ethnic conflicts, particularly among the Kurdish minority. This situation can be exacerbated by turmoil in neighboring countries like Iraq.

Iran is estimated to have the fourth largest reserves of oil in the world. It also boasts the world's largest reserves of natural gas. As in many other countries, these resources have been both a boon and a curse. It was oil that drew imperial attention at the start of the twentieth century and helped foster modernization—as well as external intervention, domestic corruption, and eventually revolution. Oil has also helped to keep the current regime in power. However, a negative consequence of Iran's oil-derived wealth has been stagnation in other parts of the economy. The nuclear deal has allowed for a dramatic increase in oil exports and foreign direct investment. Whether this will translate into economic growth and greater employment remains to be seen.

Historical Development of the State

The Persian Legacy and the Islamic Empire

Iranians trace their national and political origins back thousands of years, at least to the second millennium B.C.E. Around that time, a number of people migrated into the region from Central Asia, and among them was the ethnic group we now know as the Persians. Outside Iran, Persian continues to be a common name used to describe the majority population of the country. Until 1935, the country itself was officially known as **Persia.**

During the first millennium B.C.E., the Persians were able to extend their influence throughout the region, subduing other groups and creating the Achaemenid Empire in the process. Under the emperors Cyrus, Darius, and Xerxes, the empire grew vast, stretching from modern-day India across much of the Middle East, and becoming a major foe to the Greek city-states. The Achaemenid Empire was noted for its wealth, technical sophistication, and relative political and religious tolerance, and it is an important symbol of Iranian might that still resonates with

Iranians today. Although the empire was destroyed by Alexander the Great in 334 B.C.E., the country continued to develop under a series of ruling dynasties. These kings, or shahs, ruled through the sixth century C.E.

The most dramatic transformation of Persia by outside forces occurred in the seventh century with the arrival of Islam, brought by Arabs from the Middle East. Shortly after the death of the prophet Muhammad in 632 C.E., his successors began to spread the faith through the region by military conquest. The new empire under the Umayyad dynasty (661–750 C.E.) and its successors brought Persia into the Islamic fold. Although the conquerors adopted many Persian practices and institutions, differences between Persian and Arab culture remained. Arabic became the language of the state and religion; Farsi, however, remained the tongue of the people, though it adopted many Arabic loan words and the Arabic script.

The population slowly converted from Zoroastrianism (a native monotheistic faith) to Islam.[1] Up through the eleventh century, Persia was part of several powerful Islamic dynasties that stretched across Central Asia and the Middle East. From the thirteenth to the fifteenth century, Persia, like much of the region, was devastated by the Mongols, not only economically but also because of depopulation. Only with the death of the last major Mongol leader did a new independent Persian dynasty emerge.

Dynastic Rule and the Adoption of Shiism

The period from the sixteenth to the early twentieth century saw the rise of two long-standing Iranian dynasties: the Safavids (1502–1736) and the Qajars (1794–1925). Under the Safavids, the country adopted Shiism as the state religion as a way to differentiate the country from its Ottoman rivals, who were Sunni.

Shiism differs from dominant Sunni Islam by arguing that leadership within the Islamic community has been entrusted by God to the family and bloodline of the prophet Muhammad. From Muhammad's son-in-law Ali on down, according to the Shia, the **imams** are the true leaders of the faith, though these descendants have been repeatedly deprived of power by other Muslim leaders. The last of these imams, known as the **Mahdi**, or "guided one," has in fact been concealed by God and is expected by the Shia to reappear at the end of time to restore justice and equality to a corrupted world. In this regard, Shiism resembles Christianity. Moreover, it emphasizes the martyrdom of these descendants of Muhammad, many of whom died at the hands of Sunni rivals.

In particular, the Shia venerate Hussein, the grandson of the Prophet, who carried out a failed uprising against the corrupt Umayyad caliphate in 680 C.E.

Surrounded by enemy forces on the plains of Karbala (in modern-day Iraq), Hussein and most of his family were killed by this much larger force. His battle against overwhelming odds and his willingness to sacrifice himself for the larger cause of a more just Islam became a cornerstone of Shia belief. **Ashura**, the most important Shia religious holiday, commemorates Hussein's death with lamentation and prayer. Contemporary political and religious struggles for Shia are thus often viewed in the context of Hussein's martyrdom and the need to live by his standards, as captured in the famous quote from Iranian political thinker Ali Shariati: "Every day is Ashura, and everywhere is Karbala."[2]

Another interesting comparison between Shiism and Christianity has been the relationship between faith and state. In Shiism, the particular emphasis on the descendants of Ali returning at the end of time to rule has made worldly politics in some ways secondary to the faith. This view may seem the complete opposite of what we understand about Iran's "Islamic Republic," but it also indicates that for many Shia, an Islamic Republic is a contradiction in terms. We will explore this important perspective later in the chapter.

However, Shiism has long been connected to, if not directly involved in, politics. The Safavids cultivated within Shiism's religious leaders (or *ulema*) a higher clergy, who came to be known as **ayatollahs.** This structure, too, differs from the more decentralized Sunni Islam, and these high ranking clergy have become a central institution in modern Iranian religion and politics. Yet while Iran's supreme leader has sought to place himself above other clerics, various high-ranking ayatollahs inside and outside of Iran have their own followers and issue their own fatwas (religious rulings) independent of any political leaders.

Although Iran during the Safavid and Qajar eras was able to maintain its power in the face of regional rivals, such as the Ottoman Empire, it inevitably came under pressure from other expanding states. In the early nineteenth century, Russia squeezed Iran from the north, seizing territories, while the United Kingdom conquered neighboring India and attempted to gain control over Afghanistan. Thus, by the mid-nineteenth century, Iran faced a crisis that extended across the region: How could it confront the Western powers, given their superiority in military and economic might? How could Iran modernize and preserve its sovereignty?

Failed Reforms and the Erosion of Sovereignty

In the last decades of the Qajar dynasty, the monarchy enacted various, albeit halfhearted, reforms. They borrowed these reforms from the West, intending to use them in modernizing the weak state. The monarchy experimented with Western-style economic and political institutions even as it surrendered ever more sovereignty to the British and the Russians. Public animosity grew in the face of government weakness and the perception that the monarchy, ineffectual and corrupt, was selling off the country to Westerners.

In 1906, religious leaders, intellectuals, and members of the merchant class protested in favor of limitations on the powers of the Qajar monarchy in what came to be known as the **Constitutional Revolution**. The protest resulted in an elected assembly that drew up the country's first constitution and legislative body, known as the **Majlis**. For Iranians, the Constitutional Revolution signifies the country's first attempt at republicanism and democracy, akin to the American Revolution. Unlike other revolutions, however, it lacked a clear ideology or consensus other than weakening or removing the monarchy, and tellingly, secularists came into conflict with some ayatollahs over the future of the regime.

The Constitutional Revolution, while important, did not live up to expectations. The monarchy quickly sought to abolish the constitution, relying in part on the Russian military to attack the Majlis. Ongoing battles between monarchists and constitutionalists (and between secularists and members of the clergy) opened the way for the United Kingdom and Russia to divide the country into formal spheres of influence in 1907, all but eliminating Persian sovereignty.

With the outbreak of World War I, Iran became entangled in the conflict as troops from the Russian, British, German, and Ottoman empires fought one another and supported various Persian factions that were vying for power; about a quarter of the population was killed. Following World War I and the collapse of the Ottoman and Russian empires, the United Kingdom became the dominant foreign power and occupied much of the country.

The embattled Majlis continued to oppose British imperialism, however, rejecting a 1919 agreement that would have granted the United Kingdom significant control over the state and the economy, including Iran's growing oil industry. Modern Iranian history is thus tightly connected to British imperialism. Even though Iran never formally became part of the British Empire, these unequal relations sowed the seeds of Iranian animosity toward Britain.

Amid the ongoing political turmoil in Iran, a relatively obscure military officer came to political power. Born to a poor family, Reza Khan had distinguished himself as a superior military figure, rising rapidly through the ranks. In 1921, he marched into Tehran as part of a wider group of coup plotters, but he quickly outmaneuvered his allies (including the Majlis, who initially gave him their support)

TIMELINE OF POLITICAL DEVELOPMENT

YEAR	EVENT
1905–6	Constitutional revolution seeks to limit power of the monarchy.
1921	Reza Khan seizes power.
1925	Reza Khan is proclaimed shah and changes his name to Reza Shah Pahlavi.
1941	British and Soviet forces occupy Iran; the shah is forced to abdicate in favor of his son, Mohammad Reza Pahlavi.
1951	Parliament votes to nationalize the oil industry.
1953	Struggle between the shah and Prime Minister Mohammad Mosaddeq culminates in Operation Ajax, in which Mosaddeq is overthrown with U.S. help.
1963	White Revolution begins.
1979	Iranian Revolution takes place: the shah is deposed; Ayatollah Ruhollah Khomeini returns from exile; U.S. embassy is seized and hostages are held for 444 days.
1980	Iraq invades Iran.
1988	Iran-Iraq War ends.
1989	Ayatollah Khomeini dies; Ayatollah Khamenei is elected supreme leader.
1997	Reformer Mohammad Khatami is elected president.
1999	Pro-reform student protests lead to rioting and mass arrests.
2002	Russia begins work on Iran's first nuclear reactor, at Bushehr.
2005	Mahmoud Ahmadinejad is elected president.
2009	Ahmadinejad wins a second presidential term in a disputed election.
2013	Hassan Rouhani is elected president.
2017	Rouhani is reelected for a second term.

and consolidated his rule. Although the United Kingdom did not directly plan the coup, it was pleased to see a military "strongman" establish control of the country, which could make their influence over Iran that much easier. Thus, from the outset, most Iranians considered the coup the direct result of an imperialist plot—a view that continues to this day.

In contrast, during this same period many Persians saw the United States as an important supporter of Iranian independence. An American served as the country's treasurer in 1911, and U.S. diplomats and missionaries generally backed Iranian independence and republicanism. In time, the view of the United States as a supporter of Iranian independence would change.

Consolidation of Power under the Pahlavi Dynasty

Reza Shah Pahlavi, as Reza Khan renamed himself, proved to be more than a mere puppet of the British. Upon becoming head of the armed forces, he quickly moved to consolidate his power, removing his fellow conspirators from office and neutralizing threats within and outside Iran. By centralizing the military, he was able to quell several regional rebellions and to limit British and Soviet interference in the country's affairs.

In 1923, the last shah of the Qajar dynasty appointed Reza Khan prime minister and promptly went into exile in Europe; in 1925, the Majlis formally deposed the Qajar dynasty and appointed Reza Khan the new shah. Surprisingly, Reza Khan initially did not want to be monarch. He favored instead a republican form of government with a powerful unelected president, along the lines of post-Ottoman Turkey. However, many of the clergy saw a secular republican government as dangerous to the faith (an issue that first emerged in the Constitutional Revolution) and thus pressed for a traditional form of rule. Ironically, then, this quest for modernization by Reza Khan left Iran with a powerful monarchy up until 1979, when most other monarchs around the world had long been removed from office or stripped of their powers.

As a monarch with few constraints on his power, the shah pursued a course of dramatic Westernization and state building. That included reforming the bureaucracy, instituting primary and secondary education and a university system, developing road and rail systems, establishing a number of state-owned businesses to develop monopolies in important domestic and export-oriented markets, and abolishing the aristocracy (other than the shah himself).

Iran also exerted greater (if still limited) control over its burgeoning oil industry, which Britain had dominated since its inception. In addition, Reza Shah instituted national conscription as part of his effort to centralize military might and extend state control over what had been a fractious and tribal country. The shah complemented this political centralization with efforts to build a modern national identity by promoting the idea of a single people whose glory extended back thousands of years and drawing on the country's pre-Islamic history. For example, he demonstrated this concept by taking the name Pahlavi, a pre-Islamic word. While the idea of an Iranian people was an old one, both the Constitutional Revolution and the Pahlavi dynasty helped foster a strong sense of national identity.

Finally, as part of his modernization, the shah greatly extended the rights of women, giving them access to education, including at the university level. He also sought to root out traditional customs which he believed were holding back their emancipation. Two important symbols were the head scarf (hijab) and cloak (chador), which women wore in public as a sign of modesty and privacy. In 1934, inspired by similar reforms in Turkey, Iran forbade the wearing of the head coverings in schools, a proscription that was later extended to other public facilities. The shah's efforts were part of a broader attack on Shiism and Islamic religious and educational institutions, which were seen as backward and of foreign (that is, Arab) origin. In 1935, the name of the country itself was changed, from Persia (as it had been called by the outside world) to Iran, the traditional name of the country used by its inhabitants.

Young women near Tehran University. Although Iranian laws require women to wear the hijab, many do not fully cover their hair as required and otherwise dress in Western clothes.

Modernization came at the expense of democratization as well as traditional practices and religious beliefs. Democratic institutions, such as the press and the Majlis, were curtailed, and religious and political opponents were jailed, exiled, or killed. The power of the clergy was similarly curtailed as the state set its own standards for social norms. Yet the regime lacked any substantive ideology beyond nationalism and the shah's own exercise of power. By the eve of World War II, Iran had made significant progress in establishing modern political institutions and independence from foreign interference. Yet progress had come at the cost of increased repression of civic life.

World War II again drew the country into international conflict. Reza Shah's friendly relations with Germany raised fears in the United Kingdom and Russia; in 1941, the two countries invaded Iran to open a land corridor between them and to prevent Iran (and its oil) from falling under Axis control. Reza Shah was forced to abdicate in favor of his son, **Mohammad Reza Pahlavi**, and to go into exile. As World War II gave way to the Cold War, the United States, the United Kingdom, and the Soviet Union all sought to consolidate their power over the country and its oil supplies. Political and religious activity resurfaced in the face of the weakened state and regime.[3]

The Nationalist Challenge under Mosaddeq and the U.S. Response

In the aftermath of Reza Shah's abdication, republican and religious activity began to reassert itself; the new monarch, Mohammed Reza, was unable to thwart these advances. The Majlis and the ulema promoted the removal of Western influence over Iran, and many supported nationalization of the oil industry, which was under joint Iranian and British ownership.

Nationalization was advocated in particular by the new prime minister, **Mohammad Mosaddeq**, who represented the **National Front**, a republican party that favored reducing the power of the monarchy or eliminating it altogether. The shah reluctantly conceded to nationalization in 1951, which provoked British anger and led to the withdrawal of Britain's technical support, essentially halting oil production. As the crisis deepened, Mosaddeq relied on political allies such as the Marxist Tudeh Party to reduce the powers of the monarchy.

Mosaddeq's actions were directed toward the goals of national sovereignty and modernization. However, his nationalization of oil generated deep British animosity, while his secularism and republicanism alienated much of the ulema. His alliance with Tudeh similarly raised fears within the United States that Iran faced a Communist takeover (as had happened in Eastern Europe only years earlier).

Indeed, immediately after World War II, the Soviet Union supported an independent pro-Soviet government in the north of the county. The United States had long been sympathetic to republican views, and Mosaddeq saw it as an ally. Instead, the United States viewed these developments as yet another battle against communism, as in Europe.

With the shah's support, the United States and the United Kingdom moved to overthrow Mosaddeq through a covert program known as **Operation Ajax**. Several days of conflict between supporters of the prime minister and supporters of the shah, including republicans and the military, finally culminated in a victory for the shah and his backers. In the aftermath of Operation Ajax, hundreds of National Front and Tudeh leaders and supporters were arrested, and several key leaders were executed. Mosaddeq was placed under house arrest, where he stayed until his death in 1967.

Much of the ulema, however, welcomed Mosaddeq's overthrow because they feared he would impose secularism on Iran. While the United States and the United Kingdom were clearly major actors in the overthrow, domestic factors, too, were central to bringing down Mosaddeq.[4] In many ways, Mosaddeq's actions—his calls for greater national sovereignty in the face of Western imperialism and his opposition to the shah—can be seen as a forerunner to the 1979 revolution. However, since 1979, he has been a problematic figure for Iranian leaders due to his unstinting secularism—a reminder of a political path that Iran did not take.

The shah wasted little time in concentrating his power along his father's lines. Reza Shah had expended much of his energy developing an Iran independent of Western power, but his son balanced his quest for sovereignty with a new alliance with the United States. The United Kingdom receded as the United States became central to the development of Iran's economy, education, military, culture, and civic life. Democracy, however, was deemed not worthy of emulation. The shah repressed opposition parties and built a powerful secret police (known by its acronym, **SAVAK**); he also marginalized the prime minister and Majlis. The short-lived and turbulent period of democracy thus ended, and its destruction became forever associated with the United States.

Authoritarianism and Modernization during the White Revolution

After bringing the political system under his control, the shah revived the policy of top-down modernization that his father had promoted earlier. Once again, the policy had the effect of marginalizing the ulema. Its reforms, starting in 1963, were known as the **White Revolution**.[5]

The shah's modernization policies included land reform, privatization of state-run industries, a literacy campaign, and the enfranchisement of women. Some reforms, in particular land reform and female enfranchisement, were strongly opposed by religious leaders. In June of 1963, the reforms led to rioting, which the government suppressed violently. A subsequent protest in 1964, over Iran's growing alliance with the United States, was also quickly quelled.

Associated with both protests was Ruhollah Khomeini, an ayatollah based in the holy city of Qom. Khomeini was already known for his writings linking worldly politics to spiritual issues, an interest that extended back to the 1940s and set him apart from most Shia clerics. Khomeini quickly became an important symbol of opposition to the shah. Just as quickly, he rose to the rank of Grand Ayatollah, a position held by only a very few ayatollahs deemed worthy of emulation. Khomeini's growing power led the shah to expel him from the country (execution was too dangerous a move). Khomeini settled in neighboring Iraq and later went to France. From abroad, he continued to criticize the Iranian regime for its corruption, inequality, and reliance on the United States. Khomeini articulated a vision of an Iran governed by Islam, creating a country that could be a lodestar for revolution across the Middle East. Given the failures of democratization in 1953, a religious alternative drew many supporters, even those with little interest in or understanding of the implications of Khomeini's ideas.

For the next 15 years, the shah would rule without serious challenge. All remaining pretenses of democracy were swept away, leaving a state with power concentrated in the hands of the monarchy and enforced by the military and SAVAK. Rapid, if uneven, modernization continued, fostered by state policy and by rising oil revenues (upward of $20 billion a year by the mid-1970s). Iran built a huge military in response to the shah's desire to project the country as a major regional force and a "great civilization" to be reckoned with on the world stage. Tens of thousands of Americans came to work in Iran, helping to foster rapid social change but also generating resentment thanks to their often patronizing treatment of Iranians. Parts of Iran began to superficially resemble the United States, widening the differences between modern and traditional institutions, religious and secular. At the same time, the shah's rule became increasingly autocratic as he cracked down on religious institutions and a growing civil society.

All these rapid changes did little to legitimize or support the shah's rule. Billions of dollars in oil revenue flowed into Iran, helping to create a middle class. But much of the money also disappeared into the pockets of those in power, either to build the military or to support the lavish lifestyle of the shah and his family.

Economic improvements were not experienced widely across the population, and the influx of oil money led to inflation that increased economic insecurity. That so much disruption and misery was tied to oil, and that so much of the oil industry was directed and run by foreigners, helped foster the sentiment that the United States and other Western powers were simply plundering the nation—as many observers felt they had done for the past century.

Opposition to the Shah and the Iranian Revolution

The worsening of Iran's economy during the mid-1970s coincided with a growing, highly educated urban youth and increased state repression. Eventually, the situation led to open conflict. In 1977, the new U.S. president, Jimmy Carter, whose administration placed greater emphasis on human rights, began to criticize the shah for his repressive practices. Hoping to pacify his ally, the shah carried out a limited set of reforms, freeing some political prisoners and allowing banned organizations such as the National Front to reorganize. The Carter administration did not press the shah further and, in the eyes of many hopeful Iranians, even seemed to retreat from its earlier criticisms in favor of political stability.

As U.S. pressure on the shah flagged, Iranians found a second source of external opposition to his repressive rule: the Ayatollah Khomeini. Still living in Iraq, in the Shiite holy city of Najaf, Khomeini had through his works elaborated a vision of an Islamic political system for Iran quite at odds with that of much of the Shia clergy. These ideas culminated in his work *Islamic Government: The Governance of the Jurist*. In this work, he argued that Islamic government should be constructed around the concept of **velayat-e faqih**, or clerical rule; whereas a monarchy was a usurpation of Allah's rule on earth, a system of government by a clergy trained in Islamic jurisprudence would be a continuation of the political system first established by the prophet Muhammad. The clergy could serve as a regent in place of the Mahdi, who would someday return to reestablish religious and political righteousness. Since such a form of government was the only regime consistent with the will of God, secular forms, such as those of the shah, should be overthrown. Khomeini's writings began to attract a large following in Iran, where, despite his absence, his popularity continued to grow.[6]

The shah, Khomeini, and the United States were now on a collision course. In 1978, the Iranian government attempted a smear campaign against Khomeini, which only increased support for the ayatollah and touched off a series of protests. The government responded harshly, but this in turn sparked a new round of conflict, linked to a 40-day cycle of mourning traditionally undertaken in Islam. Finally, three important events turned public protest into revolution. First, in August 1978, a fire at Cinema Rex in Abadan killed some 400 people. Many Iranians latched onto the rumor that SAVAK had torched the theater in an attempt to frame the religious opposition (in reality Islamic radicals started the fire). The funerals for the victims became another flashpoint for massive public protest.

Second, in response to the public protests, the shah declared martial law. Yet the protests continued, resonating with the imagery of Ashura and Hussein. In September, a massive protest in Tehran in defiance of martial law called for the end of the monarchy and the return of Ayatollah Khomeini. The army fired on the protesters, and some protesters fired back. Scores were killed, and the violence continued to flow with increasingly religious symbolism, including allusions to martyrdom and the coming of the Mahdi.

Third, the shah, realizing that even in exile Khomeini was a dangerous force, persuaded the Iraqi government to remove him to France. Rather than isolating him, however, the move to Europe only improved Khomeini's connections to Iran, the outside world, and the international media. By November, Tehran was racked by widespread public violence, and the shah, while increasing his reliance on force, feared for his political survival. A series of crackdowns and attempts at co-opting the opposition had no effect. The United States, too, vacillated in its support for the shah, criticizing the use of violence while continuing to give him its support.

By late 1978, the shah's power had slipped away. In December, millions of protesters took to the streets of Tehran in defiance of a government ban on such public gatherings. Military units began to defect. The seemingly unshakable Pahlavi dynasty rapidly fell apart, and the shah fled, replaced by a provisional government with a tenuous hold on the country. On February 1, 1979, millions gathered to welcome the Ayatollah Khomeini as he returned to Iran.[7]

The Consolidation of an Islamic Republic

The revolution did not automatically mean that Iran would have an Islamic regime. As in Russia in 1917, many observers expected a democratic republic, not simply a change from one form of authoritarianism to another. Although most Iranian citizens did call for an "Islamic republic," it is not clear that those supporters agreed with, or even fully grasped, the kind of political system Khomeini was proposing. However, by capitalizing on the political turmoil and drawing on his own charismatic authority, Khomeini was able to undermine the secular provisional government that had replaced the shah. Outflanking the various political and religious factions that had sprung up during the revolution, he gained control of the government and oversaw the drafting of a new constitution that allowed for not only a president and prime minister but also a faqih (a religious leader with expertise in Islamic law) who would have supreme political authority. Khomeini filled this position until his death in 1989.

The **Islamic Republic of Iran** had a violent birth. The new government suppressed all opposition, including monarchists, members of Marxist and other secular political groups, ethnic minorities, and members of other faiths. From 1979 to 1980, perhaps thousands were executed in the name of "revolutionary justice." The course of Iran's relationship with the international community was also transformed when student radicals seized control of the U.S. embassy and held much of its staff hostage for more than a year. While Khomeini did not initially support the students, he came to back them as a way to marginalize more liberal elements who favored maintaining some relationship with the United States. The hostage crisis eventually led to an ill-fated rescue attempt by the Carter administration and to the severing of diplomatic relations between the two countries, which continues to this day.

The convulsions of the revolution were soon compounded by the **Iran-Iraq War**. As the Iranian Revolution unfolded, Iraq's authoritarian leader, Saddam Hussein, perceived these developments as a threat to his own rule over a country in which more than half the population was Shiite. Khomeini himself hoped to spread his Islamic Revolution beyond Iran's borders, and Iraq was the logical next choice. At the same time, Iraq saw in Iran's chaos an opportunity to extend its power in the region and seize Iranian territory that contained many of the country's oil fields. In September 1980, Iraq launched a full-scale invasion of Iran, initiating the Iran-Iraq War, which lasted until 1988.

The war caused widespread destruction on both sides. Iraq had significant firepower and the open or tacit support of most of the Arab world and the United States, which feared the spread of the Iranian Revolution. While Iran's massive military hardware was hobbled by Western sanctions, it benefited from a revolutionary fervor that united the public in a way not seen in Iraq. Iranians rallied to defend the homeland, helping to institutionalize the revolution.

In 1982, realizing that he had miscalculated his chance of success, Hussein sought to end the war; Khomeini refused, believing that this was the opportunity to carry his revolution across the Middle East. Indeed, at one point a regime slogan stated that "the road to Jerusalem runs through Baghdad," thus framing the Iranian revolution as part of a greater struggle for Arabs and Palestinians against Israel. In 1988, after years of war that involved the use of chemical weapons by Iraq, the conflict finally ended in a stalemate. Iran had exhausted its military force and could not remove Saddam Hussein from power. Hundreds of thousands of Iranians and Iraqis were dead. Shortly thereafter, Khomeini himself died, leaving the Islamic Republic without its founder and spiritual guide.

Political Regime

Since 1979, the Islamic Republic of Iran has sought to follow the ideas of Khomeini in creating a political system built around his notion of *velayat-e faqih*, which would replace the sovereignty of men and women with the sovereignty of God as transmitted by the clergy. Yet Khomeini came to power in the wake of a popular revolution driven by the public's demand for a political system that responded to their needs and desires, influenced by republican, democratic, Marxist, and liberal values. The new regime would thus have to reconcile the will of the people with what was viewed as the will of God.

Since Khomeini's death, however, the regime has faced the challenge of what Max Weber termed "the routinization of charisma." That is, how does a nation maintain the ideals and authority of its leader once that leader is gone? How are the ideas of a leader institutionalized as part of a new regime? How does a revolution remain true to its ideals? In Iran, the result has been a political system quite unlike any other, a mixture of institutions that seek to balance popular rights with the word of God.

Political Institutions

THE CONSTITUTION

The Iranian constitution is a product of the 1979 revolution. Since that time, the only major changes to the document were made 10 years later, when Khomeini sought to ensure that the principles of the Islamic Republic would be maintained after his death. In its preamble, the constitution lays out the origins of the current regime, which is viewed as a revolt against the "American conspiracy" of the White Revolution.

According to the constitution, the Islamic Republic exists not to serve the individual but to guide the people toward God. The Koran (the holy book of Islam) therefore serves as a spiritual text as well as the foundation for a unified national ideology that is embodied in the political system. God is sovereign over the Iranian people and state, and all political acts are expected to flow from the word of God.

As the constitution itself states, "All civil, penal, financial, economic, administrative, cultural, military, political, and other laws and regulations must be based on Islamic criteria." This concept is consistent with religious fundamentalism in general, which challenges secular notions of statehood and democracy as practices where humans arrogate to themselves powers and rights that should reside only with God. It is God's law (**Sharia**) that should reign supreme. As such, the Iranian constitution and political institutions are (at least in theory) an attempt to express God's will. At the same time, however, the constitution reflects the fact that the overthrow of the shah was a revolution primarily led by the people, not Khomeini or the ulema. The constitution thus also embodies strongly republican (if not democratic) elements. The result is ongoing political tension between republicanism and theocracy.

The Branches of Government

THE SUPREME LEADER AND THE PRESIDENT

The particular nature of the Iranian constitution has resulted in a set of political institutions that are quite bewildering to outsiders but consistent with the *velayat-e faqih*. We can see this most clearly in the executive branch of the government. As

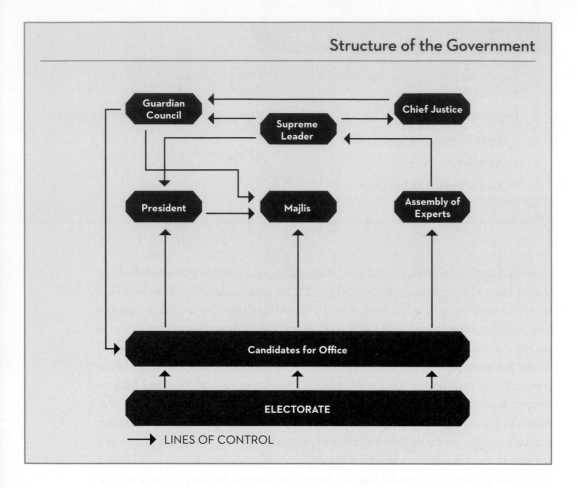

in many other countries, Iran has a dual executive that divides power between two offices. In most other cases, such divisions fall between the head of state—a monarch or president—and the head of government, usually a prime minister. The former reigns while the latter rules.

Iran's executive does not follow this pattern. The dominant executive is the **supreme leader**, a position created for Khomeini following the revolution as an expression of his charismatic power and political ideology. As befits the title, the supreme leader is the most powerful office in Iran, created to ensure that a senior cleric is at the helm of Iranian politics, directing both political and spiritual life. The supreme leader serves for life, though in theory he can be removed for incompetence or failure to uphold his religious duty.

The supreme leader has numerous, if often indirect, powers; many of these are not formally vested in the constitution but derive from practices institutionalized under Khomeini. The supreme leader is commander in chief of the armed forces and appoints the heads of the various branches of the military. He also wields control over the Guardian Council (discussed later), which has the ability to vet candidates for presidential and legislative elections. The supreme leader also appoints the chief justice and thus has significant influence over the judicial system. Finally, the supreme leader also maintains control over significant state-owned economic assets that are not subject to review by other branches of government.

In some ways, the supreme leader may be seen as the head of state, embodying the people and serving as its religious guide. But unlike other ceremonial heads of state, his role in policy is much greater. If anything, the supreme leader looks much more like a traditional monarch than any corresponding modern political executive.

Following Khomeini's death, the office of supreme leader was to be held by a high-ranking ayatollah, just as Khomeini had been. Even at the time of the revolution, however, few of the grand ayatollahs accepted Khomeini's notion of the *velayat-e faqih*. Khomeini's heir apparent, Grand Ayatollah Hussein Ali Montazeri, was sidelined for his criticism of the regime's dictatorial nature and placed under house arrest.

Since 1989, the supreme leader has been Ali Khamenei, who previously served as the president of the country from 1981 to 1989. Before his appointment as supreme leader, Khamenei was not a grand ayatollah, or even an ayatollah, as the constitution stipulated. A revision to the constitution and quick promotion of Khamenei to ayatollah resolved this problem. This raises the question of why a lesser cleric would have risen to such a prominent office. Many leaders in the Iranian government apparently believed that after Khomeini's death, the office would lose much of its power. Khamenei was viewed as unthreatening, someone whose long-standing loyalty to Khomeini and the revolution would make him an acceptable placeholder. He lacks the charismatic or intellectual power of Khomeini or the religious authority of Iran's most senior clerics. Despite this, Khamenei has wrong-footed many of his rivals, slowly consolidating power within the office by allying himself with individuals within the ulema and military.

How is the supreme leader chosen? In theory, the role falls to the **Assembly of Experts**—a body of 88 members, all men and Islamic scholars, who are themselves popularly elected for eight-year terms. According to the constitution, the assembly may also remove the supreme leader if he fails to discharge his constitutional duties, creating at least in theory the capacity for the body to oversee the supreme leader. However, candidates for the assembly are vetted by the Guardian Council in advance of elections, limiting the people's choice and ensuring that membership is dominated by clerics who accept the political status quo (that said, moderates did make inroads in the 2016 Assembly of Experts election). Since Khamenei has been the only supreme leader to come to power after Khomeini, it is difficult to say how powerful a role this body will play once he passes away. Indeed, Khamenei's ascension to power in 1989 resulted from backdoor negotiations among leaders in the Iranian government, and it is uncertain how the next transfer of power will occur.

If the supreme leader functions as a powerful head of state, the **president** is (confusingly) more akin to a head of government. Unlike the supreme leader, the president is directly elected and can serve only two 4-year terms. Within his scope of responsibilities lie drafting the state budget, initiating legislation, and selecting a cabinet of ministers charged with directing various facets of policy. However, he cannot veto legislation, nor may he dissolve the legislature and call for elections—both basic powers among executives. The president is also technically in charge of foreign policy, appointing ambassadors, signing treaties, and helping to foster diplomatic relations. Given the president's lack of control over the military, however, his powers in this area remain circumscribed, and the supreme leader clearly sets the parameters of acceptable foreign policy. In general, the president is charged with the task of executing the laws, making certain that specific policies are carried out.

After 1979, the expectation was that the president would be a nonreligious figure, more in keeping with an office concerned with "worldly" affairs. From 1981 to 2005, however, the position was held primarily by clerics. The 2005 election of President Mahmoud Ahmadinejad, whose background was in higher education and local government rather than theology, was a departure from this trend. Ahmadinejad's emphasis on social justice, religious piety, and confrontation with the West over the country's nuclear program built him a base of support that appeared to rival Khamenei's. But over the course of Ahmadinejad's second term, the supreme leader was able to check much of the president's power. Since 2013, President Hassan Rouhani, a cleric, has pursued a more reformist and less confrontational agenda. This was critical to the success of the 2016 nuclear deal and Rouhani's subsequent reelection to a second term in 2017, but similar attempts at domestic liberalization have been stymied.

THE LEGISLATURE

The Islamic Republic retains one political institution from Iran's past. The legislature, or Majlis, is a unicameral body whose members are directly elected on the basis of universal suffrage of men and women over the age of 18. Its 290 members serve four-year terms and must be at least 30 years of age.

As might be suspected, the Majlis, like its predecessors, has a limited amount of authority. Its powers include initiating and passing legislation, overseeing the budget, and approving members of the president's cabinet. Cabinet members may also be removed by a vote of no confidence, though the Majlis's power in this area does not extend to the president or to the supreme leader. The Majlis was dominated by clerics in the early years of the revolution, but their participation has declined, while that of members associated with the paramilitary Revolutionary Guard (see "Other Institutions," p. 532) has risen. There are single seats set aside for the Zoroastrian and Jewish communities, and three seats are for Christians. (None of these communities makes up more than 1 percent of the population.) Finally, there are currently 17 women in the Majlis (more than there are clerics).

The inherent supremacy of God's law in the Iranian constitution raises questions about the functioning of the legislature. Since human-made laws are liable to deviate from God's will, the role of the Majlis is technically to legislate in accordance with divine law, and its legislation can be struck down for failing on this account. Despite this limitation, the Majlis is an important actor. While it does not challenge the supreme leader, conflicts between the Majlis and the president over national policy are common, especially with regard to the budget. The Majlis is also an important instrument of local politics, used by representatives to gain resources for their constituents through the kind of "pork barreling" seen in most parliaments around the world.

The broader limitations of the Majlis are best seen in the presence of two additional bodies, the **Guardian Council** and the **Expediency Council**. The Guardian Council is made up of 12 individuals who serve six-year phased terms: 6 are lawyers nominated by the chief justice and approved by the Majlis; 6 are clerics specializing in religious law and are appointed by the supreme leader. The powers of the Guardian Council are significant; among them is the power to review all legislation that derives from the Majlis, to "ensure its compatibility with the criteria of Islam and the Constitution."[8] It may send legislation back to the Majlis for revision if it finds the legislation incompatible; if the Majlis is unable to revise the legislation to the Guardian Council's satisfaction, a third body, the Expediency Council, mediates.

Members of the Expediency Council are appointed by the supreme leader for five-year terms; until his death in 2017 the council was headed by **Ali Akbar Hashemi Rafsanjani**, a long-standing rival to Khamenei who served as the country's president from 1989 to 1997. The final decision of the Expediency Council cannot be overturned. The Guardian Council (and, to a lesser extent, the Expediency Council) serves as a kind of unelected upper house with substantial powers to restrict the work of the Majlis.

When political authority stems from religious tenets, they naturally have a profound effect on the nature of the law itself. The legal system in Iran is derived from religious law, or Sharia. The notion of a "rule of law" as understood in liberal democracies is viewed as an attempt by people to assume legal authority where God should be sovereign.

Since 1979, the legal system has thus been transformed to make it consistent with the objectives of Islamist ideology. At the apex of this branch of government is a **chief justice**, a single figure whose qualifications include an understanding of Sharia (making the appointment of a cleric necessary). The chief justice is appointed by the supreme leader for a five-year term. His role is to manage the judicial institutions and oversee the appointment and removal of judges.

Beneath the chief justice is the Supreme Court, which serves as the highest court of appeal. Like the position of chief justice, this office is entirely staffed by high-ranking clerics chosen for their familiarity with religious law. This role for clerics in the judicial system extends down to the lowest level; only clerics (and, therefore, only men) may serve as judges. As a result of this structure, judges often assert a high degree of independence in interpreting the law, which frequently leads to contradictory opinions across the courts. For this reason, some observers, both inside and outside Iran, view the courts as the most dysfunctional set of institutions in the country.[9]

Further compounding these difficulties is the fact that in addition to civil and criminal courts, Iran also has so-called revolutionary courts. They are a legacy of the immediate postrevolutionary period, when elements of the monarchy and opponents of Khomeini were tried and often executed. These revolutionary courts deal with cases involving national security, such as the public protests following the 2009 presidential elections, in which numerous individuals were tried and sentenced on the grounds of *moharebeh* (meaning "rebellion against God"). Iran executes the second-highest number of individuals in the world after China—over 500 in 2016, mostly for criminal offenses such as murder and drug smuggling. In comparison, during the same period, the United States executed 20.

The Electoral System

Despite the theocratic limitations, Iran seems to enjoy some elements of democratic participation. In particular, there are direct elections for the Majlis, the Assembly of Experts, and the presidency. Over 70 percent of eligible voters turned out for the 2017 presidential election. This result indicates that even with its restrictions, much of the Iranian republic takes political participation seriously when the people believe they can truly affect politics. Nevertheless, the public is highly constrained in its choices for representation.

The constitution gives the Guardian Council the power to oversee all elections, which as mentioned earlier means that this unelected body may reject any candidate for elected office. In the 2016 Majlis elections, the Guardian Council barred nearly half of candidates for office as "unsuitable" for elections, the highest number since 1979. In the 2017 presidential election, the Guardian Council rejected more than 1,000 individuals who applied to run for president. This included all 137 female candidates and even former president Ahmadinejad. The power of the Guardian Council to block candidates, or even remove standing representatives from running for reelection, has been a major factor in the consolidation of conservative control over the Majlis and the presidency. Still, the election of President Rouhani indicates that the vetting of candidates does not always prevent reformists from coming to office, and in spite of restrictions the most recent Majlis and Assembly of Experts elections resulted in increased representation by individuals favoring reform.

For the Majlis, Iran uses a combination of single-member and multimember districts. In the single-member districts, the candidate with the largest share of the vote (so long as it is over 25 percent) wins the seat. If no one candidate reaches that threshold, a runoff is held among the top candidates. In multimember districts with more than one seat, voters cast votes for each seat, with similar runoffs if needed. The Assembly of Experts uses a single-member district system, though with no runoff; the candidate who has secured the largest number of votes wins. For the presidency, a simple two-round runoff is held between the top two vote-getters unless one candidate wins a majority outright in the first round (as did Rouhani in both 2013 and 2017).

Local Government

Iran's history, like that of many countries, has been one of a struggle by the state to centralize power. Though the country is currently divided into 31 *ostan*, or provinces, these bodies, like the local institutions below them, have limited authority—a condition that existed long before the current regime. Although the Constitutional Revolution of 1905–6 was driven in part by the goal of creating representative local government, that goal was never realized. The 1979 revolution similarly made claims about the need for local government, though after taking initial steps in that direction, the regime moved away from devolving power. The demands of institutionalizing the regime, going to war with Iraq, nationalizing industry, and quelling ethnic unrest drove the regime to centralize power even more. It rejected any notions of regional autonomy or federalism and suspended elections to the local and regional councils.

As part of a wave of reforms in 1997, the government passed a law on decentralization that moved power away from the Ministry of the Interior. Before then, the ministry had been responsible for local affairs such as appointing regional governors and mayors. After the new law was passed, local councils were created at the village, city, district, and provincial levels to manage local politics and the indirect election of mayors. In a further departure from the past, these councils— more than 100,000 offices in all—were directly elected.

The first elections to the newly created council positions took place in 1999, when more than 500,000 candidates competed at the local level for the first time in Iranian history.[10] Candidates must be approved by the Majlis; while this review is not as onerous as that conducted by the Guardian Council, it remains a barrier. However, in the 2017 local elections (which take place simultaneously with the presidential elections) reformists gained control over the important Tehran city council.

Other Institutions

THE REVOLUTIONARY GUARD AND THE BASIJ

In addition to the institutions discussed earlier, Iran also has several powerful political institutions. Of these, two merit particular mention: the Revolutionary Guard, or Pasdaran, and the Basij, or People's Militia.

The **Revolutionary Guard** is a paramilitary force that emerged from the 1979 revolution. It originally comprised several thousand men from various militias and groups that had sprung up around the revolution and was independent of the armed forces, which Khomeini mistrusted because of their role during the Pahlavi dynasty. As a "corps of the faithful," the Revolutionary Guard was assigned the immediate task of defending the new regime and destroying rival groups and movements, such as Marxists and supporters of greater ethnic autonomy.

Later, during the Iran-Iraq War, the Revolutionary Guard expanded in size to fight on the front lines as a military force. It did this in part by relying on a large people's volunteer militia, known as the **Basij**, which had been formed shortly after the revolution as a grassroots civil defense force. Its members were poorly trained and ill-equipped but imbued with religious and nationalist fervor, and the Basij was known for its "human wave" attacks against the Iraqi front lines.

The end of the war and the consolidation of the revolution undercut the justification for the Revolutionary Guard and the Basij, but both organizations continued to play an influential and growing role in Iranian politics. Though both groups are controlled only by the supreme leader and his allies, the Revolutionary Guard has become an increasingly independent and direct player in Iranian domestic and international affairs as well; its top leaders have taken on important additional roles in the state and government.

The Guard has its own ministry, army, navy, and air force units as well as an unclear role in the development of Iran's nuclear program. It has been active in the region, providing training and some troops in the ongoing conflicts in Iraq and Syria, and has been associated with past acts of terrorism. At home, the Guard has become deeply involved in the Iranian economy. It has significant economic assets and is involved in various aspects of national development, such as construction, banking, and telecommunications. But the Guard leadership is also highly factionalized. Its various elements contend for economic and political power and the support of the supreme leader.

In contrast, the Basij is no longer a significant military force, though it has maintained its importance in other ways. Like the Revolutionary Guard (which has authority over the Basij), the organization has developed substantial economic assets. More disturbing has been its role as a public morality force, often taking responsibility for such things as preventing public displays of affection and seizing illegal satellite dishes. In the 2009 protests, the Basij was widely deployed to break up demonstrations. Basij members tend to come from poorer backgrounds, and membership is an opportunity to gain access to certain benefits, such as higher education.

In general, the Guard has become a more active player in politics and is an important tool of the supreme leader in maintaining power. At the same time, its factionalization and economic interests generate a good deal of rivalry within the institution. President Rouhani has attempted to limit the Guard's economic power, though so far with little success. This remains a significant obstacle to domestic reform and improved relations with the international community.[11]

Political Conflict and Competition

For many reasons, political competition in Iran is a confusing matter to outside observers (and insiders as well). The nature of the revolution and the role of religion constitute one factor, because they helped create political differences that do not fit easily onto our usual palette of ideologies. In addition, Iran lacks institutionalized political parties or even a single-party system. This environment is partly a reflection of the regime's populism and its suspicion of traditional party politics. As a result, Iranian politics is frequently described as factionalized and clientelist, dominated by an array of loose political and economic groups that continuously struggle for power. This battle often gives the impression of a democratic system, but in reality political struggles tend to be around competing elites within the authoritarian regime.

This factionalization was not an inevitable or a necessary function of Iranian political culture. Following the 1979 revolution, there was an outburst of new political activity. Previously suppressed groups, such as the National Front and the Tudeh Party, reemerged. Out of this activity, two dominant parties came into being. The first, the Islamic Republican Party (IRP), was closely allied with Ayatollah Ruhollah Khomeini and his desire to establish a theocracy. The second, the Liberation Movement, was more pro-Western and favored a limited role for religion in politics. Numerous parties stood for the first postrevolutionary elections in 1980, but the electoral system eliminated virtually all groups but the IRP, which gained a majority of seats.

Some independent parliamentarians and members of the Liberation Movement sought to resist this consolidation of power. Other, more radical groups turned their weapons on the IRP, much of whose leadership was killed in a bombing in 1981. The government responded with increased repression of opposition groups, imprisoning and executing thousands of political activists while marginalizing the increasingly critical Liberation Movement. With the 1984 and 1987 elections, the hold of Khomeini's supporters on the Majlis was made complete. In advance of the 1984 elections, all parties other than the IRP were banned. In 1987, even the IRP itself was eliminated.

The Challenges of Political Reform

After 1987, political debate within the Majlis was limited primarily to economic concerns. Those who favored a more free-market economic approach competed with those who supported more statist policies (see "Society" on p. 540 for a discussion of these different political tendencies). Debates on the nature of the political system itself were not allowed. Liberalization was afoot, however, made possible by the death of Khomeini in 1989 and a worsening economy. In 1992, Majlis elections saw a victory for the free-market faction, many of whom in turn supported the 1997 presidential candidacy of the pro-reform Mohammad Khatami. His victory, in which he won over 70 percent of the popular vote, was a surprise to Iranians and outside observers alike.

The reform period of the 1990s saw a dramatic diversification in political views and organizations. Many groups called for improved relations with the outside world, democratic change, and improvement of women's rights (which had been significantly reduced after 1979). These arguments were spearheaded by intellectuals, students, and a number of clerics who had long opposed the idea of the *velayat-e faqih*.

In 2000, reform groups coalesced to form the **Second Khordad Front** (named after the date in the Iranian calendar for Khatami's 1997 election) to compete in the following year's Majlis elections. This coalition went on to win a stunning 189 of the 290 parliamentary seats. In 2001, President Khatami was again overwhelmingly reelected and won over 70 percent of the vote. Many expected that these twin victories would solidify reformist power and pave the way for a political transition like that of the Soviet Union in the 1980s.

That belief was short-lived. While reformers controlled the Majlis and the presidency, these were relatively weak political institutions. Conservatives still controlled or had the support of the Guardian Council and the Expediency Council, the Revolutionary Guard and Basij, and of course the supreme leader. Soon after the elections, a wave of repression was directed against reformists. Numerous journalists and pro-democracy activists were arrested or assassinated, and a number of pro-reform newspapers were shut down. In the Majlis, while reformers passed a wide array of legislation to limit state power and increase democratic rights, the bills were mostly vetoed by the Guardian Council. Meanwhile, President Khatami lacked the power and the political skills to contend with the conservatives. In the 2004 Majlis elections, the Guardian Council banned large numbers of Khordad candidates (including 80 standing members of parliament), and reformers called for an election boycott. The 2016 elections saw a return of reformists to the Majlis on the heels of President Rouhani's election, but as in the 1990s their impact has so far been limited.

The other battlefield in the struggle over reform has been the presidency. When Khatami stepped down in 2005, many expected that former president and Khatami backer Ali Akbar Hashemi Rafsanjani would return to power. However, Rafsanjani was trounced by the mayor of Tehran, Mahmoud Ahmadinejad. Ahmadinejad benefited from the absence of many pro-reform voters, who had stayed away from the polls because they were dismayed by the conservative counteroffensive in the Majlis and repelled by Rafsanjani, who was widely regarded as corrupt. But there was also widespread support for Ahmadinejad, especially among the poor and more conservative, who were attracted by his obvious piety and modesty. Ahmadinejad also had the support of many in the Revolutionary Guard and Basij, with whom he had close ties.

Ahmadinejad's two terms in office were characterized by several trends. The first was a more populist approach to politics, akin to values seen in the early years of the Islamic Republic. Ahmadinejad focused on public programs aiding the poor, emphasizing that the government and state address their needs. This policy was in many ways a clear challenge to government and clerical elites, many of whom have grown rich since 1979 through their roles in both politics and the market. In addition, Ahmadinejad pursued a more openly confrontational relationship with the United States, an approach abetted by the wars in neighboring Afghanistan and Iraq. He raised the international profile of Iran, frequently traveling and speaking against the United States, Israel, and the inequities of global politics and economic relations. He also made the development of nuclear technology a cornerstone of his policies, though he did not have direct authority over this area. His rising profile eventually put him at odds with the supreme leader.

The 2009 presidential elections pitted Ahmadinejad against several rivals, among them Mir Hossein Mousavi, former prime minister from 1981 to 1989. Long out of power, he campaigned on a strongly pro-reformist agenda, calling for such things as a liberalized press, greater rights for women, and more power for the Majlis. Young people in particular rallied around Mousavi, forming a "Green Wave" movement in favor of his election. It was widely expected that Mousavi and Ahmadinejad would face a runoff; instead, the government announced that, in fact, Ahmadinejad had won over 60 percent of the vote, thus eliminating the need for a second round. This dubious result sparked mass demonstrations around Iran and a ferocious response by the police and Basij, resulting in perhaps 150 dead, more than 1,000 detained, and an unknown number given long sentences or executed. Mousavi came under house arrest, where he remains.

The reelection of Ahmadinejad was both a victory and a loss for conservatives in Iran. The widespread demonstration of public hostility toward him weakened the president's position, which until then had seemed to be eclipsing that of the supreme leader himself. Ahmadinejad's attempt to anoint a successor also failed; his associates came under attack from the judiciary and supreme leader, who opposed his attempt to build an independent base of power. Many expected that the next president would be someone close to the supreme leader and unlikely to challenge his views. Indeed, as the Guardian Council weeded out candidates for the 2013 presidential election, it even rejected Rafsanjani, who had already served as president from 1989 to 1997 and ran against Ahmadinejad in 2005. The supreme leader himself, while not openly supporting any candidate, made it clear from his comments that he supported a close confidant and lead negotiator on Iran's nuclear program.

Yet despite all expectations, the election campaign quickly turned in favor of Hassan Rouhani. Why? Several factors are involved. First, Rouhani ran a much more aggressive campaign than many expected, calling openly for a release of Mousavi and implicitly siding with the Green Wave movement. Second, Rouhani matched these calls with more practical critiques of Iranian politics, such as the economic difficulties that had resulted from international sanctions and the erratic economic policies of Ahmadinejad. Third, Rouhani's earlier experience as a negotiator on the nuclear issue gave credibility to his claim that he could cut a deal with the West that could help improve living conditions at home. These claims stood in sharp contrast to the other conservative candidates, who were loath to admit to the difficulties the country faced abroad and at home.

Immediately following Rouhani's elections, expectations were high both inside and outside Iran that a sea change was under way. In September 2013, President Rouhani even spoke directly with President Obama—the first such contact between leaders of the two countries since 1979. Rouhani also stepped away from Ahmadinejad's anti-Israel stance. Moving forward from these gestures, negotiations on the nuclear issue resulted in an international agreement in 2016 that froze Iran's nuclear program in return for an end to sanctions (see "Current Issues in Iran," p. 551). Iran's international economic relations have subsequently improved to some extent, though this has been coupled with numerous arrests of reformers and civil society activists reminiscent of the 1990s. The hope for a new wave of liberalization under Rouhani discounted the power of the supreme leader and those around him, and many of the president's supporters are deeply disappointed in the lack of dramatic change.

Civil Society

As might be expected, civil society in Iran has mirrored the changes and challenges of political competition. Over the past century, Iran has seen the rise of organized civil activity during periods when the state was weak, as during the constitutional revolution in 1905–6, immediately after World War II, and during the 1979 revolution.

After the creation of the Islamic Republic of Iran, the nascent civil society was again stifled, viewed as anathema to the supremacy of religious rule and a threat to national unity during the war with Iraq. Most civic organizations were either absorbed into the state or outlawed. This move was consistent with the theocracy's particular interpretation of the concept of the *ummah*, or community, whose members were expected to act as a unified group that embodied and served the revolution. Plurality and autonomy were seen as running counter to religious rule and revolutionary ideals. Ironically, however, the desire to co-opt as much of civil society as possible contributed to the factionalization and clientelism of the regime as various forces within the state battled for power and resources.

After Khomeini's death and the end of the war, however, civil society began to reemerge, though it remained marginal and beleaguered. A handful of intellectuals, clerics, and others questioned the current regime and advocated reform, but this activity was frequently met with arrest, torture, and even death. One notable example was Ayatollah Hussein Ali Montazeri, whom Khomeini had handpicked to serve as supreme leader upon his death. Montazeri eventually fell out of favor, however, having criticized the government for human rights abuses, and for many years was under house arrest.

In the 1990s, President Khatami made the invigoration of Iran's civil society a major plank of his campaign platform, and the media soon took up this cause. New publications rapidly proliferated at all levels of society, from academic journals and independent publishers to magazines and newspapers. Numerous civic organizations also sprang up, dealing with such issues as local government, human rights, the environment, women's rights, and poverty. These developments were driven by a younger generation that was better educated and had no memory of the country under the shah or the revolution itself.

The women of this younger generation also made their presence felt. While we assume that since 1979 Iranian women have been deprived of all rights, Iranian women have much higher levels of education than they did under the shah. Most of the college students in Iran are now women. However, political and economic opportunities remain limited, and edicts regarding personal morality (including public dress) strongly affect women's autonomy in the public sphere. Accordingly, the place of women in society remains central to any discussion of liberalization and civic life in Iran.

The flowering of civil society in the 1990s soon came under sustained attack. Supreme Leader Khamenei excoriated the press as "the base of the enemy," and numerous publications were closed or physically attacked by government-sponsored militants. When a 2000 law restricted the ability of the press to operate, many publications were closed, and journalists were arrested and in some cases killed. Iran's press freedom, according to Reporters without Borders, ranks 165th out of 180 countries.[12]

Similar pressure was directed against nongovernmental organizations (NGOs). Many of them were attacked, their offices destroyed, and their members detained. This intensified after the 2009 and 2013 presidential elections. In 2016, several civil society activists and even individuals close to the president were arrested on charges of espionage and "propaganda against the state."

While the public sphere has come under increased repression in Iran, one area of civic activity that has persevered is electronic communication. Over the past decade, Iran has been an Internet pioneer in the Middle East. Many Internet users have eagerly embraced each new innovation, from blogs to text messaging to social media. Because the government cracked down on traditional media outlets, the Internet has become an important environment for expression of alternative views. Many have remarked on the role of social media to galvanize public protest. Most notable was the cell phone video footage of the death of Neda Agha Soltan, a young woman shot during protests following the 2009 presidential elections. The video was distributed worldwide via the Internet.

However, it is incorrect to say that the Internet represents some liberated space that the Iranian state cannot control. A number of individuals have been arrested in Iran for Internet activism, or even for posting "immoral" content such as Iranian women not wearing a head scarf. The regime has also taken steps to limit access to important sites like Facebook, YouTube, and Twitter and is filtering various content from non-Iranian websites (and even the sites of Iranian reformists). While President Rouhani, Supreme Leader Khamenei, and other political officials rely on Twitter and Facebook to disseminate their views to the outside world, these applications are actually blocked inside Iran itself. Iranians often get around this restriction by using a virtual private network, but such activity is illegal and the government takes frequent steps to block such tools as they become widespread. Equally important, the Iranian government controls Internet speeds; until recently, the country had one of the slowest Internet services in the world. This step helps prevent access to video sites like YouTube, which are of particular concern to the government after the 2009 protests. Iran is seeing the expansion of 3G and 4G mobile Internet access, but its Internet remains among the most restricted, surpassed only by China.

Society

Ethnic and National Identity

As we noted at the start of this chapter, Iran is distinct from other Islamic states in the Middle East, not only because it embraces the minority Shia branch of Islam but also because the majority population is ethnically Iranian (or Persian) rather than Arab. With their distinct language, history, and culture, ethnic Iranians view themselves as quite separate from people in the Arab states of the Middle East. This perspective contributes to a sense of nationalism in many ways much stronger than that found elsewhere in the region. It was the people's nationalism that helped sustain Iran in its long war against Iraq, which was portrayed by both sides as part of a struggle between Persians and Arabs going back thousands of years.

In fact, as the legitimacy of the Islamic regime has waned, a form of Iranian nationalism has resurfaced that builds upon the myths of the pre-Islamic era. It also draws on the history of the Achaemenid Empire and Zoroastrianism, a largely extinct religion that predates Islam by over a thousand years. Many Iranians, particularly the young, have embraced the symbols of Zoroastrianism and pre-Islamic ceremonies such as Nowruz (New Year). These practices emphasize a distinct "Iranian Islam" that goes against the idea of the faith as a universal set of values that transcends national identities.

At the same time, Iran is not the homogeneous state that its nationalism or distinctive identity might lead us to believe it is. Although Persians make up a majority, much of the population is composed of other ethnic groups. Some of the groups are closely related to the Persian majority; others are not. Among these groups, the two largest are the Azeris and the Kurds. They are particularly important not only because of their size but also because of their connection to ethnic kin outside Iran. In both cases, turmoil and political change in surrounding countries have affected these ethnic minorities and, as a result, the way in which Iran deals with its neighbors.

The largest minority ethnic group in Iran is the Azeri, who comprise around 16 percent of the population (perhaps more) and are concentrated in the north of the country. Like the majority Persians, the Azeris follow Shiism, but they speak a language related to those spoken in Turkey and much of Central Asia.

Historically, the Azeris resided entirely within the Persian Empire; but with the expansion of Russia in the nineteenth century, their region was divided between the two countries. However, an independent Azerbaijan emerged from the collapse of the Soviet Union in 1991. The country's newfound independence

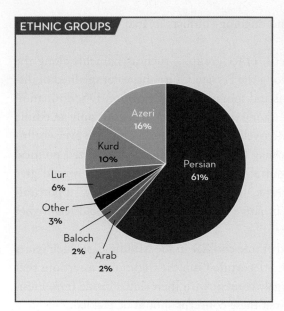

ETHNIC GROUPS

Persian 61%
Azeri 16%
Kurd 10%
Lur 6%
Other 3%
Baloch 2%
Arab 2%

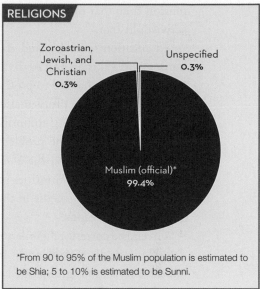

RELIGIONS

Zoroastrian, Jewish, and Christian 0.3%
Unspecified 0.3%
Muslim (official)* 99.4%

*From 90 to 95% of the Muslim population is estimated to be Shia; 5 to 10% is estimated to be Sunni.

helped foster a stronger ethnic identity among Iranian Azeris, and the Azeris in Iran have occasionally protested against discrimination by the Persian majority (though some high ranking leaders, including Khamenei, are of Azeri descent). The Republic of Azerbaijan itself has strained foreign relations with Iran, helping to increase ethnic tension. However, for now there is relatively little support for greater regional autonomy or unification with Azerbaijan, and Azeris have historically played a prominent role in all facets of Iranian life. Nevertheless, future political changes could bring such questions to the fore, much as they have in countries such as Scotland or Ukraine.

The state's relationship with the Kurds, who comprise 10 percent of the population, is more complicated. The Kurds carried out an armed revolt against the new Islamic Republic of Iran in 1979, gaining some control of parts of northwest Iran. This revolt was ultimately suppressed by military force, though sporadic guerrilla activity continued during the 1980s and 1990s. The rise of a largely autonomous Kurdish region in Iraq following the U.S. invasion raised hopes and fears of a sovereign Kurdish state, something reinforced by the rise of the Islamic State in Iraq and Syria and the de facto emergence of an independent Kurdistan in Iraq. These developments make Iran nervous. Kurds inside Iran have conducted both peaceful and violent political activism, including guerilla warfare and terrorist attacks, often in connection with Kurdish groups in Iraq or Turkey. In general, the relationship between Kurds and the countries in which they reside generates more tension than that of the Azeris, and ongoing conflicts in Iraq will shape Kurdish activism in Iran.[13]

In addition to Kurds and Azeris, other groups—such as Baluchis along the border with Pakistan and Arabs along the Persian Gulf—have complained of discrimination that has led to protests and sporadic acts of violence. Discrimination has been particularly problematic among those groups that are not only an ethnic minority, but a religious minority as well: Baluchis, for example, are overwhelmingly Sunni. Part of the problem may be that Iran's highly centralized political system has not allowed for a significant devolution of power that would give ethnic and religious minorities greater rights. Non-Persians have few opportunities for education or media in their native language, and Sunnis hold few higher government positions.

Given the current religious and ethnic conflict in the Middle East, such issues should not be dismissed lightly. In a departure from the traditional assertions that ethnic and religious groups are largely content with their status inside Iran, President Rouhani has acknowledged that these concerns should be tackled.

Ideology and Political Culture

In the absence of institutionalized political parties and free expression, it is hard to speak of any coherent spectrum of ideologies in Iran. A confusing array of terms is used: *hard-liners, radicals, conservatives, traditionalists, reformers, pragmatists, principalists, technocrats.* This problem is exacerbated by the factionalized and clientelist nature of the system, in which personal relationships are often more important than political ideas. Despite this confusion, we can speak of several loose political attitudes or tendencies, some of them more ideologically coherent than others. As in other countries, the divisions tend to fall along the lines of freedom and equality, though religion exerts an important influence on how both of those values are understood.

One major division is over the relationship between religion and the state. As we might expect, those known as "reformists" in Iran, whose political power rose and fell under the Khatami presidency, call for a reduced or modified role for Islam in politics in favor of the rule of law and democratic reform. This group, whose orientation is more secular, also has unexpected allies among many clerics. For many Shiite religious leaders, the very notion of the *velayat-e faqih* runs counter to the basic tenets of Shiism. Their **quietist** vision, which dominated Iranian Shiism before the revolution, emphasizes that worldly political power cannot be reunited with Islam until the return of the Mahdi. This belief holds that the role of the faith is to act as an intermediary between the state and society in the meantime, influencing spiritual and social values but not getting directly involved in politics. Politics is viewed as a corrupting influence on faith and thus something to be kept at a distance.

In contrast, political conservatives ("**principalists**," as they have recently called themselves) support the *velayat-e faqih* and oppose democratization or the return of faith to a primarily social, as opposed to political, role. In their view, faith must be a central institution within the state, guiding politics and society toward God's intent. In some ways, this vision implies that pious rule can hasten the Mahdi's return. Both liberals and principalists enjoy the support of various high-ranking ayatollahs who can operate independently of the supreme leader so long as they do not openly challenge the regime's legitimacy. Principalists have a significant advantage in their support by the Revolutionary Guard, which makes the prospects for liberalization much more daunting.

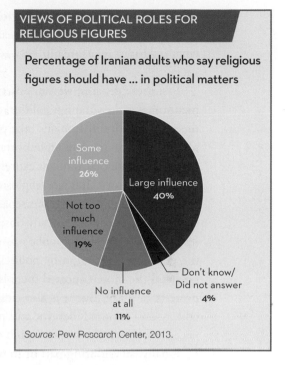

VIEWS OF POLITICAL ROLES FOR RELIGIOUS FIGURES

Percentage of Iranian adults who say religious figures should have … in political matters

Some influence 26%

Large influence 40%

Not too much influence 19%

Don't know/ Did not answer 4%

No influence at all 11%

Source: Pew Research Center, 2013.

The second area of contention is over the relationship between the state and market. At the inception of the Islamic Republic, there was a schism between those who saw the primary role of the revolution as bringing about a moral order and those who saw the revolution as a means of ensuring economic justice. Khomeini emphasized both of these issues, viewing the revolution as a way to create a just social order that integrated faith, politics, and the economy.

As we shall discuss shortly, however, just as religion has clashed with politics, so, too, it has led to divisions over the economy. There are those, such as former president Rafsanjani and President Rouhani, who favor economic liberalization and better relations with the international community to increase trade and investment. The supreme leader and many principalists take a more skeptical view of economic reform and liberalization, especially if it is predicated on improved relations with the United States. Quietists and reformers, too, while at times in agreement on political change, do not necessarily see eye to eye on economic changes. Support for or hostility to capitalism does not necessarily conform to an individual's religious position (many high-ranking clerics, for example, are very wealthy). There remain very real divisions over what a proper relationship between state and market should be in an Islamic society.[14]

Past these debates, we can observe more fixed elements of political culture. As mentioned earlier, Iranian political culture is highly nationalist. Surveys show that the vast majority of Iranians take pride in their nationality. In addition, Iranians say that religion remains an important part of their lives while at the same time the surveys indicate that Iranians express support for more democracy. These views are not contradictory; Iranian religiosity tends more toward the traditional, quietist view that would favor a greater separation between faith and state. This perspective is important to consider. Many observers of Iranian politics have assumed that one result of the Islamic Republic's fundamentalism would be effectively to alienate the public from religion by politicizing it. Certainly among the younger generation and the more educated there is disaffection, as evidenced in the Green Wave protests of 2009. But it is also clear that Islam remains a central part of Iranian culture and national identity, and political change or democratization would not necessarily mean the secularization of the country along Western lines.

Finally, an enduring part of Iranian political culture is a complicated relationship with the West. Iranian history and consequent national identity are tightly linked to the rise of the West, going back 2,000 years to when Iran, Greece, and, later, Rome all commanded power and respect. In this way, Iranians may see

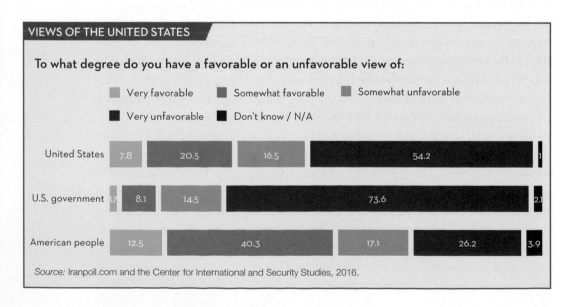

VIEWS OF THE UNITED STATES

To what degree do you have a favorable or an unfavorable view of:

- Very favorable
- Somewhat favorable
- Somewhat unfavorable
- Very unfavorable
- Don't know / N/A

United States: 7.8 | 20.5 | 16.5 | 54.2 | 1

U.S. government: 1.7 | 8.1 | 14.5 | 73.6 | 2.1

American people: 12.5 | 40.3 | 17.1 | 26.2 | 3.9

Source: Iranpoll.com and the Center for International and Security Studies, 2016.

themselves as equal participants in, and contributors to, Western history in a way other peoples may not. At the same time, the frequent Western (and Arab) interventions in modern Iranian history have created a strong tendency toward viewing international politics in conspiratorial terms, such that every political event is the product of foreign powers with seemingly limitless power.

For example, while Iranians will blame the United Kingdom and the United States for the rise of the Pahlavi dynasty, they may also argue that the West was "behind" the 1979 Islamic Revolution. The United States (or Israel) is also viewed by many as the mastermind behind Al Qaeda, September 11, or the Islamic State. Some Iranians continue to believe that the United Kingdom remains the dominant world power, concealed behind its "puppet," the United States. Indeed, Supreme Leader Khamenei singled out the United Kingdom, rather than the United States, as a mastermind of the 2009 protests.

One criticism made of Iranians by outsiders is their tendency for shifting blame to external actors rather than seeing themselves as also responsible for their political destiny. Even so, such views do not mean that average Iranians are opposed to better relations with the United States, even if they view American power with justifiable suspicion.

Political Economy

Iran's economic system reflects the dilemmas of late modernization, authoritarianism, and war. It is also a good example of what is sometimes called the "resource trap," the situation that occurs when a national resource paradoxically makes a country poorer rather than richer.

Iran's modern economic development lagged well behind that of the West—it did not begin until the 1920s, under the Pahlavi dynasty. This effort was not a late embrace of liberalism, but rather an attempt at top-down industrialization that followed the mercantilist pattern adopted by many countries in the less-developed world. Nor should such a path have been surprising; an attempt by the state to generate domestic wealth was a logical response and not unlike the Western powers' own history. Iran's

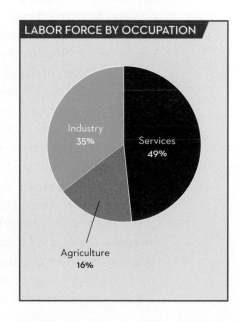

LABOR FORCE BY OCCUPATION

Industry 35%

Services 49%

Agriculture 16%

mercantilist policies helped modernize the country, such that by the 1970s half the population was living in urban areas. At the same time, it led to social dislocation as the country made a rapid jump from an agrarian, isolated, and religiously conservative society in just a few decades.

Top-down mercantilist development led to similar problems in other less-developed countries, though in Iran, the problems were compounded by the discovery of oil. At first glance, it might be expected that oil reserves would be the salvation of any country, providing it with the resources to develop its infrastructure and generate new industries. In reality, the opposite can be the case. Oil can be more a curse than a blessing, especially when controlled by the state. Rather than directing resources toward the goal of development, leaders give in to a seemingly irresistible temptation, which leads to corruption as they siphon off the wealth to line their own pockets or serve their own policy predilections. Moreover, since the public is eliminated as the major source of state revenue, those in power can effectively ignore the public and repress or co-opt any opposition.

The resource trap may also explain the degree of women's rights; where oil is strong, the private sector is weak, limiting women's participation in the workforce and their economic independence. The issue of "taxation without representation," for both women and men, thus becomes meaningless—the state can do without either and is able to avoid having to make the trade-off. This problem became evident during the time of the White Revolution, when economic development coincided with growing inflation, inequality, and increased repression. Development, built on oil exports and Western imports, also fueled hostility toward Western materialism, or what one critical Iranian scholar of the era called "Westoxication" or "Weststruckness."[15]

As a reflection of the economic factors that helped bring about the 1979 revolution, the new constitution explicitly stated that "the economy is a means, not an end." This position stood in contrast to liberal capitalist systems, in which the quest for wealth and profit becomes "a subversive and corrupting factor in the course of man's development." The oil and other state-owned industries were to remain in the state's hands, and the profits were redirected toward presumably more equitable goals. In addition, numerous private industries were nationalized after their owners fled the revolution.

In many cases, the private industries' assets were turned over to several **bonyads**, or parastatal foundations. The objective of the *bonyads* is ostensibly to help the disadvantaged, such as war veterans and the poor. Over time, however, the *bonyads* have become major economic players and often monopolies, controlling substantial assets and industries (for example, construction, pharmaceuticals, housing, and food) while operating independently of government oversight or taxation.[16] The Revolutionary Guard is one major actor with significant assets entrusted with its own *bonyad*. Compared with oil, the *bonyads*, and the state, the private sector is relatively small and dominated by small-scale businesses.

Another important distinction in Iran's economic system is its history of autarky, or economic independence. Opponents of the Qajar and Pahlavi dynasties accused their leaders of selling the country to foreigners and exporting their oil wealth for the benefit of a few. Just as the 1979 constitution describes profit and wealth as corrupting influences, the postrevolutionary government has had an ambivalent relationship to international economic ties. Oil could be exported to develop the economy, but the government, at least initially, sought a policy of greater self-sufficiency and more state ownership to secure the country from the effects of Westoxication.

During the 1990s, some in the Iranian political leadership took a greater interest in foreign direct investment, particularly to improve the aging technology of the oil sector, but international sanctions have until recently driven away most investment. This may now be changing with an influx of foreign direct investment in the wake of the 2016 nuclear deal, though many investors remain hesitant about investing. Conservatives, including the supreme leader, also continue to emphasize a "resistance economy," independent of the international economy. A similar argument has been used to justify Iran's nuclear program.

The results of the post-1979 economic model have been poor. To be fair, Iran's economy was devastated by the long war with Iraq, which destroyed infrastructure, drained the national treasury, and killed many of the country's young men. By 1988, when the war ended, Iran's per capita gross domestic product (GDP) had fallen to just over half its 1979 level. Oil production, while rising of late, remains only around half of its peak levels of the 1970s.

The official unemployment rate in Iran is around 11 percent (though it may be higher), and the country has long suffered from a high rate of inflation that erodes pensions and savings. Perhaps most striking are the difficult circumstances for Iranian youth, with around 30 percent of those under 24 unemployed. The figures are worse for women and those with higher education, indicating not just high levels of discrimination against women, but lack of opportunities in the private sector for young, well-educated Iranians. These difficulties in the labor market have led many young Iranians, especially women, to seek work in the informal (unregulated) economy. And lacking jobs or job security, many educated Iranians have left the country, leading to one of the world's highest rates of "brain drain." Others who have remained are delaying marriage, contributing to one of the lowest birthrates in the region.[17]

Solving Iran's economic problems is not easy. Iran can expect that ongoing revenues from its oil reserves and the development of natural gas will help sustain the state budget, though recent declines in world prices have hurt. Yet even high oil prices will not diversify the economy or provide new sources of employment. President Rouhani has sought better relations with the international community, in part to increase trade and investment, but the supreme leader and many principalists are concerned that a reintegration into the world economy will bring Iran back into a neocolonial relationship. Meanwhile, groups such as the Revolutionary Guard seek to defend their role in the economy. Improving international relations is an important step to economic development, but Iran has critical economic problems and obstacles that only domestic reforms can address.

Foreign Relations and the World

Iran's foreign relations are a function of the country's revolutionary aspirations, the limits of that revolution, and the nature of power at the international level. After 1979, Iran's leaders believed that theirs was the first in a series of revolutions that would sweep the Islamic world. Like the Russian and Chinese revolutions before it, the Iranian Revolution was thought to be the vanguard of a political movement that would extend beyond Iran's borders. In the early postrevolutionary years, Iran served as a beacon for Muslims everywhere, helping to give voice to their grievances against the West and against their own despotic rulers.

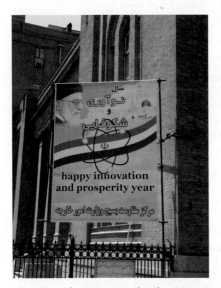

This Basij banner outside the Iranian Foreign Ministry in Iran links nuclear technology to national prestige and autarky.

Iran also became associated with terrorism, largely due to its support for the armed Shiite group Hezbollah (Party of God) in Lebanon. Hezbollah, trained by members of the Iranian Revolutionary Guard, carried out a suicide attack against American and French forces in Lebanon in 1983. The terrorists killed over 300 people and launched numerous attacks against occupying Israeli forces. Later, Iran would become a sponsor to Palestinian groups like Hamas and Islamic Jihad.

But Iran's hope to spread its vision of political Islam to the rest of the world faced several major obstacles. The first was Shiism itself, which most Muslims view at best as an incorrect interpretation of the faith. For many

Sunnis, Shiism's emphasis on the bloodline of the prophet Muhammad and the notion of the Mahdi is heretical, and thus it is in some ways worse than Judaism or Christianity. These theological differences have limited the ability of the revolution to spread among the majority Sunni Muslim population worldwide. Only in a few countries, such as Bahrain, Iraq, Lebanon, and Afghanistan, do Shiites exist in significant numbers.[18] In recent years, other countries where Shia reside (such as Saudi Arabia and Pakistan) have faced increasing discrimination as Sunni fundamentalism has grown.

A second major obstacle to Iran's international vision was ethnicity. The obvious goal of Iranian revolutionary policy was to spread the revolutionaries' vision across the Middle East, helping to overthrow secular leaders, establish Islamic states, and drive out Western influence in the process. But Iranians are not Arabs. Just as the revolution had difficulties with speaking in terms of one Islam, it could not speak in terms of one Middle Eastern people.

Here, too, Iran was the outlier. This status was further reinforced by the Iran-Iraq War, in which Iran relied in part upon nationalistic fervor to maintain public support, and Iraq's Shiite Arab majority sided with their government against Iran. Although Iran failed to serve as the lodestar for revolution, many of the ideas and symbols of the revolution influenced a wave of political conflict, beginning with the war in Afghanistan in 1980 and continuing through the emergence of Al Qaeda. Ironically, though many Islamist terrorist groups view Shiism as heretical, it can be argued that they owe much of their ideological justification for violence to the Islamic Revolution.

Over the past 20 years, Iranian relations with the outside world, particularly the West, have oscillated between reconciliation and conflict. In the late 1990s, President Mohammad Khatami actively sought to improve international relations, speaking of a "dialogue of civilizations" in contrast to a "clash of civilizations." Greater domestic liberalization and an easing of tensions led to more international contact, in areas ranging from diplomatic relations and civil society to Western tourism. In addition, the terrorist attacks on the United States in 2001 and the invasion of Afghanistan on Iran's border also seemed to provide an opportunity for engagement. While President George W. Bush spoke of Iran as part of an "Axis of Evil," the Iranian government also strongly opposed the Taliban in Afghanistan (who were hostile to that country's Shia population) and their old nemesis Saddam Hussein, who had invaded Iran in 1980.

However, both domestic and international factors brought Iranian-Western rapprochement to an end. Despite Khatami's call for improved relations, the supreme leader and many others inside the state were opposed to better relations with the United States, which they had long viewed as the "Great Satan." This position limited the extent to which the Iranian president could realize his foreign policy. Second, Iran's ongoing pursuit of nuclear technology (discussed in "Current Issues in Iran," on p. 551) became of increasing concern after 2001, when many leaders in the international community began to worry that such technology could be transferred to terrorist or other nonstate actors. This situation led to increased pressure on Iran from the international community, heightening tension. Third, the election of President Ahmadinejad further changed the tenor of Iran's relations with the outside world because Ahmadinejad took a more confrontational line, using nuclear technology as a symbol of national pride while simultaneously taking a more openly hostile line against Israel. Fourth, the U.S. invasion of Afghanistan and Iraq, and hostile rhetoric from the U.S. government, convinced many Iranian leaders that they were the next to be targeted—and that only a nuclear threat would deter U.S. aggression.

Iran now finds itself in an uneasy international situation. At one level, its presence in the international community is greater now than perhaps at any time since

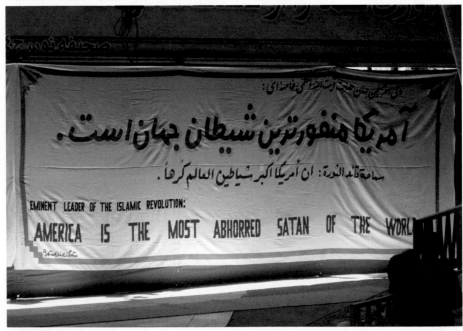

A banner at Friday prayers, Tehran University, with a quote from Ayatollah Khomeini. Anti-Americanism remains a key facet of the Iranian regime, making diplomatic relations difficult at best.

1979. Its pursuit of nuclear technology and the recent nuclear accord have raised its profile dramatically and generated international concern and debate over how best to engage it. In addition, while the U.S.-led invasions of Afghanistan and Iraq put the "Great Satan" on Iran's border, the end result of these conflicts has given Iran much greater leverage than many expected. Indeed, early in the Iraq and Afghanistan wars, some observers expected that Iran would be next in the wave of regime change. Instead, the Iraq War in particular seemed to play directly into Iran's hands. Not only was Saddam Hussein eliminated, but the war brought into power the majority Shiite population, who had long been under the thumb of the Sunni minority. Shiite exile groups in Iran returned to Iraq and quickly dominated politics, while domestic Shiite insurgents benefited from Iranian funding and training. This shift in power, combined with the nuclear standoff and growing Iranian influence in places such as Lebanon and Syria, has led some commentators to warn of a possible Iranian hegemony over the region. This has scared Saudi Arabia in particular, and relations between the two countries have grown openly hostile.

While Iran's possible reintegration into the global economy may mean a richer, and thus more powerful country, Iran is more isolated now, and has less to offer ideologically, than at any time since 1979. This does not mean the regime will reform any time soon. But it does mean that confrontation, rather than engagement, is one of the few tools Iran can still use to bolster its claim that the Islamic Revolution still matters.

CURRENT ISSUES IN IRAN

The Nuclear Program

One of the most critical issues confronting the international community at present is Iran's nuclear program. The resolution of this issue will have profound repercussions, and any long-term solution will be complicated by Iranian domestic politics.

Before going any further, we should recall the difference between a nuclear energy program and a nuclear weapons program. There are similarities but also important differences. In both cases, it is necessary to process, or "enrich," natural uranium, separating the uranium atoms with different numbers of neutrons (isotopes). Natural and low-enriched uranium is made up mostly of U-238 isotopes, and only a small amount is composed of U-235—the fissile isotopes, or those that can sustain a chain reaction. Commercial nuclear programs enrich natural uranium to about 20 percent U-235 in order to create nuclear fuel. At this low level of enrichment, uranium can be fashioned into fuel rods, which can then be placed in a nuclear reactor to generate electricity. Weapons-grade uranium, however, requires enrichment of up to around 90 percent U-235. In other words, while peaceful nuclear programs require enriched uranium, this stockpile can be further enriched to produce a nuclear weapon. This distinction is not simply a matter of degree. Enriching uranium up to weapons grade is a major project that requires a huge number of sophisticated centrifuges operating far beyond what is necessary for nuclear fuel. Once uranium is enriched to weapons grade, the next challenge is turning that uranium into an actual device small enough that it can be fitted onto a missile.

Even before the 1979 revolution, as part of an extensive plan to develop nuclear energy for peaceful purposes, Iran also showed interest in developing a nuclear weapon. This work was mostly halted by the revolution, the Iran-Iraq War, and international sanctions. By the early 1990s, however, Iran sought to

Iran's Nuclear Capabilities

Do you approve or disapprove of each of the following?

	APPROVE	DISAPPROVE	DON'T KNOW/ REFUSED
Iran developing its own nuclear power capabilities for military use	34%	41%	25%
Iran developing its own nuclear power capabilities for nonmilitary use	56%	21%	24%

Note: Question asked of Iranian adults. Based on surveys conducted May 24–June 6, 2013.

Source: "Iranians Mixed on Nuclear Capabilities," Gallup, October 14, 2013, www.gallup.com/poll/165413/iranians-mixed -nuclear-capabilities.aspx (accessed 9/20/16).

actively restart its nuclear program, mining uranium and reaching out to various countries (such as Pakistan and North Korea) for technology and assistance in such areas as centrifuge technology. These developments began to raise alarms in the international community, especially given Iran's related development in missile technology (provided in part by North Korea). Iran appeared to be on the path to becoming a "virtual" nuclear state, meaning that it would have the capacity to make a bomb within a matter of months if it chose to do so (though this does not mean it could necessarily place that bomb onto a missile).[19]

Over the past decade, both international negotiations and sanctions have attempted to halt Iran's nuclear program. The international community placed increasingly restrictive sanctions on Iran, meaning to harm the Iranian economy and deprive the government access to needed technology by limiting trade and other economic opportunities. This move, unfortunately, also served to strengthen the position of actors such as the Revolutionary Guard, who benefited from the sanctions by developing their own smuggling networks and illicit economic activities. In addition, international actors have relied on espionage to slow down Iran's nuclear program. Best known is the Stuxnet computer virus, which was apparently designed by the United States and Israel to attack Iran's centrifuge system. Several assassinations of top nuclear specialists in Iran also appear to have been the work of Israel. The danger of a preemptive military attack by the United States or Israel has been very real, though few believed this would do more than simply delay the nuclear program.

The election of President Rouhani initiated a new round of negotiations seeking an end to the nuclear impasse. In 2013, Iran and members of the international community (the United States, United Kingdom, France, Germany, China, and Russia) agreed to temporarily halt enrichment and place Iranian nuclear facilities under the inspection of the International Atomic Energy Agency (IAEA). In return, the international community relaxed sanctions on oil exports and certain imports. A final deal in 2016 stipulated that Iran would reduce its centrifuges and limit uranium enrichment for 15 years, and place the program under IAEA oversight. In return, sanctions would be suspended and funds frozen overseas would be returned.[20]

As we have suggested elsewhere in this chapter, the deal so far has led to mixed results. The greatest disappointment has been on the Iranian side; in spite of the deal, remaining sanctions over charges of terrorism have limited improvements in such important areas as international banking. Foreign direct investment, while improved, has also been deterred by concerns that businesses will run afoul of remaining American restrictions. Surveys suggest that most Iranians have not felt that their economic situation has yet benefited from the agreement. Finally, there appear no signs that as a result of the agreement diplomatic relations between the United States and Iran will improve. A concern is that barring significant improvement, Iran might pull out of the nuclear agreement. However, the longer the deal remains in place, the greater the likelihood the country will feel the benefit of improved international ties.

Alcohol and Drugs in the Islamic Republic

Alcohol and drugs have a long history in Iran. Iranian pre-Islamic history is associated with wine production, and Sufi poets such as Rumi draw frequent parallels between love and drunkenness. It is also from Iran that we get the word *assassin*, or "hashish taker," which was coined to describe a twelfth-century political and religious group, split off from Shiism, that targeted and killed a number of Sunni political leaders. (Opponents of the group claimed that its followers' fanaticism was drug induced.[21]) Opium, too, has a long Iranian pedigree. Many Iranian monarchies, especially the Qajar dynasty of the nineteenth century, are remembered for the drug use of their shahs (and for their prodigious consumption of wine). But such intoxicants are forbidden in Islam. Iran has veered back and forth between trying to restrict intoxicants and accepting them as an inescapable part of modern society.

In 1979, the Islamic Republic reversed the more permissive attitude that had characterized Iran over the past century and ushered in a prohibitive regime, among the strictest in the Middle East. Alcohol was banned, with limited exceptions for the country's non-Muslim minorities, such as Christians and Jews. The government also cracked down on opium, heroin, hashish, and other drugs. Penalties for drug and alcohol use were severe, including jail time, lashings, and even execution for drug and alcohol dealers, who may make up the largest share of those executed in Iran.

Despite this pressure, drug and alcohol use continues in Iran and has perhaps even grown over time. In the case of alcohol, the destruction of Iran's own industry has simply given rise to a large smuggling network. Since the invasion of Iraq and the opening of borders between Iraq and Iran, large amounts of alcohol are brought illegally into the country, and it is easy to purchase. While the total number of Iranians who drink may be small, the World Health Organization reports that Iran is among the top 20 consumers of alcohol in the world—a percentage higher than in Russia, France, Germany, or the United States.[22]

As a public health concern, drug addiction is a far bigger problem. According to the United Nations, Iran has more than a million drug-dependent users and represents one of the most severe addiction problems in the world. As with alcohol, this problem, too, has a regional source: drugs are coming in from Pakistan as well as from Afghanistan, which is the world's biggest producer of opium. As a result, Iran has the highest rate of opium, heroin, and morphine seizures in the world, and nearly 4,000 police officers have been killed over the past three decades in counternarcotics operations. Many of these drugs only pass through Iran, because Europe is their final destination. However, domestic crystal meth production and consumption is rapidly becoming a new problem as it overtakes heroin use.

A banner in Sarein, Iran, warning of the dangers of drug addiction.

The drug problem in Iran is one of the reasons the country has one of the highest rates of capital punishment in the world; in 2016, the majority of those put to death were convicted on drug charges. This directly counters international law, which restricts capital punishment to crimes involving intentional killing. It is not easy to determine whether the social repression under the Islamic Republic is a main driver of drug addiction in Iran or if this is a more intractable cultural problem that will remain unaffected by any future political changes.[23]

NOTES

1. Michael Axworthy, *A History of Iran: Empire of the Mind* (New York: Basic Books, 2008).
2. For a discussion of Shiism in Iran and elsewhere, see Heinz Halm, *Shi'ism* (New York: Columbia University Press, 2004), and Moojan Momen, *An Introduction to Shia Islam* (New Haven, CT: Yale University Press, 1985).

3. For a discussion of this period and the increasing U.S. influence in Iranian politics, see Kenneth M. Pollack, *The Persian Puzzle: The Conflict between Iran and America* (New York: Random House, 2004).

4. Stephen Kinzer, *All the Shah's Men: An American Coup and the Roots of Middle East Terror* (New York: John Wiley & Sons, 2003).

5. Ali M. Ansari, "The Myth of the White Revolution: Mohammad Reza Shah, 'Modernization,' and the Consolidation of Power," *Middle Eastern Studies* 37, no. 3 (July 2001): 1–24.

6. Ruhollah Khomeini, *Islamic Government* (Tehran: Institute for Compilation and Publication of Imam Khomeini's Works, n.d.); see also Karen Armstrong, *The Battle for God* (New York: Alfred A. Knopf, 2000).

7. For an analysis of these events, see Charles Kurzman, *The Unthinkable Revolution in Iran* (Cambridge, MA: Harvard University Press, 2004).

8. From International Constitutional Law, www.servat.unibe.ch/icl/ir__indx.html (accessed 10/20/14).

9. Hadi Ghaemi, "The Islamic Judiciary," *The Iran Primer*, U.S. Institute of Peace, http://iranprimer.usip.org/resource/islamic-judiciary (accessed 9/20/16).

10. Kian Tajbakhsh, "Political Decentralization and the Creation of Local Government in Iran: Consolidation or Transformation of the Theocratic State?" *Social Research* 67, no. 2 (Summer 2000), pp. 377–404, and Hossein Alekajbaf and Jayum A. Jawan, *Decentralization and Local Government in Iran* (Shah Alam, Indonesia: Karisma Publications, 2009).

11. Frederic Wehrey, Jerrold D. Green, Brian Nichiporuk, Alireza Nader, Lydia Hansell, Rasool Nafisi, and S. R. Bohandy, *The Rise of the Pasdaran: Assessing the Domestic Roles of Iran's Islamic Revolutionary Guards Corps* (Santa Monica, CA: RAND Corporation, 2009), www.rand.org/pubs/monographs/MG821 (accessed 9/20/16).

12. Reporters without Borders Press, Freedom Index 2016, https://rsf.org/en/ranking (accessed 9/20/16).

13. "Iran: Human Rights Abuses against the Kurdish Minority," London: Amnesty International Publications, 2008; see also Rasmus Christian Elling, *Minorities in Iran: Nationalism and Ethnicity after Khomeini* (New York: Palgrave Macmillan, 2013).

14. A good discussion of different political values and positions in Iran can be found in Ray Takeyh, *Guardians of the Revolution: Iran and the World in the Age of the Ayatollahs* (New York: Oxford University Press, 2009).

15. Jalal Al Ahmad, *Weststruckness*, trans. John Green and Ahmad Alizadeh (Costa Mesa, CA: Mazda, 1997).

16. David E. Thaler, Alireza Nader, Shahram Chubin, and Jerrold D. Green, *Mullahs, Guards, and Bonyads: An Exploration of Iranian Leadership Dynamics* (Santa Monica, CA: RAND Corporation, 2010), www.rand.org/content/dam/rand/pubs/monographs/2009/RAND_MG878.pdf (accessed 5/1/17).

17. Djavad Salehi-Isfahani and Daniel Egel, *Iranian Youth in Times of Crisis*, Working Paper, Belfer Center for Science and International Affairs, Harvard Kennedy School, September 2010, http://belfercenter.ksg.harvard.edu/files/Salehi-Isfahani_DI-Working-Paper-3_Iran-Youth-Crisis.pdf (accessed 9/20/16); see also Bijan Khajehpour, "Can Rouhani Reverse Iran's Brain Drain?," *Al Monitor*, January 12, 2014.

18. A nuanced discussion of the role of Shia politics in the region can be found in Vali Nasr, *The Shia Revival* (New York: W. W. Norton, 2007).

19. J. Reardon, *Containing Iran: Strategies for Addressing the Iranian Nuclear Challenge* (Santa Monica, CA: RAND Corporation, 2012).

20. Joint Comprehensive Plan of Action, U.S. Department of State, http://www.state.gov/e/eb/tfs/spi/iran/jcpoa/ (accessed 9/20/16).
21. Farhad Daftary, *The Assassin Legends: Myths of the Isma'ilis* (London: IB Tauris, 1994), 91.
22. World Health Organization, *Global Status Report on Alcohol and Health*, 2014, www.who.int/substance_abuse/publications/global_alcohol_report/en/ (accessed 9/20/16).
23. "Iran's 'Staggering' Execution Spree: Nearly 700 Put to Death in Just Over Six Months," Amnesty International, July 23, 2015, https://www.amnesty.org/en/latest/news/2015/07/irans-staggering-execution-spree/ (accessed 9/20/2016).

KEY TERMS

Ahmadinejad, Mahmoud President of Iran from 2005 to 2013

Ashura The most important Shia religious holiday, commemorating the death of Hussein, the grandson of the prophet Muhammad

Assembly of Experts Elected body that chooses the supreme leader

ayatollah In Shiite Islam, a title in the religious hierarchy achieved by scholars who have demonstrated highly advanced knowledge of Islamic law and religion

Basij "People's militia," which serves as a public morals police

bonyads Parastatal foundations made in part from assets nationalized after the Iranian Revolution

chief justice Head of the judiciary

Constitutional Revolution 1906 uprising against Qajar dynasty by secular and religious leaders to limit the power of the monarchy and resist Western imperialism

Expediency Council Appointed body that mediates between the Majlis and the Guardian Council over legislative disputes

Farsi Language of Iran

Guardian Council Appointed body that vets candidates for office and can overturn legislation

imams Descendants of the prophet Muhammad, considered by Shia to be true political and religious leaders of Islam

Iran-Iraq War The 1980–1988 conflict between the two countries, started by Iraq

Islamic Republic of Iran Name for postrevolutionary Iran

Islamism, or Islamic fundamentalism The belief that Islam should be the source of the political regime

Khamenei, Ayatollah Ali Current supreme leader of Iran, as of 1989

Khatami, Mohammad President of Iran from 1997 to 2005

Khomeini, Ayatollah Ruhollah First supreme leader of Iran, from 1980 to his death in 1989

Koran Central holy book of Islam

Mahdi In Shiism, a term for the "hidden imam," the descendant of Muhammad who will return to earth to usher in a new age

Majlis Legislature of Iran

Mosaddeq, Mohammad Prime minister of Iran; deposed in 1953 by Operation Ajax

Muhammad Main prophet of Islam

National Front Political party in Iran following World War II; it opposed the monarchy and favored greater Iranian control over natural resources; outlawed after Operation Ajax

Operation Ajax U.S.- and UK-backed overthrow of Iranian prime minister Mosaddeq in 1953

Pahlavi, Mohammad Reza Monarch of Iran from 1941 to 1979

Pahlavi, Reza Shah Monarch of Iran from 1925 to 1941

Persia Name for Iran before 1935

president In Iran, the head of government

principalists Term for political conservatives in Iran who oppose liberalization and political reform

quietist Description of view within Shiism that rejects theocracy and the direct role of religion in the state

Rafsanjani, Ali Akbar Hashemi President of Iran from 1989 to 1997; current head of the Expediency Council

Revolutionary Guard Paramilitary force charged with defending the regime from domestic and internal enemies

Rouhani, Hassan President of Iran since 2013

SAVAK Secret police of prerevolutionary Iran

Second Khordad Front Reformist alliance that emerged in Iran to contest 2000 Majlis elections

Sharia Religious law of Islam

Shiism Minority sect of Islam that differs from Sunnism over the rightful heir and proper descendants of the prophet Muhammad

supreme leader Chief spiritual and political leader of Iran

theocracy Rule by religion or religious leaders

ummah Literally, "community"; meant to refer to the nation or Islamic communities everywhere

velayat-e faqih Rule by Islamic jurists; also, Islamic Republic's political system, which places power in the hands of clerics

White Revolution Policy of reforms enacted by Reza Shah, beginning in 1963, to rapidly modernize and Westernize Iran

WEB LINKS

- The Iran Primer (http://iranprimer.usip.org/)
- Islamic Republic News Agency (www.irna.com/en)
- Ministry of Foreign Affairs, Islamic Republic of Iran (www.mfa.gov.ir)
- Press TV (www.presstv.ir/)
- Website of President Hassan Rouhani (president.ir)
- Website of the Supreme Leader Ayatollah Khamenei (www.leader.ir)

11

Javier Duarte, former governor of the Mexican state of Veracruz, after his arrest in Guatemala in April 2017. Duarte was charged with embezzling funds and involvement in organized crime. At least six former Mexican governors are being investigated on corruption charges, an example of the endemic corruption that plagues Mexican politics.

MEXICO

Why Study This Case?

Mexico offers a fascinating case study of three challenges to a young democracy that are of particular interest to students of comparative politics: the need for the state to establish political order, the need to implement the most effective and fair strategy for economic development, and the need to establish political transparency and the rule of law.

The first challenge, the need to achieve political order and to avoid the violence and disruption associated with a lack of order, was the subject of Samuel Huntington's classic *Political Order in Changing Societies*.[1] No country illustrates this challenge better than Mexico. Mexico's first spurt of economic development took place under Porfirio Díaz's brutal authoritarian regime in the late nineteenth and early twentieth centuries. That regime was displaced by the Mexican Revolution (1910–17), an extended period of cataclysmic mass violence and political anarchy. The chaos was finally ended by a unique and remarkably flexible semi-authoritarian regime governed by a dominant political party, the **Partido Revolucionario Institucional (PRI)**.

Unlike the political atmosphere of most other developing countries, Mexico's post-1917 politics was relatively peaceful: after 1920, power was transferred between leaders through regular elections; and after the late 1930s, the military was thoroughly subordinate to civilians. Since 2000, Mexico has been governed by its first democratic regime but has struggled to impose order. Mexico's first two democratic presidents waged a war against Mexico's increasingly powerful drug cartels and unleashed the most serious wave of violence the country has seen since the Mexican Revolution. The violence has traumatized Mexican society, raised serious questions about the capacity and autonomy of the Mexican state, and led some domestic and foreign observers to wonder

MEXICO

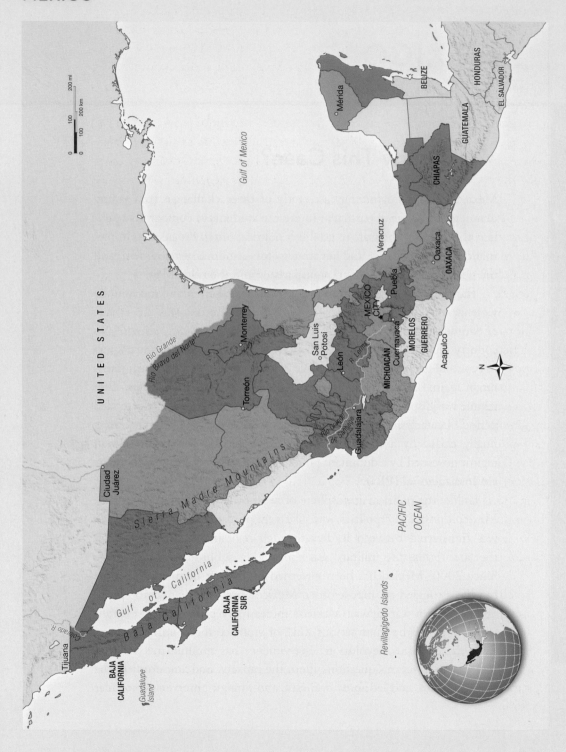

whether Mexico could become a failed state. In the context of an escalating drug war, in 2012 Mexican voters returned the presidency to the PRI, hoping that its young and charismatic leader, **Enrique Peña Nieto**, could stem the violence. However, the PRI's control of the presidency has raised questions about whether Mexico's old authoritarian political machine can transform itself into a democratic political party.

A second challenge facing Mexico is determining the appropriate role for the state in economic development. Modern Mexican history has seen radical shifts between free-market political-economic systems and a more statist political economy. Today, Mexico is one of Latin America's most open economies. Its embrace of neoliberal economics since the 1990s has made Mexico a middle-class society that is far more affluent than it was during the decades of statist economics, and it has experienced an export boom. But the dislocations caused by Mexico's opening to the global economy worsened inequality, devastated its most vulnerable citizens, and fueled a massive wave of immigration to the United States. These dislocations have also launched a debate within Mexico about proposals to dismantle the last vestiges of statism—most notably the state ownership of oil, Mexico's major natural resource.

A final challenge facing Mexico is the struggle between the rule of law and transparency on the one hand and the endemic corruption cultivated by decades of one-party rule on the other. Those who believed that Mexico's embrace of democracy and a more open economy would reduce corruption and improve accountability have been sorely disappointed to date. Decades of authoritarian rule under the PRI weakened the rule of law and left Mexico with a police force and judiciary with low capacity, little accountability, and vulnerability to corruption. The inability of the Mexican state to defend its citizens from the violence unleashed by drug cartels has raised doubts about the competence of its corruption-riddled security apparatus and judiciary. The violence has also given rise to a powerful vigilante movement by frustrated citizens, a phenomenon that may itself prove a challenge to the rule of law.

The return to power of the PRI in 2012 has renewed both hope and skepticism about each of these three dilemmas. President Enrique Peña Nieto pledged to strengthen democracy through a series of political reforms, but many Mexicans are skeptical about such claims from a politician of the PRI, a party associated with over six decades of authoritarian rule. Peña Nieto criticized his predecessors' war against the drug cartels but has broadly continued their policies. Can the PRI have more success in reducing violence in Mexico while shoring up its democratic institutions?

Peña Nieto has also pledged to further open Mexico's economy as a way of stimulating economic growth, increasing oil revenue, and modernizing the economy. Since taking office, he has enacted some ambitious and controversial reforms of the oil sector, and he has pledged to break up powerful monopolies that dominate much of the economy. However, given that the PRI presided over a statist economy that sanctioned powerful monopolies in exchange for political support, many question whether the Peña Nieto administration can face down those on the left—and those within his own party—who oppose many of those reforms. Can Peña Nieto shepherd these reforms through the Mexican political system, and can he improve Mexico's sluggish and unequal economy?

Peña Nieto's success with these first two challenges will likely depend largely on his ability to improve transparency, empower Mexico's feeble judiciary, strengthen the rule of law, and reduce systemic corruption. Can he distance himself and his party from the PRI's reputation as a bastion of patronage, corruption, and opacity?

Major Geographic and Demographic Features

Mexico's stunningly diverse geography includes tropical rain forests, snowcapped volcanoes, and rich agricultural regions. Historically, the two major mountain ranges that divide Mexico, the eastern and western Sierra Madres, have made transportation and communication difficult. Only 12 percent of Mexico's land is arable, and the most productive agricultural areas are in northern Mexico, close to the U.S. border. There, large and highly mechanized export farms provide much of America's winter produce. The proximity of Mexico's agricultural export to the U.S. market has been a major boost to Mexico's economic growth. Agriculture in southern Mexico is characterized by smaller farms and less efficient production. Mexico is well endowed with minerals and has major oil reserves.

With 114 million people, Mexico has the second-largest population in Latin America (after Brazil). Its population is racially quite diverse: about 60 percent are **mestizos**, people of mixed Spanish and indigenous blood; another 30 percent, living primarily in the central and southern parts of the country, are considered indigenous because they speak an indigenous language. The largest indigenous groups are the **Maya**, located in Mexico's far south (along the Guatemalan border), and the **Nahuatl**, concentrated in central Mexico.

Nearly three-quarters of Mexico's population lives in an urban setting, a relatively recent change. Mexico City has long dwarfed all other Mexican cities: the Federal District of Mexico now has about 18 million residents. Population growth has slowed with economic development, but Mexico's large population still strains the country's resources. As a result, Mexicans continue to migrate in very large numbers. Many have left the impoverished countryside for the cities, often leaving the poor south for the wealthier north, especially the factory towns along the U.S. border. At the same time, a steady stream of Mexicans has migrated across the border to the United States.

Historical Development of the State

The history of the modern Mexican state can be viewed as a struggle between political order, which has almost always been achieved by authoritarian rulers, and periodic outbursts of violence and political anarchy.[2]

When the Spanish conquistador **Hernán Cortés** arrived in Mexico in 1519, he encountered well-established and highly sophisticated indigenous civilizations. The country had long been home to such peoples as the Maya, Aztecs, and Toltecs, who had relatively prosperous economies, impressive architecture, sophisticated agricultural methods, and powerful militaries. Within three years of their arrival, the Spanish conquerors had defeated the last Aztec leader, **Cuauhtémoc**; destroyed the impressive Aztec capital, Tenochtitlán; and decimated the indigenous population. By the early seventeenth century, the indigenous population had been reduced from about 25 million to under 1 million. The surviving indigenous peoples of Mexico, concentrated in the central and southern parts of the country, became a permanent underclass of virtual slaves and landless peasants.

The Aztec Empire was replaced by the equally hierarchical, authoritarian, and militaristic Spanish Empire, which created a legacy very different from that imparted to the United States by British colonialism. Mexico was the richest of Spain's colonial possessions (indeed, it was far richer at the time than Britain's territories to the north), and Spain ruled the distant colony with an iron fist, sending a new viceroy to the colony every four years. Colonial viceroys were absolute dictators: armed with the terror of the Spanish Inquisition, they were able to stamp out most political dissent. Without any civilian oversight, rampant corruption thrived in the colonial administration.

Independence and Instability: The Search for Order

The struggle for independence can be viewed as a conflict over control of the state between the aristocracy loyal to Spain and the increasingly powerful and wealthy **criollos** (Mexican-born descendants of the Spanish colonists). Though inspired by the

French and American revolutions, the Mexican independence movement was mostly a response to the sudden blow that Napoleon's invading armies delivered to Spain. When Spain adopted a progressive-liberal constitution in 1812, conservative Mexican elites accepted independence as the only means to preserve order and the status quo. The leading rebels and political conservatives agreed that an independent Mexico, declared in 1821, would preserve the role of the Catholic Church and implement a constitutional monarchy with a European at the head. **Mexico's War of Independence** was extremely violent, lasted 11 years, and cost over half a million lives.

Because Mexico's independence was dominated by political conservatives who sought to preserve the economic and social status quo, it did nothing to alleviate the poverty of Mexico's indigenous people and its large mestizo population. Indeed, the violence of the War of Independence and the elimination of the minimal protections of the Spanish Crown worsened their plight. The power of the large landholders, or *latifundistas*, grew with independence, and the newly independent Mexico became more unequal and politically unstable. Much of the turmoil and political chaos that plagued Mexico over the next half-century was caused by a dispute between conservatives who wanted to maintain a monarchy and liberals who wanted a U.S.-style democracy. With the end of Spanish rule and the strong centralized government of the viceroy, Mexico was dominated by local military strongmen, known as **caciques**. Mexico's weak central state could not impose its authority.

Independent Mexico's first leader, Colonel Agustín de Iturbide, had himself crowned emperor in 1822. He was overthrown by **General Antonio López de Santa Anna**, Mexico's first in a series of **caudillos** (national military strongmen), and was executed two years later. Santa Anna dominated Mexican politics for the next 30 years; despite his considerable power, however, he was unable to impose his authority over the local caciques or to prevent the secession of Texas in 1836. The impotence of a fragmented Mexico became even more apparent in the 1840s when a rising imperial power, the United States, defeated the country in the **Mexican-American War** (1846–48) and claimed half of Mexico's territory (present-day Arizona, California, Colorado, Nevada, New Mexico, Texas, and Utah). In the aftermath of the defeat, Mexico's weakened government faced a massive uprising, known as the **War of the Castes**, by the indigenous Mayan population in the south. It took several years of fighting to subdue the rebellion.

Over the next several decades, liberals who were led by a Zapotec Indian, **Benito Juárez**, attempted to centralize, modernize, and secularize Mexico. Juárez, who occupied the presidency on three separate occasions, imposed a fairly progressive constitution in 1857 and is today considered one of Mexico's first proponents

TIMELINE OF POLITICAL DEVELOPMENT

YEAR	EVENT
1810–21	War of Independence fought against Spain.
1846–48	One-half of Mexico's territory lost in war with the United States.
1910–17	Mexican Revolution takes place.
1917	Revolutionary constitution adopted.
1929	Official revolutionary party created, later becoming the PRI.
1934–40	Presidency of Lázaro Cárdenas, during which land reform is promoted, the oil industry is nationalized, and the state is given a larger role in the economy.
1939	The PAN formed as a conservative opposition to the revolution.
1968	Student protest movement against the Mexican government violently repressed.
1981–82	Economic collapse caused by sudden drop in oil prices and Mexico's inability to pay its foreign debt.
1988	President Carlos Salinas de Gortari assumes power after elections widely viewed as fraudulent.
1994	NAFTA put into effect. Zapatistas, indigenous peasants in the southern state of Chiapas, rebel. PRI presidential candidate Luis Donaldo Colosio assassinated while campaigning; replaced by Ernesto Zedillo.
2000	PAN candidate Vicente Fox elected, marking the first defeat of the PRI in 71 years.
2006	Felipe Calderón, of the PAN, is elected president and escalates the war against Mexico's drug cartels.
2012	Enrique Peña Nieto begins a six-year term as president, marking the return to power of the PRI.

of democracy. Juárez was unable to bring stability to Mexico, however. In 1864, Mexican conservatives, backed by French troops, imposed an ill-fated and short-lived monarchy ruled by an Austrian emperor, Maximilian, who was captured and executed in 1867. Juárez regained power, but his reforms alienated Mexican conservatives, and Mexico soon succumbed to a long dictatorship.

The Porfiriato: Economic Liberalism and Political Authoritarianism

From 1876 to 1910, Mexican politics was dominated by **Porfirio Díaz**. General Díaz had backed the liberal reforms of Juárez and fought to expel the French-imposed monarchy but then embraced conservative ideas to gain the support of elites and maintain power. He assumed power in 1876 and had himself reelected for much of the period up until 1910. He imposed a brutal authoritarian regime (known as the *Porfiriato*) and gave Mexico its first taste of stability since independence. Díaz was also responsible for Mexico's first real economic development and was the first Mexican ruler to impose the power of the state on remote areas.

The Revolution

The **Mexican Revolution** (1910–17) can be viewed as a struggle between two groups attempting to seize control of the state. The first included middle-class Mexicans resisting the dictatorship of Díaz, who sought a more democratic political system with a capitalist economy. The second included radical social reformers who proposed, among other things, agrarian reform. Both groups sought to weaken the role of the Catholic Church.

In the first phase of the revolution, middle-class political reformers, led by the landowner **Francisco Madero**, defeated the Díaz dictatorship. Madero's victory promised democratic reforms and minimal economic change. The second phase of the revolution involved a struggle between these moderate political reformers and advocates of radical socioeconomic change. The most famous revolutionary advocate of the poor was **Emiliano Zapata**, a young mestizo peasant leader. Zapata organized a peasant army in Morelos, south of Mexico City, to push for agrarian reform. In the north of Mexico, **Francisco (Pancho) Villa** organized an army of peasants and small farmers.

Different social forces saw the Mexican Revolution as a means to accomplish very different types of goals, which helps explain why the conflict was so protracted and so bloody. After the initial uprising, Mexico soon descended into political chaos—armed bands led by regional caciques fought one another over a period of 10 years. About 1.5 million Mexicans (about 7 percent of the total population) died in or as a result of the conflict, and thousands more fled north to the United States. Order was restored only in 1917, under the leadership of a northern governor, **Venustiano Carranza**. He defeated not only those who wanted a return to a dictatorship but also Zapata and Villa, the more radical voices of the revolution.

The **Constitution of 1917** reflected some of the contradictions of the revolution. The document was written not by peasants and workers but by middle-class mestizo professionals who had suffered under the Díaz dictatorship. That some of their values were largely "liberal" explains provisions that call for regular elections as well as harsh measures to weaken the Catholic Church. The constitution sought to prevent the reemergence of a dictatorship by devolving political power to Mexico's states, adopting federalism, and barring presidents, governors, mayors, and federal legislators from reelection. Reflecting the power of the emerging mestizo class and the role played by indigenous Mexicans in unseating the dictatorship, the 1917 constitution provided elaborate protection for indigenous communal lands and called for land reform. It was also a nationalist document, prohibiting foreign ownership of Mexican land and mineral rights.

Although Carranza successfully seized power and fostered the new constitution, he was unable to implement many of the reforms or to stem Mexico's endemic political violence. His government was responsible for the murder of Zapata in 1919, and Carranza himself was assassinated by political opponents in 1920.

Mexico's next two elected presidents, Álvaro Obregón (1920–24) and Plutarco Elías Calles (1924–28), finally put an end to the political bloodshed and developed a political system capable of maintaining order. Obregón promoted trade unions but brought them under state control. He also promoted land reform while tolerating the presence of large landed estates. He managed to gain the support and recognition of the United States, which had feared the revolution as a socialist experiment. Most significantly, he purged the army and weakened the revolutionary generals who had continued to meddle in politics.

President Calles consolidated state power by imposing the first income tax and investing in education and infrastructure. He vigorously enforced the constitution's limit on the power of the Catholic Church. The church was a major landowner, and its support for the dictatorship of Díaz and the enemies of the revolution made it a prime target for reform. Religious processions were banned, clergy could not appear in public in religious garb, the church could not own any property, and control over education was given to the state. Attempts by the revolutionary leadership to impose these reforms provoked a major social upheaval, the Cristero Rebellion (1926–29), a bloody conflict that claimed about 90,000 lives. The conflict ended when revolutionary leaders agreed not to enforce some of the anticlerical provisions of the constitution and to restore some of the privileges enjoyed by the Catholic Church.

After Calles left power, he created, in 1929, his most enduring legacy: the Partido Nacional Revolucionario, later renamed the Partido Revolucionario Institucional (PRI). From the outset, the PRI was conceived as a party of power and a party of the state. Its colors (red, white, and green) are the colors of the Mexican flag. Its goal was to encompass all those who had supported the revolution, and its members thus ranged from socialists to liberals. Moreover, it was designed to incorporate and co-opt the most important organizations and interest groups in Mexican society, starting with the army. The PRI's main purpose was to end political violence by controlling the political system and the process of presidential succession. After decades of instability and violence, the revolution's leaders brought Mexico an unprecedented period of political peace.

Stability Achieved: The PRI in Power, 1929–2000

For decades, the PRI provided Mexico with the much-desired political stability that its founders had sought. Under the PRI, Mexico held presidential elections every six years, and presidents assumed office without violence or military intervention. The PRI regime featured a strong president, directly elected for a single six-year term. Though not stipulated in the 1917 constitution, PRI presidents claimed the power to name their successors by officially designating the PRI candidate for the presidency; for more than 80 years, no official PRI candidate lost a presidential election. During most of the PRI's tenure in office, the Mexican president enjoyed the reverence and aloofness of monarchical heads of state while possessing far more power than the typical democratic president. Most important, until 2000, Mexican presidents controlled the vast machinery of the PRI and used the state to dispense patronage. Unlike U.S. presidents, they faced no effective check on their power from the legislature, judiciary, or state governments, all of which were controlled by the PRI.

Under the PRI, regular elections were held for national, state, and local offices, and opposition parties actively contested these elections. During most of this period, there was no formal censorship of the press, and Mexicans were free to voice their opinions and criticize the government. Mexicans were also free to live where they wanted, and according to their constitution, they were living in a democratic state.

But under its surface, the Mexican regime had clear authoritarian tendencies. The PRI held an inordinate amount of power. Between 1929 and 2000, the PRI controlled the presidency and the vast majority of seats in the legislature and at the state and local level. The PRI dominated major trade unions and peasant organizations. Through its control of the state, the PRI controlled major pieces of the economy, including Mexico's vast oil wealth. The PRI became expert at co-opting possible sources of opposition, including the press and the weak opposition parties. Unlike many authoritarian regimes, the PRI did not often need to revert to harsh measures of repression; when necessary, however, the regime used a variety of tactics to stifle the opposition. Most notorious were the massacre of peaceful student demonstrators in Mexico City in 1968 and the increasing use of electoral fraud to preserve its political dominance in the 1970s and 1980s as its grip on power began to erode.

Since the Mexican Revolution, scholars have struggled to characterize the Mexican regime. It is perhaps most accurate to view Mexico under the PRI as an authoritarian regime dominated by a single political party, but one that afforded far more civil liberties than its authoritarian counterparts elsewhere. Mexico held regular (though not always free and fair) elections, tolerated and even encouraged political parties (although those parties began to win state and local races only in the 1980s), and formally protected basic civil liberties. Compared with most other authoritarian regimes, the PRI kept human rights abuses to a minimum. It maintained its power almost exclusively through co-optation, inclusion, and corruption. Its unparalleled success meant that it did not often need to resort to brute repression. The Peruvian novelist Mario Vargas Llosa aptly described the PRI regime as the "perfect dictatorship."

Just as Mexico's political system contained a mixture of democratic and authoritarian features, its political-economic model was also contradictory. Some goals of the more radical supporters of the revolution, like land reform and the nationalization of oil and mineral wealth, were promoted during the presidency of Lázaro Cárdenas (1934–40). But his successors were far more willing to accommodate the Mexican elite that the revolution had left largely intact.

The Slow Erosion of PRI Power, 1980–2000

By the early 1980s, the vaunted stability of the Mexican regime was called into question by a series of interrelated economic and political challenges to PRI rule. The economic crises of the 1980s (due mainly to Mexico's massive foreign debt) and mid-1990s (caused by a sudden devaluation of Mexico's currency, the peso) unleashed numerous challenges to the party's political hegemony. The conservative opposition in northern Mexico, long an advocate of free-market economic policies, began to seriously contest and occasionally win local and state elections.

The PRI was then forced to revert to ever-increasing and ever-more-overt electoral fraud to deny power to the opposition.

The 1988 election of PRI president Carlos Salinas de Gortari was possible only through electoral fraud, and the popular outrage that resulted led to reforms of the electoral system that would eventually benefit the opposition. Salinas continued the PRI's gradual adoption of a neoliberal economic program by signing the **North American Free Trade Agreement (NAFTA)** with the United States and Canada, and by eliminating the last remnants of the revolution's more radical agenda (such as Mexico's commitment to land reform). Mexico's economy was opened to foreign investment, and the political system began a process of liberalization. As a result of the economic crisis, and due in part to the electoral reforms enacted under Salinas, the watershed election of July 2000 ended the PRI's 71-year control of the presidency. **Vicente Fox**, candidate of the conservative **Partido Acción Nacional (PAN)**, handily defeated **Francisco Labastida** of the PRI, despite an expensive and elaborate PRI campaign.

Since 2000, Mexico has operated under the same constitution adopted after the Mexican Revolution. President Fox and his PAN successor, **Felipe Calderón**, were Mexico's first two democratically elected presidents, and they operated in a much more pluralistic and competitive political system. The election of Enrique Peña Nieto in 2012 marked the PRI's return to power at the national level (it had maintained considerable power at the state and local level).

Political Regime

Political Institutions

Political scientists describe Mexico as democratic after 2000 because that is when the PRI, and its vast network of patronage and clientelism, was first dislodged from the presidency. The democratic political regime—initially established by the Mexican Revolution and subsequently manipulated by the PRI's authoritarian regime—remains in place today.

THE CONSTITUTION

On paper, the Mexican regime does not differ markedly from that of the United States. The Constitution of 1917 calls for a presidential legislative–executive

- **Legislative–executive system**: Presidential
- **Legislature**: Congreso de la Unión (National Congress)
  - **Lower house**: Cámara de Diputados (Federal Chamber of Deputies)
  - **Upper house**: Cámara de Senadores (Senate)
- **Unitary or federal division of power**: Federal
- **Main geographic subunits**: *Estados* (states)
- **Electoral system for lower house**: Mixed single-member district and proportional representation
- **Chief judicial body**: Suprema Corte de Justicia de la Nación (National Supreme Court of Justice)

system; a separation of judicial, legislative, and executive power; and a system of federalism that at least formally gives Mexico's states considerable power. The 71-year domination of the political system by the PRI, however, rendered this formidable constitution largely meaningless. Mexican presidents enjoyed near-dictatorial powers with few checks on their authority. Through their domination of the PRI, they not only controlled the judiciary but also handpicked state governors. The Mexican legislature might have served as a check on the PRI, but until July 1997 it was controlled by it. Elections at all levels were largely a charade, serving mainly to validate PRI appointments to elective offices. Even the president was not truly elected, since incumbent presidents ritually designated their successor. Campaigns were more celebrations of the PRI's power than genuine political contests.

How, then, did the opposition manage to win local and state elections in the 1980s? And how did the opposition unseat the PRI in the 2000 presidential election? Part of the answer to these questions lies in the growing illegitimacy of the regime during the 1970s, when Mexico's economy began to deteriorate. But the erosion of PRI legitimacy was also the result of widespread outrage at the PRI's blatant and unabashed disregard for the rule of law in the 1980s and 1990s. As opposition to the PRI grew, and as the PRI resorted more openly and more regularly to widespread electoral fraud, sectors of the party pushed for democratization. Seeking to polish its image, the PRI passed a number of reforms that favored the opposition.

One important set of reforms, passed in 1977, changed the electoral law (implementing some element of proportional representation, or PR) to guarantee the presence of the opposition in the legislature. Other reforms passed under the last PRI president before democratization, **Ernesto Zedillo**, gave the legislature control over judicial appointments and imposed electoral safeguards that greatly reduced the ability of a government to steal an election.

The Branches of Government

THE PRESIDENT

Because of their immense power and unchallenged authority during the long authoritarian rule of the PRI, Mexican presidents were viewed as elected monarchs. However, on paper, the 1917 constitution created a president with powers similar to those of the U.S. president and somewhat more limited than is the norm throughout Latin America. The perception that Mexico had an "imperial presidency" had more to do with the 71-year dominance of the PRI than with the provisions of the constitution. A Mexican president can issue executive decrees that have the force of law in a few areas (including international trade agreements). The president can directly introduce legislation in Congress and can veto legislation initiated by Congress. Until 1994, Mexican presidents had extensive power to appoint and remove judges. As recently as 1982, President **José López Portillo** essentially decreed the nationalization of Mexico's banking system.

However, Mexican presidents serve a single six-year term, meaning that all of them are lame ducks (and in this regard are rendered weaker than most other presidents). During the 70-year reign of the PRI, the power of the president was greatly enhanced by the tradition of handpicking his successor, who was generally chosen from among the cabinet members, but party primaries now select presidential candidates. In fact, in the last two presidential elections (2006 and 2012), the politician favored by the sitting president failed to win the nomination in the party primary election. During the authoritarian period, Mexican presidents also enjoyed enormous power because the state played a leading role in the economy. Control over key natural resources and infrastructure (for example, oil, electricity, and communications) historically put the key economic levers in the hands of the executive. However, with the economic reforms of the last decades, Mexican presidents now have far less power over the economy than they had during the 1917–2000 period.

Mexican presidents appoint and preside over a large cabinet of ministers, who oversee the various government departments. In recent decades, the **secretary of government**, which controls internal political affairs, and the **secretary of the treasury**, which oversees the economy, have been the highest-profile cabinet posts and have often been stepping-stones to the presidency. Since 2000, the Mexican cabinet has included 19 cabinet secretaries, in addition to seven policy coordinators whose job is to ease communication among ministries. Since Vicente Fox's historic victory in 2000, Mexico's presidents have lacked a majority in Congress. As a result, some of the constitutional checks on presidential power that were long absent in the Mexican system have become more effective. Presidents Fox, Calderón, and Peña Nieto have had to contend with a fragmented and increasingly assertive legislature and have thus been forced to bargain with the two major opposition parties in order to pass legislation. In recognition of this new reality, in 2013 President Peña Nieto approved the Pact for Mexico, a formal agreement with the two major opposition parties on many proposed political and economic reforms.

THE LEGISLATURE

Mexico has a bicameral legislature, called the **National Congress**, which is composed of a lower house (the **Chamber of Deputies**) and an upper house (the **Senate**).[3] The 500-member Chamber of Deputies has the power to pass laws (with a simple majority for most laws), levy taxes, and verify the outcome of elections. Mexico's upper house is composed of 128 members: 3 senators from each state and the Federal District of Mexico City, and an additional 32 senators selected from a national list on the basis of proportional representation. The upper house has fewer powers than the lower house, but it does have the power to confirm the president's appointments to the Supreme Court, approve treaties, and approve federal intervention in state matters.

Both houses have a committee system that at first glance looks much like the U.S. system. In practice, however, Mexican legislators and the legislative committees lack the teeth of their northern counterparts because of one key difference: according to Article 59 of the constitution, Mexican legislators cannot be reelected to consecutive terms. As a result, from 1970 to 1997, only about 17 percent of Mexican deputies entered the lower house with any legislative experience, effectively depriving Mexico of the kind of senior lawmakers who dominate the U.S. system. Most legislators were members of the PRI and could not afford to cross the party leadership, because they depended on the party for future political appointments.

Even after the PRI's loss of the presidency in 2000, single-term legislators were reluctant to disobey their party leadership if they hoped to be nominated

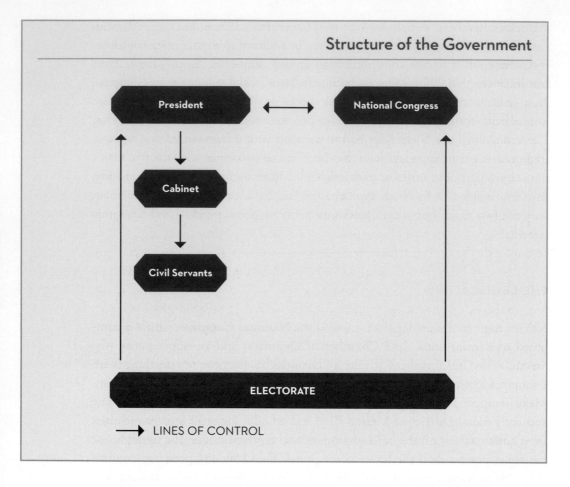

Structure of the Government

President ⟷ National Congress

President → Cabinet → Civil Servants

ELECTORATE

→ LINES OF CONTROL

for another post in local or state government. Ironically, the PRI (whose founding principle was no reelection) is now the strongest advocate of ending term limits. Since returning to power in 2012, the PRI has formally proposed amending the constitution to allow legislators to be reelected, but only with the approval of their parties. If enacted, this reform may increase the experience and prestige of legislators, but it may not make them any more willing to vote independently from their parties.

The Mexican legislature is currently in transition. Until 1988, the PRI regularly won over 90 percent of lower house seats and never lost a Senate seat. Between 1970 and 2003, it averaged 66.9 percent of the seats in the lower house, dwarfing the presence of its nearest rival, the PAN (National Action Party), which averaged about 17 percent during that period.[4] In 1997, the two main opposition parties were able to form a coalition and take control of the lower house.

Before 1997, the lower house approved about 98 percent of the legislation submitted by the executive, but that percentage has fallen steadily since then. Moreover, the number of laws originating in the legislature (instead of in the president's office) has increased dramatically. Since 2000, the lower house has successfully resisted pieces of legislation proposed by Fox, Calderón, and Peña Nieto. Because Mexican parties in the legislature have been extraordinarily well disciplined (Mexican legislators almost always vote according to the wishes of the party leadership), it has been almost impossible for presidents to poach votes from opposition legislators.

Despite his inaugural pledge to respect Congress, Fox began his term by acting very much like the PRI presidents, designing legislative proposals without any congressional input. His imperious behavior only emboldened the legislature. Congress blocked some legislation and radically altered other measures. For example, the lower house modified Fox's indigenous rights bill, which emerged from the legislature so weakened that the Zapatista guerrillas (whose rebellion it was intended to end) rejected it. Fox's proposed reform of Mexico's tax structure was torpedoed by the PRI and the leftist **Partido de la Revolución Democrática (PRD)** opposition, and Congress blocked his effort to negotiate a reduction of tariffs on imported sugar.

President Calderón faced similar legislative opposition but proved more adept at compromising with the opposition-dominated legislature. He achieved some major legislative victories as a result. President Peña Nieto has generally worked very well with the opposition-controlled legislature, and shortly after taking office he negotiated a legislative agreement called the *Pacto por México* (Pact for Mexico) to gain a majority in the legislature in support of over 90 key reforms.

THE JUDICIARY

Mexico's judiciary is structured according to the U.S. model. Like the United States, Mexico has a **National Supreme Court of Justice** as well as courts at the local and state levels. The 11 Supreme Court justices are appointed by the president and are confirmed by a two-thirds vote of the Senate. However, unlike the United States, in Mexico these justices are limited to 15-year terms.

The Mexican judiciary has important formal powers, but during the authoritarian period the Supreme Court never overturned any law, and it tended to view its jurisdiction in very limited terms. In the 1980s, dramatic changes were introduced to give the Supreme Court far greater jurisdiction and power.[5] The Supreme Court can now determine the constitutionality of legislation upon the request of one-third of the lower house, but it can strike down a law only if a supermajority of 8 out of 11 justices agrees. The reforms have increased the independence of the judiciary by creating a seven-member Federal Judicial Council to oversee the administration of justice.

During the last years of authoritarian rule and in the early years of the Fox administration, the Supreme Court assumed a much more activist role. For example, it ordered PRI President Zedillo's administration to release records relating to the banking industry, and it struck down Fox's attempt to privatize the generating of electricity. Despite this progress, Mexico's judicial system is severely hampered by a widespread perception that judges, especially at the local level, are corrupt. Presidents Fox, Calderón, and Peña Nieto have made it a priority to enhance the prestige and power of the beleaguered court system. An even more serious problem is the overall weakness of the rule of law in Mexico. According to one prominent political scientist, "Mexico is already, up to a point, a democracy, a middle-class society, and an open economy, but is nowhere near to becoming a nation of laws."[6]

Like the legislature, Mexico's judicial system is currently in transition. A number of constitutional amendments since the mid-1990s have led to significant reforms. A 2008 amendment required all state and federal judicial systems to move from a European-style inquisitorial system to an oral-based jury model by 2016. The reform's implementation is behind schedule, and by late 2016 only 23 of Mexico's 31 states and the Federal District of Mexico City had begun to implement the reforms. Mexico will have to retrain its lawyers and judges, but once implemented, the reforms will hopefully lead to a more transparent and effective legal system.[7] The new system will place greater emphasis on due process rights for those accused of crimes and will impose the presumption of innocence. A 2010 reform gave Mexicans the ability to use class action lawsuits to permit groups of citizens to sue in defense of their rights. Given the lack of resources, and training, many government officials came to believe that the new reforms were too often letting criminals go free. In 2017, the Peña Nieto administration supported a new law that would roll back many of the earlier reforms, giving more power to the police and military, allowing the use of torture to gain confessions, and placing the burden of proving innocence on the accused.

The Electoral System

During the last two decades of PRI rule, elections were widely viewed as corrupt. The 1988 presidential election was probably the zenith of PRI electoral fraud: more than

30,000 ballot boxes disappeared. In an effort to cover up the thievery, the federal government declared the final ballots a state secret. Only in 1996 did the PRI succumb to pressure and create a truly independent **Federal Electoral Institute**, taking power away from the government-controlled secretary of government. It also created the Federal Electoral Tribunal to adjudicate all electoral disputes. Mexico now has a sophisticated and transparent electoral system featuring a national electoral register and voter identification cards, public funding for electoral campaigns, and strict limits on private contributions. Nevertheless, the bitterly contested presidential election of 2006 raised new concerns about Mexico's electoral system and generated calls for further reform.

Voting is compulsory in Mexico, although this law is sporadically enforced. In part because of this law and in part because the PRI traditionally used its power to encourage electoral turnout, Mexican elections under the PRI had high turnout, usually between 60 and 70 percent. Since 2000, turnout has been closer to 60 percent (it was about 63 percent for the 2012 presidential election), which is high by U.S. standards but low in relation to the rest of the Latin American countries where voting is mandatory.

Mexican presidents are directly elected, but unlike in many Latin American political systems, there are no provisions for a second round of voting if a candidate fails to win a majority of the vote. In the context of Mexico's political party system, in which three main parties have each won about a third of the vote, this has meant that all recent elections have produced presidents with a relatively small plurality of the vote, and with a legislature dominated by the opposition. Indeed, each of the last three Mexican presidents won successively smaller percentages of the popular vote, and Calderón won the disputed 2006 election with only about 36 percent of the vote. President Calderón introduced legislation in December 2009 to create a two-round voting system, but it failed to gain legislative support.

Mexico's current electoral system for the legislature dates from reforms implemented by PRI president Miguel de la Madrid Hurtado in 1986. Mexico now has a mixed electoral system for the lower house, which includes 300 single-member districts and 200 proportional representation seats. Deputies in the lower house serve three-year terms. Mexico's electoral system for the upper house is unique. Senators serve six-year terms, and three are elected from each state and the federal district. The party with the most votes wins two Senate seats, and the party finishing second is automatically awarded the third seat. An additional 32 seats are allocated according to PR. Elections to the Senate take place at the same time as the presidential elections. Parties must get at least 2 percent of the national vote in order to win seats from the PR lists.

Mexico's electoral law also has provisions that make it difficult for a party to win a majority of the seats in either house of the legislature. A party's total number of seats in the lower house cannot exceed the percentage of the party's PR vote by more than 8 percent. In effect, this means that to gain a legislative majority, a party would need to get at least 42 percent of the PR vote and then win a large number of single-member contests to push the total number of seats over 50 percent. In Mexico's system of three major political parties, legislative majorities have, to date, been elusive. This means that, in stark contrast to the 1917–2000 period of PRI dominance, divided government is likely to be the rule in the future.

President Peña Nieto, with the support of the conservative PAN, has recently reformed the Federal Electoral Institute. It now has power over local elections, where fraud has been more widespread, as well as the power to annul the results in close elections where candidates have overspent the legal limits.

Local Government

Despite being formally federal, Mexico operated very much like a unitary political system during authoritarianism. Excessive localism and a history of instability and political violence caused by the absence of a weak central authority favored the PRI's centralizing tendencies, despite the federalist constitutional rhetoric. Federal authorities controlled local elections, local budgets, local police forces, and so forth. Until 1997, the mayor of Mexico City was a cabinet member appointed directly by the president.

Mexico currently has 31 states and a Federal District of Mexico City, each with its own constitution and unicameral legislature.[8] States are subdivided into *municipios* (similar in some ways to county governments in the United States). State governors, county councils, and county presidents are now elected directly. Until 1988, all governors were from the PRI, although in the 1980s only widespread electoral fraud prevented opposition victories. Indeed, some of the first serious opposition to PRI hegemony came at the local level, especially in Mexico's prosperous north, where unpopular PRI local leaders and state governors were successfully defeated by opposition candidates. The PRI's use of electoral fraud at the local level helped ignite regional opposition to the party's heavy-handed centralist policies. The first opposition governor took power in 1989, in the state of Baja California. In the 1990s, the PRI began to accept opposition victories in numerous local elections, and by the end of that decade opposition parties controlled seven governorships.

Mexican states have important powers, but their sovereignty is far more circumscribed by federal authorities, especially the federal bureaucracy, than is state sovereignty in other federal systems such as Brazil, Germany, and the United States. The PRI regime limited local autonomy by retaining tight control over public funds, and today the federal government collects about 90 percent of all tax revenue. Since the return to democracy, an increasing portion of government spending—currently about half of the total—has been delegated to state and local governments, often as the result of horse trading between presidents and the opposition majority in the legislature.

In the 1980s and 1990s, state and local politics provided the first opportunities for Mexico's anti-PRI opposition, although some local and state offices (especially in rural areas) remained PRI strongholds long after the party lost the presidency in 2000. A good example is the rural west coast state of Guerrero, where the PRI retained a lock on state government until being ousted by the leftist PRD in the gubernatorial elections of 2005. Another example is the southern state of Oaxaca, where a PRI governor was accused of repression and corruption, and where the PRI lost power only in 2010, when the two main opposition parties joined forces.

Following the U.S. model, Mexican states and localities have their own police forces, but these forces have been widely viewed as bastions of corruption. Since 2006, local police have been replaced in some areas by federal forces to root out corruption. The investigation surrounding the shocking disappearance of 43 university students at a rural teacher's college in September 2014 revealed that the local government, the local police, and drug traffickers had worked together to kidnap the students. Still, Mexicans have more confidence in their local governments than in the federal government (see "Confidence in Mexican Institutions," p. 601).

Political Conflict and Competition

The Party System

During Mexico's long authoritarian period following the Mexican Revolution, opposition parties were mostly tolerated; some were even encouraged to exist, to give superficial legitimacy to the PRI-dominated system. The PRI skillfully cultivated and selectively co-opted all the opposition parties, which were generally weak and divided until the 1980s. The PRI also periodically altered the election laws to increase the presence of the opposition in the legislature while using its ties with big business to outspend its rivals. And, when necessary, the PRI employed electoral fraud to retain control of the presidency and key governorships.

The PRI was founded in 1929 as a way of ending Mexico's often-violent struggle for political power. From the start, the PRI was viewed as a party representing the interests of the Mexican state. During its long rule, the PRI became increasingly indistinguishable from the state, and the immense power of Mexico's presidents resulted from their effective control over both the party and the state.

A key element of the PRI's exercise of power was the use of **patron-client relationships**, in which powerful government officials delivered state services and access to power in exchange for the delivery of political support. The patron-client relationships operated from the top of the hierarchy, dominated by the PRI-controlled presidency, down to the very poorest segments of society. At the elite level, vast informal networks of personal loyalty known as **camarillas** (political cliques) were far more important than ideology.

The PRI also maintained control over the state, as a result of its ability to mobilize and control mass organizations through a system that political scientists call *corporatism*. During the presidency of **Lázaro Cárdenas**, worker and peasant organizations were created and then integrated into the PRI structure. By using the state to channel patronage to PRI mass organizations, the PRI rendered independent mass organizations marginal and impotent. Mexico's business elite duly lavished the PRI with campaign donations. One notorious example was a 1993 dinner, hosted by President Carlos Salinas, at which two dozen of Mexico's top business leaders were asked to give $25 million each to the PRI.

As a party of power, the PRI's ideology has been malleable, shifting over time to reflect the view of its presidential candidate. For example, redistributive and nationalist economic policies implemented during the Cárdenas presidency (1934–40) were directly contradicted by subsequent PRI presidents. All PRI leaders claimed to represent the legacy of the Mexican Revolution; but as we have seen, that legacy is ambiguous. While it is true that the PRI generally favored state-led capitalism and economic nationalism until the 1980s, after that time the PRI readily accepted free-market reforms and Mexico's entry into NAFTA. However, that shift did lead to a significant schism in the party and to the creation of the leftist PRD in 1989.

Given that PRI presidents supported very different types of political-economic policies, why was there not more open dissent within the PRI? In part, dissent was not strong because the PRI wrote electoral rules that made it virtually impossible for dissident PRI factions to form new parties and win elections.

The erosion of popular support for the PRI can be traced back to the 1968 repression of the student movement. In 1982, the PRI slowly but steadily began losing support in presidential, congressional, and local elections. Some of the decline was a direct result of Mexico's rapid urbanization: while rural Mexicans were particularly susceptible to local PRI bosses, urbanites were better educated, wealthier, and more politically independent. The PRI also suffered from a reduction in the state's ability to dispense patronage during tough economic times. The economic austerity policies of the 1990s, a cornerstone of the government's neoliberal policies, undoubtedly cost it a number of votes.

Ironically, the erosion of the PRI's political power in the 1990s was also a partial consequence of its attempt at democratic reform. Seeking to enhance its democratic legitimacy, the government in the 1990s spent over $1 billion to implement a high-tech electoral system that greatly reduced electoral fraud.

Even with its historic defeat in the July 2000 presidential elections, the PRI continued to wield enormous power at the state and local level, where its old-style political machines were most effective and where allegations of old-style PRI corruption were commonplace. Even before the PRI's return to the presidency in July 2012, the PRI governed 20 of Mexico's 31 states.

After losing the presidency in 2000, the PRI was rudderless. As a party designed to serve sitting presidents, it no longer had a clear leader. The official party leadership, the PRI legislative delegation, and PRI governors all wielded considerable power and produced what one observer has called "a hydra-headed behemoth."[9] Recent changes in the PRI structure, however, have led to the direct election of a party president, and by 2011 the PRI seemed poised for a political comeback. The failure of the Fox and Calderón administrations to enact badly needed reform (largely due to the stubborn opposition of the PRI) and the inconclusive drug war, combined with the internal rancor within the leftist PRD after its narrow loss in the 2006 elections, created a political opening for the PRI. The PRI and its allied parties made impressive gains in the 2009 midterm elections, winning a majority of seats in the lower house. By 2011, the PRI controlled 17 of Mexico's 31 governorships. Outgoing state of Mexico governor Enrique Peña Nieto, a young and charismatic PRI leader, completed the party's remarkable political comeback with his victory in the 2012 presidential elections. Ironically, Peña Nieto attempted to identify the "new" PRI with an ambitious agenda to reform the very system the party had created in the early twentieth century.

The PRI remains an enigmatic political party whose ideology is hard to define. Currently, it is best viewed as being located on the center-right in the Mexican party system. In 2012, about half of voters who define themselves as being on the right or in the center supported the PRI, while less than a quarter of self-defined leftists backed the PRI. Peña Nieto has tried to portray the PRI as a modern, centrist, democratic party, but the bases of the PRI's power at the state and local level are still controlled by old-style PRI machine politicians associated with corruption, co-optation, and electoral fraud.

Peña Nieto has had a mixed record in office. He has been able to negotiate a series of important economic reforms, most prominently a constitutional amendment that will allow private investment in the energy sector. He was able to pass a major reform of Mexico's educational system, and a law that would break up its telecommunications monopolies. But Peña Nieto's term in office has also been marked by a number of serious problems, most important being his failure to stem corruption, impunity, and violence. The 2014 disappearance and murder of 43 students in Guerrero state revealed a local government and police force that were deeply penetrated by drug cartels. The government proved unable to conduct a credible investigation, and international investigators blasted the government's handling of the crisis. In 2015, the dramatic escape from a high-security prison of Mexico's most notorious drug lord further damaged the president's reputation. By the summer of 2016, Peña Nieto's public approval ratings were the lowest for any Mexican president since the return of democracy.

THE MEXICAN LEFT

After the Mexican Revolution, the PRI attempted to occupy the political space traditionally occupied by leftist parties, even though it often pursued an economic model that favored big business. Because the PRI regime had its leftist phases, especially during the presidency of Lázaro Cárdenas, and because Mexico's foreign policy often supported leftist governments and leftist movements elsewhere in Latin America, leftist parties occupied little real political space.

Nevertheless, parties of the left existed in Mexico, though most of them supported the PRI. Although the Communist Party was banned until 1979, the Popular Socialist Party (a moderate socialist party) and a few other leftist parties regularly won a few seats in the legislature. A serious leftist political force emerged only in the 1980s, when a leftist faction within the PRI, led by Michoacán governor Cuauhtémoc Cárdenas, bolted from the party in protest over the PRI's embrace of neoliberal economic reforms.[10] Cárdenas, the son of the former president most famous for promoting land reform and nationalizing Mexico's oil, then led the newly formed Partido de la Revolución Democrática (PRD) in a coalition of four opposition parties in the 1988 elections.

Bolstered by the high-profile leadership of Cárdenas and boosted by the PRI's loss of popularity, the PRD performed extremely well in the 1988 elections. Many observers believe that had there not been significant electoral fraud, the PRD would have won those elections. Despite this auspicious start, the PRD struggled as a leftist opposition party. It has been plagued by internal fighting and has been unable to capture enough voters outside its strongholds in Mexico City and the south.

The PRD clearly stands to the left of the PRI and the PAN. During the 1980s and 1990s, it attacked the PRI's neoliberal reforms and neglect of poor Mexicans. It advocated more nationalist and protectionist policies than had been pursued by the PRI since the 1940s. Some PRD candidates at the state and local level have had considerable success, and the PRD has controlled Mexico City's government since 1997, but the party's performance in the 2000 presidential elections was certainly a disappointment. Cárdenas won just over 16 percent of the presidential vote, and the PRD did only slightly better in elections to Congress. The 2000 elections left the PRD as a minor political force with too few seats in Congress to build a majority, even if combined with the PAN.

The PRD's prospects improved considerably after the 2003 legislative elections. With its allies on the left, it saw its support increase moderately, to about one-quarter of the electorate; and it gained 36 seats, the biggest gain of any party. The PRD defeated the PRI in key gubernatorial elections in Guerrero and Baja California del Sur in February 2005, although the PRD still controlled only four of Mexico's 31 states as well as the Federal District of Mexico City.

The former PRD mayor of Mexico City, **Andrés Manuel López Obrador**, a charismatic populist, emerged as the front-runner in the 2006 presidential election but saw his lead slip away as the conservative opposition portrayed him as a dangerous radical who would threaten Mexico's prosperity and harm relations with the United States. Long after his defeat, López Obrador continued to claim that his razor-thin loss in the 2006 election was the result of fraud and illegal government action, despite a ruling to the contrary by Mexico's Federal Electoral Tribunal. His defiant stand, his refusal to recognize the government of Felipe Calderón, and his convening of weeks of street protests (in which he had himself "sworn in" as president) hurt the PRD's image and badly divided the party. López Obrador's postelectoral outburst (including his remark, "to hell with your corrupt institutions") seemed to cast doubt on his and his party's commitment to democracy and served only to frighten middle-class Mexicans.[11] The 2009 lower house elections reduced the PRD's presence from 123 to 71 seats, or about 14 percent of the total.

The PRD remains a weakened and divided party, split between moderates and supporters of the more radical López Obrador. A tacit recognition of its declining strength was the PRD's decision in 2010 to enter electoral alliances with the

Andrés Manuel López Obrador, of the leftist PRD, having himself sworn in as "legitimate president" after narrowly losing the 2006 presidential election.

conservative PAN in order to compete with the resurgent PRI in state and local elections. In late 2011, the PRD again selected the controversial López Obrador as its candidate for the 2012 presidential elections, thus bypassing more moderate candidates and further dividing the Mexican left.

López Obrador toned down his leftist rhetoric and performed better than expected, but he came in second with about 32 percent of the vote. He once again unsuccessfully challenged the legitimacy of the electoral process in Mexico, claiming that the PRI had bought votes and illegally funded its campaign. The PRD proved less popular in legislative elections than its presidential candidate. It received less than 20 percent of the vote for the legislature, coming in third behind the PRI and the PAN. Shortly after the elections, López Obrador resigned from the PRD. He launched a new political movement, called **MORENA (National Regeneration Movement)**, thus further dividing Mexico's left and opening the door for new leadership within the PRD. MORENA won 8 percent of the vote and 21 seats in the 2015 lower house elections, seriously weakening the PRD and positioning López Obrador for a third presidential run in 2018. The fragmentation of Mexico's left was apparent in the June 2017 gubernatorial elections in the state of Mexico, Mexico's most populous state. The PRI narrowly retained the key governorship only because the left was divided between the PRD, whose candidate won just under 18 percent of the vote, and MORENA, which won just over 30 percent of the vote.

THE MEXICAN RIGHT

The Partido Acción Nacional (PAN) was founded in 1939 by defectors from the PRI. The PAN became the only opposition party to develop a strong organizational presence, especially in its strongholds in northern Mexico and the state of Yucatán. The party emerged as a conservative response to the leftist policies of the PRI during the late 1930s and early 1940s. It advocated Christian-democratic ideas, opposing the PRI's anticlericalism and supporting pro-business policies. Since its base of power was state politics, the PAN became an early advocate of states' rights and opposed the centralization of power that was a feature of Mexican politics under the PRI.

Like many conservative parties, the PAN has been divided historically between Catholic social conservatives and more free-market-oriented business interests. The more pro-business wing has dominated the party since the late 1980s, but the PRI's adoption of neoliberal economic strategies during that decade threatened to steal the PAN's thunder. The PAN continues to be plagued by internal division, and PAN legislators have been less willing to follow their own leadership than have legislators from the PRI or PRD.

In the 1990s, the PAN won the governorship of seven states. As the PRI fought harder to deny the PAN electoral victories, it unwittingly gave the party an issue that garnered support among Mexicans of all classes: the need to end corruption and guarantee free elections. Nonetheless, the PAN suffers from its geographic concentration of the vote (mostly in northern Mexico) and its relative weakness among rural voters.

Vicente Fox was not a prototypical PAN leader and did not share much of the social conservatism that is typical of many PAN leaders. His roots were in business, and later he became active in local government, having served as governor of his home state after a stint in Congress. His charisma and his personal support network allowed him to overcome much opposition within his own party and helped expand the PAN's appeal to new voters. In the 2000 presidential campaign, Fox created his own campaign organization. That organization did not depend on the official PAN hierarchy, which was dominated by Fox's political rivals. Once in office, Fox formed a cabinet that included no members of the PAN's more conservative "traditionalist" wing, and his closest advisers were non-PAN members. He had stormy relations with the traditionalist wing of the PAN, which dominates the legislature and the party hierarchy.

Fox's record in office has been viewed as a mixed bag, but on the whole, his administration had trouble meeting the very high expectations that accompanied his historic victory in 2000.[12] It delivered on some concrete reform promises, however: Fox passed a transparency law to facilitate public oversight of government, and he restructured and purged Mexico's powerful and corruption-riddled Federal Judicial Police. He passed legislation to allow some 10 million Mexicans living abroad (many in the United States) to vote in elections. Some progress was made on health care and pension reform, and the Fox administration was praised for containing inflation. These successes, however, were outweighed by numerous policy failures, due largely to Fox's inability to work with the opposition-dominated legislature as well as the opposition within his own party. Fox failed to end the Zapatista rebellion in Chiapas, was unable to pass a badly needed tax increase to raise revenue for social spending and other public investment, and had a disappointing record on rooting out government corruption. After the PAN's drubbing in the 2003 legislative elections, when the governing party lost one-quarter of its seats in the lower house, Fox's status as a lame-duck president was exacerbated, and his government was accused of losing focus.

Fox's successor, Felipe Calderón, had been involved in conservative politics his entire adult life. His father was a founder of the PAN, and Calderón became leader of its youth wing in his twenties. He held a variety of elected political positions and twice served as a federal deputy. He served as party president in the 1990s when the PAN first began to mount a serious challenge to the PRI. Vicente Fox appointed him secretary of energy, an important cabinet post in oil-rich Mexico. In a 2005 internal party election, Calderón defeated President Vicente Fox's choice for the 2006 PAN presidential nomination. He then narrowly defeated the leftist Andrés Manuel López Obrador in the bitterly contested 2006 presidential election. In office, Calderón generally proved to be a social conservative and a supporter of free-market policies. His campaign to defeat Mexico's drug cartels delivered mixed results. The ensuing violence tarnished Calderón's previously high approval ratings in opinion polls.

For the 2012 presidential election, the PAN selected Mexico's first-ever woman presidential candidate, Josefina Vázquez Mota. She was head of the PAN's parliamentary delegation and a former cabinet minister. Vázquez Mota won the PAN primary election, defeating President Calderón's preferred candidate. Partly because of Calderón's poor image and popular frustration with the two previous PAN presidencies, and partly because she was less well known than her two competitors, Vázquez Mota did poorly in the election, winning just over a quarter of the vote.

Since the watershed 2000 election and the transition to democracy, the Mexican party system has been in flux. Beginning in the 1990s, there was a significant partisan "dealignment," in which many voters abandoned the PRI. Not all those voters have realigned themselves with other parties, however, and a large segment of the Mexican electorate remains "fluid."

This fluidity can be witnessed in the legislative elections since 2000. The 2000 presidential elections were a clear victory for Vicente Fox, but the PRI emerged from the legislative elections as the dominant political force, though it suffered setbacks in its percentage of votes and in the number of seats it won in the lower house. The big loser in those elections was the leftist PRD, which was relegated to third place. The 2003 election signaled a comeback for the left: the PRD and its allies picked up 36 seats in the lower house. The governing PAN lost 50 seats in the lower house. The PRI continued to suffer a loss of votes but was able to exploit the electoral system to win 16 additional seats. The 2006 elections led to a recovery for the PAN and a dramatic increase in support for the leftist PRD at the expense of the PRI. Like his predecessor, President Calderón had to govern without a majority in the lower house. The 2009 elections signaled another shift in direction, as the PRI made important gains at the expense of the PAN and PRD. In 2012, the PRD gained seats at the expense of both the PRI and the PAN.

Mexico's current party system is extremely competitive. There are four major parties, but in most of the country, two parties contend for power.[13] In Mexico's more prosperous north and west, the PAN and the PRI fight for votes, while in poorer southern Mexico the PRD (and MORENA) and the PRI are chief rivals. Only in Mexico City and the surrounding areas do all four parties truly compete on an equal footing. The PRI remains the only party with support in all regions, while the PRD, MORENA, and the PAN have more regionally concentrated bases of support. About 70 percent of Mexicans identify with parties of the left, center, and right, and 30 percent claim to be independent.[14]

A variety of smaller parties compete for, and regularly win, seats in the Mexican legislature. The most important of these is the Mexican Green Party (PVEM), a mislabeled and entirely opportunistic party that has almost nothing in common with its environmentally oriented European counterparts. The PVEM was allied with the leftist PRD in the 1997 elections and then backed the conservative PAN in 2000. Since then, the PVEM has run in an electoral alliance with the PRI. In the 2015 lower house elections, smaller parties, including the new leftist party MORENA, gained seats at the expense of the three major parties.

Elections

During most of the PRI's long authoritarian rule, elections were more national celebrations of PRI power than competitive electoral campaigns. Every six years, the country was decked out in the PRI's colors, patronage was dispensed on a massive scale, and the PRI nominees (in effect, the presumed winners) toured their constituencies and made speeches.

The 2000 presidential campaign broke with this tradition. The opposition candidates (Cuauhtémoc Cárdenas of the PRD and Vicente Fox of the PAN) had announced their intention to run for the presidency several years before the election, and both candidates were widely assumed to have a lock on their parties' nominations. The PRI candidate, traditionally named quite late in the six-year presidential term, was determined for the first time by a PRI primary vote. As a result, several PRI candidates began campaigning for the nomination early in Zedillo's presidential term. Francisco Labastida won the party primary in a hotly contested race.

The 2000 campaign was also the first to be governed by new electoral finance rules, which not only sharply limited private contributions but also provided candidates with public financing. Access to the media by all political parties was far more equitable than ever before. While PRI candidates still enjoyed an advantage, the playing field was more level than it had been in past elections. The first truly fair and competitive election was also the first national campaign in which U.S.-style mudslinging was widespread. The PRI portrayed Fox as a U.S. lackey; for his part, Fox questioned Labastida's "macho" credentials. Some of the most negative campaigning took place between the two PRI contestants for the nomination. The 2000 campaign was also the first truly modern campaign in Mexican history. Television took on a pivotal role. The campaign culminated in two televised presidential debates, which the charismatic and engaging Fox won handily over the more wooden Labastida and Cárdenas.

In the 2000 campaign, Mexico's three major political parties presented voters with a fairly wide range of choices. The PRI, under the campaign slogan "Power will serve the people," represented the legacy of the Mexican Revolution and nationalism. The PAN shared the PRI's enthusiasm for neoliberal reforms but offered itself as the party of democratization, as captured by its campaign slogan, "Ya!" ("Enough already!"). Only the leftist PRD criticized neoliberal economic policies and NAFTA.

The 2006 presidential campaign was Mexico's first "normal" presidential contest.[15] In 2000, the main issue had been democratization and the defeat of the PRI's semi-authoritarian regime. In 2006, Mexicans faced their first real choice between parties of the right and left. The early front-runner, Andrés Manuel López Obrador (of the leftist PRD), ran a campaign aimed at improving the plight of Mexico's poor. His main opponent, the PAN's Felipe Calderón, advocated a pro-business set of policies aimed at increasing employment. Calderón chipped away at López Obrador's initial lead by questioning his commitment to democracy and portraying him as a dangerous leftist who would threaten Mexico's

Seats in the Chamber of Deputies and Senate after the Two Most Recent Elections

PARTY	CHAMBER OF DEPUTIES SEATS (2015)		CHAMBER OF DEPUTIES SEATS (2012)		SENATE SEATS (2012)		SENATE SEATS (2006)	
	NUMBER	%	NUMBER	%	NUMBER	%	NUMBER	%
PRI*	250	50	240	48	61	48	39	30
PAN	108	22	114	23	38	29	52	41
PRD**	88	18	136	27	28	22	36	28
MORENA	21	4						
Others	33	6	10	2	1	1	1	1
Total	500	100	500	100	128	100	128	100

*The PRI includes seats for the Mexican Green Party, allied with the PRI.
**The PRD includes seats for the Mexican Labor Party and the Citizens Movement, allied with the PRD.

Key to Party Acronyms:
 PRI: Institutional Revolutionary Party
 PAN: National Action Party (conservative)
 PRD: Party of the Democratic Revolution (leftist)
 MORENA: National Regeneration Movement (leftist)

Source: http://electionresources.org (accessed 6/24/17).

economic stability. The campaign was characterized by an unprecedented level of impassioned and negative attack ads. The outcome of the 2006 election revealed a polarized and divided electorate; Calderón and López Obrador each won just over 35 percent of the vote, and Calderón won by a mere one-half of a percentage point.

The 2012 campaign was the first to take place under electoral reforms adopted in 2007 and 2008, and that reduced allowable private campaign funding by almost half. The campaign featured two lackluster debates between the main presidential candidates.[16] In some ways, each of the three major candidates had to defend their questionable records. Peña Nieto had to try to distance himself from the PRI's association with authoritarian rule while fending off attacks involving his record as governor of the state of Mexico. Peña Nieto proposed policies that largely continued the PAN's agenda of fighting organized crime and liberalizing the economy while at the same time calling for increased social spending. Josefina Vázquez Mota had the unenviable task of defending the PAN's association with the bloody war against drug cartels as well as Mexico's sluggish economic growth under two previous PAN administrations, and she was saddled by outgoing President Calderón's low popularity ratings. The leftist López Obrador sought to distance himself from what many Mexicans viewed as his irresponsible behavior in the aftermath of the 2006 presidential elections. He was the only major candidate to call for an end to Mexico's war against drug cartels, and the only one to oppose reforming Mexico's energy sector. Peña Nieto won the election with 38.2 percent of the vote (López Obrador won 31.6 percent, and Vázquez Mota of the PAN won 25.4 percent). Although the PRI won the presidency, the party lost its majority in the legislature, forcing President Peña Nieto to negotiate with the opposition in order to pass legislation.

Civil Society

During authoritarianism, Mexican groups and associations were often incorporated into the state in a system known as *corporatism*. The paternalistic PRI would then mediate among different groups while making sure that no one group challenged government power. The PRI was formally divided into three sectors (labor, peasants, and the "popular" middle class), each dominated by PRI-controlled mass organizations. It would be a mistake, however, to assume that the Mexican state could control all autonomous groups in society. To cite one example, the private-sector Confederation of Employers of the Mexican Republic (COPARMEX) became an important voice of opposition to the PRI, instead of supporting the governing party. Indeed, a variety of autonomous civil society organizations emerged in the 1980s and 1990s, mainly in response to economic crises, predating the PRI's ouster from power in 2000.[17]

Given its level of economic development, Mexican civil society remains weak compared with many other Latin American countries.[18] Eighty-five percent of Mexicans report that they belong to no civil society organization, and a similar percentage say they have never worked formally or informally with others to resolve community problems.[19] A long history of a strong and paternalistic state, and a deep-seated distrust of others, which according to opinion research far exceeds the Latin American norm, may be responsible. In the words of a former Mexican foreign minister, "It should not be altogether surprising that after nearly five hundred years of a strong state, civil society should be weak. From this perspective, Mexicans are disorganized . . . because an all-powerful state has crowded them out."[20]

Mexican civil society may be weak in comparative perspective, but in recent years increasing numbers of Mexicans have become frustrated by their government's inability to protect them against organized crime. A good example is the tiny mountain town of Cherán in the state of Michoacán, where in June 2011 citizens expelled the municipal and state police because those forces were unwilling or unable to stop the deforestation of the surrounding old-growth forest by armed criminal gangs. Villagers claimed that the police forces had been corrupted by the gangs. Heavily armed gangs had arrived in town and cut thousands of acres of timber, and they murdered or kidnapped local citizens who opposed them. In response, the townspeople removed the mayor, formed a governing council, and established a militia to guard against further encroachments.

The willingness of Mexicans to organize to defend their communities from violence may be an encouraging example of Mexican civil society in action, but it can also have potentially dangerous consequences, and it threatens to create yet another

Mexican citizens, like these members of vigilante groups in the southeastern state of Guerrero in 2014, have organized to combat violence by drug gangs.

set of armed groups beyond state control. The vigilante movement became especially prominent in the state of Michoacán, where the "Knights Templar" (a drug and extortion gang) were responsible for a wave of violence that intimidated local government and police. At their peak, in 2014, vigilante groups had gained control of 26 of the state's 113 municipal districts.[21] That year, the Mexican government sought to integrate the vigilante groups into a new police force called the Rural Force. Some vigilante members have refused to cooperate until the Mexican state proves that it can stop the violence, arrest gang members responsible for the violence, and purge the police who have been corrupted by the gangs.[22] Moreover, vigilantes and the federal police engaged in armed clashes that threatened to escalate. After 43 college students disappeared in September 2014 after peacefully protesting discriminatory hiring practices, demonstrations took place throughout Mexico demanding that the federal government take action against corrupt local governments.

BUSINESS

Although the PRI successfully co-opted Mexico's private sector for decades, it can be argued that business groups later emerged as the most powerful source of opposition to authoritarian rule. During authoritarianism, most private-sector interests were channeled into a variety of semi-official organizations including the National Chamber of Industries and the National Chamber of Commerce. Until 1996, private-sector membership in these organizations was mandatory. Even though the PRI never gave business organizations formal representation within the governing party, business interests wielded power through more informal organizations and channels. The secretive Business Coordinating Council (CCE), which represents some of Mexico's wealthiest capitalists, had close ties to the Fox government.

In the PRI-led authoritarian regime, the relationship between the business sector and the PRI was complex and often contradictory. The PRI's policies generally favored the private sector, especially big business. At the same time, business leaders bitterly opposed attempts by some PRI presidents to enact the social agenda of the Mexican Revolution. In the 1970s, presidents Luis Echeverría Álvarez and José López Portillo sought to expand the role of the state in the economy, and their policies damaged business-government relations. Although those policies were short-lived, they served to garner opposition to the PRI among northern business interests. Moreover, they were an important factor in the business sector's early support for the conservative PAN in the last decades of PRI authoritarianism and after the return of democracy in 2000. The prospect of a PRD victory in 2006 clearly alarmed much of the business sector, which feared that the election of the leftist López Obrador would damage Mexico's business climate. Their situation encouraged many business leaders to rally behind PAN candidate Felipe Calderón.

Since returning to power in 2012, the PRI relationship with big business has been strained. President Peña Nieto has actively sought to weaken the power of monopolies that dominate key areas of the Mexican economy, like the media, telecommunications, and the banking sectors. These reforms are popular with Mexican citizens who are tired of paying higher prices that result from the monopolies, but the business sector attacked the reforms as an attempt by the PRI government to strengthen state regulation of the private sector. The Peña Nieto government passed reforms making it harder for businesses to block government regulation in the courts. The business community opposed his plans to raise sales taxes.

LABOR

After the Mexican Revolution, the PRI actively supported the unionization of Mexican workers. However, the unions were thoroughly integrated into and controlled by the governing party. They received massive subsidies from the state, which made them politically pliant. They enjoyed privileged treatment under the PRI, in part because they were never able to incorporate much of the workforce (about 16 percent, at their peak) and because one-third of their members were government employees. The labor movement in Mexico was highly centralized. The dominant labor organization, the **Confederation of Mexican Workers (CTM)**, was created by the PRI and became one of the main supporters of the governing party. Until his death in 1997, Fidel Velázquez Sánchez served as a pillar of PRI authoritarianism and dominated the CTM for more than 50 years.

Unions independent of the PRI are a relatively new phenomenon. In 1997, Mexico's independent unions formed the National Union of Workers (UNT) to compete with the CTM. Since the mid-1990s, a series of laws and court decisions have weakened the grip of the formerly official unions. Neoliberal economic policies that have been implemented over the last three decades have created challenges for the CTM. Its membership has clearly suffered from the economic reforms, and its leadership no longer benefits from government patronage. On the one hand, democratic reforms are likely to give labor unions more autonomy and a greater ability to contest government policy. On the other hand, the recent reforms passed by the Calderón and Peña Nieto governments were aimed at weakening the power of important unions. For example, in 2013 the legislature passed a reform of Mexico's education system that broke the control of the powerful teacher's union over the hiring and evaluation of teachers. Earlier that year, the government jailed Esther Gordillo, the longtime leader of the National Union of Education Workers (SNTE). The SNTE is also the largest labor union in Latin America and was a key piece of the PRI's patronage network for decades. Gordillo became wealthy as the SNTE leader, and the union has long been considered a bastion of corruption.

THE MEDIA

The PRI-dominated authoritarian regime maintained a political lock on the media through co-optation more than coercion. Rather than imposing censorship, the government courted the favor of Mexico's media by purchasing advertisements in pro-PRI media outlets, giving supportive media voices cheap access to infrastructure, and bribing reporters outright. Mexico's largest media conglomerate, **Televisa**, was extremely close to the PRI.

By the early 1990s, the PRI had loosened its control over the media somewhat. The government stopped bribing reporters, and the wave of privatizations created a more competitive media environment, allowing for criticism of the PRI. Since the return of democracy in 2000, Mexico has had a more vibrant media that is often critical of the government. Still, the power of Mexico's two main television networks, which are historical bastions of PRI support, was left largely intact. In the 2012 elections, these networks were criticized for coverage that favored the PRI. The leftist candidate Andrés Manuel López Obrador, backed by a social media protest movement, claimed that the Mexican media had unfairly favored its old patron, the PRI. However, as we have seen, since taking office the Peña Nieto administration has enacted reforms to weaken conglomerates like Televisa.

While Mexico's media has flourished in the democratic era, Mexico's journalists have often been targeted by drug cartels after reporting on the violence that has plagued Mexico.[23] At least 16 journalists were murdered over the last decade, and the Committee to Protect Journalists ranked Mexico as the seventh most dangerous country for journalists. This violence against the media was highlighted by the May 2017 murder of Javier Valdez, a legendary investigative reporter who covered Mexico's organized crime problem and who won the Committee to Protect Journalists International Press Freedom Award in 2011. Much of the Mexican media are still heavily dependent on government advertising and access to information. In some cases, these factors have led to the return of the type of self-censorship that was common during the decades of authoritarian rule.

Do you use the Internet, at least occasionally? Percentage saying yes:

COUNTRY	PERCENTAGE
United Kingdom	85
Germany	80
United States	79
France	75
Japan	66
Russia	58
China	50
Brazil	49
Mexico	37
India	7

Note: Data for Iran, Nigeria, and South Africa not available.
Source: Pew Center for the People and the Press, 2012.

One positive trend has been the growing importance of social media in Mexico. During the 2012 electoral campaign, a student movement, called #YoSoy132, used Twitter and Facebook to call attention to what the protesters viewed as uncritical media coverage of the PRI's candidate Peña Nieto, eventually persuading the major networks to televise the second presidential electoral debate. However, the impact of social media may be limited by the very low levels of Internet access; in 2013, only 18 percent of Mexicans reported using the Internet daily, and only 37 percent said they used the Internet at least occasionally (see "In Comparison: Internet Access" above).[24]

Society

Ethnic and National Identity

The journalist Alan Riding has described Mexico as a nation proud of its indigenous past but ashamed of its indigenous present.[25] After the Mexican Revolution, the PRI glorified and embraced its indigenous ancestry and inculcated pride in the *mestizaje*, or "blending of cultures," produced by the Spanish Conquest. Indigenous peoples who have not assimilated into mestizo Mexico have been politically marginalized and become victims of Mexico's worst poverty, whereas Mexico's wealthy elite have tended to be lighter skinned and of European origin.

The PRI's success in perpetuating the myth of *mestizaje* may help explain how it avoided the kind of ethnically based violence that has plagued Guatemala, its neighbor to the south, and other Latin American nations. But that myth was violently shattered on January 1, 1994, when a rebel army made up mostly of ethnic Mayans, the **Zapatista Army of National Liberation (EZLN)**, occupied several towns in Mexico's southernmost state of Chiapas.[26]

Many viewed the EZLN as solely an indigenous group seeking greater autonomy for Mexico's long-neglected native population. It soon became clear, however, that the EZLN included among its demands the democratization of the Mexican political system and an end to the neoliberal reforms that had ravaged the indigenous poor. Chief among the EZLN's concerns was the abrogation of Article 27 of the Constitution of 1917, which had mandated land reform. On a more general level, the EZLN was reacting to the devastation caused by neoliberal trade policies that had exposed the inefficient peasant farmers to competition from cheaper foreign imports. The call for democratization was partly a response to the political lock that the PRI maintained on some of Mexico's poorest and most heavily indigenous regions.

The Zapatista uprising was surprisingly popular within Mexico and, together with the economic crisis, helped erode PRI political dominance and accelerate electoral reforms. In 1996, the Zedillo government signed the **San Andrés Peace Accords** with the EZLN, promising protection of indigenous languages and granting indigenous communities political autonomy. These provisions were never implemented, however, and Vicente Fox, who claimed he could resolve the Chiapas conflict "in fifteen minutes," was unable to make peace with the Zapatistas. Fox's proposed constitutional amendment aimed at addressing some Zapatista demands was watered down by Congress, and the Zapatistas rejected the outcome. As of 2017, the standoff between the government and the Zapatistas continues; the EZLN is controlling some remote communities, and its demands remain largely unmet.

Ideology and Political Culture

Perhaps the most important aspect of Mexican political culture is a profound distrust of the state and the government. Opinion research demonstrates that Mexicans have a far more negative view of their political system and state than do

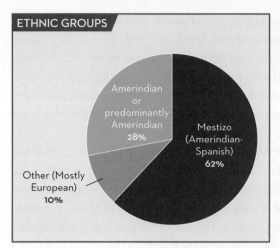

ETHNIC GROUPS

Amerindian or predominantly Amerindian
28%

Mestizo (Amerindian-Spanish)
62%

Other (Mostly European)
10%

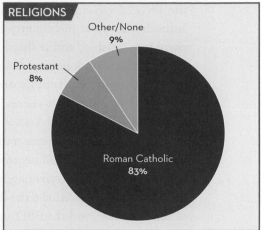

RELIGIONS

Other/None
9%

Protestant
8%

Roman Catholic
83%

their counterparts in Europe, the United States, and even Latin America. A 2015 poll showed that only about a fifth of Mexicans were very or somewhat satisfied with the way democracy works; this was the lowest assessment of any of the 18 Latin American countries polled.[27]

Mexicans' high level of disenchantment with their state and political system has been exacerbated by the government's poor response to many national crises over the past two decades. A high-profile split within the PRI, the massive electoral fraud of 1988, corruption charges against former president Carlos Salinas de Gortari, the Chiapas uprising, and the economic crisis of the 1980s and 1990s were all factors that helped to erode popular confidence in the Mexican system. More recently, the bitterly disputed 2006 presidential election, the inconclusive and bloody war against drug traffickers, and the government's weak response to crime and violence have contributed to the disenchantment.

These scandals and decades of authoritarian rule may explain why over 70 percent of Mexicans express little or no interest in politics, notwithstanding a temporary surge of interest during the historic 2000 presidential elections.[28] Mexican men express far more interest in politics than do women, and interest in politics increases with levels of education and income. Mexicans on the left of the political system (supporters of the PRD) generally express much higher levels of interest in politics than do Mexicans in the center and on the right.

Unlike communist regimes, which actively promote political mobilization, Mexican authoritarianism sought to contain and limit popular participation in politics through a variety of methods, notably co-optation. Trade unions, the media, and even some opposition political parties were for decades co-opted by the PRI. Mexico's political culture continues to show the effects of decades of authoritarian rule: the country has very low levels of participation in politics, party membership, and political activism. Although there is some evidence of a steady increase in popular political activity since the 1980s, declining voter turnout is still a concern. Turnout declined to 59 percent in 2006, but rebounded to 65 percent in 2013. In midterm legislative elections, turnout has hovered around 50 percent.

During authoritarianism, most Mexicans professed sympathy for no political party. The erosion of PRI hegemony in the 1980s and 1990s and the increasing competitiveness of elections led far more Mexicans to identify with a political party. By 2000, the PRI and the PAN each enjoyed the support of about one-third of the electorate, and the PRD was supported by about 10 percent. Opinion data show quite clearly that the Mexican electorate is anchored on the center right. The leftist PRD suffers because only about 20 percent of Mexicans identify themselves as being on the left, versus 23 percent who view themselves as being on the right.[29] Although more Mexicans define themselves as being on the left or right than do U.S. respondents, Mexicans have been steadily gravitating toward the center, where 41 percent of Mexicans now place themselves.

The erosion of PRI political hegemony has also been accompanied by a dramatic shift in the social class basis of Mexico's parties. Wealthy and middle-class Mexicans abandoned the PRI in droves between 1989 and 2000. By 2000, the PRI depended mostly on the support of lower-class Mexicans, though the PAN had nearly the same amount of support among poor voters. Indeed, one of the remarkable changes between 1989 and 2000 was the PAN's ability to garner support from all classes. In the 2006 election, the leftist PRD did best among poorer voters, while the PAN was clearly favored by wealthier and more educated voters. But region more than any other factor best explains party support in Mexico.

In 2011, political scientist (and former Mexican foreign minister) Jorge Castañeda published a controversial book in which he argued that Mexico's political culture was ill-suited to the conditions of democratic politics, a middle-class society, and an increasingly globalized economy.[30] Castañeda identifies excessive individualism, an exaggerated aversion to any form of conflict, disdain for the rule of law, and a xenophobic attitude toward the United States as signal features of Mexican culture that are likely to hamper its future development. He argues that these cultural traits have a long history, and he views the authoritarian regime of the PRI as a reflection of Mexican culture rather than a cause for it. For Castañeda, this deep-seated culture helps explain a plethora of ills afflicting Mexican

Confidence in Mexican Institutions, 2015

	A LOT	SOME	A LITTLE	NONE	DON'T KNOW/ N/A
Church	36.5	25.7	21.6	15.2	1.0
Armed forces	25.9	32.8	27.7	12.3	1.1
Police	5.0	19.0	34.7	40.8	0.5
Judiciary	4.7	19.2	35.8	38.0	2.3
Congress	4.4	19.9	34.6	36.8	4.4
Federal government	3.9	17.1	35.2	42.4	1.3
Political parties	2.0	13.8	34.2	48.8	1.2

Source: www.latinobarometro.org (accessed 6/24/17).

society, including a weak civil society, the widespread lack of respect for political institutions, and Mexico's endemic corruption. His critics attacked the book as overly simplistic, filled with stereotypes, and reflective of the values of a wealthy Mexican who spent much of his life outside of Mexico.

Opinion research reveals that most Mexicans favor democracy over authoritarianism, but their levels of support for democratic rule are below average for Latin America. In 2015, about 47 percent stated that democracy was preferable to any other kind of government, among the lowest levels of support in Latin America.[31] If there is positive news, it is that only 15 percent said that authoritarian rule might be preferable in some circumstances. This figure has dropped from a high of 43 percent in 2000 and has remained fairly constant even as the public's attachment to democracy has eroded. When compared with U.S. respondents, however, Mexicans are far more likely to define democracy in terms of equality than in terms of freedom. The inability of democracy to remedy Mexico's staggering inequality or halt the violence of its drug wars could further undermine Mexican support for democracy.

Political Economy

The leaders of the Mexican Revolution had a complex and often contradictory set of goals. Some of the revolutionaries were middle-class landowners who sought greater political democracy, others sought major socioeconomic (especially land) reform, and others were mostly interested in restoring political order while eliminating the dictatorship of Porfirio Díaz.

Between 1917 and 1980, leaders of the PRI agreed on some main features of the Mexican economy. First, Mexico's industrialization would be encouraged through **import substitution industrialization (ISI)** policies, which employed high tariffs to protect Mexican industries and agriculture. Government policies provided Mexican entrepreneurs with subsidized credit and energy and very low taxes. The PRI's ability to control labor, and therefore labor costs, also benefited Mexico's entrepreneurs. Second, Mexico was to have a capitalist economy, but the Mexican state played an important role in key sectors of the economy, though far less than in socialist economies.

Despite this general consensus, economic policies of the PRI presidents between 1917 and 2000 fluctuated a great deal. The nationalists, usually associated with the left wing of the PRI, placed more emphasis on redistribution of income, plenty of state social spending, and a strong state presence in the economy. Their economic policies tended to be strongly nationalistic, and they sought greater economic independence from the United States.

President Lázaro Cárdenas, who served from 1934 to 1940, was the most important advocate of economic nationalism. Cárdenas was a mestizo revolutionary general who became governor of the state of Michoacán. He used the PRI to organize and mobilize Mexico's workers and peasants, and he was the first president to implement the land reform called for in the Constitution of 1917. Cárdenas gave 180,000 peasant communities grants of land, called *ejidos*, that provided land to some 750,000 landless Mexicans. He integrated peasants and workers into state-controlled unions, and he strengthened the Mexican state by nationalizing the foreign-dominated oil industry and creating a state oil monopoly (**PEMEX**). More than any other Mexican president, Cárdenas embodied the socialist aspects of the Mexican Revolution. At the same time, his policies won the PRI the enduring political loyalty of Mexico's workers and peasants. Future Mexican presidents never addressed the socioeconomic aspirations of the Mexican constitution as much as Cárdenas did, but the presidencies of Adolfo López Mateos (1958–64) and Luis Echeverría Álvarez (1970–76) followed policies that mirrored the views of the PRI nationalist left.

The economic liberals—including Miguel Alemán Valdés (1946–52), Gustavo Díaz Ordaz (1964–70), Miguel de la Madrid Hurtado (1982–88), and Carlos Salinas de Gortari (1988–94)—favored economic growth over redistribution. They tended to favor freer trade, increased foreign investment in the Mexican economy, and better relations with the United States. President Díaz Ordaz enacted policies that favored big business and agricultural exporters. Presidents de la Madrid and Salinas undertook a major change in Mexico's political-economic policies by liberalizing its statist, ISI-oriented economy, abandoning long-entrenched social commitments (such as land reform), and entering the General Agreement on Tariffs and Trade (GATT) in 1986 and NAFTA, with the United States and Canada, in 1994. Since 2000, presidents Fox, Calderón, and Peña Nieto have continued these neoliberal economic policies.

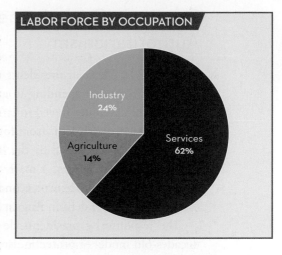

LABOR FORCE BY OCCUPATION

Industry 24%

Agriculture 14%

Services 62%

Dimensions of the Economy

In aggregate wealth, Mexico is a prosperous developing country, and compared with other developing countries, it is fairly industrialized. Industry accounts for about one-quarter of its gross domestic product (GDP), and agriculture now accounts for around 14 percent. The country is also rich in natural resources, especially oil, which is its chief economic asset. Since the presidency of Lázaro Cárdenas, Mexican oil has been controlled by the state monopoly, PEMEX.

From the 1940s to about 1980, the Mexican economy grew spectacularly in what has often been called the **Mexican miracle**. Bolstered by the peace and stability of the authoritarian regime, and benefiting from a steady increase in U.S. investment, Mexico became more industrialized, urban, and educated. Its economy also became more heavily dependent on the United States. By 1962, the United States accounted for 85 percent of all foreign investment in Mexico. Mexico sent two-thirds of its exports to the United States, and the same percentage of its imports came from the United States. The U.S.-Mexico economic relationship, however, was (and remains) asymmetrical: the U.S. economy is far more vital to Mexico than Mexico's is to the United States.

Economic Crises in the Twilight of PRI Authoritarianism

In the 1970s, Mexican presidents used the country's vast oil wealth to support massive government spending in an attempt to alleviate chronic inequality and poverty. The spending fueled inflation and began to erode the value of the peso. Mexico incurred vast debts from foreign lenders, who viewed the oil-rich country as a trustworthy borrower. By the 1980s, oil accounted for over two-thirds of the value of Mexico's exports. A major drop in world oil prices in 1981 exposed the shaky foundation of Mexico's economy, and the country came close to defaulting on its international debt in August 1982.

The response by presidents de la Madrid and Salinas was to abandon the decades-old model of protectionism and state interventionism and embrace neoliberal economics, thus beginning a reversal of the country's political economy. By terminating the constitution's promise of land reform and opening up Mexico to a flood of cheap agricultural imports, the government in effect devastated many of Mexico's poorest peasants. The country's steady economic recovery in the late 1980s and early 1990s was upset in 1994 and 1995 by its most severe economic depression since the 1930s. In December 1994, the value of the Mexican peso collapsed, and the Mexican economy was saved only by the International Monetary Fund's largest bailout ever. Between 1994 and 1996, real wages dropped 27 percent, and an estimated 70 percent of Mexicans fell below the official poverty line.[32] Mexico had abandoned ISI policies and embraced free trade and globalization as a response to the economic crisis of the early 1980s, but this response had made it even more vulnerable to economic instability.

NAFTA and Globalization

NAFTA has drastically reduced most tariffs on agricultural goods traded among Mexico, Canada, and the United States. Between 1993 and 2012, trade between the United States and Mexico increased by over 500 percent. As a result, Mexico has been flooded by U.S. products (such as corn and pork) that cost one-fifth as much to produce as similar Mexican products. NAFTA has doubled the amount of food Mexico imports from the United States, thereby lowering food prices for consumers but creating a massive crisis for millions of Mexico's farmers. About one-fifth of Mexicans work in agriculture, the vast majority poor subsistence farmers who have been hurt the most by NAFTA competition. As a result, Mexico has eliminated millions of jobs in agriculture. NAFTA has also exacerbated the gap between the wealthy north and the impoverished south.[33]

In many other ways, however, NAFTA benefits Mexico. Manufacturing exports to the United States have skyrocketed, growing at an average rate of 75 percent annually since the agreement went into effect.[34] Overall, Mexican exports rose sevenfold between 1994 and 2011. Greater access to U.S. markets has also been a boon to Mexico's fruit and vegetable producers, who now supply much of the U.S. winter market, although exports of agricultural goods have grown very modestly compared with those of manufactured goods. Cheaper imports have benefited a wide variety of Mexican producers and consumers.

Mexico's embrace of NAFTA clearly created a more diversified economy. In the 1980s, oil made up about two-thirds of the country's exports. Mexico now exports a wider variety of goods, but it remains extremely dependent on the U.S. market, to which it sends over 80 percent of all its exports.

Mexico's entry into NAFTA has attracted more direct U.S. investment in Mexico. Much of that investment has gravitated toward **maquiladoras**, factories that import materials or parts to make goods that are then exported. These factories, concentrated along the Mexico-U.S. border, account for about half of all Mexico's exports. They now generate more foreign exchange for Mexico than does any other sector, including oil. The maquiladoras have added half a million jobs to Mexico's north, but some critics argue that the operations add relatively little to the Mexican economy because most materials and technology are imported. Average maquiladora wages are above Mexico's minimum wage but far below the average wage in the manufacturing sector. The concentration of maquiladoras in Mexico's wealthier north has exacerbated the country's severe north-south income gap.

Whether NAFTA has created more winners than losers is a hot topic of debate within Mexico. One result of the new pressures created by NAFTA has been the increased flow of Mexicans to the United States in search of employment. It is clear, however, that NAFTA has dislocated millions of Mexicans and will create new political and economic challenges for future Mexican administrations.

Economic Policies and Issues

Despite the commitment to greater equality brought about by the Mexican Revolution and the efforts of some reformist presidents to help the poor, Mexico was and is a country of massive inequality. The Mexican novelist Carlos Fuentes has called Mexico a country "where 25 people earn the same as 25 million."[35] The pre-1980s statist policies were unable to address the persistence of massive poverty in Mexico, and the more recent shift to neoliberal policies has only increased the gap between rich and poor. In 2008, the poorest 40 percent of the population earned about 12 percent of Mexico's income, while the wealthiest 10 percent earned about 40 percent, and the gap has not changed significantly since the 1980s.[36] In 2017, *Forbes* listed 15 Mexicans as billionaires, including the world's sixth wealthiest individual, entrepreneur and media mogul Carlos Slim.[37]

Poverty continues to be a serious problem for Mexico, despite significant improvements in the last two decades. Between 1992 and 2008, extreme poverty declined from about 21 percent to about 18 percent of the population, and the overall poverty rate dropped from 53 percent to 47 percent.[38] Poverty in Mexico is most pronounced in rural areas, still home to some 23 million people. Despite the legacy of land reform, most rural Mexicans cannot support themselves on their tiny plots of land, and many are forced to seek work as migrant laborers. Millions have migrated to already overcrowded urban areas, seeking employment and a better life, and millions more have immigrated to the United States for the same reasons.

Mexico's wealth is also geographically unequal. Northern Mexico is far wealthier than the central and southern regions. While the north is characterized by large-scale export agriculture (benefiting from proximity to the U.S. market), land use is much more fragmented in the south. Southern Mexico has a far poorer infrastructure, lower levels of education, and more poverty.

Another indicator of the degree of inequality in Mexico is the tremendous size and importance of the **informal sector**. It is estimated that well over one-quarter of the labor force is employed in the underground economy as informal vendors of goods and services, producing about 13 percent of Mexico's GDP. Mexican cities are full of *ambulantes* (street vendors), which local governments have fought unsuccessfully to regulate. These workers pay no taxes on their earnings but enjoy few protections or benefits.

Despite these problems Mexico has been able to decrease its levels of poverty since democratization in 2000 due to steady increases in social spending as a percentage of GDP. But efforts to increase social spending even further have been hampered by Mexico's inability to collect taxes, especially when compared with wealthier industrialized countries. Attempts to raise taxes meet with widespread skepticism, in part because Mexico's traditionally corrupt state is simply not trusted. President Peña Nieto campaigned on a platform that included a major tax reform proposal, but the PRI's failure to win a majority in the legislature forced him to water down those proposals; he eventually struck a deal with the leftist PRD to gain passage for the measure. The reform, passed into law in November 2013, includes an increase in income tax on the wealthiest Mexicans, a tax on stock market profits, new taxes on high-calorie foods, and reduction of a whole host of tax breaks.

Despite the myriad problems facing Mexico's economy, we would be remiss if we failed to point out the biggest change in Mexico's political economy over the last two decades. Since its recovery from the economic crisis of the mid-1990s, and under the presidencies of Zedillo, Fox, Calderón, and Peña Nieto, about half of Mexico's population has entered the middle class. Several factors are responsible for this dramatic shift.[39] First, economic stability since the mid-1990s, and especially the containment of inflation, has benefited the middle class. Second, government antipoverty programs have kept many Mexicans from falling out of the middle class. The conditional cash transfer program called *Oportunidades* (Opportunities) gives payment to about a quarter of all Mexican families in exchange for pledges that their children remain in school and get preventive medical care. Finally, Mexico's entry into NAFTA has created a more competitive economy, lowering prices of food and consumer goods for Mexicans.

The Battle over Oil

State ownership of oil and President Lázaro Cárdenas's slogan, "The oil is ours!" became important symbols of the Mexican Revolution and Mexico's independence from foreign domination of its economy. PEMEX, the state oil company founded by Cárdenas in 1938, has played an enormous role in Mexico's economy. It is Mexico's biggest company and its biggest source of tax revenue (in 2013, taxes on its revenue funded a third of the federal budget). But PEMEX has been losing money (in 2016, it lost about $14 billion), in part because it lacks the capital and expertise to explore deep-water oil reserves in the Gulf of Mexico. As a result, oil production has steadily declined.

In December 2013, President Peña Nieto signed into law a bitterly contested constitutional reform that would permit foreign and private investment in the Mexican gas and oil sector for the first time in over 70 years. In March 2014, he called the energy reform "the most important economic change in Mexico in 50 years."[40] PEMEX lost its monopoly over the sale of gasoline but now pays lower taxes to the government The powerful National Union of Mexican Oil Workers, whose strict control over labor has hampered PEMEX's ability to hire skilled labor, no longer has seats on the PEMEX governing board. A company that for decades was run as a government agency (it was chaired by the energy minister) now has a more independent board of directors. The hope is that Mexico will attract billions of dollars of foreign investment into the energy sector and increase exploration and development of oil and gas, and that PEMEX will once again become profitable.

Foreign Relations and the World

Mexico's foreign relations have always been heavily molded by the country's complex relationship with the United States. In the political turmoil of the nineteenth century, Mexico lost half its territory to an expanding United States. Indeed, Mexico's humiliation at U.S. hands has been a major theme in the Mexican psyche. Even Porfirio Díaz, whose dictatorship promoted closer ties to the United States, is reported to have lamented, "Poor Mexico! So far from God and so close to the United States."

One goal of the Mexican Revolution (and the aim of much of its official rhetoric) was to restore the sovereignty and power of Mexico on the global stage. During authoritarianism, the PRI leadership clearly sought a system that would restore stability to the Mexican system and prevent future attacks on Mexican sovereignty. In the early years of the revolution, foreign economic interests were sharply curtailed and foreign oil companies were nationalized. Mexico began to assert itself as an independent and autonomous state, gradually gaining the status of a regional power within Latin America.

During and after World War II, Mexico became a closer ally of the United States while still asserting an independent voice in its foreign policy. From the 1960s through the 1980s, it opposed U.S. foreign policy in Latin America, fostered a close relationship with Fidel Castro's Cuba (a U.S. archenemy), and supported revolutionary movements in the region that often opposed the United States.

Many Mexicans were proud that their country could act so independently of the United States in the arena of foreign policy. However, the economic catastrophe of the 1980s and Mexico's decision to abandon revolutionary economic policies and liberalize its economy made clear the limits of Mexican independence in foreign affairs. In exchange for massive economic aid in the 1980s, Mexico was pressured to curtail its opposition to U.S. foreign policy in Latin America. The peso crisis of the mid-1990s only further served to emphasize Mexico's fundamental dependence on the United States.

After the election of Vicente Fox in 2000, Mexico moved closer to the United States on most foreign policy issues. Fox sought to work closely with President George W. Bush, in the hope of gaining new agreements on immigration and trade. Since NAFTA, Mexico's increased economic dependence on the United States has clearly limited its international assertiveness. However, this did not stop the Fox administration from opposing the U.S. invasion of Iraq in 2003, a stance that led to a cooling of U.S.-Mexico relations. Immediately after taking office in 2009, U.S. president Barack Obama and his administration took steps to improve relations with Mexico and collaborate to stem growing drug violence in Mexico.

Though Mexico and the United States have grown closer since the end of PRI rule, the relationship remains, in the words of the *Economist*, "exquisitely sensitive," a reflection no doubt of the gigantic gap between the two partners' power.[41] Mexicans continue to resent what they view as heavy-handed intervention in Mexican domestic affairs as well as unfair treatment. These feelings are well illustrated by some recent conflicts between the two neighbors.[42] In 2009, a U.S. military report raised the specter that Mexico could become a failed state. The report triggered an angry diplomatic response from Mexican officials and prompted U.S. secretary of state Hillary Clinton to travel to Mexico to help calm the crisis. In March 2011, the U.S. ambassador to Mexico was forced to resign after cables released by WikiLeaks quoted him as questioning the Mexican government's strategy in the drug war. In July 2011, the United States finally agreed to allow Mexican trucks to carry shipments within the United States, thus observing a provision of NAFTA that the United States had refused to honor for 17 years. For years, Mexico had expressed frustration with the U.S. refusal to honor such commitments, and in 2001 it imposed over $2 billion in retaliatory tariffs on imported U.S. goods. Mexican public opinion, however, remains largely favorable to the United States. A survey published in 2014 reported that 66 percent of Mexican respondents had a favorable view of the United States, and 70 percent said that economic ties with the United States were good for Mexico.[43]

Decades of very close cooperation between Mexico and its northern neighbor were put in jeopardy with the inauguration of Donald Trump as U.S. president in 2017. Trump's desire to renegotiate or abolish NAFTA, his desire to build a wall along the U.S.-Mexico border, and his negative portrayal of Mexicans in the United States are likely to worsen a relationship that is crucial for Mexico.

Mexico's Drug War: Can the Mexican State Contain Organized Crime?

The Mexican Revolution successfully strengthened state power and autonomy and ended endemic violence in Mexico. Yet the long domination of the PRI, its dependence on patron-client relations, its co-optation, and its electoral fraud all helped perpetuate a culture of corruption and lawlessness that now increasingly threatens the state and its capacity, autonomy, and legitimacy.

Over the past two decades, Mexico has seen an alarming rise in drug trafficking, driven by the growing market for illegal drugs north of the border and facilitated by a Mexican legal system that is both weak and corrupt. Mexico has experienced a dramatic growth of drug-related violence and a steady stream of corruption scandals involving drug money. The drug cartels are well funded, heavily armed, and often protected by local police forces and state governments. They intimidate local governments and have brutally executed politicians, police, and journalists who stand in their way. A series of investigations in 2008 implicated federal antidrug officials in the drug trade and further damaged the government's image.

Shortly after his inauguration, President Calderón called on the army to combat the cartels, and in 2009 he sent troops to replace corrupt local police forces in some cities along the U.S. border. The military response only emboldened the drug cartels, which initiated a campaign of assassination aimed at the police and antidrug authorities. The United States has been alarmed by the growing drug traffic across the U.S.-Mexico border: authorities estimate that about 70 percent of all marijuana and cocaine entering the United States arrives through Mexico. U.S. attempts to undertake antinarcotics operations in Mexico have been attacked as abridging Mexico's sovereignty, and U.S. criticism of Mexico's lackluster antinarcotics efforts has often raised tensions between the two neighbors. Mexican officials counter that drug cartels take advantage of lax U.S. gun control laws to purchase most of their weapons north of the border. In 2009, the Obama administration acknowledged that Mexico's drug wars are a shared problem and vowed to work with Mexico to address the threat.

By 2017, the drug war had claimed at least an estimated 80,000 lives. Almost 90 percent of those deaths have been execution-style killings. In some areas, the rise in violent deaths has been dramatic. For example, Ciudad Juárez, on the U.S. border, had a 2010 murder rate of 229 per 100,000 inhabitants, making it more dangerous than Kandahar (Afghanistan) or Baghdad (Iraq).[44]

The Calderón and Peña Nieto administrations can boast of apprehending a number of top drug cartel leaders, including the 2014 arrest of Joaquín Guzmán, the head of the Sinaloa cartel, and the world's most-wanted drug lord. Guzmán's subsequent escape from Mexico's highest security prison through a mile-long tunnel revealed the extent to which drug cartels had thoroughly penetrated Mexican law enforcement. When the drug lord was recaptured in 2016, the government announced that he would be extradited to the United States. There is a vigorous debate in Mexico about

MEXICO'S DRUG CARTELS

A map of the areas controlled by Mexico's drug cartels. Much of Mexico is plagued by drug crime.

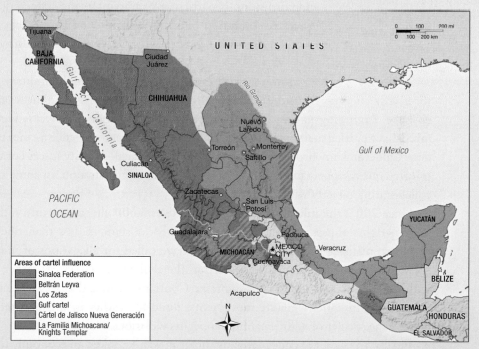

Source: "A Glimmer of Hope," *Economist*, November 24, 2012, www.economist.com/news/special-report/21566774-after-five-years-soaring-murder-rates-killings-have-last-begun-level/print (accessed 6/6/14).

The disappearance of 43 students in September 2014 shocked Mexican society. Their disappearance and murder appear to have been the result of collaboration between local government, police, and drug gangs, highlighting the problem of corruption and impunity in Mexico.

whether the drug war is being or ever can be won.[45] Opinion polling in 2014 revealed strong public support for the military campaign against drug traffickers but also showed a decline in the percentage of Mexicans who think that the campaign is making progress (only 37 percent of Mexicans now share this view).

The drug war is also compromising human rights. Although most attention in Mexico has focused on the battle between the Mexican state and drug traffickers, concern is growing about the impact of that conflict on human rights. When the mayor of a rural community cooperated with drug traffickers in the kidnapping (and presumed murder) of 43 college students in September 2014, even the most jaded observers of Mexican politics were alarmed by organized crime's penetration of local politics and law enforcement. Mexico has never had a professional, reliable police force, and corruption is particularly rampant at the state and local level.[46] As a result, presidents Calderón and Peña Nieto have relied on the armed forces to carry out their war against drug gangs.

However, with the increased reliance on the military have come thousands of allegations of human rights abuses against civilians. According to a 2015 Human Rights Watch report, "Mexico's security forces have participated in widespread enforced disappearances since former president Calderón launched a 'war on drugs.' Members of all security forces continue to carry out disappearances during the Peña Nieto administration, in some cases, collaborating directly with criminal groups."[47]

Since 2007, the military has investigated over 3,600 allegations into military human rights abuses against civilians, but only 15 soldiers (less than one half of 1 percent) have been convicted. Critics have called for allegations of military abuse against civilians to be investigated in the civilian justice system rather than within the military, and Mexico's Supreme Court has echoed that view. The rapid growth of anti-cartel vigilante movements, discussed earlier in this chapter, has created the specter of additional human rights violations.

Finally, the violence engendered by the drug war has taken an economic toll. A leading business organization reported in 2013 that the climate of insecurity was costing Mexican business almost $6 billion dollars annually. It claimed that almost 40 percent of Mexican businesses had suffered attacks by organized crime.[48]

Migration

Mexicans have a long history of emigrating across the 2,000-mile border between Mexico and the United States. Mexicans have argued that the United States depends on Mexican immigrants and that the latter's right to work in the United States should be guaranteed through bilateral agreements. But many Americans have focused on the negative effects of Mexican immigration to the United States.

Why has there been such a steady flow of Mexicans into the United States? Most of them are seeking the higher standard of living in the United States, although the first wave of immigrants in the early twentieth century were also fleeing the violence of the Mexican Revolution. During the severe labor shortages of World War II, the United States established the **Bracero Program**, which allowed more than 4 million Mexicans to work temporarily in the United States between 1942 and 1964. Today, almost 11 million Mexicans live in the United States (about 10 percent of Mexico's total population and 4 percent of the U.S. population).

From 1965 to 1986, an estimated 5.7 million Mexicans immigrated to the United States, 81 percent of them undocumented.[49] The United States operated a de facto guest-worker program whereby border enforcement was tough enough to prevent a flood of immigration but not so strict as to prevent a steady flow of cheap and undocumented labor. The costs of illegal immigration were raised just enough that only about one in three undocumented Mexicans could be caught and returned. Most immigrants who tried to enter the United States succeeded, although not on the first try. The U.S. attempt to enforce border control was largely symbolic, and it never threatened the availability of cheap labor. The dramatic growth of undocumented Mexican immigrants, especially after the economic crisis in Mexico during the early 1980s, became a political crisis in the United States during the 1980s and 1990s. The result was the 1986 U.S. **Immigration Reform and Control Act (IRCA)**, which imposed sanctions on employers of undocumented immigrants and toughened the enforcement of immigration laws. At the same time, it provided amnesty for longtime undocumented workers and legalized about 2.3 million Mexican immigrants. In the late 1990s, however, illegal immigration continued to skyrocket. In 2006, the U.S. administration of George W. Bush proposed tougher border controls as well as measures aimed at giving legal status to more Mexicans living in the United States.

The issue of migration continues to be a sore point in the relationship between Mexico and the United States. President Bush's promise to overhaul U.S. immigration policy fell victim to a changed U.S. domestic political atmosphere after the attacks of 9/11, and Obama's attempt to reform immigration failed due to political polarization. The policies of some U.S. states aimed at curtailing illegal emigration from Mexico have exacerbated the tensions. By 2011, a growing Mexican economy, a continuing recession in the United States, tighter border patrols, and a worsening atmosphere in the United States for Mexican immigrants had led to a dramatic reduction in the rate of illegal border crossings. Still, in a recent survey 35 percent of Mexicans said they would move to the United States if they could, and 15 percent of those respondents said they would be willing to do so illegally.

It is a near certainty that immigration will continue to be a point of contention between the United States and Mexico for years to come. Proposals by U.S. president Donald Trump to build a wall along the U.S.-Mexico border, and to force Mexico to pay for it (with a tax on Mexican exports to the United States), raised the ire of Mexican leaders. Mexico's treasury secretary, Luis Videgaray, retorted, "to build a wall between Mexico and the United States is a terrible idea. It is an idea based on ignorance, that has no basis in the reality of North American integration."[50] In January 2016, President Peña Nieto canceled a trip to Washington to protest Trump's proposals.

NOTES

1. Samuel Huntington, *Political Order in Changing Societies* (New Haven, CT: Yale University Press, 2006).
2. For a good overview of the development of the Mexican state, see Alan Knight, "The Weight of the State in Modern Mexico," in *Studies in the Formation of the Nation State in Latin America,* ed. James Dunkerley (London: Institute of Latin American Studies, 2002), 212–52.
3. For the best English-language overview, see Luis Carlos Ugalde, *The Mexican Congress: Old Player, New Power* (Washington, DC: Center for Strategic and International Studies, 2000).
4. Ugalde, *The Mexican Congress*, 146.
5. Jodi Finkel, "Judicial Reform as Insurance Policy: Mexico in the 1990s," *Latin American Politics and Society* 47, no. 1 (Spring 2005): 87–111.
6. Jorge Castañeda, *Mañana Forever? Mexico and the Mexicans* (New York: Alfred A. Knopf, 2011), xvi.
7. José Antonio Caballero, "Judiciary: The Courts in Mexico," in *Americas Quarterly*, Spring 2013, www.americasquarterly.org/judiciary-courts-mexico (accessed 5/27/13).
8. Wayne Cornelius, Todd Eisenstadt, and Jane Hindley, eds., *Subnational Politics and Democratization in Mexico* (San Diego, CA: Center for U.S.-Mexican Studies, 1999); R. Andrew Nickson, *Local Government in Latin America* (Boulder, CO: Lynne Reinner, 1995), 199–209.
9. Pamela Starr, "Fox's Mexico: Same as It Ever Was?" *Current History*, February 2002: 62.
10. Kathleen Bruhn, *Taking on Goliath: Mexico's Party of the Democratic Revolution* (University Park: Pennsylvania State University Press, 1997).

11. Kathleen Bruhn, "López Obrador, Calderón, and the 2006 Electoral Campaign," in *Consolidating Mexico's Democracy*, eds. Jorge Domínguez, Chappell Lawson, and Alejandro Moreno (Baltimore, MD: Johns Hopkins University Press, 2009), 169–88.

12. For a good overview, see Chappell Lawson, "Fox's Mexico at Midterm," *Journal of Democracy* 15 (2004): 339–50.

13. Joseph Klesner, "Electoral Competition and the New Party System in Mexico," paper presented at the annual meeting of the Latin American Studies Association, Washington, DC, September 6–8, 2001; and Joseph Klesner, "A Sociological Analysis of the 2006 Elections," in Domínguez, Lawson, and Moreno, eds., *Consolidating Mexico's Democracy*, 50–70.

14. D. Xavier Medina Vida, Antonio Ugues, Shaun Bowler, and Jonathan Hiskey, "Partisan Attachment and Democracy in Mexico: Some Cautionary Observations," in *Latin American Politics and Society* 52, no. 1 (January 2010): 66–87.

15. An outstanding edited volume on the 2006 presidential elections is Domínguez, Lawson, and Moreno, eds., *Consolidating Mexico's Democracy.*

16. An excellent treatment of the 2012 elections is Gustavo Flores-Macías, "Mexico's 2012 Elections: The Return of the PRI," *Journal of Democracy* 24, no. 1 (January 2013): 128–41. For a translated video of the second Mexican presidential candidate debate, see www.c-span.org /video/?192963-1/mexican-presidential-debate (accessed 11/22/14).

17. Joseph L. Klesner, "Who Participates? Determinants of Political Action in Mexico," *Latin American Politics and Society* 51, no. 2 (Summer 2009): 59–90.

18. Alberto J. Olvera, "The Elusive Democracy: Political Parties, Democratic Institutions, and Civil Society in Mexico," *Latin American Research Review* (Special Issue, 2010): 79–107.

19. Castañeda, *Mañana Forever?*, 9.

20. Castañeda, *Mañana Forever?*, 12.

21. *Economist*, "Dallying with a Monster," March 15, 2014, www.economist.com/news/americas /21598976-failing-snuff-out-vigilantism-mexico-running-big-risks-dallying-monster (accessed 6/4/14).

22. A magnificent photo essay on the vigilante phenomenon is Alan Taylor, "Mexico's Vigilantes," *Atlantic*, May 13, 2014, www.theatlantic.com/infocus/2014/05/mexicos-vigilantes/100734/ (accessed 6/4/14).

23. The Committee to Protect Journalists has information about violence against Mexican journalists, available at http://cpj.org/americas/mexico/2014/?page=1 (accessed 6/4/14).

24. Data from the 2013 Latinobarómetro Survey, available at www.latinobarometro.org (accessed 6/5/14).

25. Alan Riding, *Distant Neighbors* (New York: Vintage, 1989), 199.

26. Three excellent overviews are Tom Hayden, ed., *The Zapatista Reader* (New York: Thunder's Mouth Press, 2002); Lynn Stephen, *Zapata Lives: Histories and Cultural Politics in Southern Mexico* (Berkeley: University of California Press, 2002); and Chris Gilbreth and Gerardo Otero, "Democratization in Mexico: The Zapatista Uprising and Civil Society," *Latin American Perspectives* 28, no. 4 (July 2001): 7–29.

27. See www.latinobarometro.org (accessed 6/5/16).

28. In 2009, 72 percent of Mexicans expressed little or no interest in politics, according to the Latinobarómetro Survey at www.latinobarometro.org (accessed 7/6/11).

29. From the 2015 Latinobarómetro Survey. See www.latinobarometro.org (accessed 6/5/16).

30. Castañeda, *Mañana Forever?*

31. See www.latinobarometro.org (accessed 6/5/16).

32. Paul Cooney, "The Mexican Crisis and the Maquiladora Boom: A Paradox of Development or the Logic of Neoliberalism?" *Latin American Perspectives* 28, no. 3 (May 2001): 55–83.

33. Rafael Tamayo-Flores, "Mexico in the Context of the North American Integration: Major Regional Trends and Performance of Backward Regions," *Journal of Latin American Studies* 33 (2001): 377–407.

34. Tamayo-Flores, "Mexico in the Context of the North American Integration," 377–407.

35. Quoted in Nicolas Wilson, "What's Wrong with This Picture?" *Business Mexico* 4 (April 1997): 22.

36. World Bank, www.worldbank.org (accessed 12/17/11).

37. See www.forbes.com/wealth/billionaires/list/17/#version:static (accessed 6/27/17).

38. Castañeda, *Mañana Forever?*, 34.

39. See the discussion in Castañeda, *Mañana Forever?*, 61–62.

40. Quoted in Andrew Williams, "Pemex, Mexico's State Oil Giant, Braces for the Country's New Energy Landscape," *Washington Post*, June 6, 2014, www.washingtonpost.com/business /pemex-mexicos-state-oil-giant-braces-for-a-the-countrys-new-energy-landscape/2014/06/04 /07d171d6-ea69-11e3-93d2-edd4be1f5d9e_story.html (accessed 6/6/14).

41. "A State of Insecurity," *Economist*, March 22, 2011, www.economist.com/blogs/americas view/2011/03/mexican-american_relations (accessed 6/24/17).

42. A good overview of U.S.-Mexico relations is Shannon O'Neil, *Two Nations Indivisible: Mexico, the United States, and the Road Ahead* (New York: Oxford University Press, 2013).

43. "U.S. Image Rebounds in Mexico," Pew Research Survey report, www.pewglobal.org /2013/04/29/u-s-image-rebounds-in-mexico/ (accessed 6/6/14).

44. Latin American Regional Report: Mexico and NAFTA, February 2011 (ISSN 1741-444); Howard Campbell, "No End in Sight: Violence in Ciudad Juárez," in *NACLA Report on the Americas* 44, no. 2 (May/June 2011): 19–24.

45. A very critical view of the drug war is from Jorge Castañeda, "What's Spanish for Quagmire?" *Foreign Policy* 177 (January/February 2010): 76–81.

46. See an interview with George Grayson, December 23, 2011, www.coha.org/professor-grayson -on-mexico's-drug-war/ (accessed 6/24/17).

47. Human Rights Watch, "World Report 2015: Mexico," www.hrw.org/world-report/2015 /country-chapters/mexico (accessed 6/5/15).

48. *Latin American Weekly Report*, June 5, 2014, 11.

49. Douglas Massey, Jorge Durand, and Nolan Malone, *Beyond Smoke and Mirrors: Mexican Immigration in an Era of Economic Integration* (New York: Russell Sage Foundation, 2002), 45.

50. Available at http://ktla.com/2016/03/03/no-scenario-where-mexico-will-pay-for-donald-trumps -wall-treasury-secretary-says/ (accessed 6/5/16).

KEY TERMS

Bracero Program World War II program that allowed millions of Mexicans to work temporarily in the United States

caciques Local military strongmen who generally controlled local politics in Mexico during the nineteenth century

Calderón, Felipe Mexico's conservative president from 2006 to 2012; he was responsible for waging a war against drug cartels that led to a major increase in violence

camarillas Vast informal networks of personal loyalty that operate as powerful political cliques

Cárdenas, Lázaro Mexican president from 1934 to 1940 who implemented a radical program of land reform and nationalized Mexican oil companies

Carranza, Venustiano Mexican revolutionary leader who eventually restored political order, ended the revolution's violence, and defeated the more radical challenges of Zapata and Villa

caudillos National military strongmen who dominated Mexican politics in the nineteenth and early twentieth centuries

Chamber of Deputies The lower house of Mexico's legislature

Confederation of Mexican Workers (CTM) Mexico's dominant trade union confederation, which was a main pillar of the PRI's authoritarian regime

Constitution of 1917 Document established by the Mexican Revolution that continues to regulate Mexico's political regime

Cortés, Hernán Spanish conqueror of Mexico

criollos Mexican-born descendants of Spaniards during the period of Spanish colonial rule

Cuauhtémoc Aztec military leader defeated by the Spanish conquerors

Díaz, Porfirio Mexican dictator who ruled from 1876 to 1910 and was deposed by the Mexican Revolution

Federal Electoral Institute Independent agency that regulates elections in Mexico; created in 1996 to end decades of electoral fraud

Fox, Vicente Mexico's president from 2000 to 2006 and the first non-PRI president in more than seven decades

Immigration Reform and Control Act (IRCA) U.S. immigration legislation (1986) that toughened American immigration laws while granting amnesty to many longtime undocumented workers

import substitution industrialization (ISI) Political-economic model followed during the authoritarian regime of the PRI, in which the domestic economy was protected by high tariffs in order to promote industrial growth

informal sector A sector of the economy that is not regulated or taxed by the state

Juárez, Benito The nineteenth-century Mexican president who is today considered an early proponent of a modern, secular, and democratic Mexico

Labastida, Francisco The first-ever PRI candidate to lose a presidential election; he was defeated in 2000 by Vicente Fox of the PAN

latifundistas Owners of *latifundia* (huge tracts of land)

López Obrador, Andrés Manuel Mexican leftist politician who lost the presidential elections of 2006 and 2012; he has challenged the legitimacy and integrity of the Mexican electoral process

López Portillo, José Mexican president from 1976 to 1982; he increased the role of the state in the economy and nationalized Mexico's banking system in an attempt to avert a national economic crisis

Madero, Francisco An initial leader of the Mexican Revolution and a landowner who sought moderate democratic reform

maquiladoras Factories that import goods or parts to manufacture goods that are then exported

Maya Mexico's largest indigenous group, concentrated in the south of the country

mestizos Mexicans of mixed European and indigenous blood, who make up the vast majority of Mexico's population

Mexican-American War The conflict between Mexico and the United States (1846–48) in which the United States gained half of Mexico's territory

Mexican miracle The spectacular economic growth in Mexico from the 1940s to about 1980

Mexican Revolution Bloody conflict in Mexico between 1910 and 1917 that established the long-lived PRI regime

Mexico's War of Independence The 11-year conflict that resulted in Mexico's independence from Spain in 1821

MORENA (National Regeneration Movement) New leftist political party formed by Andrés Manuel López Obrador, a two-time presidential candidate for the PRD

municipios County-level governments in Mexican states

Nahuatl Mexico's second-largest indigenous group, concentrated in central Mexico

National Congress Mexico's bicameral legislature

National Supreme Court of Justice Mexico's highest court

North American Free Trade Agreement (NAFTA) Trade agreement linking Mexico with the United States and Canada

Partido Acción Nacional (PAN) Conservative Catholic Mexican political party that until 2000 was the main opposition to the PRI

Partido de la Revolución Democrática (PRD) Mexico's main party of the left

Partido Revolucionario Institucional (PRI) Political party that emerged from the Mexican Revolution to preside over an authoritarian regime that lasted until 2000

patron-client relationships Relationships in which powerful government officials deliver state services and access to power in exchange for the delivery of political support

PEMEX Mexico's powerful state-owned oil monopoly

Peña Nieto, Enrique Mexico's current president and the first PRI member to be elected president since the return of democracy in 2000

San Andrés Peace Accords A 1996 agreement that promised to end the Zapatista rebel uprising but was never implemented by the PRI government

Santa Anna, General Antonio López de Mexico's first great *caudillo*, who dominated its politics for three decades in the mid-nineteenth century

secretary of government A top cabinet post that controls internal political affairs and was often a stepping-stone to the presidency under the PRI

secretary of the treasury Mexico's most powerful economic cabinet minister

Senate The upper house of Mexico's legislature

Televisa Mexico's largest media conglomerate, which for decades enjoyed a close relationship with the PRI

Villa, Francisco (Pancho) Northern Mexican peasant leader of the revolution who, together with Emiliano Zapata, advocated a more radical socioeconomic agenda

War of the Castes Massive nineteenth-century uprising of Mexico's indigenous population against the Mexican state

Zapata, Emiliano Southern Mexican peasant leader of the revolution most associated with radical land reform

Zapatista Army of National Liberation (EZLN) Largely Mayan rebel group that staged an uprising in 1994, demanding political reform and greater rights for Mexico's indigenous people

Zedillo, Ernesto Mexico's president from 1994 to 2000; he implemented political reforms that paved the way for fair elections in 2000

WEB LINKS

- *El Universal*, a Mexican daily newspaper (www.eluniversal.com.mx/english)
- *La Jornada*, a Mexican daily newspaper (www.jornada.unam.mx)
- Latin American Network Information Center, Mexico, an encyclopedic collection of links maintained by the University of Texas, Austin (www.lanic.utexas.edu/la/mexico)
- Mexican government offices and agencies (www.mexonline.com/mexagncy.htm)
- *Reforma*, a Mexican daily newspaper (www.reforma.com)

12

Though its economy has grown significantly in recent years, Brazil continues to face extreme economic inequality. In São Paulo, Parque Real, a favela (or slum), sits next to the upscale Morumbi neighborhood.

BRAZIL

Why Study This Case?

What a difference five years can make! In 2011, Brazil was being hailed as a model for Latin American development. Its economy was booming, driven by commodity exports and the promise of newly discovered oil reserves. Its two-term president, **Luiz Inácio Lula da Silva**, of the leftist Workers' Party (PT), could boast real progress in reducing poverty and inequality due to a series of market-friendly welfare measures. Between 2002 and 2009, over 20 million Brazilians were lifted out of poverty. Brazil appeared to have weathered the 2008 global financial crisis better than most countries. Da Silva's success and popularity allowed him to anoint his protégée **Dilma Rousseff** as his successor, and she was elected Brazil's first female president in 2010. Brazilians were proud of the country's progress and confident about its future. Brazil became an important leader of the developing world, and its global profile was enhanced when it was announced that Brazil would host the 2014 World Cup and the 2016 Summer Olympic Games.[1]

By 2016, all of that progress was called into question. Brazil's economy began to stumble due to a major drop in global commodity prices and economic mismanagement, and it was mired in its most serious economic recession since the return of democracy in the 1980s. A series of corruption scandals and protests over government spending on the World Cup and Olympic Games rocked the Rousseff government. Rousseff narrowly won reelection in 2014, but her government soon floundered amid new charges of endemic corruption, massive protests, and continued economic decline. By the spring of 2016, Rousseff's approval ratings had dropped below 10 percent. In August 2016, she was impeached by Brazil's legislature on charges of manipulating government finances in order to win reelection, and she was replaced by Brazil's conservative vice president, **Michel Temer**, who has also been

BRAZIL

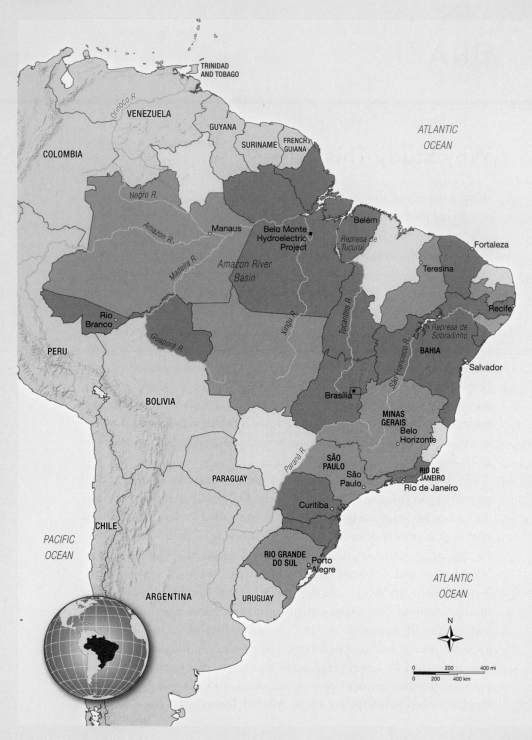

TRINIDAD
AND TOBAGO

VENEZUELA

COLOMBIA

GUYANA

SURINAME

FRENCH
GUIANA

Orinoco R.

Negro R.

Amazon R.

Manaus

Belo Monte
Hydroelectric
Project

Belém

ATLANTIC
OCEAN

Madeira R.

Amazon River
Basin

*Represa de
Tucuruí*

Fortaleza

Teresina

Rio
Branco

PERU

Guaporé R.

Xingu R.

Tocantins R.

São Francisco R.

*Represa de
Sobradinho*

Recife

BOLIVIA

Brasília ★

BAHIA

Salvador

MINAS
GERAIS

Belo
Horizonte

Paraná R.

SÃO
PAULO

São
Paulo

RIO DE
JANEIRO

Rio de Janeiro

PARAGUAY

Curitiba

CHILE

PACIFIC
OCEAN

RIO GRANDE
DO SUL

Porto
Alegre

ARGENTINA

URUGUAY

ATLANTIC
OCEAN

N

0   200   400 mi
0   200   400 km

dogged by corruption allegations. To make matters worse, Brazil's image as host of the Summer Olympic Games was damaged by construction delays, budget constraints, and the outbreak of the Zika virus.

Indeed, Brazil is a country full of paradoxes and surprises. It is the seventh-largest economy in the world and has a dynamic industrial sector. It has strikingly modern cities, such as São Paulo and Rio de Janeiro. According to the International Monetary Fund (IMF), Brazil will soon have a larger economy than the United Kingdom and is poised to become the sixth-largest economy in the world.[2] But Brazil is also plagued by some of the worst poverty, inequality, and indebtedness on the planet, and its cities are burdened by sprawling slums and violence. One Brazilian economist dubbed Brazil **Belindia** to denote this odd combination of Belgium's modernity and India's underdevelopment.[3]

Brazil is a highly urbanized society—over 80 percent of its population lives in its cities (six of which have more than 2 million residents). However, the sparsely populated **Amazon Basin** occupies about half of the country. The Amazon rain forest is often considered to be the lungs of the world, and its rapid destruction has become a major concern for environmentalists. Within Brazil, the Amazon has until recently been viewed most often as a rich resource that needs to be more efficiently exploited to help reduce inequality and poverty and to enhance Brazil's *grandeza* ("national greatness").

Given Brazil's history of extreme inequality and endemic poverty, it might have been expected to experience a mass revolution along the lines of those in Russia, Mexico, and China. At the very least, we might have assumed a history of political violence similar to that of South Africa during apartheid. But while violence has punctuated its history, Brazil has avoided cataclysmic revolutions or civil war. For over 150 years following its independence from Portugal in 1822, Brazil alternated between weak democratic regimes dominated by economic elites and authoritarian rule, usually presided over by the military.

From 1964 to 1985, a military dictatorship quashed a growing mass movement and suspended most political freedoms. Nevertheless, Brazil experienced a gradual and remarkably peaceful transition to a more effective democracy in the mid-1980s, and today it is the world's fourth-largest democracy. Brazilian democracy is characterized by regular elections and broad civil liberties and has enabled a peaceful succession of power.

The 2002 election of da Silva produced Brazil's first working-class president. Despite fears surrounding his election, democracy proved remarkably durable. His political heir, Dilma Rousseff, was elected as Brazil's first female president in 2010, and she was reelected in 2014 in Brazil's seventh democratic election since the end of military rule. Even with the impeachment of Rousseff and the massive corruption scandals that tarnished the political class, Brazil's democracy seems well consolidated.

Despite this admirable political record, serious questions remain about the long-term viability of Brazilian democracy. Can a democratic regime persist amid extraordinarily high levels of economic inequality? Will the growing wave of crime and lawlessness erode confidence in democracy and the rule of law? Will Brazil's legacy of statism, clientelism, corruption, and political deadlock prevent democratic reforms?

Brazil is also a fascinating case because of its relatively successful multiracial society. It has the largest African-origin population outside Africa. Despite a brutal history of slavery that lasted until relatively recently (ending in 1888) as well as persistent racism and race-based inequality, race has not yet polarized Brazilian politics. Nevertheless, recent attempts to redress the legacy of discrimination against Afro-Brazilians have been extremely controversial and threaten to shatter the myth of Brazil's racial harmony.

Endowed with a gigantic and geographically insulated country and blessed with formidable natural resources, Brazilians have a strong sense of national identity that makes Brazil unlike many of its Latin American neighbors. Few would have predicted the widespread and occasionally violent movement that swept Brazil in the summer of 2013, on the eve of the World Cup. Demonstrators decried the poor quality of public services and the widespread corruption, and protested massive government spending to prepare for these international events amid continuing poverty and inequality. By 2016, that disaffection had led to the removal of the president, casting doubt about a future that once seemed so promising.

Major Geographic and Demographic Features

Brazil's immense size gives it special importance: slightly larger than the continental United States, it is the world's fifth-largest country and occupies almost half of the South American continent. With more than 200 million citizens, it is home to one-third of Latin America's population.

Brazil shares borders with 10 other South American countries, but because most of its population has always been concentrated on its east coast, until recently it has had surprisingly little interaction with them. Brazilians have often identified more with Europe than with their Latin American neighbors. (Brazil's main population centers are geographically closer to Europe than to some parts of South America.)

The concentration of the population on the coast has been a major theme in Brazilian politics. In the 1950s, Brazilian leaders sought to shift Brazil's energy westward and open its vast Amazon frontier. In 1960, the capital was moved from the cosmopolitan, coastal city of Rio de Janeiro to the barren and isolated interior location of **Brasília**, where a futuristic planned city was created. Today, Brasília has a population of about 2.5 million.

Brazil's Amazon has only 13 percent of its population but contains over 60 percent of its landmass. In the 1960s, Brazil's military government began building roads west into the Amazon jungle, seeking to promote a demographic shift westward to provide land for poor Brazilians, exploit the natural resources of the region, and extend the power of the state into the hinterlands. Waves of impoverished northeasterners migrated to the Amazon to claim land and eke out a living, but with mixed success. This colonization of the Amazon region came at a tremendous cost to the natural environment and to its indigenous inhabitants.[4]

Brazil is now overwhelmingly an urban country, but this is a fairly recent development. The economic "miracle" of the late 1960s and early 1970s drew much of Brazil's rural population into its already overcrowded cities. Immigrants from the countryside helped fuel Brazil's industrial growth but were forced to live in the sprawling **favelas** (urban shantytowns) that ring Brazil's cities. Nowhere is the phenomenon of rapid urbanization more apparent than in São Paulo, Brazil's industrial capital and largest metropolitan area, with about 20 million residents.

Industrialization in Brazil has exacerbated a geographic schism in the country's socioeconomic development. Brazil's southeast, originally the center of the coffee boom, has become wealthy, industrialized, and populous; the three southeastern states of Rio de Janeiro, São Paulo, and Minas Gerais now contain nearly half of Brazil's population, generate well over half its wealth, and contain its most important cities. Meanwhile the northeast, the old center of sugar production, has become less populated and poorer. What once was the population center of Brazil now contains only 28 percent of its inhabitants and has the lowest per capita income. The region is now plagued with depleted soil, fierce international competition in the sugar market, and periodic droughts.

Historical Development of the State

The Reluctant Colony

Pedro Álvares Cabral first arrived in Brazil in 1500, when he was blown off course on his way to India. He claimed the territory for the Portuguese Crown, but Portugal initially paid little attention to it. Unlike the Spaniards, who encountered sophisticated empires and vast mineral wealth in their Latin American colonies, the Portuguese found the land sparsely populated (by between 1 million and 6 million indigenous Americans), and it offered no apparent mineral resources. While the Spaniards focused much of their energy on populating and exploiting their newfound territories, the Portuguese Crown continued to focus on the lucrative spice trade with the East, and it built few permanent colonies.

Despite this neglect, the Portuguese established trading posts along their new territory's coast. The early explorers discovered a hardwood that produced a valuable red dye; its Latin name was *Brasile*, for which the new territory was named. In response to incursions by the French in the 1530s, the Portuguese Crown attempted to take more permanent control of Brazil. The government doled out massive territories (often larger than Portugal itself) to *donatários* (nobles) who were willing to settle the remote land and defend it from foreigners. Brazil's first capital was established in 1549 in the northeastern coastal town of Salvador.

The Portuguese Crown's decision to cultivate sugar in Brazil first transformed the colony from a backwater into a more vital part of the Portuguese Empire. Brazil had unlimited rich land on which to cultivate sugar, but it lacked the necessary labor pool. Initial attempts to enslave the indigenous population backfired: the relatively small population was quickly decimated by European-borne disease, war, and harsh treatment, and the survivors fled deep into Brazil's interior.

By the late sixteenth century, the Portuguese had come to depend on African slaves to maintain the sugar economy. From 1550 to 1850, between 3 million and 4 million African slaves were shipped to Brazil, and at that time, Brazil's African population was far larger than its tiny white minority. Almost half of all Brazilians today have some African ancestry.

Unlike the United States, Brazil soon developed a large **mulatto** population (Brazilians of a mixed white and black ancestry). Portuguese settlers also mixed with indigenous people in the interior, which resulted in a smaller but still significant *caboclo* population.

TIMELINE OF POLITICAL DEVELOPMENT

YEAR	EVENT
1500	Portuguese arrive in Brazil.
1690s	Gold is discovered.
1763	Capital transferred from Salvador to Rio de Janeiro.
1822	Pedro I declares Brazilian independence from Portugal.
1822–89	Pedro I establishes a semi-authoritarian monarchical regime.
1888	Slavery is abolished.
1889–1930	First Republic, a quasi-democratic regime, is established.
1930	Military overthrows the republic and establishes authoritarian rule.
1937–45	Rule of Getúlio Vargas's Estado Nôvo (New State), an authoritarian regime.
1945–64	Second Republic, a democratic regime, is established.
1960	The capital is transferred from Rio de Janeiro to Brasília.
1964–85	Authoritarian military regime rules Brazil.
1985	New Republic, a democratic regime, is established.
2003	Luiz Inácio Lula da Silva assumes presidency.
2011	Dilma Rousseff assumes presidency.
2016	Rousseff impeached and replaced by Vice President Michel Temer.

The institution of slavery turned Brazil into the world's first great plantation export economy. The slave-based sugar economy generated massive wealth for the white minority and established a pattern that persists today: a tiny (mostly white) elite controls the vast majority of wealth, while much of the population lives in poverty.

By the mid-seventeenth century, Brazil's sugar economy had begun a steady decline, caused in part by fierce competition from Spanish, French, and Dutch colonies in the Caribbean. The presence of the Portuguese Crown was relatively small and concentrated largely in the sugar-producing areas of the northeast coast.

The Gold and Diamond Boom and the Rise of Brazil

The discovery of gold in the 1690s and diamonds in the 1720s forever changed the fate of Brazil. Mineral wealth was concentrated in the southeast and led to a demographic shift southward that has continued to this day; the central interior region, called Minas Gerais ("General Mines"), became the country's most populous area. The Portuguese began to establish settlements in the interior, and in 1763 the capital was moved south from Salvador to Rio de Janeiro. The eighteenth-century gold boom generated massive wealth, but much of Brazil's gold ended up in Europe.

By the end of the eighteenth century, the Portuguese Empire had weakened in the face of growing British, French, and Dutch power. The Portuguese Crown reacted by attempting to tighten its control of its Brazilian colony, imposing unpopular taxes on the colonists. These measures provoked a rebellion in the gold-mining capital of Vila Rica in 1789, but unlike the outcome of U.S. rebellion against Britain, in Brazil the Portuguese quickly crushed the uprising. Moreover, the colonial elites, frightened by Haiti's slave rebellion in 1791, were too fearful of the Afro-Brazilian majority to push for outright independence.

The Peaceful Creation of an Independent Brazilian State

Although Brazilian colonial elites did not advocate independence, the economic development spurred by mineral wealth created demands for increased autonomy and helped establish a distinct Brazilian identity. Furthermore, the colonial elites in the huge territory developed strong regional identities. Ironically, events in Europe more than colonial dissatisfaction paved the way for independence.

Napoleon Bonaparte's invasion of the Iberian Peninsula (Spain and Portugal) in 1807 was the catalyst for independence movements in Spanish America. Portugal's monarchy fled the invading French and moved the royal court to Brazil, a de facto recognition that Brazil had become the center of the Portuguese Empire. The arrival of the Portuguese monarch entailed transplanting the Portuguese state bureaucracy to Brazil, and Rio de Janeiro soon became a modern, cosmopolitan capital. Recognizing the importance of its colony, King João VI designated Brazil a kingdom, coequal with Portugal. The king returned to Portugal in 1821 after the end of the Napoleonic Wars, but he left his son Pedro on the Brazilian throne with instructions to support independence.

In this unusual manner, Pedro I became the leader of Brazil's transition to independence and spared the country the kind of bloody wars experienced by much of Spanish America. Pedro I declared Brazil's independence on September 7, 1822, and Portugal offered little resistance. Without its own armed forces, and facing the prospect of rebellion by powerful regional elites, Brazil depended heavily on the British, who quickly became its major trading partner.

Emperor Pedro I promulgated a constitution in 1824 and did not behave as an absolutist monarch. Nevertheless, the constitution was essentially authoritarian with a very strong executive. In 1826, Pedro I inherited the Portuguese throne from his father, and shortly thereafter he returned to Portugal, leaving his own son, Pedro II, on the Brazilian throne. Pedro I's official abdication in 1830 greatly weakened the power of the central state and further enhanced the power of regional elites. Pedro II formally assumed the throne in 1840 from a caretaker regency when he was only 14 years old, and he ruled Brazil until 1889.

Brazil's peaceful independence movement and the presence of reasonably enlightened monarchs during the nineteenth century were crucial for solidifying the Brazilian national identity and, most important, stemming the countless regional rebellions that plagued the country during its first half-century of statehood. Under the empire (1822–89), the foundations were laid for a strong central state dominated by the monarch. Brazil was also fortunate to find a new export product to replace sugar and minerals: coffee cultivation began in the 1820s in central and southern Brazil, further drawing economic development southward toward the coffee capital of São Paulo. Bolstered by the importation of slaves (which continued until the British banned the slave trade in 1850), Brazil quickly became the world's leading coffee producer.

Although the emperor opposed slavery, the Brazilian state did little to end it, largely because the economy depended so heavily on slave labor. When the monarchy finally decreed the abolition of slavery in 1888, the conservative Brazilian rural elite begrudgingly accepted the new reality rather than risk a U.S.-style civil war. Slave labor was partly replaced by a massive influx of immigration from Europe.

Politically, Brazil was remarkably stable during the nineteenth century, especially when compared with much of South and North America. Its stability was due in part to the presence of a relatively progressive monarchy that played a moderating role in Brazilian society. The monarchy promoted competition and alternation between Brazil's main conservative and liberal political parties. Pedro II purposely kept Brazil's military weak, fearing its involvement in politics, and he actively worked to limit the power of Brazil's Roman Catholic Church.

By the 1880s, however, the monarchy had a variety of opponents. Urban intellectuals, influenced by European positivism and republicanism, saw the monarchy as antiquated. Abolitionists, frustrated by the monarchy's prolonged acceptance of slavery, viewed it as a reactionary force. Powerful interests, including the military, the Catholic Church, and some regional elites, came to resent it. Faced with a military coup d'état in 1889, Pedro II chose exile instead of war, once again sparing Brazil from the violence that plagued the rest of Latin America.

Republicanism and the Continuation of Oligarchic Democracy

Brazil's military overthrew the monarchy and established the First Republic (1889–1930), whose motto, "Order and Progress," still adorns the Brazilian flag. It turned the republic over to civilian political elites (oligarchs) but replaced the monarchy as arbiter of Brazilian politics. A new constitution, modeled almost entirely on the U.S. Constitution, established a federal system composed of powerful states, a directly elected president, and separation of power between the branches of government. Voting was restricted to literate male adults, and only 3 to 6 percent of the population voted in elections.

Although the monarchy was abolished, political power continued to be held tightly by a somewhat expanded political elite. At the state level, the governorships were controlled by economic oligarchs and their network of local bosses (known as *coronéis*, or colonels). The most powerful states—São Paulo, dominated by the coffee oligarchs, and Minas Gerais, dominated by dairy farmers—competed and cooperated to control the presidency and the national legislature in an arrangement that has been called "the politics of the governors" and "the alliance of coffee and cream." Presidents selected their successors and then used a vast web of patronage and clientelism to deliver the vote.

During the First Republic, the state governments—particularly the most important states of São Paulo, Minas Gerais, Rio de Janeiro, and Rio Grande do Sul—became more powerful at the expense of the federal government. The weak federal government and the decentralization of power suited Brazil's powerful economic interests. The republic effectively mediated and contained political conflict between and within these interests while excluding all others. But by the early twentieth century, the elitist regime had alienated people in the growing urban middle class, who sought increased participation; the nascent industrial working class in São Paulo, who sought the creation of a welfare state; and immigrants, who were inspired by radical European ideologies. Demands for political and economic reform were met with harsh repression. New forces of opposition weakened the First Republic, but the increased infighting among regional leaders was the root cause of the regime's failure.

Getúlio Vargas and the New State

In October 1930, the military once again intervened in politics, this time to end the First Republic. Military leaders installed **Getúlio Vargas**, an elite politician from Rio Grande do Sul who had been a losing candidate for the presidency. Vargas acted quickly to enhance the power of the federal government, replacing elected governors with his appointees. In 1933, a new constitution reduced the autonomy of individual states (revoking their power to tax, for example), while maintaining the elected president and Congress. Vargas broke his pledge to hold democratic elections and, in 1937, created a new dictatorial regime he called the **Estado Nôvo** (New State).

The Estado Nôvo was clearly inspired by fascist Italy and Germany, whose regimes featured a strong, authoritarian central state, and by Franklin Roosevelt's New Deal policies. But Vargas is best viewed more as a typical Latin American **populist** (similar in many respects to Argentina's Juan Perón or Mexico's Lázaro Cárdenas) than as a fascist or social democrat. Unlike both the monarchy and the First Republic, which largely catered to the agricultural elite, Vargas's bases of support included the urban industrialists, middle-class professionals, workers, and sectors of the military. Politically, Vargas favored a model of **state corporatism** whereby all sectors of society were strongly encouraged to organize within state-controlled associations. Vargas viewed this system as a way to cultivate his base of support among different sectors of society while limiting the ability of civil society to challenge the state. Unofficial unions, groups, and parties were marginalized and harassed. Vargas viewed the state as a paternalistic arbiter of societal conflict.

The authoritarian Estado Nôvo was responsible for some of the first protections and welfare benefits for Brazil's urban workers, and Vargas's regime mobilized labor and raised wages. Vargas established state firms to promote industrialization in key sectors, such as steel, and imposed protectionist policies to shield Brazilian industry from foreign competition (such as import substitution industrialization, or ISI). As a result, Brazil experienced an industrial boom after 1930. Vargas also modernized and professionalized the Brazilian military, creating the **Superior**

War College, an institution that further bolstered the confidence and autonomy of the military.

After 1945, pressure mounted for Vargas to convene free elections. In the aftermath of World War II, during which Brazil had sent troops to help defeat fascism in Europe, dictatorships fell out of favor. In October 1945, Brazil's military, emboldened by its enhanced role in the dictatorship and its successful contribution to the Allied war effort, deposed Vargas and convened elections.

The Democratic Experiment: Mass Politics in the Second Republic

During the Second Republic (1945–64), Brazilians had their first real taste of democracy, and for the first time there was real competition for control of the state. The Brazilian masses, mobilized by Vargas during the Estado Nôvo, had become a force to be reckoned with. Suffrage was expanded dramatically (though only about one-fifth of the electorate participated during elections), and new national parties, including the Communist Party of Brazil, attempted to appeal to voters.

In 1950, Vargas, the former dictator, was elected to the presidency in a deeply polarized election. He attempted to continue the populist policies of the Estado Nôvo, but a vigorous opposition that controlled the legislature and the press stymied his policy proposals. In 1954, Vargas broke the deadlock by resigning, and shortly thereafter stunned the nation by committing suicide.

In the aftermath of Vargas's death, one of his followers, Juscelino Kubitschek, was elected president. Often considered Brazil's greatest president, Kubitschek was responsible for a number of grandiose public works, including the moving of Brazil's capital from Rio de Janeiro, on the coast, to Brasília, deep in the interior.

Breakdown of Democracy and Militarization of the State

Following Vargas's dictatorship, democracy was established but never consolidated. Brazil's democracy was deeply polarized between supporters and opponents of Vargas's populist policies. Opponents of Vargas and his successors called on the military to end democracy to prevent a return to populism; they also sought to reduce the role of the state in the economy. Supporters of Vargas and

History of Brazilian Regimes

REGIME	YEARS	TYPE	OUTCOME
Empire	1822–89	Quasi-democratic constitutional monarchy	Military coup
First Republic	1889–1930	Quasi-democratic republic	Military coup
Provisional government	1930–37	Authoritarian republic	Getúlio Vargas seizes power with military backing
Estado Nôvo	1937–45	Authoritarian republic	Military coup
Second Republic	1945–64	Democratic republic	Military coup
Military regime	1964–85	Military dictatorship	Controlled, negotiated transition
New Republic	1985–present	Democratic republic	

his successors viewed Brazil's democracy as weak, ineffective, and beholden to the country's wealthy elite. They increasingly advocated leftist policies that called for a growth in the state's role in the economy through a wave of nationalizations.

This political polarization crystallized during the presidency of **João Goulart** (1961–64), a minister of labor under Vargas. In the context of the Cold War, the military and many on the right viewed Goulart as a dangerous leftist and a potential dictator who reminded them too much of Vargas. His term began inauspiciously, for the military insisted that the Brazilian legislature curtail the president's power before allowing him to take office. But Goulart spent much of his first years in power, and a great deal of political capital, in passing a national referendum that restored his full powers and deeply alarmed his opponents. A severe economic crisis caused by rampant inflation and growing debt also exacerbated political tensions. In 1964, after Goulart attempted to rally workers and peasants to his defense and after he clumsily alienated the military by backing some mutinous officers, the Brazilian military, with U.S. support, once again seized power.

The military had intervened in Brazilian politics six times since 1889, but in each instance, soldiers had quickly retreated to their barracks, leaving politics to civilian leaders. By 1964, the Brazilian military believed it was time to take control of the state and hold onto it. Encouraged by the United States and politicians on the right, Brazilian military leaders thought they possessed the leadership skills to preserve political order, the power to prevent a feared Communist revolution, and the technical skills to run the economy.

Brazilian military leaders presided over a regime that has often been described as **bureaucratic authoritarian**.[5] Military leaders suspended the constitution and then decreed a new authoritarian one, banned existing parties and replaced them with two official ones to contest local and congressional elections (eliminating direct elections for governors and the president), took control of trade unions, and severely restricted civil liberties. They sought to erase for good the populist legacy of Vargas. The office of the president, a post held by a series of military leaders, issued numerous decrees that gradually stripped the political system of its democratic features. Torture, disappearances, and exile became commonplace, though they never reached the horrific dimensions experienced during bureaucratic authoritarian regimes in Argentina or Chile.[6] One young activist who was arrested and tortured was Dilma Rousseff—the former president of Brazil.

Although it initially attempted to reduce the role of the state in the economy, the Brazilian military eventually adopted policies of state-led industrialization that were in many ways a continuation of Vargas's statism. The state spent lavishly on major infrastructure projects, including hydroelectric dams, a paved highway to penetrate the Amazon rain forest, and even a nuclear power program. Military rule coincided with a period of sustained spectacular economic growth (1968–74) that averaged over 10 percent growth annually—a period known as the "economic miracle."

Gradual Democratization and the Military's Return to the Barracks

The period immediately following the economic miracle, however, featured an economic crisis and growing domestic opposition. In response, the military slowly began to loosen its political grip on the country while maintaining ultimate control. This process, known as ***abertura*** (gradual opening), coincided with the global energy crisis that hit Brazil particularly hard, raising its already high level of international debt. Inflation skyrocketed to levels that exceeded those under Goulart. The "official" opposition party tolerated by the regime became more vigorous in its call for regime change and more successful in legislative elections.

Under the presidency of General João Figueiredo (1979–85), political prisoners were released, censorship was reduced, and political parties were allowed to reemerge. These measures and the growing economic crisis led to a surge in opposition demands for direct presidential elections and democratic reform. The military's carefully laid plans for controlling the transition unraveled in 1984, when members of the pro-military party in the legislature unexpectedly backed a civilian democratic reform candidate, Tancredo Neves. He died shortly after his election and was replaced by the more conservative José Sarney, but the momentum of political reform could not be stopped. In 1987, a constituent assembly was elected to write a new democratic constitution that was formally adopted in 1988.

Thus democratization came gradually to Brazil and began when the military sought to initiate a controlled process of reform. It was encouraged by a severe economic crisis, facilitated by political miscalculation, and supported by widespread popular fatigue with military rule.

Political Regime

Political Institutions

Brazil has been a democracy since the adoption of its current constitution in 1988. The constitution was written in the waning days of the country's authoritarian regime and made important compromises in a number of areas.

THE CONSTITUTION

In many ways, the current constitution is similar to that of the Second Republic. However, in reacting to the long period of authoritarian rule, the constitution's framers established a set of rights that could not be amended or curtailed—for example, the principles of federalism, the separation of powers, and certain individual rights. Compared with previous documents, the current constitution imposes very strict limits and controls on the government's ability to declare a state of siege and thus limit civil liberties during wartime. Constitutional amendments are possible and can be initiated by the legislature (if one-third of the members of either house agree), the state legislatures (if a majority agrees), or the president. Such amendments can pass only with the support of separate two-thirds-majority votes in both houses of the legislature.

A major debate raged during the writing of the constitution in 1987. Most members of the constituent assembly favored abandoning Brazil's traditional presidential system for a parliamentary model. The conservative president at the time did not want to see his own powers diminished, and he resisted vigorously. However, he agreed to hold a plebiscite on the issue and in 1993 voters rejected the proposed parliamentary system. Brazilians were wary of losing their ability to elect their head of government directly after a period of authoritarian rule and distrusted their political parties, the linchpin of the parliamentary model.[7]

The Branches of Government

THE PRESIDENT

As is the norm in Latin America, the Brazilian president is both head of government and head of state. The president and a vice president are elected for four-year terms and may serve a second term.[8] The Brazilian president has the power of line-item vetoes, allowing for rejection of select aspects of legislation. The president has the power to initiate and push legislation through the legislature (about

80 percent of all legislation is initiated by the president) and is the only individual capable of initiating budgetary legislation. While presidents may veto legislation, these vetoes can be overridden by a simple majority in both houses of the legislature. Presidents may issue decrees, but the legislature can overturn them; decrees become law for only 30 days unless adopted by the legislature.

However, the formal power of Brazilian presidents has to date been weakened by fragmentation of the legislature. Brazilian heads of government need to patch together legislative majorities from fractious and poorly disciplined political parties. Faced with the lack of legislative majorities, Brazilian presidents have often resorted to legislating by emergency decree, thereby circumventing the legislature altogether.[9] President Fernando Collor de Mello, for example, won the presidency in 1989 as an "outsider," and his political party held only 3 percent of the seats in Congress. In his first year in office, he used 150 such emergency decrees to pass a variety of important economic reforms that were justified by the president as a necessary response to an economic crisis and whose dubious legality went unchallenged by Brazil's highest court.[10]

Former president Dilma Rousseff (on the right) was impeached in 2016, when the legislature ruled that she had illegally concealed Brazil's budget deficits. She was replaced by her conservative vice-president Michel Temer (left), who almost immediately became the target of corruption investigations.

Since Collor de Mello's resignation in 1992, Brazilian presidents have been able to build coalitions from the numerous parties in the legislature, a system that has been dubbed **coalitional presidentialism**. Perhaps the greatest power of Brazilian presidents comes from their ability to make appointments to the cabinet and top levels of Brazil's vast bureaucracy. Brazilian presidents have used this power to build legislative coalitions, but it has also helped to reinforce Brazil's long tradition of patrimonialism and corruption. While the Brazilian model has often been portrayed as inefficient and gridlocked, some scholars have begun to take a more nuanced view. According to this new perspective, skillful presidents must be master bargainers and coalition builders, forming majority legislative support from the plethora of parties. Unlike their predecessors, the four most recent Brazilian presidents (Cardoso, da Silva, Rousseff, and Temer) have excelled at that task.[11] However, the massive corruption scandals implicating much of Brazil's political system and the impeachment of Rousseff in 2016 cast some doubt on that more optimistic view.

THE LEGISLATURE

Brazil's legislature, the **National Congress (Congresso Nacional)**, is composed of two houses with equal power. The 513-member **Chamber of Deputies (Câmara dos Deputados)** is the lower house (whose members are elected to four-year terms), and the 81-member **Federal Senate (Senado Federal)** is the upper house (whose members are elected for eight-year terms). There are no term limits for members of either house.

Both houses must approve all legislation before it is sent to the president; when the houses disagree on legislation, they convene joint committees to iron out differences. The legislature can override presidential vetoes with a majority vote of both houses and can, with a two-thirds vote in both houses, amend the constitution with the agreement of the president. As in the United States, the Senate has the power to try a president or cabinet members for impeachable offenses and must approve top presidential appointments.

The actual power of the Brazilian legislature is a complex matter. On the one hand, legislators do not play a key role in most policy making. This situation exists for many reasons, including the dominance of the president, the weakness of the political parties, the individualism of legislators, and the relatively weak committee system. A persistent problem limiting the effectiveness of the legislature has been an inability to reach a quorum on key matters. In addition, legislators often view their jobs as stepping-stones to more prestigious and lucrative occupations, such as state governorships or top bureaucratic posts.

On the other hand, the constitution allocates significant power to Congress, and Brazil's legislature has played an important if not leading role from time to time.[12] Several high-profile congressional hearings (called *parliamentary commissions of investigation*) have exposed fraud and corruption, even at the highest level of government. In 1992, Congress impeached President Fernando Collor de Mello on corruption charges, forcing his resignation. In 2010 and 2011, Congress conducted several high-profile investigations of government behavior.[13] Most recently, the Chamber of Deputies voted for impeachment hearings against President Dilma Rousseff, and the Senate convicted her by a 61–20 vote.

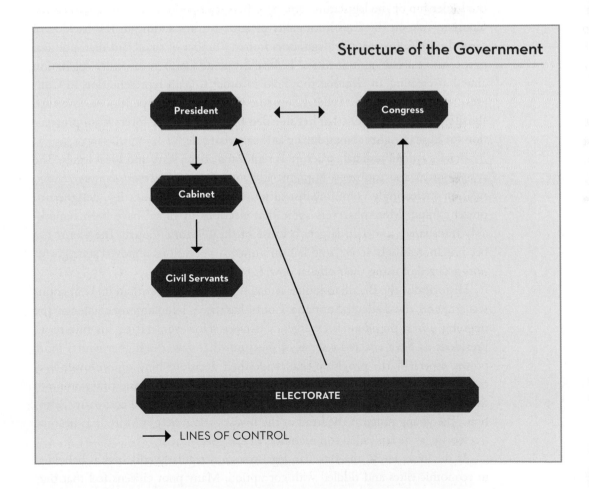

Structure of the Government

President ↔ Congress

President → Cabinet → Civil Servants

ELECTORATE

→ LINES OF CONTROL

Along with the legislature and executive branches, the judiciary is the third branch of government in Brazil. At the highest level is the **Federal Supreme Court (Supremo Tribunal Federal)**, whose 11 justices are appointed by the president and approved by a majority vote in the Senate for a term not to exceed 30 years. This court has the final say on all constitutional questions. The 30 judges of the Supreme Court of Justice, Brazil's highest criminal court, are similarly appointed and approved, and they also serve no more than 30 years.

The Federal Supreme Court has gained a reputation for independence since the return of democracy, but it has also been swamped by a huge caseload. (Recent reforms have attempted to ameliorate this problem by limiting the scope of cases that the Federal Supreme Court can consider.) The president, state governors, and the leadership of the legislature, among others, can petition the Federal Supreme Court to rule on the constitutionality of laws, further adding to the backlog of cases. In 2006, for example, legislators from a number of small Brazilian political parties successfully petitioned the Federal Supreme Court to overturn legislation aimed at creating an electoral threshold in order to gain representation in Congress. More recently, the Federal Supreme Court rejected a petition to overturn Brazil's 1979 amnesty law that has shielded Brazilian security forces from prosecution for human rights abuses during authoritarian rule.

Brazil's federal judicial structure is replicated at the state and local levels. The court system also features a Supreme Electoral Court (*Tribunal Superior Eleitoral*), an increasingly common institution in developing countries, designed to prevent fraud. Most observers agree that elections in Brazil have been remarkably transparent and fair, largely because of the Electoral Court. The Court has become increasingly active, and has on numerous occasions removed state governors accused of using their official powers to win reelection.

Historically, the Brazilian judiciary has enjoyed less power than its U.S. counterpart, and the Federal Supreme Court has been reluctant to challenge the ongoing use of presidential emergency decrees. However, during his first term, President da Silva enacted a series of measures that gave the higher courts more power, especially the provision that made their decisions binding on lower-level courts. Brazil's judiciary has taken the lead in the investigation and prosecution of those involved in the massive corruption scandal at the state oil company, Petrobras. The young judge at the head of the investigation, Sérgio Moro, has become a celebrity, as he has jailed top members of the government.

At the lower levels, the Brazilian legal system is regularly criticized as beholden to economic elites and riddled with corruption. Many poor citizens feel that they cannot be fairly represented within the system, and most Brazilians think there is little or no equality before the law.[14] In rural areas, for example, powerful landowners are often successful at influencing legal decisions to the detriment of the peasants. An old Brazilian expression summarizes this unequal access to the judicial system: "For my enemies, the law; for my friends, anything." Particularly harsh criticisms, backed by reports from international human rights organizations, have derided the judiciary's inability to hold Brazil's numerous security forces responsible for a host of human rights abuses. One survey reported that about 40 percent of Brazilians believe it is possible to bribe a judge.[15] Brazil's judiciary is overworked and underfunded, and it has been estimated that two-fifths of prison inmates are awaiting trial.[16]

The Electoral System

Brazil is an excellent example of how an electoral system can fundamentally influence the way in which legislatures and executives interact. Brazil's democracy is characterized by a multiplicity of relatively weak and loosely disciplined parties. This has made it difficult for Brazilian presidents to gain the support of a stable legislative majority and has created a built-in conflict between the executive and the legislature. As we will see, the electoral system is largely to blame.

All Brazilians over the age of 16 can vote, and since 1988 illiterate citizens have been allowed to vote. Voting is mandatory for all citizens between the ages of 18 and 70. Partly as a result, Brazil has regularly enjoyed a turnout of around 70 percent in legislative and presidential elections. Presidents, state governors, and mayors of large cities must receive a majority of the vote in a first round of voting or face their strongest opponent in a second round. For senate races, the three candidates with the most votes win seats.

Most controversial, though, is the electoral system used for Brazil's lower house (and for all state legislatures). In this highly unusual system, called **open-list proportional representation (PR)**, citizens vote for a specific individual on a party list (rather than simply for the entire party list, as is done in normal closed-list PR systems). Votes for each party (and for candidates associated with each party) are then tallied, and seats are allocated to each party proportionally. However, the determination of how seats are allocated to individual party members is based on the number of votes those members receive. Candidates must therefore campaign under their own names (not just their party labels) and have an incentive to promote their own candidacies at the expense of their party colleagues.

The open-list PR system weakens the power of political parties and the ability of those parties to enforce internal discipline. The parties are further fragmented because state-level parties, not the federal party hierarchy, determine the composition of party lists. The tendency has been for individual candidates to seek the backing of powerful state-level politicians, further enhancing Brazil's tradition of clientelism and pork-barrel politics. Moreover, unlike many systems that employ PR, Brazil has no threshold for gaining seats, which means that even the smallest political parties can easily gain representation in the legislature. Indeed, according to measures of the numbers of parties and their relative size, Brazil has the world's most fragmented party system.[17] There is widespread dissatisfaction with open-list PR, but reform has proved elusive. The legislature rejected a 2007 proposal to adopt closed lists. In 2011, the Senate created a political reform committee to propose an overhaul of the electoral system. However, Brazil's major political parties are divided over what type of system to adopt.

While Brazil's electoral system for the legislature makes it hard to form legislative majorities, its system of electing presidents guarantees that presidents enjoy majority support. If no candidate wins a majority of the vote in the first round (which has been the norm since 1985), a second round of balloting takes place between the top two first-round contenders.

Districts for both houses of the legislature are the 26 states plus the federal district. For the lower house, the number of legislators per district is determined roughly according to population and ranges from a low of 8 to a maximum of 70. This minimum allocation has overrepresented the least populated (and most conservative) sectors of Brazil and has underrepresented urban Brazil, but attempts to change the allocation have been blocked by representatives of all parties from the overrepresented regions.[18] Because each Brazilian state also sends three senators to Congress, this system has, as in the United States, added to the overrepresentation of sparsely populated, rural, and generally more conservative states.

Local Government

Brazil is a large and diverse country, and since colonial times there has been tension between control by the federal government and the desire for regional autonomy. For much of Brazil's history, local authorities have enjoyed considerable autonomy, but during the Estado Nôvo and the military regime, the pendulum swung decisively toward the federal government. During the transition to democracy, Brazil's first directly elected heads of government were the state governors chosen in 1982. Brazil's new democracy has firmly reestablished the principle of **robust federalism**, and Brazilian federalism devolves more power to the states than most other federal systems.[19]

Each of Brazil's 26 states (plus the federal district) has an elected governor and a unicameral legislature. Since 1997, governors can be reelected to a second term. Brazilian states are further divided into more than 5,000 *municípios* ("municipalities"), similar to U.S. counties, that are governed by elected mayors and elected councils. Brazilian states have historically owned their own banks and have even run some industries. The constitution allocates to state and local governments a huge chunk of all federal tax revenue. State governors have been largely free to spend as they please, and many states have run up huge debts with the federal government. In 1998, the governor of the powerful state of Minas Gerais, former president Itamar Franco, stopped repayment of his state's massive debt (over $15 billion) to the federal government, thereby provoking a severe budgetary crisis. Brazil differs from most other federal systems in that the constitution of 1988 does not spell out specific spending responsibilities in areas such as health and education. Nor did the constitution regulate the spending of state banks, which have historically funded excessive spending at the state level.

Governors and mayors of big cities thus have a lot of money to use to help federal legislators gain election. Those legislators, in turn, work at the federal level to promote pork-barrel federal spending on infrastructure projects for their states. Some of those expenditures have ended up in the pockets of corrupt local officials.

Beginning in the Collor de Mello administration, the federal government began to reassert itself vis-à-vis the states, intervening in (and in some cases privatizing) the state banking systems. The federal government forced some states to sell state-owned utilities and rein in state spending. During the two terms of President Cardoso, states and municipalities were forced to assume a greater portion of welfare spending. The 2000 Fiscal Responsibility Law further limited state and local spending by specifically preventing the federal government from refinancing state government debt.[20] Nevertheless, much of Brazilian politics can still be seen as the politics of the governors; Brazilian presidents must negotiate with powerful state governors, much as they must bargain with Brazil's fractious legislature.

Other Institutions

THE MILITARY AND THE POLICE

We have seen that Brazil's military played an important role in its domestic politics. From the late nineteenth century until 1964, the military acted mainly as an arbiter, intervening in politics to depose leaders it found unacceptable and then returning to the barracks, handing power over to the civilians.

By the mid-1960s, however, the military no longer saw itself as a simple arbiter of domestic conflict. Its officer corps, trained at the influential U.S.-supported Superior War College during the Cold War, began to view its role as a domestic guardian of order against the "foreign" ideological threats of socialism and communism. Many of these ideas were fused into a national security doctrine, which focused the military's attention domestically and deflected it from threats on Brazil's borders. Not only were the military elite trained in war strategy, but increasingly they also gained expertise in public administration and economics. By 1964, military leaders believed that Brazil's democratic regime, with its weak and polarized parties, had become chaotic and would be susceptible to communist subversion. Between 1964 and 1985, Brazil's military held power directly, in an alliance with conservative business elites and technocrats and, at least initially, with the tacit support of the upper and middle classes. Military officials participated directly in key sectors of the economy, such as the nuclear industry and arms production.

Indeed, Brazil's democratic transition in the 1970s was led mostly by the military, which after two decades of rule was eager to leave economic problems to the civilians to solve. Because military leaders controlled the transition to democracy, there were no attempts to bring Brazilian military officials to justice for destroying democracy or for engaging in widespread human rights abuses. The military was able to pressure the transitional government to pass a widespread amnesty for members of the armed forces.[21]

As a result, Brazil's military continues to be a powerful arm of the state and has far more autonomy than the military in most other advanced democracies. Article 142 of the constitution calls on the military to guarantee law and order. At the same time, democratic governments, beginning with that of President Collor de Mello, have cut military budgets (which are now among the lowest in Latin America), purged military leaders most closely connected to the authoritarian regime, redeployed troops away from population centers, and removed the military from cabinet and top bureaucratic posts. The military's national security doctrine was replaced by a new policy that focuses almost entirely on foreign threats, especially to Brazil's vast and porous Amazon borders. Some Brazilians who were victims of the military's human rights abuses have received compensation, and the resulting publicity has further eroded the image of the military.

The two Cardoso administrations continued to assert state control over the armed forces by creating a single civilian Ministry of Defense to replace ministries that had existed for each branch. Upon his election, President da Silva tested the loyalty of the armed forces by canceling the costly purchase of fighter jets, which had been a pet project of the military. But overall, he increased military spending and committed Brazilian troops to high-profile UN peacekeeping missions. In 2009, da Silva signed a decree establishing a Truth Commission to investigate torture, killings, and disappearances during the military regime. The military leadership reacted angrily, and the heads of the three branches of Brazil's armed forces (along with the civilian defense minister) threatened to resign, forcing the president to scrap his proposal. President Dilma Rousseff, who was jailed and tortured during the military regime, swore in a seven-member Truth Commission in 2011. In December 2014, the Commission produced a final report documenting 434 political murders and thousands more cases of torture and other abuses. It recommended that 100 military perpetrators still living be tried for human rights violations, but these recommendations have not been acted upon, and the Brazilian military refuses to apologize for its behavior during the military dictatorship.

Brazil's police forces, however, have continued to be a subject of concern among human rights experts, who have noted the high levels of "state violence" perpetrated against Brazil's poorest citizens. State governments control their own civil police forces (which mainly investigate crimes) and military police forces (which are uniformed and armed). The military police, like the military itself, are governed by their own judicial system, which has in practice allowed the police to act outside the law. Off-duty officers are often hired by business owners to kill homeless street dwellers, and many of the dead have been children. The large number of such killings has exceeded the number of deaths caused by the military during the two decades of authoritarian rule, leading one observer to call Brazil an "ugly democracy."[22] There are also serious concerns about the ability of Brazil's police to maintain order. Brazil's murder rate is twice that of the United States, and private security guards outnumber the almost 500,000 military police. A wave of gang violence has further eroded public confidence in the police. In 2015, only about a third of Brazilians surveyed expressed confidence in the police.[23]

Political Conflict and Competition

The Party System and Elections

Brazil's party system has perhaps been the most vilified aspect of the country's democratic regime. Brazil has a fragmented multiparty system with weak and fickle political parties, due largely to the electoral laws described earlier.[24]

Twenty-eight parties currently hold seats in the lower house of the legislature, and seven gained over 5 percent of the vote in the 2014 election. Opinion research consistently shows extremely low levels of party identification and low public confidence in parties.[25] The weakness of political parties complicates presidents' attempts to find a majority to support their legislative proposals. Before she was forced to step down in 2016, President Rousseff presided over an informal coalition of nine parties. The president's need to bargain regularly with a number of parties has only increased the pork-barrel aspects of the Brazilian political system and has often made it hard to implement tough decisions, such as reductions in state spending. It has also contributed to the numerous corruption scandals that have plagued the legislature. Since her party had so few seats in the legislature, when Rousseff lost the support of her major coalition partners, she was easily impeached.

Historically, Brazil's parties have been highly personalistic—based on the leadership of a powerful or charismatic individual instead of on an ideology. The military regime attempted to create a "modern" two-party system by fiat, but the two official parties did not survive the transition to democracy. Instead, the transition gave rise to an even greater proliferation of political parties. Today, the weakness of those parties' ideological components is evident in the large number of party members who, after being elected, change affiliation or leave to create new parties.[26] This activity has occurred most often after the election of a president from another party, prompting legislators to switch to the governing party to ensure their access to patronage. In the legislature elected in 2002, for example, 195 of 413 deputies switched parties, and over the past 16 years, 36 percent of legislators switched parties. In 2007, Brazil's courts upheld rules that will limit the ability of parliamentarians to switch parties.

Another serious problem is the sheer number of political parties and their lack of internal discipline. In 2014, the biggest party, President Rousseff's Workers' Party (PT), was in fact quite small: it won only 14 percent of the vote and about the same percentage of seats in the Chamber of Deputies. Legislators respond far more to local barons, government incentives, and pork-barrel opportunities than to their party leadership. Since Brazilian electoral laws allow candidates to run as members of a party without approval of the party leadership (in Brazil, any elected member of the legislature is guaranteed a place on the ballot in the following election), there is little incentive for party loyalty. Moreover, Brazil's powerful federalism further weakens party cohesion: it is common for legislators to vote across party lines with members of their state delegations to support legislation of local interest. President Rousseff discovered firsthand how difficult it can be to govern with such an unwieldy

Composition of the Brazilian Legislature after the 2014 Elections

PARTY	CHAMBER OF DEPUTIES		SENATE	
	# OF SEATS	% OF SEATS	# OF SEATS	% OF SEATS
PT*	70	13.6	12	14.8
PMDB*	66	12.8	18	22.2
PSDB	54	10.5	10	12.3
PSD*	37	7.2	3	3.7
PP*	36	7.0	5	6.1
PR*	34	6.6	4	4.9
PSB	34	6.6	7	8.6
DEM	22	4.2	5	6.1
Others	160	31.5	17	21.3
Total	513	100	81	100

*Parties that supported the government of President Dilma Rousseff until her impeachment.

Key to Party Acronyms:
 DEM: Democrats
 PMDB: Party of the Brazilian Democratic Movement
 PP: Progressive Party
 PR: Party of the Republic
 PSB: Brazilian Socialist Party
 PSD: Social Democratic Party
 PSDB: Brazilian Social Democracy Party
 PT: Workers' Party

Sources: www2.camara.leg.br/camaranoticias/noticias/POLITICA/475427-PT-E-PMDB-ELEGEM-NOVAMENTE-AS
-MAIORES-BANCADAS.html and http://g1.globo.com/politica/eleicoes/2014/blog/eleicao-em-numeros/post/pt-e-pmdb
-encolhem-mas-mantem-maiores-bancadas-no-congresso-psdb-cresce-na-camara.html (accessed 12/3/14).

coalition when most of her allies abandoned her in May 2011 to approve measures weakening Brazil's protection of the Amazon rain forest.

Given the large number of political parties, it is not surprising that Brazilian parties run the gamut from right to left.

The **Workers' Party (PT)** is Latin America's most important party of the left and has been the most important Brazilian political party since the election of da Silva in 2002.[27] It was founded in 1980 mainly among unionized industrial workers but has grown to incorporate landless workers, rural unions, and other disaffected Brazilians. It has also attracted significant support from educated middle-class Brazilians. It claims to represent Brazil's poor, and it advocates social democracy. Compared with most of Brazil's parties, the PT has practiced a high degree of internal democracy and has had fewer defections and splits, although the party has always had radical and more moderate factions. Da Silva was elected in 2002 partly on the PT's reputation for honesty and clean government. That reputation was badly tarnished, however, by a series of corruption scandals in 2005 and 2006. The party lost some seats in Congress as a result, but it rebounded spectacularly in 2010. A large number of corruption scandals, discontent over public spending to support Brazil's hosting of the World Cup and Olympic Games, and a slowing economy led voters to punish the PT again in 2014. Not only did the party lose votes and seats in elections to both houses of Congress, but President Rousseff also won reelection by a very narrow margin over her center-right opponent. The future of the PT is very much in doubt since Rousseff was impeached in 2016, and her predecessor, da Silva, was convicted on charges of corruption in 2017.

The dominant cleavage in the Brazilian electorate has been region, rather than social class. The rural, conservative northeast is often pitted against the more progressive and urban south and southeast. The 2002 presidential election generally followed this pattern: da Silva was most strongly supported in Brazil's southeastern urban areas, and his opponent, José Serra, drew his vote disproportionately from the rural northeast. Interestingly, Brazil's severe class inequality does not appear to have affected the outcome of that race. Da Silva did equally well among poor and wealthy Brazilians. In the 2006 presidential elections, poor northeasterners shifted their support to da Silva, due mainly to his targeted social spending. In legislative elections, however, the PT has been slower to make inroads in the northeast. This pattern has remained stable through the 2014 elections, when the PT's Rousseff won a majority of the vote in Brazil's poorer north and fared much worse in its more prosperous south.

Despite its roots as a radical working-class party, the PT has clearly established itself in government as a moderate center-left force. Given the fragmentation of the Brazilian party system, presidents da Silva and Rousseff were forced to ally with parties to the right of the PT, and this helped pull the PT to the political center.

Although some had hoped that the major parties were beginning to consolidate and become more disciplined, the party system is still very badly fragmented. The PT never won anywhere near a majority in the legislature despite winning four consecutive presidential elections. With Rousseff's 2016 impeachment and da Silva's conviction on corruption charges, the PT's future is very much in question.

Brazil has numerous other leftist parties, and only some have supported the PT. For example, the Democratic Labor Party (PDT) was founded late in the Brazilian military dictatorship by the brother-in-law of João Goulart, the leftist president deposed by the military in 1964, and it has been a steady ally of the PT.

THE BRAZILIAN CENTER

The two main centrist parties are the Party of the Brazilian Democratic Movement (PMDB) and the Brazilian Social Democracy Party (PSDB). Both parties include a mix of free-market conservatives and social democrats, and neither has a clear ideological orientation. The PMDB was the most important pro-democracy opposition party in the years of the transition and played a critical role in the move toward direct elections and a new constitution. Today, the PMDB is a classical "catchall" political party, best viewed as a pragmatic coalition of regional party bosses. More than any Brazilian party, it is a party based on clientelism. It is currently the biggest party in the legislature; it has almost twice as many members as the PT; and it controls the largest number of governorships, state legislatures, and local governments. The PMDB has had cabinet positions in most governments since the return of democracy and was an important, though ultimately unreliable, ally of presidents da Silva and Rousseff. Under Rousseff, the vice president and the heads of both houses of Congress were PMDB members. Vice President Michel Temer became acting president in April 2016, when PMDB members of the legislature supported impeachment proceedings against Rousseff. Despite the tremendous political clout of the PMDB, Temer is the first PMDB member to become president since 1985. However, like the PT, the PMDB has been dogged by allegations of corruption. In July 2016, the PMDB's Eduardo Cunha was forced to resign as speaker of the lower house over allegations that he had accepted millions of dollars in bribes (he was sentenced to 15 years in prison in 2017), and numerous other party members, including President Temer, have been accused of corruption. Since taking office, Temer has had some success passing economic austerity measures, but he has also been accused of being out of touch with Brazilian society, and his cabinet included no women or Afro-Brazilians. By June 2017, his approval rating had plummeted to 7 percent, lower than any approval rating given to his predecessor, Dilma Rousseff.

The PSDB is the party of former two-term president **Fernando Henrique Cardoso**. Cardoso and other prominent PMDB members bolted to form the PSDB in protest over the PMDB's patron-client politics. The PSDB initially distinguished itself as a social-democratic alternative to the PMDB, but since Cardoso's two terms in office, it has been more closely associated with free-market reforms. Its presidential candidates in the 2010 and 2014 presidential election lost to Dilma Rousseff in the second round of voting. The PSDB is the third biggest party in the legislature, and it controls five governorships. Together with the DEM, discussed next, the PSDB has become a mainstay of the opposition.

THE BRAZILIAN RIGHT

The most important party of the right, the Democrats (DEM; called the Liberal Front Party until 2007) grew out of the two "official" parties tolerated during the military regime. The DEM is a free-market, pro-business party, differing from parties of the center mainly in its opposition to land reform and its conservative stand on social issues. The DEM is currently the fourth-largest party in the legislature and in recent years has been in opposition, allied with centrist parties. It has been one of the strongest critics of the center-left governments of the PT.

In 2011, a faction of the party broke away to form the Social Democratic Party (PSD), and while it is a center-right party like the DEM, since its creation it has formed part of the government's legislative majority. A number of smaller parties of the right regularly win seats in the legislature. The Progressive Party (PP) has its roots among the supporters of Brazil's military regime and is a free-market, pro-business party. Nevertheless, like the PSD, the PP has been a willing legislative ally of the current leftist government. The Party of the Republic (PR) has drawn a lot of support from Brazilian evangelicals.

OTHER PARTIES

Many citizens of advanced democracies think about Brazil mainly because of concern about its large Amazon rain forest. However, environmentalism has yet to become a strong movement in Brazil. The Green Party (PV), led by Marina Silva, won under 4 percent of the vote and 15 deputies in the lower house in 2010. Silva is a well-known environmental activist who was President da Silva's minister of the environment from 2003 to 2008, when she resigned in protest over the PT's weak commitment to environmental issues. More recently, Silva joined the center-left Brazilian Socialist Party (PSB) and agreed to run for vice president in 2014 on the PSB ticket. When the PSB's presidential candidate died in a plane crash, she took his place and won almost a quarter of the vote in the first round of elections. The Green Party suffered from Silva's defection, winning only 2 percent of the vote and losing almost half its lower house seats in the 2014 legislative elections.

Civil Society

Democratization in Brazil led to a mushrooming of civil society, which had been stifled during the military regime. Membership in urban and rural trade unions grew quickly. The growth of decentralized Protestant religious groups, many with a conservative political agenda, helped to reinvigorate civil society. A host of environmental, human rights, and women's groups emerged as well. Opinion research shows that well over half of Brazilians say they belong to some sort of civil society organization.[28] In short, Brazil has a vibrant civil society.

Although the return of democracy gave rise to women's rights groups, women remain fairly marginal in Brazilian politics. Brazil's rapid industrialization has greatly increased the percentage of women in the workforce (now estimated at about 40 percent), but women are still paid far less than their male counterparts. Laws have been passed to try to increase women's representation in government. In 1998, Congress stipulated that 20 percent of the seats in the federal legislature must be held by women. The presidency of da Silva, whose PT integrated numerous women's groups, inspired new hopes for more equal representation, as did the election of Brazil's first female president in 2010.

Brazil's largest social movement is the **Landless Workers Movement (MST)**, a peasant organization that has fought for land reform. It has advocated legal change but has often supported and even organized peasant seizure of uncultivated, privately owned land.[29] This activism has been opposed, often violently, by Brazil's powerful landlords, often with the support of the police forces and the tacit tolerance of the rural courts. Hundreds of MST workers have been killed for trying to address Brazil's extremely unequal landholding patterns. Still, MST pressure has resulted in a major redistribution of land to peasants.

Despite centuries of church support for the most conservative elements of Brazilian society, the Roman Catholic Church in Brazil played an essential role in mobilizing civil society to protest the military regime. Spurred by changes in Rome, especially the Second Vatican Council (1962–65), much of the Brazilian Catholic Church, including some of the hierarchy, embraced a new interpretation of the role of religion. **Liberation theology**, which developed in the 1960s among a group of Catholic intellectuals that included numerous Brazilians, held that the church should use its power and prestige to teach the poor how to improve their lives immediately, in both physical and spiritual terms. Liberation theology advocated organizing small neighborhoods called **Christian base communities**, often in rural areas or urban favelas, not only for prayer but also to learn about and advocate for political and social justice. These base communities were often led by "lay priests" who directly challenged the traditional church hierarchy. The National Conference of Brazilian Bishops was for a time a leading advocate of liberation theology and was a major advocate of democratization, land reform, and human rights.

Former president Rousseff laments that widespread protests in the summer of 2013 hurt Brazil's image as it prepared to host the 2014 World Cup.

Society

Ethnic and National Identity

Brazil has an extremely diverse population that has emerged from a blending of Native Americans, African slaves, and Europeans. Unlike much of Spanish America and the United States during their colonial periods, a significant amount of intermarriage took place among racial groups in Brazil. Today, around 40 percent of Brazilians consider themselves to be of mixed race, and 80 percent claim some African ancestry.

Brazilians have a complex vocabulary to describe the rainbow of skin colors, ranging from *preto* ("black") to *mulato claro* ("light brown"). Despite the Brazilian myth of racial democracy, there is an extremely strong association between skin color and wealth. Wealthy Brazilians tend to be lighter skinned, and blacks are disproportionately present among Brazil's poor.[30] Relatively few blacks are found at the highest level of business or government. Blacks or mixed-race Brazilians are twice as likely to be unemployed, and whites earn on average 57 percent more than do Brazilians of color.[31]

Race was not a prominent political topic in Brazil until President Fernando Henrique Cardoso brought it to the national agenda in the 1990s. Cardoso was a sociologist whose doctoral dissertation focused on race in Brazil. Claiming that "Brazilians live wrapped in the illusion of racial democracy," he began a national

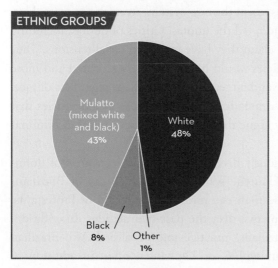

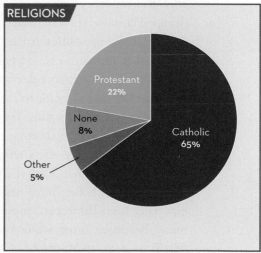

dialogue on affirmative action before and during his administration. Cardoso enacted measures to redress the problem, including quotas for Afro-Brazilians in some government ministries and the diplomatic corps. President da Silva redoubled this effort, creating a cabinet-level "secretary for the promotion of racial equity" and appointing a record number of Afro-Brazilians to government posts, including the first-ever black Supreme Court justice.

The most controversial aspect of affirmative action in Brazil has been the imposition of admissions quotas for Afro-Brazilians at some public universities.[32] Admissions to Brazilian universities are fiercely competitive (only about 8 percent of college-age Brazilians attend university), and traditionally about 65 percent of those admitted attend the exclusive private high schools that better prepare students for grueling college entrance exams. As a result, two-thirds of those admitted typically come from the wealthiest 20 percent of the population.[33]

Racially based admissions quotas were first attempted in 2001, when the state of Rio de Janeiro adopted a 40 percent quota for state universities. More than 300 lawsuits were filed, alleging that applicants with higher test scores were being denied application in favor of those with lower scores. A federal Law of Social Quotas passed in 2012 required all federal universities to reserve spots for students of African descent. Today, over 70 percent of public universities have some sort of affirmative action policy.

Racial quotas have provoked fierce debate within Brazil. Critics say it is virtually impossible to know who is black in a country where 80 percent of Brazilians have some African ancestry. Some black students with high enough test scores to enter the university without quotas resent the new system. Average test scores have dropped at universities that have adopted the quotas. Critics of quotas, including the two major opposition parties, claim they have increased racial tensions. They believe that affirmative action policies would be more widely accepted and more effective if they were more flexible and targeted poor Brazilians regardless of race. Defenders of quotas point to the dramatic increase in blacks at universities that formerly were mostly white. They argue that the debate about racial discrimination is healthy and long overdue.

Brazil has also become a religiously diverse country after centuries of domination by the Roman Catholic Church. While the vast majority of Brazilians claim to be Catholic, Brazil has seen an extraordinary explosion of Protestants, especially from Pentecostal movements, over the past two decades. In addition, many Brazilians (even white Brazilians) practice one of several Afro-Brazilian religions, such as Macumba, Candomblé, or Umbanda, often in addition to Catholicism.

Ideology and Political Culture

Has Brazil developed a democratic political culture in its almost three decades of post-military democratic rule? In the early years of Brazilian democracy, surprisingly large percentages of Brazilians expressed support for authoritarian rule, but the economic growth and redistribution over the last decade has changed the way Brazilians view democracy. In 2015, despite massive corruption scandals and widespread protests against the government, 69 percent of Brazilians reported that democracy was preferable to any other system; this figure has increased from only 30 percent in 2001.

Brazilians have fluctuated in their overall satisfaction with democracy. In 2001, only 20 percent were very or somewhat satisfied with democracy in Brazil, but that figure rose to 50 percent in 2010.[34] More recently, however, satisfaction with democracy has plummeted—in 2015, only 21 percent of Brazilians surveyed expressed satisfaction. Since then, numerous corruption scandals and the impeachment of President Rousseff have led to even more dissatisfaction with Brazil's democracy.

Despite massive inequalities, Brazil's citizens are not deeply polarized in terms of their ideology. Relatively few Brazilians identify themselves as being on the far left or right, and the vast majority of Brazilians locate their ideology as being center, center-right, or center-left.[35]

Confidence in Brazilian Institutions, 2015

INSTITUTION	PERCENTAGE EXPRESSING A LOT OF CONFIDENCE
Church	37.8
Armed forces	18.8
Judiciary	5.6
Congress	3.4
Government	3.1
Political parties	1.0

Source: www.latinobarometro.org (accessed 7/6/16).

Political Economy

Beginning with Estado Nôvo and continuing through the military regime, Brazil's political economy could be described as capitalist but also heavily statist. Over the years, Brazil's state, through the implementation of import substitution industrialization policies, has played a major role in the economy by limiting imports, regulating credit and wages, controlling the currency, and even owning and operating sectors of the economy. Statist policies have often resulted in spectacular economic growth, as was the case during the so-called economic miracle (1967–73), when annual growth rates averaged 11 percent. But statist policies have also been blamed for a number of problems that have long plagued the Brazilian economy.

Perhaps the most serious problem is inflation. An inflation rate of 90 percent was a major reason for the breakdown of democracy in 1964. The military regime was initially successful at reducing the inflation rate, but inflation still averaged 20 percent during the military period. The rate began to skyrocket in the 1970s due to a rise in oil prices, high interest rates, and heavy state spending. Inflation eroded wages and hurt Brazil's poorest disproportionately.

Another serious problem has been Brazil's debt. Brazil's military regime borrowed heavily from international lenders, and despite rapid growth rates, its foreign indebtedness grew. After the return of democracy, Brazil continued to be burdened by high levels of foreign debt. In 2002, to avoid defaulting on its debt, Brazil was forced to borrow heavily from the International Monetary Fund (IMF). However, in recent years Brazil's export-led rapid growth has reduced its indebtedness significantly. President da Silva paid off Brazil's debt to the IMF early, saving the country almost a billion dollars in interest payments. In 2008, international credit rating agencies judged Brazil's debt to be "investment grade" for the first time in the country's history, a sign that Brazil was moving rapidly toward financial stability. In 2011, Brazil's finances were so healthy that it pledged to loan money to the IMF to help struggling economies.

Finally, there is the problem of unemployment. Brazil's rapid economic growth has reduced unemployment, but a large sector of the population remains jobless. And joblessness is a chief cause of the country's endemic poverty and inequality. As a result, a large portion of Brazil's population (perhaps as much as two-thirds of the active workforce) makes its living in the informal sector.[36] As recently as 1995, one survey reported that over half of Brazil's workers did not contribute to the national social security system because they were not employed in a legally regulated job. The persistence of such a large informal sector deprives the state of needed tax revenue and, more important, deprives informal-sector workers of many welfare benefits.

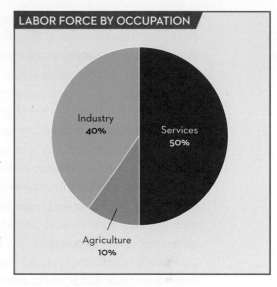

LABOR FORCE BY OCCUPATION

Industry 40%

Services 50%

Agriculture 10%

Democratization has addressed some but certainly not all of Brazil's economic problems. Democratic governments began a gradual reduction of the role of the state in Brazil's economy, but liberalization in Brazil has not been as extensive as it has been in much of the rest of Latin America. Compared with its Latin American neighbors, the Brazilian state still has a relatively large presence in the economy. However, starting with the presidency of Fernando Collor de Mello (1989–92), the role of the state in the economy has been curtailed and protective tariffs have been reduced. During Fernando Henrique Cardoso's two terms (1995–2002), the country undertook a major policy of privatization of state assets, ending the state monopoly in a number of key economic sectors, including energy and telecommunications. Under Cardoso, rules governing foreign investment in the Brazilian economy were liberalized. During the presidencies of da Silva (2003–10) and Rousseff (2011–16), virtually all of those market-friendly policies were continued.

By 2013, after a decade of steady growth and low inflation, the Brazilian economy had begun to stagnate, inflation began to increase, and Brazil's public debt began to grow. The economy was a central issue in the 2014 presidential elections. The two main opponents to President Rousseff were trained economists, and both were critics of Rousseff's handling of the economy. By 2016, Brazil's inflation rate was over 12 percent, its gross domestic product (GDP) had shrunk for two consecutive years, and the unemployment rate approached 7 percent.

Overall, aggregate economic growth in the early years of democratization did not attain the spectacular rates achieved during the economic miracle. Between 1980 and 1990, average GDP per capita fell 0.41 percent; and between 1990 and 2000, it grew by an average rate of 1.13 percent. However, during the two Cardoso administrations, inflation was eventually reduced to single digits (8.5 percent on average between 1995 and 2002). During the da Silva administration, continued fiscal conservatism and skyrocketing commodity export prices helped strengthen the economy.

Despite impressive records of aggregate growth, the most troublesome feature of Brazil's economy is its endemic poverty and persistently high levels of inequality. In recent years, Brazilian governments have enacted policies that have slowly but steadily reduced Brazil's infamous inequality, but Brazil is still among the world's most unequal countries. Brazil's ranking in the 2016 UN Human Development Index now stands at 79th, below Iran (69th), Mexico (77th), and Russia (49th).

Nowhere are Brazil's poverty and inequality more evident than in education. In the first decade of Brazilian democracy, the average number of school years completed was only 3.8, and the vast majority of Brazilians never completed primary school. Only 1 percent of Brazilians attended university. The Cardoso, da Silva, and Rousseff administrations increased spending on Brazil's education system and produced marked improvement, but a disproportionate amount of state spending continues to be directed toward a higher education system that benefits the economically advantaged.

Brazil's health care system also reflects the country's massive poverty and inequality. Since 1987, all Brazilians have been formally entitled to public health care, but access and quality are very uneven. Brazil still has one of the highest infant mortality rates in the world—higher than those in China, Mexico, and Russia. Its life expectancy is lower than China's and Mexico's. About one-third of the population lacks access to clean water.

Inadequate housing is yet another symptom and cause of poverty and inequality. The military regime did little to address housing needs, and despite increased spending on housing under the democratic governments, it is estimated that Brazil has more than 3,500 favelas, whose populations range from several thousand to half a million. Cardoso's administrations attempted to alleviate the housing crisis by distributing land to over half a million landless Brazilians, but the crisis remains acute.

The severe economic crisis of 1999, immediately following Cardoso's election to a second term, almost pulled Brazil into an economic depression. The Brazilian currency, the real, suffered 42 percent devaluation; Brazil lost $8 billion of its foreign reserves in one month; and inflation began to reemerge. The economy was rescued by two events: the International Monetary Fund provided a massive aid package, and Cardoso was finally able to pass a social security and pension reform package.

Despite a legacy of significant economic reform, Cardoso was less successful in other areas. His attempt to slim down Brazil's badly bloated state bureaucracy ran into serious opposition in the legislature. Public servants who run the state bureaucracy are relatively privileged labor elites, and their costly pension system strains the Brazilian budget. Brazilians bear a relatively heavy tax burden that is nearly at European levels (about 40 percent of GDP) but has not yet been used to create a European-style welfare state. Brazil does have a national social security system, but it does not cover the large number of informal-sector workers.

The 2002 election of President da Silva raised hopes for a fundamental resetting of economic priorities. Da Silva campaigned on a pledge to end hunger in Brazil. In office, he steered a more cautious course. He rejected further tax increases, though his administration improved tax collection, and his ability to increase social spending was constrained by Brazil's huge debt burden, commitments to state and local governments, and his inability and reluctance to reduce the state bureaucracy.

Despite these obstacles, da Silva's policies to reduce poverty clearly had

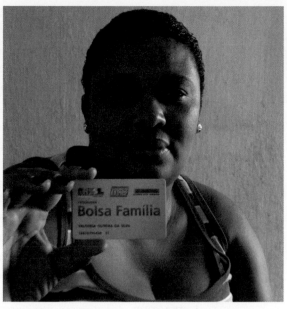

Brazil's poorest citizens use a government-issued ATM card to collect the monthly stipend that is part of the Bolsa Família program.

dramatic success. Between 2003 and 2010, the percentage of Brazilians living in extreme poverty dropped from 15 percent to 7 percent, and 20 million Brazilians were lifted out of poverty.[37] Most important in this regard was the establishment of the **Bolsa Família (Family Fund)**, a conditional cash transfer program.[38] In 2003, da Silva merged several antipoverty programs into the Bolsa Família, which pays monthly small cash stipends to Brazil's poorest families on the condition that recipients' children attend school and receive medical attention. The federal government makes payments directly to a family debit card that is usually held by the mother of the family. By the end of 2013, the program had reached almost 14 million families (a quarter of Brazil's population) and is currently the largest targeted welfare program in the world. Together with other policies such as a 50 percent increase in the minimum wage, the result was a dramatic drop in poverty and a steady reduction in inequality.

The program paid political dividends as well. Da Silva's political base was traditionally in the wealthier and more industrialized southeast of Brazil, and residents of the impoverished north and northeast usually voted for conservative parties dominated by machine politicians. After 2006, however, voters in the north and northeast (where the Bolsa Família benefited about half the population) overwhelmingly supported da Silva and his successor, Rousseff. President Rousseff continued to fund the program, and acting president Michel Temer, a conservative, approved increases in the program in 2016.[39]

Brazil has become a major exporter and currently has a large trade surplus. In 2009, its biggest exports were transport equipment and parts and metallurgical products, followed by soybeans, bran, and oil. Its export markets are fairly diversified; the United States, China, and Argentina are the top three export destinations.[40] Fueled by high commodity export prices, the center-left governments of da Silva and Rousseff were able to maintain market-friendly political-economic policies while dramatically increasing social spending. As a result, Brazil has become a more prosperous and more equal society over the last two decades. According to a 2010 poll, over 60 percent of Brazilians were confident that their country was making economic progress—the highest rate in all Latin America.[41] By 2013, that figure had dropped almost 20 percentage points, partly explaining the outbreak of political protests in the summer of that year. By 2015, only 16 percent of Brazilians expressed confidence that the economy was making progress.

When the conservative Michel Temer became president in 2016, after Rousseff's impeachment, he moved quickly to address Brazil's worsening economic crisis. Temer proposed a package of austerity measures, including a dramatic cut in public spending and a major pension reform.

Our discussion of Brazil's political economy would be incomplete without some mention of the environment, since Brazil's leadership has often viewed economic development and the environment as incompatible. Brazil's military regime made economic development a clear priority over environmental protection, and it promoted a policy of harnessing the vast Amazon interior for agricultural development.

The election of President da Silva, who proclaimed himself Brazil's first green president, was viewed as a watershed event. Once in power, however, da Silva's government bitterly disappointed environmentalists while angering pro-development forces. To the chagrin of the business sector, da Silva appointed Marina Silva, a lifelong advocate of rain forest preservation, as environment minister. The government established more than 60 forest reserves, putting vast tracts of forest off-limits to development. Laws against illegal logging were more effectively enforced. Brazil proposed a plan in which the international community would pay Brazil to preserve the area.

Yet environmentalists argued that deforestation actually increased during the da Silva administration, and they noted that forest preserves were created that could not be policed. They warned that agricultural interests increasingly

Reducing Inequality and Poverty in Brazil, 1990–2016

	1990	2000	2016
Average number of years of schooling	3.8	5.6	7.7
GDP growth rate	-4.4	4.3	-3.8
Gini index	61	59	52
Infant mortality rate per 1,000 live births	51.4	28.9	12.3
Life expectancy	66.3	70.2	75.5
Literacy rate	74.6	90.0	92.6
Percentage of population below international poverty line	16.2	10.2	3.8
Poverty rate	41.9	35.2	21.4
Unemployment rate	3.7	9.3	7.5

Note: Data provided are for the year indicated or the closest year for which data are available.
Sources: United Nations Development Indicators, http://hdr.undp.org (accessed 6/29/16); CIA World Factbook; and http://ipeadata.gov.br (accessed 5/24/17).

dominated policy making, too readily yielding to pressure by powerful governors of pro-agricultural states. Marina Silva resigned as environment minister in 2008, to protest what she viewed as insufficient government support for environmental protection. She ran for president in 2010 as the candidate for the Green Party, winning almost 20 percent of the vote in the first round.

While Dilma Rousseff pushed for policies to stem the deforestation of the Amazon, she oversaw a major rural electrification program as energy minister during President da Silva's first term. She became a strong advocate for the controversial Belo Monte Hydroelectric Dam, which would be the world's third-largest dam (after Brazil's Itaipu and China's Three Gorges dams). The project has drawn criticism from environmental and indigenous rights groups because it will flood 500 square kilometers of land and displace 20,000 mostly indigenous Brazilians.

The PT governments of da Silva and Rousseff were torn by the struggle among ministers with very different environmental agendas. The legislative coalition supporting those governments included many who favored more rapid development of the Amazon in order to promote agricultural exports. The rapid rise in agricultural commodity prices in 2008, which allowed the da Silva government to spend lavishly on very popular social programs, may have tilted the balance within the administration toward those who favor economic development over environmental protection. In 2014, after a decade of declining rates of deforestation, a spike in illegal logging and cattle ranching led to a 16 percent increase in the rate of deforestation, alarming Brazil's environmental community.[42]

Foreign Relations and the World

Until fairly recently, Brazil did not play the type of role in world politics that might be expected given the size of its territory and economy.[43] Perhaps even more counterintuitive is Brazil's historically somewhat detached attitude toward its Spanish-speaking neighbors. With democratization, and especially since the presidency of Fernando Henrique Cardoso, the country's foreign policy has assumed a higher profile, and Brazil has become an informal leader of the developing world.

The biggest issue in Brazil's foreign affairs is trade relations. Brazil is a major exporter and has sought to create free-trade agreements with its neighbors and with Europe and the United States. To date, the most important trade agreement is **MERCOSUR** (Common Market of the South; MERCOSUL in Portuguese), founded in 1991 by Argentina, Brazil, Paraguay, and Uruguay. Brazil has supported the enlargement of MERCOSUR, and Chile and Bolivia are now associate members. These countries have virtually eliminated tariffs, and within the first decade of MERCOSUR's existence, trade among its members increased spectacularly. Given the power of its industrial sector, Brazil has reaped a windfall with this increased trade, and its trade with MERCOSUR members now accounts for about 11 percent of its total exports. The economic crisis in Argentina and Argentine-Brazilian disputes over currency valuation slowed the momentum of MERCOSUR in the late 1990s, but since then, MERCOSUR trade has slowly recovered.

Brazil has emerged as a world leader in attempts to create international agreements on nuclear proliferation, women's rights, environmental protection, and human rights. The Cardoso administration's successful effort to confront major multinational drug companies and to produce cheap generic medicines to treat HIV/AIDS has been a model for countries in Africa and elsewhere.

The election of da Silva to the presidency in 2002 created new strains in what have been normally strong U.S.-Brazilian relations. The administration of U.S. president George W. Bush was wary of da Silva's socialist ideology and irritated by his warm relations with the populist Venezuelan president Hugo Chávez. As we have seen, U.S. fears about a possibly socialist Brazil proved unfounded; da Silva's administration acted moderately and continued the fiscally conservative policies of his predecessor. Da Silva honored all Brazil's debt commitments, and in December 2002 he made an official state visit to the United States. The two countries worked together to address the political crisis in Venezuela and even collaborated with regards to Colombia despite da Silva's strong opposition to U.S. policy there. In November 2004, Brazil sent 1,200 troops to Haiti as part of a Brazilian-commanded UN peacekeeping mission. It was the biggest Brazilian military deployment since World War II. Brazil has also campaigned for a permanent seat on the UN Security Council.

Despite his moderate domestic policies, da Silva clearly sought to maintain his independence from the United States and to enhance Brazil's global profile. He helped torpedo the U.S.-backed plan for a Free Trade Area of the Americas, preferring to strengthen multilateral organizations such as MERCOSUR, UNASUR (Union of South American Nations, an attempt to create a trading bloc that encompasses all of South America), and **BRICS**—an organization of developing countries including Brazil, Russia, India, China, and South Africa. Da Silva called for a major reform of the United Nations and became a spokesperson for developing countries. He successfully brought a case against the United States in the World Trade Organization to protest U.S. cotton subsidies. Da Silva also refused to criticize Cuba, North Korea, and Iran for human rights violations. In 2009, Brazil faced off with the United States over how to respond to the military coup against the president of Honduras. Da Silva invited Iran's leader, Mahmoud Ahmadinejad, to Brazil and then angered the United States and the European Union when, in May 2010, he attempted to broker an agreement with Iran to resolve the standoff over Iran's nuclear program.

While Dilma Rousseff was a close ally of President da Silva and shared many of his political views, as president she distanced herself from some aspects of da Silva's foreign policy. Rousseff made the promotion of human rights a priority and vocally criticized human rights abuses in Cuba and Iran. When U.S. president Barack Obama visited Brazil in March 2011, many Brazilians saw his visit as an endorsement of Rousseff's more moderate foreign policy stance and a harbinger of improved relations between Brazil and the United States. However, that honeymoon ended in 2013 thanks to revelations that the U.S. National Security Agency had spied on Brazilian government officials (including President Rousseff) and the state oil company. Rousseff canceled a scheduled visit to the United States and later denounced the United States in the United Nations. Rousseff also remained a staunch ally of Venezuela's increasingly authoritarian president, Nicolás Maduro, who is a fierce critic of the United States. By 2015, the U.S.-Brazil relationship had improved, and Rousseff made a state visit to the United States. Rousseff and U.S. president Obama found points of agreement on climate change and new U.S. diplomatic overtures to Cuba and Iran.

CURRENT ISSUES IN BRAZIL

Economic Inequality and Crime

Despite its many advances, Brazilian democracy faces a litany of challenges. First among them is the inequality and poverty that persist even as Brazil has taken enormous economic strides. It remains to be seen whether Brazil's state, especially under the leadership of conservative president Temer, can continue to redirect its energy to improve the lot of its poor majority.

A related challenge is the epidemic of crime, which Brazilians regularly name as one of the country's most serious problems. Brazil's murder rate has doubled since democratization, and Brazil now has one of the highest rates of homicide by guns in the world (about 40,000 Brazilians die from gun violence each year). To a considerable extent, crime is a symptom of Brazil's endemic poverty, persistent inequality, and stubborn unemployment. Much crime in Brazil can be linked to the drug trade that has infested Brazil's favelas. For decades, Brazil's police have generally retreated from the favelas, where they are outnumbered and often

Brazilian security forces occupy the Morro do Alemão favela in Rio de Janeiro in November 2010 after battling with heavily armed drug traffickers.

outgunned. In recent years, however, the government has successfully reasserted control over some of the most notorious favelas.

In July 2004, President da Silva enacted a tough new gun control law, passed by Brazil's legislature after fierce opposition from the country's powerful arms manufacturers. The law tightened rules on gun permits, created a national firearms register, and imposed strict penalties (including a four-year prison term) for possessing an unregistered gun. To reduce gun violence, the Brazilian government has begun purchasing handguns turned in by civilians, and it called a referendum in October 2005 on a proposed ban on handgun sales. The measure was rejected, however, by 63 percent of voters.

In November 2010, 2,700 members of the Brazilian police and military entered Complexo do Alemão, a group of 12 favelas in Rio de Janeiro that were controlled by drug gangs. The security forces dislodged the traffickers, arrested top leaders, and established "pacifying police units" to patrol the favelas. The murder rate has plummeted in favelas where the police have reasserted control, though concern remains that criminals are just being shunted to other communities.

Political Corruption

Even in the context of Latin America, where political corruption is commonplace, Brazilian democracy has been plagued by a nonstop series of high-profile corruption scandals.[44] In the early 1990s, President Fernando Collor de Mello resigned rather than face impeachment for corruption. President Fernando Henrique Cardoso's administration, in an attempt to garner support for an amendment that would allow Brazilian presidents to run for a second term, was found to have offered bribes to legislators. The amendment passed, and Cardoso was reelected.

When da Silva assumed the presidency in 2003, however, there were high hopes that the era of political corruption was over, since his PT enjoyed a reputation as a party of "clean government." Those hopes were soon dashed as the minority PT scrambled to achieve legislative support for the president's agenda. In the notorious *mensalão* ("monthly stipend") scandal of 2005 and 2006, the governing party was found to have paid opposition legislators to vote for the PT agenda, using funds from state-owned enterprises. President da Silva's chief of staff, communications director, and the entire top leadership of the PT were forced to resign (and in 2013 were finally sentenced to prison), but da Silva emerged unscathed and won reelection (though his party lost seats in the legislature). Corruption charges continued into da Silva's second term. In December 2007, the president

A March 2016 demonstration against political corruption. The banner reads "Corrupt Congress."

of the Senate, a close ally of the president, was forced to give up his leadership post because of corruption charges. In 2008, a scandal erupted over misuse by top government officials of government-issued credit cards.

President Rousseff took power in 2011, vowing to attack government corruption. But in her first year in office, seven of her cabinet ministers were forced to resign over allegations of corruption; they included her ministers of the presidency (her chief of staff), defense, and labor. A new wave of corruption allegations emerged from the massive infrastructural expenditures for Brazil's hosting of the 2014 World Cup and the 2016 Olympic Games. In the aftermath of her narrow reelection in October 2014, important members of Rousseff's PT were implicated in a corruption investigation of the state-owned oil firm, Petrobras. In

---

IN COMPARISON

Perceived Corruption, 2016

COUNTRY	SCORE	RANK
Germany	81	10
United Kingdom	81	10
United States	74	18
Japan	72	20
France	69	23
South Africa	45	64
Brazil	40	79
China	40	79
India	40	79
Mexico	30	123
Iran	29	131
Russia	29	131
Nigeria	28	136

Note: On a scale of 1 to 100, a score of 1 = most corrupt; 100 = least corrupt.
Source: "Corruption Perceptions Index," Transparency International, www.transparency.org/cpi2016 (accessed 7/27/17).

February 2015, the top leadership of Petrobras was forced to resign over allegations that the oil company and much of the Brazilian political class had received bribes from Brazil's largest construction conglomerate, Odebrecht, in exchange for state construction contracts. The scandal hit very near the presidency, since at the time of the alleged bribes Rousseff was head of Petrobras. Ironically, Rousseff was impeached in 2016 not because of corruption, but rather because she illegally covered up the presence of budget deficits that might have hurt her 2014 reelection chances. Odebrecht claims that it made large, illegal donations to Rousseff's 2014 presidential campaign. Michel Temer, her replacement as president, has also been dogged by corruption charges. By 2017, a third of Temer's cabinet and almost a third of the members of Brazil's national congress were under investigation for corruption.[45] In May 2017 Brazil's leading newspaper reported that Temer had been recorded recommending the payment of hush money to a jailed fellow party member and a former speaker of the lower house. In June 2017 Brazil's top prosecutor formally charged Temer with accepting bribes in exchange for political favors, leading to calls for his impeachment. Even the highly popular former president da Silva, leading the polls in the run-up to the 2018 presidential elections, was convicted on corruption charges. With President Temer and virtually the entire political class under investigation for accepting illegal campaign contributions from Brazilian businesses (a crime that can lead to prison terms), legislators proposed in 2017 to grant themselves amnesty from charges of campaign finance violations. A former Brazilian Supreme Court chief justice called the proposal "a denial of the rule of law."[46] By 2017, it was clear that the endemic nature of political corruption poses a major threat to Brazilian democracy.

There are many possible explanations for the persistence of corruption in Brazilian politics, but many scholars blame the Brazilian electoral system, which favors a proliferation of weak parties in the legislature and a low level of accountability for individual legislators. In early 2014, Brazil adopted a tough new anticorruption law aimed at addressing the growing public anger over political corruption. It is too early to tell whether the law will have real teeth, because it depends on notoriously corrupt local authorities to enforce its provisions.

NOTES

1.   Two recent overviews of Brazilian politics and society that emphasize Brazil's accomplishments and challenges are Alfred Montero, *Brazil: Reversal of Fortune* (Cambridge, UK: Polity Press, 2014), and Michael Reid, *Brazil: The Troubled Rise of a Global Power* (New Haven, CT: Yale University Press, 2014).

2. "Brazilian Economy Overtakes UK's, Says CEBR," www.bbc.co.uk/news/business-16332115 (accessed 7/5/17).

3. Marshall Eakin, *Brazil: The Once and Future Country* (New York: St. Martin's Press, 1998), 1.

4. Binka Le Breton, *Voices from the Amazon* (Hartford, CT: Kumarian Press, 1993).

5. For an excellent overview, see Alfred Stepan, ed., *Authoritarian Brazil* (New Haven, CT: Yale University Press, 1973).

6. The first attempt to document the abuses under military rule was conducted secretly by the Catholic Church and published as a book titled *Brazil, Never Again,* or *Brasil: Nunca Mais* (São Paulo: Archdiocese of São Paulo, 1985). It became an instant best seller.

7. A number of prominent political scientists have argued that presidentialism has not served Brazil's relatively young democracy well, because it is less flexible and responds less well to crises. See, for example, Juan Linz, "Presidential or Parliamentary Democracy: Does It Make a Difference?" in *The Failure of Presidential Democracy*, ed. Juan Linz and Arturo Valenzuela (Baltimore, MD: Johns Hopkins University Press), 3–87.

8. In 1997, President Fernando Henrique Cardoso was able to push a constitutional amendment through the legislature that allows presidents and state governors to run for a second term. Cardoso became the first president to avail himself of that opportunity and was reelected in 1998.

9. Scott Mainwaring, "Multipartism, Robust Federalism, and Presidentialism in Brazil," in *Presidentialism and Democracy in Latin America*, eds. Scott Mainwaring and Matthew Soberg Shugart (New York: Cambridge University Press, 1997), 55–109.

10. Bolivar Lamounier, "Brazil: An Assessment of the Cardoso Administration," in *Constructing Democratic Governance in Latin America*, ed. Jorge Dominguez and Michael Shifter (Baltimore, MD): Johns Hopkins University Press, 2003), 281.

11. Leslie Armijo, Philippe Faucher, and Magdalena Dembinska, "Compared to What? Assessing Brazil's Political Institutions," *Comparative Politics* 39, no. 6 (2006): 759–86.

12. Angelina Cheibub Figueiredo and Fernando Limongi, "Congress and Decision-Making in Democratic Brazil," in *Brazil since 1985: Economy, Polity, and Society*, eds. Maria D'Alva Kinzo and James Dunkerley (London: Institute of Latin American Studies, 2003), 62–83.

13. Juan Linz and Alfred Stepan, "Crises of Efficacy, Legitimacy, and Democratic State Presence: Brazil," in *Problems of Democratic Transition and Consolidation*, eds. Juan Linz and Alfred Stepan (Baltimore, MD: Johns Hopkins University Press, 1996), 166–89.

14. Latinobarómetro, online data analysis available at www.latinobarometro.org/latino/LATAnal izeQuestion.jsp (accessed 6/24/11). On the Brazilian judiciary, see Fiona Macaulay, "Democratization and the Judiciary: Competing Reform Agendas," in Kinzo and Dunkerley, eds., *Brazil since 1985: Economy, Polity, and Society*, 93–96.

15. Latinobarómetro, online data analysis available at www.latinobarometro.org/latino/LATAnal izeQuestion.jsp (accessed 6/24/11).

16. *Economist,* "Weird Justice," www.economist.com/node/21679861/print (accessed 7/1/16).

17. Michael Reid, *Brazil: The Troubled Rise of a Global Power* (New Haven, CT: Yale University Press, 2014), 267.

18. In 1989, the vote of one citizen of Roraima, a poor northern state, was the equivalent of 33 votes in São Paulo, Brazil's largest state. Timothy Power, "Political Institutions in Democratic Brazil," in *Democratic Brazil: Actors, Institutions, and Processes*, eds. Peter Kingstone and Timothy Power (Pittsburgh, PA: University of Pittsburgh Press, 2000), 27.

19. Scott Mainwaring, "Multipartism, Robust Federalism, and Presidentialism in Brazil," in Mainwaring and Shugart, eds., *Presidentialism and Democracy in Latin America*, 55–109.

20. David Samuels, *Ambition, Federalism, and Legislative Politics in Brazil* (Cambridge, UK: Cambridge University Press, 2003). See p. 161, on spending levels of federal and state governments.

21. Wendy Hunter, *Eroding Military Influence in Brazil: Politicians against Soldiers* (Chapel Hill: University of North Carolina Press, 1997), 42–71.

22. Anthony Pereira, "An Ugly Democracy? State Violence and the Rule of Law in Postauthoritarian Brazil," in Kingstone and Power, eds., *Democratic Brazil: Actors, Institutions, and Processes*, 217–35.

23. See www.latinobarometro.org (accessed 7/6/16).

24. Scott Mainwaring and Timothy Scully, "Introduction: Party Systems in Latin America," in *Building Democratic Institutions: Parties and Party Systems in Latin America*, eds. Scott Mainwaring and Timothy Scully (Stanford, CA: Stanford University Press, 1995), 1–35.

25. A comparative survey in 1997 found that Brazil had the lowest level of party identification in Latin America. See J. Mark Payne, Daniel Zovatto, Fernando Cavillo-Flórez, and Andrés Allamand Zavala, *Democracies in Development: Politics and Reform in Latin America* (Washington, DC: Inter-American Development Bank, 2002), 136.

26. Scott Mainwaring, *Rethinking Party Systems in the Third Wave of Democratization: The Case of Brazil* (Stanford, CA: Stanford University Press, 1999), 140–45.

27. On the Workers' Party, see William Nylen, "The Making of a Loyal Opposition: The Worker's Party (PT) and the Consolidation of Democracy in Brazil," in Kingstone and Power, eds., *Democratic Brazil: Actors, Institutions, and Processes*, 126–43.

28. Latinobarómetro online data analysis, based on a 2008 survey, www.latinobarometro.org /latino/LATAnalizeQuestion.jsp (accessed 6/24/11).

29. On the MST, see Miguel Carter, "The Landless Rural Workers Movement and Democracy in Brazil," *Latin America Research Review* 45 (Special Issue 2010): 186–217.

30. A good overview of race relations is Bernd Reiter and Gladys Mitchell, eds., *Brazil's New Racial Politics* (Boulder, CO: Lynne Rienner, 2010).

31. Jon Jeter, "Affirmative Action Debate Forces Brazil to Take Look in the Mirror," *Washington Post*, June 16, 2003, A1.

32. João Feres Júnior, Verônica Toste Daflon, and Luiz Augusto Campos, "Lula's Approach to Affirmative Action and Race," *NACLA Report on the Americas* 44, no. 2 (March/April 2011): 34–35.

33. Rodrigo Davies, "Brazil Takes Affirmative Action in Higher Education," *Guardian*, August 4, 2003, 4.

34. As reported in *Economist*, December 2, 2010, www.economist.com/node/17627929 (accessed 7/5/17).

35. Based on 2008 survey data from Latinobarómetro, www.latinobarometro.org/latino/LAT AnalizeQuestion.jsp (accessed 6/24/11).

36. Timothy Power and J. Timmons Roberts, "The Changing Demographic in Context," in Kingstone and Power, eds., *Democratic Brazil: Actors, Institutions, and Processes*, 246.

37. Data on extreme poverty were downloaded from the Instituto de Pesquisa Econômica at www. ipeadata.gov.br (accessed 11/24/14). Data on overall poverty reduction appear in Aaron Ansell, "Brazil's Social Safety Net under Lula," *NACLA Report on the Americas* 44, no. 2 (March/April 2011): 23–26.

38. For an excellent overview, see Fábio Veras Soares, Rafael Perez Ribas, and Rafael Guerreiro Osório, "Evaluating the Impact of Brazil's *Bolsa Família*: Cash Transfer Programs in Comparative Perspective," *Latin American Research Review* 45, no. 2 (2010): 173–90.

39. Simone R. Bohn, "Social Policy and Vote in Brazil: *Bolsa Família* and the Shifts in Lula's Electoral Base," *Latin American Research Review* 46, no. 1 (January 2011): 54–79.

40. *Economist* fact sheet on Brazil, 2009, www.economist.com/node/13564342 (accessed 6/25/11).

41. As reported in *Economist*, December 2, 2010, www.economist.com/node/17627929 (accessed 7/5/17).

42. David Sims, "Brazil: Amazon Deforestation Increases for the First Time in Ten Years," *International Business Times*, December 4, 2014, www.ibtimes.co.uk/brazil-amazon-deforestation-increases-first-time-ten-years-photo-report-1476352#slideshow/1411262 (accessed 12/3/14).
43. A good overview of Brazilian foreign policy is Sean W. Burges, *Brazilian Foreign Policy after the Cold War* (Gainesville: University of Florida Press, 2009).
44. On corruption in Brazil, see Matthew M. Taylor, "Brazil: Corruption as Harmless *Jeitinho* or Threat to Democracy?" in *Corruption and Politics in Latin America*, eds. Stephen D. Harris and Charles Blake (Boulder, CO: Lynne Reiner, 2010), 89–111.
45. For an overview of the corruption charges, see "Disillusionment Grows as Graft Probe Deepens," *Latin American Weekly Report*, April 20, 2017, 8.
46. Simon Romero, "Brazil's Leaders See Way Out of Scandal: Amnesty," *New York Times*, March 15, 2017, www.nytimes.com/2017/03/15/world/americas/brazil-congress-amnesty.html?smprod=nytcore-ipad&smid=nytcore-ipad-share&_r=0 (accessed 3/16/17).

KEY TERMS

abertura The gradual opening of Brazilian politics by the military during the 1970s, a process that eventually led to democratization

Amazon Basin The vast and sparsely populated area of Brazil's interior that is home to the world's largest tropical rain forest

Belindia A term combining *Belgium* and *India*; used to describe Brazil's unique combination of modernity and underdevelopment

Bolsa Família (Family Fund) A Brazilian social welfare program that pays monthly stipends to families when their children receive education and health care

Brasília Brazil's futuristic capital city, created in the barren interior during the 1960s by urban planners

BRICS An organization of emerging developing countries that includes Brazil, Russia, India, China, and South Africa

bureaucratic authoritarian A form of authoritarian rule, common in Latin America during the 1960s and 1970s (in Brazil, in 1964–85), in which military leaders and civilian technocrats presided over conservative anticommunist regimes

caboclo Brazilian of mixed European and indigenous ancestry

Cardoso, Fernando Henrique Brazil's president from 1995 to 2002; he was responsible for significant economic and political reform

Chamber of Deputies (Câmara dos Deputados) The lower house of Brazil's legislature

Christian base communities Small neighborhood groups of progressive Catholics who promoted liberation theology and political activism starting in the 1960s

coalitional presidentialism Term used to described Brazil's political system, in which presidents must cobble together legislative majorities from Brazil's fractious legislature, doling out cabinet and other government posts to coalition members

da Silva, Luiz Inácio Lula Brazil's two-term president from 2003 to 2010 and a member of the leftist Workers' Party (PT); convicted on corruption charges in 2017

Estado Nôvo The populist authoritarian regime of Getúlio Vargas between 1937 and 1945

favelas Brazil's sprawling urban shantytowns

Federal Senate (Senado Federal) The upper house of Brazil's legislature

Federal Supreme Court (Supremo Tribunal Federal) Brazil's highest judicial body

Goulart, João The Brazilian leftist president (1961–64) whose removal by the military began a long period of authoritarian rule

Landless Workers Movement (MST) The large Brazilian social movement that has fought for land reform

liberation theology A radical doctrine within the Catholic Church advocating that the church should act to improve the social and political power of the poor

MERCOSUR (Common Market of the South) A free-trade organization that includes Brazil and some of its neighbors

mulatto A Brazilian of mixed white and black ancestry

National Congress (Congresso Nacional) Brazil's legislature

open-list proportional representation (PR) Brazil's electoral system for legislative elections; allows voters to select individual candidates instead of a party list

populist A type of leader who appeals to the masses and attacks elements of the established elite; in Brazil, the term applies to Getúlio Vargas

robust federalism A system established by Brazil's current constitution, in which states enjoy very strong power

Rousseff, Dilma Brazil's first female president (2011–16), who was impeached in 2016

state corporatism A political system in which citizens are encouraged to participate in state-controlled interest groups

Superior War College The elite Brazilian military academy that professionalized the Brazilian military

Temer, Michel Brazil's conservative president, and vice president under Rousseff, who ascended to the presidency after the impeachment of Rousseff

Vargas, Getúlio The Brazilian populist dictator who presided over the Estado Nôvo (1937–45) and was later elected to office during the Second Republic

Workers' Party (PT) Brazil's most important leftist party, and the party of former president da Silva

WEB LINKS

- IESP-UERJ—Instituto de Estudos Sociais e Politicos, Instituto Universitário de Pesquisas do Rio de Janeiro—an excellent source of online data (www.iesp.uerj.br/welcome-to-iesp-uerj)
- Landless Workers Movement (www.mst.org.br)
- Latin American Network Information Center, an encyclopedic collection of links maintained by the University of Texas, Austin (lanic.utexas.edu/la/brazil)
- Links to major Brazilian periodicals (newslink.org/sabra.html)
- The Workers' Party (www.pt.org.br)

Nelson Mandela's death in December 2013 led to a nationwide outpouring of appreciation for democratic South Africa's founding father. While his funeral was a time to celebrate his legacy, it was also an opportunity for some South Africans to reflect on the failures to implement some of Mandela's vision for a rainbow nation. During his eulogy for Mandela, President Jacob Zuma, who was mired in corruption scandals and faced with charges that his government was neglecting South Africa's impoverished majority, was booed by some audience members.

SOUTH AFRICA

Why Study This Case?

True to its remarkable modern history of tragedy and triumph, South Africa is a nation of paradoxes. The contradictions that constitute South African history and the remarkable capacity of South Africans to face and resolve them make this an intriguing case to study.

South Africa is fascinating for several other reasons as well. Like Russia, it presents two cases in one. Before the early 1990s, South Africa's politics, society, and economy were dominated by the racist authoritarian system known as **apartheid**, or "separateness." In **Afrikaans**, the language spoken by the descendants of the first white settlers, the term refers to policies imposed by the ruling minority regime from 1948 to 1994 that systematically segregated races and privileged white South Africans. But with the collapse of the apartheid regime, the "new" South Africa of the past two decades has been a fascinating petri dish of unfolding multicultural democracy.

South Africa's remarkable and relatively peaceful transition from oppressive minority rule to a broad-based democracy is an even more compelling reason to study this case. Refuting the mid-1990s doomsday predictions of incendiary race wars, the overwhelming majority of South African citizens chose reconciliation over revolution, opting for ballots over bullets as a means of resolving seemingly intractable political differences. This political miracle not only stands in contrast to Africa's dismal record of failed democracies and even failed states but also offers a powerful example to other nations of the world that are plagued by racial, ethnic, and religious strife.

South Africa has taken noteworthy strides since its return to democracy in 1994. Politically, its democratically elected legislature approved a constitution with broad political rights and civil liberties, and its government has convened regular nationwide elections. Socially, South

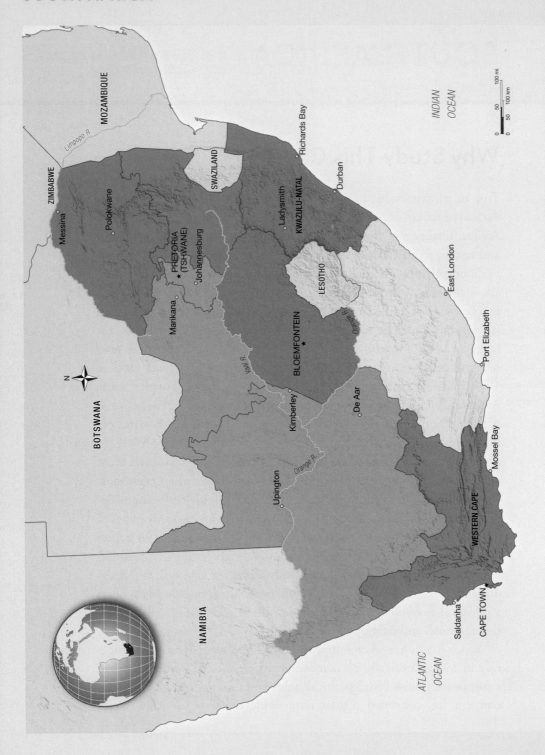

SOUTH AFRICA

Africans vanquished the world's most elaborate and overtly racist authoritarian regime and forged a common nation from its ashes. Economically, the government confounded its critics by avoiding the "easy" path of populist redistribution, instead cutting government expenditures and debt while delivering impressive gains in access to basic necessities for the country's poorest citizens. South Africa's rising international profile was evidenced when, in 2010, it became the first African country to host the FIFA World Cup and again, in 2011, when it became a member of the group of rising developing powers known as **BRICS** (Brazil, Russia, India, China, and South Africa).

Make no mistake, however; this tale of two South Africas cannot yet boast a fairy-tale ending. The decades of political violence, social partition, and economic deprivation that victimized over 80 percent of the population left some horrible and lasting scars. Compounding the legacies of racism and authoritarianism is a host of pernicious social problems, such as rampant violent crime, brooding racial tension, endemic corruption, and the pandemic of HIV/AIDS. As if these challenges were not enough, the remarkable regime change created unmet expectations for rapid economic change and social equality, and there are concerns that democracy has been successful only because post-apartheid governments have faced no serious opposition.

South Africa's leaders must attempt to satisfy rising expectations and must balance decades of pent-up social and economic demands with the requirements of lenders and investors to maintain fiscal discipline and free markets. Without economic growth, the government will lack the means to address South Africa's social and economic problems. The political inclination to promote affirmative action in the workplace must be weighed against the demands of the marketplace. Safeguarding the political rights of all groups in South Africa can at times necessitate overruling the will of the poor majority and resisting the temptation to dispense with democratic niceties.

How can a democratic government fare under such challenging circumstances? As one editorial asked, "How can a . . . revolutionary movement, forged by 40 years of struggle against white supremacy, transform itself into a multiracial ruling party, to run a sophisticated industrial economy? How can a new generation of leaders, without the aura of struggle, restrain the pressures towards populism and maintain a tolerant democracy when so many African governments have so noticeably failed?"[1] This case seeks to address these questions and the historical puzzle of why apartheid, enforced by such a small minority, managed to persist so successfully for so long and how its collapse and replacement came about under relatively peaceful circumstances.

Twenty years after South Africa's transition to a multiracial democracy, there are growing concerns about the lack of political alternation. In May 2014, the African National Congress (ANC) party won its fifth consecutive majority in the legislature, and South Africa's democratic opposition remains relatively weak and fragmented. Can South Africa avoid the negative consequences of single-party political domination (corruption, lack of accountability, and an unequal political playing field) that have plagued other "dominant-party" systems examined in this text (for example, Japan, Mexico, Russia, and China)?

In short, despite its unique history and political experience, South Africa faces many of the same issues and dilemmas as other developing countries. These include coping with the legacies of colonialism and racism, dealing with the policy trade-offs between freedom and equality, and managing the social and economic consequences of crime, poverty, disease, and political corruption. The case of South Africa offers insights into these fundamental issues.

Major Geographic and Demographic Features

Historically, South Africa has been a harsh and isolated region. Ocean currents and the dearth of natural harbors impeded early European settlement of its coastline. Much of western South Africa (with the notable exception of the area around Cape Town) remains drought stricken and unsuitable for agriculture. South Africa's eastern coast and interior are subtropical and more suitable for agriculture, though the soil quality is generally poor. South Africa has no navigable waterways; thus, until modern times, transportation and communication over the vast region were very difficult. These factors limited the growth of a large population in precolonial South Africa.

Today, South Africa has about 49 million inhabitants. Unlike much of the rest of Africa, South Africa has seen its birth rates decline dramatically over the past 25 years, though emigration from South Africa's impoverished neighbors has contributed to considerable population growth. About half of South Africa's population is 24 years of age or younger, explaining why very high rates of youth unemployment (over half of 15- to 24-year-olds are unemployed) have become such a politically charged issue.

Due to the experience of apartheid, it is common to think of South Africa's population as being neatly divided between blacks and whites. This gross simplification obscures a much more heterogeneous ethnic makeup. Eighty percent of South Africans are black, but the ethnic composition of the black population is extremely diverse. About 25 percent of black South Africans are Zulus (the ethnic group of current president **Jacob Zuma**), another 20 percent are Xhosa (the ethnic group of former presidents **Nelson Mandela** and **Thabo Mbeki**), and about 18 percent are Sotho. The Tswana and Tsonga (and to a lesser extent the Venda and Ndebele) groups also have a significant presence in the South African population. Each of these ethnic groups has a different language and is concentrated in a different area. For example, Xhosas predominate in the western part of the country and in Cape Town and Port Elizabeth. Zulus are the dominant group in Durban.

Whites constitute about 9 percent of the overall population, and that population is also divided ethnically. Over 50 percent of whites are **Afrikaners**, descendants of the Dutch, French, and German colonists who arrived in the seventeenth century and developed their own language (Afrikaans) and cultural traditions. Another 40 percent of South Africa's white population is made up of descendants of English settlers who arrived in the eighteenth century. Even today, these "English whites" favor English over Afrikaans and view themselves as somewhat distinct.

South Africans of mixed race account for 9 percent of the population. This group, largely concentrated in the Western Cape Province and KwaZulu-Natal, is widely referred to as **colored**. While colored South Africans would be considered "black" in many countries, including the United States, in the context of South Africa's complex racial history many colored South Africans view themselves as a distinct racial group. Unlike most blacks, for example, most colored South Africans speak Afrikaans as their first language. South Africans of Asian descent, for which South Africans often use the term **Indians**, make up about 2.5 percent of the overall population.

This diversity of the people is also shaped by urbanization. About half of South Africans (including most whites, Asians, and colored people) live in an urban setting. South Africa has five cities with more than 1 million inhabitants: Johannesburg (3.6 million), Cape Town (3.5 million), Durban (2.8 million), Pretoria (1.4 million), and Port Elizabeth (1.1 million). Soweto, a large black township outside Johannesburg, has 1.3 million inhabitants.

South Africa is truly a complex, polyglot nation. According to a 2011 survey, Zulu is the most common language spoken at home (23 percent), followed by Xhosa (17 percent), Afrikaans (11 percent), and English (10 percent), but seven other African languages were used at home by smaller percentages of respondents.[2] The 1994 constitution recognizes 11 languages, nine of which (Ndebele, Northern Sotho, Sotho, Swazi, Tsonga, Tswana, Venda, Xhosa, and Zulu) are spoken exclusively by blacks and some of which are very closely related to one another. One characteristic of several of the languages is the distinct clicking sound that eludes nonnative speakers. Quite a few blacks speak more than one African language.

If there is a common language among South Africans, it is, increasingly, English. Virtually all whites, Asians, educated blacks, and coloreds can speak at least some English. Almost all Afrikaners are bilingual in Afrikaans and English, and many South Africans of English descent also speak some Afrikaans. But language has often bitterly divided the South African people. Blacks long resisted the imposition of Afrikaans by Afrikaners, and the 1976 Soweto Uprising was ignited by the Afrikaner authorities' attempt to make Afrikaans the official language of instruction in schools. Colored South Africans, on the other hand, along with Afrikaners, have recently fought to preserve the role of Afrikaans in the schools.

South Africa's neighbors have also been an important focal point for many South Africans. South Africa is bordered to the north by Zimbabwe (formerly Rhodesia). Zimbabwe's transition to black majority rule in 1980 was an inspiration to black South Africans, and its political crisis in recent years has created major challenges for South Africa's leaders and society. Botswana, also to the north, has been one of the most economically successful and politically stable African nations. On South Africa's eastern border, Mozambique and Swaziland are extremely poor. Throughout much of the twentieth century, apartheid leaders frequently pointed to these neighbors (and much of the rest of Africa) as proof that blacks were incapable of governing themselves. Sparsely populated Namibia, a former German colony and later a UN protectorate, was long dominated by apartheid South Africa.

Historical Development of the State

The telling of history often reflects the perspective of those in power, so it is not surprising that South Africa's history has usually been told from the perspective of whites. Afrikaners often contend that southern Africa was largely uninhabited when their Dutch ancestors arrived at the Cape of Good Hope in 1652. The truth is far more complex. Hunters and herders populated South Africa when the Dutch arrived in the mid-seventeenth century. The Dutch East India Company officials who first established a fort in what is today Cape Town encountered tribes of Khoisans, whom they soon enslaved. When these native Africans died of disease and slavery, the Dutch settlers imported slaves, mostly from Southeast Asia.[3]

In the interior of South Africa, a variety of Bantu-speaking tribes were ending their centuries-long migration southward from central Africa, integrating with the hunters and herders who had long inhabited the region. Among the largest of these tribes were the Zulu, the Sotho, and the Swazi kingdoms.

Dutch Rule

While most of the colonial "scramble for Africa" took place in the nineteenth century, European domination of South Africa began almost two centuries earlier. Cape Town was initially settled by the Dutch East India Company to resupply ships heading to and from Dutch colonies in Indonesia. The early Dutch settlers, known as **Boers** (Afrikaans for "farmer"), quickly seized the fertile land of the Cape of Good Hope. The European residents of the cape developed their own culture, based on their conservative Protestant **Dutch Reformed Church** and their unique language. The small and isolated Cape Colony was fairly prosperous until it was seized by the British Empire in 1795. The Dutch ceded formal control of the region to the British in 1814.

Boer Migration

As Britain quickly began to integrate this new colony into its burgeoning empire, the arrival of waves of British settlers was seen as a threat to Boer society. Bristling under British rule, many Cape Colony Boers (and their slaves) undertook a migration into the interior of southern Africa after the British banned slavery. That migration, the **Great Trek** of 1835, would later gain the status of heroic myth. Beginning in 1835 and over the following decade, thousands of **Voortrekkers** (Afrikaans for "pioneers") drove their wagons northeast to regain their autonomy and preserve their way of life. They met strong initial resistance from the Xhosa and other Bantu kingdoms, though whites had important technological advantages in these conflicts and were able to exploit the numerous divisions among the indigenous tribes.

A number of bloody battles ensued, most famously the 1838 Battle of Blood River between Zulu tribesmen and Afrikaners. During that conflict, a group of heavily outnumbered Afrikaners defeated the Zulus; the legend claims that no whites were killed. Afrikaners still consider the Blood River anniversary an important religious holiday and celebrate it each year on December 16. By the early 1840s, Afrikaners were firmly ensconced in South Africa's interior.

The exhausting exodus to escape British domination, along with the bitter fighting between Boers and blacks, was in the short term a Boer success. The Boers created two states, known as the Boer republics, in which slavery, strict segregation of races, the Afrikaans language, and the Dutch Reformed Church were protected by law.

Initially, the British grudgingly tolerated the interior Boer republics. However, the discovery there of massive deposits of diamonds (in 1870) and gold (in 1886) changed everything. English speakers flooded into the interior, and the city of Johannesburg quickly became an English-speaking enclave in the Boer-controlled state of Transvaal. Transvaal president Paul Kruger attempted to limit the influence of the English by denying them the vote. In 1895, English diamond magnate Cecil Rhodes used the pretense of Boer discrimination against English settlers and the presence of slavery in the Boer republics to incite a rebellion among the English. President Kruger declared war on England in 1899.

Defeat of the Afrikaners in the Boer Wars

Though outnumbered five to one, the Boers fought tenaciously to defend their independence during the **Boer Wars** of 1880–81 and 1899–1902. To defeat the well-armed and disciplined Afrikaners, the British pioneered the use of concentration camps, in which as many as 20,000 Afrikaners and 15,000 blacks perished. By 1902, the Boers had been defeated, and the Boer republics had become self-governing British colonies. In exchange for signing a peace treaty, the Boers were promised full political rights, protections for their language and culture, and the ability to deny blacks the vote in the former Boer republics. In 1910, these agreements were formalized in the **Union of South Africa**.

The Renaissance of Afrikaner Power

English and Afrikaners worked together to create a single British colony, and the first prime minister of the Union of South Africa was a former Afrikaner military leader. The Native Land Act of 1913 prevented blacks from owning land except in designated "reserves" (less than 10 percent of the total land of South Africa). Discrimination against blacks continued in the former Boer republics. Only in the largely English Cape Colony were coloreds and a small number of blacks allowed to vote. Nowhere in South Africa were rights for the black majority granted, and

TIMELINE OF POLITICAL DEVELOPMENT

YEAR	EVENT
1652	The Dutch arrive at the Cape of Good Hope.
1795	Cape Town captured from the Dutch by the British.
1880–81; 1899–1902	Boer Wars fought between the Afrikaners and the British.
1910	The Union of South Africa formed, dominated by English-speaking South Africans.
1948	Afrikaner National Party elected and apartheid begins.
1960	African National Congress banned.
1964	Nelson Mandela imprisoned.
1990	Mandela released from prison.
1990–93	Transition made to democracy as the result of negotiations between Mandela and President F. W. de Klerk.
1994	After historic multiracial elections, ANC majority government established under Nelson Mandela.
1996	Democratic constitution approved.
1999	Legislative elections won by ANC; Thabo Mbeki named president.
2008	Thabo Mbeki replaced as president by Kgalema Motlanthe.
2009	Jacob Zuma becomes president.
2014	Jacob Zuma reelected after the ANC wins its fifth consecutive election.

racial discrimination was the rule even in English-governed areas. In the face of this institutionalized racial oppression, the **African National Congress (ANC)** was founded in 1912 as a nonviolent advocate for multiracial democracy.

The first elections in the united country brought to power the South African Party (SAP), which included both English speakers and Afrikaners. But many

Afrikaners, especially those in the former Boer republics, continued to resent the English deeply. The Afrikaners enjoyed full political rights, but the English controlled most of the country's wealth, especially its mineral profits and budding industry.

As has so often been the case throughout their history, the Afrikaners resisted being marginalized, but this time they did so within the political system. The formation of the **National Party (NP)** in 1914 was the most important step in their attempt to organize and mobilize the Afrikaner population. The NP demanded that Afrikaans be recognized alongside English, and it called for South Africa to secede from the British Empire.

In the mid-1930s, NP leader Daniel Malan articulated the policies of white supremacy that later became the hallmark of apartheid. At the same time, Malan called for Afrikaner control of the state so that wealth held by the English could be redistributed to Afrikaners. Malan's goals appealed to the mass of poor white Afrikaner workers, who felt threatened by the better-off English and by the growing number of even poorer black workers (who vied for their jobs). The NP realized that if Afrikaners could be unified, they could not be denied power. In 1948, the NP was elected to office.

The Apartheid Era

The apartheid era is distinguished by the NP's two goals: consolidating Afrikaner power and eliminating all vestiges of black participation in South African politics. To a considerable degree, apartheid simply codified and intensified the racial segregation that existed in the mid-twentieth century. During an era when racial discrimination was being challenged in virtually every other country, Afrikaner leaders sought to construct elaborate legal justifications for it. According to Hendrik Verwoerd, the leading ideologue of apartheid (and prime minister from 1958 to 1966), South Africa was composed of four distinct "racial groups" (white, African, colored, and Indian). He argued that whites, as the "most civilized" of the four groups, should have absolute control of the state.

The Population Registration Act of 1950 divided South Africa into these four racial categories and placed every South African into one of those categories. Once Africans were divided into races, the apartheid architects argued that blacks (about three-quarters of the population) were not citizens of South Africa. Blacks were deemed to be citizens of 10 remote "tribal homelands" (dubbed **Bantustans**) whose boundaries and leaders were decreed by the government. The Bantustans, somewhat akin to Native American reservations, constituted only around 13 percent of South Africa's territory and were usually made up of noncontiguous parcels of infertile land separated by white-owned farms. The NP chose black leaders (often tribal chiefs) loyal to the party goals to head the Bantustan governments. All blacks in South Africa, therefore, were in effect "guests" and did not enjoy any of the rights of citizenship. The 1971 Bantu Homelands Citizenship Act allowed the government to grant "independence" to any Bantustan, and though government propagandists defended the measure as an act of "decolonization," in reality it had little impact. Over the next decade, many Bantustans became "independent," though no foreign government would recognize them as sovereign states.

Racial segregation in the rest of South Africa went even further. Members of each of the four racial groups were required to reside in areas determined by the government. The vast majority of blacks who lived and worked in white areas were required to carry internal visas at all times. Each year, failure to carry such a pass resulted in hundreds of thousands of deportations to a "homeland" that, more often than not, the deportee had never before set foot in. The apartheid authorities created new racial categories and designed separate residential areas for South Africans of Asian descent, or of mixed race, often forcibly relocating them. Other infamous laws reinforced racial segregation. The Prohibition of Mixed Marriages Act (1950) banned relations across racial lines, and the Reservation of Separate Amenities Act (1953) provided the legal basis for segregating places as diverse as beaches and restrooms.[4]

The apartheid system retained many of the trappings of a parliamentary democracy. Apartheid South Africa had regular elections, a fairly vigorous press, and a seemingly independent judiciary. The vast majority of South Africans, however, were disenfranchised and utterly powerless. The regime tolerated mild opposition on some issues but ruthlessly quashed individuals and groups who actively opposed apartheid itself.

The Building of Apartheid and the Struggle against It

Among the pillars of South African apartheid was the 1950 **Group Areas Act**, which prohibited South Africans of different races from living in the same neighborhoods. The practical implications were immediate and devastating: nonwhites were forcibly relocated to areas outside South African cities. The most infamous example was Sophiatown, a vibrant black community in Johannesburg (often compared to New York City's Harlem) that was bulldozed in 1955. Its inhabitants were relocated 13 miles outside of the city to a settlement that later became known as **Soweto**. Another example was District Six, a multiracial neighborhood in Cape Town with a large mixed-race (or colored) population. It was destroyed in 1966, and its colored inhabitants were relocated to the dusty Cape Flats 15 miles outside of the city.

The apartheid regime met resistance from its very inception. The most important organization resisting racial discrimination was the African National Congress (ANC), a largely black organization that sought suffrage for blacks. The ANC was initially nonviolent and politically moderate in its calls for multiracial democracy. Under the leadership of Nelson Mandela, it led a series of nonviolent civil disobedience campaigns against apartheid laws.[5]

Fierce repression of this protest by the apartheid regime had two major consequences. First, some blacks, tiring of the nonviolent, gradualist approach of the ANC, advocated a more confrontational opposition to apartheid. The growing repression (especially the government slaughter of protesters during the 1960 Sharpeville Massacre) persuaded the ANC to ally with the South African Communist Party and to initiate military action against the apartheid regime. Second, the apartheid leaders, alarmed by the growing resistance, banned the ANC and other anti-apartheid groups. The government countered by arresting Nelson Mandela and other top ANC leaders in 1963 and sentencing them to life in prison. The ongoing repression led to the incarceration and murder of thousands of South Africans who actively resisted apartheid.

Although not all whites supported the apartheid system, the NP skillfully retained the majority's allegiance. For Afrikaners, the NP dramatically improved their political and economic status, making them dependent on the perpetuation of the status quo. The NP played on English-speaking whites' fears of black rule. Moderate white critics of apartheid were mostly tolerated because they generally held little sway among the white population at large.

Though the NP subdued most domestic resistance to apartheid, the system faced growing hostility from abroad. The end of colonialism created independent African states that supported the ANC, and the United Nations condemned apartheid as early as 1952 and imposed an arms embargo on South Africa in 1977. Nevertheless, in the context of the Cold War, South Africa was able to gain support (from the United States, in particular) by portraying its fight against the ANC as a struggle against communism. Moreover, the world's major capitalist powers had lucrative investments in South Africa and were ambivalent about promoting black rule.

Transition to Democracy

There was nothing inevitable about South Africa's transition from apartheid to majority rule. In this section, we discuss five categories of factors that need to be considered to explain the momentous political shift that culminated in South Africa's first free elections in 1994.

DEMOGRAPHIC PRESSURE AND GROWING UNREST

The growth of opposition to apartheid had at its core a demographic component. The proportion of whites in the population had dropped from a high of 21 percent in 1936 to only 10 percent in 1999. The black population was growing more quickly, and it was increasingly concentrated in urban areas, which were more subject to political mobilization. Most of these newly urban blacks lived in squalid conditions in South Africa's townships, which doubled in population between 1950 and 1980. These demographic trends meant that despite largely successful efforts to deny blacks political power, their economic power and significance were rapidly expanding.

These changes caused opposition to apartheid during the 1980s to assume dimensions previously unknown in South Africa. The creation of the **United Democratic Front (UDF)** in 1983 effectively united trade unions and the major black and white anti-apartheid groups. The number of protests, strikes, boycotts, and slowdowns grew, requiring ever-greater levels of repression by the apartheid regime. In July 1985, the government imposed a virtually permanent state of emergency, which led to massive arrests of suspected opposition members. In 1988, it banned the UDF and the largest trade union confederation. The ANC, whose leadership was either in prison or in exile, waged a guerrilla war against the apartheid regime. That struggle was never able to dislodge the heavily armed white regime, but neither could the regime destroy the ANC or stop the escalating violence.

ECONOMIC DECLINE

By the 1980s, the deficiencies in the apartheid economic model had become increasingly apparent. During this decade, South Africa's economy was among the most stagnant in the developing world, growing at an average annual rate of only about 1 percent. The apartheid economic system had raised the standard of living for South Africa's whites, especially Afrikaners, but it had also led to serious distortions that were by now beginning to take a toll.

The apartheid state, with its convoluted and overlapping race-based institutions and its subsidies to the entirely dependent black "homelands," was costly and inefficient. The mercantilist apartheid policies of self-sufficiency and protectionism led to the creation of industries and services that were not competitive. The system of racial preferences and job protection that was a cornerstone of apartheid clearly hindered economic development and economic efficiency.

INTERNAL REFORMS

By the mid-1970s, even leading Afrikaner politicians were convinced that apartheid was an anachronistic system that needed reform if it was to survive. The reforms that followed paved the way for a future transition to democracy.

Prime Minister P. W. Botha, who took power in 1978, promised to dismantle apartheid and enacted some minor reforms that liberalized some aspects of apartheid. However, he was unwilling to push the reforms very far. The next leader, President **F. W. de Klerk** (1989–94), repealed the Reservation of Separate Amenities Act, the Group Areas Act, and the Population Registration Act. He also legalized black political parties, including the ANC and the PAC, and freed their leaders. The crisis of apartheid served to split the traditionally unified Afrikaner leadership, opening the window to even greater reform.

THE CHANGING INTERNATIONAL CONTEXT

During the 1980s, many countries imposed embargoes on South Africa, limiting trade and foreign investment, though powerful nations such as the United States and the United Kingdom continued to trade with the regime into the 1990s. Of greater importance was the winding down of the Cold War in the 1980s. On the one hand, it deprived the South African regime of a key source of international legitimacy: the decline of communism weakened its claim that it was facing a communist insurgency. On the other hand, the collapse of the Soviet Union and the Soviet bloc weakened the ANC sectors that promoted communist revolution in South Africa.

SKILLED LEADERSHIP

South Africa's transition to democracy likely would not have occurred (or at the very least would not have been as peaceful or successful) without skilled leaders. F. W. de Klerk's role in forcing Prime Minister Botha's resignation and his courageous decisions in 1990 to free Mandela and legalize the ANC were essential to the peaceful regime change. De Klerk used his unblemished credentials as an NP stalwart to persuade NP die-hards to accept democratic reform and convince most Afrikaners that their interests would be safeguarded under majority rule.

Likewise, Nelson Mandela risked a great deal by negotiating the terms of the transition with the NP government. Mandela and the ANC leadership agreed to power sharing and numerous guarantees to assuage white fears, and they were able to restrain radicalized blacks who wanted quick redress for decades of abuse under apartheid. Mandela's knowledge of Afrikaner language and culture (gained through

Nelson Mandela greets supporters after his release from prison in February 1990. Upon being released, he immediately became the representative of the black majority in negotiating for a democratic transition. Mandela received the Nobel Peace Prize in 1993. In 1994, his ANC won a landslide victory in the country's first multiracial elections and Mandela became South Africa's first black president. He died in late 2013.

decades of study in prison) undoubtedly helped him negotiate with his Afrikaner opposition. His ability to eschew bitterness and revenge after his 27-year prison term impressed even his strongest opponents. Still, negotiations between the black leadership and the NP were protracted and difficult. De Klerk and Mandela faced serious opposition from radical sectors of their own camps. Nevertheless, an interim constitution was approved in 1993, paving the way for democratic elections and majority rule in 1994. In recognition of their important role in the South African transition, de Klerk and Mandela were awarded the 1993 Nobel Peace Prize.

Political Regime

Political Institutions

During the apartheid regime, South African whites enjoyed relatively democratic institutions. Nonwhites had much more limited political rights, or none whatsoever. As a result, few considered the country to be democratic. After the political transition in 1994, however, political rights were extended to the population as a whole, regardless of race. South Africa is now a democracy with broad political rights and civil liberties commensurate with those found in advanced democracies. South Africa's long tradition of democratic institutions, albeit highly restrictive ones, helped smooth the transition to multiracial democracy. The architects of the 1994 transition did not need to create an entirely new democratic system from scratch but merely reformed existing democratic institutions and extended them to the entire population.

THE CONSTITUTION

The new democratic regime is fundamentally enshrined in the South African constitution, approved in 1996. This document reflects the delicate nature of the country's transition to democracy, in which new democratic rights had to be provided to the black majority while those of the white minority had to be protected.

The constitution attempts to balance majority and minority concerns carefully, affirming the basic values of human rights regardless of "race, gender, sex, pregnancy, religion, conscience, belief, culture, language and birth," a list far more detailed than that of most democratic constitutions. Eleven official languages are recognized. The constitution also upholds citizens' rights to housing, health care, food, water, social security, and even a healthy environment. Reacting to decades of apartheid authoritarianism, the constitution includes unusually detailed provisions limiting the powers of the state to arrest, detain, and prosecute individuals. Finally, it enshrines the principle of affirmative action, stating that to achieve greater equality, laws and other measures can be used to promote or advance individuals who have been discriminated against.

The constitution also firmly protects the rights of private property, a provision added to assure the white population that their property would not be seized by a black-majority government. Perhaps most important, the constitution defines itself as the supreme law of the land: parliament must act within its confines, and a Constitutional Court can now strike down unconstitutional behavior. This is a departure from the past, when the legislature and the government reigned supreme and, with no higher legal power to restrain them, could change and reinterpret laws as they saw fit. Despite these successes, and largely because of the ANC's dominance in the South African political system, many scholars have begun to question the health of South Africa's political institutions. One recent report concluded that "weak institutions, a significant characteristic of South Africa's democracy, struggle to promote the effective functioning of the state, and fail to provide the checks and balances necessary for democracy to flourish."[6]

The Branches of Government

The South African government is based on British institutions, though with some variations. For most of the apartheid period, South Africa had a bicameral parliament, a prime minister, and a ceremonial president as head of state. Since 1994, the South African system has been transformed into one similar to those in many other democracies—a bicameral parliament and a Constitutional Court.

Interestingly, because of historic compromises between Afrikaner and English-speaking whites, South Africa has three capitals. The seat of government is located in Pretoria, the traditional heart of Afrikaner power and the center of the former Boer republics. Cape Town, where English influence was historically strongest, is the legislative capital. South Africa's judicial capital is located in Bloemfontein.

THE PRESIDENT

The chief executive of South Africa is the president. This title is rather confusing, however. Like a typical prime minister, the president is chosen from, and by, members of the National Assembly—the lower house of the legislature—and can be removed by a vote of no confidence. But unlike in most parliamentary systems, the South African president serves as both head of state and head of government. Like most prime ministers, the president chooses a cabinet of ministers, signs or vetoes legislation presented by the National Assembly, and can refer legislation to the Constitutional Court as necessary. The president may also call national referenda, dissolve the National Assembly, and (in some situations) call new elections. If the president wishes to dissolve the National Assembly, a majority of the lower house must support the dissolution and three years must have passed since it was first elected. The president is unable to call snap elections as in most other parliamentary systems.

The president is stronger than a typical prime minister. As head of state and head of government, the president not only exerts authority over the cabinet (which he/she selects and which he/she can dismiss) and government policy (like a typical head of government) but also speaks on behalf of the nation and represents the country on the world stage (as a head of state does). As is common in parliamentary systems, motions of no confidence require the support of a majority of the members of the National Assembly, and if successful require that the president and entire cabinet resign. President Jacob Zuma faced six unsuccessful motions of no confidence between 2009 and 2017, easily defeating the first five motions. In August 2017 a motion of no confidence against Zuma was narrowly defeated, as some legislators from the president's party voted against him.

However, the limits to the power of the president were evident in 2008, when President Thabo Mbeki was forced to resign after he failed to win reelection to the ANC leadership. Mbeki was replaced by Kgalema Motlanthe, a caretaker president who served until the 2009 general elections. As in all parliamentary systems, South Africa's head of government serves at the behest of his or her political party

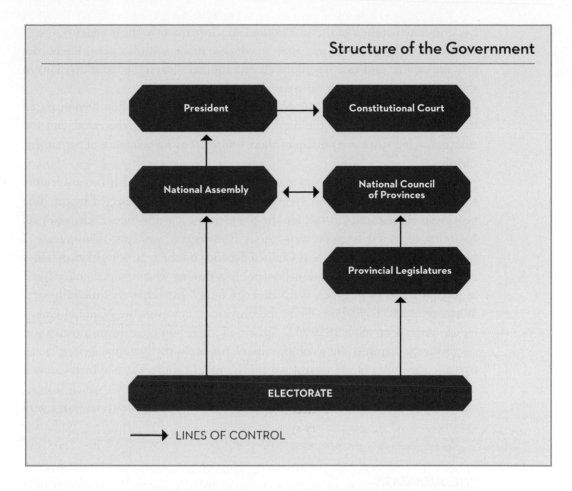

Structure of the Government

President → Constitutional Court

National Assembly ↔ National Council of Provinces

Provincial Legislatures

ELECTORATE

→ LINES OF CONTROL

and can be replaced by the party at any time. After Zuma's surprisingly narrow victory in the motion of no confidence against him in August 2017, there was speculation that the ANC might decide to remove its increasingly unpopular leader before the next election.

THE LEGISLATURE

South Africa has a bicameral parliament. The lower and more powerful of its two houses, the **National Assembly**, currently has 400 members. Members serve for five-year terms, and they are charged with electing and removing the president, preparing and passing legislation, and approving the national budget. As in the United Kingdom, the lower house has a weekly "question time," when members can question members of the cabinet (and very infrequently, the president). Question time can become a heated affair in which members of the opposition parties grill the cabinet and cast aspersions on one another. Given the racial divisions in the country, however, such debate is also limited.

For a variety of reasons, the National Assembly has not often demonstrated its independence vis-à-vis the president. The dominance of the ANC and the rules enforcing strict party discipline have limited the independence of parliament members.[7]

The upper house is the National Council of Provinces, and it is considerably weaker than the lower house. Its 90 members are indirectly elected by the nine provincial legislatures and include the premier of each province. Each province, regardless of its size or population, sends 10 delegates, who cast their votes as a bloc. The power of the National Council depends on the type of legislation under consideration. When the National Assembly is dealing with national policy (such as foreign affairs or defense), the National Council has relatively little influence. When proposed legislation affects the provinces, however, the National Council can amend or reject measures, forcing the two houses to form a mediation committee to hammer out a compromise. Ultimately, the National Assembly can override the upper house with a two-thirds vote. In short, the National Council exists to ensure that local interests are heard at the national level, which is especially important when the provinces are distinguished by ethnicity, language, and culture.

THE JUDICIARY

Another important component of the transition to democratic multiracial rule in South Africa is the Constitutional Court. This body hears cases regarding constitutional issues. Its 11 members serve 12-year terms and are appointed by the president on the basis of the recommendations of a judicial commission. The commission is made up of government and nongovernment appointees who evaluate candidates' qualifications and take racial and gender diversity into account.

To date, the court has shown a tendency for activism and independence. In 1997, for example, it struck down the country's death penalty despite public sentiment in favor of capital punishment. In 2002, the court ruled that the government was obligated to provide treatment for persons with HIV/AIDS.[8] In 2011, the Constitutional Court overturned several key decisions by President Zuma and issued a ruling that Zuma's disbanding of the elite anticorruption force known as the "Scorpions" was unconstitutional. In response, Zuma warned the judiciary against encroaching on the powers of the executive and the legislature.[9] In 2015, the Chief Justice of the Constitutional Court, an appointee of President Zuma, held a press conference in which he accused the government of trying to interfere in the judiciary. In April 2016, the Constitutional Court ordered Zuma to pay back public money that he had spent to remodel his private home. At a time of growing concern about the ruling party's monopoly of political power, the South African judiciary has proven to be a crucial check on the government. In contrast to the legislature, and the presidency, a majority of South Africans continue to express trust in the judiciary (see "The Evolution of Levels of Trust in South Africa, 2006–15," p. 712).

The Electoral System

The current electoral rules in South Africa mark a significant departure from the past. Under apartheid, the country used the British single-member district, or plurality, system. As part of the transition to democracy, South Africa had to decide what election method would best represent the needs of a diverse public and help consolidate democratic legitimacy by creating an inclusive system. The result was the creation of an electoral system based on pure proportional representation (PR).

Voters now cast their votes not for individual candidates, but for a party that is designated on the ballot by name, electoral symbol, and a picture of the head of the party (so that illiterate voters are not excluded). To ensure the greatest possible proportionality, representatives are elected from a single nationwide constituency, and there is no minimum threshold for receiving seats in the legislature. The number of seats a party wins is divided proportionally to reflect the percentage of the total vote it receives. At elections, voters are given two ballots: one for the national legislature and one for their provincial legislature.

Overall, the electoral system in South Africa has successfully created an inclusive political atmosphere and has averted conflict and violence. Electoral turnout has been very high; in the 2014 elections, turnout was over 73 percent of registered voters (about 80 percent of eligible voters registered). However, voter turnout dropped 4 percent from the 2009 general elections.

Some critics have argued that the use of PR has created a disconnect between the National Assembly and the citizens. Because members of parliament are tied to their party instead of their constituency, they are not accountable to local communities. Political parties, most notably the governing ANC, have stifled internal dissent and limited the independence of legislators by threatening to remove them from the party electoral list if they stray too far from the party's wishes. Critics inside South Africa, including the Congress of the People (COPE), a party that split from the ANC in 2009, have suggested that the country consider adopting a mixed electoral system, in which some percentage of the seats are filled by plurality while the remaining are filled by PR. This would give voters a local representative with whom they could identify as well as the ability to cast their vote for a particular party. However, after some discussion on electoral reform in recent years, such suggestions have faded and the current system has become institutionalized. The ANC, in particular, has been unwilling to change an electoral system that has so far delivered it a huge majority.

Local Government

Below the national level, South Africa is divided into nine provinces, each with its own elected assembly. Members are elected for a term of five years, and elections for the national and provincial legislatures occur simultaneously. In turn, the members of each assembly elect a premier to serve as the province's chief executive. The provincial assemblies have their own constitutions, pass legislation, and send delegates to the National Council of Provinces.

It is difficult to call South Africa a federal state, however, and the concept itself is a politically charged issue. During the transition to democracy, the ANC in particular was skeptical of federalism. At that time, the NP, the architects of apartheid, favored federalism as a way to limit the ANC's power. Meanwhile, some Afrikaners hoped that a federal right to self-determination could pave the way for outright secession. The Zulu-based **Inkatha Freedom Party (IFP)** also called for self-determination—and an independent Zulu state. The 1996 constitution reflects these concerns by supporting regional and ethnic diversity. Still, the constitution gives the central government the ability to overturn local legislation relatively easily, and any powers not delimited by the constitution reside with the central, not the local, government. Provinces also have limited power to levy taxes, giving them little financial autonomy.[10]

Since democratization, municipal governments have become increasingly important. The ANC has suffered its most important defeats at the local level, where complaints about the delivery of services have boosted the fortunes of the opposition. In the 2009 provincial elections, the ANC lost control of Western Cape

Province, and **Democratic Alliance (DA)** leader Helen Zille became premier. An increasing number of protests against ineffective local governments, some of which turned violent, set the stage for a major increase in the DA vote in the May 2011 municipal elections. In addition to retaining control of the Western Cape Province, the party won almost a quarter of the national vote and made its first inroads into areas that had previously been bastions of ANC support. In the 2016 local elections, the DA beat the ANC in Pretoria, deprived the ANC of a majority in Johannesburg, and made significant gains elsewhere. A public opinion study conducted by the country's Independent Electoral Commission showed that South Africans held local governments in lower esteem than any other level of government, and other studies show that over half of South Africans view local governments as corrupt.[11]

Political Conflict and Competition

The Party System and Elections

During apartheid, few political parties existed, and the NP dominated politics from 1948 until 1994. The main opposition was the weak Progressive Federal Party (PFP), which peacefully opposed apartheid laws and favored multiracial democracy within a federal framework. The enfranchisement of the nonwhite population has dramatically changed the political spectrum, though as in the past it remains dominated by one major party.

THE AFRICAN NATIONAL CONGRESS (ANC)

The dominant party since 1994 has been the African National Congress (ANC), which led the struggle against white rule starting in 1912.[12] During the ANC's long period underground and in exile, it developed an ideology strongly influenced by Marxism, favoring the nationalization of land and industry. Economic equality was seen as a necessary mechanism for overcoming racial discrimination. The ANC cultivated relations with communist countries, such as the Soviet Union and China, and at home formed an alliance with the much smaller South African Communist Party, the SACP (which still operates within the framework of the ANC).

Many white South Africans, including some opponents of apartheid, were troubled by the ANC's demands for radical political and economic change. Since winning power in 1994, the ANC has stood for racial and gender equality and a strong state role in the expansion of economic opportunities for nonwhites. But it has also embraced property rights that it views as essential for economic growth and a prerequisite for the provision of jobs, education, and social services to the poor black majority. As such, its ideology is unclear and often contradictory, encompassing a mixture of social-democratic and liberal views, a lingering radicalism, and an emphasis on unity. The ANC increased its share of the vote in each of the first three democratic elections and has won a large majority of the vote in each of the five elections since 1994, but its share of the vote dropped in 1999 and 2014.

The preponderance of ANC power raises concerns. Some observers fear that the party so easily embraced democracy after its long struggle in part because it has done so well in a democratic system. Were the ANC to face losing power, it might not look upon the democratic process so favorably. These concerns were heightened in particular by Thabo Mbeki's tenure in office (1999–2008), when his rhetoric and that of the ANC grew increasingly intolerant of those who challenged it. ANC leaders, including current president Jacob Zuma, have at times made statements that portray the ANC as the only truly patriotic political party and that envision the ANC as the only party capable of governing.[13]

In general, however, the ANC's record in office has been positively evaluated by most South Africans, who give it high scores for managing the economy, improving health care, and promoting racial equality. South Africans have been most critical of the ANC's record on creating jobs, reducing crime, narrowing the gap between the rich and poor, and fighting corruption.

Over the past decade, the ANC has increasingly suffered from internal political discord. A political schism emerged in late 2007 between ANC "populists," led by trade unions and the party rank and file, and the more technocratic wing, dominated by former president Mbeki. The populist challenge within the party helped propel Jacob Zuma's victory over Mbeki in the bitterly contested party leadership election of December 2007. After winning the ANC leadership, Zuma began to replace Mbeki loyalists with his own supporters in key party posts. Although Zuma was able to force Mbeki to resign in September 2008, Zuma could not become president because he was not a member of the legislature. The ANC appointed Kgalema Motlanthe, an ally of Zuma, as a caretaker president to serve until the 2009 general elections.

South Africa's current president is a striking contrast from his aloof, intellectual predecessor, Thabo Mbeki. Jacob Zuma is the ANC's most prominent Zulu politician. Unlike the scholarly Mbeki (or Nelson Mandela, who was a lawyer),

Zuma grew up poor and received no formal education. He became involved in the ANC in the 1960s and was sentenced to 10 years in prison in 1963. (He served time at Robben Island prison with Nelson Mandela.) After his release, he became a top ANC leader in exile. After the return of democracy, Zuma quickly rose within the ANC hierarchy, an ascent that culminated in his 1997 appointment as executive deputy president (Mbeki's number two). While often portraying himself as the victim of the ANC power elite, Zuma is the consummate ANC insider.

Zuma's rise to power within the ANC was clouded in controversy. In 2005, he was charged with raping a young woman in his home. He admitted to having unprotected sex with the woman, whom he knew to be HIV-positive, but claimed the relationship was consensual. Zuma was acquitted of the charges, but his statement under oath that he had showered after the intercourse to reduce his risk of contracting HIV infuriated many South Africans.

President Jacob Zuma is portrayed here as a leader plagued by corruption charges.

In 2005, Zuma was fired from his position as deputy president after being accused of corruption and racketeering in a government arms-procurement scandal. Charges were brought against him in 2007, but they were dropped in April 2009, shortly before the general election. Zuma has claimed that the corruption charges were politically motivated. He rose to power with strong support from South Africa's labor unions, those frustrated with the pace of change under Mandela and Mbeki. Some feared that Zuma might become an economic populist who could reverse the pro-business and pro-growth economic policies long pursued by the ANC. In December 2007, Zuma easily defeated Thabo Mbeki in elections for the ANC presidency, which virtually guaranteed that he would become president after the April 2009 general election.

Zuma's personal life continues to be the source of some contention. Zuma is a polygamist who married his fifth wife in 2010. After taking office, he apologized for fathering a child with a friend's daughter to whom he was not married. In short, Zuma's outward image appears to be a dramatic departure from those of Mandela and Mbeki. His less-polished image has helped South Africa's poor majority relate to him. But appearances can be deceiving. Below the surface, there is considerable continuity between Zuma's policies and those of his two more circumspect predecessors.

In the run-up to the 2014 election, controversy continued to dog Zuma. In 2013, opposition parties in the legislature alleged that he had used public funds for improvements to his personal residence—charges that were upheld in a 2016 Constitutional Court ruling. In December 2013, Zuma was heckled during his eulogy for Nelson Mandela. Nevertheless, a public opinion survey carried out in late 2011 gave Zuma a 66 percent approval rating, and the ANC won a resounding victory in the 2014 elections. By 2016, however, Zuma's approval rating had dropped from a high of 64 percent to 36 percent, damaged by continuing allegations of corruption and a stagnant economy.[14] In the local elections of August 2016, the ANC received 54 percent of the vote nationwide, its lowest percentage since the return to democracy in 2016. Opinion research shows that the ANC has experienced a dramatic loss of trust among voters (see "The Evolution of Levels of Trust in South Africa, 2006–15," p. 712) over the last decade.

President Zuma's 2017 firing of his well-respected finance minister, who was known for his opposition to corruption, threatened to further divide the governing party. Zuma's deputy president, the head of the ANC, and quite a few ANC members of parliament blasted the decision. The ANC's growing internal divisions were highlighted in 2017 when Zuma narrowly survived a motion of no confidence despite the fact that the ANC enjoyed a large majority in the legislature.

OTHER PARTIES

Zuma's rise to the leadership of the ANC, and his ability to force Mbeki's resignation, prompted the creation of the Congress of the People (COPE). This breakaway party, led by Mosiuoa Lekota, a former defense minister under Mbeki, had the potential to become the first genuine black opposition party to the ANC. Despite internal divisions, a flawed political campaign, and lack of funds leading up to the 2009 elections, COPE was able to win more than 7 percent of the vote and 30 seats in the legislature, making it South Africa's third-largest political party. However, COPE suffered a stunning setback in the 2011 municipal elections, when it won under 3 percent of the vote, and in the 2014 general elections it won under 1 percent of the vote and only three seats in the legislature.

A second party to break away from the ANC was Agang South Africa. It was formed in 2013 by Mamphela Ramphele, a black female physician and scholar who was a former managing director of the World Bank. Ramphele's new party sought to attract black voters frustrated over corruption and cronyism within the ANC. Despite a promising start, the new party made a series of strategic errors and won only two seats in the 2014 elections.

The most interesting new party to emerge from the ANC is the **Economic Freedom Fighters (EFF)**, led by the young and radical firebrand Julius Malema. Malema, the former head of the ANC youth organization, was expelled from the ANC for making radical and incendiary statements that contradicted ANC policy. Malema and the EFF represent the radical and Marxist left of the ANC, fostered during decades of anti-apartheid armed struggle. Since its inception in 2013, the EFF has been a fierce critic of what it views as the overly pro-business and excessively free-market orientation of the ANC. Most controversially, it calls for expropriation of white-owned land and the nationalization of South Africa's banks and mines. The new party's base is overwhelmingly made up of young and black South Africans. The party won just over 6 percent of the vote, and 25 seats, in the 2014 elections, making it South Africa's third largest political force, but for the moment, it has failed to provide a real challenge to the ANC from the left. After the ANC lost its majority in the local elections in Johannesburg, the EFF refused to join a coalition with the ANC, and instead negotiated with the centrist Democratic Alliance (DA).

Legislators from the Economic Freedom Fighters Party protest during President Zuma's state of the nation address in February 2016.

To date the most important opposition party in South Africa is the Democratic Alliance (DA). The DA is the successor to the pre-1994 white anti-apartheid party, the Progressive Federal Party (PFP). In the early years of the transition to democracy, the DA entered into alliance with the remnants of the now defunct National Party (most former National Party members now support the DA). It is primarily a liberal party that favors a small state, individual freedoms, privatization of state-run firms, and greater devolution of power to local governments. In the 2004 elections, the DA won 12 percent of the votes and 50 seats. In the 2006 local elections, it beat the ANC in Cape Town (at the time, the only local municipal council not controlled by the ANC), and won about 15 percent of the vote nationally.

Helen Zille, a liberal journalist during apartheid and the white mayor of Cape Town, became DA leader in 2007. Under her leadership, the DA has been an increasingly outspoken opponent of the ANC. Public support for the DA has grown since the 1994 elections, but its primary base of support remains the white, colored, and Indian population. In 2008, just under 8 percent of South Africans said they identified with the DA. In the 2009 elections, the DA increased its vote share to over 16 percent and won control of Western Cape Province (the only province not controlled by the ANC). The DA performed well in the 2011 municipal elections. In the 2014 general elections, it won just over 22 percent of the vote and 89 seats, solidifying its role as the leading party of the opposition.

However, to become a serious challenger to the ANC, the DA will have to broaden its appeal to black voters (it won only 22 percent of black voters in 2014), and it will need to change the perception that it is the party of whites. Survey data show that South Africans who identify with the DA tend to be Afrikaans speakers, wealthy, white, highly educated, and older.[15] In May 2015, **Mmusi Maimane** became the DA's first black leader, and he is currently South Africa's leader of the opposition in the National Assembly. Maimane would appear to be well positioned to attract more black voters to the DA. In his mid-30s, he grew up poor in the black township of Soweto and has a white wife and mixed-race children. Maimane's first electoral campaign came in the 2016 local and regional elections, and the DA won almost a third of the vote. It retained control of the Western Cape, and it gained control of two additional urban municipalities

South Africa's fourth largest party, the Inkatha Freedom Party (IFP), played an ambiguous role in apartheid and post-apartheid politics. The IFP, founded in 1975 by Zulu chief Mangosuthu Buthelezi, challenged apartheid institutions but also participated in local government in the KwaZulu "homeland," one of the remote areas created to remove blacks from desirable areas and deprive them of basic citizenship.

During the 1980s, animosity grew between the IFP and the ANC: the ANC saw the IFP as having been co-opted by the government, while the IFP viewed the ANC as dominated by ethnic Xhosas who did not represent Zulu interests. The animosity soon erupted into violence that was abetted by the apartheid regime as a way to weaken both sides. After the first democratic elections, however, the ANC was careful to bring members of the IFP into the government cabinet, which helped to diffuse much of the tension between the two parties.

The IFP was embarrassed in 2004 after failing to do well even in the elections for KwaZulu's provincial legislature, and the party left the national government. Fears that the IFP could threaten the stability of the country have disappeared. The long-term viability of a Zulu political party is doubtful since Jacob Zuma, a Zulu, became president in 2009. Since then, the IFP has steadily declined. In the 2014 general elections, it was hurt by internal divisions and thus won only 2.4 percent of the vote and 10 seats.

Aided by South Africa's proportional representation election system, a number of small parties regularly win seats in the legislature. But the dominance of the ANC, which has never held less than 60 percent of the seats in the legislature, dwarfs the opposition. However, in recent general elections the steady growth of the opposition, and especially the gains made by parties to the right and left of the ANC (the DA and the new EFF), have deprived the ANC of a two-thirds majority in the lower house. As a result, the ANC will need to work with the opposition if it wants to amend the constitution and pass certain types of legislation.

We have seen that despite its slow and steady decline in electoral support, the ANC has retained a large majority of the electorate since 1994, and South Africa remains a dominant-party system. Does the continued dominance of a single party threaten democracy in South Africa, as has been argued by some scholars?[16] Other democracies, such as Japan, have been dominated by a single political party. Nevertheless, the dominance of a single party may threaten democracy in the long run by encouraging corruption, contributing to political apathy, and insulating the governing party from public criticism. Moreover, some observers have argued that the ANC's internal structure is particularly centralized and hierarchical, and they point out that many in the ANC view its opposition as unpatriotic and disloyal.[17]

National elections are held at least every five years, and according to survey data from 2008, about 68 percent of South Africans identify with a political party. Since 1994, South African political parties have been heavily influenced by race. In the words of one leading scholar, "Post-apartheid South African elections bear an unmistakable racial imprint: Africans vote for one set of parties, whites support a different set of parties, and, with few exceptions, there is no cross-over voting between these groups."[18] In the 1999 elections, for example, 95 percent of blacks

South African National Assembly Elections, 2004, 2009, and 2014

PARTY	2004		2009		2014	
	% VOTE	# SEATS	% VOTE	# SEATS	% VOTE	# SEATS
ANC	70	279	66	264	62	249
DA	12	50	17	67	22	89
EFF	–	–	–	–	6	25
IFP	7	28	5	18	2	10
COPE	–	–	7	30	1	3
NNP	2	36	–	–	–	–
Others	9	7	5	21	7	24
Total	100	400	100	400	100	400

Key to Party Acronyms:
 ANC: African National Congress
 COPE: Congress of the People
 DA: Democratic Alliance
 EFF: Economic Freedom Fighters
 IFP: Inkatha Freedom Party
 NNP: New National Party

Source: Electoral Commission of South Africa, www.elections.org.za (accessed 6/1/14).

voted for the ANC, IFP, or other predominantly black parties, while 81 percent of whites supported the DA or other mostly white parties. Only colored and Indian voters more evenly split their votes among black and white parties (40 percent of coloreds and 34 percent of Indians backed white parties).[19]

Civil Society

The exclusionary nature of the apartheid regime was built upon the policy of destroying black opposition, which it carried out by weakening any form of organized resistance. Black civil society in South Africa was crushed to an extent not seen elsewhere in colonial Africa: traditional institutions were undermined, co-opted, and repressed wherever possible. Yet even with such pressure, anti-apartheid nongovernmental organizations (NGOs) continued to form and were vital in organizing the resistance that would help bring about democracy.

Since democratization, South Africa has developed a civil society that one scholar describes as "vigorous, effective, and shallow."[20] After 1994, the ANC attempted to co-opt many civil society groups, bringing them under its direction. Nevertheless, a whole host of groups has formed to pressure ANC-led governments on a gamut of issues, from providing basic services to protecting minority groups. Perhaps the best example of an effective civil society group is the Treatment Action Campaign (TAC), which successfully pressured the government into an about-face in its HIV/AIDS policies. Founded in 1998 by HIV-positive activists, the TAC used a variety of tactics, ranging from legal action to civil disobedience.

Despite the proliferation of civil society groups, some see South African civil society as shallow because engagement is still restricted to the relatively well-off minority. Moreover, from a comparative perspective, and with the exception of political protest, other forms of public activism (including membership in pressure groups) remain low in South Africa. A 2010 study of 20 African countries showed that South Africans' civic and political participation was among the lowest in the region.[21]

One major actor in civil society is organized labor—in particular, the **Congress of South African Trade Unions (COSATU)**, formed in 1985 to promote workers' rights and oppose apartheid. In post-apartheid South Africa, COSATU remains powerful in defending labor interests.[22] Like many other organizations that were involved in the battle against apartheid, COSATU is strongly tied to the ANC through what is known as the Triple Alliance, which links COSATU, the ANC, and the SACP.

Despite this alliance, COSATU has been openly hostile to the ANC's liberal economic policies, and this hostility has generated friction. COSATU has complained about the consistently high rate of unemployment that has weakened the union movement. (Only a small minority of South Africa's workforce is unionized.) It has also been vocal in opposing the government's weak criticism of the Mugabe regime in neighboring Zimbabwe. COSATU has considered severing its ties to the ANC, but like other civic actors, it fears that doing so will result in its political marginalization. While COSATU backed Jacob Zuma's challenge to Thabo Mbeki, relations between Zuma and COSATU soon soured. A wave of COSATU-led strikes in 2010, mainly over demands for higher wages, crippled

South Africa's economy. COSATU eventually compromised over the issue, sensitive to criticisms that excessive wage demands might worsen South Africa's very high unemployment rate. Another wave of strikes in South Africa's mines in 2012 turned violent, leading some top COSATU leaders to call for nationalization of the mines. In 2014, COSATU expelled its largest member union, the National Union of Metalworkers of South Africa (NUMSA), after NUMSA's leadership called on COSATU to end its alliance with the ANC. NUMSA members made up about 15 percent of COSATU membership, and other COSATU unions left the organization in support of the metal workers.

A second important element of civil society is the media. Since 1994, electronic and print media have expanded substantially, making for a relatively well-informed public. South Africans place a high degree of trust in the media, more so than they place in any of the state institutions, perhaps due in part to the ethnic integration of television and other outlets. In 2008, concerns were raised when individuals close to the ANC leadership purchased one of South Africa's four main media groups, and in 2010, the ANC introduced and passed proposals aimed at countering what it viewed as an excessively critical media. Some of those measures were interpreted as attempts to muzzle South Africa's vibrant and independent media. Over the next year, the bill was heavily amended. The version approved in November 2011, called the Protection of State Information bill, limited the ability to classify documents to police, security, and intelligence services, and it significantly reduced prison sentences for most illegal disclosures of information. But the ANC rejected calls to include an exception protecting the release of information that could be shown to be in the public interest.

After decades of apartheid authoritarianism, South Africans are sensitive to any perceived erosion of their hard-won civil liberties. The Protection of State Information bill and the ANC's plan to create a special tribunal to adjudicate complaints about unfair media coverage are signs of the governing party's increasingly defensive posture vis-à-vis South Africa's media. But the controversy also reveals a number of strengths in South Africa's democracy. The government was forced to heavily amend the legislation. Public protest and debate were vigorous and indicated that South African civil society is not easily intimidated by the government. President Zuma, yielding to public protest, refused to sign the bill and sent it back to the legislature for more deliberation. Finally, opponents have vowed to challenge the new law in South Africa's Constitutional Court if Zuma were to sign the bill. That body has shown its willingness to overturn legislation.

Society

Given the ethnic diversity of South Africa's inhabitants and the colonial and national policies of systematic racial discrimination, it is no surprise that South African society has been (and in many ways remains) significantly divided along racial and ethnic lines. In fact, one of the most tragic effects of apartheid was that the social policy of racial segregation was compounded—indeed, reinforced—by political persecution and economic discrimination.

What is surprising is the extent to which both groups and individuals in contemporary South Africa identify with the South African nation and express patriotism toward the state. A recent public opinion survey found that 83 percent of respondents express pride in being South African, and about half of South Africans claim a primary identification as South African, versus about 10 percent of South Africans who identify primarily with an ethnic group. Unfortunately, this shared national identity has not easily been translated into domestic peace or tolerance among the country's various groups. Despite South Africa's ability to avoid much of the ethnic violence and civil war that plagues other portions of the continent, there is much truth to former president Thabo Mbeki's indictment that South Africa remains in many ways two nations: one is wealthy and largely white; the other, poor and largely black. And, alarmingly, the percentage of South Africans who express confidence that South Africa can achieve racial harmony, though still a majority, has been declining.

Racism in the Rainbow Nation

Race relations have come a long way since Nelson Mandela issued his famous call for a multiethnic "rainbow nation." Public opinion research demonstrates that in the first decade of democracy, most South Africans thought that race relations had improved. However, since democratization a number of highly publicized incidents have challenged the idea of a rainbow nation.

In 2008, after the administration of the formerly all-white Afrikaner University of the Free State decided to integrate dormitories, angry white students produced a video of a mock initiation in which black students (portrayed by black staff members) were humiliated. A discovery of a whites-only restroom in a police station, a shooting rampage by a racist youth gang (in which four blacks were killed), and a number of anti-Afrikaner slogans employed by Julius Malema, the former leader of the ANC Youth League, have all been disturbing examples of the fact that racism and racial tensions have not been eradicated. Malema, who was closely associated with President Jacob Zuma, made a series of statements that appeared to incite violence against Afrikaners leading to his 2010 conviction on charges of issuing hate speech and his expulsion from the ANC in 2012.

Ethnic and National Identity

As we have discussed, South Africa is truly a multiracial and multiethnic society. Under apartheid, the government not only enforced policies of separate racial development but also used its "homelands" policy to divide and conquer the country's many ethnic and tribal groups. Although Bantustans (homelands) were legally dissolved in 1994, many citizens (particularly urban blacks) had never identified with or even visited their alleged homeland. Nonetheless, black Africans, particularly rural blacks, retain strong ethnic identities.

Like black South Africans, the white population has a long history of ethnic division, stemming from the colonial-era conflict between the Afrikaners and the British. A century of sporadic violence between the Afrikaners and the English culminated in the 1910 establishment of the Union of South Africa. The English minority dominated the Union politically, economically, and culturally. In fact, it was the fear of English dominance that inspired the formation and growth of the Afrikaner National Party and its policies of cultural and racial purity during the first half of the twentieth century. Apartheid allowed Afrikaners to separate the minority whites from the majority blacks and to culturally dominate the white English subculture.

But whereas ethnic groups were fastidiously segregated under apartheid, language has rendered the multiethnic fabric of South Africa far more complex. Indeed, linguistic differences have brought groups together and pushed them apart. Nine languages spoken exclusively by blacks are now enshrined in the constitution. Though violently resisted by blacks during apartheid, Afrikaans remains the preferred tongue of Afrikaners as well as most colored South Africans. As is true in many polyglot former colonies, the English language unifies the country's citizens somewhat. However, because most blacks do not speak English as their first language, the more dominant it becomes in South Africa, the greater the disadvantage blacks will have vis-à-vis the white minority.

Similarly, religion has both unified and divided South African society. From a comparative perspective, South Africa remains a religious society. More than two-thirds of all South Africans, including most whites and coloreds and nearly

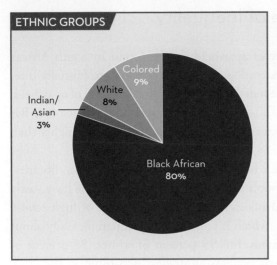

ETHNIC GROUPS

Indian/
Asian
3%

White
8%

Colored
9%

Black African
80%

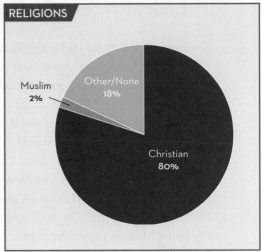

RELIGIONS

Muslim
2%

Other/None
18%

Christian
80%

two-thirds of blacks, identify themselves as Christian. Over 70 percent report that religion is very important to them, and 64 percent consider themselves religious.[23] However, the percentage of South Africans who claim to be religious dropped 19 percent from 2005 to 2012, and the 2011 census was the first to omit questions about religiosity.[24] The Dutch Reformed Church (sometimes called "the National Party in prayer") had a particularly important role in unifying Afrikaners (first against the British, then against black Africans) and providing divine justification (at least in the eyes of its members) for their separate and superior status.

As with racial discrimination in the United States, the dismantling of legal racism in South Africa and the national strides taken toward reconciliation have not fully eliminated racial prejudice or distrust. Levels of black-on-white violence and even black-on-black violence climbed during the 1990s, particularly in the townships. Murder rates in South Africa are now nearly nine times higher than those in the United States.

Despite persistent racial tensions, South Africans enjoy a remarkably high level of national identity and patriotism. And while the apartheid state essentially excluded all nonwhites from political life, citizenship is now universally shared. However, the legacies of division and exclusion, combined with the perceived inability of the ANC government to deliver socioeconomic benefits, have dampened citizen participation and increased levels of political apathy since apartheid ended. Recent polls show that support for democracy remains very strong in South Africa, but trust in government and satisfaction with government policy have declined in recent years.

Education as a Source of Inequality

Perhaps the most enduring legacy of apartheid can be found in South Africa's woefully inadequate education system.[25] Although its schools are formally integrated, de facto segregation by race remains the norm. Since the end of apartheid, the percentage of black South Africans receiving no schooling whatsoever has dropped from 24 percent to 10 percent, but that figure is still much higher than for whites, coloreds, or Asians.

Most schools serving blacks lack basic amenities such as textbooks, libraries, and science laboratories, while schools serving mostly white students have vastly superior facilities. Half of all students in South Africa drop out of high school before taking their "metric" exam, which is required for graduation. Only about half of blacks pass their metric exams, but 99 percent of whites, 92 percent of Indians, and 76 percent of coloreds get passing grades. According to the 2011 census, 8.3 percent of blacks received some sort of higher education—over double the percentage in 1996, two years after apartheid ended—but the percentage for white South Africans was over 36 percent. In 2015, nationwide protests on college campuses throughout South Africa called attention to the fact that blacks make up only a very small percentage of the total university population, and most university faculty members are white. This massive education deficit has created a major shortage of skilled black labor and is a serious impediment to the ANC's goal of integrating blacks into South Africa's business elite.

Ideology and Political Culture

Although it may be troubling for the future of South African democracy, a relative decline in levels of political interest since the tumultuous early 1990s should not be surprising. Since the fall of apartheid, political ideologies have also become less pronounced and more pragmatic. In the old South Africa, Afrikaner politicians and intellectuals combined and refined political and theological ideas to form an ideology of racist authoritarianism. Like many other movements of resistance in colonial and postcolonial settings, the ANC and other revolutionary opponents of apartheid (including the South African Communist Party) adopted radical socialist principles of economic egalitarianism and revolutionary political violence. Now the ANC government has reached out to both white capitalists and black voters, embracing liberal capitalism, promoting electoral democracy, and handily winning four national elections.

Likewise, differences among the very disparate political cultures of apartheid South Africa—between the ruling whites and oppressed blacks, the subcultures of Afrikaners and English, and even the Zulu and the Xhosa—have narrowed. Many South Africans have genuinely embraced the new culture of social inclusion and political participation and have supported efforts to integrate former adversaries and divided communities.

Certainly the highest-profile effort of bridge building was the **Truth and Reconciliation Commission**. Convened in 1995 and led by **Archbishop Desmond Tutu**, the commission was charged with two goals: first, establishing the "truth" of crimes committed (on all sides) from the time of the 1960 Sharpeville Massacre through the outlawing of apartheid in 1994; and second, using that truth as the essential foundation for healing the deep wounds of the era. The commission was given the authority to hear confessions, grant amnesty to those who were deemed to have told the complete truth, and provide recommendations for promoting long-term reconciliation (including reparation payments). While the commission uncovered a great deal of horrific "truth," much controversy surrounded the final report (some alleged it was too critical of apartheid, others suggested it was too quick to condemn actions by the ANC). Though it is not surprising, given the enormity of the crimes, genuine reconciliation has remained elusive. In February 2015, the Justice Ministry ordered the release of former police colonel Eugene de Kock, a self-confessed apartheid-era death squad leader responsible for over 100 acts of torture and murder. His release rekindled the debate over reconciliation. De Kock, whose nickname was "Prime Evil," had confessed his horrific crimes to the Truth and Reconciliation Commission and had received amnesty for many of them. South African courts nevertheless sentenced him to multiple life sentences until the ANC government decided to release him "in the interest of nation building and reconciliation."

Nonetheless, many observers remain optimistic that ANC-governed South Africa can overcome the tragedies of the country's history and its current social and economic woes, including endemic crime and violence. They argue that both the South African people and political culture have shown a remarkable capacity to avoid conflict even in the face of serious economic and social problems. Scholars note "countervailing sources of stability" in South Africa's political culture, including a pervasive tradition of collective decision making (known as *ubuntu*), the ANC's proven pragmatism and political discipline, and the "prudential caution" of whites and blacks that was forged during the period of transition. Perhaps most important, with the rise of a new black capitalist class, the country has seen the gradual emergence of a multiracial elite.

The Evolution of Levels of Trust in South Africa, 2006–2015

Percentage expressing a lot or some trust in:

	2006	2011	2015
Courts	68	56	57
Electoral agency	57	62	56
Police	48	49	45
Ruling party	61	61	41
Parliament	55	66	39
President	69	69	32

Source: www.afrobarometer.org (accessed 8/19/16).

South Africa's political culture shows many signs of supporting democracy. According to a 2011 public opinion study, about 60 percent of South Africans are satisfied with how democracy works (down from about 65 percent in 2006), and most of them think democracy is preferable to all other systems.[26] South Africans express strong support for the protection of civil liberties and minority rights, and a large majority of South Africans reject the notion of one-party rule. South Africans are split fairly evenly between those who believe that the government is responsible for improving the well-being of the population and those who believe that individuals are primarily responsible for themselves.

Political Economy

The political and social challenges confronting South Africa today cannot be separated from its economic challenges. Having vanquished the demon of apartheid, South Africa faces massive unemployment, growing income inequality, and persistent poverty among its poorest citizens.[27]

The challenge facing the ANC government has been to adopt policies that can ameliorate these problems without alienating its broad and disparate constituencies as well as to preserve South Africa's nascent democracy and civil liberties. Moreover, successful democratic political transition has not guaranteed the social and economic transformation of South Africa. In fact, it has in some ways made it more problematic, as issues of equality—delayed in the name of promoting political freedom—have taken on more significance.

To its credit, for two decades ANC governments were able to improve the economy by curtailing debt, reversing inflation, and expanding exports. They also improved employment opportunities and income for the growing black middle class; for South Africa's poor, they greatly expanded access to basic necessities, such as water, electricity, and housing (see "What Difference Did Democracy Make?," p. 715). By African standards, the South African economy is highly developed, and its companies have become major investors elsewhere in the region. South Africa's economy is also highly diversified although still fairly dependent on the country's large mineral resources, particularly gold and diamonds.

Historically, both British- and Afrikaner-controlled governments sponsored political-economic systems that favored their own ethnic constituents. In the early twentieth century, government policy facilitated English ownership and control of mines and other industries, even in Afrikaner-dominated regions of the country. Squeezed by wealthier and more highly skilled English workers from above and by cheaper black labor from below, Afrikaners sought political power largely to redress what they saw as economic oppression.

With this power, the NP government promoted essentially mercantilist policies of import substitution to promote local and, more specifically, Afrikaner industry. Though those policies were initially adopted to nurture an Afrikaner capitalist class, by the 1970s the international economic sanctions imposed on South Africa gave the state little option but to substitute local production and markets for those lost abroad. During its tenure, the NP government intervened extensively in the marketplace, imposing high tariffs and other trade barriers on imports; bestowing lucrative government contracts on favored firms; establishing state-owned enterprises (SOEs)

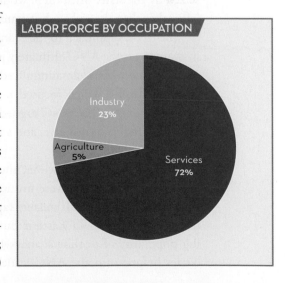

LABOR FORCE BY OCCUPATION

Industry 23%

Agriculture 5%

Services 72%

in such key industries as weapons, steel, and energy production; and using oligopolistic profits from industries ranging from gold and diamond exports to fuel industrialization.

Throughout the 1970s, the South African economy thrived and Afrikaners prospered. At the same time, the absence of economic opportunity for black Africans and the prohibition against the formation of black trade unions kept black labor costs artificially low, encouraging foreign investors eager to take advantage of the cheap labor and relative stability that authoritarian South Africa promised. During the 1980s, however, foreign firms and countries faced growing moral and legal pressures to divest their South African interests. At that time, too, multiracial trade unions (including COSATU) were legalized and began demanding higher wages. Finally, the government began to face a shortage of skilled labor. Limiting access to education for blacks meant that the economy could not depend on a large pool of educated workers. These pressures dealt severe—and some would say ultimately fatal—economic blows to the apartheid regime.

Given the history of policies benefiting the English and the Afrikaners, many observers expected the victorious ANC to adopt statist policies to redress the discrimination and exclusion that blacks had experienced for generations. Not only would such policies have promised to be popular with the ANC's majority black constituency, but this kind of progressive state intervention, designed to redistribute wealth and promote greater equality, would also have been in harmony with the long-standing socialist ideological heritage of the ANC and its allies. White property owners feared that a great share of their economic assets would simply be seized by the state. This, then, would be state manipulation of the market by the left rather than the right—but state intervention all the same.

The ANC's approach to the economy was much less radical than expected, and in many ways the ANC ultimately pursued a liberal political-economic model. In 1994, Nelson Mandela announced the Reconstruction and Development Programme (RDP), which focused on meeting the basic needs of South Africans living in poverty. The ANC argued that housing, electricity, jobs, safe drinking water, affordable health care, and a safe environment had to take precedence over economic growth.

Within two years, however, the ANC government had recognized that the huge costs of the RDP were unsustainable in the absence of substantially more foreign investment and greater, rapid economic growth. In addition, the failure of communism in Eastern Europe and the Soviet Union and the increasing popularity of neoliberal market solutions within international development circles helped turn the ANC leadership away from its socialist roots. In 1996,

What Difference Did Democracy Make?

% HOUSEHOLDS WITH	BLACK AFRICAN			COLORED			WHITE		
	1996	2001	2011	1996	2001	2011	1996	2001	2011
Formal dwelling	54	60	73	89	89	90	99	99	99
Tap water	74	80	89	95	97	98	97	99	99
Electricity	45	41	81	84	82	94	99	97	99
Flush toilets	78	78	90	88	89	92	99	99	99

Source: Statistics South Africa, based on national census data, www.statssa.gov.za/census/census_2011/census_products/Census_2011_Fact_sheet.pdf (accessed 7/10/17).

the government adopted a plan of liberal macroeconomic structural adjustment known as **Growth, Employment, and Redistribution (GEAR)**. GEAR called for opening trade, privatizing SOEs, and otherwise limiting the state's role in the marketplace in an effort to stimulate growth and attract foreign investment. These policies have paid dividends: growth rates under the ANC have been steady, if not spectacular, and are a vast improvement over apartheid-era governments.

Not surprisingly, this dramatic shift in redistributive priorities and interventionist policies has angered the ANC's longtime allies on the left, COSATU and the SACP. In labor protests against GEAR, COSATU leaders have called the GEAR privatization of the SOEs "born-again apartheid" and predicted devastating consequences for South Africa's working poor. The government has found itself in the position of being praised by the International Monetary Fund for promoting GEAR privatization and delivering steady rates of economic growth and at the same time being attacked by its erstwhile anti-apartheid allies. The 2013 creation of the Economic Freedom Fighters (EFF) Party by former ANC youth leader Julius Malema created a new electoral rival to the ANC's left. The EFF called for a dramatic increase in redistribution of South Africa's wealth and nationalization of some of the private sector.

In facing this catch-22, the government is trying to please all sides. The ANC remains committed to land reform and basic health care, and it funds programs to provide water, electricity, phones, and housing to the poor. It also continues to woo foreign investment by cutting inflation, lowering taxes, and keeping a lid on its spending to promote economic growth. It has targeted key industries and manufacturing sectors, offering low-interest loans and other incentives for investment. As in other developing economies, the government has promoted microcredit, or small-loan, initiatives designed to assist the very poorest in starting businesses. So far, GEAR and related policies have borne some fruit in the form of increased growth rates that, it is hoped, will help reduce unemployment over the coming decade. But there are still serious obstacles to be overcome.

Chief among these is persistent income inequality (see "In Comparison: Gini Index of Economic Inequality," p. 717). Despite the ANC government's affirmative action efforts and the emergence of a small but growing black middle and upper class, the white minority still dominates the economy. South Africa has one of the highest levels of income inequality in the world. Moreover, while the rising income of some blacks and the government's redistribution efforts have led to a decline in inequality among races, overall inequality among all South Africans continues to increase. The danger is that a white economic elite will simply be replaced by a black one, and income redistribution will be no better (and perhaps worse) than before apartheid.

The ANC has been especially unsuccessful in redistributing land, which remains overwhelmingly concentrated in the hands of the white minority. By 2016, less than 10 percent of land had been redistributed to blacks—a figure far short of the goal of 30 percent initially established by the ANC.[28] Until recently, the ANC has supported a system of voluntary land reform, in which the state purchased land for redistribution from willing sellers. In 2016, the ANC passed an Expropriation Bill, which allows the state to expropriate land from private owners as long as it pays fair market value for the property.

South Africa continues to suffer from extremely high rates of unemployment. By 2016, unemployment had risen to 26 percent, and the rate was much higher for young and black South Africans. Some have blamed South Africa's rigid labor laws, but COSATU and others have questioned the government's commitment to job creation. South Africa's growth rate has simply not been high enough to generate enough employment. The persistence of massive levels of poverty is an equally vexing problem facing South Africa. About half of all South Africans are below the official poverty level. When asked to identify the greatest problem facing South Africa, the largest percentage of survey respondents cited unemployment.[29]

Gini Index of Economic Inequality (Most Recent Year for Which Data Are Available)

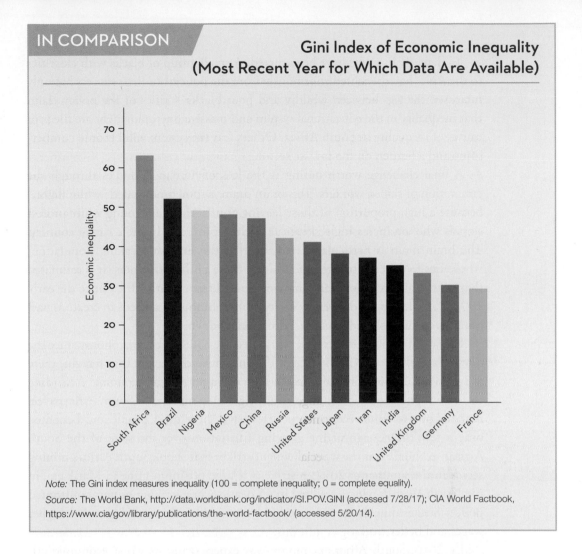

Note: The Gini index measures inequality (100 = complete inequality; 0 = complete equality).

Source: The World Bank, http://data.worldbank.org/indicator/SI.POV.GINI (accessed 7/28/17); CIA World Factbook, https://www.cia/gov/library/publications/the-world-factbook/ (accessed 5/20/14).

The ANC's main approach to affirmative action has been its policy of **Broad-Based Black Economic Empowerment (BEE)**. The goal of BEE is to increase the presence of disadvantaged South Africans (including coloreds and Asians) in a number of areas of the economy, including ownership of business, access to corporate management and training, and access to government procurement. Beginning in 2007, the government adopted a number of codes creating targets for each of these areas. State organizations and enterprises, and private-sector firms that want to do business with the state, must show progress on meeting some combination of these goals. New state agencies have been developed to rate organizations and enterprises, using "scorecards" that award points for meeting individual targets.

To date, BEE results have been mixed. A small group of blacks with close ties to the ANC have benefited enormously from the policy, but their success has only increased the gap between wealthy and poor blacks. Critics of the policy claim that inequality in the educational system and massive unemployment are the root causes of inequality in South Africa. Others fear the system will become cumbersome and a burden on the private sector.

A final challenge worth noting is the loss of human resources through the emigration of skilled workers. This brain drain is sometimes called "white flight," because a high proportion of those leaving South Africa are young white professionals who are increasingly skeptical of their prospects in their native country. The brain drain is particularly noticeable in the English-speaking population, whose ties to the country are not as old as those of the Afrikaners. It is estimated that nearly 20 percent of whites have emigrated from South Africa since the early 1990s.[30] To develop and diversify its economy, South Africa needs to create as well as retain its most skilled workers, both black and white.

Democratic governments have reoriented the South African economy since the days of apartheid. But in the face of the enormous challenges that remain, there is a growing disillusionment with the state of South Africa's economy. According to a recent public opinion study, a steadily growing number of South Africans feel that the government's economic policies have "hurt most people and benefited only a few."[31] One sign of the growing frustration over the state of the South African economy was the wave of violent strikes that shook South Africa's mining sector in the summer of 2012. A strike at a large platinum mine in Marikana, in the North West Province, resulted in 45 deaths when striking miners confronted police. Strikes quickly spread to other mines, where workers demanded higher wages and better working conditions.

By 2016, South Africa's economy was experiencing its worst economic crisis in decades. Growth was anemic and had declined for four consecutive years, South Africa's public debt increased dramatically, and its credit rating was lowered. Much of the downturn was caused by a sharp decline in prices for key export commodities. But President Zuma's inability to stem government spending and corruption, and his sometimes erratic governing style, have also contributed to the crisis. In March 2017, Zuma fired his finance minister, Pravin Gordhan, who had a reputation as a fierce anticorruption advocate. Gordhan was replaced by a Zuma loyalist with little economic expertise. The firing raised fears that Zuma might embrace a more populist political-economic orientation, and South Africa's international bond rating was downgraded to junk status as a result.

South African workers protest the deaths of 45 miners during clashes with police in 2012. The workers were striking for better pay, and the violence, which the press described as a massacre, increased tensions between the ANC government and South Africa's powerful National Union of Mineworkers.

Foreign Relations and the World

Under apartheid, South Africa was largely isolated from the outside world, limited in its economic and diplomatic ties. This isolation helped reinforce a siege mentality among the white population and directed much of the politics of the country inward. Relations with the rest of Africa were particularly hostile, often limited to military skirmishes with neighboring countries that harbored or supported the ANC. With the move to multiparty rule, South Africa was able to break out of its isolation, rebuilding ties in the region and in the international community as a whole.

As can be expected, however, the realities of this transition have been somewhat more complicated. For most observers, this complexity has been most obvious in the often prickly relationship between the ANC and members of the international community, whether they are other governments, intergovernmental organizations, or NGOs.

Former president Thabo Mbeki bristled at suggestions that his government was derelict in its response to the HIV/AIDS crisis and in addressing some of the main issues involved, such as sexual assault. ANC leaders have accused the international community of double standards and racism, and of treating South Africa as if it were still a colony of the imperial powers. Ironically, in some ways this defensiveness is reminiscent of the rhetoric of the apartheid-era NP, which also angrily rejected criticism from the international community.

Yet when we shift our focus from the international community to Africa alone, our perspective of South Africa changes. In the international community, South Africa is still a struggling country that confronts a series of major obstacles. In Africa, however, South Africa is a regional powerhouse with the continent's most powerful economy. By virtue of its large gross domestic product (GDP) and the country's vibrant private sector, South Africa has become central to trade and investment on the continent. South African exports to other African countries have risen substantially over the past decade, fostered in part by the lowering of trade barriers across the region. South Africa has also become a major investor in many neighboring countries. South African multinationals now play an important role in retail, banking, telecommunications, and other sectors in the region. This dominant economic presence has resulted in growing resentment of what is seen as a kind of South African imperialism whose effects are thought to be undermining local African businesses and increasingly controlling the regional economy. Inside South Africa, these actions have also been criticized as running counter to the goals of economic development within South Africa itself. Furthermore, at the other end of this relationship, the far better economic conditions in South Africa have attracted millions of illegal immigrants over the past decade, fueling xenophobia among the South African population and mistreatment of immigrants by the police, immigration officials, and the public as a whole.

South Africa's regional power has expanded in the diplomatic sphere as well. An important element of this growing influence is the country's role in the formation of the **African Union (AU)**, which replaced the Organization of African Unity (OAU) in 2002. In many ways inspired by the European Union, the AU seeks to depart from the OAU in pursuing greater political and economic integration across the continent. As the first head of the AU, Thabo Mbeki sought to position the organization as a mediator between African states and the advanced democracies. The AU's top official is currently Nkosazana Dlamini-Zuma, an ex-wife of President Zuma, a former cabinet minister, and the first woman to head the organization. South Africa has also helped create the **Southern African**

Development Community (SADC), a 15-member body that is also concerned with regional economic integration and cooperation in southern Africa.

A cornerstone of regional integration and cooperation has been the **New Partnership for Africa's Development (NEPAD)**. NEPAD proposes that the developed world's support for African countries, unlike past aid or loan programs, be tied to commitments to the rule of law and democracy. Progress toward this goal is to be monitored by the AU. If the AU is able to show progress in tying aid to economic and political progress in the region, it will no doubt boost its own power, and with it the regional and international authority of South Africa.

Finally, South Africa has been directly involved in peacekeeping and peacemaking efforts in the region. In recent years, the South African government has worked at brokering an end to civil conflicts in Angola, Burundi, Congo, and Liberia, and it has troops on the ground as peacekeepers or observers in several African countries.

Thus South Africa's role in the region has been transformed from pariah to continental leader and mediator with the advanced democracies. But this power has its own costs. In many ways, South Africa has become a regional hegemon—a dominant power able to set the rules for the region, adjudicate disputes between countries, and punish those who fail to go along. South Africa's authority is further reinforced because it has the most powerful army on the continent as well as a sophisticated arms industry (as a legacy of apartheid).

Any important actor in the international system knows that power comes with a certain degree of contradiction. In that respect, South Africa is no different from any other country with more power than its neighbors. What complicates matters for South Africa, however, is that its new regime has been built on moral authority—the need for democracy, multiethnicity, and tolerance. As a result, South Africa has been at the forefront of promoting democracy in the region through its own diplomatic efforts as well as its participation in the AU and the SADC. Yet its efforts have often been viewed in the region as patronizing, not unlike the behavior of the advanced democracies toward South Africa that Mbeki often condemned. This view is reinforced by the perception of double standards. In the economic realm, some observers see South Africa's economic relations with the continent as those of domination. The formation of NEPAD, too, has been criticized by some Africans as an attempt to bring a neoliberal version of GEAR to the rest of Africa, thereby primarily benefiting South African economic interests.

In the diplomatic sphere as well, South Africa's calls for greater democracy in the region have rung hollow in the face of the country's support for Zimbabwe, whose deepening authoritarianism was facilitated, in part, by South African diplomatic and economic support. The ANC leadership has long had close ties with Zimbabwe's authoritarian leader, Robert Mugabe. His Zimbabwe African National Union (ZANU), which ended white rule in 1980, was initially a role model and later a source of support for the ANC. As Mugabe's rule became increasingly repressive, and as Zimbabwe became a pariah state, ANC presidents continued to support Mugabe. As Zimbabwe's economy deteriorated, and as a flood of Zimbabwean refugees threatened to overwhelm South Africa, many within the ANC and organized labor have begun to demand more support for democratic change in Zimbabwe. Like many other countries around the world, South Africa has found that its increased international power has led to a clash of morality, stability, and self-interest.

However, there can be little doubt that democratization has enhanced the international power and prestige of South Africa. In 2007, and again in 2010, South Africa was elected as a nonpermanent member of the UN Security Council. In April 2011, it was formally inducted into the BRIC group of emerging regional powers, which is now known as BRICS (Brazil, Russia, India, China, and South Africa).

Under President Zuma, South Africa's foreign policy has continued to be difficult to predict. Zuma called for the resignation of Egyptian president Mubarak in 2011 and was one of the few government leaders to congratulate Chinese dissident Liu Xiaobo for his Nobel Peace Prize. However, his government denied the Dalai Lama a visa to attend a meeting of Nobel Peace Prize laureates in South Africa, maintained good relations with Libyan dictator Muammar Gaddafi, welcomed Sudan's Omar al-Bashir (indicted by an international tribunal for war crimes), and continued to take a conciliatory approach to the Mugabe government in Zimbabwe.

CURRENT ISSUES IN SOUTH AFRICA

Crime and Corruption

South Africans regularly cite crime as among the most serious problems facing the country. Crime rates skyrocketed after the transition to democracy but have steadily dropped after peaking in 2003. The rate of violent crime in South Africa, including murder, rape, and carjacking, is extremely high. Nearly 15,000 South

Africans are murdered each year, a rate nine times greater than the U.S. average. Carjacking, often resulting in death or serious injury, is commonplace and has increased dramatically since 1994. Pernicious inequality, unemployment, and poverty, particularly in the townships, and corruption in the police force have exacerbated the serious crime problem. Crime not only undermines the social fabric but also deters domestic and international investment and diverts security resources that could be spent elsewhere.

South Africa also faces a serious problem of deep-seated government corruption. According to South Africa's auditor general, graft and cronyism have led to massive waste and have hampered the government's ability to deliver services and reduce inequality.[32] Public opinion research has shown a steady growth in public concern about corruption since 1994, fueled in part by a number of high-profile corruption scandals that affected the governing ANC. By 2011, a quarter of South African respondents told researchers that corruption was one of the most important problems facing the country; this figure was double the one in 2002.[33] The data show that provincial local governments in particular are viewed as corrupt (over half of respondents view them as corrupt), while about 40 percent of respondents view the president and legislators as corrupt.

Faced with growing public concern over corruption, in 1999 President Mbeki established an elite crime-fighting unit: the Directorate of Special Operations, popularly known as the Scorpions. The unit, whose motto was "loved by the people, feared by the criminals," was well funded, highly trained, and had its own staff of investigators and prosecutors. It quickly became a popular and highly effective unit, achieving conviction rates much higher than those of the regular police force. The Scorpions ran into trouble, however, when the force began to investigate corruption within the ANC government. When they brought corruption charges against then former deputy president Jacob Zuma that led to his firing, Zuma's supporters claimed that the Scorpions were merely attempting to limit opposition within the ANC. A bitter political rivalry and turf war broke out between the police and the Scorpions. Despite widespread public opposition in 2008, Zuma's supporters passed legislation that reintegrated the Scorpions into the police force, effectively disbanding the unit.

Once in office, Zuma pledged to crack down on corruption by creating a performance, monitoring, and evaluation cabinet post within the government. Nevertheless, in recent years the ANC has been rocked by numerous scandals that call into question Zuma's commitment to fighting corruption. Zuma has attempted to weaken the power of the National Prosecuting Authority, the government prosecution office that has raised over 700 charges of corruption, fraud,

Demonstrators protest the perceived corruption of President Jacob Zuma in April 2017.

and tax evasion. Allegations that the president is corrupt and a 2016 court ruling that he used public funds to remodel his personal residence, have contributed to the concern about a growing lack of transparency. Zuma's 2017 firing of a well-respected anticorruption finance minister led to nationwide protests against the perceived corruption of the ANC.

The Devastation of HIV/AIDS

South Africa is believed to have the highest number of HIV-positive citizens in the world (estimated in 2015 at about 7 million people, or 18 percent of the population), and at the height of the epidemic 1,000 South Africans died of AIDS every day.[34] Despite increased access to affordable drugs, most of those infected will die of the disease. Besides being a human and social tragedy, this situation will have, and already has had, huge consequences for the economy. The HIV/AIDS pandemic has damaged South Africa's economy, and South Africans' life expectancy has dropped from age 60 to age 50 in the past two decades. The health care system is underfunded and grossly inadequate, and corporations are increasingly wary of investing in personnel, given the mortality odds their employees face.

Compounding this problem is a high degree of stigma attached to those with HIV/AIDS, not to mention the questionable handling of the issue by Thabo Mbeki and other ANC politicians. They cast doubt on the causal link between HIV and AIDS and resisted conventional drugs and drug protocols prescribed in the West, citing scientifically dubious theories and charging the West with racist views of African sexuality. Pressure from international and domestic activist groups and from Nelson Mandela (whose son died of AIDS) is slowly raising awareness and the level of treatment, but treatment remains limited in the face of this devastating epidemic.

Under President Zuma, South Africa is beginning to make gains in the fight against HIV/AIDS. His government has initiated the world's largest HIV testing and treatment program. (Zuma publicly announced that he had been tested.) There is now evidence that the rate of HIV/AIDS infections has leveled off, but attempts to stem the tide are hampered by the reluctance of South African men to use condoms as well as the alarmingly high rate of rape. Rumors that President Zuma favors Nkosazana Dlamini Zuma to be his successor has alarmed some public health advocates. She is a former wife of Zuma, and current chair of the African Union, who, as South Africa's health minister from 1994 to 1999, rejected advice from the scientific community about the best way to treat HIV/AIDS.

NOTES

1. Anthony Sampson, "Men of the Renaissance," *Guardian* (London), January 3, 1998, 19.
2. "Summary of Results," Afrobarometer, Round Five, 2012, www.afrobarometer.org (accessed 5/20/14).
3. For a discussion of South African history, see Leonard Thompson, *The History of South Africa* (New Haven, CT: Yale University Press, 2001).
4. "Apartheid Legislation 1850s–1970s," *South African History Online*, www.sahistory.org.za/article /apartheid-legislation-1850s-1970s (accessed 7/12/17); contains a detailed explanation of the apartheid legislative acts.
5. For more on the emergence of the struggle against apartheid and Mandela's role in it, see Nelson Mandela, *Long Walk to Freedom: The Autobiography of Nelson Mandela* (Boston: Little, Brown, 1996).
6. Neeta Misra-Dexter and Judith February, eds., *Testing Democracy: Which Way Is South Africa Going?* (Cape Town: ABC Press, IDASA, 2010), vii.
7. Pierre de Vos, "Key Institutions Affecting Democracy in South Africa," in Misra-Dexter and February, eds., *Testing Democracy*, 94–116.

8. J. L. Gibson and J. A. Caldeira, "Defenders of Democracy? Legitimacy, Popular Acceptance, and the South African Constitutional Court," *Journal of Politics* 65, no. 1 (February 2003): 1–30.

9. *Economist*, "President v Judges," December 10, 2011, www.economist.com/node/21541450 (accessed 12/23/11).

10. Vinothan Naidoo, "The Provincial Government Reform Process in South Africa: Policy Discretion and Developmental Relevance," *Politikon* 36, no. 2 (August 2009): 259–74.

11. Celia Dugger, "South Africa Exults Abroad but Frets at Home," *New York Times*, April 19, 2011, 4; and Iris Wielders, "Perceptions and Realities of Corruption in South Africa," Afrobarometer Briefing Paper 110, January 2013, www.afrobarometer.org (accessed 5/20/13).

12. On the ANC, see Roger Southall, "From Liberation Movement to Party Machine? The ANC in South Africa," *Journal of Contemporary African Studies* 32, no. 3 (2014): 331–48.

13. For one account, see Andrew Feinstein, *After the Party: A Personal and Political Journey through the ANC* (Johannesburg: Jonathan Ball Publishers, 2007).

14. Paul Graham and Carmen Alpin, "Public Attitudes towards the President of the Republic of South Africa, Jacob Zuma," Afrobarometer Briefing Paper 104, October 2012, www.afrobarometer.org (accessed 5/26/14).

15. Paul Graham, "Party Identification in South Africa: Profiles for the ANC and the DA," Afrobarometer Briefing Paper 108 December 2012, www.afrobarometer.org (accessed 6/6/17).

16. See, for example, Alex Boraine, *What's Gone Wrong? South Africa on the Brink of Failed Statehood* (New York: NYU Press, 2014).

17. Kebapetse Lotshwao, "The Lack of Internal Party Democracy in the African National Congress: A Threat to the Consolidation of Democracy in South Africa," *Journal of African Studies* 35, no. 4 (December 2009): 901–14.

18. Karen E. Ferree, "Framing the Race in South Africa: The Political Origins of Racial-Census Elections (New York: Cambridge University Press, 2011), 1.

19. The data are taken from Karen Ferree, "The Microfoundations of Ethnic Voting, Evidence from South Africa," Afrobarometer Working Paper 40, June 2004, www.afrobarometer.org (accessed 12/17/11).

20. Steven Friedman, "Beneath the Surface: Civil Society and Democracy after Polokwane," in Misra-Dexter and February, eds., *Testing Democracy*, 117.

21. Ann-Sofie Isaksson, "Political Participation in Africa: Participatory Inequalities and the Role of Resources," Afrobarometer Working Paper 121, September 2010, www.afrobarometer.org (accessed 6/3/11).

22. On COSATU, see Sakhela Buhlungu, "Gaining Influence but Losing Power? COSATU Members and the Democratic Transformation of South Africa," *Social Movement Studies* 7, no. 1 (May 2008): 31–42.

23. Misra-Dexter and February, eds., *Testing Democracy*, 153.

24. Gallup International, Global Index of Religiosity and Atheism, 2012, www.wingia.com/web/files/news/14/file/14.pdf (accessed 5/23/14).

25. *Economist,* "South African Schools: Desegregation and Investment Have Yet to Boost Black Schoolchildren," January 13, 2011, www.economist.com/node/17913496 (accessed 7/10/17).

26. "Summary of Results," 2006 and 2011, www.afrobarometer.org (accessed 5/21/14).

27. An excellent overview is Charles Simkins, "South African Disparities," *Journal of Democracy* 22, no. 3 (July 2011): 105–19.

28. *Economist*, "Land Reform in South Africa," December 3, 2009, www.economist.com/node/15022632 (accessed 7/10/17).

29. Afrobarometer data, www.afrobarometer.org (accessed 5/21/14).
30. Dominic Griffiths and Maria L. C. Prozesky, "The Politics of Dwelling: Being White in South Africa," *Africa Today* 56, no. 4 (summer 2010): 28.
31. Misra-Dexter and February, eds., *Testing Democracy*, 162.
32. Lydia Polgreen, "South Africans Suffer as Graft Saps Provinces," *New York Times*, February 18, 2012, www.nytimes.com/2012/02/19/world/africa/south-africans-suffer-as-graft-saps-social-services.html?ref=southafrica&pagewanted=print (accessed 5/22/14).
33. Iris Wielders, "Perceptions and Realities of Corruption in South Africa," Afrobarometer Briefing Paper 110, January 2013, www.afrobarometer.org (accessed 5/20/14).
34. Estimate by the United Nations AIDS Organization, http://www.unaids.org/en/regionscountries/countries/southafrica (accessed 6/6/17).

KEY TERMS

African National Congress (ANC) South Africa's major anti-apartheid liberation movement; also the governing party since the return of democracy in 1994

African Union (AU) An organization of African nations pursuing greater political and economic integration across the continent

Afrikaans The language of South Africa's Dutch settlers (Afrikaners)

Afrikaners White South Africans who speak Afrikaans and are descendants of Dutch, French, and German colonists

apartheid The policy of segregation put in place by the Afrikaner-dominated racist authoritarian regime in South Africa that was in power from 1948 to 1994

Bantustans Tribal "homelands" established by the apartheid regime to deprive the black majority of South African citizenship

Boers The early Dutch settlers in South Africa; the term is also used to describe Afrikaners

Boer Wars The two epic wars fought between the Boers and the British that culminated in the defeat of the Afrikaners and their integration into the Union of South Africa

BRICS An organization of emerging countries in the developing world; members include Brazil, Russia, India, China, and South Africa

Broad-Based Black Economic Empowerment (BEE) South Africa's affirmative action program that aims to create a new class of black owners and management through a series of quotas and targets

colored Widely used term in South Africa to describe citizens of mixed race, largely concentrated in and around Cape Town

Congress of South African Trade Unions (COSATU) South Africa's most important trade union confederation, closely linked to the governing ANC

de Klerk, F. W. Final president of the apartheid regime; he negotiated the transition to democracy with the ANC

Democratic Alliance (DA) South Africa's main opposition party

Dutch Reformed Church Conservative Protestant Church that has historically been central to Afrikaner culture

Economic Freedom Fighters (EFF) A leftist political party that broke away from the ANC in 2013; it is led by the former head of the ANC youth, Julius Malema

Great Trek The epic migration of Afrikaners (Voortrekkers) into the interior of South Africa in 1835 to escape British colonization

Group Areas Act The centerpiece of apartheid legislation that divided South Africans into four racial categories and required strict segregation of housing along racial lines

Growth, Employment, and Redistribution (GEAR) The 1996 liberal macroeconomic structural adjustment plan that moved the ANC toward a more market-friendly political policy

Indians The term used by South Africans to describe citizens of Southeast Asian origin

Inkatha Freedom Party (IFP) The small Zulu political party that is currently a party in opposition to the ANC

Maimane, Mmusi The current leader of the Democratic Alliance and leader of the opposition in the National Assembly; he is the party's first black leader

Mandela, Nelson The long-imprisoned leader of the ANC who became South Africa's first post-apartheid president

Mbeki, Thabo South Africa's former two-term president who was forced to resign in 2008 when he failed to win the election as the ANC leader

National Assembly South Africa's legislature

National Party (NP) The now-defunct party that created apartheid and dominated politics during the apartheid era

New Partnership for Africa's Development (NEPAD) The African Union program that attempts to tie foreign development aid to a commitment to democracy and the rule of law

Southern African Development Community (SADC) A 15-member African regional economic and cooperation community, of which South Africa was a founding member

Soweto A township created during apartheid to house blacks who were forcibly removed from Johannesburg

Truth and Reconciliation Commission The post-apartheid body established to document apartheid-era human rights abuses and to give reparations to victims and amnesty to perpetrators who confessed to crimes

Tutu, Archbishop Desmond The anti-apartheid activist and leader of South Africa's Anglican Church who chaired the Truth and Reconciliation Commission

Union of South Africa The 1910 name given to the British colony that integrated British and Afrikaner colonists after the Boer Wars

United Democratic Front (UDF) The unified anti-apartheid coalition created in 1983 from the major black and white opposition groups

Voortrekkers The Afrikaner pioneers who migrated into South Africa's interior to escape British colonists

Zuma, Jacob South Africa's current president, as of 2009

WEB LINKS

- African National Congress (www.anc.org.za)
- African Studies Internet Resources: South Africa, Columbia University Libraries (www.columbia.edu/cu/lweb/indiv/africa/cuvl/SAfr.html)
- Afrobarometer (www.afrobarometer.org)
- Democratic Alliance (www.da.org.za)
- Inkatha Freedom Party (www.ifp.org.za)
- *Mail and Guardian* (www.mg.co.za)
- South African Broadcasting Corporation (www.sabcnews.co.za/portal/site /SABCNews/)
- South African government (www.gov.za)

14

Nigeria's vast oil resources have been a source of great wealth, but this "resource curse" has also fostered endemic corruption and violence, exacerbated income inequality, and caused untold environmental damage.

NIGERIA

Why Study This Case?

Nigeria stands out in ways both impressive and disheartening. First, this "giant of Africa" is noteworthy for its sheer size: it is the most populous country in Africa and is predicted by midcentury to trail only India and China as the world's third-most-populous nation. Second, in 2014, Nigeria passed South Africa as the continent's largest economy. And third, unlike many other African countries, Nigeria is blessed with enormous natural wealth, from oil to agriculture. Following independence from British rule in 1960, these assets were expected to make Nigeria a major regional, if not global, actor.

Yet exactly the opposite happened. Nigeria has become renowned for all that can go wrong with political misrule, social unrest, economic inequality, and environmental degradation. For much of the time since independence, the country has been under military rule. These long periods of military dictatorship have coincided with widespread corruption, and substantial portions of the country's oil revenues and other resources have been channeled to those in power. Even as Nigeria earns billions of dollars in oil exports each year, it has become one of the poorest and least-developed countries in the world. Nigeria offers an excellent example of a country whose natural resources have been used by those in power to buy supporters and repress the public.

However, the long era of military rule may now be at an end. In 1999, Nigeria returned to civilian rule, and since then a fragile democratic system has taken hold. Still, much remains to be done. Nigeria lacks effective rule of law and continues to be recognized as one of the most corrupt countries in the world. The state lacks the capacity to carry out many basic tasks and also has questionable control over the monopoly of violence, in terms of both civilian authority over the military and the ability to contain the country's widespread political and criminal

NIGERIA

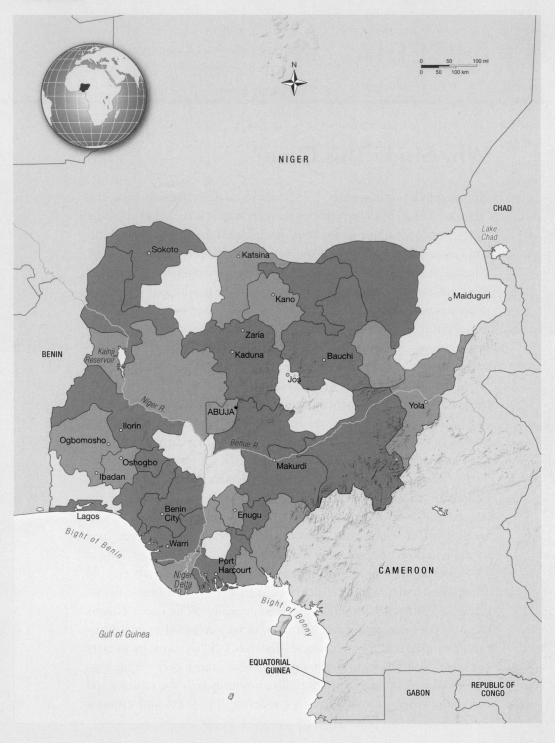

violence. The standard of living for the average Nigerian remains very low—more than three-fourths of the population survives on less than two dollars per day, which is far below what the country's wealth should ensure. And despite the return of democratic governance, levels of corruption, economic underdevelopment, income inequality, political violence, and environmental damage have increased rather than declined.

These legacies of political misrule may seem challenging enough for Nigeria, but the country's sheer size and diversity are another concern. Nigeria is made up of more than 250 ethnic groups, whose local interests and differences have been sharpened by a perniciously corrupt form of federalism. Although nearly three decades of military rule kept this fractiousness in check, democratic rule has allowed tensions and violence to surface. Most disturbing are the growing ethnic rifts between the Muslim north and the Christian and animist south as well as the rise of an Islamic insurgency in the former region associated with the terrorist organization **Boko Haram**. At a time when many global conflicts center on religion and religious fundamentalism, the prospect of increasing tension among faiths in Nigeria leads some observers to worry that in the long run, the country will be ungovernable and will return to authoritarianism, civil war, or both. Is Nigeria doomed to be a failed or even partitioned state?

Nigeria provides a fascinating, if daunting, example of the possibilities and potential limits of state power and democracy under conditions of postcolonialism and a vast wealth of natural resources. Can the most recent transition from military rule to democracy help bring stability and prosperity to Nigeria? Or are the problems of state capacity and autonomy such that democracy cannot help improve them—and might even make them worse? We will consider these tensions as we investigate Nigeria's political heritage, current institutions, social challenges, and economic and political prospects.

Major Geographic and Demographic Features

One of Nigeria's most impressive features is its sheer size. With over 181 million inhabitants, Nigeria has the largest national population in Africa and currently ranks seventh in the world. Lying along the western coast of the continent, Nigeria has a diverse climate and geography. The Niger-Benue river system divides the country into distinct regions. The north is relatively arid and known for its grasslands, while the south is characterized by tropical forests and coastal swamps.

Nigeria's geography and climate (particularly in the south) favor agriculture. Nearly a third of the land is arable, compared to only 15 percent of the land in China and 20 percent in the United States. Until oil became a major export commodity in the 1960s, cocoa and nuts were a major source of foreign trade. Recent droughts and ongoing desertification in the north have hampered agricultural production and, combined with the growing threat of terrorist violence in the region, have prompted southern migration, placing increasing demands on the already densely populated south.

Nigeria's best-known region is the **Niger Delta**. The Niger River enters the sea at that point, creating a vast, swampy area of over 5,000 square miles. It is the third-largest wetland in the world, after the Netherlands and the Mississippi Delta, and host to an enormous range of plants and animals. The Niger Delta is also home to over 30 million people, who have traditionally been engaged in farming and fishing. The complicated topography of the area has limited interaction, integration, and assimilation, thus fostering a large variety of ethnicities. By some estimates, over a dozen groups speaking some 25 languages inhabit the Delta. It is also one of the poorest regions of the country thanks to limited infrastructure and development.

But the Niger Delta is also the source of Nigeria's oil, which in most years comprises over 90 percent of the country's exports. And while oil production in the Delta has been a mixed blessing at best for the country as a whole, contributing to both national wealth and national corruption, its local consequences are just as profound but almost entirely negative. The first and most commonly cited local effect is environmental degradation. In the half century since oil production began, accidents, poor maintenance, and sabotage have caused many thousands of spills and leaked millions of gallons of oil into this highly biodiverse region. Their effects on the wetland ecosystem and human population are a source of intense domestic and international controversy.[1] Oil production has also abetted ethnic conflicts in the region. Groups compete for access to siphoned oil and occasionally attack oil facilities to draw attention to their demands or to seek ransoms. Finally, oil production has exacerbated intergroup hostility in the Delta, for some groups have perceived others as having benefited disproportionately from the industry.[2] Given the importance of oil to Nigeria, the problems of this region significantly affect the security of the country as a whole.

The diversity marking the Delta is mirrored across the country. Nigeria is home to some 250 ethnic groups. Dominant among them are the **Hausa** and the **Fulani**, who are overwhelmingly Muslim and concentrated in the north; the **Igbo** (also spelled *Ibo*), who are predominantly Christian and concentrated in the southeast; and the **Yoruba**, who inhabit the southwest and whose members are divided among Christian, Muslim, and local animist faiths.

Nigeria's large population is a function of its fertility rate. In the past 20 years, the country's population has doubled, and nearly half the population is now under the age of 14. A recent United Nations study projects that Nigeria's population will more than double by 2050, making it the third most populous country in the world behind China and India.[3] The presence of a large, rapidly growing, ethnically and religiously diverse population will continue to complicate development, stability, and governance.

Historical Development of the State

Like many other developing countries, Nigeria's history progressed from local political organization to imperial control to more recent independence and instability. Contrary to common assumptions, precolonial Nigeria was neither undeveloped nor poorly organized. Rather, the region contained varying degrees and kinds of political and social organizations, some of which were highly complex and wide ranging. Although we cannot explore each of them in depth, we can point to some of the earliest and most powerful examples.

Nigeria was the setting for several early kingdoms. Over 2,000 years ago, the members of the Nok society, located in what is now central Nigeria, fashioned objects out of iron and terra-cotta with a degree of sophistication unmatched in West Africa, though little else is known about their civilization. As the roots of today's dominant ethnic groups began to take shape, new forms of political organization emerged. Around 1200 C.E., the Hausa to the north established a series of powerful city-states that served as conduits of north–south trade. In the southwest, the Yoruba kingdom of Oyo extended its power beyond the borders of modern-day Nigeria into present-day Togo. This kingdom grew wealthy through trade and the exploitation of natural resources, facilitated by its location along the coast. In the southeast, the Igbo maintained less-centralized political power, though they too had a precedent of earlier kingdoms and would come to play a central role in modern Nigerian politics.

Islam and the Nigerian North

The fortunes of these three dominant ethnic groups (the Hausa, Yoruba, and Igbo) and other peoples in what is now Nigeria changed dramatically as contact with peoples, politics, and ideas from outside West Africa increased. The first important impact came not from Europe, however, but from the Middle East, with the spread of Islam.

By the eleventh century, Islam had found its way into the Hausa region of northern Nigeria, carried along trade routes linking the region to North Africa and beyond. By the fifteenth century, Islam had brought literacy and scholarship to the region through the Arabic language, though the religion and its influences remained largely confined to the Hausa elite. By the late eighteenth century, however, expanding contact with Islamic regions led to increasing conversions to the faith. The religion's growing influence was solidified by the leadership of Usman dan Fodio (1754–1817).

A religious scholar, Usman played an important role in spreading Islam among the Hausa and Fulani. He found widespread support among the peasantry, who felt oppressed under the city-states' warring monarchies and who saw in Islam's message a promise of greater social equality. Their embrace of Islam in turn alarmed those in power, eventually precipitating a conflict between the city-states and Usman. Following an initial conflict, Usman declared jihad against the Hausa city-states in 1804 and by 1808 had overthrown the ruling monarchs, establishing what became known as the **Sokoto Caliphate**. The Sokoto Caliphate became the largest empire in Africa at the time, providing a uniform government to a region previously wracked by war. Islam would now play a central role in western Africa and in the eventual establishment of an independent Nigerian state.

European Imperialism

As Islam and centralized political organization spread across the north, the south experienced similarly dramatic effects with the arrival of the European powers. As far back as the late fifteenth century, Europeans had begun arriving along Nigeria's coast, purchasing from indigenous traders agricultural products and slaves (often captives from local wars). From the seventeenth to the nineteenth century, Europeans established several coastal ports to support the burgeoning trade in slaves, and the United Kingdom became the major trading power. During that time, more than 3 million slaves were shipped from Nigeria to the Americas.

In 1807, the United Kingdom declared the slave trade illegal and established a naval presence off Nigeria's coast for enforcement, though illegal trade continued for another half century. The precipitous decline in the region's major export contributed to the collapse of the Yoruba's Oyo Empire and to divisions and warfare among its people. This disunity in turn paved the way for an expanded British presence in the interior. The colonial presence further expanded as British industrialization generated ever-greater demand for resources, such as palm oil, cocoa, and timber. That demand radically changed the nature of agricultural production and encouraged greater reliance on local slavery to produce these goods. At the same time, British missionaries began to proselytize in the coastal and southern regions, converting large numbers of Igbo and Yoruba to Christianity.

By 1861, the British had established a colony at Lagos. By the time of the 1884–85 Berlin Conference, other European powers had recognized the United Kingdom's "sphere of influence" along the coast. Fearing French and German encroachment in the interior, the United Kingdom quickly joined the European powers' **scramble for Africa** by asserting its authority far inland. Through a combination of diplomacy, co-optation, and force, Britain established control over both the north and the south.

In many areas, the British relied upon a policy of indirect rule. For example, as the Sokoto Caliphate was brought under British control, local leaders were allowed to keep their positions and so were absorbed into the new state bureaucracy. Furthermore, the British colonial administration respected **Sharia**—Islamic law—in noncriminal matters and prohibited Christian proselytizing in the region. Such policies helped limit local resistance but increased the power of some ethnic groups over others, giving them greater authority within the imperial administration. In areas where indirect rule was less successful, as among the Igbo, resistance was much more significant. In 1914, the various protectorates in the area under British control were unified under the name *Nigeria*. However, as a reflection and reinforcement of its distinct regional differences, the country remained highly decentralized administratively.

Following unification, Nigeria experienced dramatic change under British imperial rule. The British developed a modern infrastructure including ports, roads, and railways to facilitate economic development and extraction. Agricultural production continued to play an important role in exports. Within Nigerian society, development meant establishing Western educational policies and institutions, especially in regions where Christian missionaries were active. In general, indirect rule meant the development of a new local elite group that was more Westernized and more conscious of the complexities of imperialism. The creation of a colonial legislative council, with local elections for some of the seats, introduced the idea of democratic representative institutions, no matter how limited.

It might be thought that the development of a Westernized elite would help perpetuate imperial control. Instead, as in other British colonies such as India, exposure to Western ideas served as the foundation for resistance as Nigerians embraced what had once been alien concepts of nationalism, sovereignty, and self-rule. Such ideas, however, were not easily planted in Nigeria's complex political and cultural terrain. For some activists, anticolonialism meant a greater role for Nigeria and other African states in the Commonwealth of Nations (the loose affiliation of former British colonies opposed to complete independence). For others, it meant reassertion of precolonial political structures destroyed or weakened by British rule. As economic development, urbanization, and state centralization increased the integration of Nigeria as a whole, however, the tentative notion of a Nigerian nation and state that could be independent from colonial rule began to emerge.

Following World War II, Nigeria saw the rapid expansion of various civil society organizations, ranging from political parties and ethnic movements to labor unions and business movements. Among the numerous political leaders who emerged during that time was **Benjamin Nnamdi Azikiwe** (1904–96). Born in northern Nigeria, Azikiwe studied and taught in the United States before returning to Nigeria in 1938. He established a daily newspaper and in 1944 helped found what later came to be known as the National Council of Nigerian Citizens (NCNC), which advocated national unity and self-government. While the NCNC sought to appeal to all Nigerians, it drew heavily from the Igbo. Other political parties, such as the Northern People's Congress (NPC) and the Action Group Party (AGP), were backed by Hausa Muslims and the Yoruba, respectively.

The British government attempted to deal with the rising tide of Nigerian activism, strikes, and competing demands by reforming the local constitution, creating regional assemblies, and formalizing the decentralized nature of imperial rule through a system of federalism. Executive power remained in the hands of a British governor, but increasingly authority devolved to the local level. Thus, while Nigerian nationalism became a potent force among some political elites, at the same time the devolution of power reinforced regional tendencies.

By the late 1950s, a great wave of independence was sweeping across Africa. The British government took measures to move Nigeria toward full independence. The British legislated an array of constitutional reforms that effectively created autonomous regions in the north, west, and east with the goal of ensuring the country's eventual national independence while remaining within the British Commonwealth. The new federal political structure consisted of three regions (Northern, Western, and Eastern), a directly elected House of Representatives, a Senate whose members were indirectly elected by the regional assemblies, a prime minister, and a governor-general who served as the representative of the British monarchy. Azikiwe was appointed governor-general.

TIMELINE OF POLITICAL DEVELOPMENT

YEAR	EVENT
1100s	Hausa kingdom is formed in the north; Oyo kingdom is formed in the southwest.
1472	Portuguese navigators reach the Nigerian coast.
1500s–1800s	Slave trade develops and flourishes.
1809	Sokoto Caliphate is founded.
1861–1914	Britain acquires Lagos and establishes a series of Nigerian protectorates.
1960	Nigeria achieves independence and creates the First Republic.
1967–70	In Nigerian Civil War, Biafra fails to win independence.
1976	Olusegun Obasanjo comes to power, initiating transition to civilian rule.
1979	Elections bring Shehu Shagari to power, establishing the Second Republic.
1983–93	Military rulers again seize power.
1993	Transition to civilian rule (the Third Republic) fails; Sani Abacha seizes power.
1995	Activist Ken Saro-Wiwa is executed.
1998	Abacha dies; Abdulsalami Abubakar succeeds him as the military head of government.
1999	Military rule ends and the Fourth Republic is established; Obasanjo is elected president.
2000	Sharia criminal law is adopted by 12 northern states.
2007	Obasanjo steps down; Umaru Yar'Adua comes to power in a fraudulent election, marking Nigeria's first civilian transfer of power.
2009	Yar'Adua negotiates an amnesty with Niger Delta militants, and Boko Haram launches its Islamic insurgency in the north.
2010	Yar'Adua dies in office, and Vice President Goodluck Jonathan is named president.
2011	Jonathan is elected president in a relatively clean democratic election.
2015	Former military ruler Muhammadu Buhari is elected, marking the first democratic transfer of power between civilians from different parties.

On October 1, 1960, Nigeria formally gained its independence, creating what is known as the **First Republic**. Without much of the violence and destruction that plagued decolonization elsewhere, Azikiwe was named the first head of the new government. The new nation also enjoyed ongoing industrialization, strong exports, and the promise of oil revenues whose potential was just beginning to be explored.

Independence, Conflict, and Civil War

The relative peace and the promises of an independent Nigeria quickly experienced rougher waters, however. Elections in 1959 had given the NPC nearly half the seats in the House of Representatives, leading it to form a coalition with the NCNC. That coalition battled over some of the most essential questions regarding Nigerian statehood, including the scope of central versus local powers and national versus regional identity. Meanwhile, the AGP fragmented because of internal disputes and electoral setbacks. The infighting eventually spread across the Western Region, which the AGP controlled, and led to riots, the collapse of the regional legislature, and the central government's imposition of emergency rule over the region.

The dynamics and divisions of the Action Group crisis were not unique to the Western Region. Various groups across Nigeria demanded that the federal system be further decentralized to make way for additional states. Meanwhile other groups and leaders opposed such tactics, fearing these actions would undermine their own territorial authority or even lead to the breakup of the country. Fragmentation was of particular concern to the NPC. Because the Northern Region held over half the seats in the House of Representatives, the NPC feared that any restructuring of federalism would undermine its position of relative superiority. Such concerns even extended to the national census, which each side hoped would bolster its allotment of seats. Sharply contested elections and electoral alliances were marked by ethnic tensions and electoral discrepancies. Economic disparities sharpened the ethnic conflict, and each group viewed the state as a means to siphon off wealth for its own people.

In the violent aftermath of the contentious 1965 regional assembly elections in the Western Region, 2,000 people died. Amid the increasing disorder, a group of army officers, primarily Igbos, staged a coup d'état, assassinating the prime minister, the leaders of several political parties, and a number of military officials from the north. The coup leaders suspended the constitution, banned political parties, and called for a unitary government and the end to northern domination. But the coup failed to impose order, setting off civil war instead. Conflict erupted between northern and Igbo troops; the coup leaders were in turn overthrown, and many of them were killed. Many Igbo living in the north were also massacred, and Igbo leaders who had supported the coup and an end to federalism as a way to weaken northern power now believed that their people and region had no future in a multiethnic Nigeria.

In May 1967, the Igbo-dominated Eastern Region seceded from Nigeria, declaring itself the **Republic of Biafra**. Although the Biafrans were outnumbered and outgunned, they held off the Nigerian military for three years, aided in part by international supporters who believed the Nigerian government was conducting a genocidal war against the Igbo. Azikiwe, who had been dismissed from his post by the military government and was himself an ethnic Igbo, became a prominent supporter of Biafran independence. In 1970, Biafra was defeated. Although the defeat did not lead to the Igbo extermination that many had feared, the war itself exacted huge costs in military and civilian life: estimates range from 500,000 to 3 million fatalities.[4]

The Military Era

The armed forces brought an end to the Nigerian Civil War, but their role in the politics of Nigeria was just beginning. The 1966 countercoup in response to the takeover by Igbo army officers established the Federal Military Government (FMG), which initially claimed that it would soon return power to civilian control.

General Yakubu Gowon, who came to head the FMG in 1966, argued that in advance of any such transition, Nigeria needed to undergo dramatic political and economic reform. Dominated by none of the three main ethnic groups, the FMG broke Nigeria into a number of federal states, hoping to weaken regional and ethnic power. The government also sought to move the country away from its reliance upon agriculture by stimulating industrialization through a policy of import substitution. This shift was made possible in part because agricultural exports were declining in favor of oil, which was emerging as a major source of revenue. By the 1970s, Nigeria had become one of the top 10 oil-producing countries in the world. The result was rapid if uneven development of the country in numerous areas.

The FMG had come to power with a certain degree of public support, given its call for an end to divisive ethnic-based politics and the creation of an effective state. Yet in reality, military rule simply replaced one form of patronage with another, tapping oil revenues as a way to enrich those in power and their supporters—a theme that would recur again and again with subsequent regime changes, both military and civilian. By the mid-1970s, Gowon's political authority had deteriorated in the face of public animosity in reaction to widespread corruption, crime, and stagnating economic development. In 1975, he was overthrown in a bloodless coup that brought General Murtala Muhammed to power. Muhammed began to crack down on corruption and took the long-delayed steps necessary for the return of civilian rule, thereby earning widespread popular support. But within a year, he was assassinated in a failed coup attempt, which brought to power General **Olusegun Obasanjo**, who continued Muhammed's plans for the restoration of civilian rule.

A new constitution enacted in 1979 ushered in the **Second Republic**, under which the old parliamentary system was replaced by a presidential system in the hope of strengthening central authority and preventing a breakdown like the one that had occurred a decade earlier. Democratic elections were held in 1979, and Obasanjo willingly retired from political and military life. He subsequently became active with various intergovernmental and nongovernmental organizations (NGOs) such as the World Health Organization and Transparency International. Obasanjo's apparent respect for the rule of law while in power and his prominent international role thereafter made him one of the most popular Nigerians and favored his return to politics.

The 1979 presidential elections resulted in a victory for the northerner Shehu Shagari (who narrowly defeated the perennial candidate Azikiwe) and the reemergence of several traditional parties that had dominated Nigeria before military rule. From the outset, Shagari's civilian government faced numerous obstacles. In addition to the ethnic factionalism that continued to plague politics, state revenues declined dramatically in 1981 after a drop in oil prices. The resultant economic recession fostered unrest, which the government sought to quell with increased public spending and corrupt payments to potential detractors. Inflation and foreign debt increased, and capital fled. When the Shagari government sought to stay in power in 1983 by rigging elections, the military once again left its barracks and reentered the political scene, led by a young general, **Muhammadu Buhari**.

After 1983, Nigeria experienced another decade and a half of military rule, a period dominated by two men: General **Ibrahim Babangida** and General **Sani Abacha**. Babangida, an ethnic Gwari and a Muslim, had the unenviable task of dealing with Nigeria's mounting economic crisis. Backed by the International Monetary Fund and the World Bank, he implemented a neoliberal structural-adjustment program that made drastic cuts in public spending and dramatically worsened the lives of average Nigerians. In politics, too, while Babangida asserted that he would restore civilian rule, he increased tension by packing the military government with northerners, which only deepened regional and ethnic resentments. In the late 1980s, he sought to initiate a civilian transition under his control, even to the point of creating new political parties and platforms. Under growing public pressure, presidential elections for this **Third Republic** were held in 1993, but Babangida quickly annulled the results. That action set off a wave of public protests, strikes, and the fear of a new civil war. Babangida stepped down in the face of the unrest, installing a caretaker civilian government. Within three months, his second-in-command, Sani Abacha, a northerner, had taken the reins of power for himself in yet another military coup.

Abacha's government lacked many of the skills that had allowed Babangida to remain in power for such a long time. While Babangida sought to co-opt his opponents as much as possible, using force only as a last resort, Abacha regularly employed violence as a means of public control. Political leaders and activists involved in the 1993 elections and ensuing crisis were arrested, and Abacha used his North Korean–trained Special Bodyguard Unit to repress and murder critics of the regime. In 1995, a number of civilian and military officials were imprisoned for allegedly plotting against Abacha, among them former President Obasanjo. The writer and environmentalist **Ken Saro-Wiwa**, a critic of the regime and of the Shell Oil Company's role in Nigeria, was also arrested, and later executed, for his opposition to the regime.

Saro-Wiwa's execution led to Nigeria's expulsion from the Commonwealth of Nations and the imposing of sanctions by the United States and the European Union. Not only did Abacha repress the Nigerian people, he also stole an estimated $6 billion from the state. This dark period ended suddenly in 1998, when he died of a heart attack. (Some observers suspect that he was poisoned.) Perhaps realizing the dangers of military rule, General Abubakar, who succeeded him, rapidly carried out a democratic transition and released all political prisoners. In 1999, free presidential elections were held, bringing Obasanjo to power again as the first head of state in the current **Fourth Republic**.

Political Regime

Nigeria presents a compelling study of political regimes and a sober lesson in the challenges facing postcolonial countries struggling to institutionalize stable government and a capable state. Nigeria has experimented with an assortment of political regimes and experienced more than its share of political turmoil in its nearly six decades of independence. The country has vacillated between authoritarian military regimes and democratic civilian republics (both parliamentary and presidential) and has had a variety of federal, state, and local political arrangements.

The most prominent form of governance in independent Nigeria has been **patrimonialism**, in which personal rule by both authoritarian and democratic leaders has been shored up by the economic privileges those leaders bestow upon a coterie of loyal followers. Not surprisingly, the divisiveness, corruption, and illegitimacy of patrimonialism have meant that the bullets of military coups, rather than the ballots of electoral democracy, have more frequently determined Nigerian regime shifts and changes in government. These regime shifts have shared at least two features: each new regime has come to power promising improved governance, and each has largely failed to deliver on its promise. Whether military or civilian, no regime has worked particularly well in Nigeria.

On a brighter note, the current Fourth Republic, ushered in with the transition back to civilian democracy in 1999, has successfully sponsored five elections (including four peaceful transitions from one civilian government to another), kept the military in its barracks, and survived longer than any of its democratic predecessors. Significantly, the most recent presidential election in 2015 yielded Nigeria's first electoral defeat of an incumbent and transition to an opposition candidate. Perhaps most important, Nigerians seem willing to keep trying. As one observer noted, "Although they have badly botched it up when they achieve democratic rule, Nigerians refuse to settle for anything less."[5]

Because of that tenacity, even though military regimes have ruled Nigeria as frequently as civilian republics, over the years Nigerians have developed a number of important components of successful democracy. These include diverse and vigorous media, an educated and often critical elite, outspoken human rights organizations, a growing middle class, and a respected legal profession and judiciary. In short, Nigerians have sought to establish the rules and procedures of an effective political regime, but political instability, ethnic disunity, and political and bureaucratic corruption persist. Long periods of authoritarian oppression have alternated with shorter periods of what appears to be democratic chaos.

The primary focus of the following discussion is the nature of the current civilian democratic regime, but we also touch on the authoritarian regimes that preceded it. For, like its two predecessors, if this democratic regime is unable to deliver on its promises and devolves into corruption and chaos, history has shown that authoritarian rule will likely replace it. Nigerians may dislike military rule, but their patience for bad democracy also has its limits.

Political Institutions

THE CONSTITUTION

Since independence, Nigeria has been governed by six constitutions (after having been governed by four during the colonial era). While successive military juntas simply dispensed with the rule of law, democratic regimes have not fared much better, discarding and rewriting the rules of government on average every four years. Not to be outdone, the government recently announced plans to hold a national convention to rewrite the most recent 1999 constitution, arguing that the current document was hurriedly drafted by the last military junta. With some justification, critics complain that the problem for Nigerian political leaders has not been coming up with rules of good governance, but rather abiding by them.[6] Well-meaning leaders have oftentimes sought in good faith to revise legal norms to better accommodate both the developmental and the democratic aspirations of the Nigerian people and the realities of their ethnic and religious differences. Too often, however, neither military rulers nor civilian elites (nor foreign corporations or domestic insurgents, for that matter) have felt bound by those rules.

The British established colonial Nigeria's first constitution in 1922 and then rewrote it three times to reflect the decentralized federal arrangements they imposed to accommodate the colony's regional economic and ethnic divisions and facilitate their "divide and rule" strategy. Nigeria's first national constitution, promulgated in 1960, reflected the colonial imprint in at least two important ways. First, like all former British colonies, independent Nigeria established itself as a constitutional monarchy with a Westminster-style parliamentary democracy: the British

ESSENTIAL POLITICAL FEATURES

- **Legislative-executive system**: Presidential

- **Legislature**: National Assembly
  - **Lower house**: House of Representatives
  - **Upper house**: Senate

- **Unitary or federal division of power**: Federal

- **Main geographic subunits**: States

- **Electoral system for lower house**: Single-member district plurality

- **Chief judicial body**: Supreme Court

monarch remained the head of state, legislative authority was placed in the hands of a bicameral parliament, and executive power was vested in a prime minister and cabinet. Second, the federal nature of the Nigerian state was further institutionalized with the codification of the regional division of Nigeria into the Hausa- and Fulani-dominated north, the Igbo-dominated east, and the Yoruba-dominated west.

In 1963, after only three years of independence, Nigeria reconstituted itself as a republic, replacing the queen of England as head of state with its own elected but largely ceremonial president. The revised parliamentary system ostensibly remained in place over the next decade and a half, though military rule for most of that period precluded its functioning. When the military finally acceded to civilian rule in 1979, the constitution of the Second Republic established an American-style presidential system with a directly elected president (as both head of state and head of government), a bicameral legislature, and a separate constitutional court. Subsequent constitutions (of 1989, 1995, and 1999) have retained the presidential system. Nigeria's current Fourth Republic, established in 1999, is thus a federal democratic republic with a presidential executive and a bicameral legislature.

The Branches of Government

THE EXECUTIVE

Nigeria's frequent leadership changes are largely a consequence of the substantial social, economic, and political challenges facing this postcolonial country. Those changes and challenges have in turn fostered the personal rule of authoritarian leaders and hampered efforts to institutionalize more legitimate executive rule. As the table "Nigerian Heads of Government" (see p. 748) indicates, in its nearly six decades of independence, Nigeria has been ruled for fully half of this time by patrimonial strongmen. Until the past decade, elected civilian rule was much less frequent, consistently giving way to military rulers. Generally speaking, military and civilian rulers alike have possessed substantial, if frequently short-lived, political power.

Nigeria's current president, Muhammadu Buhari, is only the sixth democratically elected executive to govern Nigeria and the first to defeat an incumbent in a democratic election. A former general and northern Hausa Muslim, Buhari first came to power in a military coup in 1983 and ruled Nigeria with an iron fist before being ousted in another coup in 1985. During his 20-month rule, Buhari arrested hundreds of corrupt officials and businessmen, executed drug dealers, and expelled thousands of illegal immigrants. He was elected president in 2015 as a

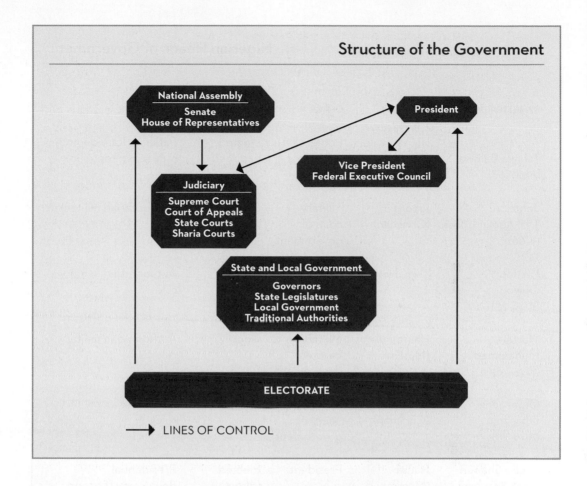

Structure of the Government

National Assembly
Senate
House of Representatives

President

Vice President
Federal Executive Council

Judiciary
Supreme Court
Court of Appeals
State Courts
Sharia Courts

State and Local Government
Governors
State Legislatures
Local Government
Traditional Authorities

ELECTORATE

→ LINES OF CONTROL

self-avowed democrat, having competed unsuccessfully in three previous presidential elections. He replaced **Goodluck Jonathan**, an ethnic Ijaw Christian from southern Nigeria, who first assumed the presidency in 2010, after President Umaru Yar'Adua died in office. The president of Nigeria is directly elected by the people and nominates his or her own running mate, who automatically becomes vice president if the president is elected. The president also appoints ministers to the Federal Executive Council, or cabinet, which is charged with initiating and implementing the policies and programs of the federal government. In a nod to Nigeria's ethnic challenges and in an effort to avoid favoritism (if not clientelism), the constitution requires the president to appoint ministers from each of the states of the Nigerian republic. This quota system, which Nigerians refer to as the **federal character principle**, is also used with federal appointments and civil service positions in the government bureaucracy.[7] Each ethnic group is allotted a certain portion of federal

Nigerian Heads of Government

NAME (TENURE)	ETHNICITY (RELIGION)	OFFICE	PATH TO POWER	REGIME TYPE
Abubakar Tafawa Balewa (1960–66)	Hausa-Fulani (Muslim)	Prime minister	Elected (indirectly)	Parliamentary democracy (First Republic)
Johnson T. U. Aguiyi-Ironsi (1966)	Igbo (Christian)	Military head of government	Coup	Authoritarian military rule
Yakubu Gowon (1966–75)	Tiv (Christian)	Military head of government	Coup	Authoritarian military rule
Murtala Muhammed (1975–76)	Hausa-Fulani (Muslim)	Military head of government	Coup	Authoritarian military rule
Olusegun Obasanjo (1976–79)	Yoruba (Christian)	Military head of government	Coup	Authoritarian military rule
Shehu Shagari (1979–83)	Hausa (Muslim)	President	Elected (directly)	Presidential democracy (Second Republic)
Muhammadu Buhari (1983–85)	Hausa (Muslim)	Military head of government	Coup	Authoritarian military rule
Ibrahim Babangida (1985–93)	Gwari (Muslim)	Military head of government	Coup	Authoritarian military rule
Ernest Shonekan (1993)	Yoruba (Christian)	Interim head of government	Appointed	Civilian puppet rule (proposed Third Republic)

NAME (TENURE)	ETHNICITY (RELIGION)	OFFICE	PATH TO POWER	REGIME TYPE
Sani Abacha (1993–98)	Kanuri (Muslim)	Military head of government	Coup	Authoritarian military rule
Abdulsalami Abubakar (1998–99)	Gwari (Muslim)	Military head of government	Assumed power	Authoritarian military rule
Olusegun Obasanjo (1999–2007)	Yoruba (Christian)	President	Elected (directly)	Presidential democracy (Fourth Republic)
Umaru Yar'Adua (2007–10)	Fulani (Muslim)	President	Elected (directly)	Presidential democracy (died in office)
Goodluck Jonathan (2010–15)	Ijaw (Christian)	President	Appointed/ Elected (directly)	Presidential democracy
Muhammadu Buhari (2015–)	Hausa (Muslim)	President	Elected (directly)	Presidential democracy

positions based on its regional population. Unfortunately, though the federal character principle may have eased ethnic rivalries by spreading the spoils of office among the various groups, it has exacerbated corruption. Bribery, waste, and corrupt ties between political patrons and clients in the private sector remain the norm in Nigeria's largely dysfunctional civil service, which "absorbs most of the budget but delivers little in the way of service."[8]

THE LEGISLATURE

Although in practice, the president and his or her cabinet initiate budgetary legislation and most other important bills, the constitution designates the National Assembly, Nigeria's federal legislature, as the highest lawmaking body. This bicameral legislature consists of a lower House of Representatives and an upper Senate, in which both representatives and senators serve four-year renewable terms.

Former military ruler Muhammadu Buhari casts his vote in the 2015 presidential election that brought him to power, marking Nigeria's first electoral contest in which an opposition candidate defeated an incumbent.

The **House of Representatives** contains 360 seats, and each member represents an individual district. The 109 seats in the Senate are divided among Nigeria's 36 states (three seats each) and the federal district of Abuja (one seat). Despite their appointed constitutional roles, both chambers of the National Assembly have served as little more than rubber stamps for the executive branch, even during periods of democratic rule. This circumstance is in part due to the same party controlling both branches of government for most of Nigeria's democratic history, but it is also due to (and related to) the legislature's lack of experience, expertise, and staff support. In recent years, however, the National Assembly has demonstrated less compliance in passing budgetary bills and has become more vocal in expressing the demands of regional and even local interests.

These regional disagreements speak to the huge political challenge an increasingly democratic Nigeria faces in overcoming its seemingly intractable ethnic divisions, as we discuss later in this chapter. Some critics have argued that a parliamentary system might better address Nigeria's challenges of cultural pluralism by reducing conflict between the executive and legislative branches. Others have called for a unicameral legislature or even the distribution and rotation of key executive posts among the dominant ethnic groups, as is done with civil service appointments (and, informally, with presidential candidates; see "The Electoral System," p. 752).

Nigeria inherited a colonial legal system that combined British common law with an assortment of traditional or customary laws that the colonial government had permitted to handle local matters (including Sharia, which predominated in the Northern Region). This legacy fostered a court system and rule of law that historically, even during periods of military rule, retained a degree of independence and legitimacy. However, the Abacha military dictatorship (1993–98) flouted this independence, routinely ignoring legal checks and using an intimidated judiciary to silence and even eliminate political opponents. Although Abacha frequently used the courts to persecute many of his enemies (including those alleged to have plotted coups against him in 1995 and 1997), the most infamous case of "judicial terrorism" was the 1994 Abacha military tribunal that resulted in the aforementioned execution of the noted playwright and activist Ken Saro-Wiwa.[9]

A member of the Ogoni ethnic minority from the oil-rich Niger Delta, by the 1980s Saro-Wiwa became internationally famous not just for novels and plays, but also for his political efforts. His agenda was to force the Shell Oil Company and the Nigerian government to take greater responsibility for the Delta's environment and share a greater portion of the oil wealth with the Ogoni, whose lands the oil rigs were despoiling. In 1990, with others, Saro-Wiwa founded the **Movement for the Survival of the Ogoni People (MOSOP)**. MOSOP challenged the government's revenue-sharing formulas, which kept the bulk of the oil wealth flowing to national government coffers. With allied groups, MOSOP also disrupted production, compelling Shell first to curtail oil extraction in the Ogoni region and ultimately to abandon its operations there altogether. By interfering in this "stream of petroleum revenues that fed the dictatorship,"[10] MOSOP raised the ire of General Sani Abacha's military government, which in 1994 ordered a brutal crackdown on Ogoni activists and sympathetic Ogoni villages. Saro-Wiwa and other activists were arrested on trumped-up charges and brought before a special military tribunal. The show trial returned a verdict of guilty, and in November 1995 the government hanged all nine of the defendants, despite an international outcry and the efforts of international human rights groups and the leaders of dozens of countries to intervene.

With the return to democratic rule, an effort has been made to reestablish the legitimacy and independence of the judiciary. The 1999 constitution established a Supreme Court, a Federal Court of Appeals, and a single unified court system at the national and state levels. The rule of law has been further strengthened under the Fourth Republic, with successive governments launching anticorruption campaigns, most recently with President Buhari's pledges to launch an "anticorruption war." But although the courts have had some success in prosecuting former state officials for enriching themselves while in office and addressing electoral fraud, these anticorruption efforts have typically faltered as they have drawn closer to those who are still in office or who remain politically influential.

Nigeria's federal constitution also permits individual states to authorize traditional subsidiary courts, giving these customary legal systems significant judicial clout. The most controversial of the traditional systems have been the Islamic Sharia courts, which now function in 12 of the predominantly Muslim northern states.[11] As discussed later in this case, Nigerians have debated heatedly and, in some cases, violently over the role and jurisdiction of the Sharia courts.

The Electoral System

As in other presidential systems, Nigerians directly elect their president and separately elect members of both chambers of their legislature, the National Assembly. But unlike the U.S. system, in Nigeria, presidents, senators, and representatives all serve four-year terms, with elections for all three offices held in the same year. In an effort to ensure that the president serves with a national mandate, Nigeria's constitution requires that the winning presidential candidate obtain both an overall majority of votes nationwide and at least 25 percent of the ballots cast in at least two-thirds of the states.[12] This distribution requirement became an issue of contention in the 1979 election, when the Supreme Court was called upon to determine what constituted two-thirds of Nigeria's then 19 states (there are now 36). Ultimately, the court ruled that Shehu Shagari's victory in 12 states—not the 13 demanded by the opposition—sufficed, and Shagari was named president. The constitution holds that if no candidate succeeds in winning a majority of total votes and obtaining the two-thirds threshold in the first round, a second round of voting takes place a week later, pitting the top two candidates against each other in a runoff.

Nigeria's dominant **People's Democratic Party (PDP)** put in place another informal arrangement designed to enhance the legitimacy of presidential elections when the country returned to democracy in 1999. Christian politicians from the south feared that democracy would always favor the more numerous Muslim population in the north and that southern candidates would thereby be shut out of power. As reassurance, PDP leaders established an informal system of presidential rotation known as **zoning**, in which the party would alternate every two terms nominating candidates from the north and the south. While this agreement facilitated support for reestablishing democratic rule, it limited the pool of qualified presidential candidates and exacerbated ethnic divisions by framing issues and policy priorities in terms of alternating regions and religions. Moreover, this plan also ran into problems when President Yar'Adua (a northern Muslim who succeeded a southern Christian) died in office in 2010. As directed by the constitution, he was succeeded by the vice president, Goodluck Jonathan, who happened to be a Christian from the south. Jonathan's successful bid for a full second term in 2011 angered many northern politicians, who saw it as a violation of the zoning system, which should have given a northern president a full two terms. Jonathan's election prompted substantial protest and violence in the north, and anticipation that he would seek reelection led to the 2013 merger of the three largest opposition parties into the **All Progressives Congress (APC)** Party and the defection of a sizable number of northern PDP politicians to the APC. This strengthened opposition agreed upon Buhari, a northern Muslim, as its candidate and elected him to office in the 2015 contest, thus preserving the informal zoning rotation.

All 360 seats in the House of Representatives are contested in single-member districts (SMDs) apportioned roughly equally by population. The 109 members of the Senate are also elected from single-member districts, with each of 36 states divided into three districts. The federal district, or "capital territory," of Abuja elects one senator in a single-seat constituency for the 109th seat. These winner-take-all, single-member districts historically favored the dominant PDP and one or two smaller opposition parties, allowing them to dominate both chambers of the National Assembly. However, Buhari's commanding win in the 2015 presidential election carried many APC legislative candidates in on his coattails, giving the APC a majority in both chambers. Several other smaller parties have managed on occasion to win seats in the House. The success of the smaller parties reflects the geographic concentration of ethnic groups willing to vote in blocs large enough to win a plurality of votes in the less-populous lower-house electoral districts, such as the districts dominated by the Kanuri minority of northeastern Nigeria.

Local Government

Constitutionally, Nigeria is a federal republic with national, state, and local levels of governance. Although Nigeria's military governments sought to establish a unitary system, the gaping ethnic divisions within the country have prevented governments of all stripes from truly unifying the nation and centralizing political authority. These divisions reflect the ethnic diversity of Nigeria and the legacy of colonial rule.

In 1970, the Federal Military Government divided the republic into 12 states following the Nigerian Civil War, which nearly split the country permanently. The number of states grew to 19 in 1976, 30 by 1991, and 36 by 1996, plus the Federal Capital Territory. The number of local government units has varied even more substantially, reflecting the uncertainty of how federalism should be constituted in Nigeria. The democratic government elected in 1979 doubled the number of local authorities to more than 700. In 1983, the military government downsized the number to 300, but it has since increased once again to nearly 800. At the same time, over three-fourths of these local government councils have been replaced by "temporary" caretaker committees appointed by state governors. These patronage appointments guarantee both the longevity and the loyalty of local government in delivering votes for the state and national party organizations.

With a history of interregional instability and suspicion and relatively weak state capacity, Nigeria will certainly see the countervailing demands of centralization and devolution persist. On the one hand, the national government's control of the bulk of oil revenues has provided the patrimonial glue that keeps the local regions dependent upon the center. But as increasingly diverse and articulate voices have entered a progressively democratic political arena, the calls for enhanced state and local autonomy have grown louder. Those demands range from expanded state control over the budget (and for the oil-rich Niger Delta, local control over its oil revenues), to a separate military for each region, to full-fledged dismemberment of Nigeria.

To date, local and even state governments have enjoyed little autonomy from the national government and have no means of generating revenue. Put simply, the central government controls the purse strings, and the Nigerian purse depends almost completely upon oil revenues. (The non-oil sector makes up just 4 percent of the private sector.) Not surprisingly, as oil revenues have expanded, so has the public sector at all levels, as have the degrees of corruption associated with that patronage. At the same time, the expansion of oil revenues has led to increased disputes over the national distribution of these funds—known as the **derivation formula**—and the percentage of revenues that should accrue to the oil-producing localities.[13]

Other Institutions

THE MILITARY

Although the Fourth Republic has managed to sponsor four successive and relatively peaceful democratic elections, independent Nigeria's tumultuous history cautions us not to become too confident that the military will remain in its barracks. Nigeria's nearly three decades of experience with military rule (1966–79 and 1983–99) left a deep impression on Nigerian politics. It is not a coincidence that most of Nigeria's most powerful leaders (including the current and former coup leaders and elected presidents Buhari and Obasanjo) boast a military background. As is the case elsewhere in postcolonial Africa and in much of the developing world, the military has served as one of the few stable avenues of meritocratic social mobility; it has long been able to attract many of Nigeria's best, brightest, and most ambitious. This avenue has been particularly important for the ethnic Muslims of northern Nigeria, who have been educationally and economically disadvantaged compared with southern Nigerians. Although the south is the source of Nigeria's oil, for many years the north controlled the army and used that control, in the form of military dictatorships, to redistribute oil wealth.

Scholars have offered a number of explanations for the military's nonintervention in Nigeria's Fourth Republic.[14] They point to President Obasanjo's legislation in the early 2000s requiring the retirement of all military officers who previously held political offices during the period of military rule. They also note the government's seizure of senior military officers' corruptly acquired money and properties and the growing professionalization of the younger cohorts of officers. The military's dismal performance in its fight against Boko Haram insurgents in the north and efforts to curtail widespread oil theft in the south have also tarnished its image. That said, a military coup plot was preempted in 2004, and persistent corruption and the inefficacy of civilian rule, combined with the vast spoils of office, remain tempting justifications for the military once again to try to usurp control. Only time will tell if Nigeria's military is prepared to make its recent withdrawal from public life permanent.

Political Conflict and Competition

The Party System

Politics in oil-rich, patrimonial Nigeria has been described as a "contest of self-enrichment."[15] Whether these political contests have been fought with ballots or bullets, the stakes have indeed been high, the competition fierce, and corruption and violence all too common. Not surprisingly, political parties and the party system have fared best under democratic regimes and have withered during periods of military rule. Political parties first began forming during the colonial period and did so quite naturally along ethnic lines, even as early advocates of democracy sought to establish multicultural and issue-based platforms. Although the names of the dominant parties have changed over time, those that emerged during each era continued to reflect the ethnic divisions of identity politics, despite efforts of democratic and even some military regimes to establish cross-ethnic national parties.

Because of this, it has made more sense to discuss Nigeria's parties in terms of their ethnic identity and, therefore, their geographic location than to try to place them on a left–right political continuum. This regional party identity has exacerbated ethnic tensions and complicated efforts to establish democratic institutions and legitimize national party politics. Moreover, most state and local contests have been dominated by the region's leading party, typically permitting that party to control the governor's office, the state assembly, and local councils. This control, in turn, allows the party to marshal sufficient votes to capture the seats in the national Senate and House of Representatives as well. This reminds us that in Nigeria, all politics are in the first instance local, and that in these local communities, ethnicity and clientelist networks have been very important.

Although recent democratic elections under Nigeria's Fourth Republic have offered some hope for the establishment of cross-ethnic parties with national appeal, strengthened democracy has also given stronger voice to persistent sectarian and even local separatist demands. The upsurge in Islamist terrorism and communal violence in the north and ongoing contention over the spoils of the oil-rich Niger Delta continue to threaten the relevance of national electoral contests too often plagued by political corruption and ethnic-based patronage networks.

Elections

Colonial-era parties survived through the First Republic (1960–66), but were banned from the onset of military rule until Olusegun Obasanjo came to power in 1976. Obasanjo legalized the establishment of political parties in 1978, and some 150 parties were formed in that year alone.

In 1979, Obasanjo's elected successor, Shehu Shagari, sought to impose order on this political cacophony by compelling the formation of nationwide parties. The constitution of the Second Republic established that any successful presidential candidate must win at least one-fourth of the vote in at least two-thirds of the states. The election commission required that all parties open membership to all Nigerians and that the parties' leadership come from at least two-thirds of the states. In all, five parties were deemed viable contenders in the 1979 and

1983 elections. Military coups in 1983 and 1985 (in part the result of the widespread corruption and failure of the Second Republic) once again banned political parties.

Ibrahim Babangida, the military ruler from 1985 to 1993, charged his National Election Commission with reforming the party system to produce a two-party system. But fears that such a system would lead to a dangerous political division between the Muslim north and the Christian south led the commission once again to approve five parties. Dissatisfied, Babangida dissolved the commission and established two national parties, one neatly placed "a little to the left of center and one a little to the right."[16] The government built headquarters for each party, gave each one start-up funds, and even named them (the Social Democratic Party and the National Republican Convention). Babangida called for local elections in 1990 and announced plans to hand over power to civilians with a presidential election in 1992.

Although the election was postponed until 1993, it took place fairly. But because the winner was a southern (Yoruba) civilian distrusted by the northern military generals, the military nullified the results and charged the apparent victor with treason. The military installed an interim puppet president, who was quickly pushed aside by General Sani Abacha. Abacha called for elections in 1996, and his military government certified five parties—all loyal to him. Not surprisingly, all five nominated Abacha as their candidate for president.

Abdulsalami Abubakar, Abacha's military successor, dissolved the five parties and called for presidential elections in 1999. In another effort to foster political parties with a national, or "federal," character, the election commission approved only parties that maintained well-established national organizations. Nine parties qualified for local elections, and the three parties with the highest votes in those elections were permitted to participate in the national legislative and presidential elections. Not surprisingly, each of those parties once again reflected its regional base in one of the country's main ethnic groups: the People's Democratic Party (PDP), representing the northern Hausa; the All People's Party (APP), representing the eastern Igbo; and the Alliance for Democracy (AD), representing the western Yoruba.

Democracy advocates are hopeful that the 1999 election marked a watershed for Nigerian national politics. In that election, PDP supporters—with strength in the Muslim north, home of many of Nigeria's military leaders—chose to support Obasanjo, a retired general but a southern Christian Yoruba. The AD chose to throw its support behind the APP contender rather than field its own candidate. Obasanjo won with nearly two-thirds of the vote, and a "relieved public" overlooked the many flaws in the election and largely accepted the results that ushered in the Fourth Republic.[17]

The subsequent four elections have followed this trend of growing democracy and declining regional basis for party affiliation, but have continued patterns of electoral corruption and (until the most recent election) PDP dominance. The 2003 election, the first sponsored by a civilian government in 20 years, returned Obasanjo to office. In 2007, he stepped down as required by the constitution, marking the first ever succession of democratically elected executives in Nigerian history. This cleared the way for Umaru Yar'Adua, Obasanjo's handpicked candidate, to succeed him, winning a landslide victory with purportedly 70 percent of the vote. As in the 2003 elections, the PDP swept not only the presidential election but also contests for the two chambers of the legislature and state assembly races, held in the same month. The victory was marred, however, by opposition and foreign observer charges of widespread corruption and fraud in electoral contests at all levels. Yar'Adua's two chief rivals for the presidency sought to annul the election results,[18] and even foreign observers concluded that the elections were so badly rigged that they "lacked even the pretense of democratic plausibility."[19] After a nearly yearlong investigation, an appeals court concluded the margin of victory was wide enough that, despite shortcomings, even a fully clean election would still have brought Yar'Adua to office.

Coming to office thanks to what was arguably Nigeria's most corrupt election, Yar'Adua in many ways redeemed himself in the eyes of the electorate. He battled political corruption and negotiated a cease-fire in the Niger River Delta, but fell ill and died in his third year in office. His vice president, Goodluck Jonathan, assumed the presidency and the right to finish out Yar'Adua's four-year term. As a southern Christian, Jonathan was initially seen as simply a caretaker until the 2011 election would permit the PDP's northern political bosses to resume their "turn" in the rotating "zoning" system. But he lost no time in pursuing his predecessor's reform agenda and promising to tackle three of Nigeria's biggest problems: rigged elections, woefully inadequate electricity, and the insurgency in his native Niger Delta. Significantly, Jonathan sacked the powerful but corrupt head of the Nigerian election commission and replaced him with an impeccably honest academic, who oversaw Nigeria's cleanest elections in both 2011 and 2015.

In the run-up to the 2015 election, as it became clear that Jonathan would again flout the PDP's zoning arrangement and pursue reelection, the three largest opposition parties (with a faction from a fourth party) put aside their differences and in 2013 merged to form a broad coalition party, the All Progressives Congress (APC). Later that same year, a group of prominent national PDP leaders

Despite a succession of democratic elections, political violence—among other problems—threatens Nigerian democracy.

and state governors, dissatisfied with Jonathan's reelection plans and the poor performance (and declining popularity) of the Jonathan government, defected from the PDP. They first formed a breakaway faction they labeled the "New PDP," but by year's end had combined their forces with the opposition APC. As a southern Christian facing a united opposition, with little positive to show for his five years in office, Jonathan was handily defeated by the APC's candidate, popular northern former military leader Buhari (see the table "Results of Recent Nigerian National Elections," p. 761). This APC victory, the first peaceful passing of power from one elected political party to another, marks a significant watershed in Nigeria's efforts to consolidate a two-party democratic electoral system that can offer a legitimate choice to Nigerian voters.

Even after this apparent step forward and five consecutive affirmations of the democratic electoral process, Nigerians' patience for democratic rule continues to be tested by endemic government corruption, political and gangster violence, and persistent economic misery. Much of the half-trillion dollars in oil revenues earned during the PDP's quarter-century control of government was neither invested nor distributed. Rather, it found its way into the hands of both regional and national political elites, despite the professed and at times genuine efforts of top leaders to stem this corruption. Oil has generated immense wealth in their country, but over three-fourths of Nigerians still live on less than two dollars a day, and critics of the former ruling PDP labeled it the "Poverty Development Party."

Nigeria's ethnic and religious fault lines also remain starkly apparent. In the 2015 election, Buhari earned nearly 54 percent of the popular vote, but won only 5 of the 17 southernmost states. Jonathan won nearly 45 percent of the vote, but captured only 3 of the northernmost states. When asked in 2015 how satisfied they were with how democracy works in Nigeria, nearly 70 percent of respondents indicated they were not very or not at all satisfied, compared with 63 percent of respondents in 2008 and only 14 percent in 2000.[20] Support for a democratic system remains strong, but governments of the Fourth Republic must start delivering on promises of better times if they hope to avoid the fate of earlier republics.

Winston Churchill once famously concluded that democracy had proven to be "the worst form of government, except for all those other forms that have been tried from time to time." Having suffered through decades of brutal military authoritarianism, Nigerians might seem to have been equally cursed under democratic regimes. Rather than delivering good governance, Nigerian democracy has

An election worker marks the finger of a Nigerian voter. Observers judged the 2015 presidential election Nigeria's cleanest polling to date.

Results of Recent Nigerian National Elections

PARTY:	PDP	APP/ANPP/CPC*	AD/ACN†	OTHER PARTIES	TOTAL
ELECTION YEAR		**PRESIDENTIAL VOTE (%)**			
1999	62.8	37.2	No candidate	—	100
2003	61.9	32.2	No candidate	5.9	100
2007	69.8	18.7	7.5	4.0	100
2011	58.9	31.9	5.4	3.8	100
2015	45.0	APC‡ 54.0	—	1.0	100
		SENATE SEATS			
1999	65	24	20	0	109
2003	73	28	6	0	107§
2007	87	14	6	2	109
2011	71	14	18	6	109
2015	49	APC 60	—	0	109
		HOUSE SEATS			
1999	212	79	69	0	360
2003	213	95	31	7	346§
2007	260	61	31	4	356§
2011	199	64	69	22	354§
2015	125	APC 225	—	10	360

*The APP renamed itself the All Nigeria People's Party (ANPP) after a merger with a smaller independent party in 2003. The Congress for Progressive Change (CPC) formed in 2009 to support Buhari's candidacy and drew most of its supporters from the ANPP, though the latter has continued as a separate party.
†The Action Congress of Nigeria (ACN) is the result of the 2006 merger of the Alliance for Democracy and several smaller parties.
‡The All Progressives Congress (APC) is a merger of the ACN, ANPP, CPC, and defectors from the PDP.
§Contested returns from some districts reduced the total number of candidates seated in some Senate and House elections.

too often brought clientelist corruption, ethnic violence, and generally weak and incompetent leaders.

Not surprisingly, oil revenues have been the primary lubricant in making democracy "work" in this postcolonial state comprising some 250 highly diverse ethnic groups. National political leaders have co-opted regional and local elites with promises of cash and political appointments in exchange for delivering votes. This patronage system has given a great electoral advantage to the incumbent party, which has had control of the "excess crude account," a giant slush fund of surplus oil revenues. During the notoriously corrupt 2007 elections, this fund of some $20 billion practically evaporated as President Obasanjo worked to ensure that the governing PDP and his handpicked successor, Yar'Adua, would secure victory.

But things are improving. If the 2007 elections were Nigeria's most corrupt, the two subsequent elections in 2011 and 2015 were arguably Nigeria's cleanest. In 2010, President Jonathan sacked the corrupt director of Nigeria's election commission, who was largely responsible for rigging past elections, and replaced him with a highly respected academic who pledged to clean up Nigeria's electoral politics. In the run-up to the 2011 elections, the newly led commission fingerprinted all 73.5 million eligible voters, required that all ballots be printed abroad, and established an "open secret ballot system" in which voters' fingerprints were scanned at the polls and voters were asked to remain at the polling stations until all votes were tallied locally. Although the process cost nearly $600 million, outside observers and voters alike have concluded it was worth the cost. In addition, the government established the Nigerian Sovereign Investment Authority in 2011. This trust is designed to insulate oil revenues from the hands and pockets of politicians, instead directing the funds toward economic development. Addressing Nigeria's poverty, inequality, and unemployment will likely do more to consolidate democracy than any other measures.

If Nigeria's elections are becoming more transparent, sadly, they remain quite violent. A journalist reporting on Nigeria's 2011 presidential election concluded that the tallies for Nigerian elections "come in two separate columns. One records the votes cast at polling stations; the other the number of people killed around the time of the election."[21] In the weeks leading up to that election, several politicians arranged to have their opponents murdered, while others hired gangs to intimidate rivals' campaigns. On election day, groups threw hand grenades to dissuade would-be voters, and others stole ballot boxes or snatched tally sheets. The worst period was that immediately following the election, as dissatisfied voters, in many cases stirred up (or even paid) by losing candidates, went on looting and killing sprees. Some 800 Nigerians died in just the first week after the elections, as simmering ethnic and religious tensions merged with electoral disappointment and economic deprivation. The greatest violence occurred (and persists) in Nigeria's Muslim north, where incomes and literacy rates are a fraction of those in the south and where poverty drives young men into the arms of criminal gangs and militant Islamic groups.[22]

Encouragingly, the 2015 elections improved in these regards, with far fewer casualties than in previous elections. Observers attribute much of this relatively peaceful outcome to outgoing President Jonathan's quick and gracious concession of defeat. On the day the results were announced, Jonathan urged his supporters to reject violence, stating "nobody's ambition is worth the blood of any Nigerian." But more must be done. As with corruption, solving electoral and ethnic violence and promoting democracy will require in the first instance alleviating Nigerian poverty. Perhaps Nigerians are patient enough to wait for this. When asked about the corruption and violence that accompanied a recent election, one voter concluded, "We have anger, but we have even more hope."

Civil Society

Neither the British colonial government nor the series of post-independence military authoritarian regimes was able to squelch Nigeria's rich tradition of activism and dissent. Even Abacha's oppressive dictatorship in the 1990s could not fully muzzle what one foreign observer referred to as Nigerian citizens' "defiant spunk."[23] In Nigeria's relatively short postcolonial history, a wide variety of formal interest groups and informal voluntary associations have emerged and persisted. Under the relaxed environment of the Fourth Republic, these groups and organizations have proliferated and strengthened. Some of them, particularly professional associations and other NGOs, have risen above Nigerians' identity politics, drawn their support from across Nigeria's cultural spectrum, and functioned in ways that promote national integration. Others, particularly those based on ethnic and religious identities, are among the most resilient of groups and in some cases serve to fragment Nigerian society.

Formal and informal ethnic and religious associations have always played an important role in Nigerian society. Some of these groups have long served as important vehicles of mutual trust for promoting the economic interests of their members, for example, by mobilizing savings or investing in a business. Others formed to protect or promote the ethnic or local interests of a particular minority group. In the early years of independence, some groups provided the foundation for the subsequent formation of political parties.

Among the most important of these issue-based minority associations were those that emerged in the Niger Delta to protect the interests of ethnic and other groups in the region. The Movement for the Survival of the Ogoni People (MOSOP), established by Ken Saro-Wiwa in the 1990s to defend the interests of the Ogoni, employed a variety of legal and extralegal political tactics to secure more financial benefits with fewer environmental costs from foreign-operated oil interests in the Niger Delta. As conditions in the region have worsened and more and broader constituencies feel they have a right to a portion of the oil revenues, groups in the Niger Delta have more readily turned to violence.

Many of these militant groups are more or less loosely connected to the **Movement for the Emancipation of the Niger Delta (MEND)**, an umbrella organization that claims to act on behalf of the Delta's oppressed peoples and exploited environment. Numerous militant subgroups have engaged in "bunkering" (illegally siphoning off) oil, kidnapping foreign oil workers and sailors, ransoming captured ships, and even launching daylight attacks on oil pipelines and facilities in the region. Former president Yar'Adua negotiated a 2009 truce and amnesty that his successor Jonathan, who came from the Delta region, continued. While this truce, unlike previous efforts, brought a significant drop in violence in the region, President Buhari, a northerner, has been less sympathetic to the regional concerns, and rebel and criminal violence has increased since 2015. The lines dividing ethnic and environmental political associations, insurgent separatist movements, youth fraternities (or cults), and common criminal gangs are blurring in this complex and troubled region.

Tragically, growing political violence in the Niger Delta has been eclipsed by rising terrorism in Nigeria's northern interior and ongoing sectarian and ethnic conflict elsewhere in this patchwork country. The radical Islamist sect known as Boko Haram (loosely translated from the Hausa as "Western education is forbidden") has waged a seven-year insurgency designed to root out Christian and Western influence and establish an Islamic Caliphate. This group has presented the single largest threat to peace in Nigeria, claiming responsibility for hundreds of terrorist attacks and the deaths of tens of thousands of Nigerians, particularly in the northeast. These assaults included a series of bombings and shootings during Christian religious services in the region, brutal attacks on government buildings and schools, and in 2014, the kidnapping of hundreds of schoolgirls. A single attack in 2015 left as many as 2000 dead, and in the same year, Boko Haram pledged its allegiance to the Islamic State, raising fears about the group's ties to

Choosing between a Good Democracy and a Strong Economy

If you had to choose between a good democracy or a strong economy, which would you say is more important?

	GOOD DEMOCRACY (PERCENTAGE)	STRONG ECONOMY (PERCENTAGE)
Nigeria	59	40
India	56	41
Mexico	53	41
China	50	44
Brazil	50	46
South Africa	40	58
Russia	15	74

Source: Pew Center for the People and the Press, 2007.

organized terrorist organizations outside of Nigeria (for more details, see "Boko Haram," p. 776). In addition, Muslims and Christians frequently engage in riots in several northern and central states, and farmers and herders regularly clash in the same areas.

But despite this growing insurgency and rising tensions between Muslims and Christians, it is important to note that sectarian conflict has been mitigated by the numerous divisions and differences within each religious tradition. Although Muslims of the north share a common faith and have banded together in defense of certain interests (such as the maintenance and expansion of the scope of Sharia law), numerous schisms exist within the faith as well. For example, the particular variety of Sufi Islam practiced among lower-class Hausa Muslims is quite distinct from and in many ways at odds with the orthodox Sunni Islam practiced by the Hausa and Fulani Muslim elite or the radical extremism of Boko Haram.

In fact, some liberal Muslim groups favor secular government and oppose the implementation of Sharia. Christian-based politics in the south is similarly far from monolithic.

Modern civic associations such as trade unions and professional organizations played a prominent role in the anticolonial struggle and have been relatively active in promoting their particular, and at times more collective, interests since the time of independence. Unions representing workers in the all-important petroleum industry—for example, the National Union of Petroleum and Natural Gas Workers (NUPENG)—have used their strategic position to exert influence on the political process. Formal associations such as those representing legal, medical, and journalism professionals have also begun to articulate the political interests of Nigeria's growing professional class. Particularly since the end of military rule and the establishment of the Fourth Republic, NGOs promoting issues such as development, democracy, and civil rights have exerted more influence in Nigerian politics. Most active among these latter groups have been those organizations engaged in monitoring Nigeria's elections.

Society

Ethnic and National Identity

It should be quite clear by now that one of the central factors defining Nigerian politics is group identity. Ethnicity is a powerful force, given the historical rivalry among the Yoruba, Igbo, Hausa, and Fulani peoples. In addition, nearly a third of the population belongs to none of these groups, further complicating the ethnic map. Nigeria can claim more than 250 separate ethnic groupings with many more languages.

This diversity has created significant problems for the consolidation of democracy, because each group has temptations to see politics in zero-sum terms. An electoral victory by a Hausa candidate, for example, is viewed as a blow to the interests of the Yoruba, and vice versa. Such ethnic divisions were largely responsible for the collapse of civilian government in 1966 and of course for the Nigerian Civil War. Subsequent military leaders often sought to play on fears of ethnic conflict as a justification for authoritarianism, arguing that democracy only exacerbated the fault lines between regions and peoples. Changes in the federal structure (creating more territorial divisions), the executive system (replacing a parliamentary system with a presidential one), and the

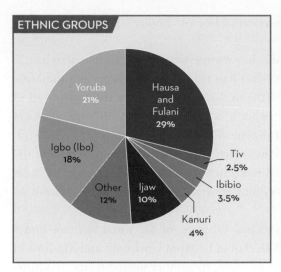

ETHNIC GROUPS

Hausa and Fulani 29%
Yoruba 21%
Igbo (Ibo) 18%
Other 12%
Ijaw 10%
Kanuri 4%
Ibibio 3.5%
Tiv 2.5%

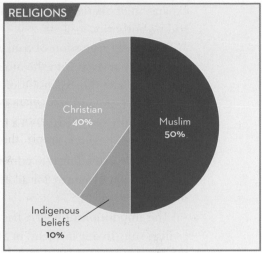

RELIGIONS

Muslim 50%
Christian 40%
Indigenous beliefs 10%

party system (the effort to ban ethnic parties) similarly reflected the desire to weaken local authority and shift more power to the center. In 1991, even the capital was moved—it went from Lagos to Abuja, a city built from scratch in the center of the country.

How has the transition to democracy affected ethnic relations? Since the end of military rule, communal violence has risen. The state is no longer able to suppress the public as it pleases, and the struggle for control over the state has returned to the populace. Since the return to civilian rule in 1999, ethnic conflicts have taken thousands of lives and displaced millions of Nigerians. This violence, which often has economic motives, originates in conflicts over access to state funds, oil revenues, jobs, and other resources. Incomes in the country's northeast are half those in the south, and fewer than 5 percent of women in some northeast states are able to read and write. Moreover, with the return to democracy, political elites often capitalize on these conflicts as a way to build their local bases of support, even to the point of inciting conflict by paying supporters to attack rival groups.

As we have noted, the conflicts also have a religious component, with deepening fissures separating the Muslims concentrated in the north and the Christians and animists concentrated in the south. This sectarian division has been exacerbated by the growing influence of Sharia law in the northern states. Under British rule, Islamic law was preserved in the north, where it was permitted an important if limited role. The practice continued under independent Nigeria, and by the 1980s, Islamic groups had begun pressuring the government to allow for the expansion of Sharia in the north to criminal law and higher courts, where it then had no authority.

While the repression of Sani Abacha's regime froze much of that activism, it was quickly revived with the onset of civilian rule. Muslim leaders and the Muslim public saw the expansion of Sharia as a way to overcome the corruption of the military era and reassert their rights in a democratic system. Some political leaders clearly saw the issue in a more cynical light: as a way to garner public support. Shortly after the 1999 elections, a dozen northern states made Sharia the primary law, extending it to criminal and other matters. This legal system includes an extreme punishment for adultery and apostasy (leaving the faith)—death by stoning.

The imposition of Sharia has touched off some of the worst violence under civilian rule. In one incident, in 2000, clashes between Christians and Muslims in the town of Kaduna left 2,000 dead. In 2006, in another northern city, 16 Christian churches were burned down during a riot; in recent years, bombings and shootings during Christmas Day services have left hundreds more people dead. The tension over Sharia also grabbed international attention when two women were sentenced to be stoned to death for committing adultery. Although higher courts eventually overturned the women's verdicts, the seeming incompatibility between secular national law and an expansive regional use of Sharia remains a serious and potentially destabilizing issue.

Ideology and Political Culture

Could the conflicts between north and south, Christian and Muslim, lead to civil war, another military coup, or the dissolution of the country itself? Perhaps. As we have seen, political parties in Nigeria tend to be built around individual leaders and ethnic groups. In this case, ideology plays a limited role compared with more narrow communal concerns; by contrast, in a country like South Africa, ideology plays a more significant role in the party system. Similarly, it is commonly asserted that Nigerians have a low sense of patriotism or pride in their state, presumably a result of their stronger local identity and the legacy of military rule. The Nigerian novelist and political activist Chinua Achebe once described Nigerians as "among the world's most unpatriotic people," which, he argued, was a serious impediment to prosperity and democracy.[24]

Despite these concerns, however, some aspects of Nigerian political culture continue to lend support to the state and the democratic regime. A 2012 survey of Nigerians showed that even with the tensions and disappointments that have followed the return of civilian rule, 69 percent continue to support democracy and reject military rule (though this figure is down from 72 percent in 2008 and a high of 84 percent in 2000). Nigerians also strongly oppose a political system dominated by a single party or leader, an attitude quite different from that in many other African democracies, where such domination is common. Over time, Nigerians have come to base their support for democracy less on economic performance and more on trustworthy leaders and similar factors—quite the opposite of what is expected in less-developed countries with weakly institutionalized democracy.[25] Moreover, while Achebe may be right to assert that Nigerians do not express great patriotism (political pride in the Nigerian state), surveys nonetheless show that Nigerians exhibit a high degree of pride in a national identity (pride in their people) broader than a particular ethnic group. Those views, if sustained, may help limit communal tension and build ties across ethnic and religious divisions.

Political Economy

The misfortune of the Nigerian economy has been a constant theme throughout our discussion. The economic difficulties Nigeria has faced since independence are not unusual among less-developed countries, but they are particularly egregious given Nigeria's position as Africa's largest economy and one of the world's largest oil producers. The country earns some $30 to $40 billion each year in oil export revenues, which make up 90 percent of its foreign currency earnings. However, its economic difficulties exist not so much in *spite* of its oil resources but largely *because* of them.

Nigeria's predicament is an excellent example of what scholars sometimes refer to as the **resource curse**. Natural resources that are abundant and state-controlled often serve to support nondemocratic rule. Rather than being beholden to a public that it depends upon for tax revenues, these ruling regimes can employ state-controlled resources to co-opt or buy off key stakeholders and pay for the repression of others. In fact, much of the state machinery functions to siphon off this oil wealth.

Political corruption, as one observer has noted, is not a flaw in Nigeria's political economic system; rather, it *is* the system.[26] And oil revenue is at the heart of what may be called a "70 percent system." In a country where over 70 percent of the population lives on less than $2 per day and where oil accounts for over

70 percent of the government's revenue, more than 70 percent of Nigeria's overall wealth is held by less than 1 percent of the population. And nearly this entire "top million" who count themselves among the wealthy elite are more or less closely connected to the Nigerian state or government.

Nigerian politicians are among the highest paid in the world. As recently as 2012, members of the Nigerian legislature received over $1 million in salary and allowances each year, making them the highest paid lawmakers in the world. President Jonathan's air fleet boasted 10 separate airplanes, and his government's aviation minister purchased two armored luxury cars for $1.4 million. Construction costs for the vice president's official residence were set at $20 million, and the same budget included $6.5 million for meals at the presidential and vice presidential residences.[27] And these were the "legitimate" expenditures. In addition, conservative estimates place the amount of stolen or "missing" oil revenues since the discovery of oil in the 1970s at over $400 billion. In the year leading up to the 2011 presidential and legislative elections, it is estimated the central government and ruling PDP distributed up to $10 billion under the table to national, regional, and local political elites. The Buhari government's anticorruption investigation concluded in 2016 that some $7 billion was stolen from government coffers between 2006 and 2013.

Furthermore, this preoccupation with natural resource wealth tends to distort the economy by diverting it from other forms of development. This situation can be seen in other states with oil-producing economies, such as Iran. Until the 1970s, Nigeria led the world in peanut and palm oil exports, and agriculture is still Nigeria's largest employer (primarily subsistence farming). But Nigeria is now the world's largest importer of rice, and although the country each day produces over 2 million barrels of oil and exports hundreds of thousands of barrels of oil, it imports nearly all of its gasoline. It is estimated that nearly half a million barrels of oil are stolen each day.

Each of these factors is evident in the development of Nigeria's political-economic system. Like other less-developed countries, in the years following independence Nigeria opted for a system of import substitution, creating tariff barriers and parastatal industries with the objective of rapidly industrializing the country. This ambitious program was made possible by oil sales, which during the 1970s benefited from high prices. However, these programs suffered from policies that directed resources toward certain industries for political reasons without having a clear understanding of whether the investments would be profitable. For example, $8 billion was spent in the attempt to create a domestic steel industry that in the end produced barely any steel.[28] The decline in oil prices in the 1980s and the consequent economic crisis and spi-raling foreign debt led Nigeria to initiate a policy of structural adjustment that moved the country away from import substitution, although the economy remained highly regulated and closed to trade.

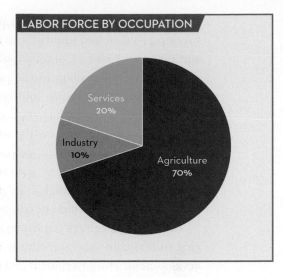

LABOR FORCE BY OCCUPATION

Services 20%

Industry 10%

Agriculture 70%

The limited reforms also did not address the fact that Nigeria remained highly dependent upon oil exports and that the revenues from those exports were in the hands of the military government. While the public suffered from the effects of structural adjustment, such as unemployment and inflation, the Babangida regime used its financial resources to co-opt some opponents while repressing others. Economic reforms only facilitated this patronage, because newly liberalized markets and privatized state assets could be doled out in return for political support—a situation not unlike the "insider privatization" that plagued Russia in the 1990s.

By the time of Sani Abacha's government, corruption had reached such heights as to be described by one scholar as outright "predation" under an "avaricious dictatorship."[29] The Nigerian economy not only suffered from the outright theft of state funds but also became a center for illicit activity, including narcotics trafficking, human trafficking, money laundering, and, perhaps best known, the so-called 419, or advance-fee, scams. One might argue that corruption should not be a central concern if it has helped provide funds for economic development, but the reality is that far too little of this wealth has ever been reinvested in the country. Nigeria ranks 152nd out of 188 countries in the Human Development Index. In Nigeria, great oil wealth and endemic corruption, inequality, and poverty are intimately and tragically interrelated.

In fairness, successive elected governments under the current Fourth Republic have taken steps to break with the corrupt practices of the previous regimes and improve Nigeria's prospects for economic development. These steps included the development of a wide-ranging reform program launched in 2003 and known as the **National Economic Empowerment and Development Strategy (NEEDS)**. The NEEDS program addressed several important areas. First, it increased the transparency of government finances by auditing the accounts of various levels of government to oversee how money was being spent and by making the findings available to the public. Second, it prompted the government to address the corruption problem and improve the rule of law, in part by creating an Economic and Financial Crimes Commission to pursue theft and money laundering—and seizing over $500 million in the process.[30] Under the Yar'Adua administration, this commission took some impressive steps to tackle Nigeria's endemic corruption, arresting seven former state governors for the misappropriation of funds. NEEDS has also focused on the country's inadequate infrastructure, seeking to boost electricity production, improve transportation, increase telecommunications, and expand access to sanitation and clean drinking water. The NEEDS program, which ran through 2007, made some significant headway in addressing some of Nigeria's thorniest development challenges.

Although pledging to continue these efforts, the Jonathan government struggled to maintain this momentum in either stemming corruption or promoting development. His government did restructure Nigeria's foreign debt, modernize its heavily indebted banking system, privatize electrical production, and begin to address the country's dismally inadequate economic infrastructure in areas such as power generation and transportation. The Jonathan government also attracted more foreign direct investment than any previous (or subsequent) government and more than any other African country in those years of high oil prices. Nigeria today boasts nearly 150 million mobile phone subscribers and has a growing service sector, including a prosperous "Nollywood" entertainment industry. And yet, Africa's largest economy still produces only one-tenth of South Africa's electrical output with three times the population.

The Buhari government came to power with a mandate to root out Nigeria's endemic corruption and invest reclaimed revenues in fighting terrorism and creating jobs. President Buhari's war on corruption has made significant strides, with the arrest of a number of former government officials (predictably all from the opposition party) and the recovery of nearly $1.5 billion during his first year in office. President Buhari and his vice president have both taken a 50 percent pay cut and are taking measures to further expose illicit ties between the oil industry and political leaders.

Of course, the long-term success of any developmental efforts will hinge on the critical factor of oil. Increased tampering with oil facilities by insurgents in the Niger Delta combined with plummeting oil prices in recent years have cut both oil production and government revenues. These blows to the Nigerian economy have been cushioned somewhat by the launching in 2012 of the Nigerian Sovereign Investment Authority (NSIA). Designed largely to insulate oil revenues from the grasp of national and regional politicians, the fund channels profits from crude oil sales to the independent NSIA, which invests these monies in funds designed to enhance infrastructure, aid development, and manage fluctuations in oil prices. Since 2013, significant investments have been made in all three areas, providing key support during a time of economic hardship. Still, huge problems remain, reflecting the enormous impact that the oil industry will continue to have on the Nigerian political economy.

Foreign Relations and the World

Since gaining independence half a century ago, Nigerian policy makers have viewed and prioritized their country's foreign policy as a series of concentric circles. Nigeria is the innermost circle, followed by successive rings including West Africa, Africa as a whole, and finally the world beyond the African continent. Within this context, Nigeria's foreign policy has undergone several shifts in emphasis since independence, reflecting a variety of international and domestic influences and a growing sense of state sovereignty and regional influence.

The country's gradual transition from colonialism has meant that it did not undergo revolution or a protracted war of independence, either of which might have dramatically reshaped its relationship with the outside world. As a result, during the Cold War, Nigeria remained clearly within the pro-Western camp and retained its ties to the United Kingdom through membership in the Commonwealth of Nations. However, Western sympathy for the Biafran independence movement during the 1967–70 Nigerian Civil War, and the West's refusal to provide arms to defeat Biafra, steered Nigeria toward nonalignment. During the 1970s, Nigeria played an activist anticolonial role and provided diplomatic and material support to a number of communist movements throughout Africa.

Nigeria has also sought to play an important regional role by helping to lead several international governmental organizations focused on Africa. One such body is the Economic Community of West African States (ECOWAS), whose membership includes 16 West African countries. ECOWAS was established in 1975 as an instrument of regional integration, not unlike the European Union in its early stages. The process of economic integration has been slow, however, although ECOWAS has actively met its obligation to intervene in armed conflicts in member states. Thus it has dispatched peacekeeping troops to help resolve civil conflicts in Liberia, Sierra Leone, Côte d'Ivoire, Togo, and Mali.

As the largest ECOWAS member state by far, Nigeria has borne the brunt of the peacekeeping efforts. It has similarly been active in deploying peacekeepers for far-flung UN missions, as in Lebanon and along the India-Pakistan border. Despite these important responsibilities, Nigeria's international relations declined steadily under the Sani Abacha regime, and by 1995 the country had been suspended from the Commonwealth and subjected to sanctions by the European Union and the United States following the execution of Ken Saro-Wiwa. Since the reestablishment of democracy under the Fourth Republic, however, Nigeria has once again gained status as a regional and, increasingly, global actor.

In the coming decades, Nigeria is likely to become more important on the international scene. Whether this change will contribute to global security and prosperity, however, is an open question. One main reason Nigeria will continue to grow in importance takes us back to the recurrent theme of oil. It is estimated that Nigeria has some 34 billion barrels of oil reserves, and the country has been a member of the Organization of the Petroleum Exporting Countries (OPEC) since 1971. Whereas that is only a fraction of the reserves of the largest oil-producing states, such as Saudi Arabia, this capacity nevertheless makes Nigeria the largest oil producer in Africa and the world's fifth-largest oil exporter. Moreover, Nigeria's crude oil is both "light" (low density) and "sweet" (low sulfur), making it highly prized for its ease of refinement. The vast majority of Nigerian oil is exported to Europe, Asia, and North America, making it an important trading partner.

Instability in the Middle East and economic development in Asia will likely further push Nigeria to the forefront of energy production. For example, China has not only invested heavily in oil extraction efforts in Nigeria but more recently has also funded refinement and power generation projects. (Nigeria currently imports roughly 70 percent of its refined petroleum.) As in other African countries, in Nigeria resource-hungry China has become the largest trade and development partner, supplanting both Europe and the United States. Although this trade and investment has brought inevitable friction and fears of overdependence, Chinese trade and investment has come with less economic or political strings or "conditions" than Western assistance, and at least for the present, has been considered mutually beneficial.

A second factor in Nigeria's growing international importance is regional. Despite its many domestic challenges, Nigeria's growing prominence as the most populous country and largest economy in Africa means that it stands to play a key role on the continent in helping to bolster democracy and stability. In addition to its role in ECOWAS, it has long been an important player in the Organisation of African Unity (OAU), which was created in 1963. Within the OAU, Nigeria was a strong opponent of white rule in Rhodesia (now Zimbabwe) and South Africa. And, with its own transition to democracy, Nigeria has stressed its commitment to democratic rule in Africa. This attitude can be seen in the recent transformation of the OAU. In 1999, its members agreed that the body should broaden its responsibilities to actively pursue a process of greater regional integration (not unlike the original intentions of ECOWAS in West Africa). In 2002, the OAU officially renamed itself the African Union (AU) and declared a new mandate for its member states, known as the New Partnership for Africa's Development, or NEPAD. The primary goals of NEPAD are to eradicate poverty, sustain growth, integrate Africa into the process of globalization, and empower African women. To that end, the AU and NEPAD have broken with past practices by serving as intermediaries between international donors and African states and holding the latter accountable for enforcing the rule of law and making certain that foreign aid is properly spent.

Nigeria and South Africa have become the leading members of the African Union, and Nigeria is taking a strong line on supporting democracy on the continent. For example, as Zimbabwe's government under Robert Mugabe slid deep into authoritarian rule over the past decade, Nigeria supported the country's suspension from the Commonwealth of Nations, and its elected leaders have been openly critical of Mugabe's dictatorial rule. Both Nigeria and South Africa can be expected to grow in influence across the continent, with the former benefiting from its size and the latter from its more developed economy. Some observers have called Nigeria and South Africa the China and Japan of Africa. Recognizing this increased status, Nigeria has been pushing for representation as a permanent member of the UN Security Council, which currently has no permanent African member. (The permanent members are China, France, the Russian Federation, the United Kingdom, and the United States.) And although Nigeria was overlooked for inclusion in the group of fast-growing BRICS (Brazil, Russia, India, China, and South Africa), it has been included in the more recently recognized group known as MINT (Mexico, Indonesia, Nigeria, and Turkey) as an up-and-coming middle-income economy.

Finally, Nigeria's presence in the international system will greatly depend on how its democracy fares. A shift toward authoritarian rule would undoubtedly weaken the country's regional and international moral authority and, in the process, damage regional institutions such as the AU and NEPAD. Another worry is that the growing insurgency of Boko Haram will exacerbate the long-standing conflict between northern and southern Nigeria and embroil the country in the regional and global struggles against violent Islamic extremism. Regional cooperation between Nigeria and its three neighbors to the north and east—Niger, Chad, and Cameroon—since 2015 has had some measure of success in tackling the Boko

Haram terrorist insurgency. But Nigeria's weak state capacity and long-standing ethnic and religious tensions have made the country a valued regional platform for terrorist activity, especially attacks on the country's oil facilities. These terrorist concerns will only be heightened if state capacity further weakens under ineffectual democracy or illegitimate authoritarianism. Because of these concerns, the United States has significantly increased its military support for West African countries, including Nigeria. Closer ties with the United States increase the risk of exacerbating tensions in Nigeria's Muslim community, however, and could play directly into the hands of terrorists.[31] Nigeria will undoubtedly become more connected to the globalizing world in the coming decade, but such a connection will require balancing domestic tensions with regional and international pressures. It will not be easy.

CURRENT ISSUES IN NIGERIA

Boko Haram

Although only a tiny fraction of the roughly 100 million Nigerian Muslims embrace the extremism of radical Islam, Nigeria now confronts a violent group of Islamic insurgents that seems to be gaining strength in recent years even as its terrorist activities have become more violent and indiscriminate. The group's formal name translates as "People committed to the propagation of the prophet's teachings and jihad," but it is known as Boko Haram (which interpreted roughly from the Hausa language means "Western education is forbidden").

The Boko Haram movement began as a peaceful Islamic splinter group in 2002 based in Nigeria's northeastern state of Borno. But when its charismatic leader, Mohammed Yusuf, was captured by the military in 2009 and publicly executed on the spot, he was replaced by a far more radicalized leader, Abubakar Shekau. Since 2009, Shekau has led increasingly frequent, deadly, and coordinated terrorist attacks with the vague goal of rooting out Western influences, destabilizing and overthrowing the government, and establishing an Islamic caliphate in northern Nigeria.

Boko Haram initially targeted primarily state institutions such as police stations, government buildings, and military installations, but its targets have become increasingly "soft." Attacks have been made on Christian churches, bus stations, schools, refugee camps, and even mosques. Of the more than 20,000 casualties linked to this violence since 2009, most of the victims have been Muslims. Moreover, it is estimated that nearly half of these casualties have come at the hands of the military and police, whose use of force has in many cases been as indiscriminate as that of the terrorists. The state's seeming inability to prevent the terrorist acts as well as its resort to extrajudicial killings and other human rights violations have angered local citizens and driven recruits into the terrorists' ranks. In addition, while the overwhelming majority of Nigerians have little sympathy for Boko Haram, the growing economic disparity between the Christian south and Muslim north and the generally ineffectual and corrupt performance of the federal government have strengthened the social welfare role of Islam and increased popular support for the enforcement of Sharia law as an attractive alternative to the state's inability to impose the rule of law or maintain a monopoly of violence.

In fact, while clashes between Muslims and Christians have impetus in disputes dating back many generations, today many cases stem from more immediate frustrations felt by northern Muslims concerning economic inequality and political exclusion. Nearly three-fourths of northerners live on less than $200 a year. And while the literacy rate in Lagos, the commercial capital on the southern coast, is over 90 percent, in the state of Borno—where Boko Haram is based—it is 15 percent. Northerners also have felt politically marginalized since the transition to democracy. During periods of military rule, northerners dominated the state and ensured that significant portions of the south's oil wealth were redistributed to the north. For well over half of the nearly two decades since the transition to democracy, southerners have held the office of president.

Boko Haram's brazen kidnapping of nearly 300 schoolgirls in 2014 and its threat to sell them into slavery put the international spotlight on both the brutality of the insurgency and the incompetency and indifference of the government. And by 2015, as in other parts of the world, this local ethnic conflict had become not only radicalized but also internationalized and drawn into the loose network of the Islamic State and its supporters. Extremist Islamic groups pledging allegiance to the Islamic State have gained footholds in several African countries in recent years. Moreover, Boko Haram has taken its insurgency on the road, attacking targets in neighboring Niger, Chad, and Cameroon.

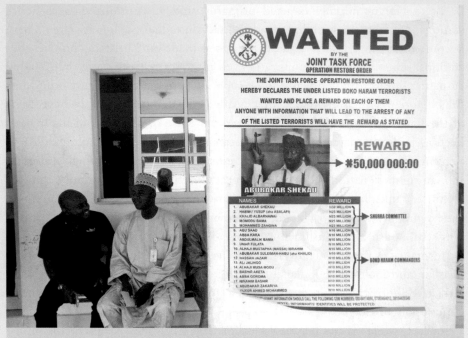

The insurgent Islamist group Boko Haram has been the source of much controversy in Nigeria. Here in Baga Village, a poster advertises the search for Boko Haram leader Abubakar Shekau.

As is the case with unrest in the Niger Delta to the south, any long-term solution to this northern insurgency will require carrots as well as sticks. Before 2009, most political violence in Nigeria occurred in the Delta region. Thousands were killed at the hands of insurgents, and criminal gangs fed on the poverty, corruption, and inequality that marked the area. A 2009 amnesty deal (discussed in the next section) brought pardons, cash payouts, and opportunities for vocational training. While this program certainly did not solve many of the region's problems and has been cut back recently in the face of declining government revenues, it did greatly quell the violence. Boko Haram, like the dominant militant group MEND in the Niger Delta, has become more of an umbrella organization that has split over time into factions and attracted assorted criminals and other opportunists, some not even Muslim, who have taken advantage of the franchise name and reputation. Beginning in 2014, there has been talk of negotiating with at least some of these factions and offering amnesty, counseling, education, and organized sports programs for those willing to renounce violence and their affiliation with

Boko Haram. Critics argue that while this kind of "hearts and minds" campaign is admirable, it may be too little, too late.

Oil and the Niger Delta

It is fitting to conclude this chapter with a final discussion of oil. And nowhere do Nigeria's multitude of complex political, social, economic, and environmental problems and prospects converge more acutely than in the oil-producing Niger Delta. Home to some 31 million Nigerians who comprise more than 40 distinct ethnic groups and speak more than 250 dialects, this region also typically produces over 2 million barrels of crude oil a day and has the potential to produce up to 3 million barrels. Tragically, as much as half a million barrels a day are stolen by local militias and gangsters, who also kidnap oil workers, pirate tankers, and wreck production facilities. Corrupt national and local politicians steal or squander the lion's share of revenues from the oil that is not stolen. The country's four refineries function well below capacity, compelling Nigeria to import most of its fuel and to subsidize the price of imported fuel it sells to its citizens.

Meanwhile, millions of gallons of oil and other effluents contaminate the Niger's delicate tropical ecosystem. A 2013 report estimated that drinking water in certain areas of the Delta contains some 900 times the amount of benzene (a carcinogen) deemed safe by the World Health Organization and further predicted that cleaning the crude oil residue in the area will take decades and billions of dollars. The wasteful and illegal "flaring," or burning off, of natural gas alone is by some estimates the world's single largest contributor of greenhouse gas and wastes $500 million in potential gas revenues each year.

Although the region has been troubled for many decades, in recent years impoverished communities in the Delta have become increasingly angry, organized, and restive. With the reestablishment of democracy in 1999, politicians began to arm local gangs to rig elections for them. International oil producers who operate in Nigeria, such as Shell and Chevron, have worsened matters by providing regular payments to local leaders as tribute for operating in their communities. This practice has increased conflict and competition among ethnic groups in the Delta and between community leaders and unemployed youth, as each group vies for a share of the funds. A result has been the spread of armed militias—frequently linked to political parties—that battle, often violently, over oil. Among their activities are "bunkering" (illegally siphoning oil from pipelines, taking easily 10 percent of all that is produced), seizing or destroying facilities, kidnapping foreign oil industry workers for ransom, and staging attacks on rival groups. The militant group MEND has become the largest and best organized of these groups, launching frequent and increasingly brazen attacks since 2006.

Both authoritarian and elected governments have tried a variety of schemes to calm the region, including military operations and offers of amnesty. Most successful of these was a truce negotiated in 2009 in which thousands of militants surrendered in exchange for unconditional pardon, a monthly stipend, and the promise of retraining and education. The government also promised to adjust the derivation formula, allocating more oil revenues directly to Delta communities. However, the promised retraining was slow to materialize, and violence in the region has once again been on the rise with the electoral defeat of Jonathan, an Ijaw—the largest ethnic group in the Delta—who grew up in the region and had made broad promises of rehabilitation and redress. As violence increased and as oil prices and government revenues have fallen, Jonathan's successor Buhari—a northern Hausa—slashed the budget for the program by 70 percent, practically ensuring increased violence and declining oil production. A lasting solution to this conflict will not be easy; it will require more effective policing, local governance, central control over the actions of foreign oil producers, and acknowledgment of the economic and environmental demands of the local population most directly affected and deeply harmed by these activities. As this chapter has shown, for all the potential benefits this resource windfall could offer to the country and its people, the curse of Nigerian oil expresses itself in myriad ways and will not be easily lifted.

NOTES

1.   Judith Burdin Asuni, *Blood Oil in the Niger Delta* (Washington, DC: United States Institute of Peace, 2009).
2.   *The Niger Delta: No Democratic Dividend* (New York: Human Rights Watch, 2002).
3.   United Nations, *World Population Prospects: The 2012 Revision* (New York: United Nations, 2013).
4.   Charles R. Nixon, "Self-Determination: The Nigeria/Biafra Case," *World Politics* 24, no. 4 (July 1972): 473–97.
5.   Blaine Harden, *Africa: Dispatches from a Fragile Continent* (Boston: Houghton Mifflin, 1990), 247.
6.   For a useful discussion of the Nigerian constitutional process, see Julius O. Ihonvbere, "How to Make an Undemocratic Constitution: The Nigerian Example," *Third World Quarterly* 21 (2000): 343–66.

7. The 1999 constitution states that the "composition of the Government of the Federation or any of its agencies and the conduct of its affairs shall be carried out in such a manner as to reflect the federal character of Nigeria and the need to promote national unity, and also to command national loyalty thereby ensuring that there shall be no pre-dominance of persons from a few states or from a few ethnic or other sectional groups in that government or in any of its agencies." See E. Ike Udogu, "Review of Rotimi T. Suberu's *Federalism and Ethnic Conflict in Nigeria*," *Journal of Third World Studies* (Spring 2004): 296–300.

8. "A Reporter's Tale," *Economist*, February 26, 2004.

9. For the term *judicial terrorism*, see Shu'aibu Musa, "Shades of Injustice: Travails of Muslim Activists in Nigeria in the Hands of Successive Regimes," paper presented at the International Conference of Prisoners of Faith, London, February 17, 2002 (London: Islamic Human Rights Commission, 2002), www.ihrc.org.uk/attachments/7668_02feb17drmusaSHADES%20OF%20INJUSTICE.pdf (accessed 7/20/17).

10. Howard French, *A Continent for the Taking* (New York: Alfred A. Knopf, 2004), 38.

11. For a useful discussion of Sharia and asymmetrical federalism, see M.H.A. Bolaji, "Shari'ah in Northern Nigeria in the Light of Asymmetrical Federalism," *Journal of Federalism* 40, no. 1 (2009): 114–35.

12. Matthijs Bogaards, "Ethnic Party Bans and Institutional Engineering in Nigeria," *Democratization* 17 (August 2010): 730–49.

13. Udogu, "Review of Rotimi T. Suberu's *Federalism and Ethnic Conflict in Nigeria*."

14. William Ehwarieme, "The Military Factor in Nigeria's Democratic Stability, 1999–2009," *Armed Forces & Society* 37 (2011): 494–511.

15. French, *A Continent for the Taking*, 27.

16. Harden, *Africa: Dispatches from a Fragile Continent*, 306.

17. Peter M. Lewis, "Nigeria: Elections in a Fragile Regime," *Journal of Democracy* 14 (2003): 133.

18. These two opposition candidates were Muhammadu Buhari from the All Nigeria People's Party (formerly the APP) and Atiku Abubakar from the Action Congress (a party resulting from the 2006 merger of the Alliance for Democracy and other small parties).

19. "It All Looks Horribly the Same," *Economist*, February 28, 2008.

20. Michael Bratton and Richard Houessou, "Demand for Democracy Is Rising in Africa, but Most Political Leaders Fail to Deliver," *Afrobarometer Policy Paper* 11 (April 23, 2014): 10; "Summary of Results for Nigeria, 2015," *Afrobarometer Round 6* (Practical Sampling International, 2015), http://afrobarometer.org/sites/default/files/publications/Summary%20of%20results/nig_r6_sor_en.pdf (accessed 7/16/16).

21. "Ballots and Bullets: Political Violence Reaches New Heights," *Economist*, April 14, 2011.

22. Brandon Kendhammer, "Talking Ethnic but Hearing Multi-Ethnic: The PDP in Nigeria and Durable Multi-Ethnic Parties in the Midst of Violence," *Commonwealth & Comparative Politics* 48 (February 2010): 48–71.

23. French, *A Continent for the Taking*, 42.

24. Chinua Achebe, *The Trouble with Nigeria* (London: Heinemann, 1983), 15.

25. Bratton and Houessou, "Demand for Democracy Is Rising in Africa," 10; Michael Bratton and Peter Lewis, "The Durability of Political Goods? Evidence from Nigeria's New Democracy," *Afrobarometer Working Paper* 48 (April 2005), 1–43 (accessed 6/20/17).

26. Adam Nossiter, "In Nigeria, Where Graft Is the System," *New York Times*, February 5, 2014.

27. Anene Ejikeme, "Nigerian Anger Boils Over," *New York Times*, January 12, 2012.

28. "A Tale of Two Giants," *Economist*, January 13, 2000.

29. Peter Lewis, "From Prebendalism to Predation: The Political Economy of Decline in Nigeria," *Journal of Modern African Studies* 34, no. 1 (March 1996): 79–103.

30. International Monetary Fund, "Nigeria: 2005 Article IV Consultation, Concluding Statement," International Monetary Fund, March 25, 2005, www.imf.org/external/np/ms/2005/032505.htm (accessed 7/20/17).
31. Princeton N. Lyman and J. Stephen Morrison, "The Terrorist Threat in Africa," *Foreign Affairs* (January/February 2004): 75–86.

KEY TERMS

Abacha, Sani Oppressive Nigerian military dictator from 1993 to 1998 who came to power in a military coup

All Progressives Congress (APC) Opposition political party formed in 2013 by merger of largest opposition parties and defections from the ruling People's Democratic Party

Azikiwe, Benjamin Nnamdi Nigerian nationalist and independent Nigeria's first head of state (1960–66)

Babangida, Ibrahim Military ruler of Nigeria from 1985 to 1993 who sought to establish the failed Third Republic

Boko Haram Islamic terrorist group based in northeastern Nigeria that since 2009 has launched a violent insurgency

Buhari, Muhammadu Former military ruler and current democratically elected president of Nigeria (2015–)

derivation formula Formula for distributing percentage of oil revenues between national and local government in Nigeria

federal character principle Nigerian quota system designed to ease ethnic tension by requiring the president to appoint ministers and civil servants from each Nigerian state

First Republic Nigerian parliamentary democratic regime that followed independence (1960–66)

Fourth Republic Nigeria's current presidential democratic regime, established in 1999

Fulani Predominantly Muslim ethnic group located in northern Nigeria

Hausa Predominantly Muslim ethnic group concentrated in northern Nigeria

House of Representatives Lower house of Nigerian parliament

Igbo (Ibo) Predominantly Christian ethnic group concentrated in southeast Nigeria

Jonathan, Goodluck President of Nigeria from 2010 to 2015

Movement for the Emancipation of the Niger Delta (MEND) Militant separatist group from the Niger Delta

Movement for the Survival of the Ogoni People (MOSOP) Ethnic association founded by Ken Saro-Wiwa to promote the interests of ethnic Ogoni in the Niger Delta

National Economic Empowerment and Development Strategy (NEEDS) A wide-ranging Nigerian reform program designed to stem government corruption and enhance economic infrastructure

Niger Delta World's third-largest wetland and source of Nigerian oil and economic and ethnic conflict

Obasanjo, Olusegun Military ruler from 1976 to 1979 and two-term elected president from 1999 to 2007

patrimonialism Arrangement whereby a ruler depends on a collection of supporters within the state who will gain direct benefits in return for enforcing the ruler's will

People's Democratic Party (PDP) Political party that has dominated Nigerian politics since its formation in 1998; its base was originally the Hausa Muslim ethnic group of northern Nigeria

Republic of Biafra Igbo-dominated Eastern Region that tried, and failed, to secede from Nigeria in 1967

resource curse Affliction caused by abundant natural resources distorting an economy by preventing diversification

Saro-Wiwa, Ken Noted Nigerian playwright and environmental activist, executed in 1995 for his defense of the land and peoples of the Niger Delta

scramble for Africa Late nineteenth-century race by European countries to expand influence and establish imperial control over the majority of African territory

Second Republic Short-lived Nigerian democratic regime, from 1979 to 1983, in which the former parliamentary system was replaced by a presidential system

Sharia System of Islamic law

Sokoto Caliphate Islamic empire founded in 1809 and centered in northern Nigeria

Third Republic Democratic regime proposed by General Ibrahim Babangida in 1993; precluded by General Sani Abacha's military coup in the same year, following annulled elections

Yoruba Ethnic group largely confined to southwest Nigeria whose members are divided among Christian, Muslim, and local animist faiths

zoning A PDP system of presidential rotation; the party would alternate every two terms in nominating candidates from Nigeria's north and south

WEB LINKS

- African Studies Internet Resources: Columbia University Libraries (http://library.columbia.edu/locations/global/africa.html)
- Economic and Financial Crimes Commission (www.efccnigeria.org)
- *Guardian* (Nigeria) (www.ngrguardiannews.com)
- IRIN News.org, a service of the UN Office for the Coordination of Humanitarian Affairs (www.irinnews.org)
- Niger Delta Development Commission (http://nddc.gov.ng/)
- Nigeria Direct: Official Government Gateway (www.nigeria.gov.ng)

CREDITS

CHAPTER 8

Page 386: Matt Mawson/Getty Images; **p. 400:** Students reading the 'Little Red Book' (photo), Chinese Photographer, (20th century)/Private Collection/Bridgeman Images; **p. 409:** Roman Pilipey/EPA/REX/Shutterstock; **p. 423:** © Tom Toles/CartoonStock .com; **p. 433:** STR/AFP/Getty Images; **p. 442:** Zhao Yuguo/Imaginechina via AP Images

CHAPTER 9

Page 450: Daniel Berehulak/© The New York Times/Redux Pictures; **p. 479:** AP Photo/ Kashif Masood; **p. 486:** © Patrick O'Neil; **p. 491:** Paresh Nath/The KhaleeJ Times, UAE/ PoliticalCartoons.com; **p. 493:** © Patrick O'Neil; **p. 499:** Lee Thomas/Alamy Stock Photo

CHAPTER 10

Page 506: Maryam Rahmanian/Redux; **p. 517:** © Patrick O'Neil; **p. 548:** © Patrick O'Neil; **p. 550:** © Patrick O'Neil; **p. 555:** © Patrick O'Neil

CHAPTER 11

Page 560: Jesus Miranda/AFP/Getty Images; **p. 586:** Daniel Aguilar/Reuters/Newscom; **p. 593:** Pedro Pardo/AFP/Getty Images; **p. 612:** Angel Boligan/Caglecartoons.com

CHAPTER 12

Page 620: Danny Lehman/Getty Images; **p. 637:** Evaristo SA/AFP/Getty Images; **p. 652:** © Chappatte in The International New York Times June 06, 2013; **p. 659:** Tyler Bridges/ MCT/MCT via Getty Images; **p. 665:** Antonio Scorza/AFP/Getty Images; **p. 666:** Miguel Schincariol/AFP/Getty Images

CHAPTER 13

Page 674: Rex Features via AP Images; **p. 689:** © Louise Gubb/CORBIS SABA/Corbis via Getty Images; **p. 699:** Hajo de Reijger, The Netherlands/Cagle Cartoons; **p. 701:** Schalk van Zuydam/AFP/Getty Images; **p. 719:** Siphiwe Sibeko/Reuters/Newscom; **p. 724:** Nic Bothma/EPA/REX/Shutterstock

CHAPTER 14

Page 730: Akintunde Akinleye/Reuters/Newscom; **p. 750:** AP Photo/Ben Curtis; **p. 759:** Paresh Nath, Courtesy of Cagle Cartoons; **p. 760:** Seyllou/AFP/Getty Images; **p. 778:** Tim Cocks/Reuters/Newscom

INDEX

Page numbers in **boldface** refer to key terms as they are called out in text.

Bangladesh, 461, 462, 495

banking system in Brazil, 643

Bank of Britain, 51

Bannockburn, battle of, 82

Bantu, 681

Bantu Homelands Citizenship Act (1971), 685

Bantustans, **684**, 684–85, 708, **727**

al-Bashir, Omar, 722

Basic Law, **228**, 230, 231–32, **272**
    electoral system in, 238–39
    head of government in, 232
    head of state in, 234
    judicial system in, 238
    legislature in, 235, 236
    local government in, 240
    party system in, 241, 249

Basij, **532**, 532–33, 535, 536, **557**

Basques, 189, 190

Bastille, storming of, 157

Bavaria, 254–55

Beijing consensus, **434**, **446**

Belarus, 379

Belgium, 155, 200, 623

Belindia, **623**, **671**

Belo Monte Hydroelectric Dam, 661–62

Benedict XVI, Pope, 255

Berlin Airlift, 228

Berlin Conference, 737

Berlin Wall, 138, 229, 243

Bharatiya Janata Party (BJP), **465**, 465–66, 467, 470, 471, 473, 477–79, *491*, **503**
    election results for, 481–83, 502

Bhopal, 483

Biafra, Republic of, **741**, **783**

bicameral legislatures, **9**, **28**
    in France, 170
    in Germany, 224, 235
    in India, 471, 473
    in Japan, 286, 296

    in Mexico, 575
    in Nigeria, 746, 749–50
    in Russia, 350, 354
    in South Africa, 691, 693–94
    in United States, 108, 112

Bill of Rights (United Kingdom), 41, 46

Bill of Rights (United States), **100**, 107, **147**

birth rate
    in Brazil, 96
    in China, 96
    in Japan, 315
    in Nigeria, 735
    in Russia, 381
    in South Africa, 678
    in United States, 96, 97

Bismarck, Otto von, 222–23

Black Economic Empowerment (BEE), **717**, 717–18, **727**

Black Lives Matter, *128*

Blair, Tony, **37**, 45, 47, 50, 51–53, 62–63, 83, **88**
    and European Union, 85
    Iraq War policy of, 82
    and local governments, 60, 74

blocked vote, **170**, **211**

Bloemfontein, 692

Blood River Battle (1838), 681

Boers, **681**, 681–82, **727**

Boer Wars, **682**, **727**

Boko Haram, **733**, 755, 764–65, 775, 776–79, *778*, **782**

Bolivia, 662

Bolsa Família, **659**, *659*, 659–60, **671**

Bonn Republic, **230**, 230–31, 252, 253, **272**

bonyads, **546**, 546–47, **557**

Bosnia, 261, 375

Boston Massacre (1770), 99

Botha, P. W., 688, 689

Chinese Communist Party (CCP), 138,
389, **396**, 396–403, 414, 415–19,
446
capitalists in, 419
challenges to, 430
and civil society, 418–19
economic policies of, 430–32
institutions and organs of, 406–8
membership in, 415, 416
parallel organization with Chinese
government, 403, *404*, *410*, 413
peasants in, 415
Taiwan policy, 438
Three Represents policy of, **416**, 419,
448
Chinese Dream, **407**, **446**
Chirac, Jacques, *168*, **169**, 174, 176, 181,
182, 183, **211**
Christian base communities, **652**, **671**
Christian Democratic Union (CDU), **228**,
241, 242, **272**
and Catholic Church, 254
economic policies of, 258
in election campaigns, 251
and Free Democratic Party coalition,
247
and Green Party coalition, 248
and Merkel, 243–44, 246
and Social Democratic Party coalition,
246, 264–65
Christianity. *See also* Catholic Church;
Protestant Church
in China, 430
compared to Shiism, 512, 513
in Iran, 529
in Nigeria, 733, 737, 753, 757
and civil society, 764–66
of heads of government, *748–49*
and regional divisions, 752–53,
767, 777

and violence, 768, 777
and zoning system, 752–53
in South Africa, 709
Christian Social Union (CSU), *241*, 242,
243, 246, 247, 254
Churchill, Winston, 760
Church of England, 55, 72
citizenship
in France, 153, 171
in Germany, 246, 255–56, 269
in Japan, 314
in Russia, 368–69
in South Africa, 709
in United Kingdom, 83
in United States, 128
Ciudad Juárez, 611
The Civic Culture Revisited (Almond and
Verba), 128
civil rights and liberties, 8, *8*
in Brazil, *8*, 623, 634, 636
in France, *8*, 159, 160
in Germany, *8*, 222, 226, 246, 247
in India, *8*, 463, 472, 475
in Japan, *8*, 278, 288, 290, 317
in Mexico, *8*, 571, 578, 612
in Nigeria, *8*, 14, 766
in Russia, *8*, 349, 356, 366
in South Africa, *8*, 675, 690, 706, 712,
713
in Soviet Union, 347
in United Kingdom, 8, *8*, 47, 56, 75
in United States, *8*, 93, 103, 104–5,
119, 120, 127, 147
civil rights movement, **104**, 104–5, **147**
civil society, **16**, **28**
in Brazil, 631, 651–52
in China, 418–24
in France, 185–89
in Germany, 252–54
in India, 483–84

codetermination policy, **258**, **272**

coffee cultivation in Brazil, 625, 629, 630

cohabitation, 166, **169**–170, 177, **211**

Cold War era, 5, 104, 138
    France in, 200, 201
    Germany in, 215, 227, 228, 260, 261, 264, 265
    Japan in, 290
    Nigeria in, 773
    South Africa in, 688
    Soviet Union in, 337
    United States in, 104, 138

collective responsibility, **53**, **89**

collectivist consensus, **44**, 45, 51, 63, 77, **89**

Collor de Mello, Fernando, 637–38, 639, 643, 657, 666

Colombia, 137, 663

colonialism
    in Brazil, 623, 626–28
    of British Empire. *See* British Empire
    Dutch. *See* Dutch colonizers
    of France, 96, 98
    in future United States, 42, 96–99
    in India, 38, 73, 378, 458–61, 462
    in Mexico, 565–66, 598
    in Nigeria, 736–40, 773
    of Portugal, 623, 626–28
    in South Africa, 679, 680–82, 681–82
    of Spain, 96, 98, 565

Colorado, 101

colored South Africans, **679**, 680, 702, 704, 708, **727**
    affirmative action program for, 717
    in apartheid era, 684
    education of, 710
    impact of democracy on, *715*

comfort women, 323

Committee to Protect Journalists, 596

Common Agricultural Policy, 197, 199

common law, **40**, 56, **89**, 172

Common Man's Party, 481, 501–2

Commonwealth, **42**, 48, **89**

Commonwealth of Independent States (CIS), **376**, **383**

Commonwealth of Nations, 738, 743, 773, 774, 775

communism, **19**, **28**, 138

Communist Party
    in Brazil, 632
    in China. *See* Chinese Communist Party
    in France, 161, 162, **177**, 180–81, 187, **212**
    in Germany, 225, 226, 229, 238, 249
    in India, 480
    in Japan, 304
    in Mexico, 584
    in Russian Federation, 360, **362**, **383**
    in South Africa, 686, 697, 705, 710
    in Soviet Union, 337, 345–48, 349

Communist regimes, **14**, 14–15, **29**

comparative politics, **3**, **29**

competition, political. *See* political conflict and competition

concrete review, **10**, **29**

Confederate States of America, 102

Confederation Congress, 100

Confederation of British Industry, **70**, 70–71, **89**

Confederation of Employers of the Mexican Republic (COPARMEX), 592

Confederation of Mexican Workers (CTM), **595**, **617**

conflict, political. *See* political conflict and competition

Confucianism, **392**, **446**
    in China, 392–93, 394, 427–28
    in Japan, 283, 285, 316

Confucius, 427

Macartney, Lord, 395
Macron, Emmanuel, **164**, 184–85, **212**
   economic policies of, 199
   election of (2017), 164, *168*, 173, 177,
     178, 184, *185*, 204, 209
   as ENA graduate, 176
   political party of, 184–85
Madero, Francisco, **568**, **618**
Maduro, Nicolás, 664
Maginot Line, 155
Magna Carta, **40**, 41, 46, **90**, 156
Mahdi, **512**, 543, 549, **558**
Maimane, Mmusi, **702**, **728**
Majlis, **514**, 516, 518, 528–29, 531, 534,
   558
Major, John, 50
majoritarian systems, **46**, 61, **90**, 173
Malan, Daniel, 684
Malaya, 289
Malaysian Airlines, 366
Malema, Julius, 701, 707–8, 715
Mali, 773
Manchuria, 281, 288
Mandarin language, 424
Mandela, Nelson, 462, **679**, 686, *689*,
   689–90, 698, 699, 707, **728**
   death of, *674*
   economic policies of, 714
   HIV/AIDS policies of, 725
   Zuma eulogy for, *674*, 700
manifest destiny, **137**, 139, **148**
Maoism, 428–29
Mao Zedong, 15, **396**, 396–97, 398–400,
   406, 414, 417, *417*, **448**
   Cultural Revolution of. *See* Cultural
     Revolution
   danwei system under, **403**, **447**
   death of, 400, 416, 418, 427, 429,
     432
   economic policies of, 430–32

   Great Leap Forward of, **398**, 398–99,
     429, 431, **447**
   Hundred Flowers Campaign of, **398**, **447**
   political culture under, 426–27, 428–29
   political economy under, 430–32
   on role of peasants, 415
maquiladoras, **605**, **618**
Marbury v. Madison, 113
markets, **20**, **30**
   free market policies. *See* free market
     policies
Marshall Plan, 138
Marx, Karl, 71
Marxism, 244, 697, 701
Massachusetts, 97
Mauer im Kopf, 256
Maximilian I of Mexico, 567
May, Theresa, **37**, *45*, 45–46, 65, 68, 71,
   78, 86, **90**
Maya, **564**, 565, 566, 598, **618**
May Fourth movement, **396**, **448**
Mbeki, Thabo, **679**, 698, 699, 705, 707,
   721, **728**
   in African Union, 720
   anticorruption program of, 723
   HIV/AIDS policies of, 720, 725
   resignation of, 692–93, 698, 700
McGuinness, Martin, 73
media
   in India, 484
   in Iran, 538–39
   in Japan, 295, 310
   in Mexico, 596–97, 599
   in Nigeria, 744
   in Russia, 339, 345, 360, 361, 362,
     366, 377–78
   in South Africa, 706
   in United States, 123, *124*, 144
Medvedev, Dimitri, 330, 340, 351, 353,
   354, 357

rational-legal legitimacy, **5**, **32**, 106
reactionary attitudes, **18**, **32**
Reagan, Ronald, 105, 132–33, 134
Reconstruction and Development Program
   (RDP), 714
red capitalists, **419**, **448**
Red Guards, **399**, *400*, 414, **448**
Reds versus experts, **431**, **448**
referenda
   in France, 163, 174
   in Germany, 240
   in United States, 116, 118
reform and opening of China, **389**,
   400–402, 403, 413, 415, 434, 443, **448**
regimes, 7–15, **151**, **213**. *See also* political
   regimes
reich, **219**, **272**
   Second Reich, 222–24
   Third Reich, **219**, 226–27, 231, **273**
Reichsrat, 225
Reichstag, 220–21, 223, 225, 226
Reign of Terror, **160**, **213**
religion, *17*, *18*. *See also specific religions.*
   in Brazil, *17*, *191*, 629, 651, 652, *653*,
     654, *655*
   in China, *17*, 420, *428*, 430
   in France, 18, 153–54, 155, 157, 160,
     161, 189, 190–94
     compared to other countries, *17*, *191*
     Islam, 153–54, 189, 191–94, 205–7
   fundamentalism in, 20
   in Germany, 221, 227, 228, 243,
     250–51, 254, 255, 267
     compared to other countries, *17*,
       191
     Islam, 250–51, 256, 267, 268, 269
   in India, 451, 453, 455–58, 460, 464,
     485, *485*
     compared to other countries, *17*, *191*
     Hindu. *See* Hindus in India

Islam, 453, 458, 459, 460–61, 465,
   474, 478, 485, *485*, *486*
   and political parties, 477–79
in Iran, *17*, 507, 509, 525, 529, 530,
   538, *541*, 542–44
   and foreign relations, 548–49
   Islam. *See* Islam, in Iran
in Japan, *17*, 18, *191*, 279, 286, *315*,
   316
in Mexico, *17*, 569, *599*, *601*
and morality, *191*
in Nigeria, 733, 734, 736, *767*, 767, 767–68
   in British rule, 737
   Christianity. *See* Christianity, in
     Nigeria
   in civil society, 763–66
   compared to other countries, *17*,
     191
   of heads of government, *748–49*,
     752–53, 760
   Islam. *See* Islam, in Nigeria
   and regional divisions, 767, 777
   and zoning system, 752–53
in Russia, 18, 342, 365–66, 367, *367*,
   368, 369
   compared to other countries, *17*, *191*
in South Africa, *17*, *191*, 681, 708–9,
   709
in United Kingdom, 18, 40–41, 60,
   72–73, *74*
   compared to other countries, *17*,
     191
in United States, *17*, 18, 93, 97, *126*,
   130–31, *191*
renewable energy, 266, *267*
RENGO, 313
rent seeking, **15**, **32**
Reporters without Borders, 366, 539
Republican Party (France), **182**, 184, 185,
   186, **213**